The Columbia Documentary History of Religion in America Since 1945

THE COLUMBIA DOCUMENTARY HISTORY OF

Religion in America Since 1945

Edited by Paul Harvey and Philip Goff

Columbia University Press
New York

COLUMBIA UNIVERSITY PRESS

Publishers Since 1893

New York   Chichester, West Sussex

Copyright © 2005 Columbia University Press

All rights reserved

Library of Congress Cataloging-in-Publication Data

The Columbia documentary history of religion in America since 1945 /
edited by Paul Harvey and Philip Goff.

p.   cm.

Includes bibliographical references and index.

ISBN 0–231–11884–8 (alk. paper)

1. United States—Religion—1946–   I. Harvey, Paul, 1961–
II. Goff, Philip, 1964–

BL2525.R4653   2004

200'.973'09045—dc22   2004049445

Columbia University Press books are printed on permanent and
durable acid-free paper.

Printed in the United States of America

c 10 9 8 7 6 5 4 3 2 1

ॐ For Eleanor Ning and Hilary Qian Goff
and for Layne, Mark, Andrew, Jessica, Chris, Alex, and John

Contents

Expanded Contents

Introduction: Religion and American Life Since World War II

IN NEW MEXICO in the spring of 1945, upon witnessing the first test of the atomic bomb, the result of the massive Manhattan Project that he had overseen to successful completion, the physicist Robert Oppenheimer, quoting the *Bhagavad-Gita* (a Hindu sacred text), said, "I am become death, destroyer of worlds." In the 1950s, President Dwight D. Eisenhower urged Americans to go to church, endorsing advertisements that trumpeted spiritual life as vital to the American republic and to the struggle against atheistic communism. Eisenhower did not suggest one church in particular—any would do. Meanwhile, poetic dissenters from consensus-era American life, such as the beatniks, conjured up "mystical visions and cosmic dreams," as Allen Ginsberg expressed it in his poem "America."

In the 1960s, Martin Luther King Jr., captured a portion of the national imagination with his soaring religious rhetoric, rooted deeply in the black church as well as in the ideas he had imbibed in seminaries. Among young people, apocalyptic visions sprouted, utopian ideas and communal experiments much like the period of hothouse reform in the antebellum era that produced Thoreau's *Walden*, the Oneida experiment, and numerous other spiritual trends. Though written as a conventional text, Charles Reich's *The Greening of America* captured the religious promise of the counterculture, even as the mass suicide of young followers of Jim Jones in Guyana symbolized the dark side of that vision.

In the 1970s, Democrat James Earl Carter Jr., arose from modest Southern Baptist roots to the presidency, taking care to advertise his evangelical beliefs even as a coalition of conservative Christians, sometimes dubbed the "New Religious Political Right," formulated plans to make evangelicalism into a major force in national politics. In the 1980s, Republican President Ronald Reagan reigned, to the delight of those Christian conservatives, even while on television (and in a series of best-selling autobiographies) actress

Shirley MacLaine popularized what came to be called the "New Age," a descendant of eastern influences and the utopian thinking of young people in the 1960s, Theosophy and New Thought in the later nineteenth century, and Transcendentalism in the antebellum era. In the 1990s, nondenominational believers created massive "megachurches," huge structures, usually in suburban areas, that attracted throngs to services that mimicked theatrical productions. Meanwhile, the historic massive edifices of mainline Protestantism and Catholicism in urban areas sat largely empty or else marketed themselves to the black or Hispanic populations that now predominated in their area. Religious language in politics, however, was ascendant, perhaps reaching a peak in the 2000 presidential election, which featured a consciously evangelical George W. Bush and the very publicly Jewish vice-presidential candidate Joseph Lieberman. Ironically, the infusion of religious language and believers into politics accompanied a crest of criticism that religion was somehow excluded or marginalized from American public life.

That has never been true, and certainly cannot be said of recent American political or cultural life, when religion has seemed to be everywhere—not only suffusing politics from local school boards to presidential campaigns but also readily available through every type of media: on network television series like *Touched by an Angel* (and in New Age form on *The X-Files*); on the Christian Broadcasting Network and numerous other cable channels; at the movies in myriad productions ranging from *The Apostle* to *The Passion of the Christ*; on bumper stickers and billboards; in Christian bookstores and on the best-seller lists; at theme parks (sometimes called "Christian kitsch"); on religious radio stations and in Christian rap and rock music concerts and CDs; in video games and other products aimed at adolescents. Religion is visible in a variety of environments: unassuming storefronts that now house newer immigrant congregations of Thai Buddhists, Somali Muslims, Indian Hindus, Mexican Pentecostals; countless yoga and spirituality classes and workshops throughout the nation; and national memorials that serve as sites of religious reverence (including the Vietnam Veterans Memorial in Washington, the somber space of the bombed Murrah Federal Building in Oklahoma City, and ground zero, the site of the former World Trade Center in New York City).

The examples could go on and on. Just as Alexis de Tocqueville perceived during his tour of America in 1830–31, Americans are at once spiritually devout and materially entrepreneurial and even avaricious, two impulses that, while seemingly contradictory, in fact have worked in tandem, like twin ventricles in the American heart pumping blood. And yet, at gatherings of scholars in American religious history, there is a frequent query: "Is there a good book of primary documents?" Often, the answer is simply no. Existing documentary history books are out of print, overpriced, or too extensive and detailed for classroom use. There is, moreover, no collection of documents on American religious history from World War II to the present. Religion comes in for close scrutiny in works covering earlier periods of American history, when it was obviously a dominant force: among the Puritans, within the African American slave community, during the Civil War, among the social gospelers of the early twentieth century. Religion in the post–World War II era, however, remains mostly the province of sociologists studying long-term "secular" trends, or specific case studies of particular churches or religious communities.

With the passing of the twentieth century, it seems time to provide an introductory set of resources for students and scholars to use in assessing the bewildering variety and remarkable centrality of religious belief and expression in American life. Religion does not mean what it meant in earlier periods of U.S. history—a point lamented by many religious conservatives. But it means far more than many secular Americans have assumed—hence their surprise at the resurgence of politicized religious conservatism in the 1970s and 1980s. But those same conservatives have little or no comprehension of the remarkable religious impulses that suffuse American life and culture, in part because those impulses often don't fall under the category of "religion." Examples include beatnik poetry, countercultural visions, the importation of African religious ideas (such as Santeria), and the religious rhetoric that saturates the twelve-step and self-help movements. Americans' narratives about their own lives remain hugely influenced by the tradition of the spiritual autobiography, and American politicians never let their favorite son, the phrase, "city on a hill," rest for long. Religion thus remains a vital and central part of American life, even if in ways that disturb or disappoint inheritors of the Christian evangelical traditions that have long assumed themselves at the center of the culture. They no longer are in that position, but remain feisty and dogged entrants in a ferociously competitive religious marketplace that now includes far more market niches.

This book is a documentary history text that covers the full spectrum of American religious life from 1945 to the millennium. Paying attention to both the center and the margins of American religions, it provides material for studying major intersections of religion and politics, and documents that illuminate issues for courses that focus more on culture. The work devotes extended attention to race and gender while recognizing the power centers of American life. In short, it illustrates the dialectic of unity and multiplicity, homogeneity and heterogeneity, tradition and innovation, and religion and materialism in American culture.

This collection is divided into three sections, mixing a chronological and thematic format. It begins with attention to the center of power in American religious life—the Protestant, Catholic, and Jewish "mainstream" from World War II through the 1980s—in part one, "Religion in Cold War America: Cultures and Countercultures." This section explores the close relationship of religion, especially Protestantism, to the essential notions undergirding Cold War America. The first chapter examines mainstream American Protestant denominations, their bureaucratic growth and gigantic mission programs, and their struggles to redefine themselves in postmodern America. Chapter 2 examines the efflorescence in the 1950s and 1960s of countercultures that defined themselves in opposition to Cold War American assumptions (rationality, consumerism, and the technocratic state) and that exalted new forms of "consciousness" and politics. It includes material on beats and hippies, religious expressions of the antiwar movement in the 1960s, spiritual roots of what Christopher Lasch called "the culture of narcissism," and recent trends in "New Age" spirituality and attempts by baby boom-generation "seekers" to find something to replace the displaced center.

Part two, "Gender, Race, and Politics in American Religion Since 1945," explores the numerous and increasingly effective challenges to "the center" from African Americans, women, and gays, along with conservative responses from the revitalized fundamentalist and conservative evangelical movements. The central role of religion in the civil rights movement—the most significant social movement of twentieth-century American history—is the exclusive focus of chapter 3. The complex interactions of gender and religion are explored in chapter 4. This book, unlike many others, not only focuses on feminist theology but also considers some of the expressions of conservative and fundamentalist women, and religion in both the prochoice and antiabortion movements. Finally, chapter 5 addresses the very *au courant* topic of religion and the political culture wars, including battles (over abortion, gay rights, and other issues) that remain heated and unsettled to the present day.

Part three of this work provides a multidimensional examination of religion and contemporary American culture. Chapter 6, covering American life since the 1960s, shows the multitude of ways that Americans—believers and nonbelievers alike—continue to feel the influence of religion in their national culture, from T-shirts and other items of kitsch to country music lyrics to television shows to books. Chapter 7 focuses on megachurches, charismatics, and contemporary conservatives and Pentecostals, who form the fastest growing segment of American Protestantism and Catholicism. What used to be "the Right" is now often "the center." Accordingly, historians have increasingly sought to uncover and understand what happened to "everyone else" in the 1960s, to comprehend the so-called silent majority. They were certainly not unaffected by the liberal/radical social movements of the era— even conservative women often work at full-time jobs and demand equal pay—but they often defined their religion and politics against what they per- ceived as the social agenda of the 1960s. In short, this chapter is about on- going attempts to enforce and maintain a sense of religious (largely Protes- tant) homogeneity. By contrast, chapter 8 focuses on the immense impact of the "new" (post–1965) immigrant communities. For example, California is already a "majority minority" state, where Latino Catholics and Pentecostals outnumber "mainstream" Protestants. Asian Buddhists form an increasing- ly large part of the religious communities in Los Angeles and San Francisco, as one might expect, but also in Fresno and Stockton. Any effort to under- stand the future of American religion will have to start with the rapidly changing demographics of American believers. Some (admittedly disputed) statistics, for example, have suggested that there are now more Muslims than Episcopalians in America—even if those Muslims increasingly are subject to suspicion, questioning, and sometimes detention after the events of Sep- tember 11, 2001. Chapters 6, 7, and 8 exemplify the equally powerful pulls toward unity and multiplicity that have always characterized and continue to dominate American religious history.

The book concludes with a set of documents expressing some major themes of American religion at the millennium, including conservative mil- lennialism (the coming of one world shows that the end of the world is near) and New Age millennialism (the new century means the land will achieve peace and harmony), as well as excerpts that reflect more seriously on the future of religion in the United States. Although it ends with 2000, we pro- vide a brief poetic epilogue on the tragic events of September 11, 2001, a day that was hardly envisioned in any of the documents of those who looked for- ward, from the perspective of the twentieth century, to religion in America in the twenty-first century.

The second half of the twentieth century (especially the Cold War period) is passing from memory into history. Indeed, freshmen entering college in 2004 have political and cultural memories primarily of post–Cold War America. Many have little conception of notions such as a Protestant "cen- ter" to American life, and little or no understanding of the central role of re- ligion in some of the nation's pivotal struggles since World War II (includ- ing the civil rights movement, early feminism, and the counterculture). Students with religious backgrounds now often come from megachurches and other religious institutions that are detached from denominations and indeed from any historical tradition. Despite the thriving and even bewildering demographic heterogeneity of contemporary American life, it is re-markable how much of the Judeo-Christian center still holds, even if in a vestigial form. Culturally, Protestant hegemony is gone, never to return; po-litically, in terms of public power, the Protestant/Catholic/Jewish triad re-mains immensely powerful (as has been most evident since 9/11 and dur-ing the first presidential administration of George W. Bush). This book attempts to attend to both aspects of this tradition's influence.

Any work of this sort faces dilemmas common to the genre. Editors of comprehensive survey volumes want to be "inclusive," but that can mean shortening documents so much as to make them nearly incomprehensible to the nonexpert reader. Longer and more substantive excerpts make for more interesting reading and meatier classroom discussion, but inevitably require that other documents simply be cut. Editors seek a balance of polit-ical, economic, and cultural themes, of ethnic diversity, yet a recognition of the common threads that hold cultures (in this case, American religious culture) together. They must recognize power relationships, but at the same time give due credence to those left out of power. Permissions fees and oth-er obstacles may prevent some documents from inclusion at all, no matter how appropriate or perfect they may be. We have faced all these questions in assembling this collection. We sought also to select documents that work well together, that "speak" to one another as much as possible, illustrating the dialectic of unity and heterogeneity mentioned above. These documents not only stand by themselves but also make up a narrative (and counter-narrative) story.

One question was how to represent fairly the remarkable persistence of Anglo-Protestant influence, while also showing how much of this history has been altered since World War II. There were also questions about how to strike a balance between "political" and "cultural" documents. Some read-ers and students, for example, might consider New Age religions a vitally important part of American life that should be abundantly represented in a documentary history; others might think them a relative flash in the pan, and insist on documents that show religion affecting public life (such as in the abortion debates). Without slighting culture—which is indeed abun-dantly represented here—this book has an emphasis on political documents and the nexus of religion and public power, simply because religion has been so intimately involved with American political life since World War II.

In terms of representing ethnic diversity, the heavy concentration on African American religious history may appear biased, unfairly slighting other groups. But, in our judgment, the civil rights movement is the most important social movement in twentieth-century American history, and it was largely fueled by religious impulses. African American religious culture, moreover, has simply woven itself more deeply, fully, and richly into the warp and woof of American life than has Asian Buddhism or Latino Catholicism, just to name two examples (that's why, to use a trivial example, McDonald's uses black gospel music rather than Buddhist chants to sell Big Macs). At the same time, the dualistic "white/black paradigm" has broken down, and many Americans have considerable familiarity with topics that might formerly have been exotic, such as New Mexican *santos* and *retablos*, Buddhist practices of meditation, Islamic holiday traditions and food stores, and Native American shamans. Thus, we have attempted to give due credence to the absolutely central importance of African American religion while also providing documents that demonstrate the incorporation of other traditions into American life.

Americans have been and remain among the most religious people of the western world. Certainly their religiosity stands in striking contrast to the relatively low rates of religious adherence (and interest) in the United Kingdom and throughout most of Europe. But the point goes beyond such measurements, for Americans use religious language in a casual way and live in a culture suffused with religious themes. The free market of religion in America, protected by the Constitution ("Congress shall make no law respecting the establishment of religion, or prohibiting the free exercise thereof") and practiced in daily spiritual quests, means that groups use persuasion to attract and hold converts. The many traditions in America coexist in an environment of toleration and competition, of entrepreneurial drive and theological innovation, of diversity and multiplicity. We hope this book is successful in providing the reader just a small introduction to the remarkably vital story of religion in America since 1945.

Editors' Acknowledgments

FOR HIS ASSISTANCE and encouragement and patience in the preparation of this volume, we would like especially to thank James Warren of Columbia University Press. We are also grateful to Leslie Kriesel for skillful copyediting of a messy manuscript, Sue Marasco for assistance in initial tracking down of rights holders, students at the University of Colorado at Colorado Springs for offering document ideas and critiques of our interpretations, Catherine Vasko for her pursuit of nontraditional documents, Rebecca Vasko for her editorial eye, and Marilyn Pisani for her help in getting the Hubbard piece. A particular note of appreciation is due to Michele Mashburn of IUPUI for her organization of data, communication with authors and copyright holders, proofreading of primary and secondary materials, and her general helpfulness in many facets of this volume.

We also gratefully acknowledge assistance from the Jackson Fellows grant issued by the Southwest Studies Program at Colorado College, in researching documents pertaining to the American Southwest.

Our collaborative efforts in religious history are thanks in large part to Harry Stout of Yale University and John Wilson of Princeton, who provided us a most enriching time together in the 1995–96 class of Young Scholars in American Religion.

Part 1

Religion in Cold War America:
Cultures and Countercultures

Chapter 1

Mainline Religion and the Cold War

WHEN THE "iron curtain" fell across Europe following World War II, it marked a new act on the stage of world events. Long suspicious of each other's economic systems, the United States and the Soviet Union had put aside their differences long enough to defeat Adolf Hitler's Axis powers. But now they returned to their earlier distrust with renewed vigor. The stakes of world domination had been raised considerably by the creation of atomic weaponry, which the United States had used to help end the war in the Pacific theater and which the USSR acquired soon thereafter. The "Cold War," marked not by a physical battlefield but by frigid relations, an arms race, and a constant chess match on the world stage, was under way.

Not surprisingly, religion soon entered the picture, and it took many forms over the coming decades. Various chapters in this volume include themes that overlap considerably with the sort of religious responses often occasioned and sometimes even generated by the Cold War.

For instance, the rapid rise of evangelicalism and Pentecostalism is clearly connected to American fears surrounding the Cold War. Billy Graham, the foremost global evangelist of the twentieth century, earned his worldwide fame by catching the attention of virulently anticommunist publisher William Randolph Hearst through his attacks on communism's spiritual bankruptcy. Hearst instructed his editors across the country to "puff Graham," and soon the North Carolina preacher's face covered *Time* magazine and other national publications. Speaking for evangelicals of all stripes, Graham taught that "Social sins are merely a large-scale projection of individual sins and need to be repented of by the offending segment of society." By linking individual salvation to the politics of individualism through their rhetoric, evangelicals and Pentecostals worked their way into the mainstream discussions of the day, which were dominated by the fear of society taking control over individual freedoms.

Likewise, the Cold War affected policies regarding immigration. Since the 1910s, the number of immigrants from Asian countries had been miniscule. A law in 1917 had created an "Asiatic Barred Zone" that kept out those across the Pacific, most of whom belonged to very different faith traditions than most Americans. Things changed, however, when communist revolutions began occurring through Asia, starting with Mao's successful revolution in China in 1949. Throughout the 1950s turmoil spread—first in Korea, dragging the United States back into war, and later in Vietnam as the French (who had colonized the nation in the nineteenth century) battled the China-backed forces of Ho Chi Minh. Recognizing defeat, the French agreed to divide the country in 1954; but within two years the North and South began hostilities. The United States entered the fray in 1959 and began building up a military presence in earnest by 1961. Soon, with the backing of China and North Vietnam, communist rebellions spread to Cambodia and Laos. With longtime business (as well as religious) allies in jeopardy of their lives, Congress could no longer live with the ban on Asian immigration. The Hart-Celler Immigration Act of 1965 opened the door to Asian immigrants and forever altered the ethnic landscape of the United States, as thousands—and eventually, millions—of Buddhist and Hindu (as well as some Christian) Asians entered the country and became citizens. The results of this migration are addressed in a different chapter, but the cause was the Cold War.

The Vietnam conflict, in fact, also helped bring about a powerful counterculture movement in the United States. The "peace movement" that grew through the 1960s and early 1970s, while often associated with the secularization of American culture, ironically had a deeply religious element. Jesus was embraced by the youth culture as a first-century "hippie" who taught a message of peace and earned the ire of the conservative government. Even the more "hard-core hippies," who characterized the drug culture of the period, used religious language to describe their chemically induced experiences. Eschewing the materialism of American culture, many who participated in this youth-led criticism of the national culture found spiritual voice and sustenance in the folk music that highlighted peace and the treasure of the Earth rather than earthly treasures.

But the Cold War did more than open the playing field—or, better, the praying field—to more people, different from mainline Protestants. It set in motion a more traditional revival of religion across the land. By 1960, 65 percent of Americans were members of a church or synagogue, the highest level in the country's history. Just as amazing is the fact that 96 percent of the population claimed adherence to a specific group, which indicates the level of public expectation that individuals have a religious affiliation, even if they only rarely or never attended services. While the numbers would slip somewhat from their 1960 high mark, religious membership remained at historically high levels in the second half of the twentieth century.

That upsurge in church membership paralleled the increased public role of religion in national life. At times, this attempt to sacralize the nation's history and purpose appeared in official ways, as in the 1950s when the words "In God We Trust" were first emblazoned on American currency and "under God" was added to the Pledge of Allegiance. But it was most evident in a long-standing form of rhetoric that blended political and religious ideas and terms in such a way that America's goals were equated with God's purposes for the world. Expressions of American destiny under God—American mythology that could nearly deify leaders within a generation of their deaths—dated back to Puritan days, before the establishment of the American political state. Consisting of official statements and collectively accepted sacred stories of America's past, this "civil religion" affirmed and renewed in a changing world Americans' religious understanding of themselves as a people. The Cold War was but one powerful and long-lasting example of its effects.

If anyone could be called a "high priest" of civil religion during the Cold War, Dwight Eisenhower would be a powerful nominee. His speeches and actions as president during its early days set the pace for the nation in multiple ways. First, by tying religion to political freedoms, he created a fateful distinction between the United States and the growing number of communist nations. "Democracy," he would later explain, "is the political expression of a deeply felt religion." That theory became part of the nation's mentality for decades without any real debate of its merits. Further, by using his "bully pulpit" to encourage Americans to attend church—he refused to offer an opinion as to which one was best—Eisenhower extended what had been traditionally understood as religious behavior to an act of patriotism and national virtue. In public service television commercials during the mid-1950s, he promoted the role of religion in the nation's overall health. Signing into law congressional acts to place explicitly religious expressions on the federal currency and in the national pledge solidified his significant role as shaper of the culture's rhetoric and behavior.

That sort of positive reinforcement, when coupled with growing anxieties over the expanding power of communist regimes, made a powerful combination. School drills that taught public safety measures to implement during an atomic strike accompanied vehement anticommunist preaching in the daily lives of Americans. Ever watchful of trends toward collectivist thinking or action, religious leaders Billy Graham, Fulton Sheen, and Norman Vincent Peale told people to look inside their souls to root out sinful ways. The religious answer to the frightening threat of communism, according to the most popular preachers of the day, lay in the individual. A more American message cannot be imagined. Religion and democracy were as wed in the minds of citizens as atheism and communism. "If you would be a true patriot, then become a Christian," preached Graham. "If you would be a loyal American, then become a loyal Christian."

That sort of language did not end in the 1950s. While Graham eventually moderated his tone and began to give religious credence to dealing with social ills beyond the concerns of the individual, the combination of religious and political language had become part of daily life. It was used most effectively by President Ronald Reagan, who sought (and received) the support of conservative Christians who preached the value of political and spiritual individualism. His appropriation of religious terminology to explain the political standoff—the Soviet Union as "the evil empire" is an apt example—brought civil religion to a new generation, one born during the Cold War and in need of an explanation for the state of their world.

If conservative politics and religion were the beneficiaries of Cold War civil religion, then mainstream Protestants and socially engaged religious liberals were the losers. In its early days, Cold War fears brought millions of newcomers to the staid, old Protestant traditions. The amount of money spent nationally on new church buildings increased by 4,000 percent between 1945 and 1960, with mainline Protestants paying the lion's share. These traditions were solid, familiar. If American history was sacred, then these were the books on which it was written. No one saw what was to come.

The "individualism" that tied conservative politics to conservative faith was not the concern of mainline Protestants. As the purveyors of the national culture—or so they believed themselves to be—they held a corporate view of the nation. Either everyone shared in American liberties or no one truly did. Their backing of the civil rights movement is but one example of their commitment to the larger social concerns that troubled the country, problems that they felt could not be addressed by appeals to individual salvation. This community understanding of sin and redemption—social situations shape the individual, not vice versa—was part of their heritage dating back to the nineteenth century.

When Cold War religious rhetoric took hold in Washington in the 1950s, mainline Protestants committed to the "Social Gospel" were among the first casualties. "Could it be," asked J. B. Matthews, chief investigator of the congressional committee on un-American activities, "that these pro-Communist clergy have allowed their zeal for social justice to run away with their better judgment and patriotism?" Placed on the defensive—social justice versus patriotism—leaders of religious social programs were nonplussed. How could they answer a question that made them either hypocrites or communists? Ultimately, the Cold War sounded the death knell for the progressive Social Gospel movement within mainline Protestantism.

For instance, the United Methodist Church sat at the top of the Protestant ladder with 10.6 million members in 1960. A poll later that decade indicated that it was the religious group most liked by those in other denominations—it was the "middle of the road" dominant mainline church. Its positions on social issues, however, were beginning to take their toll, especially in the South. By 1996, the United Methodist Church had shrunk to 8.5 million members, despite a general rise in the nation's population. The more conservative Southern Baptists, meanwhile, had grown from 9.7 million members to nearly 16 million, the largest Protestant denomination in the United States.

Others followed the same path. The Disciples of Christ lost approximately half their members during the same period, dropping from 1.8 million to just over 900,000. While Lutherans held their ground, Presbyterians (4.1 million to 3.1 million), United Church of Christ (2.2 million to 1.7 million), and the Episcopal Church (3.3 million to 2.5 million) all lost ground. And this during a time when the U.S. population had *increased* by 85 million people.

But the story of mainline Protestantism in the second half of the twentieth century cannot be fully told by the loss of cultural capital it once enjoyed. Indeed, the fact that it lost such power means that it once held it—and used it to shape the nation in multiple ways in the postwar era. While historians and sociologists today highlight the rise of more conservative and varied religious traditions, to emphasize the decline of mainline Protestantism overlooks just how much influence it had and its present role in American society.

Various events led to the decline of the mainline Protestant denominations. Their advocacy for racial equality, women's rights, world peace, and disarmament was seen by some Americans as following in the great train of Christian activists who worked for abolition of slavery, suffrage for women, and the minimum wage. To others, however, especially those who felt themselves to be outside the halls of power, the intentions of the well-heeled Protestant mainline smacked of paternalism, too-big government, and anti-individualism.

The Protestant mainline could probably have weathered that sort of difference of opinion, but it came at a particularly bad time. The defensive Cold War mindset, with its growing distrust of attacks on capitalism, did irreparable harm to Protestantism's image. Those who had helped improve the lot of the American worker were dragged before congressional inquiries into their activities and associates. Bromley Oxnam, Methodist bishop and president of the Federal Council of Churches, requested the opportunity to defend himself after constant vilification by congressmen. He survived the incident with his reputation somewhat intact. Others were not so lucky. Harry Ward, perhaps the most liberal of the activists, had been a leading theorist of political systems as well as a devout Protestant, for years both president of the American Civil Liberties Union and a seminary professor. After his hearing, his longtime friends cut off communications and rarely spoke of him again.

With its prophetic message against the war in Vietnam as immoral, the mainline further divided itself from large portions of American culture. With its leadership on behalf of civil rights, the Equal Rights Amendment, and, in many cases, the right of a woman to choose an abortion, that was the recipe for its descent from glory during an era of distrust of foreigners (especially communists), emphasis on individual sin over social conditions, and freedom from burdensome taxes.The growing national economy further decentered power from the East Coast, giving the growing Southern Baptists and mountain Mormons greater say in political affairs.

Like many of the themes visited here, those stories are told more fully in other chapters. But it is clear that many significant developments in postwar America—from the growth of some movements and the decline of others to changes in immigration, the flowering of a counterculture, and the conservatives' mastery of the language of democracy in both politics and religion—were occasioned by the Cold War. When the Berlin Wall fell in 1989 and the Soviet Union dissolved the following year, the iron curtain lifted, and revealed a very different religious America.

1. HAROLD JOHN OCKENGA, "CONVOCATION ADDRESS FOR FULLER THEOLOGICAL SEMINARY" (1947)

The founding address of Fuller Theological Seminary, given on October 1, 1947 by one of its founders, Harold John Ockenga, directly reflects the common fear at the time that communism was a threat to Christianity and thus to western culture, particularly American culture. Ockenga, most famous as the pastor of the historic Park Street Church in Boston and the first President of the National Association of Evangelicals, in 1947 co-founded Fuller Theological Seminary with radio evangelist Charles E. Fuller in Pasadena, California. He chose the occasion of its inauguration to place the school, evangelicalism, and western culture in ever-expanding circles in order to indicate the gravity of this moment in history, as the Cold War between western Christianity and godless communism commenced.

Beginning with the Renaissance, Ockenga holds secular Europe responsible for the upheaval faced by the world in recent centuries, and goes so far as to say that the destruction wrought by World War II was a "punishment for the intellectual, moral and spiritual attitude of Europe." Ockenga sees this as a warning to America, and expresses concern over the nation's decadence and the deterioration of its moral standards, fueled by science, secularism, and the intellectual forces of the day.

Ockenga's concluding remarks warn that time is shorter than people think for redeeming western civilization, and hold that it is the mission of Fuller Seminary—an evangelical school that rejected the separateness of Protestant fundamentalism—to prepare those individuals whose task it will be to save the world. Through his writings and lectures over the following decades, he inspired thousands of evangelical ministers to understand their daily struggles within a larger context—a spiritual war waged against the unseen forces of Satan and the very apparent moral vacuum of communism.

❦

As Rome disintegrated and lost the control of political authority a new development of the inner principles of Christianity had to take place. These began to express themselves in the culture of the Middle Ages. Whatever we may think of the failures of civilization in the Middle Ages, we must agree with Matthew Spinka that there was a cultural unity in the arts, sciences, politics and economics which was created largely by the church.

To-day the west has entered a crisis which threatens the continuance of this culture. It may be seen as a rupture in the inner development of the west since the Renaissance. Pitirim Sorokin in "The Crisis Of This Age" amply substantiates the view that there was a unity of culture in the Middle Ages. Art, music, literature, politics and economics were theocentric. It was the age of Madonnas, of cathedrals, of the divine right of kings, of feudalism and chivalry. Into this the Renaissance injected the discordant element of an anthropocentric norm of judgment. Man became the measure of all things. Through the discoveries of Greek manuscripts and philosophy kept through the Middle Ages by the Arabs and returned through the fall of Constantinople and the arrival of Greek scholars in Rome, man was thus enabled not only to sit in judgment upon the church and its authority, returning as the Reformers did to the Bible and to primitive Christianity, but he also could sit in judgment upon all other things. Thus two lines of descent originated at the Renaissance; one, the Reformation of the Christian viewpoint, which simultaneously retained theocentric point of reference; and the revival of ancient rationalism which simultaneously became the forerunner of the modern secularistic spirit and of scientific naturalism. A rupture had occurred in the inner development of the west which was to bring about its ultimate crisis.

This crisis was seen by me as a member of the Commission of the United States War Department investigating the conditions in Europe. I witnessed the terrible, physical destruction in which from sixty to eighty per cent of the buildings of the great cities of Germany are destroyed, in which the population is wrecked by tuberculosis and subject to the diseases coming from malnutrition, in which there is very little clothing, shelter and fuel, in which the mental and moral outlook is that of despair and in which the prime subject of thought and action is "Where will I get my next meal?" Literally, I flew in the wake of the four horsemen who have ravaged Europe over a period of years. Millions of people are displaced. Hundreds of millions are living on a sub-marginal diet. Millions are still in slave labor. Other millions have been bereaved through mass bombings. As Charles Clayton Morrison has said, "Western civilization is not in danger of breaking up. It has broken up."

I hold this condition to be punishment for the intellectual, moral and spiritual attitude of Europe. Intellectually Germany adopted the humanistic dialectic of philosophical naturalism as it was reborn in the Renaissance. The rationalism of German enlightenment was stimulated by Kant's repudiation of God and the erection of the autonomous man who was enabled to superimpose the categories of his mind upon all experience and thus became the final norm of judgment. It was further developed by Hegel's idealism of process in which thesis, antithesis and synthesis became the ultimate order of things. Darwin's theory of evolution was quickly absorbed by the German positivists and reversed the idealistic process of Hegel to a naturalistic process of development as the ultimate order of things. Marx seized upon this to develop his theory of scientific naturalism and economic determinism. Theoretically, God, religion, immortality, the soul of man and ethical values derived therefrom were ruled out and society itself became the object of man's striving. Nietzsche added to this his doctrine of force, of the super race and super man, with his ruthless disregard of the weaker and inferior beings. It was a natural result of the development of the dialectics laid down by Kant, combined with the evolution of Darwin. The last step in the process was Spengler's view of the decline of the west as manifested in the mob rule of the various democratic or pseudo-democratic forms including the dictatorship of the proletariat. His "hour of decision" was a plea for class consciousness, race consciousness, inequalities and the willingness to initiate a new culture. The result was inevitable, namely Hitler with the Nazi ideology expressed in Mein Kamp [sic] and incorporated in the German movement which threatened to overrun Europe and the world. Here naturalism, the twilight of the west, the existence of the super race whose mission was to exterminate and rule the weak, the survival of the fittest and the supremacy of the economic question reached their epitome. The intellectual preparation for World War II and the resultant destruction was completed in Hitler.

Herein lies a warning to America, for the dominant intellectual current in America is scientific naturalism, the exclusion of God from life and action. The adoption of a pure secularism and of total concern with the social questions may well give the mental preparation for such a relativism of ethics and politics that the type of thing which emerged in Germany, tore the world apart and brought on the judgment of God may be repeated here. It is not a far leap from the intellectual forces which are working within through our national decadence to the recognition of physical forces developing in the world for our judgment.

Similarly, moral reasons for the crisis exhibited in Europe may be traced. The standards of right and wrong given in the Ten Commandments have been repudiated. Treaties were scraps of paper in Belgium, Poland, Austria, ultimately the Atlantic Charter and Potsdam. Purity was repudiated by a long process of misuse of the human body until under Hitler the highest honor was held before German woman of submitting their bodies to the troopers in order to build a stronger nation and to fulfil the destiny of the German people. The full result may be seen in what are called the "Ruin-mauschen" who are cohabiting with American soldiers in Europe to-day. As a result of this promiscuity a new generation, half-German, half-American or in other cases half-German and half-Russian or half-German and half-British is rising. But the condition is likewise only a reflection of what has taken place in America in the deterioration of moral standards, reflected in child delinquency, youth immorality and in adult divorce.

The spiritual reasons likewise lie behind the judgment of Germany. Once it was the home of the Reformation, where reform and revival originated and spread throughout Europe. Once a gigantic price was paid by princes, priests and people for freedom of worship and of conscience. Once this was guaranteed in the peace of Westphalia after Germany had been laid waste by war for thirty years in resisting a foreign ecclesiastical tyranny. But in the home of the Reformation rationalism has triumphed.

This same Germany became the source of rationalism and modernism. Higher criticism flourished in the universities and theological seminaries of Germany until the Bible as a source of authority was removed. The resultant liberalism of Ritschel, of Schleiermacher and of Harnach [*sic*] applied evolution to Christianity. Consequently the people were left prey to the pagan teachings of the Nazis based on the dialectic as explained above. Something had to command their allegiance and it became the Nazi philosophy. Not all of the people by any means abandoned Christianity. Some of them resisted the Nazi movement, but many of them did not.

This terrible destruction, therefore, and suffering of German to-day is proof of the moral nature of the universe, of the righteousness of God and of the triumph of morality among the nations. This was really expressed to us by Dean Kunneth of Erlangen University when he said that Germany had two messages to give unto the world. One is that any nation which divorces its culture from God will suffer the full depths of the wrath of God. The other is that in the midst of such suffering the grace of God is sufficient for his people.

This crisis then in western culture may be seen as the pattern of conflict and destruction threatening to engulf western civilization. John Baillie in the little work already referred to called "What Is Christian Civilization?" raised the question as to whether Christian civilization can endure without Christian truth and doctrine and then he strongly affirmed that it cannot. It is essential that we have moral foundations to western civilization and these foundations are derived from the Hebrew Christian tradition. When we divorce the Hebrew Christian tradition from our civilization then we have reached the eventide of the west.

This conflict within western culture has reached its apotheosis in Marxism, Marxism's attempt to overthrow the Christian foundations of the west. It is coinsic that Marxism originated in the west and was embraced first in the east. In the name of democracy and in the name of the common man Marxism has become the ruthless mob rule of the proletariat, which combined with brutality and atheism totally disregards the value of the individual life or the setting up of a theoretical type of state. It was Marxism that caused the creation of Hitler and Nazism. Hitler affirms in "Mein Kamp" [sic] that he created his movement with the determination that he would have a stronger force enabled to crush Marxism, but the economic materialism of Marx had nothing to resist it in Germany. It was only natural because of the abnegation of the Christian faith that some one like Hitler would create an opposing movement. This challenge of naturalism and of man as the measure of all things in the form of Communism to supernaturalism and to society and culture based upon supernatural foundations in God and God's revelation is the inner conflict of western culture to-day which causes it to enter this terrible crisis. Communistic dialectic need only be used as the extreme for purposes of illustration but the same naturalism exists in the philosophical theories of the leading educators in America as has been demonstrated in the books of Dr. Wilbur Smith, of Dr. Carl Henry of this school. . . .

The cause of the decline, however, is other than these mentioned facts. They are merely symptoms of the decline. The lives of men are connected with their theories. It is very clear from the writings of Spengler, of Toynbee, of Sorokin that the basic concepts of men have changed. They have changed to such a degree that the moral effects of a Christian civilization no longer exist where the basic theories of the Christian civilization are gone.

The content of this society will so develop as to destroy itself. It already contains the inner dialectic necessary to this end in philosophic naturalism. In proportion as our civilization repudiates the groundwork of Christian theism and revelation and the resultant law of God, it will experience the operation of a moral universe in the disintegration of that culture. It is this basic fact which fundamentalism has failed to grasp, namely the connection of our faith with the cultural question. It is often thought that our preaching has nothing to do with the social condition in the world. Fundamentalism has often shown a total disregard of questions of war, of lawlessness, of crime, of immortality, social theory, affirming that the purpose of the gospel in this age was merely to call people out for an other worldly existence. Fundamentalism is right in the fact that Christianity primarily is to prepare us for another world, but it by no means therefore implies that we are not to be concerned with this world. Christianity must develop afresh a new social theory and that social theory must be able to face the attacks of naturalism on a philosophic basis and the evils of a secularistic society on a social basis. . . .

The time is short, shorter than you think, shorter than most of us think. My impression as I went throughout Europe was that the holocast [sic] which will destroy western civilization may begin at any moment. We are now living in the economic and political stage of World War III. The Russian challenge is imminent and great. General Keyes declared that Vienna is an island in a Red Sea. Ambassador Caffrey declared that it is the Marshall Plan or the iron curtain for Europe. An Austrian minister of state declared that if war comes there will not be any uniform in Europe but a Russian within ten days. Secretary of War Royall declared that we cannot defend Europe. This means that when Russia pleases she will be on the Atlantic as she is to all intents and purposes now. The international situation is desperate. No political leader is optimistic. The atomic war may begin in the near future.

World conditions therefore reflect the challenge to the Christian. We may do a tremendous work for Europe by taking exchange students and training them to go back to be leaders among their own people. We have a period of respite which must be seized for world evangelism and to do that we must have prepared ministers. We are not to despair, but to hope. . . .

2. FULTON J. SHEEN, *PEACE OF SOUL* (1949)

Postwar America quickly moved from celebration to anxiety as war tribunals in Europe revealed the depth of human hate and its expression in the treatment of others, followed by communist advances across Eastern Europe and then Asia. While Americans had through hard work and sacrifices helped to win the war, they seemed powerless to win the peace. Bishop Fulton J. Sheen's Peace of Soul *dealt with mounting fears on the eve of the Cold War and, interestingly, reads like a jeremiad.*

Sheen, also a popular radio preacher (and soon-to-be television star) calls upon people to be more concerned about their relationship with God than with each other. He suggests that modern anxieties are misplaced. "Peace of soul," he writes, "comes to those who have the right kind of anxiety about attaining perfect happiness, which is God." He reminds his readers that individuals in "previous and more normal ages" used to be concerned about their souls, but are now more concerned with such earthly worries as security, health, social prestige, and sex, to name a few. He cites the Sermon on the Mount and calls it "a warning against the wrong kind of anxieties." And the alternative to those, according to Sheen, "consists in letting oneself go . . . by an act of proper abandonment, in which the body is disciplined and made subject to the spirit and the whole personality is directed to God." Presumably, if people are more anxious about what is their real business, i.e., the state of their souls, they will attain personal peace, even in an age of mounting anxieties.

One of the favorite psychological descriptions of modern man is to say that he has an anxiety complex. Psychology is more right than it suspects, but for a more profound reason than it knows. There is no doubt that anxiety has been increased and complicated by our metropolitan and industrialized civilization. An increasing number of persons are afflicted with neuroses, complexes, fears, irritabilities, and ulcers; they are, perhaps, not so much "run down" as "wound up"; not so much set on fire by the sparks of daily life as they are burning up from internal combustion. . . .

But modern anxiety is different from the anxiety of previous and more normal ages in two ways. In other days men were anxious about their souls, but modern anxiety is principally concerned with the body; the major worries of today are economic security, health, the complexion, wealth, social prestige, and sex. To read modern advertisements, one would think that the greatest calamity that could befall a human being would be to have dishpan hands or a cough in the T-zone. This overemphasis on corporal security is not healthy; it has begotten a generation that is much more concerned about having life belts to wear on the sea journey than about the cabin it will occupy and enjoy. The second characteristic of modern anxiety is that it is not a fear of objective, natural dangers, such as lightning, beasts, famine; it is subjective, a vague fear of what one believes would be dangerous if it happened. That is why it is so difficult to deal with people who have today's types of anxieties; it does no good to tell them that there is no outside danger, because the danger that they fear is inside of them and therefore is abnormally real to them. Their condition is aggravated by a sense of helplessness to do anything about the danger. They constantly sense a disproportion between their own forces and those marshaled by what they believe to be the enemy. These people become like fish caught in nets and birds trapped in a snare, increasing their own entanglements and anxieties by the fierceness of their disorderly exertions to overcome them.

Modern psychologists have done an admirable service in studying anxieties, revealing a phase of human nature which has been to some extent closed to us. But the cause of anxiety is deeper than the psychological. Anxiety may take on new forms in our disordered civilization, but anxiety itself has always been rooted in the nature of man. There has never been an age, there has never been a human being in the history of the world without an anxiety complex; in other times, it was studied on *all* the levels of life. The Old Testament, for example, has one book which is concerned solely with the problem of anxiety—the Book of Job. The Sermon on the Mount is a warning against the wrong kind of anxieties. St. Augustine's writings center around what he called the restless soul. Pascal wrote about human misery. A modern philosopher, Kierkegaard, bases his philosophy on dread, or *Angst*, and Heidegger has told us *Dasein ist Sorge*, "Self-existence is worry."

It is important to inquire into the basic reason and ground of anxiety, according to man's present historical condition, of which the psychological is only one superficial manifestation. The philosophy of anxiety looks to the fact that man is a fallen being composed of body and soul. Standing midway between the animal and the angel, living in a finite world and aspiring toward the infinite, moving in time and seeking the eternal, he is pulled at one moment toward the pleasures of the body and at another moment to the joys of the spirit. He is in a constant state of suspension between matter and spirit and may be likened to a mountain climber who aspires to the great peak above and yet, looking back from his present position, fears falling to the abyss below. This state of indeterminacy and tension between what he ought to be and what he actually is, this pull between his capacity for enjoyment and its tawdry realization, this consciousness of distance between his yearning for abiding love without satiety and his particular loves with their intermittent sense of "fed-up-ness," this wavering between sacrificing lesser values to attain higher ideals or else abdicating the higher ideals entirely, this pull of the old Adam and the beautiful attraction of the new Adam, this necessity of choice which offers him two roads, one leading to God and the other away from Him—all this makes man anxious about his destiny beyond the stars and fearful of his fall to the depths beneath.

In every human being, there is a double law of gravitation, one pulling him to the earth, where he has his time of trial, and the other pulling him to God, where he has his happiness. The anxiety underlying all modern man's anxieties arises from his trying to be himself without God or from his trying to get beyond himself without God. The example of the mountain climber is not exact, for such a man has no helper on the upper peak to which he aspires. Man, however, has a helper—God on the upper peak of eternity reaches out His Omnipotent Hand to lift him up, even before man raises his voice in plea. It is evident that, even though we escaped all the anxieties of modern economic life, even though we avoided all the tensions which psychology finds in the unconsciousness and consciousness, we should still have that great basic fundamental anxiety born of our creature-liness. Anxiety stems fundamentally from irregulated desires, from the creature wanting something that is unnecessary for him or contrary to his nature or positively harmful to his soul. Anxiety increases in direct ratio and proportion as man departs from God. Every man in the world has an anxiety complex because he has the capacity to be either saint or sinner.

Let it be not believed that man has an anxiety complex "because he still has traces of his animal origin"; indeed, animals left to themselves never have anxieties. They have natural fears, which are good, but they have no subjective anxieties. Birds do not develop a psychosis about whether they should take a winter trip to California or Florida. An animal never becomes less than it is; but a man can do just that, because a man is a composite of both spirit and matter. . . .

Dread arises because man becomes aware, however dimly, of his contingency and finiteness. He is not the absolute, though he wants it; he is not even all that he is or all that he could be. This tension between possibility and fact, this oscillation between wanting to be with God and wanting to be God is a deeper side of his anxiety. Alfred Adler has always emphasized that back of neuroses is the striving of man to become like God, a striving as impotent as the goal is impossible. The root of every psychological tension is basically metaphysical.

Despair and anxiety are possible because there is a rational soul. They presuppose the capacity of self-reflection. Only a being capable of contemplating itself can dread annihilation in face of the infinite, can despair either of itself or of its destiny. Despair, Kierkegaard tells us, is twofold. It is a desperate desire either to be oneself or to be not oneself; man wants either to make himself into an absolute, unconditioned being, independent, self-subsistent; or else he wants desperately to get rid of his being, with its limitation, its contingency, and its finiteness. Both these attitudes manifest the eternal revolt of the finite against the infinite: *Non serviam*. By such a revolt, man exposes himself to the awareness of his nothingness and his solitude. Instead of finding a support in the knowledge that he, though contingent, is held in existence by a loving God, he now seeks reliance within himself and, necessarily failing to find it, becomes the victim of dread. For dread is related to an unknown, overwhelming, all-powerful something—which may strike one knows not when or where. Dread is everywhere and nowhere, all around us, terrible and indefinite, threatening man with an annihilation which he cannot imagine or even conceive. Such fear is man's alone. Because an animal has no soul capable of knowing perfect love, because it has to render no account of its stewardship beyond the corridors of the grave, because it is not like a pendulum swinging between eternity and time, it is devoid of those eternal relationships which man possesses; therefore it can have only a sick body, never a sick soul. Thus a psychology which denies the human soul is constantly contradicting itself. It calls man an animal and then proceeds to describe a human anxiety which is never found in any animal devoid of a rational soul.

Since the basic cause of man's anxiety is the possibility of being either a saint or a sinner, it follows that there are only two alternatives for him. Man can either mount upward to the peak of eternity or else slip backward to the chasms of despair and frustration. Yet there are many who think there is yet another alternative, namely, that of indifference. They think that, just as bears hibernate for a season in a state of suspended animation, so they, too, can sleep through life without choosing to live for God or against Him. But hibernation is no escape; winter ends, and one is then forced to make a decision—indeed, the very choice of indifference itself is a decision. White fences do not remain white fences by having nothing done to them; they soon become black fences. Since there is a tendency in us that pulls us back to the animal, the mere fact that we do not resist it operates to our own destruction. Just as life is the sum of the forces that resist death, so, too, man's will must be the sum of the forces that resist frustration. A man who has taken poison into his system can ignore the antidote, or he can throw it out of the window; it makes no difference which he does, for death is already on the march. St. Paul warns us, "How shall we escape if we neglect . . . " (Heb. 2:3). By the mere fact that we do not go forward, we go backward. There are no plains in the spiritual life; we are either going uphill or coming down. Furthermore the pose of indifference is only intellectual. The will *must* choose. And even though an "indifferent" soul does not positively reject the infinite, the infinite rejects it. The talents that are unused are taken away, and the Scriptures tell us that, "But because thou art lukewarm, and neither cold nor hot, I will begin to vomit thee out of my mouth" (Apoc. 3:16).

Returning to the supreme alternatives, man can choose between an earthly love to the exclusion of Divine Love, or he can choose a Divine Love which includes a healthy, sacramental, earthly love. Either he can make the soul subject to the body, or he can make the body subject to the soul. Consider first those who resolve their anxiety in favor of Godlessness. They invariably end by substituting one of the false gods for the true God of Love.

This god can be the ego, or self. This happens in atheism when there is a denial of dependence on the true God, or when there is an affirmation of one's own wish and pleasure as the absolute law, or when freedom is interpreted as the right to do what one pleases. When such a false god is adored, religion is rejected as a rationalization or an escape, or even as a fear to affirm one's own self as supreme.

Atheists commit the sin of *pride*, by which a man pretends to be that which he is not, namely, a god. Pride is inordinate self-love, an exaltation of the conditional and relative self into an absolute. It tries to gratify the thirst for the infinite by giving to one's own finitude a pretension to divinity. In some, pride blinds the self to its weakness and becomes "hot" pride; in others, it recognizes its own weakness and overcomes it by a self-exaltation which becomes "cold" pride. Pride kills docility and makes a man incapable of ever being helped by God. The limited knowledge of the puny mind pretends to be final and absolute. In the face of other intellects it resorts to two techniques, either the technique of omniscience, by which it seeks to convince others how much it knows, or the technique of nescience, which tries to convince others how little they know. When such pride is unconscious, it becomes almost incurable, for it identifies truth with *its* truth. Pride is an admission of weakness; it secretly fears all competition and dreads all rivals. It is rarely cured when the person himself is vertical—*i.e.*, healthy and prosperous—but it can be cured when the patient is horizontal—sick and disillusioned. That is why catastrophes are necessary in an era of pride to bring men back again to God and the salvation of their souls.

The false god of the atheist can be *another* person, cherished, not as a bearer of human values, but as an object to be devoured and used for one's own pleasure. In such a case, the vocabulary of religion is invoked to solicit the object, such as "adore," "angel," "worship," "god," and "goddess." From it is born the sin of *lust*, or the adoration of another person's vitality as the end and goal of life. Lust is not the inevitable result of the flesh, any more than a cataract is directly caused by eyesight; it is due, rather, to the rebellion of the flesh against the spirit and of the person against God. . . .

Flesh in revolt (or lust) is related to pride. The conquest of the one desired may serve the individual's need of excessive self-exaltation; but consummated lust leads to despair (or the opposite of self-exaltation) by the inner tension or sadness resulting from an uneasy conscience. It is this effect which divorces it from a purely biological phenomenon, for in no creature except man is there any act which involves such an interactivity of matter and spirit, body and soul. It need hardly be noted that lust is not sex in the ordinary sense of the term but, rather, its deorientation—a sign that man has become ex-centric, isolated from God, and enamored of the physically good to such an excess that he is like the serpent which devours its own tail and eventually destroys itself.

The unbeliever's god can be things by which he seeks to remedy his own sense of nothingness. Some men seek this compensation in wealth, which gives them the false sense of power. External luxury is pursued to conceal the nakedness of their own souls. Such worship of wealth leads to tyranny and injustice toward others, and thus is born the sin of *avarice.*

Avarice is the material expression of one's own insufficiency and a challenge to the sublime truth that "our sufficiency is from God." Filling up its own lack at the storehouse of the earthly, the soul hopes to find at least a temporary escape from Divinity itself. All intense interest in luxury is a mark of inner poverty. The less grace there is in the soul, the more ornament must be on the body. It was only after Adam and Eve fell that they perceived themselves to be naked; when their souls were rich with original justice, their bodies were so suffused with its reflection that they felt no need for clothes. But once the Divine-internal was lost, they sought a compensation in the material, the external. Excessive dedication to temporal security is one of the ways a society's loss of eternal security manifests itself. The quest for wealth and luxury can be infinite, and for the moment it satisfies the godless souls. A man can reach a point of marginal utility in the accumulation of ice-cream cones, but not in the accumulation of credits, for there is an infinity to these ambitions. Thus does man seek to become God in gratifying limitless desires for riches, when he impoverishes himself from within. "Life wants to secure itself against the void that is raging within. The risk of eternal void is to be met by the premium of temporal insurance . . . social security, old age pensions, etc. It springs no less from metaphysical despair than from material misery."

Pride, lust, avarice; the devil, the flesh and the world; the pride of life, the concupiscence of the flesh, and the concupiscence of the eyes—these constitute the new unholy trinity by which man is wooed away from the Holy Trinity and from the discovery of the goal of life. It was these three things Our Lord described in the parable of those who offered excuses for not coming to the banquet; one refused because he had bought a farm, another because he had purchased a yoke of oxen, and the third because he had taken unto himself a woman. Love of self, love of person, and love of property are not in themselves wrong, but they do become wrong when they are made ends in themselves, are torn up from their true purpose, which is to lead us to God. Because there are some who abuse love of self and love of person and love of property, the Church has encouraged the three vows of obedience, chastity, and poverty to make reparation for those who make gods out of their opinions, their flesh, and their money. Anxiety and frustration invariably follow when the desires of the heart are centered on anything less than God, for all pleasures of earth, pursued as final ends, turn out to be the exact opposite of what was expected. The expectation is joyous, the realization is disgust. Out of this disappointment are born those lesser anxieties which modern psychology knows so well; but the root of them all is the meaninglessness of life due to the abandonment of Perfect Life, Truth, and Love, which is God.

The alternative to such anxieties consists in letting oneself go, not by a surrender of the spirit to the world, the flesh, and the Devil, but by an act of proper abandonment, in which the body is disciplined and made subject to the spirit and the whole personality is directed to God. Here the basic anxiety of life is transcended in three ways, each of which brings a peace of soul that only the God-loving enjoy: (1) by controlling desires; (2) by transferring anxiety from body to soul; (3) by surrender to the Will of God. . . .

Peace of soul comes to those who have the right kind of anxiety about attaining perfect happiness, which is God. A soul has anxiety because its final and eternal state is not yet decided; it is still and always at the crossroads of life. This fundamental anxiety cannot be cured by a surrender to passions and instincts; the basic cause of our anxiety is a restlessness within time which comes because we are made for eternity. If there were anywhere on earth a resting place other than God, we may be very sure that the human soul in its long history would have found it before this. As St. Augustine has said, "Our hearts were made for Thee. They are restless until they rest in Thee, O God."

3. REINHOLD NIEBUHR, "THE INNOCENT NATION IN AN INNOCENT WORLD" (1952)

Mainline Protestantism produced a number of public intellectuals during its heyday—learned individuals who could write for the broad American public and who were paid great respect by national publications at mid-century. Reinhold Niebuhr, his brother H. Richard Niebuhr, and Paul Tillich were among the most admired thinkers in the nation, able to put into larger philosophical and theological contexts many of the issues facing the country and the world. Theirs were often "prophetic voices" that indicated both the heights and the failings of American culture during the early Cold War era. Reinhold Niebuhr, born in 1892 and educated at Yale Divinity School, was a leading advocate of "religious socialism" during the Great Depression and spent much of his life trying to reconcile Marxist and Christian values before developing his idea of "Christian realism." Such books as Moral Man and Immoral Society *and* The Nature and Destiny of Man *brought him great attention—both from an admiring public and from a suspicious government worried about his association with alleged communists.*

In this excerpt from his book The Irony of American History, *published in 1952, Niebuhr provides a neo-orthodox critique of American civil religion and its pride of self. It is an exploration of national political, ideological, and religious struggles, through the lens of American guilt in an "innocent world." Not only a powerful message about American religious culture, this piece also embodies the sort of prophetic voice the Protestant mainline thinkers could muster to critique their own society in an age of particular patriotism.*

⎯⎯⎯⎯⎯ ◌◖◗◌ ⎯⎯⎯⎯⎯

[1]

Practically all schools of modern culture, whatever their differences, are united in their rejection of the Christian doctrine of original sin. This doctrine asserts the obvious fact that all men are persistently inclined to regard themselves more highly and are more assiduously concerned with their own interests than any "objective" view of their importance would warrant. Modern culture in its various forms feels certain that, if men could be sufficiently objective or disinterested to recognize the injustice of excessive self-interest, they could also in time transfer the objectivity of their judgments as observers of the human scene to their judgments as actors and agents in human history. This is an absurd notion which every practical statesman or man of affairs knows how to discount because he encounters ambitions and passions in his daily experience, which refute the regnant modern theory of potentially innocent men and nations. There is consequently a remarkable hiatus between the shrewdness of practical men of affairs and the speculations of our wise men. The latter are frequently convinced that the predicament of our possible involvement in an atomic and global conflict is due primarily to failure of the statesmen to heed the advice of our psychological and social scientists. The statesmen on the other hand have fortunately been able to disregard the admonition of our wise men because they could still draw upon the native shrewdness of the common people who in smaller realms have had something of the same experience with human nature as the statesmen. The statesmen have not been particularly brilliant in finding solutions for our problems, all of which have reached global dimensions. But they have, at least, steered a course which still offers us minimal hope of avoiding a global conflict.

But whether or not we avoid another war, we are covered with prospective guilt. We have dreamed of a purely rational adjustment of interests in human society; and we are involved in "total" wars. We have dreamed of a "scientific" approach to all human problems; and we find that the tensions of a world-wide conflict release individual and collective emotions not easily brought under rational control. We had hoped to make neat and sharp distinctions between justice and injustice; and we discover that even the best human actions involve some guilt.

This vast involvement in guilt in a supposedly innocent world achieves a specially ironic dimension through the fact that the two leading powers engaged in the struggle are particularly innocent according to their own official myth and collective memory. The Russian-Communist pretensions of innocency and the monstrous evils which are generated from them, are the fruit of a variant of the liberal dogma. According to the liberal dogma men are excessively selfish because they lack the intelligence to consider interests other than their own. But this higher intelligence can be supplied, of course, by education. Or they are betrayed into selfishness by unfavorable social and political environment. This can be remedied by the growth of scientifically perfected social institutions.

The communist dogma is more specific. Men are corrupted by a particular social institution: the institution of property. The abolition of this institution guarantees the return of mankind to the state of original innocency which existed before the institution of property arose, a state which Engels describes as one of idyllic harmony with "no soldiers, no gendarmes, no policemen, prefects or judges, no prisons, laws or lawsuits."

The initiators of this return to innocency are the proletarian class. This class is innocent because it has no interests to defend; and it cannot become "master of the productive forces of society except by abolishing their mode of appropriation." The proletarians cannot free themselves from slavery without emancipating the whole of mankind from injustice. Once this act of emancipation has been accomplished every action and event on the other side of the revolution participates in this new freedom from guilt. A revolutionary nation is guiltless because the guilt of "imperialism" has been confined to "capitalistic" nations "by definition." Thus the lust for power which enters into most individual and collective human actions, is obscured. The priest-kings of this new revolutionary state, though they wield inordinate power because they have gathered both economic and political control in the hands of a single oligarchy, are also, in theory, innocent of any evil. Their interests and those of the masses whom they control are, by definition, identical since neither owns property.

Even the vexatious and tyrannical rule of Russia over the smaller communist states is completely obscured and denied by the official theory. Hamilton Fish Armstrong reports Bukharin's interpretation of the relation of communist states to each other as follows: "Bukharin explained at length that national rivalry between Communist states was 'an impossibility by definition.' 'What creates wars,' he said, 'is the competition of monopoly capitalisms for raw materials and markets. Capitalist society is made up of selfish and competing national units and therefore is by definition a world at war. Communist society will be made up of unselfish and harmonious units and therefore will be by definition a world at peace. Just as capitalism cannot live without war, so war cannot live with Communism.'"

It is difficult to conceive of a more implausible theory of human nature and conduct. Yet it is one which achieves a considerable degree of plausibility, once the basic assumptions are accepted. It has been plausible enough, at any rate, to beguile millions of people, many of whom are not under the direct control of the tyranny and are therefore free to consider critical challenges of its adequacy. So powerful has been this illusory restoration of human innocency that, for all we know, the present communist oligarchs, who pursue their ends with such cruelty, may still be believers. The powers of human self-deception are seemingly endless. The communist tyrants may well legitimatize their cruelties not only to the conscience of their devotees but to their own by recourse to an official theory which proves their innocency "by definition."

John Adams in his warnings to Thomas Jefferson would seem to have had a premonition of this kind of politics. At any rate, he understood the human situation well enough to have stated a theory which comprehended what we now see in communism. "Power," he wrote, "always thinks it has a great soul and vast views beyond the comprehension of the weak; and that it is doing God's service when it is violating all His laws. Our passions, ambitions, avarice, love and resentment, etc., possess so much metaphysical subtlety and so much overpowering eloquence that they insinuate themselves into the understanding and the conscience and convert both to their party." Adams's understanding of the power of the self's passions and ambitions to corrupt the self's reason is a simple recognition of the facts of life which refute all theories, whether liberal or Marxist, about the possibility of a completely disinterested self. Adams, as every Christian understanding of man has done, nicely anticipated the Marxist theory of an "ideological taint" in reason when men reason about each other's affairs and arrive at conclusions about each other's virtues, interests and motives. The crowning irony of the Marxist theory of ideology is that it foolishly and self-righteously confined the source of this taint to economic interest and to a particular class.

It was, therefore, incapable of recognizing all the corruptions of ambition and power which would creep inevitably into its paradise of innocency.

In any event we have to deal with a vast religious-political movement which generates more extravagant forms of political injustice and cruelty out of the pretensions of innocency than we have ever known in human history.

The liberal world which opposes this monstrous evil is filled ironically with milder forms of the same pretension. Fortunately they have not result-ed in the same evils, partly because they are not as consistently held; and partly because we have not invested our ostensible "innocents" with inordi-nate power. Though a tremendous amount of illusion about human nature expresses itself in American culture, our political institutions contain many of the safeguards against the selfish abuse of power which our Calvinist fa-thers insisted upon. According to the accepted theory, our democracy owes everything to the believers in the innocency and perfectibility of man and lit-tle to the reservations about human nature which emanated from the Chris-tianity of New England. But fortunately there are quite a few accents in our constitution which spell out the warning of John Cotton: "Let all the world give mortall man no greater power than they are content they shall use, for use it they will. . . . And they that have the liberty to speak great things you will find that they will speak great blasphemies."

[2]

But these reservations of Christian realism in our culture cannot obscure the fact that, next to the Russian pretensions, we are (according to our tra-ditional theory) the most innocent nation on earth. The irony of our situa-tion lies in the fact that we could not be virtuous (in the sense of practicing the virtues which are implicit in meeting our vast world responsibilities) if we were really as innocent as we pretend to be. It is particularly remarkable that the two great religious-moral traditions which informed our early life—New England Calvinism and Virginian Deism and Jeffersonianism—arrive at remarkably similar conclusions about the meaning of our national char-acter and destiny. Calvinism may have held too pessimistic views of human nature, and too mechanical views of the providential ordering of human life. But when it assessed the significance of the American experiment both its conceptions of American destiny and its appreciation of American virtue fi-nally arrived at conclusions strikingly similar to those of Deism. Whether our nation interprets its spiritual heritage through Massachusetts or Vir-ginia, we came into existence with the sense of being a "separated" nation, which God was using to make a new beginning for mankind. We had re-nounced the evils of European feudalism. We had escaped from the evils of

European religious bigotry. We had found broad spaces for the satisfaction of human desires in place of the crowded Europe. Whether, as in the case of the New England theocrats, our forefathers thought of our "experiment" as primarily the creation of a new and purer church, or, as in the case of Jefferson and his coterie, they thought primarily of a new political community, they believed in either case that we had been called out by God to create a new humanity. We were God's "American Israel." Our pretensions of innocency therefore heightened the whole concept of a virtuous humanity which characterizes the culture of our era; and involve us in the ironic incongruity between our illusions and the realities which we experience. We find it almost as difficult as the communists to believe that anyone could think ill of us, since we are as persuaded as they that our society is so essentially virtuous that only malice could prompt criticism of any of our actions.

The New England conception of our virtue began as the belief that the church which had been established on our soil was purer than any church of Christendom. In Edward Johnson's *Wonder Working Providence of Zion's Saviour* (1650) the belief is expressed that "Jesus Christ had manifested his kingly office toward his churches more fully than ever yet the sons of men saw." Practically every Puritan tract contained the conviction that the Protestant Reformation reached its final culmination here. While the emphasis lay primarily upon the new purity of the church, even the Puritans envisaged a new and perfect society. Johnson further spoke of New England as the place "where the Lord would create a new heaven and a new earth, new churches and a new commonwealth together." And a century later President Stiles of Yale preached a sermon on "The United States elevated to glory and honor" in which he defined the nation as "God's American Israel."

Jefferson's conception of the innocency and virtue of the new nation was not informed by the Biblical symbolism of the New England tracts. His religious faith was a form of Christianity which had passed through the rationalism of the French Enlightenment. His sense of providence was expressed in his belief in the power of "nature's God" over the vicissitudes of history. In any event, nature's God had a very special purpose in founding this new community. The purpose was to make a new beginning in a corrupt world. Two facts about America impressed the Jeffersonians. The one was that we had broken with tyranny. The other was that the wide economic opportunities of the new continent would prevent the emergence of those social vices which characterized the social life of an overcrowded Continent of Europe.

Jefferson was convinced that the American mind had achieved a freedom from the prejudice which corrupted the European minds, which could not be equaled in Europe in centuries. "If all the sovereigns of Europe," he declared, "were to set themselves to work to emancipate the minds of their subjects from their present ignorance and prejudice and that as zealously as they now attempt the contrary a thousand years would not place them on that high ground on which our common people are now setting out." . . .

In common with the Enlightenment Jefferson sometimes ascribed our superior virtue to our rational freedom from traditional prejudices and sometimes to the favorable social circumstances of the American Continent. "Before the establishment of the American States," he declared, "nothing was known to history but the man of the old world crowded within limits either small or overcharged and steeped in vices which the situation generates. A government adapted to such men would be one thing, but a different one for the man of these States. Here every man may have land to labor for himself; or preferring the exercise of any other industry, may exact for it such compensation as not only to afford a comfortable subsistence but wherewith to provide a cessation from labor in old age." . . .

Every nation has its own form of spiritual pride. These examples of American self-appreciation could be matched by similar sentiments in other nations. But every nation also has its peculiar version. Our version is that our nation turned its back upon the vices of Europe and made a new beginning.

The Jeffersonian conception of virtue, had it not overstated the innocency of American social life, would have been a tolerable prophecy of some aspects of our social history which have distinguished us from Europe. For it can hardly be denied that the fluidity of our class structure, derived from the opulence of economic opportunities, saved us from the acrimony of the class struggle in Europe, and avoided the class rebellion, which Marx could prompt in Europe but not in America. When the frontier ceased to provide for the expansion of opportunities, our superior technology created ever new frontiers for the ambitious and adventurous. In one sense the opulence of American life has served to perpetuate Jeffersonian illusions about human nature. For we have thus far sought to solve all our problems by the expansion of our economy. This expansion cannot go on forever and ultimately we must face some vexatious issues of social justice in terms which will not differ too greatly from those which the wisest nations of Europe have been forced to use.

The idea that men would not come in conflict with one another, if the opportunities were wide enough, was partly based upon the assumption that all human desires are determinate and all human ambitions ordinate. This assumption was shared by our Jeffersonians with the French Enlightenment. "Every man," declared Tom Paine, "wishes to pursue his occupation and enjoy the fruits of his labors and the produce of his property in peace and safety and with the least possible expense. When these things are accomplished all objects for which governments ought to be established are accomplished." The same idea underlies the Marxist conception of the difference between an "economy of scarcity" and an "economy of abundance." In an economy of abundance there is presumably no cause for rivalry. Neither Jeffersonians nor Marxists had any understanding for the perennial conflicts of power and pride which may arise on every level of "abundance" since human desires grow with the means of their gratification.

One single note of realism runs through Jefferson's idyllic picture of American innocency. That consists in his preference for an agricultural over an urban society. Jefferson was confident of the future virtue of America only in so far as it would continue as an agricultural nation. Fearing the social tensions and the subordination of man to man in a highly organized social structure, his ideal community consisted of independent freeholders, each tilling his own plot of ground and enjoying the fruits of his own labor. "Dependence begets subservience," he wrote in extolling the life of the farmer. "It suffocates the germ of virtue and prepares fit tools for the design of ambition."

There is a special irony in the contrast between the course of American history toward the development of large-scale industry and Jefferson's belief that democracy was secure only in an agrarian economy. America has become what Jefferson most feared; but the moral consequences have not been as catastrophic as he anticipated. While democracy is tainted by more corruption in our great metropolitan areas than in the remainder of our political life, we have managed to achieve a tolerable justice in the collective relations of industry by balancing power against power and equilibrating the various competing social forces of society. The rise of the labor movement has been particularly important in achieving this result; for its organization of the power of the workers was necessary to produce the counter-weight to the great concentrations of economic power which justice requires. We have engaged in precisely those collective actions for the sake of justice which Jefferson regarded as wholly incompatible with justice.

The ironic contrast between Jeffersonian hopes and fears for America and the actual realities is increased by the exchange of ideological weapons between the early and the later Jeffersonians. The early Jeffersonians sought to keep political power weak, discouraging both the growth of federal power in relation to the States and confining political control over economic life to the States. They feared that such power would be compounded with the economic power of the privileged and used against the less favored. Subsequently the wielders of great economic power adopted the Jeffersonian maxim that the best possible government is the least possible government. The American democracy, as every other healthy democracy, had learned to use

the more equal distribution of political power, inherent in universal suffrage, as leverage against the tendency toward concentration of power in
economic life. Culminating in the "New Deal," national governments, based
upon an alliance of farmers, workers and middle classes, have used the
power of the state to establish minimal standards of "welfare" in housing,
social security, health services, etc. Naturally, the higher income groups ben-
efited less from these minimal standards of justice, and paid a proportion-
ately higher cost for them than the proponents of the measures of a "welfare state." The former, therefore, used the ideology of Jeffersonianism to
counter these tendencies; while the classes in society which had Jefferson's
original interest in equality discarded his ideology because they were less
certain than he that complete freedom in economic relations would inevitably make for equality.

In this development the less privileged classes developed a realistic appreciation of the factor of power in social life, while the privileged classes
tried to preserve the illusion of classical liberalism that power is not an important element in man's social life. They recognize the force of interest; but
they continue to assume that the competition of interests will make for justice without political or moral regulation. This would be possible only if the
various powers which support interest were fairly equally divided, which
they never are.

Since America developed as a bourgeois society, with only remnants of
the older feudal culture to inform its ethos, it naturally inclined toward the
bourgeois ideology which neglects the factor of power in the human community and equates interest with rationality.

Such a society regards all social relations as essentially innocent because
it believes self-interest to be inherently harmless. It is, in common with
Marxism, blind to the lust for power in the motives of men; but also to the
injustices which flow from the disbalances of power in the community. Both
the bourgeois ideology and Marxism equate self-interest with the economic
motive. The bourgeois world either regards economic desire as inherently
ordinate or it hopes to hold it in check either by prudence (as in the thought
of the utilitarians) or by the pressure of the self-interest of others (as in classical liberalism). Marxism, on the other hand, believes that the disbalance of
power in industrial society, plus the inordinate character of the economic
motive, must drive a bourgeois society to greater and greater injustice and
more and more overt social conflict.

Thus the conflict between communism and the bourgeois world achieves
a special virulence between the two great hegemonous nations of the respective alliances, because America is, in the eyes of communism, an exemplar of the worst form of capitalistic injustice, while it is, in its own eyes,

a symbol of pure innocence and justice. This ironic situation is heightened by the fact that every free nation in alliance with us is more disposed to bring economic life under political control than our traditional theory allows. There is therefore considerable moral misunderstanding between ourselves and our allies. This represents a milder version of the contradiction between ourselves and our foes. The classes in our society, who pretend that only political power is dangerous, frequently suggest that our allies are tainted with the same corruption as that of our foes. European nations, on the other hand, frequently judge us according to our traditional theory. They fail to recognize that our actual achievements in social justice have been won by a pragmatic approach to the problems of power, which has not been less efficacious for its lack of consistent speculation upon the problems of power and justice. Our achievements in this field represent the triumph of common sense over the theories of both our business oligarchy and the speculations of those social scientists who are still striving for a "scientific" and disinterested justice. We are, in short, more virtuous than our detractors, whether foes or allies, admit, because we know ourselves to be less innocent than our theories assume. The force and danger of self-interest in human affairs are too obvious to remain long obscure to those who are not too blinded by either theory or interest to see the obvious. The relation of power to interest on the one hand, and to justice on the other, is equally obvious. In our domestic affairs we have thus builded better than we knew because we have not taken the early dreams of our peculiar innocency too seriously.

4. "LETTER TO THE PRESBYTERIANS FROM THE GENERAL ASSEMBLY" (1953)

While most Americans feared the mounting threat of communism worldwide, many began to question the efficacy of tearing apart the fabric of American life in order to discover the identity of those with communist leanings. That sentiment grew more widespread when hundreds of public figures, many of them quite popular, were dragged before the House Un-American Activities Committee (HUAC) in the early 1950s. The Presbyterian Church was among the first religious organizations to respond to the "communist witch hunt." Written in 1953, "A Letter to the Presbyterians from the General Assembly of the Presbyterian Church" is concerned with how the church and its members should respond to McCarthyism and the general hysteria precipitated by the notion that communism represented an imminent threat to American society and culture.

The document does not downplay the aspects of communism believed by most Americans to be menacing, but it does call for a reasoned and rational response to the events of the day. It calls into question the activities of Congress and points specifically to the infringement on basic human rights taking place in congressional inquiries. Indeed, it uses much stronger language to describe this infringement, calling it both an "assault" and an "attack" and proclaiming it "utterly alien" not only to America's democratic tradition but to the Protestant religious tradition as well. Most notably, perhaps, it exhorts Presbyterians to make a distinction between hating the system of communism and hating communist-ruled peoples.

∞∞∞

Dear Fellow Presbyterians:

. . . Things are happening in our national life and in the international sphere which should give us deep concern. Serious thought needs to be given to the menace of Communism in the world of today and to the undoubted aim on the part of its leaders to subvert the thought and life of the United States. Everlasting vigilance is also needed, and appropriate precautions should be constantly taken, to forestall the insidious intervention of a foreign power in the internal affairs of our country. In this connection Congressional committees, which are an important expression of democracy in action, have rendered some valuable services to the nation.

At the same time the citizens of this country, and those in particular who are Protestant Christians, have reason to take a grave view of the situation which is being created by the almost exclusive concentration of the American mind upon the problem of the threat of Communism.

Under the plea that the structure of American society is in imminent peril of being shattered by a satanic conspiracy, dangerous developments are taking place in our national life. Favored by an atmosphere of intense disquiet and suspicion, a subtle but potent assault upon basic human rights is now in progress. Some Congressional inquiries have revealed a distinct tendency to become inquisitions. These inquisitions, which find their historic pattern in medieval Spain and in the tribunals of modern totalitarian states, begin to constitute a threat to freedom of thought in this country. Treason and dissent are being confused. The shrine of conscience and private judgment, which God alone has a right to enter, is being invaded. Un-American attitudes toward ideas and books are becoming current. Attacks are being made upon citizens of integrity and social passion which are utterly alien to our democratic tradition. They are particularly alien to the Protestant religious tradition which has been a main source of the freedoms which the people of the United States enjoy.

There is something still more serious. A great many people, within and without our government, approach the problem of Communism in a purely negative way. Communism, which is at bottom a secular religious faith of great vitality, is thus being dealt with as an exclusively police problem. As a result of this there is growing up over against Communism a fanatical negativism. Totally devoid of a constructive program of action, this negativism is in danger of leading the American mind into a spiritual vacuum. Our national house, cleansed of one demon, would invite by its very emptiness, the entrance of seven others. In the case of a national crisis this emptiness could, in the high sounding name of security, be occupied with ease by a Fascist tyranny.

We suggest, therefore, that all Presbyterians give earnest consideration to the following three basic principles and their implications for our thought and life.

I. *The Christian Church has a prophetic function to fulfill in every society and in every age.*

Whatever concerns man and his welfare is a concern of the Church and its ministers. Religion has to do with life in its wholeness. While being patriotically loyal to the country within whose bounds it lives and works, the Church does not derive its authority from the nation but from Jesus Christ. Its supreme and ultimate allegiance is to Christ, its sole Head, and to His Kingdom, and not to any nation or race, to any class or culture. It is, therefore, under obligation to consider the life of man in the light of God's purpose in Christ for the world. While it is not the role of the Christian church to present blueprints for the organization of society and the conduct of government, the Church owes it to its own members and to men in general, to draw attention to violations of those spiritual bases of human relationship which have been established by God. It has the obligation also to proclaim those principles, and to instill that spirit, which are essential for social health, and which form the indispensable foundation of sound and stable policies in the affairs of state.

II. *The majesty of truth must be preserved at all times and at all costs.*

Loyalty to truth is the common basis of true religion and true culture. Despite the lofty idealism of many of our national leaders, truth is being subtly and silently dethroned by prominent public figures from the position it has occupied hitherto in our American tradition. The state of strife known as "cold war," in which our own and other nations, as well as groups within nations, are now engaged, is producing startling phenomena and sinister personalities. In this form of warfare, falsehood is frequently preferred to fact if it can be shown to have greater propaganda value. In the interests of propaganda, truth is deliberately distorted or remains unspoken. The demagogue, who lives by propaganda, is coming into his own on a national scale. According to the new philosophy, if what is true "gives aid and comfort" to our enemies, it must be suppressed. Truth is thus a captive in the land of the free. At the same time, and for the same reason, great words like "love," "peace," "justice," and "mercy," and the ideas which underlie them, are becoming suspect.

Communism, as we know to our sorrow, is committed on principle to a philosophy of lying; democracy, in fighting Communism, is in danger of succumbing, through fear and in the name of expediency, to the self-same philosophy. It is being assumed, in effect, that, in view of the magnitude of the issues at stake, the end justifies the means. Whatever the outcome of such a war, the moral consequences will be terrifying. People will become accustomed to going through life with no regard for rules or sanctities.

A painful illustration of this development is that men and women should be publicly condemned upon the uncorroborated word of former Communists. Many of these witnesses have done no more, as we know, than transfer their allegiance from one authoritarian system to another. Nothing is easier for people, as contemporary history has shown, than to make the transition from one totalitarianism to another, carrying their basic attitudes along with them. As a matter of fact, the lands that have suffered most from Communism, or that are most menaced by it today, Russia and Italy, for example, are lands which have been traditionally authoritarian in their political or their religious life. And yet the ex-Communists to whose word Congressional committees apparently give unqualified credence are in very many instances people whose basic philosophy authorizes them now, as in the past, to believe that a lie in a good cause is thoroughly justified.

III. *God's sovereign rule is the controlling factor in history.*

We speak of "This nation under God." Nothing is more needed today than to explore afresh and to apply to all the problems of thought and life in our generation, what it means to take God seriously in national life. There is an order of God. Even in these days of flux and nihilism, of relativism and expediency, God reigns. The American-born poet, T. S. Eliot, has written these prophetic words:

Those who put their faith in worldly order
Not controlled by the order of God,
In confident ignorance, but arrest disorder,
Make it fast, breed fatal disease,
Degrade what they exalt.

Any attempt to impose upon society, or the course of history, a purely manmade order, however lofty the aims, can have no more than temporary success. Social disorder and false political philosophies cannot be adequately met by police measures, but only by a sincere attempt to organize society in accordance with the everlasting principles of God's moral government of the world. It is, therefore, of paramount importance that individuals, groups and nations should adjust themselves to the order of God. God's character and God's way with man provide the pattern for man's way with his fellow man.

That we have the obligation to make our nation as secure as possible, no one can dispute. But there is no absolute security in human affairs, nor is security the ultimate human obligation. A still greater obligation, as well as a more strategic procedure, is to make sure that what we mean by security, and the methods we employ to achieve it, are in accordance with the will of God. Otherwise, any human attempt to establish a form of world order which does no more than exalt the interest of a class, a culture, a race, or a nation, above God and the interests of the whole human family, is foredoomed to disaster. Ideas are on the march, forces are abroad, whose time has come. They cannot be repressed and they will bring unjust orders to an end. In the world of today all forms of feudalism, for example, are foredoomed. So too are all types of imperialism. The real question is how to solve the problems presented by these two forms of outmoded society in such a way that the transition to a better order will be gradual and constructive.

Let us frankly recognize that many of the revolutionary forces of our time are in great part the judgment of God upon human selfishness and complacency, and upon man's forgetfulness of man. That does not make these forces right; it does, however, compel us to consider how their driving power can be channeled into forms of creative thought and work. History, moreover, makes it abundantly clear that wherever a religion, a political system or a social order, does not interest itself in the common people, violent revolt eventually takes place.

On the other hand, just because God rules in the affairs of men, Communism as a solution of the human problem is foredoomed to failure. No political order can prevail which deliberately leaves God out of account. Despite its pretension to be striving after "liberation," Communism enslaves in the name of freedom. It does not know that evil cannot be eradicated from human life by simply changing a social structure. Man, moreover, has deep spiritual longings which Communism cannot satisfy. The communistic order will eventually be shattered upon the bedrock of human nature, that is, upon the basic sins, and the abysmal needs, of man and society. For that reason Communism has an approaching rendezvous with God and the moral order.

Nevertheless, Communists, Communist nations and Communist-ruled peoples, should be our concern. In hating a system let us not allow ourselves to hate individuals or whole nations. History and experience teach us that persons and peoples do change. Let us ever be on the lookout for the evidence of change in the Communist world, for the effects of disillusionment, and for the presence of a God-implanted hunger. Such disillusionment and hunger can be met only by a sympathetic approach and a disposition to listen and confer.

There is clear evidence that a post-Communist mood is actually being created in many parts of Europe and Asia. Let us seek to deepen that mood. Let us explore afresh the meaning of mercy and forgiveness and recognize that both can have social and political significance when they are sincerely and opportunely applied.

Let us always be ready to meet around a conference table with the rulers of Communist countries. There should be, therefore, no reluctance to employ the conference method to the full in the settling of disputes with our country's enemies. Let us beware of the cynical attitude which prevails in certain official circles to regard as a forlorn hope any negotiated solution of the major issues which divide mankind.

In human conflicts there can be no substitute for negotiation. Direct personal conference has been God's way with man from the beginning. "Come, now, and let us reason together," was the word of God to Israel through the Prophet Isaiah. We must take the risk, and even the initiative, of seeking face-to-face encounter with our enemies. We should meet them officially, whatever their ignominious record, and regardless of the suffering they may have caused us. We too have reasons for penitence and stand in need of forgiveness. In any case, talk, unhurried talk, talk which does not rule out in advance the possibility of success, talk which takes place in private, and not before reporters or microphones or television, is the only kind of approach which can lead to sanity and fruitful understanding. Let the process of conference be private, but let its conclusions, its complete conclusions, be made public.

In this connection such an organization as the United Nations is in harmony with the principles of God's moral government. American Presbyterians should remember with pride that it is the successor of a former organization which was the creation of a great American who was also a great Presbyterian. While the United Nations organization is very far from perfection and it functions today under great handicaps, it is yet the natural and best available agent for international cooperation and the settlement of disputes among nations. It is imperative, therefore, that it be given the utmost support. It stands between us and war.

While we take all wise precautions for defense, both within and outside our borders, the present situation demands spiritual calm, historical perspective, religious faith, and an adventurous spirit. Loyalty to great principles of truth and justice has made our nation great; such loyalty alone can keep it great and ensure its destiny.

May God give us the wisdom and courage to think and act in accordance with His Will.

With fraternal greetings,
THE GENERAL COUNCIL OF THE PRESBYTERIAN CHURCH IN THE U.S.A.
October 21, 1953

5. DOROTHY DAY, "OUR BROTHERS, THE COMMUNISTS" (1949, 1953)

This document is remarkable in that it was written by a woman and self-professed ex-communist in the heyday of McCarthyism. It is simply astounding that she could say, in reference to her time as a member of the Communist Party, "I loved the people I worked with and learned much from them. They helped me to find God in His poor, in His abandoned ones, as I had not found Him in Christian churches," and escape congressional questioning.

Dorothy Day claims at the outset of this piece that it is written to explain and perhaps justify her protest of the refusal of bail to eleven communists. She does that, but more significantly, she points to the many similarities between socialism and the teachings of Christ. Day herself, however, comes across more as a humanitarian than as a socialist, and as someone more interested in the message of Jesus than many who claimed to be at the time.

Day concludes with a very moving account of what she was doing (bathing her grandchildren) the evening the Rosenbergs were put to death by electrocution, and imagines that Ethel Rosenberg must have been thinking of her own "soon-to-be-orphaned" children. She describes an article in the next day's New York Times that gave details of the Rosenbergs' last two hours. Ethel's last act (embracing one of the police-women who accompanied her), Day notes, was a "gesture of love."

Women think with their whole bodies. More than men do, women see things as a whole.

Maybe I am saying this to justify myself for my recent protest of the refusal of bail to the eleven Communists, a protest which was published in the *Daily Worker*, the *American Guardian*, and other papers, much to the horror of many of our Catholic fellow workers.

It is necessary to explain if we do not wish to affront people. We sincerely want to make our viewpoint understood.

First of all, let it be remembered that I speak as an ex-Communist and one who has not testified before congressional committees, nor written works on the Communist conspiracy. I can say with warmth that I loved the people I worked with and learned much from them. They helped me to find God in His poor, in His abandoned ones, as I had not found Him in Christian churches.

I firmly believe that our salvation depends on the poor with whom Christ identified Himself. "Inasmuch as you have not fed the hungry, clothed the naked, sheltered the homeless, visited the prisoner, protested against injustice, comforted the afflicted . . . you have not done it to Me." The Church throughout the ages in all its charities, in the person of all its saints, has done these things. But for centuries these works were confined to priests, brothers, and nuns. Pius XI called on everyone to perform these works when he called for Catholic Action. The great tragedy of the century, he said, is that the workers are lost to the Church. All this has been repeated many times.

But I must speak from my own experiences. My radical associates were the ones who were in the forefront of the struggle for a better social order where there would not be so many poor. What if we do not agree with the means taken to achieve this goal, nor with their fundamental philosophy? We do believe in "from each according to his ability, to each according to his need." We believe in the "withering away of the State." We believe in the communal aspect of property, as stressed by the early Christians and since then by religious orders. We believe in the constructive activity of the people, "the masses," and the mutual aid which existed during medieval times, worked out from below. We believe in loving our brothers, regardless of race, color, or creed and we believe in showing this love by working, immediately, for better conditions, and ultimately, for the ownership by the workers of the means of production. We believe in an economy based on human needs, rather than on the profit motive.

Certainly we disagree with the Communist Party, but so do we disagree with the other political parties, dedicated to maintaining the status quo. We don't think the present system is worth maintaining. We and the Communists have a common idea that something else is necessary, some other vision of society must be held up and worked toward. Certainly we disagree over and over again with the means chosen to reach their ends, because, as we have repeated many a time, the means become the end.

As for their alleged conspiracy to overthrow the government by force and violence, I do not think that the state has proved its case. Of course, the Communists believe that violence will come. (So do we when it comes down to it, though we are praying it won't.) They believe it will be forced upon the worker by the class struggle which is going on all around us. This class war is a fact, and one does not need to advocate it. The Communists say it is forced on them and when it comes they will take part in it. In the meantime they want to prepare the ground and win as many as possible to their point of view. And where will we be on that day?

If we spend the rest of our lives in slums (as I hope we will, who work for and read *The Catholic Worker*), if we are truly living with the poor, helping the poor, we will inevitably find ourselves on their side, physically speaking. But when it comes to activity, we will be pacifists—I hope and pray—nonviolent resisters of aggression, from whomever it comes, resisters to repression, coercion, from whatever side it comes, and our activity will be the Works of Mercy. Our arms will be the love of God and our brother.

But the Communists are dishonest, everyone says. They do not want improved conditions for the workers. They want the end, the final conflict, to bring on the world revolution.

Well, when it comes down to it, do we of the *Catholic Worker* stand only for just wages, shorter hours, increase of power for the workers, a collaboration of employer and worker in prosperity for all? No, we want to make "the rich poor and the poor holy," and that, too, is a revolution obnoxious to the pagan man. We don't want luxury. We want land, bread, work, children, and the joys of community in play and work and worship. We don't believe in those industrial councils where the heads of United States Steel sit down with the common man in an obscene *agape* of luxury, shared profits, blood money from a thousand battles all over the world. No, the common good, the community must be considered.

During the first seven months of this year, 412 miners were killed at work. And as for crippling and disabling accidents there were 14,871 during these same months.

What has all this to do with signing protests, advocating bail for convicted Communists?

If people took time to think, if they had the zeal of the C.P. for school and study and meeting and planning, and with it all the thirst for martyrdom, and if Catholics delved into the rich body of Catholic liturgy and sociology, they would grow in faith and grace and change the world.

I believe we must reach our brother, never toning down our fundamental oppositions, but meeting him when he asks to be met with a reason for the faith that is in us. "We understand because we believe," St. Anselm says, and how can our brothers understand with a darkened reason, lacking this faith which would enlighten their minds?

The bridge—it seems to me—is love and the compassion (the suffering together) which goes with all love. Which means the folly of the Cross, since Christ loved men even to that folly of failure.

St. Therese said her aim was to make God loved. And I am sure that we pray to love God with an everlasting love, and yearn over our fellows in desire that He should be loved. How can they hear unless we take seriously our lay apostolate and answer them when they speak to us? We believe that God made them and sustains them. It is easier sometimes to see His handiwork here than in the Pecksniffs and Pharisees of our capitalist industrial system. We must cry out against injustice or by our silence consent to it. If we keep silent, the very stones of the street will cry out.

November 1949

——— ∞ ———

At eight o'clock on Friday, June 19, the Rosenbergs began to go to death. That June evening the air was fragrant with the smell of honeysuckle. Out under the hedge at Peter Maurin Farm, the black cat played with a grass snake, and the newly cut grass was fragrant in the evening air. At eight o'clock I put Nickie in the tub at my daughter's home, just as Lucille Smith was bathing her children at Peter Maurin Farm. My heart was heavy as I soaped Nickie's dirty little legs, knowing that Ethel Rosenberg must have been thinking with all the yearning of her heart of her own soon-to-be-orphaned children.

How does one pray when praying for "convicted spies" about to be electrocuted? One prays always of course for mercy. "My Jesus, mercy." "Lord Jesus Christ, Son of the living God, have mercy on them." But somehow, feeling close to their humanity, I prayed for fortitude for them both. "God let them be strong, take away all fear from them; let them be spared this suffering, at least, this suffering of fear and trembling."

I could not help but think of the story of Dostoevsky's *Idiot*, how Prince Myshkin described in detail the misery of the man about to be executed, whose sentence was commuted at the last moment. This had been the experience of Dostoevsky himself, and he had suffered those same fears, and had seen one of his comrades, convicted with him, led to the firing line, go mad with fear. Ethel and Julius Rosenberg, as their time approached and many appeals were made, must, in hoping against hope, holding fast to hope up to the last, have compared their lot to that of Dostoevsky and those who had been convicted with him. What greater punishment can be inflicted on anyone than those two long years in a death house, watched without ceasing so that there is no chance of one taking one's life and so thwarting the vengeance of the state. They had already suffered the supreme penalty. What they were doing in their own minds, no doubt, was offering the supreme sacrifice, offering their lives for their brothers. Both Harold Urey and Albert Einstein, and many other eminent thinkers at home and abroad, avowed their belief in the innocence of these two. They wrote that they did not believe their guilt had been proved.

Leaving all that out of account, accepting the verdict of the court that they were guilty, accepting the verdict of the millions of Americans who believed them guilty, accepting the verdict of President Eisenhower and Cardinal Spellman, who thought them guilty—even so, what should be the attitude of the Christian but one of love and great yearning for their salvation?

"Keep the two great commandments, love God and love your neighbor. Do this and thou shalt live." This is in the Gospel; these are the words of Jesus.

Whether or not they believed in Jesus, did the Rosenbergs love God? A rabbi who attended them to the last said that they had been his parishioners for two years. He followed them to the execution chamber reading from the Psalms, the Twenty-third, the Fifteenth, the Thirty-first. Those same psalms Cardinal Spellman reads every week as he reads his breviary, among those hundred and fifty psalms which make up not only the official prayers of the Church, but also the prayers which the Jews say. We used to see our Jewish grocer on the East Side, vested for prayer, reciting the Psalms every morning behind his counter when we went for our morning supplies. I have seen rabbis on all-night coaches praying thus in the morning. Who can hear the word of God without loving the word? Who can work for what they conceive of as justice, as brotherhood, without loving God and brother? If they were spies for Russia, they were doing what we also do in other countries, playing a part in international politics and diplomacy, but they indeed were serving a philosophy, a religion, and how mixed up religion can become. What a confusion we have gotten into when Christian prelates sprinkle holy water on scrap metal, to be used for obliteration bombing, and name bombers for the Holy Innocents, for Our Lady of Mercy; who bless a man about to press a button which releases death on fifty thousand human beings, including little babies, children, the sick, the aged, the innocent as well as the guilty. "You know not of what Spirit you are," Jesus said to His Apostles when they wished to call down fire from heaven on the inhospitable Samaritans.

I finished bathing the children, who were so completely free from preoccupation with suffering. They laughed and frolicked in the tub while the switch was being pulled which electrocuted first Julius and then his wife. Their deaths were announced over the radio half an hour later, jazz music being interrupted to give the bulletin, and the program continuing immediately after.

The next day, *The New York Times* gave details of the last hours, and the story was that both went to their deaths firmly, quietly, with no comment. At the last, Ethel turned to one of the two police matrons who accompanied her

and, clasping her by the hand, pulled her toward her and kissed her warm-
ly. Her last gesture was a gesture of love.

July–August 1953

6. WILL HERBERG, "PROTESTANT, CATHOLIC, JEW" (1955)

*In 1955 Drew University sociology professor Will Herberg penned one of the most in-
fluential books of the century about religion in the United States. As both a description
and a critique of American religion, it has stood the test of time, remaining a classic in
the field nearly five decades later. Pointing to the commonalities that underlay Protestantism, Catholicism, and Judaism in postwar America, he argued that the "American
Way of Life" had become the faith of the nation, which then exhibited itself in the separate religious traditions.*

*While major politicians, including Presidents Truman and Eisenhower in the 1950s,
celebrated a national mood of ecumenism and tolerance, Herberg was troubled by its
sterility. After all, those transcendent qualities that constituted Protestantism as Protestantism, Catholicism as Catholicism, and Judaism as Judaism seemed to be sacrificed
on the altar of patriotism and capitalist values. First-generation immigrants appeared
willing to resist the seductive call of the American Way of Life, but very quickly the second generation had succumbed to it. Third-generation Americans hoped to recover
some of the transcendence of the faith their grandparents held so tightly, but now it was
already wrapped in layers of American accretions.*

*Herberg's heavy-handed use of the "triple melting pot" thesis nearly belies the shrewd-
ness of his interpretation. If ecumenism and tolerance could remove the significant aspects of tradition and spirituality from an entire religion, then surely they had already
done it to mainline Protestantism. Inherently arguing that Protestantism was symbolic
of the American Way of Life—already a damning statement—he let the mainline part
of that tradition stand as the quintessential example of bland religion, bled of its power
by too much acceptance of that which once stood against it. While evangelical Protestants had made this claim for decades, it was not until such scholars as Will Herberg
and Reinhold Niebuhr castigated the spiritual impotence of the Protestant mainline that
many began to take a second look at the large ecumenical institutions it had created.*

The basic unity of American religion is something that goes deeper than the
similarities and differences of social pattern we have been examining. The
basic unity of American religion is rooted in the underlying presupposi-
tions, values, and ideals that together constitute the American Way of Life
on its "spiritual" side. It is the American Way of Life that is the shared pos-

session of all Americans and that defines the American's convictions on those matters that count most. Just as the three great religious communities are the basic subdivisions of the American people, so are the three great "communions" (as they are often called) felt to be the recognized expressions of the "spiritual" aspect of the American Way of Life. This underlying unity not only supplies the common content of the three communions; it also sets the limits within which their conflicts and tensions may operate and beyond which they cannot go.

[1]

For the fundamental unity of American religion, rooted in the American Way of Life, does not preclude conflict and tension; rather, in a way, it stimulates and accentuates it. Since each of the three communities recognizes itself as fitting into a tripartite scheme, each feels itself to be a minority, even the Protestants who in actual fact constitute a large majority of the American people. In this sense, as in so many others, America is preeminently a land of minorities.

The communal tensions in American society are of major importance in the life of the nation. So much attention is usually focused, properly, of course, on political and economic conflicts that we are only too prone to overlook or underestimate tensions on other levels of social life, particularly the religious, since religion is generally felt to be a matter that must be kept free of "controversy." Yet the religious tensions are real and significant; they have, moreover, become considerably accentuated in recent years in connection with a number of issues that have emerged into public life, centering on the problem of church and state. Such is the peculiar structure of American religious institutionalism under the constitutional doctrine of "separation" that every tension between religious communities, however deep and complex it may actually be, tends to express itself as a conflict over church-state relations. This approach is perhaps as useful a way as any of focusing the religio-communal tensions in American life.

American Catholics still labor under the heavy weight of the bitter memory of non-acceptance in a society overwhelmingly and self-consciously Protestant. Hardly a century has passed since Catholics in America were brutally attacked by mobs, excluded from more desirable employment, and made to feel in every way that they were unwanted aliens. Despised as foreigners of low-grade stock, detested and denounced as "minions of Rome," they early developed the minority defensiveness that led them to with draw into their own "ghetto" with a rankling sense of grievance and to divide the world into "we" and "they." . . .

These feelings of rejection, exclusion, and grievance, though they no longer correspond to the facts of American life, and though they are deplored by more thoughtful Catholics, are still a real force among the great mass of Catholic people in this country. It takes a long time for such wounds to heal.

Partly in the interest of corporate survival in a hostile world, though basically in line with the demands and teachings of the church, Catholics in America have built up a vast and complex system of parallel institutions, the most important and pervasive of which are the church schools operating at every academic level. Though initiated under other circumstances, these parallel institutions soon fell in rather neatly with the emerging religio-communal pattern of American life. At the same time, the development of these institutions no doubt helped accentuate that tradition of Catholic "separatism" which has recently come under the criticism of Catholics themselves. . . .

Minority defensiveness breeds aggressiveness, intensifies separatism, and accentuates prejudice. Many Catholics still, as in earlier days, attempt to sustain their corporate self-esteem by an attitude that makes Protestant almost equivalent to unbeliever, or in more modern terminology, to "secularist." But authoritative Catholic opinion is increasingly taking another line of ideological defense—that Catholicism is, in fact, a true expression of Americanism and that the genuine Catholic position on church and state, is fully in line with American tradition and experience. The extensive system of Catholic institutions is interpreted in terms of the emerging community structure of American society, involving no more separatism than any other aspect of community organization. By and large, American Catholicism has succeeded in shifting the ground of self-understanding and self-justification from the earlier negative defensiveness to a more positive affirmation of its legitimate place in the tripartite America of today. The Catholic attitude is increasingly that of a substantial minority with a strong sense of self-assurance.

Protestantism in America today presents the anomaly of a strong majority group with a growing minority consciousness. "The psychological basis of much of American Protestantism," *Social Action* (Congregational) somewhat ruefully pointed out in 1952, "lies in a negative rejection of Roman Catholicism. . . . The one emotional loyalty that of a certainty binds us [Protestants] together . . . is the battle against Rome." The fear of "Rome" is indeed the most powerful cement of Protestant community consciousness, and it seems to loom larger today than it has for some time. Discussion of Protestant communal affairs moves increasingly under the shadow of the "Catholic problem," and Protestant attitudes tend more and more to be defined in, terms of confrontation with a self-assured and aggressive Catholicism. The tension here has become really acute.

The fear of Catholic domination of the United States would seem to be hardly borne out by statistics. In the period from 1926 to 1950 church membership in this country increased 59.8 per cent, as against a 28.6 per cent increase in population. The Catholic Church grew 53.9 per cent, but in the same period Protestantism increased 63.7 per cent. Moreover, Protestant proselytism seemed to be more intensive and successful than Catholic. Most of the Protestant margin of increase, however, was accounted for by the expansion of the Baptists, especially the Southern Baptists. The churches affiliated with the National Council grew only 47 per cent, falling short of the total increase as well as of the comparable Roman Catholic growth. In those parts of the country where Protestants and Catholics come into more direct contact, particularly in the urban centers, the Catholic Church has been making considerable headway.

But it is not this numerical growth, such as it is, that so deeply disquiets the Protestant consciousness, for, after all, the Protestant-Catholic balance has remained pretty steady in the past thirty years. Neither is it entirely the mounting intellectual prestige that American Catholicism has been acquiring from the work of a number of artists, philosophers, and writers, mostly European. What seems to be really disturbing many American Protestants is the sudden realization that Protestantism is no longer identical with America, that Protestantism has, in fact, become merely one of three communions (or communities) with equal status and equal legitimacy in the American scheme of things. This sudden realization, shocking enough when one considers the historical origins of American life and culture, appears to have driven Protestantism into an essentially defensive posture, in which it feels itself a mere minority threatened with Catholic domination.

This minority-group defensiveness has contributed greatly toward turning an important segment of American Protestantism into a vehement champion of an extreme doctrine of the separation of church and state, of religion and education, despite a disturbed awareness of the growing "religious illiteracy" of the American people. This minority-group defensiveness and fear of "Rome" have tended to drive American Protestantism into a strange alliance with the militant secularist anti-Catholicism that is associated with the recent work of Paul Blanshard. It would seem to be of some significance that the contemporary Protestant case against Catholicism is not primarily religious or theological, as it was in previous centuries, but is characteristically secular: Catholicism, we are told, is un-American, undemocratic, alien to American ways, and prone to place loyalty to church above loyalty to state and nation. Particularly shocking to many Protestants is the

Catholic insistence on by-passing the public schools and educating their children in their own religious institutions. The "neutral" public school, inculcating a common national ideology above religious "divisiveness," has in fact become to large numbers of Protestants the symbol of their cause in the face of dreaded Catholic encroachment. . . .

The radical evil of a plural society, we are told, is that "it can have no common will; it makes for national instability; it puts an undue emphasis on material things; [and] it nullifies the unifying function of education." The last point, which seems most basic, again raises the question of the "divisive" parochial school. "A plural society," it is alleged, "nullifies the unifying function of education by splitting up among its constituent units the responsibility for providing education, rather than allowing the state to provide a common education for all children." In a most curious way, the authoritarian doctrine of *l'état enseignant* (the "teaching state," the state as the molder of the ideology of its citizens) has become part of the creed of a large segment of American Protestantism.

Pluralism in Furnivall's sense would indeed be a serious matter for a society such as ours. But there would seem to be little danger of it in contemporary America. Indeed, *The Christian Century* appears to have discovered the menace precisely at a time when, due to advanced acculturation and increasing mobility, American Catholics are becoming increasingly integrated into the general community rather than the reverse. But this integration is taking place in a new and characteristic fashion, in and through the religious community as one of the three "pools" in the "triple melting pot" that is America. *The Christian Century* writer apparently does not see, yet his outburst of alarm is not unrelated to the sociological process.

American Protestantism is so apprehensive at the development of religio-communal pluralism in part at least because in this kind of pluralistic situation it would seem to be at a serious disadvantage. It has been so long identified with America as a whole that it has neither the background nor the conviction necessary to build up its own Protestant community institutions in the same way that Jews and Catholics have built up theirs. Jews and Catholics have their own war veterans' associations, but it would probably appear strange and unwholesome to Protestants to establish a Protestant war veterans' organization; aren't the "general" war veterans' organizations sufficiently Protestant? Once they were, just as until the last quarter of the nineteenth century the public schools were virtually Protestant "parochial" schools, but they are no longer such today. Protestants, particularly the old-line Protestant leadership, cannot seem to reconcile themselves to this primary fact. Nor do they seem capable of overcoming, in many cases even of mitigating, the fragmentation of denominationalism, which places

Protestantism at another disadvantage in the face of an ecclesiastically united Catholicism. All this contributes to the Protestant distaste for "pluralism" and adds fuel to Protestant defensive resentment against "Rome."

It would be gravely misleading, however, to leave the impression that this attitude is universal among Protestants or that there are no Protestant voices urging other counsels. There is, in the first place, a striking difference in outlook between the older and the younger generations of Protestants in America. The older generation, still thinking of America as the Protestant nation of their youth, cannot help feeling bitter and resentful at what must appear to them to be menacing encroachments of Catholics in American life; the younger generation, accustomed to America as a three-religion country, cannot understand what the excitement is all about: "After all, we're all Americans . . . " On the other side, theologically concerned Protestants find it difficult to go along with the kind of negative "anti-Romanism" current in many Protestant circles; they find it both too sterile and too secularist, too reminiscent of cultural totalism, for their taste. Reinhold Niebuhr, John C. Bennett, Robert McAfee Brown, Angus Dun, Liston Pope, Henry P. Van Dusen, and other Protestant theologians, while criticizing what they regard as erroneous views and abuses of power among Catholics, have been particularly insistent on the necessity of a new Protestant orientation more in conformity with the facts of American life and more faithful to its own religious tradition.

Minority consciousness is, of course, particularly strong among American Jews, and it is among American Jews that the "philosophy" and strategy of minority-group defensiveness has been most elaborately developed. "Defense" activities play a major part in American Jewish community life: the "defense" is against "defamation" (anti-Semitism) on the one hand, and against the intrusion of the "church" into education and public life on the other. Spokesmen of American Jewish institutions and agencies—no one, of course, can speak for American Jewry as a whole—have almost always displayed an attitude on matters of church and state, religion and public affairs, more extreme even than that of the Protestant champions of the "wall of separation." Their alliance with secularism is even closer; perhaps it would be more accurate to say that they have themselves taken over the entire secularist ideology on church-state relations to serve as defensive strategy.

It is not difficult to understand why an extreme secularism and "separationism" should appeal to so many American Jews as a defensive necessity. At bottom, this attitude may be traced to the conviction, widely held though rarely articulated, that because the Western Jew achieved emancipation with the secularization of society, he can preserve his free and equal status only so long as culture and society remains secular. Let but religion gain a significant place in the everyday life of the community, and the Jew, because he is outside the bounds of the dominant religion, will once again be relegated to the margins of society, displaced, disfranchised culturally if not politically, shorn of rights and opportunities. The intrusion of religion into education and public life, the weakening of the "wall of separation" between religion and the state, is feared as only too likely to result in situations in which Jews would find themselves at a disadvantage—greater isolation, higher "visibility," an accentuation of minority status. The most elementary defensive strategy would thus seem to dictate keeping religion out of education and public life at all costs; hence the passionate attachment of so many American Jews to the secularist-Protestant interpretation of the principle of "separation" and to the general "Blanshardite" position.

The defensive necessities of Jewish minority interests do not, in the case of most Jews, seem to imply any particular tension with Protestants, especially the more "liberal" Protestants in the big cities where Jews are to be found; suspicion and tension emerge, however, more obviously in Jewish-Catholic relations. A recent survey indicated that more than three times as many Jews felt themselves "interfered with" by Catholics as by Protestants, almost twice as many Jews felt they were "looked down upon" by Catholics as by Protestants, and three times as many Jews confessed to harboring "ill feeling" toward Catholics as toward Protestants. Catholicism represents, to many Jews, a much more aggressive form of religion than Protestantism (most Jews never come into contact with the militant fundamentalism of rural and small-town America); deep down, it is the Catholic Church that is suspected of untoward designs and Catholic domination that is feared.

The precarious minority position of the American Jew in a non-Jewish world also impels him to strenuous, and what to some might seem extravagant, efforts at corporate self-validation. The extensive building programs that are being feverishly pursued by Jewish communities throughout the land are not merely the reflection of unparalleled prosperity and a rising level of synagogue affiliation; these programs serve a public relations function which is never entirely unconscious. Indeed, public relations seems to be more anxiously, and skillfully, cultivated by American Jewry than by either the Catholics or the Protestants; nothing that any Jewish community agency does, whatever may be its intrinsic nature or value, is ever without its public relations angle. A curious manifestation of this concern with corporate self-validation in the face of the "outside" world is the extraordinarily high salaries Jewish rabbis receive in comparison with those received by Protestant ministers of equal status and service. The salary and style of life of the rabbi is, to a Jewish community outside the very big cities, a significant form of vicariously defining and enhancing its corporate status in the larger society. It is felt to be humiliating to the entire Jewish community if the rabbi cannot maintain a manner of life that would make him at home in the upper strata—something that would never occur to the average Protestant community, which hardly expects its minister to achieve equal standing with the social elite. Considerations of minority-group validation and defense thus enter into every phase and aspect of Jewish life in America.

7. THE CHURCH LEAGUE OF AMERICA, "A MANUAL FOR SURVIVAL" (1961)

J. B. MATTHEWS, *CERTAIN ACTIVITIES OF CERTAIN CLERGYMEN* (1963)

Those who drew connections between communism and secularism on the one hand and American political and moral problems on the other were quick to assert that the nation's foundations were under attack. More dangerous than the growing number of missiles aimed at the United States, according to these critics, were the threats to "Americanism" from liberal politics, increased secularization, and Marxist brainwashing in public schools. As J. B. Matthews, chief researcher for the House Committee on Un-American Activities, put it during a radio interview in 1939, "Americanism is a spiritual force, working, economically, in a system of private property and free enterprise; embodied, politically, in a government of checks and balances; and expressing itself culturally in tolerance, religious liberty, and freedom of thought." With religion holding such a prominent place in this definition of "Americanism," those agreeing with Matthews saw their anticommunist stance as nothing less than a holy war.

The excerpt from A Manual for Survival *published by* The Church League of America *is most notable for its unbridled hubris. J. Edgar Hoover is the only authority cited to cover its many claims, which demonize communists and cast suspicion on "thousands" of people as "sympathizers" and "dupes" who are more effective in furthering the communist agenda than card-carrying party members. It is a good example of the period's well-written (although poorly documented) propaganda.*

While the introduction to J. B. Matthews's book, Certain Activities of Certain Clergymen, *also calls upon the authority of J. Edgar Hoover, Matthews's research, if not his conclusions, is more respectable. A former Methodist missionary and later a college professor, during part of the 1930s he sympathized with socialist theories before breaking with the communists and becoming a leading voice against them. Matthews asserts that certain U.S. clergymen, and by extension, their respective churches, are communist "fronts." He offers no real evidence or proof but rather suggests, ironically, that the lack thereof is what makes these "fronts" so dangerous. While today the piece sounds like anticommunist cant, something to lampoon rather than take seriously, it reminds us of*

the deep fears of tens of millions that their families and faith were endangered by spir-
itual and political forces.

A MANUAL FOR SURVIVAL

Since the end of World War II, more than 900,000,000 people have been taken behind the "Iron Curtain" by the Soviet Union. The U.S.S.R. has conquered more people and has seized more territory than Adolph Hitler conquered in all of his years of active military campaigns on the continent of Europe and in North Africa.

The remarkable part about this accomplishment is that the Soviet Union has done it without committing one single Russian military division to battle.

The gains of World Communism have been made by means of a new conception of warfare—that of deceit, subterfuge, lies and internal subversion.

Few individuals, in what remains of the Free World, are able to recognize the enemy even when he is working in their midst. He appears in various forms and clever disguises. He uses the same words they use but with different meanings.

For too long a time the free citizen has had the idea that the Communist is some wild-looking character with long red hair and beard, ragged clothing, and a bomb in one hand, a pistol in the other, standing on a soap box on a street corner; jumping up and down, and shouting: "Comes the Revolution!"

Such a picture is far from the truth! This was the typical caricature of the old Bolshevik in the 1920's, or shortly after the Russian Revolution of 1917.

Many people still have the misconception that World Communism is led by ignorance and poverty-stricken persons. That idea is also quite false.

The leaders of Communism are individuals of high intelligence, very clever, and they are supported with a great deal of money earned under a capitalistic or free enterprise system. Many of them are in the "intellectual class."

They have an extreme sense of dedication to a cause—the cause of overthrowing the present society and replacing it with one in which they will be the planners and the controllers. They have a lust for power and position.

The peoples of the Free World will never be able to combat the Red menace until they learn to recognize it and to understand its strategy and tactics. . . .

Karl Marx put the materialistic interpretation of history (Feurbach's theory) together with the dialectic (struggle theory) of Dr. Hegel and produced his concept of dialectical materialism, or Marxian Socialism. He called it "Scientific Socialism."

Marx believed that a great struggle was taking place in the world. He stated that the masses of the people were struggling for a more abundant life. What kind of abundant life? Spiritual? No! Material!

Marx said that only greed stood between the masses and the realization of the abundant life. Greed was represented by the ownership class—the holders of private property and production—the capitalists. He said that the Capitalist Class must be eliminated and their holdings distributed equally among the people before the perfect world society could be realized. The state, representing the people, would be an instrument in accomplishing this, and then the state itself would be eliminated, and the masses would be supreme—no one ruling over anyone else. All would be equal. All would have all things in common. Greed would be eliminated forever. Paradise would be restored on earth. Utopia would have arrived on the human scene.

This was the so-called intellectualism of Marx—prophet of falsehoods—son of the Father of lies—Satan, who was to plunge the entire world into fear and chaos in a little more than 100 years!

God was to be left out of this Utopian dream. "Religion," said Marx, "is the tool of the Capitalists, an anesthetic to lull the masses to sleep so that the Capitalists can exploit them."

Materialism, humanism and rationalism were to replace God's plan of Redemption for the human race. The Bible was to be scrapped and all religious doctrine eliminated.

If anyone today wonders why so many student groups and intellectual leaders are found furthering the Communist Conspiracy then take a look at the sources of Marx's theories, and also see that he was a student with a twisted brain who produced the Communist Manifesto, the bible of World Communism, when he was only 30 years of age in 1848.

Mr. J. Edgar Hoover, director of the Federal Bureau of Investigation of the United States of America, says that Communism, in simple terms, can be defined as "a revolt against duly constituted law and order." It is rebellion of the human heart against the divine order of things. It is basically the setting of man's will over against the will and law of Almighty God. It is the replacement of orderliness with chaos, confusion and misery by those who have a lust for power.

Mr. Hoover, in a recent report for 1960, entitled "Communist Target—Youth," warned the young people of the world to be aware of the designs of the Communists to penetrate their groups and to use them as an explosive force for World Communism. He cited recent events in Japan, Uruguay, Cuba and San Francisco, U.S.A. as examples of how the Reds could exploit young people.

One of the primary things we must understand is that the Communist

Conspiracy is not a political movement; and, if we try to treat it as such, then we will fail to stop it.

The U.S. Supreme Court and many Federal Government bodies have unanimously ruled that the Communist Party is not a political party such as the Republican or Democratic parties. It is a conspiracy to subvert genuine parties and governments. The Communist Party is not permitted on the voters' ballots in the U.S.A.

What is the Communist movement, actually? It is a disease. It is a materialistic religion. It affects the mind. It is a Satanic substitute for Christianity and the Gospel.

Turn to its instruction book—the Manifesto—and to the writings of its fanatics from Marx, Engles [sic], and Stalin, to the present day. You will find its plan for overthrowing all free societies. You will find the definite instructions to all its missionaries.

Communism is the fulfillment of the doctrines of Marx and Lenin, as advocated today by the leaders of the Soviet Union and their puppets throughout the world.

Communists believe that they have not yet reached the goal of true Communism, but that what exists in the U.S.S.R., in the Eastern Satellite states of Europe and in the Far East, is Socialism. Socialism, they believe, is an imperfect society, which is an improvement on Capitalism, but which falls short of the perfection of Communism. The objective of all Communists is the Communist society, in which all will think and act as Communists do. When this state arrives, then the world will have "peace" and government itself will wither away. Until this is achieved, however, the leaders of Communism must be the dictators and tell others what to do. So say the Red bosses.

The Communist leaders say that the transition from the imperfect society of Socialism to the perfect society of Communism cannot take place until the Free World (the United States and its allies) is defeated. The overthrow of Capitalism, then, is the prerequisite for the establishment of Communism. The Communist must use any device to accomplish this end. Infiltration of every major phase of a free society must take place: government, labor, communications, entertainment, art, literature, education and even religious institutions.

Disguises must be used in this infiltration process. While using the term "peace," or "peaceful co-existence," the Communist must understand that these are only terms of convenience to lull the unsuspecting and trusting citizens of the Free World into a false state of security.

Such devices as "cultural exchanges" and "summit conferences," "trade pacts" and "agricultural talks" must be used by the Reds to soften the free nations.

Once their agents have infiltrated every sphere of a free society, then they will condition or brainwash the people into believing that Communism is a good thing and the only solution to the world's chronic ills such as hunger, greed, wars, misunderstandings, and even sickness!

You see, Communists teach that even sickness and disease are products of this "terrible" thing called "Capitalism," and that when the perfect Communist society finally appears, all infirmities will be prohibited!

The Communists are few in number compared to the total population of the world, but they are dedicated fanatics. Of great importance is the fact that they seek opinion-molding positions in all spheres of society. As Mr. Hoover has often stated: it is not a case of how many Communists there are, but rather where are they located.

The Communists have already successfully penetrated every major phase of free societies and are recruiting thousands of sympathizers and just plain dupes who never join the Communist Party, but who carry out the Communist objectives far more effectively than do the Communist Party members themselves. . . .

The United States has a Christian civilization. Communism is the sworn enemy of this nation. That is why the Communists, their sympathizers, and dupes carry on an incessant campaign to smear, to distort the truth, and to call their opponents names similar to the ones mentioned by Mr. Hoover, such as 'fascist.'

Christianity is the strongest force in the Free World to turn back the Red Tide and prevent the destruction of the bodies and souls of men.

Our nation has the truth on its side. We must declare it boldly no matter what our enemies try to do to suppress it. We must educate our people to be able to recognize the Red enemy when he appears in our midst, and to expose him and oppose him with the truth which comes from God.

Our Lord Jesus Christ said: "Ye shall know the truth and the truth shall make you free."

He then declared: "I am the Way, the Truth and the life. No man cometh to the Father but by me."

The Communists have no god but Materialism. Their false prophet is a dead Marx. Their evil spirit is Satan.

We have a great God and Heavenly Father. On our side with Him is His only begotten Son Jesus Christ, and our teacher of all truth, the Holy Spirit.

We are engaged in a spiritual warfare for the souls of men. The Holy Trinity versus the unholy three.

Volunteers are needed to join in this spiritual warfare against the greatest enemy of mankind. Our weapons are powerful but they must be used. Let us instruct free people everywhere how to use them.

Totalitarianism thrives on keeping the people in the dark as to what is happening. Freedom and Liberty thrive on bringing all things unto the light.

A free people is an enlightened people.

CERTAIN ACTIVITIES OF CERTAIN CLERGYMEN

. . . The organization of Communist propaganda, aimed at influencing and controlling the minds of a people, is like the concentric circles of water caused by the dropping of a rock. The center of all Communist propaganda and agitation is in the Kremlin. From there it spreads out to encompass the thinking of millions all over the world. Nothing closely akin to it was ever before organized in the history of the world.

The Communist conspirators know all about this; but millions of non-Communists and even anti-Communists are as unaware of the source which sways their judgments as is the blade of grass at the water's edge which bends in response to the force of the outermost circle.

Now, let us take a concrete case of how this technique of the concentric circles is applied by the Communist conspiracy.

Several years ago, orders went out from the Kremlin high command to all the national units of the international Communist conspiracy, to launch a world-wide peace agitation. The Kremlin was the point of origin; the national units of the Communist movement were the first of the concentric circles.

Several world congresses on peace were held—in Stockholm, in Paris, in Warsaw. World-wide publicity for these tightly Communist-controlled gatherings was the first order of business. Petitions were circulated in practically every country in the world. Hundreds of millions of people affixed their signatures to these petitions.

Regional peace congresses were held. In Mexico City, a gathering was called under the name of the American Continental Congress for World Peace. This was in September, 1949. The gathering was sponsored in the United States by professors, lawyers, clergymen, artists, and scientists. In March, 1952, the Communists called the American Inter-Continental Peace Conference to meet in Brazil. . . .

From the central conspiratorial apparatus from far-away Moscow, through international couriers and congresses, through national Communist Party headquarters in New York, through state Communist Party headquarters in a midwestern state, through the local Communist Party leaders, through a non-Communist doctor who acted as intermediary between local party leaders and "conservative" sponsors, through the "conservative" sponsors, through willing stooges who rang doorbells and did other menial chores for the enterprise, through a mass meeting (possibly in a school auditorium), through local newspaper publicity, a whole American community of respectable citizens finally felt the impact of subversive Communist propaganda. Multiply this single instance of the midwestern community a thousand times over in all of the 50 states and the District of Columbia, and you will begin to comprehend the techniques by which the Communists reach the minds of millions of Americans and warp the judgments of these "innocent" Americans to suit the purposes of the Communist conspiracy.

When attention is called to the support they have given the Communist-front apparatus, many notables seem to think they are being accused of harboring Communist sympathies and reply with great indignation that they are *not* Communists. Far from proving that they are Communists, the presence of their names on the sponsors' list of a Communist front is substantial, though not necessarily conclusive, evidence to the contrary. When the sponsors of an organization or the signers of a petition are predominantly Communists, proof is conclusive that the enterprise is *not* a front. In order to be a front, that is, to perpetrate a deception, an organization's group of supporters must be composed predominantly of non-Communists and preferably of those who think of themselves as anti-Communists.

The essence and most distinctive characteristic of the Communist-front organization is its deceitfulness.

Behind an often impressive facade of non-Communist notables who serve as sponsors, signers, or nonfunctioning officers of a front organization lurk unseen directors, manipulators, and functioning executives who are agents of the Communist conspiracy. For its deceptive purposes, a clergyman is the ideal national chairman of a Communist front; and the record discloses that at least a score of the party's front organizations have been headed by clergymen.

Behind the title of a front organization coils a conspiratorial reality which strikes savagely at the ideals of those who neglect to immunize their humanitarian impulses with sound judgment and a healthy skepticism.

Behind announced objectives which may be wholly praiseworthy lie unannounced and shrewdly concealed aims which are calculated to advance—however slightly—the cause of the Communist conspiracy.

The conspiring totalitarian entices the unsuspecting humanitarian into his web, and fattens on the gullibility of his victim. The spider-and-fly analogy is weak at one point: the humanitarian cannot be held altogether blameless for his credulity, and his credulity is believable in direct ratio to the number and seriousness of the front organizations he has supported.

The Communist-front organization, to change the figure, is a whited sepulcher, outwardly beautiful but full of dead bones within. The facade belies the interior.

No more succinct statement of the deceitfulness of the Communist-front organization has been written in official documents than that which appeared in the United States Supreme Court brief of the Department of Justice in its case for the deportation of Harry Bridges, in May 1942. The brief said: "Testimony on front organizations showed that they were represented to the public for some legitimate reform objective, but actually used by the Communist Party to carry on its activities, pending the time when the Communists believe they can seize power . . ."

It is unfortunately a common error to ascribe conscious disloyalty to all Communist Party members on the one hand, and to ascribe nothing more than misguided idealism to all supporters of the Communist-front apparatus on the other. There are unwitting dupes, as well as witting subverters, among both party members and fronters.

In the case of the overwhelming majority of professional groups—educators, clergymen, lawyers, artists, novelists, and the like—who have been affiliated in one way or another with the Communist movement in the United States, the Communist-front apparatus has been their only point of contact.

The information presented in this book is not intended to suggest or imply Communist Party membership to any of the persons named, unless explicitly so stated.

8. J. WILLIAM FULBRIGHT, "THE ARROGANCE OF POWER" (1966)

"The causes of the malady are not entirely clear but its recurrence is one of the uniformities of history: power tends to confuse itself with virtue and a great nation is peculiarly susceptible to the idea that its power is a sign of God's favor, conferring upon it a special responsibility for other nations—to make them richer and happier and wiser, to remake them, that is, in its own shining image."

In this excerpt from his book, The Arrogance of Power, Arkansas Senator J. William Fulbright questions both the right and the ability of a powerful western nation like the United States to wage war on smaller countries and then attempt to create stable, democratic, honest governments where none has ever before existed. Writing in the heat of public debates over Vietnam, Fulbright makes the point that the Vietnamese resent American strength in spite of their dependence upon it, likely because they fear that their own culture and traditions can never survive American influence. Running headlong into the civil religion that seemed to excuse any American action around the world, Fulbright's jeremiad calls Americans back to a humbler understanding of their place, one that makes difficult their confusion of military might with God's call to remake the world in America's image.

America is the most fortunate of nations—fortunate in her rich territory, fortunate in having had a century of relative peace in which to develop that territory, fortunate in her diverse and talented population, fortunate in the institutions devised by the founding fathers and in the wisdom of those who have adapted those institutions to a changing world.

For the most part America has made good use of her blessings, especially in her internal life but also in her foreign relations. Having done so much and succeeded so well, America is now at that historical point at which a great nation is in danger of losing its perspective on what exactly is within the realm of its power and what is beyond it. Other great nations, reaching this critical juncture, have aspired to too much, and by overextension of effort have declined and then fallen.

The causes of the malady are not entirely clear but its recurrence is one of the uniformities of history: power tends to confuse itself with virtue and a great nation is peculiarly susceptible to the idea that its power is a sign of God's favor, conferring upon it a special responsibility for other nations—to make them richer and happier and wiser, to remake them, that is, in its own shining image. Power confuses itself with virtue and tends also to take itself for omnipotence. Once imbued with the idea of a mission, a great nation easily assumes that it has the means as well as the duty to do God's work. The Lord, after all, surely would not choose you as His agent and then deny you the sword with which to work His will. German soldiers in the First World War wore belt buckles imprinted with the words "*Gott mit uns.*" It was approximately under this kind of infatuation—an exaggerated sense of power and an imaginary sense of mission—that the Athenians attacked Syracuse, and Napoleon and then Hitler invaded Russia. In plain words, they overextended their commitments and they came to grief.

I do not think for a moment that America, with her deeply rooted democratic traditions, is likely to embark upon a campaign to dominate the world in the manner of a Hitler or Napoleon. What I do fear is that she may be drifting into commitments which, though generous and benevolent in intent, are so far-reaching as to exceed even America's great capacities. At the same time, it is my hope—and I emphasize it because it underlies all of the criticisms and proposals to be made in these pages—that America will escape those fatal temptations of power which have ruined other great nations and will instead confine herself to doing only that good in the world which she *can* do, both by direct effort and by the force of her own example.

The stakes are high indeed: they include not only America's continued greatness but nothing less than the survival of the human race in an era when, for the first time in human history, a living generation has the power of veto over the survival of the next. . . .

When the abstractions and subtleties of political science have been exhausted, there remain the most basic unanswered questions about war and peace and why nations contest the issues they contest and why they even care about them. . . .

Many of the wars fought by man—I am tempted to say most—have been fought over such abstractions. The more I puzzle over the great wars of history, the more I am inclined to the view that the causes attributed to them—territory markets, resources, the defense or perpetuation of great principles—were not the root causes at all but rather explanations or excuses for certain unfathomable drives of human nature. For lack of a clear and precise understanding of exactly what these motives are, I refer to them as the "arrogance of power"—as a psychological need that nations seem to have in order to prove that they are bigger, better, or stronger than other nations. Implicit in this drive is the assumption, even on the part of normally peaceful nations, that force is the ultimate proof of superiority—that when a nation shows that it has the strongest army, it is also proving that it has better people, better institutions, better principles, and, in general, a better civilization.

Evidence for my proposition is found in the remarkable discrepancy between the apparent and hidden causes of some modern wars and the discrepancy between their causes and ultimate consequences. . . .

We are engaged in a war to "defend freedom" in South Vietnam. Unlike the Republic of Korea, South Vietnam has an army which fights without notable success and a weak, dictatorial government which does not command the loyalty of the South Vietnamese people. The official war aims of the United States government, as I understand them, are to defeat what is regarded as North Vietnamese aggression, to demonstrate the futility of what the communists call "wars of national liberation," and to create conditions under which the South Vietnamese people will be able freely to determine their own future. . . .

In the spring of 1966 demonstrators in Saigon burned American jeeps, tried to assault American soldiers, and marched through the streets shouting "Down with American imperialists," while a Buddhist leader made a speech equating the United States with the communists as a threat to South Vietnamese independence. Most Americans are understandably shocked and angered to encounter expressions of hostility from people who would long since have been under the rule of the Viet Cong but for the sacrifice of American lives and money. Why, we may ask, are they so shockingly ungrateful? Surely they must know that their very right to parade and protest and demonstrate depends on the Americans who are defending them.

The answer, I think, is that "fatal impact" of the rich and strong on the poor and weak. Dependent on it though the Vietnamese are, American strength is a reproach to their weakness, American wealth a mockery of their poverty, American success a reminder of their failures. What they resent is the disruptive effect of our strong culture upon their fragile one, an effect which we can no more avoid having than a man can help being bigger than a child. What they fear, I think rightly, is that traditional Vietnamese society cannot survive the American economic and cultural impact. . . .

Sincere though it is, the American effort to build the foundation of freedom in South Vietnam is thus having an effect quire different from the one intended. "All this struggling and striving to make the world better is a great mistake," said George Bernard Shaw, "not because it isn't a good thing to improve the world if you know how to do it, but because striving and struggling is the worst way you could set about doing anything."

One wonders how much the American commitment to Vietnamese freedom is also a commitment to American pride—the two seem to have become part of the same package. When we talk about the freedom of South Vietnam, we may be thinking about how disagreeable it would be to accept a solution short of victory; we may be thinking about how our pride would be injured if we settled for less than we set out to achieve; we may be thinking about our reputation as a great power, fearing that a compromise settlement would shame us before the world, marking us as a second-rate people with flagging courage and determination.

Such fears are as nonsensical as their opposite, the presumption of a universal mission. They are simply unworthy of the richest, most powerful, most productive, and best educated people in the world. One can understand an uncompromising attitude on the part of such countries as China or France: both have been struck low in this century and a certain amount of arrogance may be helpful to them in recovering their pride. It is much less comprehensible on the part of the United States—a nation whose modern history has been an almost uninterrupted chronicle of success, a nation which by now should be so sure of its own power as to be capable of magnanimity, a nation which by now should be able to act on the proposition that, as George Kennan said, "there is more respect to be won in the opinion of the world by a resolute and courageous liquidation of unsound positions than in the most stubborn pursuit of extravagant or unpromising objectives."

The cause of our difficulties in Southeast Asia is not a deficiency of power but an excess of the wrong kind of power, which results in a feeling of impotence when it fails to achieve its desired ends. We are still acting like Boy Scouts dragging reluctant old ladies across streets they do not want to cross. We are trying to remake Vietnamese society, a task which certainly cannot be accomplished by force and which probably cannot be accomplished by any means available to outsiders. The objective may be desirable, but it is not feasible. As Shaw said: "Religion is a great force—the only real motive force in the world; but what you fellows don't understand is that you must get a man through his own religion and not through yours."

With the best intentions in the world the United States has involved itself deeply in the affairs of developing nations in Asia and Latin America, practicing what has been called a kind of "welfare imperialism." Our honest purpose is the advancement of development and democracy, to which end it has been thought necessary to destroy ancient and unproductive modes of life. In this latter function we have been successful, perhaps more successful than we know. Bringing skills and knowledge, money and resources in amounts hitherto unknown in traditional societies, the Americans have overcome indigenous groups and interests and become the dominant force in a number of countries. Far from being bumbling, wasteful, and incompetent, as critics have charged, American government officials, technicians, and economists have been strikingly successful in breaking down the barriers to change in ancient but fragile cultures.

Here, however, our success ends. Traditional rulers, institutions, and ways of life have crumbled under the fatal impact of American wealth and power but they have not been replaced by new institutions and new ways of life, nor has their breakdown ushered in an era of democracy and development. It has rather ushered in an era of disorder and demoralization because in the course of destroying old ways of doing things, we have also destroyed the self-confidence and self-reliance without which no society can build indigenous institutions. Inspiring as we have such great awe of our efficiency and wealth, we have reduced some of the intended beneficiaries of our generosity to a condition of dependency and self-denigration. We have done this for the most part inadvertently: with every good intention we have intruded on fragile societies, and our intrusion, though successful in uprooting traditional ways of life, has been strikingly unsuccessful in implanting the democracy and advancing the development which are the honest aims of our "welfare imperialism." . . .

The "Blessings-of-Civilization Trust," as Mark Twain called it, may have been a "Daisy" in its day, uplifting for the soul and good for business besides, but its day is past. It is past because the great majority of the human race is demanding dignity and independence, not the honor of a supine role in an American empire. It is past because whatever claim America may make for the universal domain of her ideas and values is balanced by the communist counter-claim, armed like our own with nuclear weapons. And, most of all, it is past because it never should have begun, because we are not God's chosen saviour of mankind, but only one of mankind's more successful and fortunate branches, endowed by our Creator with about the same capacity for good and evil, no more or less, than the rest of humanity.

An excessive preoccupation with foreign relations over a long period of time is more than a manifestation of arrogance; it is a drain on the power that gave rise to it, because it diverts a nation from the sources of its strength, which are in its domestic life. A nation immersed in foreign affairs is expending its capital, human as well as material; sooner or later that capital must be renewed by some diversion of creative energies from foreign to domestic pursuits. I would doubt that any nation has achieved a durable greatness by conducting a "strong" foreign policy, but many have been ruined by expending their energies in foreign adventures while allowing their domestic bases to deteriorate. The United States emerged as a world power in the twentieth century, not because of what it had done in foreign relations but because it had spent the nineteenth century developing the North American continent; by contrast, the Austrian and Turkish empires collapsed in the twentieth century in large part because they had so long neglected their internal development and organization.

If America has a service to perform in the world—and I believe she has—it is in large part the service of her own example. In our excessive involvement in the affairs of other countries we are not only living off our assets and denying our own people the proper enjoyment of their resources, we are also denying the world the example of a free society enjoying its freedom to the fullest. This is regrettable indeed for a nation that aspires to teach democracy to other nations, because, as Edmund Burke said, "Example is the school of mankind, and they will learn at no other."

The missionary instinct in foreign affairs may, in a cautious way, reflect a deficiency rather than an excess of national self-confidence. In America's case the evidence of a lack of self-confidence is our apparent need for constant proof and reassurance, our nagging desire for popularity, our bitterness and confusion when foreigners fail to appreciate our generosity and good intentions. Lacking an appreciation of the dimensions of our own power, we fail to understand our enormous and disruptive impact on the world; we fail to understand that no matter how good our intentions—and they are, in most cases, decent enough—other nations are alarmed by the very existence of such great power, which, whatever its benevolence, cannot help but remind them of their own helplessness before it.

Those who lack self-assurance are also likely to lack magnanimity, because the one is the condition of the other. Only a nation at peace with itself, with its transgressions as well as its achievements, is capable of a generous understanding of others. Only when we Americans can acknowledge our own past aggressive behavior—in such instances, for example, as the Indian wars and the wars against Mexico and Spain—will we acquire some perspective on the aggressive behavior of others; only when we can understand the human implications of the chasm between American affluence and the poverty of most of the rest of mankind will we be able to understand why the American "way of life" which is so dear to us has few lessons and limited appeal to the poverty-stricken majority of the human race.

It is a curiosity of human nature that lack of self-assurance seems to breed an exaggerated sense of power and mission. When a nation is very powerful but lacking in self-confidence, it is likely to behave in a manner dangerous to itself and to others. Feeling the need to prove what is obvious to everyone else, it begins to confuse great power with unlimited power and great responsibility with total responsibility: it can admit of no error; it must win every argument, no matter how trivial. For lack of an appreciation of how truly powerful it is, the nation begins to lose wisdom and perspective and, with them, the strength and understanding that it takes to be magnanimous to smaller and weaker nations.

Gradually but unmistakably America is showing signs of that arrogance of power which has afflicted, weakened, and in some cases destroyed great nations in the past. In so doing we are not living up to our capacity and promise as a civilized example for the world. The measure of our falling short is the measure of the patriot's duty of dissent.

9. NATIONAL CONFERENCE OF CATHOLIC BISHOPS, "THE CHALLENGE OF PEACE" (1983)

Not surprisingly, the crescendo of the cry for nuclear disarmament was reached at the height of atomic weapons construction—or at least the threat thereof. During the 1980s, President Ronald Reagan embarked on a military buildup that included plans for advanced nuclear weaponry and a still-unproven defense system based in space. Soviet military spending replicated American spending, thus ratcheting up the arms race to new levels. Those who feared what this might mean for the future took to the streets in massive demonstrations around the world.

In a very thoughtful call for national leaders of both sides to reexamine their assumptions, the National Conference of Catholic Bishops in America in 1983 met, discussed the situation, and finally wrote a pastoral letter. Before them were ideas that had governed international relations for centuries, including just war and nonviolent theories. Placing squarely on the table the American and Soviet shared response of "mutual deterrence" through the threat of nuclear annihilation, the bishops attempted to hew a middle course between just war teachings and nonviolence. Understanding that many would disagree, they prefaced their long letter with an explanation of the dire situation the world was in, one that could explode at any minute and literally destroy the planet.

The bishops' letter marks an important moment during the dénouement of the Cold War, when those representing the largest Christian tradition in the United States dispensed with one-sided arguments and called upon Americans to think clearly through the issues at hand. By the end of the decade, the Soviet Union had collapsed under the debt of its military buildup, thus ending the argument of deterrence, but still leaving in place thousands of nuclear warheads.

∞

122. Both the just-war teaching and non-violence are confronted with a unique challenge by nuclear warfare. This must be the starting point of any further moral reflection: nuclear weapons particularly and nuclear warfare as it is planned today, raise new moral questions. No previously conceived moral position escapes the fundamental confrontation posed by contemporary nuclear strategy. Many have noted the similarity of the statements made by eminent scientists and Vatican II's observation that we are forced today "to undertake a completely fresh reappraisal of war." The task before us is not simply to repeat what we have said before; it is first to consider anew whether and how our religious-moral tradition can assess, direct, contain, and, we hope, help to eliminate the threat posed to the human family by the nuclear arsenals of the world. Pope John Paul II captured the essence of the problem during his pilgrimage to Hiroshima:

> In the past it was possible to destroy a village, a town, a region, even a country. Now it is the whole planet that has come under threat.

123. The Holy Father's observation illustrates why the moral problem is also a religious question of the most profound significance. In the nuclear arsenals of the United States or the Soviet Union alone, there exists a capacity to do something no other age could imagine: we can threaten the entire planet. For people of faith this means we read the Book of Genesis with a new awareness; the moral issue at stake in nuclear war involves the meaning of sin in

its most graphic dimensions. Every sinful act is a confrontation of the creature and the creator. Today the destructive potential of the nuclear powers threatens the human person, the civilization we have slowly constructed, and even the created order itself.

124. We live today, therefore, in the midst of a cosmic drama; we possess a power which should never be used, but which might be used if we do not reverse our direction. We live with nuclear weapons knowing we cannot afford to make one serious mistake. This fact dramatizes the precariousness of our position, politically, morally, and spiritually.

125. A prominent "sign of the times" today is a sharply increased awareness of the danger of the nuclear arms race. Such awareness has produced a public discussion about nuclear policy here and in other countries which is unprecedented in its scope and depth. What has been accepted for years with almost no question is now being subjected to the sharpest criticism. What previously had been defined as a safe and stable system of deterrence is today viewed with political and moral skepticism. Many forces are at work in this new evaluation, and we believe one of the crucial elements is the Gospel vision of peace which guides our work in this Pastoral Letter. The nuclear age has been the theater of our existence for almost four decades; today it is being evaluated with a new perspective. For many the leaven of the Gospel and the light of the Holy Spirit create the decisive dimension of this new perspective.

A. THE NEW MOMENT

126. At the center of the new evaluation of the nuclear arms race is a recognition of two elements: the destructive potential of nuclear weapons, and the stringent choices which the nuclear age poses for both politics and morals.

127. The fateful passage into the nuclear age as a military reality began with the bombing of Nagasaki and Hiroshima, events described by Pope Paul VI as a "butchery of untold magnitude." Since then, in spite of efforts at control and plans for disarmament (e.g., the Baruch Plan of 1946), the nuclear arsenals have escalated, particularly in the two superpowers. The qualitative superiority of these two states, however, should not overshadow the fact that four other countries possess nuclear capacity and a score of states are only steps away from becoming "nuclear nations."

128. This nuclear escalation has been opposed sporadically and selectively but never effectively. The race has continued in spite of carefully expressed doubts by analysts and other citizens and in the face of forcefully expressed opposition by public rallies. Today the opposition to the arms race is no

longer selective or sporadic, it is widespread and sustained. The danger and destructiveness of nuclear weapons are understood and resisted with new urgency and intensity. There is in the public debate today an endorsement of the position submitted by the Holy See at the United Nations in 1976: the arms race is to be condemned as a danger, an act of aggression against the poor, and a folly which does not provide the security it promises. . . .

132. To say "no" to nuclear war is both a necessary and a complex task. We are moral teachers in a tradition which has always been prepared to relate moral principles to concrete problems. Particularly in this letter we could not be content with simply restating general moral principles or repeating well-known requirements about the ethics of war. We have had to examine, with the assistance of a broad spectrum of advisors of varying persuasions, the nature of existing and proposed weapons systems, the doctrines which govern their use, and the consequences of using them. We have consulted people who engage their lives in protest against the existing nuclear strategy of the United States, and we have consulted others who have held or do hold responsibility for this strategy. It has been a sobering and perplexing experience. In light of the evidence which witnesses presented and in light of our study, reflection, and consultation, we must reject nuclear war. But we feel obliged to relate our judgment to the specific elements which comprise the nuclear problem.

133. Though certain that the dangerous and delicate nuclear relationship the superpowers now maintain should not exist, we understand how it came to exist. In a world of sovereign states, devoid of central authority and possessing the knowledge to produce nuclear weapons, many choices were made, some clearly objectionable, others well-intended with mixed results, which brought the world to its present dangerous situation.

134. We see with increasing clarity the political folly of a system which threatens mutual suicide, the psychological damage this does to ordinary people, especially the young, the economic distortion of priorities—billions readily spent for destructive instruments while pitched battles are waged daily in our legislatures over much smaller amounts for the homeless, the hungry, and the helpless here and abroad. But it is much less clear how we translate a "no" to nuclear war into the personal and public choices which can move us in a new direction, toward a national policy and an international system which more adequately reflect the values and vision of the Kingdom of God. . . .

136. Precisely because of the destructive nature of nuclear weapons, strategies have been developed which previous generations would have found unintelligible. Today military preparations are undertaken on a vast and sophisticated scale, but the declared purpose is not to use the weapons produced. Threats

are made which would be suicidal to implement. The key to security is no longer only military secrets, for in some instances security may best be served by informing one's adversary publicly what weapons one has and what plans exist for their use. The presumption of the nation-state system, that sovereignty implies an ability to protect a nation's territory and population, is precisely the presumption denied by the nuclear capacities of both superpowers. In a sense each is at the mercy of the other's perception of what strategy is "rational," what kind of damage is "unacceptable," how "convincing" one side's threat is to the other.

137. The political paradox of deterrence has also strained our moral conception. May a nation threaten what it may never do? May it possess what it may never use? Who is involved in the threat each superpower makes: government officials? or military personnel? or the citizenry in whose defense the threat is made?

138. In brief, the danger of the situation is clear; but how to prevent the use of nuclear weapons, how to assess deterrence, and how to delineate moral responsibility in the nuclear age are less clearly seen or stated. Reflecting the complexity of the nuclear problem, our arguments in this Pastoral must be detailed and nuanced; but our "no" to nuclear war must, in the end, be definitive and decisive. . . .

MORAL PRINCIPLES AND POLICY CHOICES

178. Targeting doctrine raises significant moral questions because it is a significant determinant of what would occur if nuclear weapons were ever to be used. Although we acknowledge the need for deterrent, not all forms of deterrence are morally acceptable. There are moral limits to deterrence policy as well as to policy regarding use. Specifically, it is not morally acceptable to intend to kill the innocent as part of a strategy of deterring nuclear war. The question of whether U.S. policy involves an intention to strike civilian centers (directly targeting civilian populations) has been one of our factual concerns.

179. This complex question has always produced a variety of responses, official and unofficial in character. The NCCB Committee has received a series of statements of clarification of policy from U.S. government officials. Essentially these statements declare that it is not U.S. strategic policy to target the Soviet civilian population as such or to use nuclear weapons deliberately for the purpose of destroying population centers. These statements respond, in principle at least, to one moral criterion for assessing deterrence policy: the immunity of non-combatants from direct attack either by conventional or nuclear weapons. . . .

182. The location of industrial or militarily significant economic targets within heavily populated areas or in those areas affected by radioactive fall-out could well involve such massive civilian casualties that, in our judgment, such a strike would be deemed morally disproportionate, even though not intentionally indiscriminate.

183. The problem is not simply one of producing highly accurate weapons that might minimize civilian casualties in any single explosion, but one of increasing the likelihood of escalation at a level where many, even "discriminating," weapons would cumulatively kill very large numbers of civilians. Those civilian deaths would occur both immediately and from the long-term effects of social and economic devastation.

184. A second issue of concern to us is the relationship of deterrence doctrine to war-fighting strategies. We are aware of the argument that war-fighting capabilities enhance the credibility of the deterrent, particularly the strategy of extended deterrence. But the development of such capabilities raises other strategic and moral questions. The relationship of war-fighting capabilities and targeting doctrine exemplifies the difficult choices in this area of policy. Targeting civilian populations would violate the principle of discrimination—one of the central moral principles of a Christian ethic of war. But "counterforce targeting," while preferable from the perspective of protecting civilians, is often joined with a declaratory policy which conveys the notion that nuclear war is subject to precise rational and moral limits. We have already expressed our severe doubts about such a concept. Furthermore, a purely counterforce strategy may seem to threaten the viability of other nations' retaliatory forces, making deterrence unstable in a crisis and war more likely.

185. While we welcome any effort to protect civilian populations, we do not want to legitimize or encourage moves which extend deterrence beyond the specific objective of preventing the use of nuclear weapons or other actions which could lead directly to a nuclear exchange. . . .

188. On the basis of these criteria we wish now to make some specific evaluations:

1) If nuclear deterrence exists only to prevent the *use* of nuclear weapons by others, then proposals to go beyond this to planning for prolonged periods of repeated nuclear strikes and counter-strikes, or "prevailing" in nuclear war, are not acceptable. They encourage notions that nuclear war can be engaged in with tolerable human and moral consequences. Rather, we must continually say "no" to the idea of nuclear war.

2) If nuclear deterrence is our goal, "sufficiency" to deter is an adequate strategy; the quest for nuclear superiority must be rejected.

3) Nuclear deterrence should be used as a step on the way toward progressive disarmament. Each proposed addition to our strategic system or

change in strategic doctrine must be assessed precisely in light of whether it will render steps toward "progressive disarmament" more or less likely. . . .

192. These judgments are meant to exemplify how a lack of unequivocal condemnation of deterrence is meant only to be an attempt to acknowledge the role attributed to deterrence, but not to support its extension beyond the limited purpose discussed above. Some have urged us to condemn all aspects of nuclear deterrence. This urging has been based on a variety of reasons, but has emphasized particularly the high and terrible risks that either deliberate use or accidental detonation of nuclear weapons could quickly escalate to something utterly disproportionate to any acceptable moral purpose. That determination requires highly technical judgments about hypothetical events. Although reasons exist which move some to condemn reliance on nuclear weapons for deterrence, we have not reached this conclusion for the reasons outlined in this letter.

193. Nevertheless, there must be no misunderstanding of our profound skepticism about the moral acceptability of any use of nuclear weapons. It is obvious that the use of any weapons which violate the principle of discrimination merits unequivocal condemnation. We are told that some weapons are designed for purely "counterforce" use against military forces and targets. The moral issue, however, is not resolved by the design of weapons or the planned intention for use; there are also consequences which must be assessed. It would be a perverted political policy or moral casuistry which tried to justify using a weapon which "indirectly" or "unintentionally" killed a million innocent people because they happened to live near a "militarily significant target."

194. Even the "indirect effects" of initiating nuclear war are sufficient to make it an unjustifiable moral risk in any form. It is not sufficient, for example, to contend that "our" side has plans for "limited" or "discriminate" use. Modern warfare is not readily contained by good intentions or technological designs. The psychological climate of the world is such that mention of the term "nuclear" generates uneasiness. Many contend that the use of one tactical nuclear weapon could produce panic, with completely unpredictable consequences. It is precisely this mix of political, psychological, and technological uncertainty which has moved us in this letter to reinforce with moral prohibitions and prescriptions the prevailing political barrier against resort to nuclear weapons. Our support for enhanced command and control facilities, for major reductions in strategic and tactical nuclear forces, and for a "no first use" policy (as set forth in this letter) is meant to be seen as a complement to our desire to draw a moral line against nuclear war.

195. Any claim by any government that it is pursuing a morally acceptable policy of deterrence must be scrutinized with the greatest care. We are pre-

pared and eager to participate in our country in the ongoing public debate on moral grounds.

196. The need to rethink the deterrence policy of our nation, to make the revisions necessary to reduce the possibility of nuclear war, and to move toward a more stable system of national and international security will demand a substantial intellectual, political, and moral effort. It also will require, we believe, the willingness to open ourselves to the providential care, power, and Word of God, which call us to recognize our common humanity and the bonds of mutual responsibility which exist in the international community in spite of political differences and nuclear arsenals.

197. Indeed, we do acknowledge that there are many strong voices within our own episcopal ranks and within the wider Catholic community in the United States which challenge the strategy of deterrence as an adequate response to the arms race today. They highlight the historical evidence that deterrence has not, in fact, set in motion substantial processes of disarmament.

198. Moreover, these voices rightly raise the concern that even the conditional acceptance of nuclear deterrence as laid out in a letter such as this might be inappropriately used by some to reinforce the policy of arms buildup. In its stead, they call us to raise a prophetic challenge to the community of faith—a challenge which goes beyond nuclear deterrence, toward more resolute steps to actual bilateral disarmament and peacemaking. We recognize the intellectual ground on which the argument is built and the religious sensibility which gives it its strong force.

10. RONALD REAGAN, "NATIONAL ASSOCIATION OF EVANGELICALS; REMARKS AT THE ANNUAL CONVENTION IN ORLANDO, FLORIDA" (1983)

The simultaneous rise of the religious Right and of Ronald Reagan was no coincidence. After having supported their own born-again Jimmy Carter in 1976, evangelicals turned to Reagan in 1980 and collectively dismissed Carter from office. The marriage of Reagan and the religious Right was based more on rhetoric than real policy, but the "Great Communicator" performed masterfully before an evangelical crowd. Tying a secular fear of central government to their concerns over the Antichrist's one-world government, Reagan forged an overarching language that could gather religious conservatives into the expanding tent of political conservatives.

In this speech of March 8, 1983 to the National Association of Evangelicals Annual Convention in Orlando, Florida, Reagan uses humor and personal stories to encourage evangelicals to enter the debate over escalating the arms race. Deflecting criticism that his military buildup is making the world a more dangerous place, he argues

that peace can only be achieved through strength. Employing language the audience ap-
preciates, namely, that America is a God-led country on a God-led mission, with a duty
to do something about the rise of national secularism (especially with regard to issues
like abortion and school prayer) and world communism, Reagan today might be ac-
cused of "preaching to the choir." But preaching to the choir can never be underesti-
mated—something Ronald Reagan knew better than perhaps anyone.

I can't tell you how you have warmed my heart with your welcome. I'm de-
lighted to be here today.

Those of you in the National Association of Evangelicals are known for
your spiritual and humanitarian work. And I would be especially remiss if
I didn't discharge right now one personal debt of gratitude. Thank you for
your prayers. Nancy and I have felt their presence many times in many
ways. And believe me, for us they've made all the difference.

The other day in the East Room of the White House at a meeting there,
someone asked me whether I was aware of all the people out there who were
praying for the President. And I had to say, "Yes, I am. I've felt it. I believe
in intercessionary prayer." But I couldn't help but say to that questioner after he'd asked the question that—or at least say to them that if sometimes
when he was praying he got a busy signal, it was just me in there ahead of
him. I think I understand how Abraham Lincoln felt when he said, "I have
been driven many times to my knees by the overwhelming conviction that I
had nowhere else to go." . . .

I'll tell you there are a great many God-fearing, dedicated, noble men and
women in public life, present company included. And, yes, we need your
help to keep us ever mindful of the ideas and the principles that brought us
into the public arena in the first place. The basis of those ideals and principles is a commitment to freedom and personal liberty that, itself, is grounded in the much deeper realization that freedom prospers only where the
blessings of God are avidly sought and humbly accepted.

The American experiment in democracy rests on this insight. Its discovery was the great triumph of our Founding Fathers, voiced by William Penn
when he said: "If we will not be governed by God, we must be governed by
tyrants." Explaining the inalienable rights of men, Jefferson said, "The God
who gave us life, gave us liberty at the same time." And it was George Washington, who said that "of all the dispositions and habits which lead to political prosperity, religion and morality are indispensible supports."

And finally, that shrewdest of all observers of American democracy,
Alexis de Tocqueville, put it eloquently after he had gone on a search for the

secret of American's greatness and genius—and he said: "Not until I went into the churches of America and heard her pulpits aflame with righteousness did I understand the greatness and the genius of America. . . . America is good. And if America ever ceases to be good, America will cease to be great."

Well, I'm pleased to be here today with you who are keeping America great by keeping her good. Only through your work and prayers and those of millions of others can we hope to survive this perilous century and keep alive this experiment in liberty, this last, best hope of man.

I want you to know that this administration is motivated by a political philosophy that sees the greatness of America in you, her people, and in your families, churches, neighborhoods, communities—the institutions that foster and nourish values like concern for others and respect for the rule of law under God.

Now, I don't have to tell you that this puts us in opposition to, or at least out of step with, a prevailing attitude of many who have turned to a modern-day secularism, discarding the tried and time-tested values upon which our very civilization is based. No matter how well intentioned, their value system is radically different from that of most Americans. And while they proclaim that they're freeing us from superstitions of the past, they've taken upon themselves the job of superintending us by government rule and regulation. Sometimes their vices are louder than ours, but they are not yet a majority. . . .

During my first press conference as President, in answer to a direct question, I pointed out that, as good Marxist-Leninists, the Soviet leaders have openly and publicly declared that the only morality they recognize is that which will further their cause, which is world revolution. I think I should point out I was only quoting Lenin, their guiding spirit, who said in 1920 that they repudiate all morality that proceeds from supernatural ideas— that's their name for religion—or ideas that are outside class conceptions. Morality is entirely subordinate to the interests of class war. And everything is moral that is necessary for the annihilation of the old, exploiting social order and for uniting the proletariat.

Well, I think the refusal of many influential people to accept this elementary fact of Soviet doctrine illustrates an historical reluctance to see totalitarian powers for what they are. We saw this phenomenon in the 1930s. We see it too often today.

This doesn't mean we should isolate ourselves and refuse to seek an understanding with them. I intend to do everything I can to persuade them of our peaceful intentions, to remind them that it was the West that refused to use this nuclear monopoly in the forties and fifties for territorial gain and which now proposes a 50-percent cut in strategic ballistic missiles and an entire class of land-based, intermediate-range nuclear missiles.

At the same time, however, they must be made to understand we will never compromise our principles and standards. We will never give away our freedom. We will never abandon our belief in God. And we will never stop searching for a genuine peace. But we can assure none of these things America stands for through the so-called nuclear freeze solutions proposed by some.

The truth is that a freeze now would be a very dangerous fraud, for that is merely the illusion of peace. The reality is that we must find peace through strength.

I would agree to a freeze if only we could freeze the Soviet's global desires. A freeze at current levels of weapons would remove any incentive for the Soviets to negotiate seriously in Geneva and virtually end our chances to achieve the major arms reductions which we have proposed. Instead, they would achieve their objectives through the freeze.

A freeze would reward the Soviet Union for its enormous and unparalleled military buildup. It would prevent the essential and long overdue modernization of United States and allied defenses and would leave our aging forces increasingly vulnerable. And an honest freeze would require extensive prior negotiations on the systems and numbers to be limited and on the measures to ensure effective verification and compliance. And the kind of freeze that has been suggested would be virtually impossible to verify. Such a major effort would divert us completely from our current negotiations on achieving substantial reductions.

A number of years ago, I heard a young father, a very prominent young man in the entertainment world, addressing a tremendous gathering in California. It was during the time of the cold war, and communism and our own way of life were very much on people's minds. And he was speaking to that subject. And suddenly, though, I heard him saying, "I love my little girls more than anything—" And I said to myself, "Oh, no don't. You can't—don't say that." But I had underestimated him. He went on: "I would rather see my little girls die now, still believing in God, than have them grow up under communism and one day die no longer believing in God."

There were thousands of young people in that audience. They came to their feet with shouts of joy. They had instantly recognized the profound truth in what he had said, with regard to the physical and the soul and what was truly important.

Yes, let us pray for the salvation of all of those who live in that totalitarian darkness—pray they will discover the joy of knowing God. But until they do, let us be aware that while they preach the supremacy of the state, declare its omnipotence over individual man, and predict its eventual domination of all people on the Earth, they are the focus of evil in the modern world.

It was C. S. Lewis who, in his unforgettable *Screwtape Letters*, wrote: "The greatest evil is not done now in those sordid 'dens of crime' that Dickens loved to paint. It is not even done in concentration camps and labor camps. In those we see its final result. But it is conceived and ordered (moved, seconded, carried and minuted) in clear, carpeted, warmed, and well-lighted offices, by quiet men with white collars and cut fingernails and smooth-shaven cheeks who do not need to raise their voice."

Well, because these "quiet men" do not "raise their voices," because they sometimes speak in soothing tones of brotherhood and peace, because, like other dictators before them, they're always making "their final territorial demand," some would have us accept them at their word and accommodate ourselves to their aggressive impulses. But if history teaches anything, it teaches that simple-minded appeasement or wishful thinking about our adversaries is folly. It means the betrayal of our past, the squandering of our freedom.

So, I urge you to speak out against those who would place the United States in a position of military and moral inferiority. You know, I've always believed that old Screwtape reserved his best efforts for those of you in the church. So, in your discussions of the nuclear freeze proposals, I urge you to beware the temptation of pride—the temptation of blithely declaring yourselves above it all and label both sides equally at fault, to ignore the facts of history and the aggressive impulses of an evil empire, to simply call the arms race a giant misunderstanding and thereby remove yourself from the struggle between right and wrong and good and evil.

I ask you to resist the attempts of those who would have you withhold your support for our efforts, this administration's efforts, to keep America strong and free, while we negotiate real and verifiable reductions in the world's nuclear arsenals and one day, with God's help, their total elimination.

While America's military strength is important, let me add here that I've always maintained that the struggle now going on for the world will never be decided by bombs or rockets, by armies or military might. The real crisis we face today is a spiritual one; at root, it is a test of moral will and faith.

Whittaker Chambers, the man whose own religious conversion made him a witness to one of the terrible traumas of our time, the Hiss-Chambers case, wrote that the crisis of the Western World exists to the degree in which the West is indifferent to God, the degree to which it collaborates in communism's attempt to make man stand alone without God. And then he said, for Marxism-Leninism is actually the second oldest faith, first proclaimed in the Garden of Eden with the words of temptation, "Ye shall be as gods."

The Western World can answer this challenge, he wrote, "but only provided that its faith in God and the freedom He enjoins is as great as Communism's faith in Man."

I believe we shall rise to the challenge. I believe that communism is another sad, bizarre chapter in human history whose last pages even now are being written. I believe this because the source of our strength in the quest for human freedom is not material, but spiritual. And because it knows no limitation, it must terrify and ultimately triumph over those who would enslave their fellow man. For the words of Isaiah: "He giveth power to the faint; and to them that have no might He increased strength. . . . But they that wait upon the Lord shall renew their strength; they shall mount up with wings as eagles; they shall run and not be weary."

Yes, change your world. One of our Founding Fathers, Thomas Paine, said, "We have it within our power to begin the world over again." We can do it, doing together what no one church could do by itself.

God bless you, and thank you very much.

Chapter 2

Religion and the Counterculture

> I saw the best minds of my generation destroyed by madness
> Starving, hysterical, naked
> Dragging through the negro streets at dawn,
> Looking for an angry fix.

WITH THESE WORDS, Allen Ginsberg announced a revolution in American poetry, one that paralleled the innovations of Jackson Pollock in painting and John Cage in music. Ginsberg read these opening lines to his poem "Howl" in 1955, in front of some friends and comrades (including Jack Kerouac, Ginsberg's friend and author of the famous novel *On the Road*) in Berkeley, California. As a Jew in a country still tinged with anti-Semitism, a political radical and son of a left-wing family in an America entering the anxieties of the Cold War era, and a gay man in a time obsessed with diagnosing and "curing" the illness of homosexuality before the communists could blackmail those afflicted into betraying the country, Ginsberg naturally felt himself an alien in the McCarthy-era United States. In a later poem, "America," addressing his country from the outside, he asks, "America, why are your libraries full of tears?" Ginsberg finishes "Howl" by invoking the ancient god of destruction, Moloch, on consumerist America: "They broke their backs lifting Moloch to Heaven." Ginsberg and others pioneered what later became known as the counterculture, seeking a way out of what they perceived to be the mindless conformism of 1950s America.

Some fourteen years after "Howl," hundreds of thousands of young people gathered at a farm near Woodstock, in upstate New York, and celebrated three days of music, food, and fellowship. On Broadway, the hit musical *Hair* proclaimed, "This is the dawning of the age of Aquarius," while in academics, Theodore Roszak explained *The Making of a Counterculture* and

Charles Reich exulted about *The Greening of America*. By that time, the counterculture was in vogue, soon to be mainstream. Indeed, corporate commercial culture soon swallowed it up, as rock songs once considered revolutionary sold shoes and soap.

American religions responded to the rise of the counterculture and the baby boomers in myriad ways, but could by no means ignore them. Mainstream religious groups sought to capture the energy of the young people who seemed to be leading the country in new directions. Many spiritual seekers, meanwhile, simply rejected mainstream Protestant, Catholic, and Jewish traditions altogether, turning their spiritual quests to eastern thought, meditation, psychedelic drugs, and neopaganism. They sought access to heightened states of awareness, to what many of them called a new or "expanded" consciousness. To them, mainstream American religions seemed just part of the "system," with churches preaching as empty a message as American businessmen practiced. In the selection below from *The Greening of America*, Charles Reich interprets the counterculture as representing the rise of "Consciousness III," open, flexible, adaptive, nonhierarchical modes of thinking and living that would (he believed) replace the rigid, authoritarian structures of corporate capitalist America. Reich's work appeared toward the end of the flowering of the counterculture, and represents the most utopian (and dated) expression of its ideals.

The religious ferment of the time was so pronounced that one distinguished scholarly commentator saw it as another Great Awakening. At times in American history, William McLoughlin wrote in his book *Revivals, Awakenings, and Reforms*, the old ideas and institutions by which society regulated itself suddenly became ossified. First the seers and visionaries, and later the populace as a whole, grew weary of them and sought alternatives. In place of order and structure, they yearned for communitas, that feeling of being at one with fellow man in a search for life's meaning. These so-called Great Awakenings had taken the form of large-scale revivals in the mid-eighteenth century and in the early and mid-nineteenth century. The first responded to the disintegration of the old Puritan order; the second was a response to the market revolution and the rise of early industrialism. Both were sparked by societal changes.

So was the Great Awakening of the 1960s and beyond, McLoughlin continued. Americans in the 1950s married earlier and went to church more often than the several generations preceding them. Mainstream churches were simply part of the established order of the time. President Eisenhower's famous television commercial urging Americans to go to church—any church—signified how much democracy, free enterprise, and religious faith were tied together. But a new generation born to parents coming out of the

Depression and World War II found that the suburban nuclear-family "happy days" of the 1950s, and the Cold War assumptions and paranoia that lay beneath that structure, no longer sufficed to define their world.

The social revolutions beginning in that decade—the civil rights movement, the antiwar crusade, feminism, gay rights, and others—unraveled the close connection of organized religious expression to fundamental "American" values. Americans now valued self-expression and personal quests for fulfillment. Certainly religious institutions were not alone. Government, universities, and corporate bureaucracies came under the same scrutiny and intense questioning. But American religion was a perfect place for the counterculture to blossom, for it always has been about the freedom of the individual conscience in spiritual expression.

Religious themes emerge clearly in the literature produced by the beat generation of the 1950s, including Allen Ginsberg, Jack Kerouac, and Gary Snyder; this chapter provides a few excerpts. In "Howl," Ginsberg's part religio-political-sexual primal scream, the poet had equated the insanity of the "best minds" of his generation with a kind of religious ascension, with the pilgrims (the beatniks whose real-life personal exploits he chronicled) wandering the deserts of contemporary America like the ancient lost sages in the wilderness, searching for truth and beauty. In "A Blake Experience," based on interviews over a period of years, Ginsberg traces his mystical communion with poets past, with whom he felt he shared "mystical visions and cosmic dreams," as he later wrote in "America."

Some extracts of essays by Gary Snyder invoke the gods of ancient and extinct bands of Native Americans as a requiem for the contemporary American landscape. In the 1960s, self-styled visionaries used psychedelic drugs to expand their consciousness (and that of others). For decades prior to that, natural hallucinogens quietly had become part of Native American religious expression, namely in the form of the peyote buttons taken by members of the Native American Church as part of all-night rituals. And for generations before that, mushrooms and other botanicals were part of the religions of many indigenous groups in the Americas. White Americans, however, remained largely ignorant of those traditions.

Drugs—marijuana, speed, and lysergic acid (LSD)—entered the counterculture originally through a variety of sources, from the black jazzmen emulated by the beats to the controlled hallucinogenic experiments conducted by psychology professors such as Timothy Leary and Richard Alpert. LSD in particular developed a small following in the early 1960s, when Leary conducted LSD "trials" on groups of academics and (especially) divinity students who came to his home to ingest the drugs and report on what happened to them.

Coming from a background of behavioralist psychology, Leary originally had little use for the religious terminology that would come to be associated with LSD. But he quickly was intrigued by the fact that it was divinity students, ministers, and others from religious backgrounds who were attracted to consciousness expansion through acid. Leary placed himself in the tradition of William James and others earlier in the century who had been intrigued by the varieties of religious experience, including psychical phenomena such as hypnotism and mesmerism. He was joined by the well-known interpreter of the Zen Buddhist tradition, Alan Watts, who in the selections below reports on his personal experience with LSD, and more generally on his religious quests (as well as his disappointment with what he saw as the philosophical and aesthetic crudities of the early counterculture).

One of Leary's other coenthusiasts, another Harvard psychologist named Richard Alpert, tried LSD, several hundred times. Like Watts, he eventually decided that the chemical was a temporary expedient needed to introduce followers to new realms of consciousness, but that other religious traditions could produce the same effect without the need for drugs. Alpert set off for India and Nepal to discover these traditions, just as the poet Gary Snyder had done in the 1950s during his twelve-year period of Zen Buddhist study in Japan. Alpert's stay was much shorter, but profoundly life-changing. After taking the new name Ram Dass, he returned to the United States to spread the new gospel of natural enlightenment. His 1971 book *Remember, Be Here Now*, excerpted below, tells of his spiritual quest. This work was enormously influential, particularly the latter section, "Cookbook for a Sacred Life," which explained in easy steps practices such as meditation and yoga to Americans who sought user-friendly introductions to such foreign spiritual practices.

At its best, religious expression in the counterculture introduced many Americans to previously unfamiliar traditions, including the wisdom of the East. At its worst, the counterculture encouraged narcissistic individualism, characterized by personal amalgamations of beliefs not understandable or recognizable by anyone else. As the veterans of the movement grew up in the 1970s, their quest for individual fulfillment took on increasingly programmatic forms, such as the vogue in the 1970s for EST (Erhard Seminars of Training)—expensive retreats during which middle-class baby boomers learned how to reconcile spiritual seeking with desires for material goods and success in the corporate workplace. The 1960s, in popular understanding, now stands as an emblem of activism for social causes. By contrast, the 1970s were famously tagged by social essayist Tom Wolfe as the "me decade," a parody description of the proliferation of trendy programs for self-fulfillment, from jogging to primal scream therapy.

Evangelicals responded to the counterculture, in part to rebuff charges that they were "squares." Since the 1950s, young evangelicals had worked for Campus Crusade for Christ and Youth for Christ, two organizations run with militarylike discipline by Bill Bright. Mostly these groups reached out to audiences already receptive, generally conservative and clean-cut college students, many of whom came from church backgrounds. By the later 1960s, it was clear that new methods, styles, and rhetoric would be needed to win and keep young adherents. As was usual in American history, religious entrepreneurs and innovators (as well as charlatans and cultish figures) filled the vacuum. Duane Pederson worked in California among "street people," a term that then referred not to the homeless but to young people who lived outside the norms of conventional society. Pederson started a free paper with a Christian message that in style mimicked the many alternative free papers (including *Ramparts* and the *Berkeley Barb*) that were the intellectual forums of the counterculture. He also coined (and later copyrighted) the term "Jesus People," sometimes called "Jesus Freaks." Pederson sought the young men and women who would be rejected from mainstream churches because of their hairstyle or dress, who would find little of relevance in "square" churches, cooperating and competing with a number of other religious entrepreneurs, including Richard Alamo, who organized The Children of God as a cult of personality.

Many of the new religious trends blurred the lines between movement, sect, and cult. Christians joined in the numerous experiments in communal living that sprang up in the 1960s. Most were short-lived and unsuccessful, although they led to interesting innovations in food preparation, organic farming, and environmental consciousness. Some communes directly descended from the Jesus People, such as The Children of God, allowed members almost no personal freedoms and required constant volunteer labor, the proceeds of which went into the pockets of the leaders.

The logical extreme and human calamity of such experiments came with the horrific mass suicide of members of the People's Temple, followers of the former Disciples of Christ minister Jim Jones, in November 1978. The People's Temple started as an experiment in religiously based activism for racial reconciliation in the Bay area of California and ended as a grotesque cult of personality in the jungles of Guyana. When authorities and the press came to investigate, three of them (including a congressman) were murdered, and Jones's remaining followers—938 of them—drank poisoned Kool-Aid. The horror of Jonestown fed into a national hysteria about "cults," as American adults came to fear their children were being captured by charismatic but evil individual personalities (such as Reverend Sun Myung Moon and the Unification Church) who would brainwash them into slavish robots.

In response to the cults and new religious movements springing from the counterculture, conservative evangelicals established centers to save imperiled youths from psychological kidnapping. They wrote countless pamphlets, magazine articles, and books publicizing what they perceived as the dangerous rise of extremist religious sects. A number of evangelicals formed the Cult Awareness Network, a coalition mostly of conservative Christians who specialized in "deprogramming," a term coined to describe the process of trying to reverse the effects of the "brainwashing" supposedly performed in cult settings. Later, in the 1990s, the Cult Awareness Network would emerge as a primary adviser to the government in dealing with the Branch Davidians in Waco, Texas, a confrontation that ended in another horrific tragedy (an event discussed in chapter 7).

The commercialization and trivialization of the counterculture in the 1970s and after inevitably, if ironically, proceeded from the same assumptions that its adherents thought would transform American culture. But if the counterculture failed to bring the revolution, it succeeded in popularizing new spiritual concepts and practices that would be taken up by millions of Americans in the coming years. In the 1980s, the New Age movement, promoted by figures such as Marilyn Ferguson (author of the best-seller *The Aquarian Conspiracy*) and Shirley MacLaine, emerged as one of its descendants. For many Americans, the counterculture profoundly influenced the very language in which they described and explained to themselves their spiritual quests—whether or not they recognized it. Certainly alternative sources of wisdom and esoteric lore had found advocates in the United States prior to that time, among intellectuals and writers such as Ralph Waldo Emerson, Henry Steel Olcott, spiritualists, and other religious experimenters. What the counterculture ultimately did was to popularize these sources and apply them to contemporary American life. Religion in the counterculture, then, was not really about revolution. It was about popularization and democratization of alternative traditions.

1. ALLEN GINSBERG, "A BLAKE EXPERIENCE" (1966)

Beatniks of the 1950s, predecessors of and an inspiration to the hippies of the 1960s, self-consciously and flamboyantly rejected the dominant values and mores of 1950s America. Where middle-class Americans sought security, comfort, domesticity, the beatniks valued freedom, spontaneity, open living. Poets, novelists, and free spirits such as Allen Ginsberg, Gary Snyder, Jack Kerouac, and others experimented with new literary and artistic forms, smoked marijuana, and in some cases risked mental institutional-

ization because of their uncloseted homosexuality. In his poem "America," Ginsberg queried the monolith that he saw before him, 1950s U.S. culture, and asked, "America, why are your libraries full of tears?"

In the fall of 1955, Ginsberg first read his masterpiece "Howl" before a small crowd of poetic supporters who pounded the tables and shouted "Go" in between the lines. "Howl" depicts Cold War America and mechanical consumer culture as a destroyer, and calls on Moloch, a Canaanite fire god whose worship was marked by parents burning their children as propiatory sacrifice, as an emblem of the soul-deadening culture that Ginsberg despised: "Moloch! Moloch! Robot apartments! Invisible suburbs! Skeleton treasuries! Blind capitals! Demonic industries! Spectral nations! . . . They broke their backs lifting Moloch to heaven."

In the following interview excerpts, done for the Paris Review *in 1966, Ginsberg traces his mystical communion with poets past, with whom he felt he shared "mystical visions and cosmic dreams." His "Blake experience" was akin to a religious conversion for a poet in search of his voice.*

INTERVIEWER: What was the Blake experience you speak of?

GINSBERG: About 1945 I got interested in Supreme Reality with a capital S and R, and I wrote big long poems about a last voyage looking for Supreme Reality. . . . I'd been in a very lonely solitary state, dark night of the soul sort of, reading Saint John of the Cross, maybe on account of that everybody'd gone away that I knew. . . . And I figured I'd never find any sort of psychospiritual sexo-cock jewel fulfillment in my existence! . . .

So, in that state therefore, of hopelessness, or dead-end, change of phase, you know—growing up—and in an equilibrium in any case, a psychic, a mental equilibrium of a kind, like of having no New Vision and no Supreme Reality and nothing but the world in front of me, and of not knowing what to do with *that* . . . there was a funny balance of tension, in every direction. And just after I came, on this occasion, with a Blake book on my lap—I wasn't even reading, my eye was idling over the page of "Ah, Sun-flower," and it suddenly appeared—the poem I'd read a lot of times before, over familiar to the point where it didn't make any particular meaning except some sweet thing about flowers—and suddenly I realized that the poem was talking about *me* "Ah, Sun-flower! weary of time, / Who countest the steps of the sun; / Seeking after the sweet golden clime, / Where the traveller's journey is done . . . " Now, I began understanding it, the poem while looking at it and suddenly, simultaneously with understanding it, heard very deep earthen grave voice in the room, which I immediately assumed, I didn't think twice, was Blake's voice; it wasn't any voice that I knew, though I had previously had a conception of voice of rock, in a poem, some image like that—or maybe that came after this experience.

And my eye on the page, simultaneously the auditory hallucination, or whatever terminology here used, the apparitions voice, in the room, woke me further deep in my understanding of the poem, because the voice was so completely tender and beautifully . . . ancient. Like the voice of the Ancient of Days. But the peculiar quality of the voice was something unforgettable because it was like God had a human voice, with all the infinite tenderness and anciency and mortal gravity of a living Creator speaking to his son . . . and simultaneous to the voice there was also an emotion, risen in my soul in response to the voice, and a sudden *visual* realization of the same awesome phenomena. That is to say, looking out at the window through the Window at the sky, suddenly it seemed that I saw into the depths of the universe, by looking simply into the ancient sky. The sky suddenly seemed very *ancient*. And this was the very ancient place that he was talking about, the sweet golden clime, I suddenly realized that *this* existence was *it*! And, that I was born in order to experience up to this very moment that I was having this experience, to realize what this was all about—in other words that this was the moment that I was born for. This initiation. Or this vision or this consciousness, of being alive unto myself, alive myself unto the Creator. As the son of the Creator—who loved me, I realized, or who responded to my desire, say. It was the same desire both ways. . . .

. . . My body suddenly felt *light*, and a sense of cosmic consciousness, vibrations, understanding, awe, and wonder and surprise. And it was a sudden awakening into a totally deeper real universe than I'd been existing in. . . .

It's taken me all these years to manifest it and work it out in a way that's materially communicable to people. Without scaring them or me. Also movements of history and breaking down the civilization. To break down everybody's masks and roles sufficiently so that everybody has to face the universe *and* the possibility of the sick rose coming true and the atom bomb. So it was an immediate messianic thing. . . .

So. Next time it happened was about a week later walking along in the evening on a circular path around what's now I guess the garden or field in the middle of Columbia University, by the library. I started invoking the spirit, consciously trying to get another depth perception of cosmos. And suddenly it began occurring again, like a sort of breakthrough again, but this time—this was the last time in that period—it was the same depth of consciousness or the same cosmical awareness but suddenly it was not blissful at all but it was *frightening*. Some like real serpent-fear entering the sky. The sky was not a blue hand anymore but like a hand of death coming down on me—some really scary presence, it was almost as if I saw God again except God was the devil. The consciousness itself was so vast, much more vast than any idea of it I'd had or any experience I'd had that it was not even human anymore—and was in a sense a threat, because I was going to die into that inhuman ultimately. Don't know *what* the score was there—I was too cowardly in pursue it. To attend and experience completely the Gates of Wrath—there's a poem of Blake's that deals with that, "To find a Western Path / Right through the Gates of Wrath." But I didn't urge my way there, I shut it all off. And got scared, us thought, I've gone too far. . . .

The confrontation with a society—or a family, for that matter—which is going in a different direction, and the ineptness of the initiate, who is totally dependent during those confrontations on the blissful will of others, at knowing how to handle his perception without becoming fearful or blowing his cool. Knowing how to feel human and holy and not like a madman in a world which is rigid and materialistic and all caught up in the immediate necessities. Like if it's time to cook supper and you're busy communing, the world says there must be something wrong with you. Or like, after my Blake vision, when I tried to evoke the sensations of the experience myself, artificially, by dancing around my apartment chanting a sort of homemade mantra: "Come, spirit. O spirit, spirit, come. Come, spirit. O spirit, spirit, come." Something like that. There I was, in the dark, in an apartment in the middle of Harlem, whirling like a dervish and invoking powers. And everybody I tried to talk to about it thought I was crazy. Not just that psychiatrist. The two girls who lived next door. My father. My teachers. Even most of my friends. Now, in a society which was open and dedicated to spirit, like in India, my actions and my address would have been considered quite normal. Had I been transported to a street-corner potato-curry shop in Benares and begun acting that way, I would have been seen as in some special, holy sort of state and sent on my way to the burning grounds, to sit and meditate. And when I got home, I would have been like gently encouraged to express myself, to work it out, and then left alone. I would have been understood.

2. ALAN WATTS, "BEGINNING A COUNTERCULTURE" (FROM *IN MY OWN WAY*, 1972), "PSYCHEDELICS AND RELIGIOUS EXPERIENCE" (FROM *DOES IT MATTER?*, 1971)

If Timothy Leary was the sacred clown and enthusiast of drug-induced changes in consciousness, Alan Watts, an English-born scholar and proponent of eastern religious traditions in the United States, was its popularizing theoretician. Watts was known primarily for his lectures on Zen in the 1950s and 1960s, which introduced many Americans to this particular Asian religious philosophy. But Watts also led an incredibly varied religious life over several decades, including time as an Episcopal priest at Northwestern University in Chicago, leadership of Asian studies institutes on the West Coast, and world-famous lectures delivered to acolytes all over the country. In the first selection, from his autobiography In My Own Way, *Watts reflects on "beginning a counterculture," a time when his own religious experimentation drew interest from a growing body of fellow seekers. He saw his work "simply as one of philosophical and spiritual stimulation," more as a physician than as a minister.*

In the 1960s Watts also experimented with psychedelics, seeing their use as a continuation of the psychical experiments of the late nineteenth century and the religious explorations of William James in the early twentieth. Much like Leary, only with more self-consciously serious prose and manner, Watts saw drugs as one means to mystical experience. If this was not "practical" in the western sense, if the new consciousness broke down hierarchies and encouraged unorthodox visions, so much the better. Religious resistance to drug use, Watts argued, came in part because "our own Jewish and Christian theologies will not accept the idea that man's inmost self can be identical with the Godhead." Watts later turned away from psychedelic experiments, seeing them as one baby step in western man's attempt to shed techno-rational culture and attain spiritual enlightenment.

BEGINNING A COUNTERCULTURE

I am more often considered a popularizer of Zen, Vedanta, and Taoism, who often twists the facts to suit his own views. One reason for this impression is that my style of writing does not lend itself to the tortuous course of interminable qualifications, reservations, and drawing of fine distinctions. But I am well aware of them when I leave them out, and can (and do) refer those who want the fine points to the proper sources, and can, furthermore, produce the necessary scholarly evidence for my conclusions if asked. . . .

It is therefore also said—perhaps with truth—that my easy and free-floating attitude to Zen was largely responsible for the notorious "Zen boom" which flourished among artists and "pseudointellectuals" in the late 1950s, and led on to the frivolous "beat Zen" of Kerouac's *Dharma Bums*, of Franz Kline's black and white abstractions, and of John Cage's silent concerts. . . .

What I saw in Zen was an intuitive way of understanding the sense of life by getting rid of silly quests and questions. . . . It is thus that almost every morning, when I first awaken, I have a feeling of total clarity as to the sense of life, a feeling of myself and the universe as a matter of the utmost simplicity. "I" and "That which is" are the same. Always have been and always will be. I could say that what constitutes me is the same jazz that constitutes the cosmos, and that there is simply nothing special to be achieved, realized, or performed. . . .

One could say it with music, but this is expressive, not descriptive, and the trouble with industrially civilized people is that they have no gift for spontaneous music. Our music is so counted out, scaled, metered, and trickily calculated that no one but an expert may have the nerve to indulge in it lest he be accused of making a nasty noise. But we would understand the sense of life if we would sing more and say less.

I have for years been trying to show people that it is extremely important to chant spontaneously, or at least to hum, and also to dance. I have offended people who, on attending seminars to hear an internationally famous philosopher, were simply encouraged to breathe effortlessly and allow their voices to hum along a line of least resistance, like water. . . . Chanting, flute or drum playing, and dancing in demilitarized patterns are ideally natural forms of yoga-meditation, because they silence the hypnotic chattering of thought and give one a direct feeling of *shabda*—the basic energy or vibration of the universe. This is why Gregorian chant, for example, gives the sense of eternity so absent from metered hymns. . . .

Among our students at this time there were also Michael Murphy and Richard Price, who together founded the Esalen Institute at Big Sur; Richard Hittleman, who subsequently taught Yoga to the nation on television; and on occasion, Gary Snyder the poet, who first appeared unaccountably and amazingly dressed in a formal black suit, British style, with a neatly rolled umbrella, but who later emerged in history as Japhy Ryder—the Buddhist-beatnik hero of Kerouac's *Dharma Bums*—in a characterization which hardly begins to do him justice. I am not Gary's teacher. He studied Chinese at the University of California with Shih-hsiang Chen and Zen at Daitokuji in Kyoto with Goto and Oda; but when I am dead I would like to be able to say that he is carrying on everything I hold most dearly, though with a different style. To put it in another way, my only regret is that I cannot formally claim him as my spiritual successor. He did it all on his own, but nevertheless he *is* just exactly what I have been trying to *say*. For Gary is tougher, more disciplined, and more physically competent than I, but he embodies these virtues without rubbing them in, and I can only say that a universe which has manifested Gary Snyder could never be called a failure. . . .

Now I am writing of the year 1960, and it will be remembered that this was when—in San Francisco in particular—there were the first signs of an astonishing change of attitude among young people which, despite its excesses and self-caricatures, had spread far over the world by the end of the decade. In a way, it started with the Beat Generation, and though I appear under a pseudonym in Kerouac's *Dharma Bums*, Jano and I were *in* this milieu rather than *of* it, and I was somewhat severe with it in my essay *Beat Zen, Square Zen, and Zen* which had appeared in the *Chicago Review* in 1958. But Jack Kerouac, Lawrence Ferlinghetti, and especially Gary Snyder and Allen Ginsberg, were now among our friends. . . . Allen is a rabbinic *sadhu* who can at need transform himself into an astute and hardheaded lawyer, and only this combination of fearless holiness, blazing compassion, and clear intellect has prevented him from being jailed or shot long ago. There was a night in Gavin's apartment when we chanted sutras together for hours, Allen ringing the time with his little Indian finger-cymbals, and through this purely sonic communion, with the glee that Allen puts into it, we somehow reached each other more deeply than in verbal exchanges. There was a time, too, when we chanted the *Dharani of the Great Compassionate One* all the way down New York's Second Avenue in a Volkswagen bus.

For some reason OM and the chanting of OM has always struck the press and Middle Americans as something to be laughed off—like the Islamic prayer rug and the Tibetan praying wheel—and it may be that the boys in Cairo speak with equal flippancy of some of their weird brethren who turn Christian and go and get themselves watered—as if *that* would do any good. But when the musical *Hair* opened in San Francisco I was invited on stage before the curtain went up to lead the cast in mantra-chanting, and today most of my college audiences are disappointed if I do not give some time to exercises in meditation and the chant. No one is more astonished at this than I. In my work of interpreting Oriental ways to the West I was pressing a button in expectation of a buzz, but instead there was an explosion. . . .

The power of something so apparently simple—and so seemingly absurd—as mantra- and OM-chanting is that it fosters a relaxed concentration on pure sound, as distinct from words, ideas, and abstractions, and thus brings attention to bear on reality itself. Now the ears bring reality to us entirely as process, as flowing vibration, and we hear this energy emerging from silence in the immediate moment and then echoing away into memory and the past; just as the world itself emerges instantly and spontaneously from space and no-thingness, which is as essential to energy as negative electricity to positive. To the eyes and the fingers the world seems more static, rendering it less easy to understand that a mountain is actually a vibration. . . .

But in the circles in which we were then moving—in San Francisco, Los Angeles, and New York—something else was on the way, in religion, in music, in ethics and sexuality, in our attitudes to nature, and in our whole style of life. We took courage and began to swing. For there was an energy in the air that cannot entirely be attributed to the revelations of LSD, an energy which manifested itself on the surface as color and imagination in clothing, in a rebirth of poetry, in the rhythms of rock-and-roll and in fascination for Hindu music, in social gatherings where people were no longer afraid to touch one another and show affection (so that even men greeted one another with embraces), and in a general letting down of hair, both figurative and literal. . . .

PSYCHEDELICS AND RELIGIOUS EXPERIENCE

The experiences resulting from the use of psychedelic drugs are often described in religious terms. They are therefore of interest to those like myself who, in the tradition of William James, are concerned with the psychology of religion. For more than thirty years I have been studying the causes, consequences, and conditions of those peculiar states of consciousness in which the individual discovers himself to be one continuous process with God, with the Universe, with the Ground of Being, or whatever name he may use by cultural conditioning or personal preference for the ultimate and eternal reality. We have no satisfactory and definitive name for experiences of this kind. The terms "religious experience," "mystical experience," and "cosmic consciousness" are all too vague and comprehensive to denote that specific mode of consciousness which, to those who have known it, is as real and overwhelming as falling in love. . . .

The idea of mystical experiences resulting from drug use is not readily accepted in Western societies. Western culture has, historically, a particular fascination with the value and virtue of man as an individual, self-determining, responsible ego, controlling himself and his world by the power of conscious effort and will. Nothing, then, could be more repugnant to this cultural tradition than the notion of spiritual or psychological growth through the use of drugs. . . . There is really no analogy between being "high" on LSD and "drunk" on bourbon. True, no one in either state should drive a car, but neither should one drive while reading a book, playing a violin, or making love. . . .

I myself have experimented with five of the principal psychedelics: LSD-25, mescaline, psilocybin, dimethyltryptamine (DMT), and cannabis. I have done so, as William James tried nitrous oxide, to see if they could help me in identifying what might be called the "essential" or "active" ingredients of the mystical experience. . . .

In the course of two experiments I was amazed and somewhat embarrassed to find myself going through states of consciousness which corresponded precisely with every description of major mystical experiences I had ever read. Furthermore, they exceeded both in depth and in a peculiar quality of unexpectedness the three "natural and spontaneous" experiences of this kind which I had had in previous years.

Through subsequent experimentation with LSD-25 and the other chemicals named above . . . I found I could move with ease into the state of "cosmic consciousness," and in due course became less and less dependent on the chemicals themselves for "tuning in" to this particular wave-length of experience. . . .

Almost invariably, my experiments with psyehedelics have had four dominant characteristics. I shall try to explain them—in the expectation that the reader will say, at least of the second and third, "Why, that's obvious! No one needs a drug to see that." Quite so, but every insight has degrees of intensity. There can be obvious and obvious—and the latter comes on with shattering clarity, manifesting its implications in every sphere and dimension of our existence.

The first characteristic is a slowing down of time, a *concentration in the present*. One's normally compulsive concern for future decreases, and one becomes aware of the enormous importance and interest of what is happening at the moment. Other people, going about their business on the streets, seem to be slightly crazy, failing to realize that the whole point of life is to be fully aware of it as it happens. One therefore relaxes, almost luxuriously, in studying the colors in a glass of water, or in listening to the now highly articulate vibration of every note played on an oboe or sung by voice. . . .

The second characteristic I will call *awareness of polarity*. This is the vivid realization that states, things, and events which we ordinarily call opposite are interdependent, like back and front or the poles of a magnet. By polar awareness one sees that things which are explicitly different are implicitly One: self and other, subject and object, left and right, male and female—and then, a little more surprisingly, solid and space, figure and background, pulse and interval, saints and sinners, and police and criminals, in-groups and out-groups. . . .

The third characteristic, arising from the second, is *awareness of relativity*. I see that I am a link in an infinite hierarchy of processes and beings, ranging from molecules through bacteria and insects to human beings, and, maybe, to angels and gods—a hierarchy in which every level is in effect the same situation. . . .

I see, further, that feeling threatened by the inevitability of death is really the same experience as feeling alive, and that as all beings are feeling this everywhere, they are all just as much "I" as myself. Yet the "I" feeling, to be felt at all, must always be a sensation relative to the "other", to something beyond its control and experience. To be at all, it must begin and end. But the intellectual jump which mystical and psychedelic experience make here is in enabling you to see that all these myriad I-centers are yourself—not, indeed, your personal and superficial conscious ego, but what Hindus call the *paramatman*, the Self of all selves. As the retina enables us to see count-less pulses of energy as a single light, so the mystical experience shows us innumerable individuals as a single Self.

The fourth characteristic is *awareness of eternal energy*, often in the form of intense white light, which seems to be both the current in your nerves and that mysterious *e* which equals mc^2. This may sound like megalomania or delusion of grandeur—but one sees quite clearly that all existence is a single energy, and that this energy is one's own being. . . . At root, you are the God-head, for God is all that there is. . . .

Resistance to allowing use of psychedelic drugs originates in both reli-gious and secular values. The difficulty in describing psychedelic experi-ences in traditional religious terms suggests one ground of opposition. The Westerner must borrow such words as *samadhi* or *moksha* from the Hindus, or *satori* or *kensho* from the Japanese, to describe the experience of oneness with the universe. We have no appropriate word because our own Jewish and Christian theologies will not accept the idea that man's inmost self can be identical with the Godhead, even though Christians may insist that this was true in the unique instance of Jesus Christ. . . .

If, however, in the context of Christian or Jewish tradition an individual declares himself to be one with God, he must be dubbed blasphemous (sub-versive) or insane. Such a mystical experience is a clear threat to traditional religious concepts. The Judaeo-Christian tradition has a monarchical image of God, and monarchs, who rule by force, fear nothing more than insubor-dination. The Church has therefore always been highly suspicious of mys-tics because they seem to be insubordinate and to claim equality or, worse, identity with God. . . .

The Western man who claims consciousness of oneness with God or the universe thus clashes with his society's concept of religion. In most Asian cultures, however, such a man will be congratulated as having penetrated the true secret of life. He has arrived, by chance or by some such discipline as Yoga or Zen meditation, at a state of consciousness in which he experiences directly and vividly what our own scientists know to be true in theory. . . .

3. CHARLES REICH, *THE GREENING OF AMERICA* (1970)

By the late 1960s, experiments in consciousness-raising (through drugs or otherwise), sensational rock concerts, artistic revolt, communal living experiments, and intellectual revolutions had convinced some that a new stage of American life and thought was emerging—what Charles Reich in this excerpt from his 1970 treatise The Greening of America *refers to as "Consciousness III." In Reich's reading of American history, "Consciousness I" was, in effect, the age of radical individualism, with the man on the make and the entrepreneurial genius being the valued social types. "Consciousness II" arose with twentieth-century corporate capitalism, and taught men to achieve success by scaling corporate hierarchies. By contrast, Consciousness III "accepts no imposed system. . . . It is always in a state of becoming." It could abide no pre-existing routine, no outmoded conformist ideologies, no cookie-cutter suburban tract lifestyle. Reich's book, dedicated to his students at Yale, represented the pinnacle of the utopian hopes of 1960s visionaries, who believed strongly that they were entering the Age of Aquarius, a new realm of expanded consciousness and human freedom.*

It is upon these premises that the Consciousness III idea of community and of personal relationships rests. In place of the world seen as a jungle, with every man for himself (Consciousness I) or the world seen as a meritocracy leading to a great corporate hierarchy of rigidly drawn relations and manoeuvers for position (Consciousness II), the world is a community. People all belong to the same family, whether they have met each other or not. . . .

One quality unites all aspects of the Consciousness III way of life: energy. It is the energy of enthusiasm, of happiness, of hope. . . . Consciousness III draws energy from new sources: from the group, the community, from eros, from the freedom of technology, from the uninhibited self. . . .

Consciousness III is beginning to experiment with small communities of different sorts. Many of the communes that have sprung up in various parts of the country are based primarily on shared values, such as love of desert sunsets and use of drugs; the members get along with each other, but did not come together on the basis of personal affinity, as is the case with lifelong friendships. They are sharing a "trip." . . .

All of these are examples of means that are being used to escape patterns of thought imposed by the Corporate State—to liberate the mind. . . .

All of this search for increased consciousness culminates in an attitude that is the very antithesis of Consciousness II: a desire for innocence, for the ability to be in a state of wonder or awe. It is of the essence of the thinking of the new generation that man should be constantly open to new experience, constantly ready to have his old ways of thinking changed, constantly hoping that he will be sensitive enough and receptive enough to let the wonders of nature and mankind come to him. Consciousness II regards it as a sign of weakness to be surprised or awed; III cultivates the experience.

Consciousness III says "the full moon blew my mind" and is proud of it; II has seen the moon before and takes it in stride. . . . In *Why Are We In Vietnam?*, Norman Mailer's hero, D.J., rids himself of the machine consciousness and, in the vastness of Alaska's remote Brooks Range, rediscovers a childlike, breathless sense of wonder; this is the quality that Consciousness III supremely treasures, to which it gives its ultimate sign of reverence, vulnerability, and innocence, "Oh wow!"

4. TIMOTHY LEARY, "INTERPRETATIONS OF RELIGIOUS EXPERIENCE" (FROM *CHANGING MY MIND, AMONG OTHERS*, 1982)

As a Berkeley-trained research psychologist in the 1950s, Timothy Leary appeared destined for academic success and stardom in a prestigious post at Harvard. Instead, he initiated a series of experiments with psychedelic drugs, especially LSD. Eventually he formed the aptly named League for Spiritual Development to encourage mind-expanding drug-taking sessions in carefully controlled environments. Leary had little use for religion until he discovered that it was not scientists but Divinity School students at Harvard who truly were interested in his "new tool for expanding awareness." He agreed that his "consciousness-change experiences" should be discussed in terms of religion, on the condition that no religious rituals or priests would invade the holy houses of experimentation (usually homes in the Boston suburbs where Leary and his followers dropped LSD [acid]). In this selection, Leary explores his "experiential science of religion," tracing his own trajectory from eating sacred mushrooms in Mexico to dropping acid with ministers, priests, and other religious professionals at Harvard and elsewhere. Because of his advocacy of LSD, Harvard fired him, and later his escapades landed him in Folsom prison in California. Harkening back to the 1950s, when he and some colleagues in psychology assisted the CIA in mind-control experiments, Leary secretly offered to cooperate with the agency in exchange for a lighter prison sentence. Along with such figures as Allen Ginsberg, in the 1960s Leary called for an expansion of consciousness that was popularized in rock and roll music (especially on the West Coast) and soon outgrew its religio-scientific origins to become a youthful (and often dangerous) fad.

YOUR BRAIN IS GOD

Though it might be against the law for responsible American citizens to use psychoactive plants and drugs to change their brains, nearly 400 years of Western civilization must support the right of Americans to worship the divinity within, using sacraments that worked for them. We studied the meaning of the word *sacrament*, usually defined as something that relates one to the divinity. One of the most offensive, flaky characteristics of 1960's acid-users was their compulsion to babble about new visions of God, new answers to the Ultimate Secret of the Universe. For thousands of years individuals whose brains were activated had chattered about "ultimate secrets" in the context of mystical-personal religious revelation. We were forced to recall that for most of human history, science and philosophy were the province of religion. And most specifically, all references to what we would now call the psychoneurological were described in religious terms. Our political experiences at Harvard also pushed us in the direction of the religious metaphor. When it became known on campus that a group of psychologists was producing revelatory brain-change, we expected that astronomers and biologists would come flocking around to learn how to use this new tool for expanding awareness. But the scientists committed to external manipulations were uninterested. Instead we were flooded by inquiries from the Divinity School! . . .

The only way in which consciousness-change experiences could be discussed was in terms of philosophic-religious. Even Buddhism, an atheist method of psychological self-control, allowed itself to be classified as a religion.

So religion it was. I recall the moment of decision: During a wild, all-night LSD session in our mansion in the Boston suburbs, Richard Alpert came up to me, eyes popping, and announced, "The East! We must go back to the wisdom of the East!" *Go back?*

The lawyers agreed. There is apparently nothing in the Bill of Rights to protect scientific freedom. The Constitution was written in a horse-and-buggy pre-technological era. But there was a First Amendment protection of Freedom of Religion. After all, Catholic priests were allowed Communion wine during Prohibition. So I agreed to the religious posture on the conditions that there was to be no kneeling down, no dogmas, no holy men, no followers, no churches, no public worship, no financial offerings. . . .

THE EIGHT CRAFTS OF GOD: TOWARDS AN EXPERIENTIAL
SCIENCE OF RELIGION

Many years ago, on a sunny afternoon in a Cuernavaca garden, I ate seven so-called sacred mushrooms given to me by a scientist from the University of Mexico. During the next five hours, I was whirled through an experience which was, above all and without question, the deepest religious-philosophic experience of my life. And it was totally electric-cellular scientific, cinematographic. . . .

Since my brain-activation-illumination of August 1960, I have repeated this biochemical and (to me) sacramental ritual several thousand times, and almost every subsequent brain-opening has awed me with philosophic-scientific revelations as convincing as the first experience. During this period (1960–68) I have been lucky enough to collaborate with several hundred scientists and scholars who joined our various search and research projects. In our brain-activation centers at Harvard, in Mexico, Morocco, Almora, India, Millbrook, and in the California mountains we have arranged transcendent brain-change experiences for several thousand persons from all walks of life, including more than 400 full-time religious professionals: about half professing Christian or Jewish faiths and about half belonging to Celtic, pagan, or Eastern religions.

In 1962, an informal group of ministers, theologians, academic hustlers, and religious psychologists in the Harvard environment began meeting once a month to further these beginnings. This group was the original planning nucleus of the organizations that assumed sponsorship of our consciousness-expansion research: IFIF (1963), the Castalia Foundation (1963–66), and the League for Spiritual Discovery (1966). That our generating impulse and original leadership came from a seminar in religious experience may be related to the alarmed confusion we aroused in secular and psychiatric circles of the time. . . .

As subjects, 20 divinity students were selected from a group of volunteers and divided into 5 groups of 4 persons. To each group were assigned 2 guides with considerable psychedelic experience—professors and advanced graduate students from Boston-area colleges. . . .

Our studies, naturalistic and experimental, demonstrate that if the expectation, preparation, and setting are Protestant-New England religious, an intense mystical or revelatory experience will be admitted by 40 to 90% of subjects ingesting psychedelic drugs. These results may be attributed to the bias of our research group, which has taken the rather dangerous ACLU position that there are "experiential-spiritual" as well as secular-behavioral emotional-political potentialities of the nervous system. Five scientific studies by other investigators yield data which indicate that (1) if the setting is supportive but not spiritual, between 40 to 75% of psychedelic subjects will report intense and life-changing philosophic-religious experiences and (2) if the set and setting are supportive and "spiritual," then from 40 to 90% of the experiences will be revelatory and mystico-philosophic-religious.

How can these results be disregarded by those concerned with philosophic growth and religious development? These data are even more interesting because the experiments took place in 1962, when individual religious ecstasy (as opposed to religious piety) was highly suspect and when meditation, jogging, yoga, fasting, body-consciousness, social-dropout-withdrawal, and sacramental (i.e., organic) foods and drugs were surrounded by an aura of eccentricity, fear, clandestine secrecy, even imprisonment. The 400 professional workers in religious vocations who partook of psychedelic substances were responsible, thoughtful, and "moral," highly moral, individuals, grimly aware of the controversial nature of drugs and aware that their reputations and jobs might be undermined. Not bad, huh? Still the results read: 75% philosophic revelation. It may well be that, like the finest metal, the most intense religious experience requires fire, the "heat" of police constabulatory opposition, to produce the keenest edge. When sacramental biochemicals are used as routinely and tamely as organ music and incense the ego-shattering, awe-inspiring effect of the drugs may be diminished.

What Is a Religious Experience?

The religious experience is the ecstatic, jolting, wondrous, awe-struck, life-changing, mind-boggling confrontation with one or all of the eight basic mysteries of existence. The goal of an intelligent life, according to Socrates, is to pursue the philosophic quest—to increase one's knowledge of self and world. Now there is an important division of labor involved in the philosophic search. Religion, being personal and private, cannot produce answers to the eight basic questions. The philosopher's role is to ignite the wonder, raise the burning issues, inspire the pursuit of answers. It is science that produces the ever-changing, improving answers to the haunting questions that religious wonder poses. . . .

The Harvard Psychedelic Drug Research Project's first goal was to train scientist-technicians in the use of powerful brain-change chemicals. LSD provided us with a method of changing consciousness and brain function—the tool that philosophers and psychologists had been anticipating for centuries. . . .

When all was read and said, it seemed to us that the best "clinical," step-by-step description of a psychedelic experience yet published was *The Tibetan Book of the Dead*. This classic Buddhist text outlined the stages of the dying-rebirth process over a period of 49 days. Though couched in primitive rural language, the highs and lows, the "hallucinations" and visions were clearly similar to the altered states our Harvard subjects experienced.

During the summer of 1962 I went through *The Tibetan Book of the Living* (as we re-named it) line by line, translating Buddhist imagery into American psychedelic jargon. The mimeographed versions were "tried out" on hundreds of LSD trippers, and the polished, revised version published by University Books in 1964. Since that time, *The Psychedelic Experience* has been reissued in nine hardback editions and several paperback reprintings. Hundreds of thousands of LSD experiences have been guided by this manual. Because of mass-merchandising techniques, ironically, this book has probably turned on more persons to the Guatama's [sic] teachings than any single text since the Buddha's enlightenment 2,500 years ago—although I doubt that you could get the Buddhist professional to admit it. . . .

In September 1966, working with First Amendment lawyers, we formally founded a new religion, called the League for Spiritual Development, to provide legal protection for our own neurological investigations and to encourage others to form their own religions. We made very clear that the league was *not* a mass organization but was limited to 100 people centered around the Millbrook estate in Dutchess County, New York. We were not seeking to convert, but to show others how to do it themselves.

Our first sacramental assembling, a religious celebration at the Village Theatre in New York's Lower East Side, was based on the "Magic Theatre" sequence from Hermann Hesse's *Steppenwolf*. It was a bead-game multi-media performance deliberately designed to "blow minds," to overload nervous systems with ever-changing Niagaras of moving forms, some familiar, some novel. The sound track blasted with acid rock, Oriental chants, synthesizer whirls, body noises, heartbeats, heavy breathings—all highly amplified. A video orchestra of 9 performers manipulating slide projectors playing over double- and triple-exposed films. Psychedelic prayers . . . and a spoken narrative guided viewers through the reenactments of Harry Haller's mystical trip.

The Psychedelic Celebrations were a sensation. Enormous worldwide publicity, sold-out performances. I was nominated for best Off-Broadway actor of the year. Hollywood film people thronged to the events. . . .

When television commercials took over our techniques, we knew it was time to quit. "Turn on to Squirt. Tune in to Taste. Drop Out of the Cola rut!" We did.

LSD AS SACRAMENT

Your descriptions of the psychedelic experience sound very much like Hermann Hesse's Siddhartha. *Have you been influenced by his writings?*

Very much. Of course, in philosophic and literary interpretations of consciousness expansion, most great writers basically agree on the necessity of going out of your mind, going within, and about what you find once you get there. Metaphors change from culture to culture, but every great mystic and visionary reports the same eternal flow, timeless series of evolutions, and so forth. Our first psychedelic celebration in New York addressed the intellectual trapped in his mind. For that first celebration we were using *Steppenwolf* as our "bible." . . .

Is each celebration supposed to appeal to a different kind of believer?

Each celebration will take up one of the great religious or philosophic traditions. We attempt to turn on everyone to that religion. We hope anyone that comes to all our celebrations will discover that each of these great myths is based on a psychedelic experience, a death-rebirth sequence. But in addition, we hope that the Christian will be particularly turned on by our Catholic LSD Mass, because it will renew for him the resurrection metaphor, which for many has become rather routine and tired. The aim is to turn on not just the mind, but the sense organs, and even to talk to people's cells and ancient centers of wisdom.

A lot of your beliefs do borrow from other cultures. Wouldn't exposure to these other ways of thinking make your religion more meaningful?

. . . There are three processes involved that every spiritual teacher has passed on to humanity for the past thousand years. 1. Look within, glory in the revelation. 2. Then express it in acts of glorification on the outside and 3. detach yourself from the current tribe. After you turn on, don't spend the rest of your life contemplating the inner wonders. Begin immediately expressing your revelation in acts of beauty. That's very much a part of our religion—the glorification, the acting out, the expression of what you have learned. That's what we're doing in the Village Theatre. Every Tuesday night people come there, and we stone them out of their minds.

And all without LSD?

Well, in order to do anything new, you have to change your nervous system. You can do it through breathing, fasting, flagellation, dancing, solitude, diet; you can do it through any sense organ—visual, auditory, and so forth. There are hundreds of ways of turning on. But at present, very few people can use these methods, so drugs are almost the only specific way an American is ever going to have a religious experience. . . .

Postscript

. . . Everything we did in the 1960's was designed to fission, to weaken faith in and conformity to the 1950's social order. Our precise surgical target was the Judeo-Christian power monolith, which has imposed a guilty, inhibited, grim, anti-body, anti-life repression on Western civilization. Our assignment was to topple this prudish, judgmental civilization. And it worked! For the first time in 20 centuries, the good old basic paganism got everybody moving again. White people actually started to move their hips, let the Marine crewcuts grow long, adorn themselves erotically in Dionysian revels, tune into nature. The ancient Celtic-pagan spirit began to sweep through the land of Eisenhower and J. Edgar Hoover. Membership in organized churches began to plummet. Hedonism, always the movement of individuals managing their own rewards and pleasures, ran rampant.

Millions of Americans exulted in the old Celtic Singularity. Every woman a queen, every man a king; God within. The classic paganism now combined with the American virtues of do-it-yourself, distrust of authority. Millions of Americans writing their own Declarations of Independence: *My life, my liberty, my pursuit of happiness.*

But millions more couldn't handle the freedom or independence. The familiar hunger for authority, the recurring obsession to submit; to give responsibility to a master. . . .

But a glance at American history was comforting. Since the Pilgrims, the Quakers, the Mormons, the Emersonian Transcendentalists, our frontier country has always seethed with kooky cults and splinter messiahs. The amazing independent religiosity, the off-the-wall fervor of Americans has always been a wonderful source of eccentric individuality. There were, after all, no Jehovah's Witnesses or Hare Krishnas running around Franco's Spain or the Soviet Union. I was also comforted by the thought that the new religiosity was part of our wonderful aristocratic American consumerism, the insatiable American televoid brain demanding new sensations, new surprises, new heroes, new reality scripts.

5. RAM DASS, *REMEMBER, BE HERE NOW* (1971)

Richard Alpert was born in 1931 in Boston, received his Ph.D. in psychology at Stanford in 1957, and taught at major universities in the United States in the 1950s and 1960s. In the early 1960s he was associated with Timothy Leary's experiments in psychedelic drugs, eventually ingesting hallucinogens more than three hundred times in his quest for consciousness expansion. As he later said, "God came to the United States in the form of LSD." Later in the decade, increasingly dissatisfied with western materialism and consumerism, Alpert traveled to India and studied with a holy man in the Himalayas. After a year, he took the name Ram Dass, and was instructed by his guru to teach Americans what he had learned. Dass's 1971 book Be Here Now *did exactly that. Called the "cookbook for the counterculture," it became an enduringly popular text for spiritual seekers. In this excerpt, Dass explains his philosophy of "being fully here in the moment," soon to be a staple (and cliché) of New Age popularizers.*

OUR-STORY

There are three stages in this journey that I have been on! The first, the social science stage; the second, the psychedelic stage; and the third, the yogi stage. They are summating—that is, each is contributing to the next. It's like the unfolding of a lotus flower. Now, as I look back, I realize that many of the experiences that made little sense to me at the time they occurred were prerequisites for what was to come later. I want to share with you the parts of the internal journey that never get written up in the mass media: I'm not interested in the political parts of the story; I'm not interested in what you read in the *Saturday Evening Post* about LSD. This is the story of what goes on inside a human being who is undergoing all these experiences.

SUCCESS

In 1961, the beginning of March, I was at perhaps the highest point of my academic career. I had just returned from being a visiting professor at the University of California at Berkeley; I had been assured of a permanent post that was being held for me at Harvard, if I got my publications in order. In a worldly sense, I was making a great income and I was a collector of possessions. . . .

Something was wrong. And the something wrong was that I just didn't know, though I kept feeling all along the way that somebody else must know even though I didn't. The nature of life was a mystery to me. All the stuff I was teaching was just like little molecular bits of stuff but they didn't add up to a feeling anything like wisdom. I was just getting more and more knowledgeable. And I was getting very good at bouncing three knowledge balls at once. I could sit in a doctoral exam, ask very sophisticated questions and look terribly wise. It was a hustle.

DISSATISFACTION

Now my predicament as a social scientist was that I was not basically a scholar. I came out of a Jewish anxiety-ridden high-achieving tradition. Though I had been through five years of psychoanalysis, still, every time I lectured, I would get extraordinary diarrhea and tension. Lecturing five days a week made it quite a complex problem to keep my stomach operating. . . .

Here I was, sitting with the boys of the first team in cognitive psychology, personality psychology, developmental psychology, and in the midst of this I felt here were men and women who, themselves, were not highly evolved beings. Their own lives were not fulfilled. There was not enough human beauty, human fulfillment, human contentment. I worked hard and the keys to the kingdom were handed to me. I was being promised all of it. I had felt I had got into whatever the inner circle meant. . . .

Down the hall from my big empire, there was a little office. It had been a closet and they needed an extra office, so they cleared out the closet and put a desk in there and in that closet was Timothy Leary. He had been bicycling around Italy, bouncing checks, and David McClelland found him and brought him back as a creative gift to western science. Tim and I became drinking buddies together. Then we started to teach courses together, such as the first year clinical course—practicum—on "Existential Transactional Behavior Change."

The more time I spent with Tim, the more I realized he had an absolutely extraordinary intellect. He really knew a lot. I found him extremely stimulating and the students found him exciting to be around, because of his openness to new ideas and his willingness to take wild risks in thinking. . . .

TURNING ON

Now, what we did at first at Harvard was to tell all of our colleagues about this extraordinary thing that was happening to us, and they all shared our delight, as any scientists do when a fellow scientist finds a new avenue into the unknown. And so the first week they listened with delight. And then at the end of the first week we all went back into our experimental cell—the living room by the fire and opened the bottle again and took some more psylocybin to chart this course further. And the next week we had shared a deeper experience and we came back and we spoke to our colleagues. Now they couldn't hear us quite as well. It wasn't that they were changing, it was that we were. We were developing a language among ourselves. If Admiral Byrd and an exploratory party are going deeper and deeper into the polar region, the things they think about and are concerned about and are interested in become less and less relevant to somebody living in New York City. This was our situation. . . .

Now my own experiences were horrible and beautiful and I kept working in different environments and settings and whenever anybody that I trusted brought along some new chemical, I would open my mouth and off I'd go. I was interested in doing this exploring.

For example, at one point I had been in the meditation room in the community house we had in Newton, and I was for four hours in a state of total homogeneous light, bliss, and then I recall starting to "come down" and this huge red wave rolled in across the room. It looked like a cross between a William Blake (that picture of the wave) sketch and a Hieronymous Bosch painting, and it was all my identities, all rolling in over me. I remember holding up my hand and saying, "NO, NO, I don't want to go back." It was like this heavy burden I was going to take on myself. And I realized I didn't have the key—I didn't know the magic words, like "Abracadabra" or "Hocus Pocus" or whatever it was going to be that would stop that wave, and it rolled in over me and then . . . "Oh, here I am again—Richard Alpert—what a drag!" . . .

ENVIRONMENTAL CHANGES

Now in 1962 or 3, Tim and Ralph Metzner with him (I was just given author's credit because I took care of the kitchen) had come across the Tibetan Book of the Dead, which was a very close description of a number of these experiences. This book was 2500 years old, at least, and it had been used all those years for preparing Tibetan Lamas to die and be reincarnated. And when we opened it, we would find descriptions of the 49 days after death before rebirth, that were perfect descriptions of sessions we were having with psychedelics.

How could this be? The parallel was so close. Tim rewrote the book as a manual called "The Psychedelic Experience", a manual for psychological death and rebirth, arguing that this was really a metaphor about psychological death and rebirth and not necessarily physical death and reincarnation. . . .

And by 1966–7, I was in the same predicament. I was aware that I didn't know enough to maintain these states of consciousness. And I was aware that nobody else around me seemed to know enough either. I checked with everybody I thought might know, and nobody seemed to know.

So I wasn't very optimistic about India or psychedelics. By 1967 I had shot my load! I had no more job as a psychologist in a respectable establishment and I realized that we didn't know enough about psychedelics to use them profitably. . . .

[Alpert then traveled to India.]

We had done it all. We had gone to see the Dalai Lama, and we had gone on horseback up to Amanath Cave up in Kashmir; we had visited Benares, and finally we ended up in Katmandu, Nepal. I started to get extremely, extremely depressed. I'm sure part of it was due to the hashish. But also, part of it was because I didn't see what to do next.

I had done everything I thought I could do, and nothing new had happened. It was turning out to be just another trip. The despair got very heavy. We didn't know enough and I couldn't figure out how to socialize this thing about the new states of consciousness. And I didn't know what to do next.

It wasn't like I didn't have LSD. I had plenty of LSD, but why take it. I knew what it was going to do, what it was going to tell me. It was going to show me that garden again and then I was going to be cast out and that was it. And I never could quite stay. I was addicted to the experience at first, and then I even got tired of that. And the despair was extremely intense at that point.

We were sitting in a hippie restaurant, called the Blue Tibetan, and I was talking to some French hippies . . .

I had given LSD to a number of pundits around India and some reasonably pure men:

An old Buddhist Lama said, "It gave me a headache."

Somebody else said, "It's good, but not as good as meditation."

Somebody else said, "Where can I get some more?"

And I got the same range of responses I'd get in America. I didn't get any great pearl of wisdom which would make me exclaim, "Oh, that's what it is—I was waiting for something that was going to do that thing!"

So I finally figured, "Well, it's not going to happen." We were about to go on to Japan and I was pretty depressed because we were starting the return now, and what was I returning to? What should I do now?

I decided I was going to come back and become a chauffeur. I wanted to be a servant, and let somebody else program my consciousness. I could read holy books while I'd wait for whoever it was I was waiting for while they were at Bergdorf Goodman's and I'd just change my whole style of life around. I could just get out of the whole drama of having to engineer my own ship for a while. This is a funny foreshadowing, as you'll see.

The despair was extremely intense at that point. I was really quite sad.

BHAGWAN DASS

I was in the Blue Tibetan with my friend and these other people, and in walked this very extraordinary guy, at least extraordinary with regard to his height. He was 6'7" and he had long blonde hair and a long blonde beard. He was a Westerner, an American, and was wearing holy clothes—a dhoti (a cloth Indian men wear instead of pants) and so on, and when he entered, he came directly over to our table and sat down. . . .

I don't know how to describe this to you, except that I was deep in my despair; I had gone through game, after game, after game, first being a professor at Harvard, then being a psychedelic spokesman, and still people were constantly looking into my eyes, like "Do you know?" Just that subtle little look, and I was constantly looking into their eyes—"Do you know?" And there we were, "Do you?" "Do you?" "Maybe he . . . " "Do you . . . ?"

And there was always that feeling that everybody was very close and we all knew we knew, but nobody quite knew. I don't know how to describe it, other than that.

And I met this guy and there was no doubt in my mind. It was just like meeting a rock. It was just solid, all the way through. Everywhere I pressed, there he was! . . .

I thought, "Well, look, I came to India to find something and I still think this guy knows—I'm going to follow him."

But there was also the counter thought, "How absurd—who's writing this bizarre script. Here I am—I've come half-way around the world and I'm going to follow, through India, a 23 year old guy from Laguna Beach, California."

I said to Harish and to David, "Do you think I'm making a mistake?" And Harish said, "No, he is a very high guy." And so I started to follow him—literally follow him.

Now, I'm suddenly barefoot. He has said, "You're not going to wear shoes, are you?" That sort of thing. And I've got a shoulder bag and my dhoti and blisters on my feet and dysentery, the likes of which you can't imagine, and all he says is, "Well, fast for a few days."

He's very compassionate, but no pity.

And we're sleeping on the ground, or on these wooden tables that you get when you stop at monasteries, and my hip bones ache. I go through an extraordinary physical breakdown, become very childlike and he takes care of me. And we start to travel through temples—to Baneshwar and Konarak and so on.

I see that he's very powerful, so extraordinarily powerful—he's got an ectara, a one-stringed instrument, and I've got a little Tibetan drum, and we go around to the villages and people rush out and they touch our feet because we're holy men, which is embarrassing to me because I'm not a holy man—I'm obviously who I am—a sort of overage hippie, western explorer, and I feel very embarrassed when they do that and they give us food. And he plays and sings and the Hindu people love him and revere him. And he's giving away all my money . . .

But I'm clinging tight to my passport and my return ticket to America, and a traveler's check that I'll need to get me to Delhi. Those things I'm going to hold on to. And my bottle of LSD, in case I should find something interesting.

And during these travels he's starting to train me in a most interesting way. We'd be sitting somewhere and I'd say,

"Did I ever tell you about the time that Tim and I . . . "

And he'd say, "Don't think about the past. Just be here now."

Silence.

And I'd say, "How long do you think we're going to be on this trip?"

And he'd say, "Don't think about the future. Just be here now." . . .

But there was no conversation. I didn't know anything about his life. He didn't know anything about my life. He wasn't the least bit interested in all of the extraordinary dramas that I had collected . . . He was the first person I couldn't seduce into being interested in all this. He just didn't care.

And yet, I never felt so profound an intimacy with another being. It was as if he were inside of my heart. And what started to blow my mind was that everywhere we went, he was at home. . . .

Now, though I am a beginner on the path, I have returned to the West for a time to work out karma or unfulfilled commitment. Part of this commitment is to share what I have learned with those of you who are on a similar journey. One can share a message through telling "our-story" as I have just done, or through teaching methods of yoga, or singing, or making love. Each of us finds his unique vehicle for sharing with others his bit of wisdom.

For me, this story is but a vehicle for sharing with you the true message . . . the living faith in what is possible.

6. DANIEL BERRIGAN, "BERRIGAN AT CORNELL" (1968)

A Jesuit priest and committed antiwar activist, Daniel Berrigan came to represent a kind of homegrown liberation theology. He spoke to numerous groups, organized and participated in demonstrations, and engaged in acts of nonviolent civil disobedience, arguing that it was all a part of his religious commitment and a natural outgrowth of his immersion in the Catholic tradition. The war was a "nightmare," and heretofore the Church had not dealt with the "fact of death, mass extermination and nuclear overkill, the cold war and the despair of the developing peoples." Neither did his beloved order, the Jesuits, come to his aid during his stints in jail. Berrigan and his brother Philip, also a priest, made choices that caused conflict with conservative leaders of the Church and of their order, indicating a larger split between younger radical theologians and Church activists (increasingly associated with the counterculture of the 1960s) who were "aware of very deep sacrificial possibility" and conservative Church leaders who were concerned about priests being associated with radicals, hippies, and the political Left.

The question of the war is a very precious one to which I have given certain irreplaceable years of my life in my poetry and my relationship with others, in all those things which define me. These are years I will not have again. I can't really go back and say that I made a good or bad choice. I just chose! I chose to be here rather than elsewhere in the largest sense. So it is clear to me that I operate from a sense that all things are obscurely joined and that to be really at a point of human death or anguish or hope is to be at the center of the picture. Maybe this is the act demanded of us: to take one choice that includes many other choices.

The choice that my brother and I have made was, given the times and the Church, a choice of conflict, undoubtedly with our own communities and our own faith and the things we had grown up with. But this act resulted in a great communion with all sorts of other people, of other faiths and traditions. We found a larger meaning to being Catholic Christians. Neither of us found a serious temptation to leave our commitments in any of these absurd ways that others are speaking of. We probably have certain resources available to us which allowed us to get beyond our own needs. We didn't need to be married—and I say this humbly, it's just that we could operate as celibates. We were not in such revolt against authority that we could not communicate with it. We didn't have any personal frenzy or revenge to work out.

The war is a nightmare and the only advantage my brother and I have is that our nightmare began earlier. It began four or five years ago. So, we are better prepared to live in this nightmare, not as nightmare figures but as men who declare that it is a nightmare and, therefore, can dissolve it. Let us begin living in reality once more. This requires what it required of any period of the Church where death is in command and where society is moving to exclude more and more people through jail or the army or exclusion from benefits.

The real news is that Rome is burning. The city in which we are asked to live is in flames. I am trying to get with a much bigger thing than this little churchy thing which has been proposed as a real thing. What I am trying to suggest is that neither the Church nor the State nor the University alone has been capable of dealing with the fact of death, mass extermination and nuclear overkill, the cold war and the despair of the developing peoples.

Christianity deepens in men without violating any area in which we are requested to be human beings. Christianity does not say get the hell out of your profession or income or anything else. But it does place these things in question; which is exactly where they should be—in question.

We will try to expose our conscience to the Catholic community and listen. If they will respect us, we will go ahead. If they do not respect us, we will go ahead. But we will not cut ourselves off, though we will not foreclose the possibility of their cutting us off. . . .

I speak as a minority figure. I've always been one. I try not to be romantic or obsessive about it but that is where I am. Around me for a minority group whether Christian or Jewish or humanist or secular. We represent, perhaps, only two percent of the community. From the point of view of anything now operating in society that remains true. Mine is an embattled, impoverished minority. My brother is just out of jail; he is in official disgrace. He is a cleric facing trial in war time and I am with him. The Society of Jesus, which is my community which I love very much, which is the source of almost everything I have ever learned and valued is silent and will probably remain silent.

When I was in jail in Washington in November, I asked myself where the members of my community were. Why didn't a Jesuit come to see how I was or another member of the Catholic community. Why didn't someone come and say, "Where is Berrigan? I don't agree with what he is doing but he is my brother and, therefore, I must know how he is?" . . .

I don't want to make a great issue. I want to express my anguished longing which I am trying to be faithful to, to remain a priest in the Church and my Order. To invite my Order to a deeper understanding of itself, of the dead-end it is encountering by identifying through its silence with the structures of power, the war structures. This momentary evidence of power has nothing to do with real history, which is to say, the real Church. It may be necessary to be evicted from the Jesuits in order to do this. I have faced this and it is quite tolerable to me. I do not have any turn-off point at which I must say that my conscience must come to terms with what is officially acceptable. . . .

We are facing a mysterious kind of new form of the immanence of God with regard to young people of very deep sacrificial possibility. I don't know whether it is inevitably connected with one period, one war, one crisis; or whether the times are really forming people who can be ready for whatever is going to happen. But let us rejoice in what is here.

7. SHIRLEY MACLAINE, *GOING WITHIN* (1989)

As the social movements of the 1960s receded, Americans increasingly turned to quests for personal fulfillment—hence the satirical term "me decade" Tom Wolfe coined to describe the 1970s. Few enthusiasts of religious transformation have been more popular—or more popularly parodied—than the stage and screen actress Shirley MacLaine. In a series of best-selling books published in the 1980s, MacLaine narrated her religious pilgrimage toward "inner transformation." Her works rode the surge in popularity of the New Age movement, itself a descendant (and to some degree a bowdlerization) of the countercultural prophesying of the 1950s and 1960s. In this excerpt from Going Within, *MacLaine explains how she came to the conclusion that personal change would have to precede "transforming the world I live in," an argument ironically parallel to the long-standing evangelical call for personal salvation as the necessary prerequisite to any change in the social order. She explains her practices of meditation, chanting, and reading crystals—all in pursuit of discovering the "Higher Self" trapped within the mortal body. MacLaine's popularity peaked in the mid-1980s, with a television special touting her guru's powers of levitation and reincarnation. Following the exposure of some prominent New Age teachers as fraudulent and the acknowledgment of some practitioners that their faith in crystals was just that—faith—and not verifiable in any sense, the movement went into decline. Yet the kinds of sentiments preached here retain wide currency, even among those who know nothing of the larger "New Age movement." MacLaine's writings are part of a long American tradition of the quest for the true "higher" self.*

⸎

I came to recognize the need for personal transformation before I could address any longer the issue of participating in transforming the world I live in. So I began my personal transformation in earnest—some would say too earnest. That doesn't mean that I cut myself off from political and social activism, but it does mean that I saw the necessity for change in a clearer light because I was viewing myself more clearly.

It was at that point that I began a program of exercises of the mind which I put myself through nearly every day in order to accomplish a feeling of inner transformation. As a result, I began to feel more centered in my own power and more aligned, not only with my own destiny but with the destinies of those around me who moved in and out of my life as they pursued their own journeys toward understanding.

At the same time, I recognized how little I knew and understood. When that happened, I tried to focus on what I did know. What I understand today is a result of the knowledge I've gleaned from ancient teachers and modern students who are far more evolved than I. They have all been through their own personal fires in an attempt to understand themselves and how they fit into the great overall universal consciousness of which we are all a part. Whenever things go wrong I have learned to use these events as catalysts to help me understand how I participated in them. In that respect it is *because* of conflicts and problems and pressures that I have learned to handle both them and myself in a more balanced way. So, though the journey within has often been painful, it has reflected every area of the human condition and how I relate to my immediate world. It has helped me in the most practical ways to deal with reality. . . .

I am shifting from my feelings of helplessness about having any effect in helping to change the world, to a position that recognizes there is a power within me, and within each of us, so awesome that, when tapped, a transformation in the world could result. It is not only possible but necessary— and part of the next stage of our own evolution and development is to realize (literally "make real") that power. I am obviously not the only one conscious of this approach to bringing about change.

A great awakening is taking place. Individuals all across the world are tapping into their internal power to understand who they are and using that knowledge to elevate their lives and their circumstances to a higher octave of happiness and productivity. Sharing the search, and the techniques of searching, is only a part of the help we can give one another. . . .

As I began to go within myself more deeply, and my spiritual studies and investigations advanced, I became more and more interested in the correlation between body and spirit. I had been trained as a dancer so my approach to many of these issues was from a physical culturist's point of view. Anyone who is intensely involved with the physicality of performance knows that the body does not perform well if the spirit is gloomy. Therefore, the connection between the two needs improvement and the access to "interior light" is necessary.

I had heard a great deal about meditation from many of my friends around the world who had been doing it for years, claiming that their very survival depended upon it. "One needs to go within for concentration, balance, strength, and flexibility," they said. "You just can't get that on the outside." So I became interested in the "going within" process. In order to achieve a better and less painful physical performance, I tried my own brand of meditation. I wanted the outer results of my physical life to improve, so that meant I would have to touch the "inner results." I found the experience phenomenal.

One night, after dancing two shows on fifty-odd-year-old legs, Vita-Bath therapy and massage were not enough. In the stillness of my bedroom, I sat cross-legged on the floor and shut my eyes. I got up and put a cassette of music on the tape recorder, sat down, and shut my eyes again. I listened to a quiet tinkle of harp music and tried to allow my mind to have no thoughts at all. This wasn't easy. It required trust and a kind of passive discipline that I was not used to because I am an overachiever who is motivated by will and by thought: but thoughts were what were causing the emotional glitches that in turn manifested as pain and tension in my body.

Then I tried directing my thoughts to my body, beginning with my feet, to relax. Slowly and with care and attention, I told each area of my body to drop its tensions. . . . I allowed the tensions to drift away. And waited, consciously enjoying the growing relaxation. Then slowly I allowed myself to drift away. I drifted and floated . . . drifted and floated. If a thought bothered me, I told it to go away or evaded it by concentrating on a small muscle in a toe or finger. Slowly I realized that my body was completely relaxed. Then I shifted my focus to my interior center. It was easier than I had suspected. I found a ball of light that I'd heard was always there. It was small. I don't know whether I "found" it or whether I visualized it. It was irrelevant. It was there. . . .

I answered my own question: I had created everything myself. I had created the pain. And I had created the healing. I was in control of it all. The pain *and* the healing were inventions of mine. . . . If I had created the pain and the healing in my body, was I also creating the pain and the healing in every area of my life? And was that light inside me a tool with which i could create my reality to be whatever I desired?

This, then, was a spiritual technology worthy of examination. This was a new Soul Physics. And how did it happen?

Simply by going within. . . .

Chanting has always been believed to be very effective in experiencing "God." Murmuring over a rosary; chanting in a synagogue; repeatedly intoning a prayer in church—all are much the same process. However, all religions seem to agree that the actual naming of the deity in each respective culture gets better results. Chanting seems to be a universally accepted method of removing all thoughts and interferences from the mind, which, when emptied, can be filled with "God feeling." . . .

The Higher Self is exactly what the words imply—the best positive elements of your own being, the most reassuring aspect of your own inner strength, your personal expression of the Divine in you. It links you with everything else that exists: it is your channel to the enormous resources of the human potential. . . .

Whatever it might reveal itself as, it has no difficulty expressing itself with its God Source understanding, because the Higher Self is our link and reflection to the God energy: it is harmonious, beautiful, peaceful, and commanding. When the connection occurs, the resulting inner calm can be felt physically. You *know* you can trust it. You *know* it is your inner guide, which you always intuitively understood was there but felt too silly to trust. When you finally align with that Higher Self, you have found the guiding light and friend who has always been with you—that guide has loved you unconditionally through eternity and understands you totally. . . . It is non-physical, yet it affects us physically. It is beyond the physical, yet we know it's there. It is *metaphysical.*

8. MEDICINE STORY, "SOMEWHERE UNDER THE RAINBOW" (1991)

In this excerpt, a Native American named Manitonquat, also called Medicine Story, narrates his spiritual journey. He describes his years growing up in the Northeast, learning Native American lore from his grandfather. Following his university education, he had a career in experimental theater in New York City, and moved to San Francisco just in time for the 1967 "Summer of Love," at the apex of the counterculture. Some years later he became involved with the Rainbow Gathering, and subsequently became a writer and poetry editor in upstate New York.

The Rainbow Gathering was a major early link between the counterculture and New Age religions. The group held yearly meetings in the American West at which seekers fasted, meditated, and made pilgrimages to Native American sacred sites. Inspired by the peaceful union of young people at Woodstock in 1969 for a festival of music, art, and countercultural fellowship, the Rainbow Gathering, as Medicine Story explains, was to symbolize and cement the "unity of all people in the universal family, . . . bound together by our desire to live in peace, to be in the cathedral of nature." Native American lore held a special place among these seekers. As he writes, "I realized that there was this universal thing that all human beings must have had at one time, before civilization began to get built up on fear." Manitonquat also relates his vision quest experiences in the Native American tradition of the sweat lodge, where he came to understand enough "to be propelled outward on a spiritual journey."

⚬⚬⚬

"When I heard these stories from my grandfather, I took all of it the same way I took Robin Hood and all the other great stories. They were stories. It wasn't real life. Real life was you had to go to school and you had to go to college. You had to get a job and like that, and I didn't see any correlation. I can remember being in college at twenty-one years old, and my grandfather saying to me, 'I can't understand why you're still in school at twenty-one years old, because I was working for my family when I was ten.'"

"And I said, 'Well, you know times have changed since your day, and you can't get anywhere without a college education.' So he said, 'Well, what do I know?' And that was that. I've often thought about that conversation, and I say he really knew better than me. As I see it now, the only things that I learned that were really important I've learned from him and from other elders.

"There are those who think that everything happens by direction, and that there's a purpose to it. Well, there must be some reason why I had to go and get all that education, and why I'm in kind of a unique position of being a university-educated traditionalist. There's not many of us around, traditionalists with university backgrounds. There are a few, and I guess our job is as communicators both ways. If people can understand the old people and couch what they have to say in terms that can be understood by both modern native people and nonnative people, then I guess that's good." . . .

"That was about 1967. I had read a lot. I knew people like Paul Goodman and Alan Watts. I had a broad background in the religious and Utopian thinking of the times, so I had a sense that there was something there for human beings, but nobody had really put it together completely or satisfyingly enough to me to make sense of it. So in 1967 I went west with my brother, Jim. There were seven of us altogether. I had a girlfriend in tow who was from California, and so I had talked her into going back with me. And Jim was with his rock band, so we all went out together. We all got a big flat together in San Francisco, and I just was into everything that was going on out there—all the different exotic religions and mystic practices and humanistic psychology, and drugs and Tim Leary and the Grateful Dead and Jefferson Airplane, and the whole thing was just an explosion out there. I went from high to low, and finally had to get out of the city and into the country, 'cause I had to put my head together."

A NEW PEOPLE, A NEW WORLD

"In 1972, I went to my first Rainbow Gathering and my life turned all around again. Early in that year I received word of a great gathering that was planned to be held in the summer in the Colorado Rocky Mountains. Since it was to be people of all races, religions, nationalities, classes, and lifestyles, it was called a Gathering of the Rainbow Tribes. There was to be a walk, a pilgrimage to Table Mountain, a place sacred to the Arapaho. The people planned to fast and stay in silence all day on that mountain while praying for worlds peace and understanding.

"Now there are old prophecies that at the end of this world many people of many different nations and tribes would come together to seek a new world and a new way. This would be according to the vision the Creator placed in their hearts. Then, you know, seeing how sincerely they sought this, how deeply they desired it, the Great Spirit would hear the cries of their hearts and take pity on them. At that time, the prophecies said, the new world would be born in the midst of the old. This new world would be very small at first, like a newborn baby. But it would be full of life and learning and growth, full of trust and love, like a newborn. Because of this, the new world wouldn't hate the dying old world, but instead learn how to survive and become strong within it. It was said that the sign the Creator would send of this new beginning would be a white buffalo.

"Over twenty thousand people came to that first gathering, and everyone was treated with respect. It was wonderful. One night it rained. The next day, when we came out in the meadow, we saw that a huge patch of white snow on the side of the mountain that faced us had been eaten away and carved into the perfect shape of a buffalo. People began to cheer and sing, and many of them wept joyfully.

"Then, starting at midnight on the third of July, everybody began a walk over the eight miles to Table Mountain. All night long that line moved in silence, carrying candles and torches. At dawn, thousands of people stood still upon the mountain, people who had come from all over the world to be together and share that moment, to watch the Sun rise on a new day, a new people, a new world.

"People stayed together all day on that mountain. We fasted and stayed in silence until, sometime after noon, someone started singing an Arapaho chant. All of us took up that chant to honor the traditional caretakers of that land. When we left that gathering, everyone had the feeling that something very important had happened, and was happening all over the world. No one could say exactly what it was, or knew what to do about it. So everyone went home and went on with their business. But the next summer a lot of the people decided the only way they could learn what to do with this new energy was to gather again and keep on gathering until the spirit directed something different. That's how it's been. Ever since, the Rainbow World Family Gathering of the Tribes has been held during the first week of July.

"The rainbow is based on the recognition that we are all spiritual people. So part of the idea is a spiritual gathering with no dividing lines. There's no laws, no regulations, no hassles. It's a try at anarchy. Does it work? Yeah, it works. When problems come up we sit down and talk about them. We figure it out as we go along." . . .

"The Rainbow Gathering is an opportunity to celebrate human diversity, to venerate the Earth, to deepen connections, and to party—to share a community that is beyond the rules of violence, prejudice, and caste." . . .

"One reason my life turned around was this vision of twenty thousand people getting together on top of a mountain praying in silence for a new world to be ushered in. The whole thing was so powerful. I knew something was happening. I didn't know what, or how, but I knew I had to *be* a part of it. Also, I met a number of young Indians who, although they weren't very traditional, came from people who were traditional and had their traditions together. They invited me to their reservation, to the Sun Dance and the Sweatlodge and things like that. And so I opened up into a whole world of

traditional old ways that I knew nothing about. So those two things came together at the same time, this rainbow communal world vision, and the old
ways, finding that there were still the old ways, and going to seek them out.
I kept balancing those two things.

"Pretty soon I left the commune where I was living in the mountains and
went together with a bunch of people on a bus that we bought and called the
Rainbow Rider. We traveled all around, building barns and picking apples
and things like that, and spreading the joyous rainbow message. But at the
same time I had a little truck and I would go bopping off to Sun Dances and
peyote ceremonies, and just getting in with different people, different
teachers wherever I found them, and learning the sweatlodge ways. I was
beginning to understand the philosophy behind all of that, which to me
made the picture complete, made me understand what had really gone
wrong." . . .

RECALLING THE ORIGINAL INSTRUCTIONS

"When I listened to the chiefs of the Longhouse and to the common, ordinary people, whose language was formed by these sensibilities, I began to
put all that together with what my grandfather had told me via stories. . . .
And from all of this I began to deepen my appreciation of the Original Instructions.

"Native people refer to the Original Instructions often in speech and
prayer, but rarely attempt to say exactly what they are. They are not like the
Ten Commandments carved in stone by a stern authority figure. They are
not ideas. They are reality. They are natural law, the Way Things Are—the
operational manual for a working creation—and they cannot totally be understood in words. They must be experienced. The Original Instructions are
not imposed by human minds on the world. They are of the living spirit.
Other creatures follow them instinctively, and they are communicated to humankind through the heart, through feelings of beauty and love.

"Black Elk spoke of it very well when he said that everything we do is
done in a circle, because the power of the world always works in circles and
everything tries to be round. In the old days, when we were strong and happy people, he said all our power came from the sacred hoop of the nation.
That circle, that basic circle, fits into the larger circle of the universe. And
the universe is circles within circles, and everything is one circle, and all the
circles are connected to each other. Each family is a circle, and those family
circles connect together and make a community, and the community makes
its circle where it lives on the Earth. It cares for that part, but cares for it as
a circle—which is to say in a cooperative way and an egalitarian way, where

everybody is cared for and everybody is respected. The way of the circle is the way of respect. The way of the circle is that everybody is equal, every being is equal, everything is sacred and respected and given consideration. That's why the Longhouse prayer you'll hear me speak is, to me, one of the most powerful and meaningful, because it acknowledges everything, and it contains the whole attitude of our ways. It's basically greetings and thanksgivings to all the things that give us life." . . .

"The Original Instructions urge us to find our place in the cosmos, to know our true nature and our goal in existence. There must be a response—not an intellectual answer—but a felt understanding of the nature of this existence, of its purpose and of our part in that purpose. That is the reason for the spiritual quests, the religions, the rituals, the searches, pilgrimages, meditations, and mystic disciplines of humankind. Something in our consciousness is just not satisfied with only eating, sleeping, creating, and reproducing. Something in us wants to know what it's all about and how we fit into it."

9. SHUNRYU SUZUKI, "POSTURE" (1970)

Eastern wisdom came to the counterculture through a variety of gurus and teachers, both American and immigrant. One of the most important was Shunryu Suzuki, a Japanese Zen Buddhist priest who came to American in 1959. Suzuki's talks on the practice of Zen attracted a considerable following of American converts, leading to the establishment of the San Francisco Zen Center in 1966 (just as the counterculture was cresting), and eventually of the first Zen monastery in the United States. Suzuki taught his followers that, since they already inherently possessed enlightenment, proper sitting meditation was the expression of that enlightenment, rather than the means to accomplish it: "The state of mind that exists when you sit in the right posture is, itself, enlightenment." Suzuki's teachings were popular among countercultural seekers, in part because they tapped into a long American tradition of deep optimism about the fundamental goodness of human nature.

Now I would like to talk about our zazen posture. When you sit in the full lotus position, your left foot is on your right thigh, and your right foot is on your left thigh. When we cross our legs like this, even though we have a right leg and a left leg, they have become one. The position expresses the oneness of duality: not two, and not one. This is the most important teaching: not two, and not one. Our body and mind are not two and not one. If you think your body and mind are two, that is wrong; if you think that they are one, that is also wrong. Our body and mind are both two *and* one. . . .

You should not be tilted sideways, backwards, or forwards. You should be sitting straight up as if you were supporting the sky with your head. This is not just form or breathing. It expresses the key point of Buddhism. It is a perfect expression of your Buddha nature. If you want true understanding of Buddhism, you should practice this way. These forms are not a means of obtaining the right state of mind. To take this posture itself is the purpose of our practice. When you have this posture, you have the right state of mind, so there is no need to try to attain some special state. When you try to attain something, your mind starts to wander about somewhere else. When you do not try to attain anything, you have your own body and mind right here. A Zen master would say, "Kill the Buddha!" Kill the Buddha if the Buddha exists somewhere else. Kill the Buddha, because you should resume your own Buddha nature.

Doing something is expressing our own nature. We do not exist for the sake of something else. We exist for the sake of ourselves. This is the fundamental teaching expressed in the forms we observe. Just as for sitting, when we stand in the zendo we have some rules. But the purpose of these rules is not to make everyone the same, but to allow each to express his own self most freely. . . .

We must exist right here, right now! This is the key point. You must have your own body and mind. Everything should exist in the right place, in the right way. . . .

So try always to keep the right posture, not only when you practice zazen, but in all your activities. Take the right posture when you are driving your car, and when you are reading. If you read in a slumped position, you cannot stay awake long. Try. You will discover how important it is to keep the right posture. This is the true teaching. The teaching which is written on paper is not the true teaching. Written teaching is a kind of food for your brain. Of course it is necessary to take some food for your brain, but it is more important to be yourself by practicing the right way of life.

10. GARY SNYDER, *THE PRACTICE OF THE WILD* (1990)

If many expressions of the counterculture proved to be relatively shallow and evanescent, some of the major writers and poets that emerged from this era had considerably more staying power. Gary Snyder bridges the entire history of religious thought from "beat Zen" in the 1950s through the countercultural expressions of the 1960s to the movements for self-fulfillment of the 1970s, and finally to a reawakened social con-

sciousness in environmentalism in the 1980s and 1990s. Snyder was memorialized in
literature as Japhy Ryder in Jack Kerouac's novel Dharma Bums, *and later in the*
1950s and 1960s served a long Zen apprenticeship in Japan. In more recent years he
has produced profoundly influential poetry and essays, exploring deeper concepts of Na-
tive American spirituality and religio-environmental thought. In these excerpts from
his essay collection The Practice of the Wild, *Snyder offers words both spiritual and*
practical on how to enact the gratitude expressed in his poems.

"Wild and free." An American dream-phrase loosing images: a long-maned
stallion racing across the grasslands, a V of Canada Geese high and honk-
ing, a squirrel chattering and leaping limb to limb overhead in an oak. It
also sounds like an ad for a Harley-Davidson. Both words, profoundly political and sensitive as they are, have become consumer baubles. I hope to investigate the meaning of *wild* and how it connects with *free* and what one
would want to do with these meanings. To be truly free one must take on
the basic conditions as they are—painful, impermanent, open, imperfect—
and then be grateful for impermanence and the freedom it grants us. For in
a fixed universe there would be no freedom. With that freedom we improve
the campsite, teach children, oust tyrants. The world is nature, and in the
long run inevitably wild, because the wild, as the process and essence of nature, is also an ordering of impermanence.

The World Is Watching

The world is as sharp as the edge of a knife—a Northwest Coast saying.
Now how does it look from the standpoint of peoples for whom there is no
great dichotomy between their culture and nature, those who live in societies whose economies draw on uncultivated systems? The pathless world
of wild nature is a surpassing school and those who have lived through her
can be tough and funny teachers. Out here one is in constant engagement
with countless plants and animals. To be well educated is to have learned
the songs, proverbs, stories, sayings, myths (and technologies) that come
with this experiencing of the nonhuman members of the local ecological
community. Practice in the field, "open country," is foremost. Walking is
the great adventure, the first meditation, a practice of heartiness and soul
primary to humankind. Walking is the exact balance of spirit and humility.
Out walking, one notices where there is food. And there are firsthand true
stories of "Your ass is somebody else's meal"—a blunt way of saying interdependence, interconnection, "ecology," on the level where it counts, also a
teaching of mindfulness and preparedness. There is an extraordinary

teaching of specific plants and animals and their uses, empirical and im-
peccable, that never reduces them to objects and commodities.

It seems that a short way back in the history of occidental ideas there was
a fork in the trail. The line of thought that is signified by the names of
Descartes, Newton, and Hobbes (saying that life in a primary society is
"nasty, brutish, and short"—all of them city-dwellers) was a profound rejection of the organic world. For a reproductive universe they substituted a
model of sterile mechanism and an economy of "production." These
thinkers were as hysterical about "chaos" as their predecessors, the witch-
hunt prosecutors of only a century before, were about "witches." They not
only didn't enjoy the possibility that the world is as sharp as the edge of a
knife, they wanted to take that edge away from nature. Instead of making
the world safer for humankind, the foolish tinkering with the powers of life
and death by the occidental scientist-engineer-ruler puts the whole planet
on the brink of degradation. Most of humanity—foragers, peasants, or arti-
sans—has always taken the other fork. That is to say, they have understood
the play of the real world, with all its suffering, not in simple terms of "nature red in tooth and claw" but through the celebration of the gift-exchange
quality of our give-and-take. "What a big potlatch we are all members of!"
To acknowledge that each of us at the table will eventually be part of the
meal is not just being "realistic." It is allowing the sacred to enter and accepting the sacramental aspect of our shaky temporary personal being. . . .

We are all capable of extraordinary transformations. In myth and story
these changes are animal-to-human, human-to-animal, animal-to-animal,
or even farther leaps. The essential nature remains clear and steady through
these changes. So the animal icons of the Inupiaq people ("Eskimos") of the
Bering Sea (here's the reverse!) have a tiny human face sewn into the fur, or
under the feathers, or carved on the back or breast or even inside the eye,
peeping out. This is the *inua,* which is often called "spirit" but could just as
well be termed the "essential nature" of that creature. It remains the same
face regardless of the playful temporary changes. Just as Buddhism has chosen to represent our condition by presenting an image of a steady, solid,
gentle, meditating human figure seated in the midst of the world of phenomena, the Inupiaq would present a panoply of different creatures, each
with a little hidden human face. This is not the same as anthropocentrism
or human arrogance. It is a way of saying that each creature is a spirit with
an intelligence as brilliant as our own. The Buddhist iconographers hide a
little animal face in the hair of the human to remind us that we see with archetypal wilderness eyes as well.

The world is not only watching, it is listening too. A rude and thought-
less comment about a Ground Squirrel or a Flicker or a Porcupine will not

go unnoticed. Other beings (the instructors from the old ways tell us) do not mind being killed and eaten as food, but they expect us to say please, and thank you, and they hate to see themselves wasted. The precept against needlessly taking life is inevitably the first and most difficult of commandments. In their practice of killing and eating with gentleness and thanks, the primary peoples are our teachers: the attitude toward animals, and their treatment, in twentieth-century American industrial meat production is literally sickening, unethical, and a source of boundless bad luck for this society. . . .

THE PLACE, THE REGION, AND THE COMMONS

"When you find your place where you are, practice occurs."

DŌGEN

The World Is Places

. . . People today are caught between the remnants of the ongoing "grandmother wisdom" of the peoples of the world (within which I include several of the Ten Commandments and the first five of the Ten Great Buddhist Precepts) and the codes that serve centralization and hierarchy. Children grow up hearing contradictory teachings: one for getting what's yours, another for being decent. The classroom teacher, who must keep state and church separate, can only present the middle ground, the liberal humanistic philosophy that comes out of "the university." It's a kind of thinking that starts (for the Occident) with the Greek effort to probe the literal truth of myth by testing stories and theories against experience. The early philosophers were making people aware of the faculty of reason and the possibility of objectivity. The philosopher is required to conduct the discussion with both hands on the table, and cannot require that you ingest a drug, eat a special diet, or follow any out-of-the-way regimen (other than intelligent reflection) to follow the argument. I'd say this was a needed corrective in some cases. A kind of intellectual clarity could thus be accomplished without necessarily discarding myth. Keeping myth alive requires a lively appreciation of the depths of metaphor, of ceremony, and the need for stories. Allegorizing and rationalizing myth kills it. That's what happened later in Greek history. . . .

American society (like any other) has its own set of unquestioned assumptions. It still maintains a largely uncritical faith in the notion of continually unfolding progress. It cleaves to the idea that there can be unblemished scientific objectivity. And most fundamentally it operates under the delusion that we are each a kind of "solitary knower"—that we exist as rootless intelligences without layers of localized contexts. Just a "self" and the "world." In this there is no real recognition that grandparents, place, grammar, pets, friends, lovers, children, tools, the poems and songs we remember, are what we *think with*. Such a solitary mind—if it could exist—would be a boring prisoner of abstractions. *With no surroundings there can be no path, and with no path one cannot become free.* . . .

The poor literati, I was thinking. Have philosophers and writers and such always been ineffectual bystanders while the energetic power-players of church, state, and market run the show? In the shorter time scale, this is true. Measured in centuries and millennia, it can be seen that philosophy is always entwined with myth as both explicator and critic and that the fundamental myth to which a people subscribe moves at glacial speed but is almost implacable. Deep myths change on something like the order of linguistic drift: the social forces of any given time can attempt to manipulate and shape language usages for a while, as the French Academy does for French, trying to stave off English loanwords. Eventually languages return to their own inexplicable directions.

The same is true of the larger outline of world philosophies. We (who stand aside) stand on the lateral moraine of the glacier eased along by Newton and Descartes. The revivified Goddess Gaia glacier is coming down another valley, from our distant pagan past, and another arm of ice is sliding in from another angle: the no-nonsense meditation view of Buddhism with its emphasis on compassion and insight in an empty universe. Someday they will probably all converge, and yet carry (like the magnificent Baltoro glacier in the Karakoram) streaks on each section that testify to their place of origin. Some historians would say that "thinkers" are behind the ideas and mythologies that people live by. I think it also goes back to maize, reindeer, squash, sweet potatoes, and rice. And their songs. . . .

Grace

Everyone who ever lived took the lives of other animals, pulled plants, plucked fruit, and ate. Primary people have had their own ways of trying to understand the precept of nonharming. They knew that taking life required gratitude and care. There is no death that is not somebody's food, no life that is not somebody's death. Some would take this as a sign that the universe is fundamentally flawed. This leads to a disgust with self, with humanity, and with nature. Otherworldly philosophies end up doing more damage to the planet (and human psyches) than the pain and suffering that is in the existential conditions they seek to transcend.

The archaic religion is to kill god and eat him. Or her. The shimmering food-chain, the food-web, is the scary, beautiful condition of the biosphere. Subsistence people live without excuses. The blood is on your own hands as you divide the liver from the gallbladder. You have watched the color fade on the glimmer of the trout. A subsistence economy is a sacramental economy because it has faced up to one of the critical problems of life and death: the taking of life for food. Contemporary people do not need to hunt, many cannot even afford meat, and in the developed world the variety of foods available to us makes the avoidance of meat an easy choice. Forests in the tropics are cut to make pasture to raise beef for the American market. Our distance from the source of our food enables us to be superficially more comfortable, and distinctly more ignorant.

Eating is a sacrament. The grace we say clears our hearts and guides the children and welcomes the guest, all at the same time. We look at eggs, apples, and stew. They are evidence of plenitude, excess, a great reproductive exuberance. Millions of grains of grass-seed that will become rice or flour, millions of codfish fry that will never, and *must* never, grow to maturity. Innumerable little seeds are sacrifices to the food-chain. A parsnip in the ground is a marvel of living chemistry, making sugars and flavors from earth, air, water. And if we do eat meat it is the life, the bounce, the swish, of a great alert being with keen ears and lovely eyes, with foursquare feet and a huge beating heart that we eat, let us not deceive ourselves. . . .

> At our house we say a Buddhist grace—
> We venerate the Three Treasures [teachers, the wild, and friends]
> And are thankful for this meal
> The work of many people
> And the sharing of other forms of life.

Anyone can use a grace from their own tradition (and really give it meaning)—or make up their own. Saying some sort of grace is never inappropriate, and speeches and announcements can be tacked onto it. It is a plain, ordinary, old-fashioned little thing to do that connects us with all our ancestors.

11. DUANE PEDERSON, *THE JESUS PEOPLE* (1971)

HILEY WARD, *THE FAR-OUT SAINTS OF THE JESUS COMMUNES* (1971)

Throughout the 1960s, many American evangelicals, Catholics, and conservative Jews were frightened by the countercultural challenge to dominant values. Where the counterculture advocated consciousness expansion, evangelicals perceived brainwashing.

While the counterculture saw drugs, rock music, and alternative lifestyles as part of the American future, evangelicals feared them as the latest ruses of Satan.

Some evangelicals tried to respond to the counterculture in its own terms, adopting its language, personal dress styles, and ways of viewing the world. One of the most publicized groups of evangelicals was on the West Coast, dubbed the "Jesus People," sometimes also called "Jesus Freaks." They termed Jesus the "true revolutionary" and introduced contemporary dress and musical styles to their worship expressions. Duane Pederson, whose self-promoting autobiography Jesus People *is excerpted below, led a movement that emerged from conventional groups such as Campus Crusade for Christ. They eventually spurned the "square" styles for which evangelicals were ridiculed. Pederson began the Hollywood Free Paper, modeled after the "underground" papers of the counterculture and full of the argot ("groovy," "turned on to Jesus") of the times. In the second selection, Hiley Ward, a participant-observer of the "Jesus movement," reflects on its meaning, putting his analysis in the language of "Consciousness III" popularized by Charles Reich's* The Greening of America. *He views the Jesus People in the context of small pietistic cells that historically provided alternatives to institutionalized Christianity.*

⊶⊷

THE JESUS PEOPLE

Chapter Four
Jesus People: For Real?

Everywhere I go people ask, "Who are these Jesus People? Are they for real?"

"Is it a new denomination?"

"What's it all about?"

"How did you get involved in it?"

"What do Jesus People believe in?"

Well, to begin with, no person started the Jesus People Movement. God did that. I coined the name after I launched the *Free Paper*, but I didn't start the Movement. It was spontaneous, clearly led by the Holy Spirit. The Movement started several places at the same time: in Seattle. San Francisco. Los Angeles. And others . . .

Originally the press called us Jesus Freaks. On the street and within the Jesus Movement, the word "freak" isn't a bad word. A freak is someone who has gone to an extreme on anything—even Jesus Christ.

On the street, the word described the people who were dropping too much acid, or "speed"—or so much of something that they "freaked out." So they were called "acid freaks" or "speed freaks"—or

some other kind of "freak," depending what they were "freaked out" on.

Basically it was speed, because that would really freak them out even more than acid. Acid is more of a head trip. But speed does something complete, something totally destructive to the person. A guy who's been a speed freak for a while gets "spaced out." His mind, or part of it, gets wiped out, destroyed.

One day as I was talking to one of the newsmen he said, "Those street people who get turned on for Jesus are freaks—'Jesus Freaks.'"

I said, "They're not freaks. They're people. They're Jesus People." Somehow the name stuck, and now the movement is called the Jesus People Movement.

It started as a ministry to the street people—the thousands upon thousands of people who live on the streets. These people exist in abandoned buildings, on roof tops, in alleys, parks, on the beaches. And many of them live in VW busses. They have no other homes than the street.

According to the authorities over a million kids a year leave home and wander to Hollywood. They aren't just Californians. They are boys and girls from the farm in Iowa or Texas. From the house next door. They aren't always from the "down-and-out" neighborhood. Far from it. They are the neighbors to everybody in America.

Most of the street people are called drop-outs or runaways. But they are people. Real people. They may not matter to their own community or family. But they matter to Jesus Christ. They matter to Him very much. He came to seek and to save them. . . .

Chapter Eight
Revolutionaries!

As soon as I left the Midwest I headed for California. I was determined not to cooperate with Christians again. It seemed that each time I had done it I got stomped on. I did some work with some youth organizations, but turned down many of their invitations. . . .

I had the feeling then that anything I would do must be done alone, because I had gone through too many broken confidences by too many who professed to serve the Lord.

I became a gypsy again.

This went on for some time: school assemblies and other engagements—all of which kept me on the road all the time. My contacts with people were brief as I was in a different town every day.

But during these months I was praying, "Lord, please use me. I don't know how You are working. I don't know what Your plans are. But, Lord, I am Yours."

Often, in the wee hours of the morning as I lay awake praying I would speak to Him as though He were in the room. "Lord, it seems that I have been turned down by every group I've ever tried to be with.

"My ideas seem to be so radical and far out in left field that they're totally unacceptable to any of the religious world. But, God, I know I belong to You. I know You love me. And I know You have given me talents You can use . . . "

That was my condition when I returned to Hollywood to work on a TV series. And then in just that flash that evening when I saw all the underground papers—and not a single Christian paper—I somehow knew that here there was something for me.

Strangely enough though, even as I was publishing and distributing that first issue or two of the *Free Paper*, I did not realize . . . the thought never once entered my head . . . that this would turn into the permanent situation as it has. I thought it would be something I would do just that once, or twice, then be back on the road.

But when the responses came back—and my mailbox was jammed with letters from desperate people—I had that same feeling I had in Springfield when I was personally introducing those people to Jesus Christ.

Then the letters came pouring in. And then I knew that God was going to use me to communicate the love of Jesus Christ to those people who were searching. I realized that I had been unsuccessful in communicating with the church people and the religious world.

But now, through His infinite grace and wisdom, He was giving me an opportunity to share Jesus Christ to the rejects and castoffs of society. I felt so humbled . . .

I walked the Boulevard more than one night saying, "Thank You, Jesus. Thank You; Jesus . . . "

Maybe the reason Jesus is using me this way is because I am considered to be a sort of rebel. And Jesus Christ was Himself a rebel . . . in fact, a revolutionary!

———— ∞ ————

THE FAR-OUT SAINTS OF THE JESUS COMMUNES

But the Jesus communes seem to be more a part of the new consciousness of which Roszak talks, with some perpetuity implied. Granted, Jesus houses are closing down all the time. Try and send a survey to them, and a large percentage of the letters will be returned because the commune left no forwarding address. But that does not negate their existence. A part of the Jesus People philosophy, like that of Zinzendorf and the Moravians, is to keep on the move and establish new colonies. People in the centers that remain open, on the other hand, can tell you the addresses of several other Jesus houses you never heard of.

The Jesus People are more than a fad and have a future because:

(1) They have money working for them, as outsiders bankroll their efforts and they themselves devise new ways of paying expenses. The money of evangelists and business tycoons can help keep the movement on the map. . . .

(2) There is a wide diversity of individual religious experience that exists apart from the promoters. This experiential quality, shared with other communal and radical types, can become effective in social and political action and guarantee the movement with its communes a future influence.

(3) The Jesus People generally consist of small groups and are more durable, much like a small family, in which even if only one person works there is some assurance of paying the rent.

(4) Although there are conflicts, there is little real heresy or deviation in the movement. Of course, this could be a negative factor, for many groups are created over conflicts, quarrel internally, and derive their energy in so doing. But again, the common ground of "Jesus only," communal styles and life in the Spirit aspects of the movement might hint at the emergence already of incipient denominations. Indeed, the process has developed to the point where some consolidation among structured groups, as we will see, is also at hand. There are still heretics in the movement. Some could cite the cult groups, of which the Children of God are the biggest and most popular, that refuse cooperation with society and with most other Jesus People. But the Children of God are not the whole picture, despite their noise, their prominence on TV documentaries and their new acquisitions. . . .

(5) Most Jesus People make no demand on the individual in terms of political activism, nor does the movement demand much of society at the present (potentially, yes); the movement thus finds itself in a very favorable climate, acceptable to society (a condition that favors institutionalization if not the health of the movement).

(6) The Jesus People nevertheless remain a part of a continuing alienation—*i.e.*, alienation from family and church establishments (denominations)—which makes it difficult for them even to want to return to former milieus and structures.

(7) They are more nomadic than their fellow freaks. The network of published addresses of Jesus communes and a common cause encourage travel and visitation. The bus freaks on the secular side are settling down. . . .

(8) The Jesus People become bi- and tri-cultural. Turned off to society, they nevertheless begin to look fairly straight. Girls groom their hair immaculately, boys shave, etc. They speak and witness in straight churches. They stand with a foot in each consciousness—traditional, technical and the new, creative trying-to-emerge Consciousness III. Middle-class and generally sophisticated, many having attended college, they remain individuals, particularly as they relate to the smaller communes. . . .

Duane Pederson may not be so important as his monopoly on national distribution of his Hollywood *Free Paper*, claiming up to 400,000 circulation, would seem to indicate. . . . Yet as a coordinator and a hub nationally, if not locally, of the movement, Pederson is a man to reckon with. He has done much to give the movement a special strength by coordinating it through his newspaper. Each issue has an up-to-date (more or less) list of hundreds of Jesus houses, centers, and coffee houses, new and old. Thus, as we have noted, it encourages the mobility of the Jesus People, as they look up houses to visit in other communities, often near friends, and end up by staying. He is also responsible for introducing commercialism into the movement, by producing his own bumper stickers, etc., and carrying ads of new Jesus records and other products. You might say he is Americanizing, or westernizing, the cop-out Christians, making them quantitatively conscious again, preparing them for a role of some sort within society.

Pederson, aged thirty-three, probably looks as much like Billy Graham as anybody in the country. The similarity does not stop with just the handsome Nordic features, straight nose, keen, almost birdlike eyes, broad forehead and straight blond-brown hair. Both are national evangelists and close to a more *status quo* wing of evangelism.

Pederson has registered the name Jesus People with the United States copyright office, and gets very uptight when you talk about others using the name Jesus People on watches, as the Melodyland pentecostal-oriented center at Anaheim, California, is doing.

The six-foot two-inch Minnesota farm boy, in fairly new working jeans and matching jacket, finds himself on the quiet end of the spectrum of a movement that tends to take a fancy to speaking in tongues and shouting out songs.

Pederson, a sort of pope or archbishop without a parish, gets out and baptizes in the ocean, but he sees the kids going to various communes and centers. He is content to leave it that way. Like Graham, who also prefers to conduct rallies, Pederson likes to work with and speak encouraging words about the church. However, Pederson differs with Billy Graham about the future of the church. Graham has told Pederson and this writer that the future of the church is likely to be in small groups, as it was in the first century.

12. KEITH HARRARY, "THE TRUTH ABOUT JONESTOWN" (1992)

Jim Jones was a minister originally affiliated with the Disciples of Christ, a mainstream Protestant denomination strong in the Midwest and upper South. Caught up in the countercultural movements of the 1960s, Jones led a group of devotees to San Francisco, forming a "People's Temple" to encourage racial harmony, social action, charity, and a countercultural vision of Christianity. Jones, however, also abused his increasingly fearful followers mentally and physically. Refugees from the People's Temple began to gather at the Freedom Center in Berkeley, a safe house where escapees from abusive religious leaders shared stories and mutual support. Later, Jones took his followers to establish a utopian commune in the Central American country of Guyana. News of his doings there sparked concern. When a congressman and three members of the press went to investigate in November 1978, they were murdered. Shortly thereafter, on November 18, Jones ordered the mass suicide of his followers, over 900 of whom drank Kool-Aid laced with cyanide. Among the dead were 276 children. Jonestown soon became the symbol for the worst-case scenario of cults, a specter raised again in 1994 outside of San Diego, where several dozen followers of a group known as Heaven's Gate left their "bodily vessels" by taking poison en masse. Soon after Jonestown, "deprogramming" became big business, as parents and friends sought help in "curing" those who had been trapped by cult mind control.

⊶⊷

The old Peoples Temple building collapsed in the last, big San Francisco earthquake, leaving behind nothing but an empty plot of land to mark its passing. I'd avoided the place for nearly 10 years—it always struck me as a dark reminder of the raw vulnerability of the human mind and the superficial nature of civilized behavior. In ways that I never expected when I first decided to investigate the Jonestown holocaust, the crimes that took place within that building and within the cult itself have become a part of my personal memory. If Jim Jones has finally become a metaphor, a symbol of power-hungry insanity—if not a term for insanity itself—for me he will always remain much too human.

Suicide is usually an act of lonely desperation, carried out in isolation or near isolation by those who see death as an acceptable alternative to the burdens of continued existence. It can also be an act of self-preservation among those who prefer a dignified death to the ravages of illness or some perceived humiliation. It is even, occasionally, a political statement. But it is rarely, if ever, a social event. The reported collective self-extermination of 912 individuals (913 when Jim Jones was counted among their number) therefore demanded more than an ordinary explanation.

The only information I had about Jim Jones was what I could gather from news accounts of the closing scene at the Jonestown compound. The details were sketchy but deeply disturbing: The decomposing corpses were discovered in the jungle in the stinking aftermath of a suicidal frenzy set around a vat of cyanide-laced Flavor-Aid. Littered among the dead like broken dolls were the bodies of 276 children. A United States congressman and three members of the press entourage traveling with him were ambushed and murdered on an airstrip not far from the scene. It had all been done in the name of a formerly lesser-known cult called the Peoples Temple.

The group was started years before with the avowed vision of abolishing racism. Although it was headquartered in San Francisco, its members sought to found their own Utopia in a nondescript plot of South American jungle near Georgetown, Guyana. The commune they created was named in honor of the cult's founder and religious leader, a charismatic figure in dark glasses named the Reverend Jim Jones.

While the news media treated the Jonestown holocaust like a fluke of nature, it seemed to me a unique opportunity to learn something crucial about the fundamental weakness of the human mind. In addition to my formal education in psychology, I had recently spent four years as a suicide-prevention counselor and had helped train dozens of other counselors working in the field. But even with that experience, the slaughter that took place in Jonestown seemed incomprehensible. . . .

Had the massacre succeeded in killing all the witnesses to what occurred inside the confines of Jonestown, it would have been impossible to get a believable answer. But there were a number of survivors: An old woman sleeping in a hut slipped the minds of her fellow members who were preoccupied with dying at the time; a nine-year-old girl survived having her throat cut by a member who then committed suicide; a young man worked his way to the edge of the compound and fled into the jungle. The only other eyewitness escaped when he was sent to get a stethoscope so the bodies could be checked to make certain they were dead.

Other survivors included a man wounded by gunfire at the airstrip who managed to escape by scrambling into the bush; the official Peoples Temple basketball team (including Jones's son), which was visiting Georgetown during the holocaust; a number of members stationed at the San Francisco headquarters; and a small group of defectors and relatives of those who had remained in the cult. The last was gathered at a place called the Human Freedom Center in Berkeley—a halfway house for cult defectors founded by Jeannie and Al Mills, two Peoples Temple expatriates. . . .

There was a deliberate malevolence about the way Jones treated the members of his cult that went beyond mere perversion. It was all about forcing members to experience themselves as vulgar and despicable people who could never return to a normal life outside of the group. It was about destroying any personal relationships that might come ahead of the relationship each individual member had with him. It was about terrorizing children and turning them against their parents. It was about seeing Jim Jones as an onmipotent figure who could snuff out members' lives on a whim as easily as he had already snuffed out their self-respect. In short, it was about mind control. And, after all that, it was not incidentally about Jones's own sick fantasies and sexual perversions.

Both men and women were routinely beaten, coerced into having sex with Jones in private and with other people in public. Husbands and wives were forbidden to have sex with each other, but were forced to join other members in watching their spouses being sexually humiliated and abused. In order to prove that he wasn't a racist, a white man was coerced into having oral sex in front of a gathering of members with a black woman who was having her period. Another man was made to remove all his clothes, bend over and spread his legs before the congregation while being examined for signs of venereal disease. A woman had to strip in front of the group so that Jones could poke fun at her overweight body before telling her to submerge herself in a pool of ice-cold water. Another woman was made to squat in front of 100 members and defecate into a fruit can. Children were tortured with electric shocks, viciously beaten, punished by being kept in the bottom of a jungle well, forced to have hot peppers stuffed up their rectums and made to eat their own vomit.

Dozens of suicide drills—or "white nights" as Jim Jones called them—were rehearsed in San Francisco and in the jungle in a prelude to the final curtain he said might fall at any moment. Members were given wine to drink, then told it had been poisoned to test their loyalty and get them used to the idea that they might all be asked to take their lives as a sign of their faith. Their deaths, Jones tried to convince them, would be honored by the world as a symbolic protest against the evils of mankind—a collective self-immolation. (This would also serve to eliminate anyone who might reveal the dirty secrets of life with the Peoples Temple.) The faithful would be "transformed," Jones claimed, and live with him forever on another planet. . . .

The Human Freedom Center was a beaten-up, two-story wood-and-stucco building that had once been used as a private rest home. Its long rows of odd-size rooms filled with broken-down furniture could have served as a backdrop for a 1950s horror movie set in a sanitarium. Although most of the Peoples Temple survivors who might have taken refuge there were suddenly dead, the events in Jonestown instantly made many other organizations seem potentially as dangerous. Jeannie and Al decided to open the center to defectors from all sorts of cult groups, from the Unification Church to the Hare Krishnas. I had already decided that—whatever the pay—if they offered me the director of counseling position, I was going to take it. . . .

Most of the center's clients were people seeking help in extricating family members from various cults, or ex-cult members who were starting to put their own lives back together. Additionally, a couple of former Peoples Temple members lived on the premises, and others came periodically to talk about their present feelings and past experiences.

The first thing that struck me when I met the clients and got to know them was that, although the specific details of their belief systems and activities varied considerably, those who became involved in cults had a frightening underlying commonality. They described their experiences as finding an unexpected sense of purpose, as though they were becoming a part of something extraordinarily significant that seemed to carry them beyond their feelings of isolation and toward an expanded sense of reality and the meaning of life. Nobody asked if they would be willing to commit suicide the first time they attended a meeting. Nor did anyone mention that the feeling of expansiveness they were enjoying would later be used to turn them against each other.

Instead they were told about the remarkable Reverend Jones, a self-professed social visionary and prophet who apparently could heal the sick and predict the future. Jim Jones did everything within his power to perpetuate that myth: fraudulent psychic-healing demonstrations using rotting animal organs as phony tumors; searching through members' garbage for information to reveal in fake psychic readings; drugging his followers to make it appear as though he were actually raising the dead. Even Jeannie Mills, who later told me she knowingly assisted Jones in his faked demonstrations, said she did so because she believed she was helping him conserve his real supernatural powers for more important matters. . . .

Once thrown off balance (in the exclusive company of other people who already believe it) and being shown evidence that supports the conclusion, it is not difficult to become convinced that you have actually met the Living God. In the glazed and pallid stupor associated with achieving that confused and dangerous state of mind, almost any conceivable act of self-sacrifice, self-degradation, and cruelty can become possible.

The truth of that realization was brought home to me by one survivor who, finding himself surrounded by rifles, was told he could take the poison quietly or they would stick it in his veins or blow his brains out. He didn't resist. Instead, he raised his cup and toasted those dying around him without drinking. "We'll see each other in the transformation," he said. Then he walked around the compound shaking hands until he'd worked his way to the edge of the jungle, where he ran and hid until he felt certain it had to be over.

"Why did you follow Jim Jones?" I asked him.

"Because I believed he was God," he answered. "We all believed he was God."

A number of Peoples Temple survivors told me they viewed Jones in the same way—not as God metaphorically, but as God *literally*. They would have done anything he asked of them, they said. Or almost anything. . . .

Jim Jones did not create the human weaknesses that led so many people to follow him; he merely exploited them. Ultimate power is seductive not only to those who achieve it themselves but also to those who give up their own power in order to help others achieve it. It is the ability to answer the unanswerable questions about the meaning of life and death. And it does not matter if those answers make no sense—the belief in them and in the individual who bears them makes any sacrifice in the service of some more eternal purpose seem acceptable.

Most of us don't think of ourselves as the kind of person who could ever possibly become embroiled in a cult like the Peoples Temple. We are not at all correct in that assumption. Given an unfortunate turn of fate that leads to a moment of weakness, or a momentary lapse in judgment that expands into a shift in our perception, nearly any of us could find ourselves taking the cyanide in Jonestown—if not passing out the poison to other people.

People end up joining cults when events lead them to search for a deeper sense of belonging and for something more meaningful in their lives. They do so because they happen to be in the wrong place at the wrong time and are ripe for exploitation. They do so because they find themselves getting caught in the claws of a parasite before they realize what is happening to them.

13. FRITJOF CAPRA, "MODERN PHYSICS" (FROM *THE TAO OF PHYSICS*, 1983)

Science teaches a natural explanation of the way the world works; religion explores the supernatural basis of the world. Historically, it has been assumed that the two are in conflict. For example, scientists explain the development of the natural world through evolutionary theory, while theologians are concerned with God's presence in the world. At the same time, many scientists, from Isaac Newton forward, have been profoundly influenced by religious belief. Newton's physics came about in part because of his attempt to worship God through expressing the harmony of the universe in mathematical symbols. Albert Einstein, arguing for the fundamental order even in a non-Newtonian quantum universe, insisted that "God does not play dice." In this selection, physicist Fritjof Capra explores the parallels between modern physics and eastern mysticism, how "the two foundations of twentieth-century physics—quantum theory and relativity theory—both force us to see the world very much in the way a Hindu, Buddhist or Taoist sees it." Capra was one of many scientists and theologians who have attempted to bridge the gap between science and religion, a movement itself profoundly influenced by the counterculture's quest to find harmony between the physical/natural and the spiritual.

⟳

MODERN PHYSICS: A PATH WITH A HEART?

Any path is only a path, and there is no affront, to oneself or to others, in dropping it if that is what your heart tells you . . . Look at every path closely and deliberately. Try it as many times as you think necessary. Then ask yourself, and yourself alone, one question . . . Does this path have a heart? If it does, the path is good; if it doesn't it is of no use.

CARLOS CASTANEDA, *THE TEACHINGS OF DON JUAN*

We shall see how the two foundations of twentieth-century physics—quantum theory and relativity theory—both force us to see the world very much in the way a Hindu, Buddhist or Taoist sees it, and how this similarity strengthens when we look at the recent attempts to combine these two theories in order to describe the phenomena of the submicroscopic world: the properties and interactions of the subatomic particles of which all matter is made. Here the parallels between modern physics and Eastern mysticism are most striking, and we shall often encounter statements where it is almost impossible to say whether they have been made by physicists or by Eastern mystics. . . .

If physics leads us today to a world view which is essentially mystical, it returns, in a way, to its beginning, 2,500 years ago. It is interesting to follow the evolution of Western science along its spiral path, starting from the mystical philosophies of the early Greeks, rising and unfolding in an impressive development of intellectual thought that increasingly turned away from its mystical origins to develop a world view which is in sharp contrast to that of the Far East. In its most recent stages, Western science is finally overcoming this view and coming back to those of the early Greek and the Eastern philosophies. This time, however, it is not only based on intuition, but also on experiments of great precision and sophistication, and on a rigorous and consistent mathematical formalism. . . .

The philosophy of Descartes was not only important for the development of classical physics, but also had a tremendous influence on the general Western way of thinking up to the present day. Descartes' famous sentence "*Cogito ergo sum*"—"I think, therefore I exist"—has led Westerners to equate their identity with their mind, instead of with their whole organism. As a consequence of the Cartesian division, most individuals are aware of themselves as isolated egos existing "inside" their bodies. The mind has been separated from the body and given the futile task of controlling it, thus causing an apparent conflict between the conscious will and the involuntary instincts. Each individual has been split up further into a large number of separate compartments, according to his or her activities, talents, feelings, beliefs, etc., which are engaged in endless conflicts generating continuous metaphysical confusion and frustration. . . .

The Cartesian division and the mechanistic world view have thus been beneficial and detrimental at the same time. They were extremely successful in the development of classical physics and technology, but had many adverse consequences for our civilization. It is fascinating to see that twentieth-century science, which originated in the Cartesian split and in the mechanistic world view, and which indeed only became possible because of such a view, now overcomes this fragmentation and leads back to the idea of unity expressed in the early Greek and Eastern philosophies.

In contrast to the mechanistic Western view, the Eastern view of the world is "organic." For the Eastern mystic, all things and events perceived by the senses are interrelated, connected, and are but different aspects or manifestations of the same ultimate reality. Our tendency to divide the perceived world into individual and separate things and to experience ourselves as isolated egos in this world is seen as an illusion which comes from our measuring and categorizing mentality. It is called *avidya*, or ignorance, in Buddhist philosophy and is seen as the state of a disturbed mind which has to be overcome:

> When the mind is disturbed, the multiplicity of things is produced, but when the mind is quieted, the multiplicity of things disappears.

Although the various schools of Eastern mysticism differ in many details, they all emphasize the basic unity of the universe which is the central feature of their teachings. The highest aim for their followers—whether they are Hindus, Buddhists or Taoists—is to become aware of the unity and mutual interrelation of all things, to transcend the notion of an isolated individual self and to identify themselves with the ultimate reality. The emergence of this awareness—known as "enlightenment"—is not only an intellectual act but is an experience which involves the whole person and is religious in its ultimate nature. For this reason, most Eastern philosophies are essentially religious philosophies.

In the Eastern view, then, the division of nature into separate objects is not fundamental and any such objects have a fluid and ever-changing character. The Eastern world view is therefore intrinsically dynamic and contains time and change as essential features. The cosmos is seen as one inseparable reality—for ever in motion, alive, organic; spiritual and material at the same time.

Since motion and change are essential properties of things, the forces causing the motion are not outside the objects, as in the classical Greek view, but are an intrinsic property of matter. Correspondingly, the Eastern image of the Divine is not that of a ruler who directs the world from above, but of a principle that controls everything from within:

> He who, dwelling in all things,
> Yet is other than all things,
> Whom all things do not know,
> Whose body all things are,
> Who controls all things from within—
> He is your Soul, the Inner Controller,
> The Immortal. . . .

The further we penetrate into the submicroscopic world, the more we shall realize how the modern physicist, like the Eastern mystic, has come to see the world as a system of inseparable, interacting and ever-moving components with the observer being an integral part of this system. . . .

For most of us it is very difficult to be constantly aware of the limitations and of the relativity of conceptual knowledge. Because our representation of reality is so much easier to grasp than reality itself, we tend to confuse the two and to take our concepts and symbols for reality. It is one of the main aims of Eastern mysticism to rid us of this confusion. Zen Buddhists say that a finger is needed to point at the moon, but that we should not trouble ourselves with the finger once the moon is recognized; the Taoist sage Chuang Tzu wrote:

> Fishing baskets are employed to catch fish; but when the fish are got, the men forget the baskets; snares are employed to catch hares; but when the hares are got, men forget the snares. Words are employed to convey ideas; but when the ideas are grasped, men forget the words.

. . . What the Eastern mystics are concerned with is a direct experience of reality which transcends not only intellectual thinking but also sensory perception. In the words of the *Upanishads,*

> What is soundless, touchless, formless, imperishable,
> Likewise tasteless, constant, odourless,
> Without beginning, without end, higher than the great, stable—
> By discerning That, one is liberated from the mouth of death.

Knowledge which comes from such an experience is called "absolute knowledge" by Buddhists because it does not rely on the discriminations, abstractions and classifications of the intellect which, as we have seen, are always relative and approximate. It is, so we are told by Buddhists, the direct experience of undifferentiated, undivided, indeterminate "suchness." Complete apprehension of this suchness is not only the core of Eastern mysticism, but is the central characteristic of all mystical experience.

Part 2

*Gender, Race, and Politics
in American Religion Since 1945*

Chapter 3

Religion and the Civil Rights Movement

THIS CHAPTER presents documents that explore the close relationship of religion and the black freedom struggle of the 1950s and 1960s, as well as social justice crusades in the Latino community and churches through the
words of César Chávez and others; the rise of feminist theologies in communities of color, including "womanist theology" among black women and
"*mujerista* theology" among Latinas; the spread of liberation theologies; and
the controversy and rancor raised over issues of religion, race, and power
during the tumultuous days of the late 1960s. The chapter focuses especially on documents related to black Americans' fight for civil rights in the
1950s and 1960s, a movement that provided the impetus and model for
feminism, *la raza*, the gay rights movement, and a host of other crusades to
extend the boundaries of "freedom" in American society.

In some ways it is remarkable that such a movement sprang from the
black church. Since the early twentieth century, black churches had been severely criticized for being "otherworldly," too concerned with preaching the
joys and terrors of the afterlife to address the pressing concerns of their
members in this one. Black churches certainly were important in sustaining
communities, providing needed social, recreational, and political outlets for
people denied access to public facilities and political power. Yet, in con-
structing internal defenses against the external ravages of Jim Crow, black
churches often became depoliticized, especially compared to the central political role they had played during the heady days of Reconstruction after the
Civil War (1865–1877). Leaders raised in the church, including Martin
Luther King Jr. and John Lewis (future chairman of the Student Non-Violent
Coordinating Committee [SNCC, pronounced "Snick"]), were critical of its
relative silence and complicity in the segregationist structure—in part, they
recognized, because black ministers held a relatively privileged position in
the system.

In other ways, it is not so remarkable that the civil rights crusade drew so much of its strength from churches—or, more accurately, from church people and ministers. For it took deep religious faith to sustain the thousands of black Southerners who stood up in the face of white Southern power, endured petty daily harassment as well as more explosive acts of terrorism (beatings, bombings, kidnappings, lynchings, and the like), and sought to "redeem the soul of America," as the manifesto of the Southern Christian Leadership Conference (SCLC) proclaimed its mission to be. While many churches, through indifference or fear, closed their doors to the civil rights movement, it was church men and women who made up the majority of the rank and file who marched in the streets, filled jail cells, and engaged in acts of nonviolent civil disobedience. It was fundamentally Protestant imagery— of Exodus, redemption, salvation—that undergirded the movement. And it was ministers and church activists—most obviously Martin Luther King Jr., but also men such as Ralph Abernathy, Fred Shuttlesworth, James Lawson, and John Lewis and women such as Rosa Parks, Fannie Lou Hamer, Mary King, and Bernice Johnson Reagon—who provided much of its leadership, moral passion, and steely commitment. The documents in this section provide a glimpse of the involvement of churches and their members in a campaign that transformed American life.

Nowhere is the philosophy of the movement better articulated than in two very different sets of documents: the SNCC's freedom songs and King's "Letter from Birmingham City Jail." One represents the energy, creativity, and spiritual sustenance that empowered the movement; the latter stands as the single most concise and powerful intellectual manifesto of the philosophy of nonviolent resistance produced by a participant.

Freedom songs arose in a variety of ritual contexts. Most often, they came at the beginning and end of mass meetings, as civil rights organizers energized crowds with song. Protestant hymns, familiar especially to older black folk raised in church, often began the services. Newer freedom songs increasingly took their place. Sometimes the music was accompanied by piano or organ, sounding much like hymns on Sunday mornings. Often, especially in places dominated by students and younger participants, the singing was a capella, with spirited hand clapping and foot stomping providing the rhythmic force that propelled the music forward, a legacy of the rituals of black religious song dating from the antebellum spirituals and ring shouts. Jailhouses also served as a prime origin of and motivating force for freedom songs. As civil rights protestors filled cells through the South, they sang to each other, consciously modeling themselves on Paul and Silas in the New Testament. Prison guards threatened protestors with physical harm if they continued to sing and pray, but that only enlivened the choruses. Jail cells themselves became creative bases from which dozens of new verses to freedom songs spontaneously arose. Picket and boycott lines became another ritual center, as did mass marches down city streets in Birmingham, Selma, and dozens of other Southern locations.

More than any other tune, "We Shall Overcome" became associated with the black freedom struggle, and symbolized as well the movement's religious, interracial, and nonviolent emphasis up to 1965. The song dated from the antebellum era. South Carolina slaves sang a tune entitled "I'll be Alright," which soon entered the black sacred music repertoire. Another version, now with the words "We Shall Overcome," came out of the labor movement when striking tobacco workers used it in their Southern campaigns in the 1940s.Folk singer Pete Seeger carried the song throughout the country, and introduced it to civil rights activists at the Highlander Folk School in Tennessee in the 1940s and 1950s. Indeed, it was at Highlander that the tune became identified with civil rights. Later in the 1960s, movement activists substituted the final word "someday" with the more insistent "today." As with the other freedom songs, a seemingly infinite number of verses were added, many spontaneously. Birmingham residents in 1963 chimed in with this variation:

We shall go to jail, we shall go to jail
We shall go to jail, today. . . .

While the freedom songs provided folk music for the movement, "Letter from Birmingham City Jail" was its 95 theses nailed to the door of the white Southern churches. In his searching letter, King severely chastises his white church brethren and other Southern "moderates" who settled for order rather than fighting for justice. King also employs his theological training in his exposition of just and unjust laws, as explained in Paul's letter to the Romans. Just as Paul and Silas sat in jail for breaking unjust Roman laws, so King and his cohorts sat in jail for breaking the unjust laws of the Jim Crow South. King's letter soon achieved the status of classic American literature, just as his great speech of that August, "I Have a Dream," has assumed a canonical place in the history of American oratory. Along with it are documents from participants in the Student Non-Violent Coordinating Committee (SNCC), outlining their deeply religious commitment to nonviolence as the means to achieve civil rights and social justice.

The religious impulses of the civil rights movement soon inspired activists in other groups that had been denied first-class citizenship. César Chávez, a Latino Catholic and farm laborer, organized farmworkers in the Central Valley of California. He drew his inspiration from a highly personal and mystical folk Catholicism, both tapping and reacting to his own tradition, much like Martin Luther King did with his black Baptist upbringing. Other theologians and activists took up the mantle of liberation theology, whose most prominent advocates came from Latin America. They argued that God was in solidarity with oppressed peoples everywhere. For black theologian James Cone, this meant that God was "black," a term he meant metaphorically rather than phenotypically. For Latino Christians, God was living among the struggling farmworkers who were denied decent housing and minimal health care, exposed to pesticides and disease, paid miserable wages for long hours of uncertain seasonal work, and turned away even at the door of the one true Church. Latinos took action to desegregate the ethnically divided Catholic Church and implant notions of social justice, as recounted in some selections below from the 1970s. Native Americans responded as well, represented here through Indian scholar Vine Deloria Jr.'s *God is Red,* with a title consciously modeled on James Cone's black theology. While Deloria articulated an Indian tradition of resistance to Christianization, other Native people attempted to forge a theology that combined their tradition with Christian themes, represented in chapter 7 by Steve Charleston's essay on the Indian Old Testament.

As liberation and ethnic theologies spread among Latinos, Native Americans, and Asians, the rhetoric of the black religious experience evolved significantly. Black Christians, including those who, like Cone, had been given first-class seminary training in white institutions, gradually developed stringent critiques of the unspoken assumptions and practices of white racism that pervaded the American Christian establishment. Included here are a number of documents from the "black theology" movement of the 1960s, by James Cone, Vincent Harding, and Jacquelyn Grant. They exposed the implicit racism running through the western theological tradition. Along with these theological developments came radical acts and public displays that shocked many white Christians, who had become accustomed to the nonviolent street protests conducted by Dr. King. While "Black Power" replaced "Freedom Now" as the reigning slogan, militants such as James Forman, formerly of SNCC, ascended pulpits and demanded reparations for centuries of racist oppression of blacks in American society. Forman's reading of the "Black Manifesto" put into practice the assumptions explicit in academic black theology.

Meanwhile, many black Americans rejected Christianity altogether; some found their way into the fledgling Nation of Islam. Malcolm X soon emerged as their articulate and galvanizing spokesman. He instilled pride and defiance in his listeners (especially African Americans in Harlem and the urban North who formed his street audiences) along with fear and some loathing among whites who watched television documentaries such as *The Hate That Hate Produced* that purported to explore the world of "black cult movements" like the Nation of Islam. As Malcolm became nationally known in the 1960s, his own views rapidly evolved, from the strict black separatism of his black Islamic training to a more inclusive Islam that was still black nationalist but embraced orthodox and international Islam. Included here are excerpts from his autobiography, which became a bestseller. It traces his life from street hustling as a young man through prison and conversion to the Nation of Islam to his induction into the international community of Islam. The chapter concludes with an apology from Protestant churches in the Northwest to Native Americans. No area of American life, least of all religion, escaped racism, but religious beliefs and institutions also provided much of the moral impetus to challenge and dismantle the historically discriminatory regime of American life. The documents in this chapter explore how religious belief empowered so many people to envision a new and more racially just future for the United States.

1. MARTIN LUTHER KING JR., "LETTER FROM BIRMINGHAM CITY JAIL" (1963)

In the spring of 1963, the Southern Christian Leadership Conference (SCLC) led a series of protests in the brutally racist city of Birmingham, Alabama. Having been unsuccessful the previous year in cracking the equally segregationist stronghold of Albany, Georgia, SCLC leaders searched for a new location for an action program that could spark national interest. Birmingham fit the bill perfectly. For years, the Reverend Fred Shuttlesworth, a local Baptist minister and fearless advocate of human rights, had borne the brunt of the city's campaign of terror against civil rights activists, enduring beatings and bombings of his house with remarkable courage. Shuttlesworth invited the SCLC to town; the group organized boycotts, pickets, and other acts of nonviolence to dramatize the evils of segregation. Birmingham responded by obtaining court orders against further picketing. As the campaign seemed to falter, Martin Luther King Jr. decided to make his point by going to jail, even as SCLC planned a new stage of the campaign, the "children's crusade." While King sat in prison, Birmingham's schoolchildren marched and were arrested, filling the jails of the city. Meanwhile, that Easter weekend, responding to a newspaper advertisement from eight local clergymen suggesting that the protests were "ill-timed" (because the imminent change of city government would soon transfer power from Mayor Bull Connor to a more reasonable city council), King penned this famous letter. He explains the philosophy of nonviolence, severely critiques those who settle for "order" over justice, and outlines the theology of the movement.

My dear Fellow Clergymen,

. . . I think I should give the reason for my being in Birmingham, since you have been influenced by the argument of "outsiders coming in." I have the honor of serving as president of the Southern Christian Leadership Conference, an organization operating in every southern state, first headquarters in Atlanta, Georgia. We have some eighty-five affiliate organizations all across the South—one being the Alabama Christian Movement for Human Rights. Whenever necessary and possible we share staff, educational and financial resources with our affiliates. Several months ago our local affiliate here in Birmingham invited us to be on call to engage in a nonviolent direct-action program if such were deemed necessary. We readily consented and when the hour came we lived up to our promises. So I am here, along with several members of my staff, because we were invited here. I am here because I have basic organizational ties here.

Beyond this, I am in Birmingham because injustice is here. Just as the eighth century prophets left their little villages and carried their "thus saith the Lord" far beyond the boundaries of their hometowns; and just as the Apostle Paul left his little village of Tarsus and carried the gospel of Jesus Christ to practically every hamlet and city of the Graeco-Roman world, I too am compelled to carry the gospel of freedom beyond my particular hometown. Like Paul, I must constantly respond to the Macedonian call for aid.

Moreover, I am cognizant of the interrelatedness of all communities and states. I cannot sit idly by in Atlanta and not be concerned about what happens in Birmingham. Injustice anywhere is a threat to justice everywhere. We are caught in an inescapable network of mutuality, tied in a single garment of destiny. Whatever affects one directly affects all indirectly. Never again can we afford to live with the narrow, provincial "outside agitator" idea. Anyone who lives in the United States can never be considered an outsider anywhere in this country. . . .

In any nonviolent campaign there are four basic steps: (1) collection of the facts to determine whether injustices are alive, (2) negotiation, (3) self-purification, and (4) direct action. We have gone through all of these steps in Birmingham. There can be no gainsaying of the fact that racial injustice engulfs this community.

Birmingham is probably the most thoroughly segregated city in the United States. Its ugly record of police brutality is known in every section of this country. Its unjust treatment of Negroes in the courts is a notorious reality. There have been more unsolved bombings of Negro homes and churches in

Birmingham than any city in this nation. These are the hard, brutal and un-believable facts. On the basis of these conditions Negro leaders sought to ne-gotiate with the city fathers. But the political leaders consistently refused to engage in good faith negotiation.

Then came the opportunity last September to talk with some of the lead-ers of the economic community. In these negotiating sessions certain prom-ises were made by the merchants—such as the promise to remove the hu-miliating racial signs from the stores. On the basis of these promises Rev. Shuttlesworth and the leaders of the Alabama Christian Movement for Hu-man Rights agreed to call a moratorium on any type of demonstrations. As the weeks and months unfolded we realized that we were the victims of a bro-ken promise. The signs remained. Like so many experiences of the past we were confronted with blasted hopes, and the dark shadow of a deep disap-pointment settled upon us. So we had no alternative except that of preparing for direct action, whereby we would present our very bodies as a means of lay-ing our case before the conscience of the local and national community. We were not unmindful of the difficulties involved. So we decided to go through a process of self-purification. We started having workshops on nonviolence and repeatedly asked ourselves the questions, "Are you able to accept blows without retaliating?" "Are you able to endure the ordeals of jail?" We decided to set our direct-action program around the Easter season, realizing that with the exception of Christmas, this was the largest shopping period of the year. Knowing that a strong economic withdrawal program would be the by-product of direct action, we felt that this was the best time to bring pressure on the merchants for the needed changes. Then it occurred to us that the March election was ahead and so we speedily decided to postpone action un-til after election day. When we discovered that Mr. Connor was in the run-off, we decided again to postpone action so that the demonstrations could not be used to cloud the issues. At this time we agreed to begin our nonviolent wit-ness the day after the run-off.

This reveals that we did not move irresponsibly into direct action. We too wanted to see Mr. Connor defeated; so we went through postponement after postponement to aid in this community need. After this we felt that direct ac-tion could be delayed no longer.

You may well ask, "Why direct action? Why sit-ins, marches, etc.? Isn't ne-gotiation a better path?" You are exactly right in your call for negotiation. In-deed, this is the purpose of direct action. Nonviolent direct action seeks to create such a crisis and establish such creative tension that a community that has constantly refused to negotiate is forced to confront the issue. It seeks so to dramatize the issue that it can no longer be ignored. I just referred to the creation of tension as a part of the work of the nonviolent resister. This may sound rather shocking. But I must confess that I am not afraid of the word tension. I have earnestly worked and preached against violent tension, but there is a type of constructive nonviolent tension that is necessary for growth. Just as Socrates felt that it was necessary to create a tension in the mind so that individuals could rise from the bondage of myths and half-truths to the unfettered realm of creative analysis and objective appraisal, we must see the need of having nonviolent gadflies to create the kind of tension in society that will help men to rise from the dark depths of prejudice and racism to the majestic heights of understanding and brotherhood. So the purpose of the direct action is to create a situation so crisis packed that it will inevitably open the door to negotiation. We, therefore, concur with you in your call for negotiation. Too long has our beloved Southland been bogged down in the tragic attempt to live in monologue rather than dialogue. . . .

History is the long and tragic story of the fact that privileged groups seldom give up their privileges voluntarily. Individuals may see the moral light and voluntarily give up their unjust posture; but as Reinhold Niebuhr has reminded us, groups are more immoral than individuals.

We know through painful experience that freedom is never voluntarily given by the oppressor; it must be demanded by the oppressed. Frankly, I have never yet engaged in a direct action movement that was "well-timed," according to the timetable of those who have not suffered unduly from the disease of segregation. For years now I have heard the word "Wait!" It rings in the ear of every Negro with a piercing familiarity. This "Wait" has almost always meant "Never." It has been a tranquilizing thalidomide, relieving the emotional stress for a moment, only to give birth to an ill-formed infant of frustration. We must come to see with the distinguished jurist of yesterday that "justice too long delayed is justice denied." We have waited for more than 340 years for our constitutional and God-given rights. The nations of Asia and Africa are moving with jetlike speed toward the goal of political independence, and we still creep at horse and buggy pace toward the gaining of a cup of coffee at a lunch counter. I guess it is easy for those who have never felt the stinging darts of segregation to say, "Wait." But when you have seen vicious mobs lynch your mothers and fathers at will and drown your sisters and brothers at whim; when you have seen hate-filled policemen curse, kick, brutalize and even kill your black brothers and sisters with impunity; when you see the vast majority of your twenty million Negro brothers smothering in an airtight cage of poverty in the midst of an affluent society; when you suddenly find your tongue twisted and your speech stammering as you seek to explain to your six-year-old daughter why she can't go to the public amusement park that has just been advertised on television, and see tears welling up in her little eyes when she is told that Funtown is closed to colored children, and see the depressing clouds of inferiority begin to form in her little mental sky, and see her begin to distort her little personality by unconsciously developing a bitterness toward white people; when you have to concoct an answer for a five-year-old son asking in agonizing pathos; "Daddy, why do white people treat colored people so mean?"; when you take a cross-country drive and find it necessary to sleep night after night in the uncomfortable corners of your automobile because no motel will accept you; when you are humiliated day in and day out by nagging signs reading "white" and "colored"; when your first name becomes "nigger" and your middle name becomes "boy" (however old you are) and your last name becomes "John," and when your wife and mother are never given the respected title "Mrs."; when you are harried by day and haunted by night by the fact that you are a Negro, living constantly at tiptoe stance never quite knowing what to expect next, and plagued with inner fears and outer resentments; when you are forever fighting a degenerating sense of "nobodiness"; then you will understand why we find it difficult to wait. There comes a time when the cup of endurance runs over, and men are no longer willing to be plunged into an abyss of injustice where they experience the blackness of corroding despair. I hope, sirs, you can understand our legitimate and unavoidable impatience.

You express a great deal of anxiety over our willingness to break laws. This is certainly a legitimate concern. Since we so diligently urge people to obey the Supreme Court's decision of 1954 outlawing segregation in the public schools, it is rather strange and paradoxical to find us consciously breaking laws. One may well ask, "How can you advocate breaking some laws and obeying others?" The answer is found in the fact that there are two types of laws; there are *just* and there are *unjust* laws. I would agree with Saint Augustine that "An unjust law is no law at all."

Now what is the difference between the two? How does one determine when a law is just or unjust? A just law is a man-made code that squares with the moral law or the law of God. An unjust law is a code that is out of harmony with the moral law. To put it in the terms of Saint Thomas Aquinas, an unjust law is a human law that is not rooted in eternal and natural law. Any law that uplifts human personality is just. Any law that degrades human personality is unjust. All segregation statutes are unjust because segregation distorts the soul and damages the personality. It gives the segregator a false sense of superiority, and the segregated a false sense of inferiority. To use the words of Martin Buber, the great Jewish philosopher, segregation substitutes an "I-it" relationship for the "I-thou" relationship, and ends up relegating persons to the status of things. So segregation is not only politically, economically and sociologically unsound, but it is morally wrong and sinful. Paul Tilich has said that sin is separation. Isn't segregation an existential expression of man's tragic separation, an expression of his awful estrangement, his terrible sinfulness? So I can urge men to disobey segregation ordinances because they are morally wrong. . . .

I hope you can see the distinction I am trying to point out. In no sense do I advocate evading or defying the law as the rabid segregationist would do. This would lead to anarchy. One who breaks an unjust law must do it *openly*, *lovingly* (not hatefully as the white mothers did in New Orleans when they were seen on television screaming, "nigger, nigger, nigger"), and with a willingness to accept the penalty. I submit that an individual who breaks a law that conscience tells him is unjust, and willingly accepts the penalty by staying in jail to arouse the conscience of the community over its injustice, is in reality expressing the very highest respect for law. . . .

We can never forget that everything Hitler did in Germany was "legal" and everything the Hungarian freedom fighters did in Hungary was "illegal." It was "illegal" to aid and comfort a Jew in Hitler's Germany. But I am sure that if I had lived in Germany during that time I would have aided and comforted my Jewish brothers even though it was illegal. If I lived in a Communist country today where certain principles dear to the Christian faith are suppressed, I believe I would openly advocate disobeying these anti-religious laws. I must make two honest confessions to you, my Christian and Jewish brothers. First, I must confess that over the last few years I have been gravely disappointed with the white moderate. I have almost reached the regrettable conclusion that the Negro's great stumbling block in the stride toward freedom is not the White Citizen's Counciler or the Ku Klux Klanner, but the white moderate who is more devoted to "order" than to justice; who prefers a negative peace which is the absence of tension to a positive peace which is the presence of justice; who constantly says, "I agree with you in the goal you seek, but I can't agree with your methods of direct action"; who paternalistically feels that he can set the timetable for another man's freedom; who lives by the myth of time and who constantly advised the Negro to wait until a "more convenient season." Shallow understanding from people of good will is more frustrating than absolute misunderstanding from people of ill will. Lukewarm acceptance is much more bewildering than outright rejection.

I had hoped that the white moderate would understand that law and order exist for the purpose of establishing justice, and that when they fail to do this they become dangerously structured dams that block the flow of social progress. I had hoped that the white moderate would understand that the present tension of the South is merely a necessary phase of the transition from an obnoxious negative peace, where the Negro passively accepted his unjust plight, to a substance-filled positive peace, where all men will respect the dignity and worth of human personality. Actually, we who engage in nonviolent direct action are not the creators of tension. We merely bring to the surface the hidden tension that is already alive. We bring it out in the open where it can be seen and dealt with. Like a boil that can never be cured as long as it is covered up but must be opened with all its pus-flowing ugliness to the natural medicines of air and light, injustice must likewise be exposed, with all of the tension its exposing creates, to the light of human conscience and the air of national opinion before it can be cured. . . .

I had also hoped that the white moderate would reject the myth of time. I received a letter this morning from a white brother in Texas which said: "All Christians know that the colored people will receive equal rights eventually, but it is possible that you are in too great of a religious hurry. It has taken Christianity almost two thousand years to accomplish what it has. The teachings of Christ take time to come to earth." All that is said here grows out of a tragic misconception of time. It is the strangely irrational notion that there is something in the very flow of time that will inevitably cure all ills. Actually time is neutral. It can be used either destructively or constructively. I am coming to feel that the people of ill will have used time much more effectively than the people of good will. We will have to repent in this generation not merely for the vitriolic words and actions of the bad people, but for the appalling silence of the good people. We must come to see that human progress never rolls in on wheels of inevitability. It comes through the tireless efforts and persistent work of men willing to be co-workers with God, and without this hard work time itself becomes an ally of the forces of social stagnation. We must use time creatively, and forever realize that the time is always ripe to do right. Now is the time to make real the promise of democracy, and transform our pending national elegy into a creative psalm of brotherhood. Now is the time to lift our national policy from the quicksand of racial injustice to the solid rock of human dignity.

You spoke of our activity in Birmingham as extreme. At first I was rather disappointed that fellow clergymen would see my nonviolent efforts as those of the extremist. I started thinking about the fact that I stand in the middle of two opposing forces in the Negro community. One is a force of complacency made up of Negroes who, as a result of long years of oppression, have been so completely drained of self-respect and a sense of "somebodiness" that they have adjusted to segregation, and of a few Negroes in the middle class who, because of a degree of academic and economic security, and because at points they profit by segregation have unconsciously become insensitive to the problems of the masses. The other force is one of bitterness and hatred, and comes perilously close to advocating violence. It is expressed in the various black nationalist groups that are springing up over the nation, the largest and best known being Elijah Muhammad's Muslim movement. This movement is nourished by the contemporary frustration over the continued existence of racial discrimination. It is made up of people who have lost faith in America, who have absolutely repudiated Christianity, and who have concluded that the white man is an incurable "devil." I have tried to stand between these two forces, saying that we need not follow the "do-nothingism" of the complacent or the hatred and despair of the black nationalist. There is the more excellent way of love and nonviolent protest. I'm grateful to God that, through the Negro church, the dimension of nonviolence entered our struggle. If this philosophy had not emerged, I am convinced that by now many streets of the South would be flowing with floods of blood. And I am further convinced that if our white brothers dismiss us as "rabble-rousers" and "outside agitators" those of us who are working through the channels of nonviolent direct action and refuse to support our nonviolent efforts, millions of Negroes, out of frustration and despair, will seek solace and security in black nationalist ideologies, a development that will lead inevitably to a frightening racial nightmare.

Oppressed cannot remain oppressed forever. The urge for freedom will eventually come. This is what happened to the American Negro. Something within has reminded him of his birthright of freedom; something without has reminded him that he can gain it. Consciously and unconsciously, he has been swept in by what the Germans call the *Zeitgeist*, and with his black brothers of Africa, and his brown and yellow brothers of Asia, South America and the Caribbean, he is moving with a sense of cosmic urgency toward the promised land of racial justice. Recognizing this vital urge that has engulfed the Negro community, one should readily understand public demonstrations. The Negro has many pent-up resentments and latent frustrations. He has to get them out. So let him march sometime; let him have his prayer pilgrimages to the city hall; understand why he must have sit-ins and freedom rides. If his repressed emotions do not come out in these nonviolent ways, they will come out in ominous expressions of violence. This is not a threat; it is a fact of history. So I have not said to my people "get rid of your discontent." But I have tried to say that this normal and healthy discontent can be channelized through the creative outlet of nonviolent direct action. Now this approach is being dismissed as extremist. I must admit that I was initially disappointed in being so categorized.

But as I continued to think about the matter I gradually gained a bit of satisfaction from being considered an extremist. Was not Jesus an extremist in love—"Love your enemies, bless them that curse you, pray for them that despitefully use you." Was not Amos an extremist for justice—"Let justice roll down like waters and righteousness like a mighty stream." Was not Paul an extremist for the gospel of Jesus Christ—"I bear in my body the marks of the

Lord Jesus." Was not Martin Luther an extremist—"Here I stand; I can do none other so help me God." Was not John Bunyan an extremist—"I will stay in jail to the end of my days before I make a butchery of my conscience." Was not Abraham Lincoln an extremist—"This nation cannot survive half slave and half free." Was not Thomas Jefferson an extremist—"We hold these truths to be self-evident, that all men are created equal." So the question is not whether we will be extremist but what kind of extremist will we be. Will we be extremists for hate or will we be extremists for love? Will we be extremists for the preservation of injustice—or will we be extremists for the cause of justice? In that dramatic scene on Calvary's hill, three men were crucified. We must not forget that all three were crucified for the same crime—the crime of extremism. Two were extremists for immorality, and thusly fell below their environment. The other, Jesus Christ, was an extremist for love, truth and goodness, and thereby rose above his environment. So, after all, maybe the South, the nation and the world are in dire need of creative extremists. . . .

Let me rush on to mention my other disappointment. I have been so greatly disappointed with the white church and its leadership. Of course, there are some notable exceptions. . . . [But] I must honestly reiterate that I have been disappointed with the church. I do not say that as one of the negative critics who can always find something wrong with the church. I say it as a minister of the gospel, who loves the church; who was nurtured in its bosom; who has been sustained by its spiritual blessings and who will remain true to it as long as the cord of life shall lengthen.

I had the strange feeling when I was suddenly catapulted into the leadership of the bus protest in Montgomery several years ago that we would have the support of the white church. I felt that the white ministers, priests and rabbis of the South would be some of our strongest allies. Instead, some have been outright opponents, refusing to understand the freedom movement and misrepresenting its leaders; all too many others have been more cautious than courageous and have remained silent behind the anesthetizing security of the stained-glass windows.

In spite of my shattered dreams of the past, I came to Birmingham with the hope that the white religious leadership of this community would see the justice of our cause, and with deep moral concern, serve as the channel through which our just grievances would get to the power structure. I had hoped that each of you would understand. But again I have been disappointed. I have heard numerous religious leaders of the South call upon their worshippers to comply with a desegregation decision because it is the *law*, but I have longed to hear white ministers say, "Follow this decree because integration is morally *right* and the Negro is your brother." In the midst of blatant injustices inflicted upon the Negro, I have watched white churches stand on the sideline and merely mouth pious irrelevancies and sanctimonious trivialities. In the midst of a mighty struggle to rid our nation of racial and economic injustice, I have heard so many ministers say, "Those are social issues with which the gospel has no real concern," and I have watched so many churches commit themselves to a completely otherworldly religion which made a strange distinction between body and soul, the sacred and the secular.

So here we are moving toward the exit of the twentieth century with a religious community largely adjusted to the status quo, standing as a taillight behind other community agencies rather than a headlight leading men to higher levels of justice.

I have traveled the length and breadth of Alabama, Mississippi and all the other southern states. On sweltering summer days and crisp autumn mornings I have looked at her beautiful churches with their lofty spires pointing heavenward. I have beheld the impressive outlay of her massive religious education buildings. Over and over again I have found myself asking; "What kind of people worship here? Who is their God? Where were their voices when the lips of Governor Barnett dripped with words of interposition and nullification? Where were they when Governor Wallace gave the clarion call for defiance and hatred? Where were their voices of support when tired, bruised and weary Negro men and women decided to rise from the dark dungeons of complacency to the bright hills of creative protest?"

Yes, these questions are still in my mind. In deep disappointment, I have wept over the laxity of the church. But be assured that my tears have been tears of love. There can be no deep disappointment where there is not deep love. Yes, I love the church; I love her sacred walls. How could I do otherwise? I am in the rather unique position of being the son, the grandson and the great-grandson of preachers. Yes, I see the church as the body of Christ. But, oh! How we have blemished and scarred that body through social neglect and fear of being nonconformists. . . .

I hope the church as a whole will meet the challenge of this decisive hour. But even if the church does not come to the aid of justice, I have no despair about the future. I have no fear about the outcome of our struggle in Birmingham, even if our motives are presently misunderstood. We will reach the goal of freedom in Birmingham and all over the nation, because the goal of America is freedom. Abused and scorned though we may be, our destiny is tied up with the destiny of America. Before the Pilgrims landed at Plymouth we were here. Before the pen of Jefferson etched across the pages of history the majestic words of the Declaration of Independence, we were here. For more than two centuries our foreparents labored in this country without wages; they made cotton king; and they built the homes of their masters in the midst of brutal injustice and shameful humiliation—and yet out of a bottomless vitality they continued to thrive and develop. If the inexpressible cruelties of slavery could not stop us, the opposition we now face will surely fail. We will win our freedom because the sacred heritage of our nation and the eternal will of God are embodied in our echoing demands.

2. STUDENT NON-VIOLENT COORDINATING COMMITTEE (SNCC), "FREEDOM SONGS" (1960s)

"You sing the songs which symbolize transformation, which make that revolution of courage inside you," a civil rights activist said of the vocal expression that was an integral part of the movement. The ordinary citizens who made up the rank and file of the black freedom struggle empowered themselves through song. It sustained black protestors through years of turmoil.

The civil rights movement had legislative aims. It was, to that extent, a political movement. But it was also a religious uprising, sustained by the deeply Protestant imagery and fervor of Southern black churches. As one female sharecropper and civil rights activist in Mississippi explained her conversion to the cause, "Something hit me like a new religion." And it was a religious movement in its rituals of mass meetings, revivalistic preaching to inspire activism, and most especially in its singing. Pat Watters was a white journalist who watched, reported on, and participated in the movement. Attending the mass meetings in Albany, Georgia, as a reporter, he quickly found himself becoming a participant-observer. Even while he reported on the differences that had emerged between older ministerial leaders and students in SNCC, his thoughts kept returning to "the powerful pounding of the music of the mass meetings as a counterpoint to my words of discovery and analysis." He wrote of the "mystical, inspired and excited, ecstatic—and reverent mood of those meetings." Freedom songs were accompanied by swaying, singing, shouting, foot stomping, and other bodily movements and rhythmic accompaniment, a legacy of the rituals of black religious expression dating from the antebellum spirituals and ring shouts.

INTERVIEW WITH BERNICE REAGON (BY *EYES ON THE PRIZE* PRODUCTION TEAM)

Growing up in Albany, I learned that if you bring black people together, you bring them together with a song. To this day, I don't understand how people think they can bring anybody together without a song.

Now, the singing tradition in Albany was congregational. There were not soloists, there were song leaders.

When you ask somebody to lead a song, you're asking them to plant a seed. The minute you start the song, then the song is created by everybody there. It's almost like a musical explosion that takes place. But the singing in the movement was different from the singing in church. The singing is the kind of singing where you disappear.

The song-singing I heard in Albany I'd never heard before in my life, in spite of the fact that I was from that congregational singing culture. The only difference was that in Albany, Georgia, black people were doing some stuff around being black people. I know a lot of people talk about it being a movement and when they do a movement they're talking about buses and jobs and the ICC ruling, and the Trailways bus station. Those things were just incidents that gave us an excuse to be something of ourselves. It's almost like where we had been working before we had a chance to do that stuff was in a certain kind of space, and when we did those marches and went to jail, we expanded the space we could operate in, and that was echoed in the singing. It was a bigger, more powerful singing. . . .

After this first march, we're at Union Baptist Church, Charlie Jones [of SNCC] looks at me and said, "Bernice, sing a song." And I started "Over My Head I See Trouble in the Air." By the time I got to where "trouble" was supposed to be, I didn't see any trouble, so I put "freedom" in there. And I guess that was the first time I really understood using what I'd been given in terms of songs. I'd always been a singer but I had always, more or less, been singing what other people taught me to sing. That was the first time I had the awareness that these songs were mine and I could use them for what I needed them to. This sort of thing was important because I ended up being arrested in the second wave of arrests in Albany, Georgia. And I was in jail. And when we got to jail, Slater King was already in jail, and he said, "Bernice, is that you?" And I said, "Yeah." And he said, "Sing a song."

The voice I have now, I got the first time I sang in a movement meeting, after I got out of jail. Now I'm past that first meeting in Union Baptist, I've done "Lift Every Voice and Sing." I am a song leader, I lead every song in jail, but I did not lead the songs in jail in the voice I have now. The voice I have now I got that night and I'd never heard it before in my life. At that meeting, they did what they usually do. They said, "Bernice, would you lead us in a song?" And I did the same first song, "Over My Head I See Freedom in the Air," but I'd never heard that voice before. I had never been that me before. And once I became that me, I have never let that me go.

I like people to know when they deal with the movement that there are these specific things, but there is a transformation that took place inside of the people that needs to also be quantified in the picture. And the singing is just the echo of that. If you have a people who are transformed and they create the sound that lets you know they are new people, then certainly you've never heard it before. They have also never heard it before, because they've never been that before. . . .

What I can remember is being very alive and very clear, the clearest I've ever been in my life. I knew that every minute, I was doing what I was supposed to do. That was the way it was in jail, too, and on the marches. In "We Shall Overcome" there's a verse that says "God is on our side," and there was a theological discussion that said maybe we should say, "We are on God's side." God was lucky to have us in Albany doing what we were doing. I mean, what better case would he have? So it was really like God would be very, very happy to be on my side. There's a bit of arrogance about that, but that was the way it felt. . . .

We Shall Overcome

We shall overcome,
We shall overcome.
We shall overcome,
Someday.
Oh, deep in my heart,
I do believe, that
We shall overcome
Someday.
We'll walk hand in hand,
We'll walk hand in hand,
We'll walk hand in hand,
Someday.
Oh, deep in my heart,
I do believe, that
We shall overcome,
Someday.
We are not afraid,
We are not afraid,
We are not afraid,
Oh, no, no, no,
'Cause deep in my heart,
I do believe that

We shall overcome,
Someday.

        ∞∞∞

Keep Your Eyes on the Prize

Paul and Silas bound in jail,
Had no money for to go their bail
Keep your eyes on the prize,
Hold on, hold on.
  Hold on, hold on.
Keep your eyes on the prize,
  Hold on, hold on.

Paul and Silas begin to shout,
The jail door open and they walked out.
Keep your eyes on the prize,
Hold on, hold on.

Freedom's name is mighty sweet,
Soon one day we're gonna meet.
Keep your eyes on the prize,
Hold on, hold on.
Got my hand on the Gospel plow,
I wouldn't take nothing for my journey now.
Keep your eyes on the prize,
Hold on, hold on.

The only chain that a man can stand,
Is that chain of hand in hand.
Keep your eyes on the prize,
Hold on, hold on.

The only thing that we did wrong,
Stayed in the wilderness a day too long.
Keep your eyes on the prize,
Hold on, hold on.

But the one thing we did right,
Was the day we started to fight.
Keep your eyes on the prize,
Hold on, hold on. . . .

Ain't Gonna Let Nobody Turn Me 'Round

Ain't gonna let nobody, Lordy, turn me 'round,
Turn me 'round, turn me 'round,

Ain't gonna let nobody turn me 'round,
I'm gonna keep on a-walkin',
Keep on a-talkin',
Marching up to freedom land.

Ain't gonna let no jailhouse turn me 'round,
Turn me 'round, turn me 'round,
Ain't gonna let no jailhouse turn me 'round,
I'm gonna keep on a-walkin',
Keep on a-talkin',
Marching up to freedom land.

Ain't gonna let no sheriff turn me 'round,
Turn me 'round, turn me 'round,
Ain't gonna let no sheriff turn me 'round,
Turn me 'round, turn me 'round,
I'm gonna keep on a-walkin',
Keep on a-talkin',
Marching up to freedom land. . . .

Hallelujah, I'm A-Traveling (civil rights version)

Stand up and rejoice, a great day is here.
We're fighting Jim Crow and the vic'try is near.
(Chorus)
Hallelujah, I'm a-traveling.
Hallelujah, ain't it fine,
Hallelujah, I'm a-traveling,
Down freedom's main line.

I'm paying my fare on the Greyhound bus line.
I'm riding the front seat to Jackson this time.
(Chorus)

I'm traveling to Mississippi on the Greyhound bus lines.
Hallelujah, I'm a-riding the front seat this time.
(Chorus)
In old Fayette County, set off and remote,
The polls are now open for Negroes to vote.
(Chorus)
In Nineteen Fifty-four, the Supreme Court has said,
Looka here, Mr. Jim Crow, it's time you were dead.

(Everybody Says) Freedom (civil rights version)

(Everybody says) Freedom
(Everybody says) Freedom
(Everybody says) Freedom, freedom, freedom.

(In the cottonfield) Freedom,
(In the schoolroom) Freedom,
(In the jailhouse) Freedom, freedom, freedom.

(Everybody says) Civil rights . . .
(All across the South) Freedom . . .
(In Mississippi) Freedom . . .

Woke Up This Morning with My Mind on Freedom

Woke up this morning with my mind
(My mind it was) Stayed on freedom,
(Oh yes I) Woke up this morning with my mind
Stayed on freedom,
(Well I) Woke up this morning with my mind
(My mind it was) Stayed on freedom,
Hallelu, hallelu, hallelu, hallelu,
Hallelujah!

Ain't no harm in keep'n' your mind
In keeping it stayed on freedom. . . .
Walkin' and talkin' with my mind
My mind it was stayed on freedom . . .

Interlude:

You got to walk walk,

You got to walk walk,

You got to walk with your mind on freedom,

You got to talk talk,

You got to talk talk,

You got to talk with your mind on freedom,

Oh oh oh you got to walk walk, talk talk.

Singin' and prayin' with my mind

My mind it was stayed on freedom. . . .

3. SNCC STATEMENT OF PURPOSE (1960)

JAMES M. LAWSON JR., "WE ARE TRYING TO RAISE THE 'MORAL ISSUE'" (1960)

In the spring of 1960, four students in Greensboro, North Carolina, initiated a series of sit-ins that inspired young black people throughout the South. By sitting down at lunch counters designated for whites only, waiting to be served, remaining seated when refused service, and remaining nonviolent even when attacked by local toughs, the young people reenergized a civil rights movement that had been stalled since massive resistance to the Supreme Court's Brown v. Board of Education decision had stymied the legal strategies to end segregation. The Student Non-Violent Coordinating Committee (SNCC or "Snick") formed from a meeting of students across the South in April 1960. They gathered ostensibly under the auspices of the Southern Christian Leadership Conference (SCLC), which wanted them to form a "youth wing" of this established organization of black ministers. The students instead followed the advice of the Executive Secretary of SCLC, Ella Baker, who had long experience in organizing through the YMCA and the NAACP (National Association for the Advancement of Colored People). Baker urged the students to remain independent, not to fall in line with the wishes of their elders in SCLC.

SNCC's founding statement of purpose emerged as a collective voice of the new group but came largely through the efforts and pen of James Lawson, a Methodist minister and committed Gandhian who since 1958 had been training Nashville students in the philosophy and techniques of nonviolent civil disobedience. As Lawson explained in another setting, "Under Christian non-violence, Negro students reject the hardship of disobedient passivity and fear, but embrace the hardship (violence and jail) of obedience. . . . Non-violence in the Negro's struggle gains a fresh maturity. And the Negro gains a new sense of his role in molding a redeemed society." SNCC's state-

ment embodied the radical Christian views of James Lawson and his cohorts, includ-
ing Nashville students John Lewis and Diane Nash.

STATEMENT OF PURPOSE

We affirm the philosophical or religious ideal of non-violence as the foundation of our purpose, the presupposition of our faith, and the manner of
our action. Non-violence as it grows from Judaic-Christian traditions seeks
a social order of justice permeated by love. Integration of human endeavor
represents the crucial first step towards such a society.

Through non-violence, courage displaces fear; love transforms hate. Acceptance dissipates prejudice; hope ends despair. Peace dominates war;
faith reconciles doubt. Mutual regard cancels enmity. Justice for all over-
throws injustice. The redemptive community supersedes systems of gross
social immorality.

Love is the central motif of non-violence. Love is the force by which God
binds man to Himself and man to man. Such love goes to the extreme; it remains loving and forgiving even in the midst of hostility. It matches the capacity of evil to inflict suffering with an even more enduring capacity to absorb evil, all the while persisting in love.

By appealing to conscience and standing on the moral nature of human
existence, non-violence nurtures the atmosphere in which reconciliation
and justice become actual possibilities.

"WE ARE TRYING TO RAISE THE 'MORAL ISSUE'"

. . . Reflect how over the last few weeks, the "sit-in" movement has leaped
from campus to campus, until today hardly any campus remains unaffected. At the beginning of this decade, the student generation was "silent,"
"uncommitted," or "beatnik." But after only four months, these analogies
largely used by adults appear as hasty cliches which should not have been
used in the first place. The rapidity and drive of the movement indicates that
all the while American students were simply waiting in suspension; waiting
for that cause, that ideal, that event, that "actualizing of their faith" which
would catapult their right to speak powerfully to their nation and world.

The witness of enthusiastic, but mature young men and women, auda-
cious enough to dare the intimidations and violence of racial injustice, a wit-

ness not to be matched by any social effort either in the history of the Negro or in the history of the nation, has caused this impact upon us. In his own time, God has brought this to pass. . . .

The issue is not integration. This is particularly true for the Christian oriented person. Certainly the students are asking on behalf of the entire Negro community and the nation that these eating counters become places of service for all persons. But it would be extremely short-sighted to assume that integration is the problem or the word of the "sit-in." . . .

The Christian favors the breaking down of racial barriers because the redeemed community of which he is already a citizen recognizes no barriers dividing humanity. The Kingdom of God, as in heaven so on earth, is the distant goal of the Christian. That Kingdom is far more than the immediate need for integration. . . .

In the first instance, we who are demonstrators are trying to raise what we call the "moral issue." That is, we are pointing to the viciousness of racial segregation and prejudice and calling it evil or sin. The matter is not legal, sociological or racial, it is moral and spiritual. Until America (South and North) honestly accepts the sinful nature of racism, this cancerous disease will continue to rape all of us. . . .

The non-violent movement would convict us all of sin. We assert, "Segregation (racial pride) is sin. God tolerates no breach of his judgment. We are an unhealthy people who contrive every escape from ourselves." Thus a simple act of neatly dressed, non-violent students with purchases in their pockets, precipitated anger and frustration. Many "good" people (white and Negro) said, "This is not the way. We are already making adequate progress." Nonsense! No progress is adequate so long as any man, woman or child of any ethnic group is still a lynch victim. . . .

The choice of the non-violent method, "the sit-in," symbolizes both judgment and promise. It is a judgment upon middle-class conventional, halfway efforts to deal with radical social evil. It is specifically a judgment upon contemporary civil rights attempts. . . .

But the sit-in is likewise a sign of promise: God's promise that if radically Christian methods are adopted the rate of change can be vastly increased. This is why non-violence dominates the movement's perspective. Under Christian non-violence, Negro students reject the hardship of disobedient passivity and fear, but embrace the hardship (violence and jail) of obedience. Such nonviolence strips the segregationalist power structure of its major weapon: the manipulation of law or law-enforcement to keep the Negro in his place.

Furthermore, such an act attracts, strengthens and sensitizes the support of many white persons in the South and across the nation. (The numbers who openly identify themselves with the "sit-in" daily grow.)

Non-violence in the Negro's struggle gains a fresh maturity. And the Negro gains a new sense of his role in molding a redeemed society. The "word" from the lunch-counter stool demands a sharp re-assessment of our organized evil and a radical Christian obedience to transform that evil. Christian non-violence provides both that re-assessment and the faith of obedience. The extent to which the Negro joined by many others apprehends and incorporates non-violence determines the degree that the world will acknowledge fresh social insight from America.

4. MARY KING, *FREEDOM SONG* (1987)

One of the whites attracted to SNCC idealism was Mary King. As the daughter and granddaughter of Methodist ministers, she grew up suffused with the ideals of that faith, to which she added the progressive political ideas she developed in the 1950s and early 1960s. During her days with SNCC, King and Julian Bond worked as communications directors for the organization. They issued press releases, set up and monitored telephone lines to assist SNCC staffers in trouble, took and published photographs of civil rights activities, and publicized the brutality met by those on the front lines of the movement. King and her fellow white SNCC staffer Casey Hayden later developed a "position paper" for a SNCC meeting in 1964, which many feminists now point to as one of the origins of the feminist movement that emerged later in the decade. They made the direct connection between the oppression of black Americans and the subjugation of women.

In this passage from her memoir Freedom Song, *King explains her ideas of SNCC as a religious movement. Even if it was not understood by all participants as such, she points out that "theological terminology was commonplace and the influence of specifically Protestant thinking was pervasive, again reflecting the cultural milieu of the South."*

SNCC's distinctively idealistic belief that fortitude, determined action, and fearlessness would result in momentous social change stemmed to a great degree from the Protestant upbringings of most of its workers. Even if one were in rebellion against a church that provided insufficient witness or failed to challenge the status quo, still at work was the fundamental influence of the Christian tradition. Translated into political action, John Wesley's belief that through grace and redemption each person can be saved reinforced our belief that the good in every human being could be appealed to, fundamental change could correct the immorality of racial segregation, and new political structures could be created. This was not new. What may have been novel was the sense of timing influenced by the sweep of anti-colonialism—we wanted it now and not in the hereafter; we were not willing to wait for "the kingdom to come." Even if each SNCC field secretary did not use the term *redemption* in everyday conversation (but in the earliest days of the group I venture to say everyone did), the concept abounded in the biblical ethos of the southland, black and white, and was part of the climate in which the movement was working. . . .

SNCC was more secular than SCLC, but even within our group theological terminology was commonplace and the influence of specifically Protestant thinking was pervasive, again reflecting the cultural milieu of the South, black and white. I remember some workers talking frankly of the undertaking as a "Christian movement." We openly thought of ourselves as working toward "reconciliation" and used the phrase "the beloved community" as a golden image representing an America that would one day reject racism. For many, it was the fundamental assumption of the "redemptibility" of America that gave rise to our confidence that the appeal of nonviolence would be successful. Anyone who put himself or herself on the line, subjected to humiliation, brutality, arrests, beatings, or even torture, *had* to believe that America as a nation could experience shame and remorse and would repeal its history of oppression. . . .

SNCC was in fact radical during the period about which I write in its spirit of self-sacrifice, its vision of human worth, and its heterogeneity. Its radicalism expressed itself in its ferocious insistence that ideals should be made reality, the obstinacy of its existential position that belief and action were one, and its puritanical determination that ideas came from action and that rhetoric should never precede behavior. . . .

5. MALCOLM X, *AUTOBIOGRAPHY OF MALCOLM X* (1965)

Born Malcolm Little in Omaha, Nebraska, this orator of black power and pride grew up the hard way. Working in Boston as a young man, Malcolm, then known by his street name "Red," shined shoes, hustled, and robbed, all the while enjoying the night life of black urban America. Finally caught and sentenced for his criminal activity, while in prison in the early 1950s Malcolm engaged in an intense period of self-study that resulted in his conversion to black Islam. He became a follower of Elijah Muhammad, a black man originally from Georgia who was the prophet of the Nation of Islam movement and a protégé of its founder, Wallace Fard. As was the custom among many converts, Malcolm rejected his given "white" name of Little and took the name "Malcolm X," signifying the lost names of his black ancestors brought to the United States during the era of slavery.

Throughout the 1950s and early 1960s, Malcolm was the Nation of Islam's foremost spokesman, attracting thousands to his passionate, fiery speeches. He rejected integration as a solution, arguing that "the white man" would never accept blacks as equals. In its place he argued for black power, self-defense, and economic autonomy, and supplied his followers with the Nation of Islam's own "history" of the evil doings of the white devil in history. Critics labeled the group a "cult" and criticized Malcolm's ideas as "black supremacy" akin to the white supremacy he fought against. CBS news produced a famous documentary, "The Hate That Hate Produced," that purported to expose the workings of the cult.

Malcolm's real following, however, came not so much for his offering of orthodox Nation of Islam doctrines as for his insistence that oppressed African Americans had to defend their rights "by any means necessary." He attracted admirers throughout black America for his eloquence in defending his positions and insisting on racial pride. In the early 1960s, Malcolm was disillusioned by corruption and thievery within the Nation of Islam, as well as by Elijah Muhammad's escapades with female initiates. He broke with the formal organization, and late in his life began the Organization of Afro-American Unity. This corresponded also with a broadening of Malcolm's vision, particularly after his pilgrimage to Mecca, from one of strict black separatism to one that embraced a more universalist notion of Islam. Malcolm was assassinated in 1965, an inside job by the Nation of Islam. His funeral drew mourners from across the nation, who had come to respect his intense devotion to black Americans.

In these passages from his autobiography, Malcolm retraces his life steps, explaining how he moved from street hustling to prosletyizing for an exclusivist black version of Islam to understanding international Islam.

Wednesdays, Fridays, and Sundays were the meeting of the relatively small Detroit Temple Number One. Next to the temple, which actually was a storefront, were three slaughtering pens. The squealing of hogs being slaughtered filtered into our Wednesday and Friday meetings. I'm describing the condition that we Muslims were in back in early 1950's.

The address of Temple Number One was 1470 Freder Street, I think. The first Temple to be formed, back in 1931 by Master W. D. Fard, was formed in Detroit, Michigan. I never had seen any Christian-believing Negroes conducting themselves like the Muslims, the individuals and the families alike. The men were quietly, tastefully dressed. The women wore ankle-length gowns, no makeup, and scarves covered their heads. The neat children were mannerly not only to adults but to other children as well.

I had never dreamed of anything like that atmosphere among black people who had learned to be proud they were black, who had learned to love other black people instead of being jealous and suspicious. I thrilled to how we Muslim men used both hands to grasp a black brother's both hands, voicing and smiling our happiness to meet him again. The Muslim sisters, both married and single, were given an honor and respect that I'd never seen black men give to their women, and it felt wonderful to me. The salutations which all exchanged were warm, filled with mutual respect and dignity "Brother" . . . "Sister" . . . "Ma'am" . . . "Sir." Even children speaking to other children used these terms. Beautiful! . . .

I thought it was outrageous that our small temple still had some empty seats. I complained to my brother Wilfred that there should be no empty seats, with the surrounding streets full of our brainwashed black brothers and sisters, drinking, cursing, fighting, dancing, carousing, and using dope—the very things that Mr. Muhammad taught were helping the black man to stay under the heel of the white man here in America.

From what I could gather, the recruitment attitude at the temple seemed to me to amount to a self-defeating waiting view . . . an assumption that Allah would bring us more Muslims. I felt that Allah would be more inclined to help those who helped themselves. I had lived for years in ghetto streets; I knew the Negroes in those streets. Harlem or Detroit were no different. I said I disagreed, that I thought we should go out into the streets and get more Muslims into the fold. All of my life, as you know, I had been an activist, I had been impatient. My brother Wilfred counseled me to keep patience. And for me to be patient was made easier by the fact that I could anticipate soon seeing and perhaps meeting the man who was called "The Messenger," Elijah Muhammad himself. . . .

I was totally unprepared for the Messenger Elijah Muhammad's physical impact upon my emotions. From the rear of Temple Number Two, he came toward the platform. The small, sensitive, gentle, brown face that I had studied on photographs, until I had dreamed about it, was fixed straight ahead as the Messenger strode, encircled by the marching, strapping Fruit of Islam guards. The Messenger, compared to them, seemed fragile, almost tiny. He and the Fruit of Islam were dressed in dark suits, white shirts, and bow ties. The Messenger wore a gold-embroidered fez.

I stared at the great man who had taken the time to write to me when I was a convict whom he knew nothing about. He was the man whom I had been told had spent years of his life in suffering and sacrifice to lead us, the black people, because he loved us so much. And then, hearing his voice, I sat leaning forward, riveted upon his words. (I try to reconstruct what Elijah Muhammad said from having since heard him speak hundreds of times.)

"I have not stopped one day for the past twenty-one years. I have been standing, preaching to you throughout those past twenty-one years, while I was free, and even while I was in bondage. I spent three and one-half years in the federal penitentiary, and also over a year in the city jail for teaching this truth. I was also deprived of a father's love for his family for seven long years while I was running from hypocrites and other enemies of this word and revelation of God—which will give life to you, and put you on the same level with all other civilized and independent nations and peoples of this planet earth. . . . "

Elijah Muhammad spoke of how in this wilderness of North America, for centuries the "blue-eyed devil white man" had brainwashed the "so-called Negro." He told us how, as one result, the black man in America was "mentally, morally and spiritually dead." Elijah Muhammad spoke of how the black man was Original Man, who had been kidnapped from his homeland and stripped of his language, his culture, his family structure, his family name, until the black man in America did not even realize who he was.

He told us, and showed us, how his teachings of the true knowledge of ourselves would lift up the black man from the bottom of the white man's society and place the black man where he had begun, at the top of civilization. . . .

In the summer of 1953—all praise is due to Allah—I was named Detroit Temple Number One's Assistant Minister.

Every day after work, I walked, "fishing" . . . in the Detroit black ghetto. I saw the African features of my black brothers and sisters whom the devilish white man had brainwashed. I saw the hair as mine had been for years, conked by cooking it with lye until it lay limp, looking straight like the white man's hair. Time and again Mr. Muhammad's teachings were rebuffed and even ridiculed . . . "Aw, man, get out of my face, you niggers are crazy!" My head would reel sometimes, with mingled anger and pity for my poor blind black brothers. I couldn't wait for the next time our Minister Lemuel Hassan would let me speak:

"We didn't land on Plymouth Rock, my brothers and sisters—Plymouth Rock landed on *us!*" . . . "Give *all* you can to help Messenger Elijah Muhammad's independence program for the black man! . . . This white man always has controlled us black people by keeping us running to him begging, 'Please, lawdy, please, Mr. White Man, boss, would you push me off another crumb down from your table that's sagging with riches. . . . '

" . . . my *beautiful*, black brothers and sisters! And when we say 'black,' we mean everything not white, brothers and sisters! Because *look* at your skins! We're all black to the white man, but we're a thousand and one different colors. Turn around, *look* at each other! What shade of black African polluted by devil white man are you? You see me well, in the streets they used to call me Detroit Red. Yes! Yes, that raping, red-headed devil was my *grandfather!* That close, yes! My *mother's* father! She didn't like to speak of it, can you blame her? She said she never laid eyes on him! She was *glad* for that! I'm *glad* for her! If I could drain away his blood that pollutes *my* body, and pollutes *my* complexion, I'd do it! Because I hate every drop of the rapist's blood that's in me!" . . .

I would become so choked up that sometimes I would walk in the streets until late into the night. Sometimes I would speak to no one for hours, thinking to myself about what the white man had done to our poor people here in America. . . .

We went "fishing" fast and furiously when those little evangelical store-front churches each let out their thirty to fifty people on the sidewalk. "Come to hear us, brother, sister—" "You haven't heard anything until you have heard the teachings of The Honorable Elijah Muhammad—" These congregations were usually Southern migrant people, usually older, who would go anywhere to hear what they called "good preaching." These were the church congregations who were always putting out little signs announcing that inside they were selling fried chicken and chitlin dinners to raise some money. And three or four nights a week, they were in their store-front rehearsing for the next Sunday, I guess, shaking and rattling and rolling the gospels with their guitars and tambourines.

I don't know if you know it, but there's a whole circuit of commercial gospel entertainers who have come out of these little churches in the city ghettoes or from down South. People such as Sister Rosetta Tharpe, The Clara Ward Singers are examples, and there must be five hundred lesser lights on the same general order. Mahalia Jackson, the greatest of them all—she was a preacher's daughter in Louisiana. She came up there to Chicago where she worked cooking and scrubbing for white people and then in a factory while she sang in the Negro churches the gospel style that, when it caught on, made her the first Negro that Negroes ever made famous. She was selling hundreds of thousands of records among Negroes before white people ever knew who Mahalia Jackson was. Anyway, I know that somewhere I once read that Mahalia said that every time she can, she will slip unannounced into some little ghetto storefront church and sing with her people. She calls that "my filling station."

The black Christians we "fished" to our Temple were conditioned, I found, by the very shock I could give them about what had been happening to them while they worshiped a blond, blue-eyed God. I knew the temple that I could build if I could really get to those Christians. I tailored the teachings for them. I would start to speak and sometimes be so emotionally charged I had to explain myself:

"You see my tears, brothers and sisters. . . . Tears haven't been in my eyes since I was a young boy. But I cannot help this when I feel the responsibility I have to help you comprehend for the first time what this white man's religion that we call Christianity has *done* to us. . . .

"Brothers and sisters here for the first time, please don't let that shock you. I know you didn't expect this. Because almost none of us black people have thought that maybe we were making a mistake not wondering if there wasn't a special religion somewhere for us—a special religion for the black man.

"Well, there *is* such a religion. It's called Islam. Let me spell it for you, I-s-l-a-m! *Islam!* But I'm going to tell you about Islam a little later. First we need to understand some things about this Christianity before we can understand why the *answer* for us is Islam.

"Brothers and sisters, the white man has brainwashed us black people to fasten our gaze upon a blond-haired, blue-eyed Jesus! We're worshiping a Jesus that doesn't even *look* like us! Oh, yes! Now just bear with me, listen to the teachings of the Messenger of Allah, The Honorable Elijah Muhammad. Now, just think of this. The blond-haired, blue-eyed white man has taught you and me to worship a *white* Jesus and to shout and sing and pray to this God that's *his* God, the white man's God. The white man has taught us to shout and sing and pray until we *die*, to wait until *death*, for some dreamy heaven-in-the-hereafter, when we're *dead*, while this white man has his milk and honey in the streets paved with golden dollars right here on *this* earth!" . . .

⸺ ⧉ ⸺

MECCA

. . . At one or another college or university, usually in the formal gatherings after I had spoken, perhaps a dozen generally white-complexioned people would come up to me, identifying themselves as Arabian, Middle Eastern or North African Muslims who happened to be visiting, studying, or living in the United States. They had said to me that, my white-complexioned statements notwithstanding, they felt that I was sincerely considering myself a Muslim—and they felt if I was exposed to what they always called "true Islam," I would "understand it, and embrace it." Automatically, as a follower of Elijah Muhammad, I had bridled whenever this was said.

But in the privacy of my own thoughts after several of these experiences, I did question myself: if one was sincere in professing a religion, why should he balk at broadening his knowledge of that religion?

Once in a conversation I broached this with Wallace Muhammad, Elijah Muhammad's son. He said that yes, certainly a Muslim should seek to learn all that he could about Islam. I had always had a high opinion of Wallace Muhammad's opinion. . . .

[Malcolm then began the trip to Mecca.]

Back at the Frankfurt airport, we took a United Arab Airlines plane on to Cairo. Throngs of people, obviously Muslims from everywhere, bound on the pilgrimage, were hugging and embracing. They were of all complexions, the whole atmosphere was of warmth and friendliness. The feeling hit me that there really wasn't any color problem here. The effect was as though I had just stepped out of a prison. . . .

Packed in the plane were white, black, brown, red, and yellow people, blue eyes and blond hair, and my kinky red hair—all together, brothers! All honoring the same God Allah, all in turn giving equal honor to each other. . . .

Establishing the rapport was the best thing that could have happened in the compartment. My being an American Muslim changed the attitudes from merely watching me to wanting to look out for me. Now, the others began smiling steadily. They came closer, they were frankly looking me up and down. Inspecting me. Very friendly. I was like a man from Mars. . . .

There had never before been in my emotions such an impulse to pray— and I did, prostrating myself on the living-room rug.

Nothing in either of my two careers as a black man in America had served to give me any idealistic tendencies. My instincts automatically examined the reasons, the motives, of anyone who did anything they didn't have to do for me. Always in my life, if it was any white person, I could see a selfish motive.

But there in that hotel that morning, a telephone call and a few hours away from the cot on the fourth-floor tier of the dormitory, was one of the few times I had been so awed that I was totally without resistance. That white man—at least he would have been considered "white" in America— related to Arabia's ruler, to whom he was a close advisor, truly an international man, with nothing in the world to gain, had given up his suite to me, for my transient comfort. He had *nothing* to gain. He didn't need me. He had everything. In fact, he had more to lose than gain. He had followed the American press about me. If he did that, he knew there was only stigma attached to me. I was supposed to have horns. I was a "racist." I was "antiwhite"—and he from all appearances was white. I was supposed to be a criminal; not only that, but everyone was even accusing me of using his religion of Islam as a cloak for my criminal practices and philosophies. Even if he had had some motive to use me, he knew that I was separated from Elijah Muhammad and the Nation of Islam, my "power base," according to the press in America. The only organization that I had was just a few weeks old. I had no job. I had no money. Just to get over there, I had had to borrow money from my sister.

That morning was when I first began to reappraise the "white man." It was when I first began to perceive that "white man," as commonly used, means complexion only secondarily; primarily it described attitudes and actions. In America, "white man" meant specific attitudes and actions toward the black man, and toward all other non-white men. But in the Muslim world, I had seen that men with white complexions were more genuinely brotherly than anyone else had ever been.

That morning was the start of radical alteration in my whole outlook about "white" men. . . .

The major press, radio, and television media in America had representatives in Cairo hunting all over, trying to locate me to interview me about the furor in New York that I had allegedly caused—when I knew nothing about any of it. I only knew what I had left in America, and how it contrasted with what I had found in the Muslim world. About twenty of us Muslims who had finished the Hajj were sitting in a huge tent on Mount Arafat. As a Muslim from America, I was the center of attention. They asked me what about the Hajj had impressed me the most. One of the several who spoke English asked; they translated my answers for the others. My answer to that question was not the one they expected, but it drove home my point.

I said, "The *brotherhood!* The people of all races, colors, from all, over the world the world coming together as *one!* It has proved to me the power of the One God."

It may have been out of taste, but that gave me an opportunity, and I used it, to preach them a quick little sermon on America's racism, and its evils. . . .

I have reflected since that the letter I finally sat down to compose had been subconsciously shaping itself in my mind.

The *color-blindness* of the Muslim world's religious society and the *color-blindness* of the Muslim world's human society: these two influences had each day been making a great impact, and an increasing persuasion against my previous way of thinking.

The first letter was, of course, to my wife, Betty. I never had a moment's question that Betty, after initial amazement, would change her thinking to join mine. I had known a thousand reassurances that Betty's faith in me was total. I knew that she would see what I had seen—that in the land of Muhammad and the land of Abraham, I had been blessed by Allah with a new insight into the true religion of Islam and a better understanding of America's entire racial dilemma. . . .

I knew that when my letter became public knowledge back in America, many would be astounded—loved ones, friends, and enemies alike. And no less astounded would be millions whom I did not know—who had gained during my twelve years with Elijah Muhammad a "hate" image of Malcolm X.

Even I was myself astounded. But there was precedent in my life for this letter. My whole life had been a chronology of—*changes.*

Here is what I wrote . . . from my heart:

"Never have I witnessed such sincere hospitality and the overwhelming spirit of true brotherhood as is practiced by people of all colors and races here in this Ancient Holy Land, the home of Abraham, Muhammad, and all the other prophets of the Holy Scriptures. For the past week, I have been utterly speechless and spellbound by the graciousness I see displayed all around me by people *of all colors. . . .*"

"There were tens of thousands of pilgrims, from all over the world. They were of all colors, from blue-eyed blonds to black-skinned Africans. But we were all participating in the same ritual, displaying a spirit of unity and brotherhood that my experiences in America had led me to believe never could exist between the white and the non-white."

"America needs to understand Islam, because this is the one religion that erases from its society the race problem. Throughout my travels in the Muslim world, I have met, talked to, and even eaten, with people who in America would have been considered "white"—but the "white" attitude was removed from their minds by the religion of Islam. I have never before seen *sincere* and *true* brotherhood practiced by all colors together, irrespective of their color."

"You may be shocked by these words coming from me. But on this pilgrimage, what I have seen, and experienced, has forced me to *re-arrange* much of my thought-patterns previously held, and to *toss aside* some of my previous conclusions. This was not too difficult for me. Despite my firm convictions, I have been always a man who tries to face facts, and to accept the reality of life as new experience and new knowledge unfolds it. I have always kept an open mind which is necessary to the flexibility that must go hand in hand with every form of intelligent search for truth. . . .

" . . . as racism leads America up the suicide path, I do believe, from the experiences that I have had with them, that the whites of the younger generation, in the colleges and universities, will see the handwriting on the wall and many of them will turn to the *spiritual* path of *truth*—the *only* way left to America to ward off the disaster that racism inevitably must lead to." . . .

———— ∞∞∞ ————

1965

I must be honest. Negroes—Afro-Americans—showed no inclination to rush to the United Nations and demand justice for themselves here in America. I really had known in advance that they wouldn't. The American white man has so thoroughly brainwashed the black man to see himself as only a domestic "civil rights" problem that it will probably take longer than I live before the Negro sees that the struggle of the American black man is international.

And I had known, too, that Negroes would not rush to follow me into the orthodox Islam which had given me the insight and perspective to see that the black men and white men truly could be brothers. America's Negroes—especially older Negroes—are too indelibly soaked in Christianity's double standard of oppression.

So, in the "public invited" meeting which I began holding each Sunday afternoon or evening in Harlem's well-known Audubon Ballroom, as I addressed predominantly non-Muslim Negro audiences, I did not immediately attempt to press the Islamic religion, but instead to embrace all who sat before me:

"—not Muslim, nor Christian, Catholic, nor Protestant . . . Baptist nor Methodist, Democrat nor Republican, Mason nor Elk! I mean the black people of America—and the black people all over this earth! Because it is as this collective mass of black people that we have been deprived not only of our civil rights, but even of our human rights, the right to human dignity. . . . "

On the streets, after my speeches, in the faces and the voice of the people I met—even those who would pump my hand and want my autograph—I would feel the wait-and-see attitude. I would feel—and I understood—their uncertainty about where I stood. Since the Civil War's "freedom," the black man has gone down so many fruitless paths. His leaders, very largely, had failed him. The religion of Christianity had failed him. The black man was scarred, he was cautious, he was apprehensive.

I understood it better now than I had before. In the Holy World, away from America's race problem, was the first time I ever had been able to think clearly about the basic divisions of white people in America, and how their attitudes and their motives related to, and affected Negroes. In my thirty-nine years on this earth, the Holy City of Mecca had been the first time I had ever stood before the Creator of All and felt like a complete human being. . . .

In Mecca, too, I had played back for myself the twelve years I had spent with Elijah Muhammad as if it were a motion picture. I guess it would be impossible for anyone ever to realize fully how complete was my belief in Elijah Muhammad. I believed in him not only as a leader in the ordinary *human* sense, but also I believed in him as a *divine* leader I believed he had no human weaknesses or faults, and that therefore, he could make no mistakes and that he could do no wrong. There on a Holy World hilltop, I realized how very dangerous it is for people to hold any human being in such esteem, especially to consider anyone some sort of "divinely guided" and "protected" person. . . .

Largely, the American white man's press refused to convey that I was now attempting to teach Negroes a new direction. With the 1964 "long, hot summer" steadily producing new incidents, I was constantly accused of "stirring up Negroes." . . .

They called me "the angriest Negro in America." I wouldn't deny that charge. I spoke exactly as I felt. "I *believe* in anger. The Bible says there is a *time* for anger." They called me "a teacher, a fomentor of violence." I would say point blank, "That is a lie. I'm not for wanton violence, I'm for justice. I feel that if white people were attacked by Negroes—if the forces of law prove unable, or inadequate, or reluctant to protect those whites from those Negroes—then those white people should protect and defend themselves from those Negroes, using arms if necessary. And I feel that when the law fails to protect Negroes from whites' attack, then those Negroes should use arms, if necessary, to defend themselves.

"Malcolm X Advocates Armed Negroes!"

What was wrong with that? I'll tell you what was wrong. I was a black man talking about physical defense against the white man. The white man can lynch and burn and bomb and beat Negroes—that's all right: "Have patience" . . . "The customs are entrenched" . . . "Things are getting better."

Well, I believe it's a crime for anyone who is being brutalized to continue to accept that brutality without doing something to defend himself. If that's how "Christian" philosophy is interpreted, if that's what Gandhian philosophy teaches, well, then, I will call them criminal philosophies. . . .

I am in agreement one hundred per cent with those racists who say that no government laws ever can *force* brotherhood. The only true world solution today is governments guided by true religion—of the spirit. Here in race-torn America, I am convinced that the Islam religion is desperately needed, particularly by the American black man. The black man needs to reflect that he has been America's most fervent Christian—and where has it gotten him? In fact, in the white man's hands, in the white man's interpretation . . . where has Christianity brought this *world?*

It has brought the non-white two-thirds of the human population to rebellion. Two-thirds of the human population today is telling the one-third minority white man, "Get out!" And the white man is leaving. And as he leaves, we see the non-white peoples returning in a rush to their original religions, which had been labeled "pagan" by the conquering white man. Only one religion—Islam—had the power to stand and fight the white man's Christianity for a *thousand years!* Only Islam could keep white Christianity at bay . . .

I believe that God now is giving the world's so-called "Christian" white society its last opportunity to repent and atone for the crimes of exploiting and enslaving the world's non-white peoples. It is exactly as when God gave Pharaoh a chance to repent. But Pharaoh persisted in his refusal to give justice to those whom he oppressed. And, we know, God finally destroyed Pharaoh.

Is white America really sorry for her crimes against the black people? Does white America have the capacity to repent—and to atone? Does the capacity to repent, to atone exist in a majority, in one-half, in even one-third of American white society?

Many black men, the victims—in fact most black men—would like to be able to forgive, to forget, the crimes.

But most American white people seem not to have it in them to make any serious atonement—to do justice to the black man. . . .

A desegregated cup of coffee, a theater, public toilets—the whole range of hypocritical "integration"—these are not atonement.

6. JAMES H. CONE, "THE WHITE CHURCH AND BLACK POWER" (1969); "GOD IS BLACK" (1970)

A professor at Union Theological Seminary in New York City since 1969, James Cone is best known as an exponent of "black theology," first announced in his 1969 book Black Theology of Liberation. *Cone followed this work with a series of treatises on themes in African American religious history, including a seminal 1972 book,* The Spirituals and the Blues. *Heavily influenced originally by German modernist theologians whose works he read in his graduate training, Cone later came to reject reliance on white scholars and terminology, arguing that black Christians would have to devise their own understandings freed from a dominant theological tradition too entangled in racism and colonialism.*

In these excerpts from his works, Cone first outlines his original position, that God is black. By this, he meant not that God had a particular skin color, but rather that God always and by definition aligns himself with the oppressed and against the oppressors. Black people in the United States were thus a chosen people. In later essays, Cone reflects on his own theological contributions and suggests how much his own work fit with a rapidly evolving tradition of liberation theology, which argued many of the same points, though without the overlay of racial language. Cone also responds to "womanist" critics of his theology, who pointed out that he was in some ways simply turning a white male God into a black male God, ignoring the deeper underlying structures of patriarchy that oppressed women. Cone's own work influenced numerous other theolo-

gians and writers, including Vine Deloria Jr., Native American author of the seminal 1972 work God is Red.

―――――∞∞∞―――――

THE WHITE CHURCH AND BLACK POWER

The meaning of Black Power and its relationship to Christianity has been the focal point of our discussion thus far. It has been argued that Black Power is the spirit of Christ himself in the black-white dialogue which makes possible the emancipation of blacks from self-hatred and frees whites from their racism. Through Black Power, blacks are becoming men of worth, and whites are forced to confront them as human beings. . . .

The Church is not defined by those who faithfully attend and participate in the 11:00 a.m. Sunday worship. . . . It may have been fine for distinguishing orthodoxy from heresy, but it is worthless as a vehicle against modern racism. We must therefore be reminded that Christ was not crucified on an altar between two candles, but on a cross between two thieves. He is not in our peaceful, quiet, comfortable suburban "churches," but in the ghetto fighting the racism of churchly white people. . . .

Where is "the opening" that Christ provides? Where does he lead his people? Where indeed, if not in the ghetto. He meets the blacks where they are and becomes one of them. We see him there with his black face and his black hands lounging on a streetcorner. "Oh, but surely Christ is above race." But society is not raceless, any more than when God became a despised Jew. White liberal preference for a raceless Christ serves only to make official and orthodox the centuries-old portrayal of Christ as white. The "raceless" American Christ has a light skin, wavy brown hair, and sometimes—wonder of wonders—blue eyes. For whites to find him with big lips and kinky hair is as offensive as it was for the Pharisees to find him partying with tax collectors. But whether whites want to hear it or not, *Christ is black, baby,* with all of the features which are so detestable to white society. . . .

It is the job of the Church to become black with him and accept the shame which white society places on blacks. But the Church knows that what is shame to the world is holiness to God. Black is holy, that is, it is a symbol of God's presence in history on behalf of the oppressed man. Where there is black, there is oppression; but blacks can be assured that where there is blackness, there is Christ who has taken on blackness so that what is evil in men's eyes might become good. Therefore Christ is black because he is oppressed, and oppressed because he is black. And if the Church is to join Christ by following his opening, it too must go where suffering is and become black also.

This is what the New Testament means by the service of reconciliation. It is not smoothing things over by ignoring the deep-seated racism in white society. It is freeing the racist of racism by making him confront blacks as men. Reconciliation has nothing to do with the "let's talk about it" attitude, or "it takes time" attitude. It merely says, "Look man, the revolution is on. Whose side are you on?"

⸎

GOD IS BLACK

Many things have changed since the 1960s. The most notable change for *my* theological perspective has been the impact of the rise of liberation theologies among the oppressed in the so-called Third World countries in Asia, Africa, and Latin America. During the sixties, I was not aware of the currently well-known liberation theology in Latin America, and neither did I know of similar theological developments in Asia and Africa. My reflections on God were defined by the great contradiction of racism in the U.S. as mirrored in its history and the Civil Rights and Black Power movements of the 1950s and 60s. My chief concern then was to reconcile Martin Luther King, Jr.'s accent on divine love in race relations (which he called agape) with Malcolm X's stress on divine justice (which he identified with the destruction of the white oppressor). I also wanted to demonstrate that the God of the Christian gospel was not *white* as most Christians and non-Christians, even in the Black community, seemed to believe. On the contrary, I was determined to show, using the intellectual tools whites had taught me in seminary, that "God is Black," not. just because African-Americans are Black, but because God freely chooses to be known as the One who liberates victims from their oppression. . . .

I am more convinced today than I was during the 1960s that the God of the Christian gospel can be known only in the communities of the oppressed who are struggling for justice in a world that has no place for them. I still believe that "God is Black" in the sense that God's identity is found in the faces of those who are exploited and humiliated because of their color. But I also believe that "God is mother," "rice," "red," and a host of other things that give life to those whom society condemns to death. "Black," "mother," "rice," and "red" give concreteness to God's life-giving presence in the world and remind us that the universality of God is found in the particularity of the suffering poor. We can know God only in an oppressed community in struggle for justice and wholeness. It is because I believe that "God is Black" that I also believe that the dominant, western, male theological tradition is much too limiting to speak about God. . . .

I first encountered the God of justice and love at Macedonia A.M.E. Church in Bearden, Arkansas. It was a liberating experience which bestowed upon me the power to know that what whites said about Blacks was a lie. The power to be somebody in a world that had defined Blacks as nobody is what God meant to me and many other Black people. The Civil Rights and Black Power movements concretized in the society what many Blacks had already discovered in the spirituality of their churches. Using the tools of white theology, I, as a new seminary graduate, tried to interpret the meaning of God for the Black struggle for liberation. Although white intellectual tools were too limiting and often hampered what I felt in the deepest resources of my experience, I think that my thesis about God's blackness was adequate then and is still appropriate today if we realize that blackness is a powerful symbol of oppression and liberation among the victims in the world. . . .

Construction

Because blacks have come to know themselves as *black*, and because that blackness is the cause of their own love of themselves and hatred of whiteness, the blackness of God is the key to our knowledge of God. The blackness of God, and everything implied by it in a racist society, is the heart of the black theology doctrine of God. There is no place in black theology for a colorless God in a society where human beings suffer precisely because of their color. The black theologian must reject any conception of God which stifles black self-determination by picturing God as a God of all peoples. Either God is identified with the oppressed to the point that their experience becomes God's experience, or God is a God of racism. . . .

White theologians would prefer to do theology without reference to color, but this only reveals how deeply racism is embedded in the thought forms of this culture. To be sure, they would probably concede that the concept of liberation is essential to the biblical view of God. But it is still impossible for them to translate the biblical emphasis on liberation to the black-white struggle today. Invariably they quibble on this issue, moving from side to side, always pointing out the dangers of extremism on both sides. (In the black community, we call this "shuffling.") They really cannot make a decision, because it has already been made for them. . . .

Knowing God means being on the side of the oppressed, becoming one with them, and participating in the goal of liberation. *We must become black with God!*

It is to be expected whites will have some difficulty with the idea of "becoming black with God." The experience is not only alien to their existence as they know it to be, it appears to be an impossibility. "How can whites become black?" they ask. They know, as everyone in this country knows, blacks are those who say they are black, regardless of skin color. In the literal sense a black person is anyone who has "even one drop of black blood in his or her veins."

But "becoming black with God" means more than just saying, "I am black," if it involves that at all. The question "How can white persons become black?" is analogous to the Philippian jailer's question to Paul and Silas, "What must I do to be saved?" The implication is that if we work hard enough at it, we can reach the goal. But the misunderstanding here is the failure to see that blackness, or salvation (the two are synonymous) is the work of God, not a human work. It is not something we accomplish; it is a gift. That is why Paul and Silas said, "Believe in the Lord Jesus and you will be saved." . . .

Even some blacks will find this view of God hard to handle. Having been enslaved by the God of white racism so long, they will have difficulty believing that God is identified with their struggle for freedom. Becoming one of God's disciples means rejecting whiteness and accepting themselves as they are in all their physical blackness. This is what the Christian view of God means for blacks.

7. COMMITTEE OF BLACK CHURCHMEN, "THE BLACK MANIFESTO" (1969); "BLACK POWER" (1966)

By 1969, the Black Power movement had challenged the conventional assumptions of the Christian nonviolent phase of the civil rights crusade. Far from arguing (as had SNCC's John Lewis) from the standpoint of "redemptive suffering," black spokesmen of the late 1960s refused to take the violence meted out by whites—whether it came from Klansmen in sheets or from the boardrooms of corporate America. Instead, they would fight back, claiming pride in their African heritage and calling white institutions to account for their role in creating a racist society.

On May 4, 1969, James Forman, formerly of SNCC, stormed the pulpit of Riverside Church in New York City, one of the country's most prestigious (and socially conscious) congregations. He presented the document below, the "Black Manifesto," a product of the National Black Economic Development Conference in April of that year. In his address, Forman connects the black struggle in America to the cause of colonized people around the world. "Caution is fine," he warns, "but no oppressed people ever gained their liberation until they were ready to fight, to use whatever means necessary, including the use of force and power of the gun to bring down the colonizer." He argues that the churches are sustained "by the military might of the colonizers," and calls on "black people to commence the disruption of the racist churches and synagogues throughout the United States." In the subsequent document, the National Committee of Black Churchmen hails the manifesto as a necessary first strike in addressing the economic inequalities that result from hundreds of years of racist oppression.

THE BLACK MANIFESTO

We the black people assembled in Detroit, Michigan, for the National Black Economic Development Conference are fully aware that we have been forced to come together because racist white America has exploited our resources, our minds, our bodies, our labor. For centuries we have been forced to live as colonized people inside the United States, victimized by the most vicious, racist system in the world. We have helped to build the most industrial country in the world.

We are therefore demanding of the white Christian churches and Jewish synagogues, which are part and parcel of the system of capitalism, that they begin to pay reparations to black people in this country. We are demanding $500,000,000 from the Christian white churches and the Jewish synagogues. This total comes to 15 dollars per nigger. This is a low estimate for we maintain there are probably more than 30,000,000 black people in this country. $15 a nigger is not a large sum of money and we know that the churches and synagogues have a tremendous wealth, and its membership, white America, has profited and still exploits black people. We are also not unaware that the exploitation of colored peoples around the world is aided and abetted by the white Christian churches and synagogues. This demand for $500,000,000 is not an idle resolution or empty words. Fifteen dollars for every black brother and sister in the United States is only a beginning of the reparations due us as people who have been exploited and degraded, brutalized, killed and persecuted. Underneath all of this exploitation, the racism of this country has produced a psychological effect upon us that we are beginning to shake off. We are no longer afraid to demand our full rights as a people in this decadent society. . . .

(9) We call upon all white Christians and Jews to practice patience, tolerance, understanding, and nonviolence as they have encouraged, advised, and demanded that we as black people should do throughout our entire en-

forced slavery in the United States. The true test of their faith and belief in the Cross and the words of the prophets will certainly be put to a test as we see legitimate and extremely modest reparations for our role in developing the industrial base of the Western world through our slave labor. But we are no longer slaves, we are men and women, proud of our African heritage, determined to have our dignity.

(10) We are so proud of our African heritage and realize concretely that our struggle is not only to make revolution in the United States, but to protect our brothers and sisters in Africa and to help them rid themselves of racism, capitalism, and imperialism by whatever means necessary, including armed struggle. We are and must be willing to fight the defamation of our African image wherever it rears its ugly head. . . .

(12) To implement these demands we must have a fearless leadership. We must have a leadership which is willing to battle the church establishment to implement these demands. To win our demands we will have to declare war on the white Christian churches and synagogues and this means we may have to fight the total government structure of this country. Let no one here think that these demands will be met by our mere stating of them. For the sake of the churches and synagogues, we hope that they have the wisdom to understand that these demands are modest and reasonable. But if the white Christians and Jews are not willing to meet our demands through peace and good will, then we declare war and we are prepared to fight by whatever means necessary. . . .

Brothers and sisters, we no longer are shuffling our feet and scratching our heads. We are tall, black and proud. . . .

We are not threatening the churches. We are saying that we know the churches came with the military might of the colonizers and have been sustained by the military might of the colonizers. Hence, if the churches in colonial territories were established by military might, we know deep within our hearts that we must be prepared to use force to get our demands. We are not saying that this is the road we want to take. It is not, but let us be very clear that we are not opposed to force and we are not opposed to violence.

❈

BLACK POWER

Statement by the National Committee of Negro Churchmen, July 31, 1966
We, an informal group of Negro churchmen in America, are deeply disturbed about the crisis brought upon our country by historic distortions of important human realities in the controversy about "black power." What

we see shining through the variety of rhetoric is not anything new but the same old problem of power and race which has faced our beloved country since 1619.

We realize that neither the term "power" nor the term "Christian conscience" is an easy matter to talk about, especially in the context of race relations in America. The fundamental distortion facing us in the controversy about "black power" is rooted in a gross imbalance of power and conscience between Negroes and white Americans. It is this distortion, mainly, which is responsible for the widespread, though often inarticulate, assumption that white people are justified in getting what they want through the use of power, but that Negro Americans must, either by nature or by circumstance, make their appeal only through conscience. As a result, the power of white men and the conscience of black men have both been corrupted. The power of white men is corrupted because it meets little meaningful resistance from Negroes to temper it and keep white men from aping God. The conscience of black men is corrupted because, having no power to implement the demands of conscience, the concern for justice is transmuted into a distorted form of love, which, in the absence of justice, becomes chaotic self-surrender. Powerlessness breeds a race of beggars. We are faced now with a situation where conscienceless power meets powerless conscience, threatening the very foundations of our nation. . . .

I. To the Leaders of America: Power and Freedom
. . . From the point of view of the Christian faith, there is nothing necessarily wrong with concern for power. At the heart of the Protestant reformation is the belief that ultimate power belongs to God alone and that men become most inhuman when concentrations of power lead to the conviction—overt or covert—that any nation, race or organization can rival God in this regard. At issue in the relations between whites and Negroes in America is the problem of inequality of power. Out of this imbalance grows the disrespect of white men for the Negro personality and community, and the disrespect of Negroes for themselves. This is a fundamental root of human injustice in America. In one sense, the concept of "black power" reminds us of the need for and the possibility of authentic democracy in America. . . .

II. To White Churchmen: Power and Love
As black men who were long ago forced out of the white church to create and to wield "black power," we fail to understand the emotional quality of the outcry of some clergy against the use of the term today. It is not enough to answer that "integration" is the solution. For it is precisely the nature of the operation of power under some forms of integration which is being

challenged. The Negro Church was created as a result of the refusal to submit to the indignities of a false kind of "integration" in which all power was
in the hands of white people. A more equal sharing of power is precisely
what is required as the precondition of authentic human interaction. We
understand the growing demand of Negro and white youth for a more honest kind of integration; one which increases rather than decreases the capacity of the disinherited to participate with power in all of the structures of
our common life. Without this capacity to *participate with power*—i.e., to
have some organized political and economic strength to really influence
people with whom one interacts—integration is not meaningful. For the issue is not one of racial balance but of honest interracial interaction.

For this kind of interaction to take place, all people need power, whether
black or white. We regard as sheer hypocrisy or as a blind and dangerous illusion the view that opposes love to power. Love should be a controlling element in power, not power itself. So long as white churchmen continue to
moralize and misinterpret Christian love, so long will justice continue to be
subverted in this land.

III. To Negro Citizens: Power and Justice

Both the anguished cry for "black power" and the confused emotional response to it can be understood if the whole controversy is put in the context
of American history. Especially must we understand the irony involved in
the pride of Americans regarding their ability to act as individuals on the
one hand, and their tendency to act as members of ethnic groups on the other hand. In the tensions of this part of our history is revealed both the
tragedy and the hope of human redemption in America. . . .

Getting power necessarily involves reconciliation. We must first be reconciled to ourselves lest we fail to recognize the resources we already have
and upon which we can build. We must be reconciled to ourselves as persons and to ourselves as an historical group. This means we must find our
way to a new self-image in which we can feel a normal sense of pride in
self, including our variety of skin color and the manifold textures of our
hair. As long as we are filled with hatred for ourselves we will be unable to
respect others.

At the same time, if we are seriously concerned about power then we
must build upon that which we already have. "Black power" is already present to some extent in the Negro church, in Negro fraternities and sorori-
ties, in our professional associations, and in the opportunities afforded to
Negroes who make decisions in some of the integrated organizations of
our society.

We understand the reasons by which these limited forms of "black power" have been rejected by some of our people. Too often the Negro church has stirred its members away from the reign of God in *this world* to a distorted and complacent view of *an otherworldly* conception of God's power. We commit ourselves as churchmen to make more meaningful in the life of our institution our conviction that Jesus Christ reigns in the "here" and "now" as well as in the future he brings in upon us. We shall, therefore, use more of the resources of our churches in working for human justice in the places of social change and upheaval where our Master is already at work. . . .

Neither must we rest our concern for reconciliation with our white brothers on the fear that failure to do so would damage gains already made by the civil rights movement. If those gains are in fact real, they will withstand the claims of our people for power and justice, not just for a few select Negroes here and there, but for the masses of our citizens. We must rather rest our concern for reconciliation on the firm ground that we and all other Americans *are* one. Our history and destiny are indissolubly linked. If the future is to belong to any of us, it must be prepared for all of us whatever our racial or religious background. For in the final analysis, we *are persons* and the power of all groups must be wielded to make visible our common humanity.

8. VINCENT HARDING, "BLACK POWER AND THE AMERICAN CHRIST" (1967)

"Whatever its other sources," Vincent Harding argues in this piece for Christian Century magazine in 1967, "the ideology of blackness surely grows out of the deep ambivalence of American Negroes to the Christ we have encountered here." In his attempt to "interpret" black theology for a largely white and liberal Protestant leadership, Harding insisted that the open expression of black anger was "a far more healthy state of affairs" than the silence beneath which it had simmered for so long. It was the very fear of white Christians before the social transformation of their time that motivated Black Power rhetoric. As whites fled cities in racial transition, "leaving their stained-glass mausoleums behind them," Black Power advocates drew all the more sustenance for their critiques of white America. Ultimately, Harding suggests that, however frightening Black Power might be, it could also be "a message for all who claim to love the Lord of the church." In place of the "redemptive suffering" preached by SNCC, Black Power could be the "redemptive anger" that would bring down judgment on white "arrogance and power."

The mood among many social-action-oriented Christians today suggests that it is only a line thin as a razor blade that divides sentimental yearning over the civil rights activities of the past from present bitter recrimination against "Black Power." As is so often the case with reminiscences, the nostalgia may grow more out of a sense of frustration and powerlessness than out of any true appreciation of the meaning of the past. This at least is the impression one gets from those seemingly endless gatherings of old "true believers" which usually produce both the nostalgia and the recriminations. Generally the cast of characters at such meetings consists of well-dressed, well-fed Negroes and whites whose accents almost blend into a single voice as they recall the days "when we were all together, fighting for the same cause." The stories evoke again the heady atmosphere, mixed of smugness and self-sacrifice, that surrounded us in those heroic times when nonviolence was our watchword and integration our heavenly city. One can almost hear the strains of "our song" as men and women remember how they solemnly swayed in the aisles or around the charred remains of a church or in the dirty southern jails. Those were the days when Martin Luther King was the true prophet and when we were certain that the civil rights movement was God's message to the churches—and part of our smugness grew out of the fact that *we* knew it while all the rest of God's frozen people were asleep.

A VEIL BETWEEN THEN AND NOW

. . . The trouble with these meetings is that they are indeed becoming ritual, cultic acts of memory that blind us to creative possibilities. Because that "veil" may be a wall, not primarily for separating but for writing on— both sides of it. Or it may be a great sheet "let down from heaven"; or a curtain before the next act can begin. Most of us appear totally incapable of realizing that there may be more light in blackness than we have yet begun to glimpse. . . .

Perhaps the first and central discovery is also the most obvious: there is a strong and causative link between Black Power and American Christianity. Indeed one may say with confidence that whatever its other sources, the ideology of blackness surely grows out of the deep ambivalence of American Negroes to the Christ we have encountered here. . . .

If the American Christ and his followers have indeed helped to mold the Black Power movement, then might it not be that the God whom many of us insist on keeping alive is not only alive but just? May he not be attempting to break through to us with at least as much urgency as we once sensed at the height of the good old "We Shall Overcome" days? Perhaps he is writing on the wall, saying that we Christians, black and white, must choose between death with the American Christ and life with the Suffering Servant of God. Who dares deny that God may have chosen once again the black sufferers for a new assault on the hard shell of indifference and fear that encases so many Americans?

If these things are difficult to believe perhaps we need to look more closely both at the American Christ and the black movement he has helped to create. From the outset, almost everywhere we blacks have met him in this land, this Christ was painted white and pink, blond and blue-eyed—and not only in white churches but in black churches as well. Millions of black children had the picture of this pseudo-Nazarene burned into their memory. The books, the windows, and paintings, the filmstrips all affirmed the same message—a message of shame. This Christ shamed us by his pigmentation, so obviously not our own. He condemned us for our blackness, for our flat noses, for our kinky hair, for our power, our strange power of expressing emotion in singing and shouting and dancing. He was sedate, so genteel, so white. And as soon as we were able, many of us tried to be like him.

GLAD TO BE BLACK

For a growing edge of bold young black people all that is past. They fling out their declaration: "No white Christ shall shame us again. We are glad to be black. We rejoice in the darkness of our skin, we celebrate the natural texture of our hair, we extol the rhythm and vigor of our songs and shouts and dances. And if your American Christ doesn't like that, you know what you can do with him." That is Black Power: a repudiation of the American culture-religion that helped to create it and a quest for a religious reality more faithful to our own experience. . . .

That is Black Power: a search for roots in a land that has denied us both a past and a future. And the American Christ who has blessed the denial earns nothing but scorn.

The advocates of Black Power know this Christ well. They see his people running breathlessly, cursing silently, exiting double-time from the cities with all their suffering people. They see this white throng fleeing before the strangled movement of the blacks out of the ghettos, leaving their stained-glass mausoleums behind them. This very exodus of the Christians from the places where the weak and powerless live has been one of the primary motivating forces of Black Power.

The seekers of Black Power, seeing their poorest, most miserable people deserted by the white American Christians, have come to stand with the forlorn in these very places of abandonment. Now they speak of Black Unity, and the old Christian buildings are filled with Negroes young and old studying African history. The new leaders in the ghettos tell them: "Whites now talk about joining forces, but who has ever wanted to join forces with you? They only want to use you—especially those white American Christian liars. They love you in theory only. They love only your middle-class incarnations. But they are afraid of you—you who are black and poor and filled with rage and despair. They talk about 'progress' for the Negro, but they don't *mean you*." . . .

GROVELING NO MORE

. . . As black men they have long seen into the heart of American darkness. They have no patriotic illusions about this nation's benevolent intentions toward the oppressed nonwhite people of the world, no matter how often the name and compassion of divinity are invoked. With eyes cleared by pain they discern the arrogance beneath the pious protestations. The American Christ leads the Hiroshima-bound bomber, blesses the marines on their way to another in the long series of Latin American invasions, and blasphemously calls it peace when America destroys an entire Asian peninsula. . . .

Black people are not fooled by the churchly vestments of humility. They hear arrogant white pastors loudly counting dollars and members, and committees smugly announcing the cost of their new modern churches—hollow tombs for Christ. They hear the voices: "Negroes, oh Negroes, you must be humble, like Christ. You must be patient and long-suffering. Negroes, don't push so hard. Look at all we've given you so far." And the voices trail off: "Negroes, dear Negroes, remember our Lord taught how good it is to be meek and lowly." And then a whisper: "Cause if you don't, niggers, if you don't, we'll crush you." . . .

CHRISTIAN BLASPHEMERS

Then comes the sharpest of all moments of truth, when Christian voices are raised in hostility and fear, directing their missionary chorus to the young men drained of hope by the ghetto. "Black boys," they say, "rampaging, screaming, laughing black boys, you must love—like Christ and Doctor King. Black boys, please drop your firebombs. Violence never solved anything. You must love your enemies—if they're white and American and represent law and order. You must love them for your rotting houses and for your warped education. You must love them for your nonexistent jobs.

Above all, you must love them for their riot guns, their billy clubs, their hatred and their white, white skin."

It would be terrifying enough if the voices stopped on that emasculating note. But they go on: "Just the same, black boys, if the enemies have been properly certified as such by our Christian leaders, and if they're poor and brown and 10,000 miles away, you must hate them. You must scream and rampage and kill them, black boys." . . .

What can a nation expect in response to such vicious words? It gets the truth—far more than it deserves. For the black men reply: "Hypocrites, white hypocrites, you only want to save your skin and your piled-up treasure from the just envy-anger of your former slaves, your present serfs and your future victims. In the name of this Christ you deny our past, demean our present and promise us no future save that of black mercenaries in your assaults upon the world's dark and desperate poor." . . .

"If we must fight," they say, "let it be on the streets where we have been humiliated. If we must burn down houses, let them be the homes and stores of our exploiters. If we must kill, let it be the fat, pious white Christians who guard their lawns and their daughters while engineering slow death for us. If we must die, let it be for a real cause, the cause of black men's freedom as black men define it. And may all the white elders die well in the causes they defend." This is Black Power—the response to the American Christ.

9. JACQUELYN GRANT, "BLACK THEOLOGY AND THE BLACK WOMAN" (1980)

Advocates of "black theology" soon found themselves under critique, namely from black women who perceived the old false god of patriarchy barely hidden under the theoretically revolutionary rhetoric of Black Power. A black feminist theologian named Jacquelyn Grant has been among the most articulate advocates of black women's theology. She insists that "Black theology cannot continue to treat Black women as if they were invisible creatures who are on the outside looking into the Black experience." Given that women made up the majority of members of black churches (as they did of white Protestant churches), an "authentic theology of liberation" would necessarily have to address the liberation of black women from sexism, as well as the liberation of black people in America from racism.

What are the forces of liberation in the Black community and the Black Church? Are they to be exclusively defined by the struggle against racism?

My answer to that question is No. There are oppressive realities in the Black community which are related to, but independent of, the fact of racism. Sexism is one such reality. Black men seek to liberate themselves from racial stereotypes and the conditions of oppression without giving due attention to the stereotypes and oppressions against women which parallel those against Blacks. Blacks fight to be free of the stereotype that all Blacks are dirty and ugly, or that Black represents evil and darkness. The slogan "Black is Beautiful" was a counterattack on these stereotypes. The parallel for women is the history of women as "unclean" especially during menstruation and after childbirth. Because the model of beauty in the White male dominated society is the "long-haired blonde," with all that goes along with that mystique, Black women have an additional problem with the Western idea of "ugliness," particularly as they encounter Black men who have adopted this White model of beauty. Similarly, the Christian teaching that woman is responsible for the fall of *mankind* and is, therefore, the source of evil has had a detrimental effect in the experience of Black women. . . .

THE BLACK CHURCH AND THE BLACK WOMAN

. . . If the liberation of women is not proclaimed the church's proclamation cannot be about divine liberation. If the church does not share in the liberation struggle of Black women, its liberation struggle is not authentic. If women are oppressed the church cannot possibly be "a visible manifestation that the gospel is a reality"—for the gospel cannot be real in that context. One can see the contradictions between the church's language or proclamation of liberation and its action by looking both at the status of Black women in the church as laity and Black women in the ordained ministry of the church.

It is often said that women are the "backbone" of the church. On the surface this may appear to be a compliment, especially when one considers the function of the backbone in the human anatomy. . . . In any case, the telling portion of the word backbone is "back." It has become apparent to me that most of the ministers who use this term have reference to location rather than function. What they really mean is that women are in the "background" and should be kept there. They are merely support workers. This is borne out by my observation that in many churches women are consistently given responsibilities in the kitchen, while men are elected or appointed to the important boards and leadership positions. While decisions and policies may be discussed in the kitchen, they are certainly not made there. . . .

For the most part, men have monopolized the ministry as a profession. The ministry of women as fully ordained clergypersons has always been controversial. The Black church fathers were unable to see the injustices of their own practices, even when they paralleled the injustices in the White Church against which they rebelled. . . .

THE BLACK EXPERIENCE AND THE BLACK WOMAN

. . . The status of Black women in the community parallels that of Black women in the church. Black Theology considers the Black experience to be the context out of which its questions about God and human existence are formulated. This is assumed to be the context in which God's revelation is received and interpreted. Only from the perspective of the poor and the oppressed can theology be adequately done. Arising out of the Black Power Movement of the 1960s, Black Theology purports to take seriously the experience of the larger community's struggle for liberation. But if this is, indeed, the case, Black Theology must function in the secular community in the same way as it should function in the church community. It must serve as a "self-test" to see whether the rhetoric or proclamation of the Black community's struggle for liberation is consistent with its practices. How does the "self-test" principle operate among the poor and the oppressed? Certainly Black Theology has spoken to some of the forms of oppression which exist within the community of the oppressed. Many of the injustices it has attacked are the same as those which gave rise to the prophets of the Old Testament. But the fact that Black Theology does not include sexism specifically as one of those injustices is all too evident. It suggests that the theologians do not understand sexism to be one of the oppressive realities of the Black community. Silence on this specific issue can only mean conformity with the status quo. . . .

Notwithstanding all the evidence to the contrary, some might want to argue that the central problem of Black women is related to their race and not their sex. Such an argument then presumes that the problem cannot be resolved apart from the Black struggle. I contend that as long as the Black struggle refuses to recognize and deal with its sexism, the idea that women will receive justice from that struggle alone will never work. It will not work because Black women will no longer allow Black men to ignore their unique problems and needs in the name of some distorted view of the "liberation of total community." . . . Black men who have an investment in the patriarchal structure of White America and who intend to do Christian theology have yet to realize that if Jesus is liberator of the oppressed, all of the oppressed must be liberated.

10. CÉSAR A. CHÁVEZ, "THE MEXICAN-AMERICAN AND THE CHURCH" (1968)

While black Americans in the 1960s captured the attention of the nation through the mass protests of the civil rights movement, Hispanics, a smaller and less visible minority group, began their own movement toward freedom. The name most associated with their cause was César E. Chávez, a devoutly Catholic labor organizer in the fields of California. Chávez organized a series of farmworker strikes in the produce fields in the 1960s, where migrant laborers of Mexican descent toiled for low pay in terrible conditions. Migrant workers had briefly captured the attention of the nation in the 1930s when the "Okies," whites from the American South and Southwest, migrated to California in search of work and often ended up picking produce in the fields. Mexican migrant laborers historically had been exploited with impunity, and had difficulty organizing since farmworkers had been exempted from many of the formative labor laws of the New Deal era.

César Chávez brought the plight of the migrants to national attention by employing the same philosophy and techniques of nonviolence that had worked in the black civil rights struggle. Like the black Protestants who dominated parts of that movement, Chávez drew on the rich legacy of the Church, and of Hispanic spirituality in particular, to empower his cause. He encountered resistance from the Catholic establishment (not unlike what Martin Luther King Jr. had seen in the Protestant establishment), but knew that the Church could be a "powerful moral and spiritual force which cannot be ignored by any movement." In this selection, Chávez advocates what would come to be called "liberation theology." For him, as for liberation theologians generally, the Church was spiritually mandated to side with the poor. He concludes by asking the Church to "sacrifice with the people," to enact true servanthood.

The place to begin is with our own experience with the Church in the strike which has gone on for thirty-one months in Delano. For in Delano the Church has been involved with the poor in a unique way which should stand as a symbol to other communities. Of course, when we refer to the Church we should define the word a little. We mean the whole Church, the Church as an ecumenical body spread around the world, and not just its particular form in a parish in a local community. The Church we are talking about is a tremendously powerful institution in our society, and in the world. That Church is one form of the Presence of God on Earth, and so naturally it is powerful. It is powerful by definition. It is a powerful moral and spiritual force which cannot be ignored by any movement. . . .

In a small way we have been able, in the Delano strike, to work together with the Church in such a way as to bring some of its moral and economic power to bear on those who want to maintain the status quo, keeping farm workers in virtual enslavement. In brief, here is what happened in Delano. Some years ago, when some of us were working with the Community Service Organization, we began to realize the powerful effect which the Church can have on the conscience of the opposition. In scattered instances, in San Jose, Sacramento, Oakland, Los Angeles and other places, priests would speak out loudly and clearly against specific instances of oppression, and in some cases, stand with the people who were being hurt. Furthermore, a small group of priests, Frs. McDonald, McCollough, Duggan and others, began to pinpoint attention on the terrible situation of the farm workers in our state.

At about that same time, we began to run into the California Migrant Ministry in the camps and fields. They were about the only ones there, and a lot of us were very suspicious, since we were Catholics and they were Protestants. However, they had developed a very clear conception of the Church. It was called to serve, to be at the mercy of the poor, and not to try to use them. After a while this made a lot of sense to us, and we began to find ourselves working side by side with them. In fact, it forced us to raise the question why OUR Church was not doing the same. We would ask, "Why do the Protestants come out here and help the people, demand nothing, and give all their time to serving farm workers, while our own parish priests stay in their churches, where only a few people come, and usually feel uncomfortable?"

It was not until some of us moved to Delano and began working to build the National Farm Workers Association that we really saw how far removed from the people the parish Church was. In fact, we could not get any help at all from the priests of Delano. When the strike began, they told us we could not even use the Church's auditorium for the meetings. The farm workers' money helped build that auditorium! But the Protestants were there again, in the form of the California Migrant Ministry, and they began to help in little ways, here and there.

When the strike started in 1965, most of our "friends" forsook us for a while. They ran—or were just too busy to help. But the California Migrant Ministry held a meeting with its staff and decided that the strike was a matter of life or death for farm workers everywhere, and that even if it meant the end of the Migrant Ministry they would turn over their resources to the strikers. The political pressure on the Protestant Churches was tremendous and the Migrant Ministry lost a lot of money. But they stuck it out, and they began to point the way to the rest of the Church. . . .

Then the workers began to raise the question: "Why ministers? Why not priests? What does the Bishop say?" But the Bishop said nothing. But slowly the pressure of the people grew and grew, until finally we have in Delano a priest sent by the new Bishop, Timothy Manning, who is there to help minister to the needs of farm workers. His name is Father Mark Day and he is the Union's chaplain. *Finally,* our own Catholic Church has decided to recognize that we have our own peculiar needs, just as the growers have theirs. . . .

When poor people get involved in a long conflict, such as a strike, or a civil rights drive, and the pressure increases each day, there is a deep need for spiritual advice. Without it we see families crumble, leadership weaken, and hard workers grow tired. And in such a situation the spiritual advice must be given by a *friend,* not by the opposition. What sense does it make to go to Mass on Sunday and reach out for spiritual help, and instead get sermons about the wickedness of your cause? That only drives one to question and to despair. The growers in Delano have their spiritual problems . . . we do not deny that. They have every right to have priests and ministers who serve their needs. BUT WE HAVE DIFFERENT NEEDS, AND SO WE NEEDED A FRIENDLY SPIRITUAL GUIDE. And this is true in every community in this state where the poor face tremendous problems.

But the opposition raises a tremendous howl about this. They don't want us to have our spiritual advisors, friendly to our needs. Why is this? Why indeed except that THERE IS TREMENDOUS SPIRITUAL AND ECONOMIC POWER IN THE CHURCH. The rich know it, and for that reason they choose to keep it from the people.

The leadership of the Mexican-American Community must admit that we have fallen far short in our task of helping provide spiritual guidance for our people. We may say, "I don't feel any such need. I can get along." But that is a poor excuse for not helping provide such help for others. For we can also say, "I don't need any welfare help. I can take care of my own problems." But we are all willing to fight like hell for welfare aid for those who truly need it, who would starve without it. Likewise we may have gotten an education and not care about scholarship money for ourselves, or our children. But we would, we should, fight like hell to see to it that our state provides aid for any child needing it so that he can get the education he desires. LIKEWISE WE CAN SAY WE DON'T NEED THE CHURCH. THAT IS OUR BUSINESS. BUT THERE ARE HUNDREDS OF THOUSANDS OF OUR PEOPLE WHO DESPERATELY NEED SOME HELP FROM THAT POWERFUL INSTITUTION, THE CHURCH, AND WE ARE FOOLISH NOT TO HELP THEM GET IT. . . .

Therefore, I am calling for Mexican-American groups to stop ignoring this source of power. It is not just our right to appeal to the Church to use its power effectively for the poor, it is our duty to do so. It should be as natural as appealing to government . . . and we do that often enough.

Furthermore, we should be prepared to come to the defense of that priest, rabbi, minister, or layman of the Church, who out of commitment to truth and justice gets into a tight place with his pastor or bishop. It behooves us to stand with that man and help him see his trial through. It is our duty to see to it that his rights of conscience are respected and that no bishop, pastor or other higher body takes that God-given, human right away.

Finally, in a nutshell, what do we want the Church to do? We don't ask for more cathedrals. We don't ask for bigger churches or fine gifts. We ask for its presence with us, beside us, as Christ among us. We ask the Church to *sacrifice with the people* for social change, for justice, and for love of brother. We don't ask for words. We ask for deeds. We don't ask for paternalism. We ask for servanthood.

11. LUIS FONTÁNEZ, "THE THEOLOGY OF SOCIAL JUSTICE" (1974)

The black theology of liberation had its counterpart among Latinos. Inspired by the activism of César Chávez and the Chicanismo movement of the 1960s (the approximate Latino equivalent to Black Power), Christians of Spanish-speaking descent forged their own theological formulations. Unlike the African American struggle, which emerged within a deeply Protestant (especially Baptist) context, Latino theologians mostly lived within the realm of the Church universal, Catholicism, a fact that significantly influenced their theology. For while blacks had a long tradition of independent churches, and black Christian culture was acknowledged to be significant and distinctive unto itself, Hispanics were faced with a Church historically dominated by Euro-American (especially Irish American) priests. "Why do many want to de-Hispanicize and to Americanize us?" Luis Fontánez asks. "What crime is there in being Hispano?"

The church, in its redemptive concern, has the responsibility of liberating the person from sin, but it also has to try to liberate those structures and institutions where sin originates and flourishes. Love of neighbor does not mean avoiding confrontations, but means trying to liberate the oppressed from the oppressor, and the oppressor from ambition for power and selfishness. The church thus exists for the complete liberation of humanity from all slavery, whether motivated by hardness of heart or by the injustice of the social environment. Every conversion is influenced by socioeconomic conditions, politics, and factors which are cultural and human, wherever they occur. If these structures are not changed, true conversion is impossible. . . . The church, in its redemptive function of liberating humanity, has to consider new structures, new institutions and relations, as well as different attitudes which not only reach a conversion of hearts, but also bring about a social transformation. . . .

Justice assumes its fullness only in love, since each person is both a visible image of the invisible God and a brother or sister of Christ. The Christian has to find in each person the same God in his continuous demand for justice and love. We are not going to find this God except in our encounter with the poor, with the needy, with the oppressed, who constitute our neighbor. We have the actual presence of our neighbor around the corner: in those workers enslaved and oppressed by the power of ambition and selfishness, in those immigrants, called "illegal criminals," whose only crime has been the "exodus" from certain conditions of oppression in search of "bread" and the "staff of life," and those others, farm workers who are reduced to kissing the feet of their bosses, in order that they be permitted to breathe; this is a neighbor stripped of every sense of dignity and reduced to the condition of a slave.

This present reality of our situation, by the light of faith, has to carry us to the core of the Bible message in order that a consciousness of the authenticity of the gospel and its demands be created. This gospel of Jesus Christ demands of us a commitment to the liberation of humankind, but if this message of love and justice is not crystallized in our activity, in our works on behalf of justice, this message will lose any semblance of credibility. It is not enough to say that the love of God and the love of neighbor are inseparable. This love has to show itself in works on behalf of the oppressed.

Christ gave to the church the great mission of bringing the Good News of Salvation to everyone, the building up of the community of brotherhood, but this requires justice as base and foundation for its existence. For this reason, when the rights of its members and their salvation are violated, the church has the obligation to proclaim justice and denounce injustice. In this way, the church will be witness in the world of the message of love and justice proclaimed by the gospel. But where is the church? Why are the cries of denunciation on behalf of the helpless not heard? Our Hispano families are at the edge of despair; our children are being annihilated by those who make of youth a market place of personal profit; and our women are converted into guinea pigs in experiments to reduce and even eliminate the continuance of the Hispano family in the United States, most especially in this Northeast region. Denunciation, with all possible courage and with all our might, is indispensable against all injustice, never forgetting, however, our deepest sense of charity and our position as Christians. . . .

The church, as the presence of the liberating action of Christ, has to offer opposition to every practice of racial discrimination and discrimination against minorities. We know that great injustices have been committed against Hispanos, and that if it is to be the light and love of the world, the church has to respond to these injustices. Help for our Hispano community is imperative, as much in the spiritual order as in the material, if we are to acquire the dignity and the status that belong to us in the church. Thus we can enrich others with our rich and beautiful culture. Why do many want to de-Hispanicize and to Americanize us? What crime is there in being Hispano? We are Hispanos and we want to be Hispanos, with all the pride that it requires, because thus God the Father Almighty created us, and we love our parents and forebears.

12. VINE DELORIA JR., *GOD IS RED* (1973)

Vine Deloria, a scholar of Native American history and religions, deliberately adapted James Cone's title "God is Black" for his classic work God is Red *in 1973. The work arrived on the heels of a standoff between Indian activists in AIM (the American Indian Movement) and federal authorities at Wounded Knee. At that site in South Dakota in 1890, the U.S. Army had butchered hundreds of Indian "ghost dancers" in an incident often seen as the "last" of the Indian wars of the nineteenth century. Here, Deloria thoughtfully explores what it means for Indian people to search for meaning in their tribal religions, given their (often) Christian educations and given the secularization and techno-rationalism of the modern world. "As they search for religious experiences to make them whole again," he concludes, Indians will "discover the fascination and familiarity of tribal religions," just as whites unsettled by the social revolutions of the 1960s were seeking spiritual wholeness outside of a Christianity that could "no longer provide a comprehensible picture of either man or the world."*

⌘

We have just begun to see the revival of Indian tribal religions at a time when the central value of Indian life—its land—is under incredible attack from all sides. Tribal councils are strapped for funds to solve pressing social problems. Leasing and development of tribal lands is a natural source of good income. But leasing of tribal lands involves selling the major object of tribal religion for funds to solve problems that are ultimately religious in nature. The best example of this dilemma is the struggle over the strip-mining at Black Mesa on the Navajo and Hopi reservations. Traditional Indians of both tribes are fighting desperately against any additional strip-mining of the lands. Tribal councils are continuing to lease the lands for development to encourage employment and to make possible more tribal programs for the rehabilitation of the tribal members.

A substantial portion of every tribe remains solidly within the Christian tradition by having attended mission schools. They grew up in a period of time when any mention of tribal religious beliefs was forbidden, and they have been taught that Indian values and beliefs are superstitions and pagan beliefs that must be surrendered before they can be truly civilized. They stand, therefore, in much the same relationship to the tribal religion as educated liberals now stand to the Christian and Jewish religions. Both groups have lost their faith in the mysterious, the transcendent, the communal nature of religious experience. They depend on a learned set of ethical principles to maintain some semblance of order in their lives.

A great many Indians reflect the same religious problem as do the young whites who struggled through the last several decades of social disorder. They are somehow forced to hold in tension beliefs that are not easily reconciled. They have learned that some things are true because they have experienced them, that others are true because everyone seems to agree that they are true, and that some things are insoluble and cannot be solved by any stretch of the imagination.

One of the primary aspects of traditional tribal religious has been the secret ceremonies, particularly the vision quests, the fasting in the wilderness, and the isolation of the individual for religious purposes. This type of religious practice is nearly impossible today. The places currently available to people for vision quests are hardly isolated. . . .

If modern conditions were not sufficient to prevent the continuance of traditional ceremonies, the U.S. Supreme Court has made it almost impossible to perform some ceremonies on federal lands. In 1988 in *Lyng v. Northwest Indian Cemetery Protective Association,* the Court dealt with the question of whether the Forest Service could construct a 6-mile segment of road for the convenience of the logging industry in the high country of Northern California where the Yurok and Karok tribes traditionally conducted religious ceremonies. Relying on the American Indian Religious Freedom Resolution, the Indian demonstrated to the Forest Service and to the lower courts that to construct the road would damage the traditional religion beyond repair. Yet the Court turned away their argument noting that it could not order the government to protect a religion of this kind. The majority decision compared it to a sudden rush of religious feeling by someone who had gazed upon the Lincoln Memorial, a dreadful and perhaps deliberate misunderstanding of the religious principles involved. . . .

Tribal religions thus face the task of entrenching themselves in a contemporary Indian society that is becoming increasingly accustomed to the life-style of contemporary America. While traditional Indians speak of a reverence for the earth, Indian reservations continue to pile up junk cars and beer cans at an alarming rate. While traditional Indians speak of sharing the structure of jobs, insurance, and tribal politics, education prohibits a realistic sharing. To survive, people must in effect feed off one another, not share with each other. . . .

One of the greatest hindrances to the reestablishment of tribal religions is the failure of Indian people to understand their own history. The period of cultural oppression in its severest form (1887–1934) served to create a collective amnesia in contemporary people. Too many Indians look backward to the treaties, neglecting the many laws and executive orders that have come to define their lives in the period since their first relationship with the United States was formed. Tribal people are in the unenviable position of dealing with problems the origins of which remain obscured to them.

The disruptions of tribal religions for a period of fifty years have resulted in the loss of a well-accepted recent tradition of ceremonies, religious leaders, and other ongoing developments characterizing a living religion. Contemporary efforts to reestablish tribal religions have come at too rapid a rate to be absorbed on many reservations. In some instances ceremonials are considered part of the tribal social identity rather than religious events. This attitude undercuts the original function of the ceremony and prevents people from reintegrating community life on a religious basis.

Most tribal religions, as we have seen, have not felt that history is an important aspect of religious life. Today as changes continue to occur in tribal peoples, the immediate past history of the group is vitally important in maintaining the nature of the ceremonies. The necessary shift in emphasis to a more historical approach can be seen in the various Indian studies programs that have attempted to fill in the missing tribal history. Indian tribal religions thus find themselves in the position of earlier Christian communities that were forced to derive historical interpretations to account for unfulfilled prophecies.

We may find the incongruous situation of many Indian people leaving Christianity to return to traditional religions, creating a tribal history to solve social problems, and falling into the historical trap that has plagued Christianity. It would seem that history itself is a deceremonial process that continues to strip away the mystery of human existence and replace it with intellectual propositions. As the mainstream of Christianity begins to face ecology and the problems inherent in its traditional doctrine of creation, tribal religions are running the risk of abandoning the traditional Indian concerns about the creation in favor of a more historical and intellectual religion.

Tribal religions in the old days did not create an external ethical system. Cultural considerations involving total tribal life enabled people to merge all societal functions into a unity from which all forms of behavior derived. With tribal members spread across the country today and the conditions on the reservations subject to radical shifting at every change of federal policy, there is not that continuity of experience or homogeneous community of people present that would enable Indian people to avoid creating ethical systems based on traditional values. . . .

One of the chief past functions of tribal religions was to perform healing ceremonies. This function was impaired by lack of any rights to train new people to perform the ceremonies and a general lessening of dependence on tribal medicine men because of the presence of Public Health Service hospitals on the larger reservations. Indian healers were generally considered as superstitious magicians by the missionaries and government officials, and healing arts were lost in many tribes.

Today healing remains one of the major strengths of tribal religions. Christian missionaries are unable to perform comparable healing ceremonies, and a great many still regard Indian healers as fakers and charlatans. This particular field is thus open for Indian religious figures who have received particular healing powers, and traditional healing ceremonies are being recognized by the Public Health Service as competent complementary healing practices. Some special grants have been given to train more healers and shamans and to have them work closely with doctors trained in internal medicine.

The modern world has lost a large number of healing medicines because of the arbitrary rejection of Indian religions. Some tribes had special roots and herbs that had amazing properties. Only a few have remained in use in some tribes while the vast majority have been lost for a number of reasons. Restriction of Indian people to the reservations has meant that long trips to particular places to gather specific kinds of roots and herbs have stopped. Gradually people have forgotten which plants were used for what purpose. As the older people have died off knowledge about a substantial number of medicinal plants has also been lost. . . .

Unless there is a determined effort to gather individual knowledge of healing plants, herbs, and earths as well as a general acceptance of the necessity of rebuilding tribal use of healing people, the impact of healing on Indian religions will continue to decline in spite of temporary successes. Perhaps religious healing will lose validity as a ceremonial experience in another generation.

A counterpart of the healing ceremonies are the rites performed by the religious practitioners that allow them to predict the future in part or in whole, to give advice on courses of action, and to give general advice and admonitions on a variety of subjects. Divination and foretelling the future were once major parts of religion; with the coming of Christianity, they appear to have lost their respectability. The result of this loss has been the survival of astrology, fortune-telling through cards, and the use of the I Ching in recent years in Western civilization. Discovering the future was once a major function of tribal religious leaders. It remains today as one of the major strengths of traditional religious people.

In the last two decades traditional healers have significantly increased the scope and depth of their ability to foretell the future. The impending earth catastrophes are appearing more and more in these rituals and this prospect had meant a great increase in the number of Indians returning to traditional ways. Unlike some Western efforts to predict specific personal fortunes, the information received by Indian religious leaders generally describes situations and conditions that are likely to come to pass, given existing circumstances. There is a sophisticated principle of probability here reminiscent of modern explanations of modern physics. So this aspect of tribal religion bears watching and reflection.

One can hardly speculate on either the problems or the changes this field will experience in the immediate future. The most important aspect that stands out is the insufficient number of people who can perform this special function. In many tribes it is a power given to people only after special ceremonies have been undertaken, and it is a power not always given. It would seem to be a gift most urgently needed by Indian people, as decisions of crucial importance are being forced on Indian people daily, particularly on tribal governments. . . . The big danger is that this gift, which must remain a property of the Indian community, may become part of the popular New Age activities and the Indian religious leaders will lose this talent by secularizing it.

The rapid expansion of the New Age physic phenomena has been unusually detrimental to traditional religions. Non-Indians can pay very attractive fees to Indian shamans, and there has been a good deal of pressure on traditional healers to spend their time working with non-Indians and neglecting their own communities. Unfortunately there have also been an unusual number of Indian fakers who have invaded suburbia offering to perform ceremonies, primarily sweat lodges, for anyone with the money to pay. A regular circuit has been established that these people tour in search of gullible whites. It should be clear to non-Indians that if shamans really had significant powers, they would obtain these powers through constant ceremonial practice in their homeland, and they would not be out hustling the workshop circuits. But the hunger for some kind of religious experience is so great that whites shown no critical analysis when approaching alleged Indian religious figures. . . .

The situation, however, is far from hopeless. On the reservations we are seeing amazing resiliency in restoring the old ceremonies. A massive shift in allegiance is occurring in most tribes away from Christianity and secularism and back towards the traditional ways. A surprisingly high percentage of Native American clergy are also doing traditional ceremonies and urban area churches are often the scene of traditional healing ceremonies. The Native American clergy are to be congratulated for their efforts to bring the two religious traditions together, but it is clear that no synthesis will take place. In almost every instance the effect of merging the two traditions is to bring attention to traditional ways to the detriment of the particular Christian denomination. The result is that the semblance of a national Indian religion is being born that incorporates major Indian themes. As people are sensitized to this new religious milieu, being dissatisfied with the lack of specificity in this religious activity, they return to the more precise practices of their own tribes. Thus, it appears that traditional religions in some form will transcend the inroads that contemporary American culture has made.

13. "A PUBLIC DECLARATION TO THE TRIBAL COUNCILS AND TRADITIONAL SPIRITUAL LEADERS OF THE INDIAN AND ESKIMO PEOPLES OF THE PACIFIC NORTHWEST" (1987)

In the 1980s and 1990s, white Christians, often stricken by guilt and shame when looking at the record of their churches in race relations, offered a number of public apologies and pleas for forgiveness. In 1995, for example, the Southern Baptist Convention issued an official apology to African Americans for the convention's role in defending slavery and segregation, a move that many critics saw as too little, too late but that was defended by others as a necessary public recognition of the church's central role in sacralizing Southern racism. Another effort came in this document, signed by major Protestant and Catholic leaders in the Northwest. They acknowledged the role of churches in abetting the "destruction of traditional Native American spiritual practices" and in ignoring the impact of injurious federal policies. These leaders recognized what Native Americans in the Northwest and elsewhere long had criticized: that policies upheld by both church and state intruded on lands held sacred by Native peoples, destroyed burial sites, and interfered with the free exercise of Native religions. A few years later, a writer for Christian Century *magazine, reflecting on the legacy of white-*

*native relations and recent efforts toward reparations, called for humbly listening to na-
tive voices and "making modest, specific commitments to help recover what the church
helped to destroy."*

⎯⎯⎯∞∞∞⎯⎯⎯

November 21, 1987

A PUBLIC DECLARATION TO THE TRIBAL COUNCILS AND TRADITIONAL SPIRITUAL LEADERS OF THE INDIAN AND ESKIMO PEOPLES OF THE PACIFIC NORTHWEST: C/O JEWELL PRAYING WOLF JAMES, LUMMI

Dear Brothers and Sisters,

This is a formal apology on behalf of our churches for their long-standing
participation in the destruction of traditional Native American spiritual practices. We call upon our people for recognition of and respect for your traditional ways of life and for protection of your sacred places and ceremonial objects. We have frequently been unconscious and insensitive and not come to
your aid when you have been victimized by unjust Federal policies and practices. In many other circumstances we reflected the rampant racism and prejudice of the dominant culture with which we too willingly identified. During
this 200th Anniversary of the United States Constitution we, as leaders of
our churches in the Pacific Northwest, extend our apology. We ask for your
forgiveness and blessing.

As the Creator continues to renew the earth, the plants, the animals and
all living things, we call upon the people of our denominations and fellowships to a commitment of mutual support in your efforts to reclaim and protect the legacy of your own traditional spiritual teachings. To that end we
pledge our support and assistance in upholding the American Indian Religious Freedom Act (P.L. 95–134, 1978) and within that legal precedent affirm
the following:

(1) The rights of the Native Peoples to practice and participate in traditional ceremonies and rituals with the same protection offered all religions
under the Constitution;

(2) Access to and protection of sacred sites and public lands for ceremonial purposes;

(3) The use of religious symbols (feathers, tobacco, sweet grass, bone, etc.)
for use in traditional ceremonies and rituals.

The spiritual power of the land and the ancient wisdom of your indigenous religions can be, we believe, great gifts to the Christian churches. We offer our commitment to support you in the righting of previous wrongs: to protect your peoples' efforts to enhance Native spiritual teachings; to encourage the members of our churches to stand in solidarity with you on these important religious issues; to provide advocacy and mediation, when appropriate, for ongoing negotiations with State agencies and Federal officials regarding these matters.

May the promises of this day go on public record with all the congregations of our communions and be communicated to the Native American Peoples of the Pacific Northwest. May the God of Abraham and Sarah, and the Spirit who lives in both the cedar and Salmon People, be honored and celebrated.

Sincerely,

The Rev. Thomas L. Blevins
Bishop, Pacific Northwest Synod
Lutheran Church in America

The Most Reverend Raymond G. Hunthausen
Archbishop of Seattle
Roman Catholic Archdiocese of Seattle

The Rev. Dr. Robert Bradford
Executive Minister, American Baptist
Churches of the Northwest

The Rev. Elizabeth Knott, Synod Executive
Presbyterian Church
Synod of Alaska-Northwest

The Rev. Robert Clarke Brock
Regional Minister
NW Regional Christian Church

The Rev. Lowell Knutson
Bishop, North Pacific District
American Lutheran Church

The Rt. Rev. Robert H. Cochrane
Bishop, Episcopal Diocese
of Olympia

The Most Rev. Thomas Murphy
Coadjutor Archbishop
Roman Catholic Archdiocese of Seattle

The Rev. W. James Halfaker
Conference Minister
United Church of Christ
Washington North Idaho Conference

The Rev. Melvin G. Talbert, Bishop
United Methodist Church
Pacific Northwest Conference

Chapter 4

Religion and Gender

FOR MUCH of American history, women have made up the majority of adherents in organized religious institutions. Women, moreover, have often been assigned the "role" of religion in socialization. In the nineteenth century, for example, the "separate spheres" ideology pervasive in Victorian America placed women on a moral pedestal, with the task of instilling moral and religious values in children, while men left the home to compete in the amoral world of business. Women were the unnamed leaders of the Second Great Awakening in the early nineteenth century. They brought sons, husbands, and other male relatives to church and to the altar.

However, until recent years women generally have been denied or given extremely limited access to positions of formal religious leadership in churches, cathedrals, synagogues, temples, seminaries, and schools. Religious traditions have developed elaborate arguments about men's place as leaders and theological specialists—as pastors, priests, rabbis, and educators. Drawing on the Bible and other sacred texts, church tradition, and broader cultural ideas of what comprises "masculine" and "feminine" traits, religious leaders have restricted the roles of religious leadership and specialization. Indeed, in the early twentieth century women in many Protestant denominations fought not for pastorates but simply for "laity rights," that is, the right to attend denominational meetings as full voting participants.

Following World War II, the nuclear family and its attendant gender dualism of male-breadwinner and female-homemaker defined white American conceptions of the good life (most women of color, by contrast, did not have the luxury to indulge in the pursuits of homemaking above breadwinning). Religious and political leaders preached the gender orthodoxy,

and argued that men and women filling their proper place in American society would determine the outcome of the Cold War struggle against communism. The 1950s were a boom time for American religion. More Americans claimed a belief in God and an official religious affiliation during this
decade than during any other in U.S. history.

The social movements of the 1960s challenged these conventions and
initiated a revolution in gender and religion. Just as in the civil rights movement, in which African Americans, Latinos, and other minorities claimed
their full citizenship rights, women seized on the inspiring rhetoric of freedom and democracy to compel a rethinking of religious ideologies, doctrines, and institutions that had limited or excluded them. The civil rights
and women's struggles were deeply connected not only in rhetoric but in the
very people who participated in both movements. Mary King, the daughter
of several generations of Southern Methodist ministers, joined the Student
Non-Violent Coordinating Committee in the early 1960s, a time she recounts in her autobiography *Freedom Song*, excerpted in the previous chapter. During King's years in SNCC, she increasingly questioned the way gender oppression infected even the civil rights crusade.

This chapter includes excerpts from discussions in which American
Protestant groups debated the entrance of women into the ministry. Some
church leaders upheld the pulpit as a divinely ordained male prerogative. Increasing numbers of liberal Protestants suggested that the notion of the
"call" to the ministry was not, and could not be, divided by gender, that the
apparent biblical injunctions mandating women's "silence" in the church
were specific instructions for some churches of the biblical world but could
no longer be used to prevent women's participation in religious leadership.
Also included in this chapter is a portion of the story of Pauli Murray, the
first woman to be ordained an Episcopal priest. A black woman originally
from North Carolina, Murray was a longtime civil rights activist, friend and
confidant of Eleanor Roosevelt, and lawyer. In the 1970s, as she entered her
sixties, Murray felt the call to the ministry, took a year of training at divinity
school, and waged a struggle to receive ordination, succeeding in 1977. Her
autobiography movingly tells of her lifelong struggles, the meaning of her
religious faith, and her joy at breaking through the "stained-glass ceiling."

In the feminist movement of the 1960s and 1970s, women decried the
historically sexist use of religious tradition, the masculine language that pervaded the hymns, sermons, and liturgy, and the way that religious institutions reinforced the oppression of women in American society. Those institutions responded, slowly and often hesitantly, and women gradually
entered more leadership positions (though many complained of limited opportunities in religious organizations).

Denominational committees altered hymns, liturgies, and biblical translations to conform to nonsexist language. Seminaries opened their doors to women, and when denominational institutions (such as the Southern Baptist Convention) remained resistant to women entering the ministry, individual churches created opportunities for women seeking to fulfill their call. Ministers, priests, and rabbis were given new directions for counseling women, in an age when the language of therapy and psychoanalysis shaped consciousness and counseling techniques.

In the 1970s, feminist thinking addressed deeper questions of religion and patriarchy, as many women challenged (and some rejected) the religious traditions in which they had been raised. Radical theologians such as Mary Daly began by calling for a theology "beyond God the father," that is, beyond normative patriarchal conceptions of God as a male head of household. They then assailed "God-talk" language as hopelessly masculinist and called for entirely new theologies and languages. Daly's 1983 work *Gyn/Ecology* employed a punning language of her own construction to signify her complete break from theological terminology of the past.

Other women left their traditional religions behind altogether in exploring alternative worlds of spiritual life. Many found that reimaging the divine was a necessary first step in this process. Much like black theologians, who wrote of what it meant for God to be black, female religious thinkers and practitioners reawakened Christian traditions of "the goddess" or goddesses, arguing that since "God" had been archetypically male, new terminology was needed for women on spiritual quests. For some women, "Goddess" simply became a female term for God, one that "brought out" the feminine in the Christian divine. For others, however, goddess talk attempted to revive ancient traditions of female deities of fertility and power, to visualize women's power through goddess imagery. Included in this section are documents from witches such as Starhawk (née Miriam Somos), neopagan ritualists, Jewish feminists, and a scholar of Vodou, all of whom write about recovering divine power through the power of the Divine Feminine.

It was a short step for many from Christian-tinged goddesses to pagan goddesses, and to what has come to be called the neopagan movement. In 1939 Wicca was founded by a group of English men and women interested in reviving and developing ancient traditions of witchcraft and pagan worship rituals. Wicca came to America in the 1960s and 1970s, and blossomed in the 1980s as a primary outlet for American neopaganism. Whereas it originated with men in England, however, in America it mostly attracts women. Indeed, many Wiccans see the faith as a pagan expression of feminism, one freed of hierarchical and masculinist Christian overlays, as may be seen in abundance on "The Witches' Voice," one of many Web sites available for modern pagans. As yet another alternative model for women's spir-itual expression, we have included an essay by Karen McCarthy Brown, a scholar of traditions in the Caribbean, who writes of marrying the "war God" as part of her research on the Vodou tradition. She found in this ritu-al an outlet for the anger and hostility built up in her personal and profes-sional life.

For women of color—black, Latina, Native American, and Asian—much of the discussion about women and religion was necessary but also to some degree painfully irrelevant. For black women, to cite one example, the kinds of female ritual, language, and bonding exemplified in Mary Daly's *Gyn/Ecology* simply missed the issues raised in their lives in the United States. Black female poet and essayist Audre Lorde responds to Mary Daly's work in a letter written originally to Daly privately and later published. Lorde queries and at points chastises Daly for implicitly using white women's lives as the model for all American women's experience, and using ethnocentric models for devising her feminist theology.

Black women's responses to feminism formed a basic core of critiques that soon spread to other communities of color. Alice Walker, a black novel-ist, coined the term "womanism" to refer specifically to black women's fem-inism. In an aphorism that soon became famous enough to be a cliché, Walker wrote, "womanist is to feminist as purple is to lavender." Among Latinas, "womanist" theology was retranslated as "*mujerista* theology" in the work of the theologian Ada Maria Diaz-Stevens, who has written of the ways ordinary Latinas (that is, women of Spanish-speaking descent, whether Mexican American, Central or Latin American, Cuban, Puerto Rican, or oth-er) conceive of God, Jesus, and the saints in their personal spiritual lives. The "patriarchy" spoken of by Daly and others took a particular form in the context of Hispanic Catholicism and family life, and required a particular Latina response, as evidenced in the selection below by Teresita Basso. Na-tive American women's voices are represented through a series of oral his-tory interviews with Native women in Oklahoma who write of their experi-ences in traditional religious rituals.

In the 1970s and 1980s, the reaction of the women's liberation move-ment to the strictures of American society produced an equal and opposite reaction among conservative women. While religious feminists isolated pa-triarchal religious structures as a grounding framework for gender oppres-sion, conservative women argued that these same structures were the source of meaning and purpose in their lives. While feminists labeled the nuclear family inevitably oppressive to women, conservative women trum-peted "family values" as a source for women's true power—as a moral force in the home. While feminists saw abortion rights (following the Supreme

Court's *Roe v. Wade* decision in 1973) as fundamental to women's liberation, conservative women saw "abortion on demand" as degrading to the most central role women played, as child bearers and caregivers. While feminists formed organizations such as NOW (National Organization for Women), conservative women counterattacked with their own organizations, such as the Eagle Forum (led by conservative women's activist Phyllis Schlafly) and Concerned Women of America (led by Beverly LaHaye, wife of religious Right leader Tim LaHaye). While feminist women read books such as Betty Friedan's *Feminist Mystique,* which outlined "The Problem That Has No Name," conservative women turned to their own literature, including Marabel Morgan's *Total Woman* and other manuals on Christian marriage and home. Documents from the conservative women's critique of the women's movement excerpted here include the Southern Baptist Convention resolution on "wifely submission," passed to considerable national attention in 1997 and drafted in part by Dorothy Patterson, wife of a fundamentalist leader of the convention. Next is a document from a Jewish woman, who writes of how the Orthodox Jewish tradition honors women by allowing them their modesty and privacy. Her work enunciates a theme common to critiques of feminist women's theology: that by trying to break free of the strictures of their religious traditions, women are losing the very power they seek to claim.

1. "THE METHODIST CHURCH DEBATES EQUALITY FOR WOMEN MINISTERS" (1956)

The following documents present a variety of perspectives on women and the ministry in the post–World War II era. Although the first officially sanctioned female minister, Antoinette Blackwell, was ordained in the nineteenth century, the clergy remained an almost exclusively male profession before World War II. Women struggled for voting rights in denominations, and access to the ministry, for the most part, was denied, with the notable exception of Pentecostal and Holiness groups. In the 1950s, controversies over women's ordination again arose among Methodists, Presbyterians, Lutherans, Baptists, and other groups. Church and denominational committees explored the issues; national conventions and convocations debated them; church people earnestly examined both biblical and practical perspectives. What did the Bible's words about women's submission to their husbands mean? Could a church close down if the female pastor went on maternity leave? Would the accession of more women to the pulpit exacerbate the already unbalanced sex ratios in most churches (the preponderance of female over male parishioners)? In the process of debating these issues, American Protestants fought some early battles that would later recur more widely in the feminist movement of the 1960s and 1970s.

In 1956, during the last debate surrounding the question of whether women should have full status in the Methodist Church, the issues were practical, not theological. A halfway measure was proposed by the Committee whereby only widowed and single women would have Conference membership, but even this was unacceptable to some. J. Dewey Muir presented a minority report.

The ability to preach and to give leadership in the Church is not in any sense determined by sex. This is acknowledged. That some women have done excellent and outstanding work and service, is recognized. Ability to preach, to give leadership, have little to do with the real issue of granting Full Ministerial Rights to Women.

The General Conference has been deluged with a multiplicity of Memorials dealing with this question. Not all of these Memorials were in agreement that Full Clergy Rights should be granted to women. Without examination, however, one might assume that the multiplicity of these Memorials is a mandate from the churches and Conferences.

Upon examination of these Memorials, because of their similarity of statement, one may well conclude that they have come from a limited segment of the Church. Since the burden of these Memorials has to do with Full Clergy Rights For Women, let us raise this question: what are Full Clergy Rights and how are they constituted?

Ministerial rights we believe are vested in ordination rather than in Conference membership. Ordination is now available to the women of Methodism. We remind you that ordination, either as Deacon or elder, gives to every recipient thereof, male or female, traveling preacher or local preacher, exactly the same rights, privileges, and prerogatives. There is no ministerial function or service which can be performed by an Ordained Elder who is a member of an Annual Conference, which cannot be performed by a Local Elder, man or woman.

The issue then becomes the sole matter of Ministerial Membership in an Annual Conference. It is the judgment of the Ministerial Members of the Committee on the Ministry that such request as has come before The General Conference is based upon a general theory that basically no privilege should be granted one sex which is denied to the other. In that noble sentiment we share. However, we are facing the realistic problems of administration of the law of the Church. It is at this point that our conclusion differs from the Majority Report.

We submit to you that the proposed legislation is an admission of the administrative problems involved, for it proposes that admission to Conference Membership shall be restricted to unmarried women and widows, and further provides that upon marriage, Conference Membership of a traveling woman preacher shall be discontinued.

We remind you that our traveling ministry operates within an appointive system in which [pastors minister] to churches where appointed, and churches accept pastors appointed to them. If the proposed legislation is enacted, let us not assume that women preachers will be sent to little churches, to undesirable churches, to undesirable circuits, or places no one else wishes to fill.

Rather, let it be assumed that any church to which a Bishop sees fit to appoint a Minister will accept that appointment without raising any question as to the sex of the Minister. In other words, admitting women to the traveling ministry ought never to be restrictive as to appointment, but open the way for appointment of a woman Minister to any church in Methodism. . . .

I am keenly aware of the problems involved in appointing some men to churches, yet no church has said, "No, we just do not want a man preacher." Yet in trying to appoint even good women ministers—and I remind you that I come from one of the Annual Conferences of Methodism which has in its ministerial membership a woman member, plus our quota of women who are Approved Supply Pastors—yet in trying to appoint good women pastors, ministers, it is not uncommon for the answer to be, "We just do not want a woman minister." . . .

Although many laywomen's organizations supported the proposed change, some women did not agree. . . .

For: Bishop, first of all I would like to say that I think this is a very serious question that is before us, and although we have had some funny things happening, I think we should consider it in a very serious light.

I would also like to say that as a woman, as a Local Preacher in my Church, I have never felt that my Church has discriminated against me, but that wherever I wanted to serve, there seemed to be a door opened to me, to be able to serve.

I would remind you all of the many times that you have sat in a meeting where you have been privileged to see great groups of Missionaries coming to the platform, as well as groups of Deaconesses, and we have been impressed by the great number of years of service that they have given to our Church. But we have also been impressed with the fact that many of these women are beyond 50 years of age and we do not seem to be able to attract the younger women to fill up the ranks.

Now, if I were a young woman and God was calling me into full-time Christian service, I feel that the Ministry would be a very attractive field for me. I won't go into all of the details as to why it would; but if we open up another field of service for our younger women, when at this time we do not have enough Deaconesses to work in our institutions and when we are bereft of those we need to fill up the ranks of the older Missionaries, I feel that we are making a big mistake.

I am not impressed, Bishop and Members of The Conference, Brothers and Sisters included, by the number of Memorials that have been sent in regard to this question, because I feel that many of them were sent in without the people realizing all that would be involved if this legislation were passed. I do know that of those that I have interviewed, and some in this very Conference, they said, "Yes, we are in favor of Full Clergy Rights For Women, but I don't want a woman minister serving our church."

Now, we do not want to discriminate further against our women, but if we enact such legislation we will find ourselves in the very embarrassing position of belittling many of our women who would be very glad to serve.

Now, there is an opportunity in our great Church for women to preach and we are very thankful for that. But before we vote on this question, those of us who might be tempted to vote to change our *Discipline* would have to answer yes to three very important questions, and I submit them in all seriousness.

First of all, if I voted yes, I would be able to say to my District Superintendent, "Yes, send me a Woman Pastor."

Secondly, the Ministers as well as the Laymen would have to say, "I am willing to serve under a woman District Superintendent," for if this goes through, we are not going to discriminate.

I do not like even to use the word "discrimination" because in my mind it has always been connected with unhappiness and discontent. I have never felt that I needed as a woman to fight for equal rights with men. I feel I have more rights than the men will ever have.

Furthermore, Bishop, my last question that I believe the Delegates of this Conference would have to answer in the affirmative if they vote yes, would be this: We are willing to elect a woman Bishop. Now, you may think that is rather exaggerated, but, believe me, it is not. You have had the reference to the power of womanhood. I leave that to your own thinking.

Against: I am President of the Conference Woman's Society of Christian Service. In considering women's place in the Church, since the early days when she was not even permitted to sit in the pew with the men of her family, to say nothing of having a voice in Church policy, to the turn of the century when she was gradually given more recognition, the present time finds women being given more recognition in all areas of service and meeting the same standards as men.

Membership in our Methodist Church has increased by nearly two million in the past fifteen years, and as a result is far short of ministers to stock adequately the churches and expand its Program. The reserve of well-trained women ministers is ignored because of tradition, thus losing valuable and much needed leadership.

Women are accepted as candidates for the ministry and are permitted to graduate from seminaries. They are permitted to perform all the services that men ministers perform, and they are required to attend the sessions of Annual Conference. The Lay Delegate is permitted to sit within the bower of the church and has the privilege of the floor; but the woman minister has no privileges. . . .

The churches which have given Full Clergy Rights to women have been greatly pleased with the results. The Methodist Church has always been able to adapt itself to change and should set an example in granting equal rights and opportunities of service to all its members, regardless of sex.

2. MARY DALY, *GYN/ECOLOGY* (1983)

In her seminal 1973 work Beyond God the Father: Toward a Philosophy of Women's Liberation, *Mary Daly enunciated themes and arguments that would dominate feminist theological thought for the remainder of the twentieth century. She hoped to tear theology free "from its function of legitimating patriarchy" and show how the women's movement was a "spiritual revolution" that could spark "creative action in and toward transcendence. . . . It has everything to do with the search for ultimate meaning and reality, which some would call God." Daly argued that far more than masculine language afflicted theology. Rather, theologies of "God" historically functioned to "legitimate the existing social, economic, and political status quo, in which women and other victimized groups are subordinate."*

Always evolving and self-critiquing, Daly in her next major work, Gyn/Ecology, moved beyond her previous notions of transforming the theological project. She now saw herself as a "Postchristian." She could no longer use words such as "God," since there was no way to remove masculine imagery from them, nor could she employ terms such as "androgyny" and "homosexuality," which by their very notions of "inclusion" were exclusive of women who wanted to break from old patriarchal patterns. She discarded old theological semantic baggage "so that Journeyers will be unencumbered by malfunctioning (male-functioning) equipment." Daly wrote for "the Hag/Crone/Spinster in every living woman," not for any mythical broader theological community, using a self-invented vocabulary that both exasperates and excites readers. Daly's work provided a theoretical and theological context for women who sought to explore a spirituality not defined by church fathers.

Going beyond *Beyond God the Father* involves two things. First, there is the fact that be-ing continues. Be-ing at home on the road means continuing to Journey. This book continues to Spin on, in other directions/dimensions. It focuses beyond Christianity in Other ways. Second, there is some old semantic baggage to be discarded so that Journeyers will be unencumbered by malfunctioning (male-functioning) equipment. There are some words which appeared to be adequate in the early seventies, which feminists later discovered to be false words. Three such words in *Beyond God the Father* which I cannot use again are *God, androgyny,* and *homosexuality.* There is no way to remove male/masculine imagery from *God.* Thus, when writing/speaking "anthropomorphically" of ultimate reality, of the divine spark of be-ing, I now choose to write/speak gynomorphically. I do so because *God* represents the necrophilia of patriarchy, whereas *Goddess* affirms the life-loving be-ing of women and nature. The second semantic abomination, *androgyny,* is a confusing term which I sometimes used in attempting to describe integrity of be-ing. The word is misbegotten—conveying something like "John Travolta and Farrah Fawcett-Majors scotch-taped together"—as I have reiterated in public recantations. The third treacherous term, *homosexuality,* reductionistically "includes," that is, excludes, gynocentric be-ing/Lesbianism. . . .

The Journey of this book, therefore, is (to borrow an expression from the journal *Sinister Wisdom*) "for the Lesbian Imagination in All Women." It is for the Hag/Crone/Spinster in every *living* woman. It is for each individual Journeyer to decide/expand the scope of this imagination within her. It is she, and she alone, who can determine how far, and in what way, she will/can travel. She, and she alone, can dis-cover the mystery of her own history, and find how it is interwoven with the lives of other women. . . .

The reader/Journeyer of this book will note that it is not addressed only to those who now call themselves members of "the women's community." Many women who so name themselves are Journeyers, but it is also possible that some are not. It seems to me that the change in nomenclature which gradually took place in the early seventies, by which *the women's movement* was transformed into *the women's community,* was a symptom of settling for too little, of settling *down,* of being too comfortable. I must ask, first, just *who* are "the women"? Second, what about *movement?* This entire book is asking the question of movement, of Spinning. It is an invitation to the Wild Witch in all women who long to spin. This book is a declaration that it is time to stop putting answers before the Questions. It is a declaration/Manifesto that in our chronology (Crone-ology) it is time to get moving again. It is a call of the wild to the wild, calling Hags/Spinsters to spin/be beyond the parochial bondings/bindings of any comfortable "community." It is a call to women who have never named themselves Wild before, and a challenge to those who have been in struggle for a long time and who have retreated for awhile. . . .

THE METAPATRIARCHAL JOURNEY OF EXORCISM AND ECSTASY

. . . The radical be-ing of women is very much an Otherworld Journey. It is both discovery and creation of a world other than patriarchy. Patriarchy appears to be "everywhere." Even outer space and the future have been colonized. As a rule, even the more imaginative science-fiction writers (allegedly the most foretelling futurists) cannot/will not create a space and time in which women get far beyond the role of space stewardess. Nor does this colonization exist simply "outside" women's minds, securely fastened into institutions we can physically leave behind. Rather, it is also internalized, festering inside women's heads, even feminist heads.

The Journey, then, involves exorcism of the internalized Godfather in his various manifestations (his name is legion). It involves dangerous encounters with these demons. Within the Christian tradition, particularly in medieval times, evil spirits have sometimes been associated with the "Seven Deadly Sins," both as personifications and as causes. A standard listing of the Sins is the following: pride, avarice, anger, lust, gluttony, envy, and sloth. The feminist voyage discloses that these have all been radically misnamed, that is, inadequately and perversely "understood." They are particularized expressions of the overall use of "evil" to victimize women. Our journey involves confrontations with the demonic manifestations of evil.

Why has it seemed "appropriate" in this culture that the plot of a popular book and film (*The Exorcist*) centers around a Jesuit who "exorcises" a girl who is "possessed"? Why is there no book or film about a woman who exorcises a Jesuit? From a radical feminist perspective it is clear that "Father" is precisely the one who cannot exorcise, for he is allied with and identified with The Possessor. The fact that he is himself possessed should not be women's essential concern. It is a mistake to see men as pitiable victims or vessels to be "saved" through female self-sacrifice. However possessed males may be within patriarchy, it is *their* order; it is they who feed on women's stolen energy. It is a trap to imagine that women should "save" men from the dynamics of demonic possession; and to attempt this is to fall deeper into the pit of patriarchal possession. It is women ourselves who will have to expel the Father from ourselves, becoming our own exorcists.

Within a culture possessed by the myth of feminine evil, the naming, describing, and theorizing about good and evil has constituted a maze/haze of deception. The journey of women becoming is breaking through this maze—springing into free space, which is an a-mazing process.

Breaking through the Male Maze is both exorcism and ecstasy. It is spinning through and beyond the fathers' foreground which is the arena of games. This spinning involves encountering the demons who block the various thresholds as we move through gateway after gateway into the deepest chambers of our homeland, which is the Background of our Selves. . . .

Spinsters can find our way back to reality by destroying the false perceptions of it inflicted upon us by the language and myths of Babel. We must learn to dis-spell the language of phallocracy, which keeps us under the spell of brokenness. This spell splits our perceptions of our Selves and of the cosmos, overtly and subliminally. Journeying into our Background will mean recognizing that both the "spirit" and the "matter" presented to us in the father's foreground are reifications, condensations. They are not really "opposites," for they have much in common: both are dead, inert. This is unmasked when we begin to see through patriarchal language. . . . "Texts" are the kingdom of males; they are the realm of the reified word, of condensed spirit. In patriarchal tradition, sewing and spinning are for girls; books are for boys. . . .

Women's minds have been mutilated and muted to such a state that "Free Spirit" has been branded into them as a brand name for girdles and bras rather than as the name of our verb-ing, be-ing Selves. Such brand names brand women "Morons." Moronized, women believe that male-written texts (biblical, literary, medical, legal, scientific) are "true." Thus manipulated, women become eager for acceptance as docile tokens mouthing male texts, employing technology for male ends, accepting male fabrications as the true texture of reality. Patriarchy has stolen our cosmos and returned it in the form of *Cosmopolitan* magazine and cosmetics. They have made up our cosmos, our Selves. Spinning deeper into the Background is courageous sinning against the Sins of the Fathers. As our senses become more alive we can see/hear/feel how we have been tricked by their texts. We begin unweaving our winding sheets. The process of exorcism, of peeling off the layers of mindbindings and cosmetics, is movement past the patriarch-ally imposed sense of reality and identity. This demystification process, a-mazing The Lies, is ecstasy. . . .

A-mazing Amazons must be aware of the male methods or mystification. Elsewhere I have discussed four methods which are essential to the games of the fathers. First, there is *erasure* of women. (The massacre of millions of women as witches is erased in patriarchal scholarship.) Second, there is *reversal*. (Adam gives birth to Eve, Zeus to Athena, in patriarchal myth.) Third, there is *false polarization*. (Male-defined "feminism" is set up against male-defined "sexism" in the patriarchal media.) Fourth, there is *divide and conquer*. (Token women are trained to kill off feminists in patriarchal professions.) As we move further on the metapatriarchal journey, we find deeper and deeper layers of these demonic patterns embedded in the culture, implanted in our souls. These constitute mind-bindings comparable to the footbindings which mutilated millions of Chinese women for a thousand years. Stripping away layer after layer of these mindbinding societal mental embeds is the a-mazing essential to the journey. . . .

Patriarchy is itself the prevailing religion of the entire planet, and its essential message is necrophilia. All of the so-called religions legitimating patriarchy are mere sects subsumed under its vast umbrella/canopy. They are essentially similar, despite the variations. All—from buddhism and hinduism to islam, Judaism, Christianity, to secular derivatives such as freudianism, jungianism, marxism, and maoism—are infrastructures of the edifice of patriarchy. All are erected as parts of the male's shelter against anomie. And the symbolic message of all the sects of the religion which is patriarchy is this: Women are the dreaded anomie. Consequently, women are the objects of male terror, the projected personifications of "The Enemy," the real objects under attack in all the wars of patriarchy.

Women who are willing to make the Journey of becoming must indeed recognize the fact of possession by the structures of evil and by the controllers and legitimators of these structures. But the solution is hardly "rebirth" (baptism) by the fathers in the name of male mating. Indeed, this "rebirth"—whether it is accomplished by the officially acknowledged religious fathers or by the directors of derivative secular organizations (e.g., television, schools, publishers of children's books)—is the very captivity from which we are trying to escape, in order to find our own origins. . . .

Women moving in this way are in the tradition of Great Hags. Significantly, Hags are commonly identified with Harpies and Furies. Harpies are mythic monsters represented as having the head of a woman and the body and claws of a vulture, and considered to be instruments of divine vengeance. As Harpies, Hags are workers of vengeance—not merely in the sense of re-venge, which is only reactionary—but as asserting the primal energy of our be-ing. The Furies were believed by the Greeks and Romans to be avenging deities. As Harpies and Furies, Feminists are agents for the Goddess Nemesis.

3. BEVERLY WILDUNG HARRISON, "THE POWER OF ANGER IN THE WORK OF LOVE: CHRISTIAN ETHICS FOR WOMEN AND OTHER STRANGERS" (1981)

Mary Daly's startling and pathbreaking books drew a huge variety of responses from enthusiasts, sympathizers, and harsh critics. Following are two of the most powerful and succinct, both sympathetic and appreciative but also critical. In the first piece, from her inaugural lecture as Professor of Christian Ethics at Union Theological Seminary in New York, Beverly Harrison wonders about the efficacy of Daly's apparent retreat (in Gyn/Ecology) into a "language of otherworldliness." However metaphorical such language might be, Harrison argues, it is still "misguided," for it ignores the need "for a moral theology shaped and informed by women's actual historical struggle." Daly's "inexhaustible" anger, the fount of so much creative work, could become destructive if it led women "to portray ourselves and other women chiefly as victims rather than those who have struggled for the gift of life against incredible odds." The "incredible collective power of women," Harrison concludes, belies Daly's retreat into an "Otherworldly Womanspace." This essay shows the creative ways in which Daly's ideas could be reshaped and adapted by contemporary women's theologians.

⸘

I cannot concur with Daly's call to women to abandon processions and join the "Journey to the Otherworld" of segregated feminism. The joyful world of Womanspace, which she commends to us as a permanent habitat, can be at best only an occasional sanctuary for the feminist *for whom life itself, and the embodied world of flesh and blood,* are the true gifts of God. For this reason the turn in Mary Daly's writing, marked by a new emphasis on the language of otherworldliness, disturbs me. In contrast to Daly, my basic ethical thesis is that women, and other marginated people, are *less* cut off from the real, material conditions of life than are those who enjoy the privileges of patriarchy and that, as a result, an otherworldly spirituality is far removed from the life experience of women. Even if Daly were clear, as I hope she is, that her use of the language of otherworldliness is metaphorical, her imagery still seems misguided. Our need is for a moral theology shaped and informed by women's actual historical struggle. Women's experience, I submit, could not possibly yield an "otherworldly" ethic. Nor can feminists ignore the growing but morally dubious fascination with forms of world-denying spirituality in our culture. In light of a massive trend toward escapist religiosity, Daly's imagery, even if it stems from poetic license, is dangerous. It gives aid and comfort to those who have very strong political and economic reasons to encourage a spirituality that does not focus on in-justice and the personal suffering it generates. . . .

Daly's metaphorical leap into Otherworldly Womanspace may well come from the real agony and pain she has experienced in the face of misogyny. The inexhaustibility of her rage suggests that this is so. However, a feminist metaethics must not fail to affirm and generate . . . power to affect the ex-isting world. We must wrest this power of action from our very rightful anger at what has been done to us and to our sisters and to brothers who do not meet patriarchy's expectations. The deepest danger to our cause is that our anger will turn inward and lead us to portray ourselves and other women chiefly as victims rather than those who have struggled for the gift of life against incredible odds. The creative power of anger is shaped by owning this great strength of women and of others who have struggled for the full gift of life against structures of oppression.

We need not minimize the radicality of women's oppression in varied cultures and communities nor minimize Christianity's continuing involve-ment in that oppression, but we must not let that recognition confirm us in a posture of victimization. Let us note and celebrate the fact that "woman-spirit rising" is a *global* phenomenon in our time. Everywhere women are on the move. Coming into view now, for the first time, on a worldwide scale, is the incredible *collective* power of women so that anyone who has eyes to see can glimpse the power and strength of women's full humanity. We dare not forget, in spite of the varied forms of women's historical bondage, that we have also been, *always*, bearers of many of the most precious and special arts of human survival. The Chinese revolutionary slogan "Women hold up half the sky" is not mere hyperbole. . . .

I believe we have a very long way to go before the priority of activity over passivity is internalized in our theology and even farther to go before love, in our ethics, is understood to be a *mode of action*. In *Beyond God the Father*, Mary Daly began the necessary theological shift by insisting that a feminist theism has no place for a God understood as stasis and fixity, that out of women's ex-perience the sacred is better imaged in terms of process and movement. Her proposal that God be envisaged as Be-ing, as verb rather than as noun, struck a deep chord in her readers, and not merely in her women readers.

Even so, Daly's reformulation does not seem to me even to go far enough. . . .

A feminist moral theology needs to root its analysis in this realm of rad-ical moral creativity. Such freedom is often abused, but the power to create a world of moral relations is a fundamental aspect of human nature itself. In my opinion, the metaphor of Be-ing does not permit us to incorporate the radicality of human agency adequately. *Do-ing* must be as fundamental as *be-ing* in our theologies. Both do-ing and be-ing are, of course, only metaphors for conceptualizing our world. Both are only "ways of seeing things." However, we can never make sense of what is deepest, "wholiest," most powerfully sacred in the lives of women if we identify women only with the more static metaphor of being, neglecting the centrality of praxis as basic to women's experience. We women have a special reason to appreciate the radical freedom of the power of real, concrete deeds.

4. AUDRE LORDE, "AN OPEN LETTER TO MARY DALY" (1979)

One of the best-known responses to Mary Daly's work, especially Gyn/Ecology, *came from the black lesbian poet and essayist Audre Lorde. In this open letter, first addressed privately to Daly herself, Lorde speaks not only to Daly but also to the larger white feminist community. She praises Daly's work for opening new vistas, but criticizes her for implying that "all women suffer the same oppression simply because we are women." Such a view, Lorde argues, ignores the broader context of the racial system in which patriarchy works; deeply embedded structures of racism are so tightly woven into the patriarchal strand that the two are nearly inseparable. She asks Daly to unearth her implicit assumption "that the herstory and myth of white women is the legitimate and sole herstory and myth of all women to call upon for power and background, and that non-white women and our herstories are noteworthy only as decorations, or examples of female victimization." Lorde's critique represented a broader notion among black women writers, intellectuals, and feminists, often called "womanism," which challenged white feminism to examine its own racially exclusivist assumptions and to recognize that white women, while experiencing gender oppression, nevertheless enjoyed the social benefits of "whiteness." Black women, accordingly, suffered from a "double bind," that of race and sex, a fact that white feminists too often ignored.*

———— ∞ ————

The following letter was written to Mary Daly, author of *Gyn/Ecology*, on May 6, 1979. Four months later, having received no reply, I open it to the community of women.

Dear Mary,

. . . When I started reading *Gyn/Ecology*, I was truly excited by the vision behind your words and nodded my head as you spoke in your First Passage of myth and mystification. Your words on the nature and function of the Goddess, as well as the ways in which her face has been obscured, agreed with what I myself have discovered in my searches through African myth/legend/religion for the true nature of old female power.

So I wondered, why doesn't Mary deal with Afrekete as an example? Why are her goddess images only white, western european, judeo-christian? Where was Afrekete, Yemanje, Oyo, and Mawulisa? Where were the warrior goddesses of the Vodun, the Dahomeian Amazons and the warrior-women of Dan? Well, I thought, Mary has made a conscious decision to narrow her scope and to deal only with the ecology of western european women.

Then I came to the first three chapters of your Second Passage, and it was obvious that you were dealing with noneuropean women, but only as victims and preyers-upon each other. I began to feel my history and my mythic background distorted by the absence of any images of my foremothers in power. Your inclusion of African genital mutilation was an important and necessary piece in any consideration of female ecology, and too little has been written about it. To imply, however, that all women suffer the same oppression simply because we are women is to lose sight of the many varied tools of patriarchy. It is to ignore how those tools are used by women without awareness against each other.

To dismiss our Black foremothers may well be to dismiss where european women learned to love. As an African-american woman in white patriarchy, I am used to having my archetypal experience distorted and trivialized, but it is terribly painful to feel it being done by a woman whose knowledge so much touches my own.

When I speak of knowledge, as you know, I am speaking of that dark and true depth which understanding serves, waits upon, and makes accessible through language to ourselves and others. It is this depth within each of us that nurtures vision.

What you excluded from *Gyn/Ecology* dismissed my heritage and the heritage of all other noneuropean women, and denied the real connections that exist between all of us.

It is obvious that you have done a tremendous amount of work for this book. But simply because so little material on nonwhite female power and symbol exists in white women's words from a radical feminist perspective, to exclude this aspect of connection from even comment in your work is to deny the fountain of noneuropean female strength and power that nurtures each of our visions. It is to make a point by choice.

Then, to realize that the only quotations from Black women's words were the ones you used to introduce your chapter on African genital mutilation made me question why you needed to use them at all. For my part, I felt that you had in fact misused my words, utilized them only to testify against myself as a woman of Color. For my words which you used were no more, nor less, illustrative of this chapter than "Poetry Is Not a Luxury" or any number of my other poems might have been of many other parts of *Gyn/Ecology*.

So the question arises in my mind, Mary, do you ever really read the work of Black women? Did you ever read my words, or did you merely finger through them for quotations which you thought might valuably support an already conceived idea concerning some old and distorted connection between us? This is not a rhetorical question.

To me, this feels like another instance of the knowledge, crone-ology and work of women of Color being ghettoized by a white woman dealing only out of a patriarchal western, european frame of reference. Even your words on page 49 of *Gyn/Ecology*, "The strength which Self-centering women find, in finding our Background, is our *own* strength, which we give back to our Selves," have a different ring as we remember the old traditions of power and strength and nurturance found in the female bonding of African women. It is there to be tapped by all women who do not fear the revelation of connection to themselves.

Have you read my work, and the work of other Black women, for what it could give you? Or did you hunt through only to find words that would legitimize your chapter on African genital mutilation in the eyes of other Black women? And if so, then why not use our words to legitimize or illustrate the other places where we connect in our being and becoming? If, on the other hand, it was not Black women you were attempting to reach, in what way did our words illustrate your point for white women?

Mary, I ask that you be aware of how this serves the destructive forces of racism and separation between women—the assumption that the herstory and myth of white women is the legitimate and sole herstory and myth of all women to call upon for power and background, and that nonwhite women and our herstories are noteworthy only as decorations, or examples of female victimization. I ask that you be aware of the effect that this dismissal has upon the community of Black women and other women of Color, and how it devalues your own words. This dismissal does not essentially differ from the specialized devaluations that make Black women prey, for instance, to the murders even now happening in your own city. When patriarchy dismisses us, it encourages our murderers. When radical lesbian feminist theory dismisses us, it encourages its own demise.

This dismissal stands as a real block to communication between us. This block makes it far easier to turn away from you completely than to attempt to understand the thinking behind your choices. Should the next step be war between us, or separation? Assimilation within a solely western european herstory is not acceptable.

Mary, I ask that you re-member what is dark and ancient and divine within yourself that aids your speaking. As outsiders, we need each other for support and connection and all the other necessities of living on the borders. But in order to come together we must recognize each other. Yet I feel that since you have so completely un-recognized me, perhaps I have been in error concerning you and no longer recognize you.

I feel you do celebrate differences between white women as a creative force toward change, rather than a reason for misunderstanding and separation. But you fail to recognize that, as women, those differences expose all women to various forms and degrees of patriarchal oppression, some of which we share and some of which we do not. . . .

The oppression of women knows no ethnic nor racial boundaries, true, but that does not mean it is identical within those differences. Nor do the reservoirs of our ancient power know these boundaries. To deal with one without even alluding to the other is to distort our commonality as well as our difference.

For then beyond sisterhood is still racism.

We first met at the MLA panel, "The Transformation of Silence Into Language and Action." This letter attempts to break a silence which I had imposed upon myself shortly before that date. I had decided never again to speak to white women about racism. I felt it was wasted energy because of destructive guilt and defensiveness, and because whatever I had to say might better be said by white women to one another at far less emotional cost to the speaker, and probably with a better hearing. But I would like not to destroy you in my consciousness, not to have to. So as a sister Hag, I ask you to speak to my perceptions.

Whether or not you do, Mary, again I thank you for what I have learned from you.

This letter is in repayment.

In the hands of Afrekete,
Audre Lorde

5. CYNTHIA OZICK, JUDITH PLASKOW, ELSYE GOLDSTEIN: JEWISH FEMINIST THEOLOGY (1979, 1983, 1981)

Much like women in other ethnic and religious traditions, Jewish women faced the dilemma of celebrating the strength of their own heritage while critiquing the sexist assumptions that constrained their lives and aspirations. In the following three short excerpts, Jewish feminist writers Cynthia Ozick, Judith Plaskow, and Elsye Goldstein reflect on what it means to be Jewish and a feminist in contemporary America. For Ozick, the Holocaust demands a rethinking of Jewish traditions: "The consciousness that we are the first generation to stand after the time of mass loss is knowledge that spills inexorably—how could it not?—into every cell of the structure of our lives." She insists that Jewish feminism arose not from the "influence" of the larger secular feminist movement—"as if Jewish steadfastness could be so easily buffeted by secular winds of power and pressure." Rather, Jewish feminism was about wanting equality "as Jews with Jews," over and above as women with men. By contrast, Judith Plaskow, arguing more in the Mary Daly vein, notes that the Jewish "tradition" honored and respected in synagogues and homes is a male one, a "cause and reflection both of the Otherness of women and the maleness of God." Jewish feminism must begin, she says, with a recognition of the "profound injustice of the Torah itself," its "assumption of the lesser humanity of women." Her argument parallels that made by Daly in Beyond God the Father. Finally, Elsye Goldstein, searching for the meaning of traditional Jewish customs such as the ritual bath following menstruation, finds reason to reappropriate a practice many feminists had found degrading: "To take back the water means to see mikvah as a wholly female experience: as Miriam's well gave water to the Israelites so too will the mikvah give strength back to Jewish women." Goldstein's essay fit into an emerging argument across many traditions, that rituals could be sources of power for women.

∞

CYNTHIA OZICK, EXCERPTS FROM "NOTES TOWARD FINDING THE RIGHT QUESTION" (1979)

In the world at large I call myself, and am called, a Jew. But when, on the Sabbath, I sit among women in my traditional shul and the rabbi speaks the word "Jew," I can be sure that he is not referring to me. For him, "Jew" means "male Jew." . . .

When my rabbi says, "A Jew is called to the Torah," he never means me or any other living Jewish woman.

My own synagogue is the only place in the world where I, a middle-aged adult, am defined exclusively by my being the female child of my parents.

My own synagogue is the only place in the world where I am not named Jew. . . .

Though we read in Scripture that Deborah was a judge in Israel, under post-Biblical halachic rules a woman may not be a witness. In this debarment she is in a category with children and imbeciles.

In the halachic view, a woman is not a juridical adult.

She is exempted from liturgical and other responsibilities that are connected with observing a particular practice at a specific time. This, it is explained, is a compassionate and sensible ruling. What? Shall she be obliged to abandon the baby at her breast to run to join a prayer quorum at a fixed hour? . . .

Young girls, older women, and unmarried women do not have babies at their breasts. Where is the extenuating ideal for them? They are "exempted"—i.e., excluded, debarred—from public worship all the same.

The halachic rationale for universal female exemption, however, is not based on compassion for harried mothers, nor is it, as some erroneously believe, related to any menstrual taboo. It rests on a single phrase—*kavod ha-tsibur*—which can be rendered in English as "the honor (or self-respect) of the community." One infers that a woman's participation would degrade the community (of men).

I am not shocked by the use of this rationale. (I *am* perhaps shocked at a halachic scholar of my acquaintance who refers to the phrase "the honor of the community" as a "concept that seems to defy comprehension.") Indeed, I welcome this phrase as wonderfully illuminating: it supports and lends total clarity to the idea that, *for Judaism, the status of women is a social, not a sacred, question.*

Social status is not sacral; it cannot be interpreted as divinely fixed; it can be repented of, and repaired. . . .

That these protests and claims are occurring in this generation and not in any earlier generation is *not* due to the parallel advent of a movement. The timing is significant: now and not forty years ago: but it is not the upsurge of secular feminism that has caused the upsurge of Jewish feminism.

The timing is significant because the present generation stands in a shockingly new relation to Jewish history. It is we who have come after the cataclysm. We, and all the generations to follow, are, and will continue to be into eternity, witness-generations to Jewish loss. What was lost in the European cataclysm was not only the Jewish past—the whole life of a civilization—but also a major share of the Jewish future. We will never be in possession of the novels Anne Frank did not live to write. It was not only the intellect of a people in its prime that was excised, but the treasure of a people in its potential. . . .

To think in terms of *having lost so much and so many* is not to "use" the Holocaust, but to receive a share in its famously inescapable message: that after the Holocaust every Jew will be more a Jew than ever before—and not just superficially and generally, but in every path, taken or untaken, deliberate or haphazard, looked-for or come upon.

The consciousness that we are the first generation to stand after the time of mass loss is knowledge that spills inexorably—how could it not?—into every cell of the structure of our lives. What part of us is free of it, or can be free of it? Which regions of discourse or idea or system can we properly declare to be free of it? Who would risk supposing that the so-called "women's issue" can be free of it?

Put beside this view, how trivializing it is to speak of the "influence" of the women's movement—as if Jewish steadfastness could be so easily buffeted by secular winds of power and pressure and new opinion and new perception. The truth is that it would be a blinding mistake to think that the issue of Jewish women's access to every branch and parcel of Jewish expression is mainly a question of "discrimination" (which, if that were all, *would* justify it as a feminist issue). No. The point is not that Jewish women want equality as women with men, but as Jews *with Jews*. The point is the necessity—*having lost so much and so many*—to share Jewish history to the hilt.

<hr>

JUDITH PLASKOW, "THE RIGHT QUESTION IS THEOLOGICAL" (1983)

The Jewish women's movement of the past decade has been and remains a civil-rights movement rather than a movement for "women's liberation." It has been a movement concerned with the images and status of women in Jewish religious and communal life, and with halakhic and institutional change. It has been less concerned with analysis of the origins and bases of women's oppression that render change necessary. It has focused on getting women a piece of the Jewish pie; it has not wanted to bake a new one! . . .

Our legal disabilities are a *symptom* of a pattern of projection that lies deep in Jewish thinking. They express and reflect a fundamental stance toward women that must be confronted, addressed and rooted out at its core. While it is Jewish to hope that changes in *halakhah* might bring about changes in underlying attitudes, it is folly to think that justice for women can be achieved simply through halakhic mechanisms when women's plight is not primarily a product of *halakhah*.

. . . The Otherness of women is also given dramatic expression in our language about God. Here, we confront a great scandal: the God who supposedly transcends sexuality, who is presumably one and whole, is known to us through language that is highly selective and partial. The images we use to describe God, the qualities we attribute to God, draw on male pronouns and male experience and convey a sense of power and authority that is clearly male in character.

The female images that exist in the Bible and (particularly the mystical) tradition form an underground stream that reminds us of the inadequacy of our imagery without, however, transforming its overwhelmingly male nature. The hand that takes us out of Egypt is a male hand—both in the Bible and in our contemporary imaginations. . . . The maleness of God is not arbitrary—nor is it simply a matter of pronouns. It leads us to the central question, the question of the Otherness of women, just as the Otherness of women leads to the maleness of God. . . . If God is male, and we are in God's image, how can maleness *not* be the norm of Jewish humanity? If maleness is normative, how can women not be Other? And if women are Other, how can we not speak of God in language drawn from the male norm? . . .

Women's greater access to Jewish learning, our increased leadership in synagogue ritual only bring to the surface deep contradictions between equality for women and the tradition's fundamental symbols and images for God. While the active presence of women in congregations should bespeak our full membership in the Jewish community, the language of the service conveys a different message. It impugns the humanity of women and ignores our experience, rendering that experience invisible, even in the face of our presence. . . . The equality of women in the Jewish community requires the radical transformation of our religious language in the form of recognition of the feminine aspects of God.

ELSYE GOLDSTEIN, "TAKE BACK THE WATERS" (1981)

As a feminist, I have struggled with the Jewish menstrual taboos for many years. Leviticus 25 prohibits a menstruating woman from touching her husband or even his things for seven days; while at the same time it proscribes her husband from even sitting on the same chair upon which she has sat. . . .

There can be no doubt that the mikvah has been tied to menstruation since the destruction of the Temple and the subsequent end of other types of "impurities." Therefore, while men may occasionally go to mikvah to prepare for Shabbat or festivals, or even, among the ultra-observant, after an involuntary nocturnal emission, they are never predictably and cyclically in need of cleansing. For men, mikvah is nonobligatory and going is an act usually unconnected to their biologies or their marital status. Add to this the dirty and dark atmosphere of mikvaot in poor immigrant neighborhoods when our mothers grew up, fostering in them a fear and loathing of the whole process which we have inherited. Now add the English Biblical translation of a menstruating woman as "unclean" or "impure." Add our grandmother's "meises" about not touching a Torah during that time of month. . . . Then add one more piece of fuel to the fire: that mikvah has been the domain of married women only. It is inexorably linked to having a husband, to making oneself ready to return to sexual relations with one's male partner, to being connected to a man. Divorced and single women, even though menstruating, are not to go to mikvah, according to tradition—because no matter how we try to skirt the issue, no matter how we rewrite history or remake images, the bottom line is that mikvah is seen as the last necessary step before resuming sexual relations within a heterosexual marriage, a step commanded by God. . . .

Why then was I, a Reform rabbi and committed feminist, splashing around in the mikvah? Was I going to make myself "kosher" for my new husband? Hardly. For me, it was an experience of reappropriation. The mikvah has been taken from me as a Jewish woman by sexist interpretations, by my experiences with Orthodox "family purity" committees who run communal mikvaot as Orthodox monopolies, by a history of male biases, fears of menstruation and superstitions. I was going to take back the water.

To take back the water means to see mikvah as a wholly female experience: as Miriam's well gave water to the Israelites so too will the mikvah give strength back to Jewish women. Water is the symbol of birth—now it can be a symbol of rebirth. To take back the water means to open the mikvah up to women not attached to men. In order to do that we may have to build alternative mikvaot, run by women, for women, following women's rules, not funded or run "behind the scenes" by male rabbis with family purity laws or their own denominational territories to protect. . . .

But why bother at all to take back the water? Why not simply abandon an institution which has been used to debase us? Because we have so little that is ours. We put on a *tallis* but in doing so we share a man's ritual garb. The water is ours: it is the fluid of our own bodies and a deeply moving experience of connection to Mother Earth. We climb the top of Masada in Israel and there we see a mikvah. It is our Jewish history.

So there we were: washing away past relationships, past hurts. As we prepared, we sang; one friend washed my hair, another rubbed my feet. When I entered the water, they all entered with me. I began with a chant: May my *tevilah* (immersion) cleanse me of past wrongs. . . . May it cleanse me of grudges toward past loves. . . . May it cleanse me of pain from past loves. . . . May it cleanse me of the times I have hurt past loves. . . . May it move me in the future. . . . May my *tevilah* connect me to other women. . . . May it strengthen my commitment to women's causes. . . . May it bring out the goodness of woman in me. I dipped and sang out the traditional blessing, not meekly and with arms covering my breasts as the attendant would have liked, but in a clear, loud song. And I dipped again and again, saying "Amen, May it be Your will," as each friend offered her prayer, her wish for my future life. The attendant grew weary of what she thought were antics—yet we continued in this deeply spiritual vein long after she left. It was a moment which inspired me. It was a moment I shall never forget. It was a moment of taking back what was mine a long time ago, offering a new wisdom of the water which can be uplifting for all women.

6. SHAINA SARA HANDELMAN, "MODESTY AND THE JEWISH WOMAN" (1981)

Just as conservative Protestant and Catholic women responded to feminism and other social revolutions with a vigorous defense of orthodoxy and traditional women's roles in the home and religious institutions, here Shaina Handelman defends Jewish scripture and tradition from the critiques launched by theologians such as Judith Plaskow. Far from seeing the Torah (the Jewish scripture) as oppressive to women, Handelman insists that it teaches modesty and inwardness, prime spiritual values "in contrast to the prevailing norms of contemporary culture, where self-advertisement and public recognition are emphasized." Women who seek leadership roles, she suggests, violate the precepts of the Torah, modesty and "inward spirituality." Moreover, laws of family purity and the mikvah (postmenstrual bath) reflect "the concept of the holiness of the physical, and not the reverse." Handelman's defense of the Jewish tradition and scripture parallels arguments made by women in other religious traditions.

In the value-system of Torah, that which is most precious, most sensitive, most potentially holy is that which is most private—in the spiritual as well as the physical realms. The holiest objects, such as the scrolls of Torah, are kept covered. In Torah, "modesty," "inwardness" is a prime spiritual value in contrast to the prevailing norms of contemporary culture, where self-advertisement and public recognition are emphasized. . . .

Though men and women are both obligated in prayer, men's obligation is more rigidly and communally defined and required at certain times, and consequently the public functions of the synagogues are more men's province, for the synagogue is the place of communal worship. The synagogue, notwithstanding its importance, has not been, however, the center of Jewish life. Today in America, though, when so little of the practice of Judaism is left in the home—which has been as much if not more the "spiritual center" of Jewish life and is called a "Miniature Temple"—and when the day-to-day lives of so many Jews are devoid of Jewish observance, the synagogue has been made into the only place where Torah can be found, certainly a mistaken idea and one all too similar to non-Jewish ideas about "Houses of Worship."

Though its nature is communal, the synagogue is not a place where there should be competition for public recognition, between men or between men and women. The greatest rabbis of the past had to be begged to assume synagogue positions, so much did they shy away from all manner of public recognition. . . .

Thus, in truth, withdrawal and separation are ultimately deeper, subtler *modes of revelation*, modes through which the most profound intimacy and union is made possible, be it between G-d and the world, or woman and man. Indeed G-d's relation to the Jewish people is compared to that of husband and wife.

The Torah's laws of Family Purity and *mikvah* reflect this concept of a rhythm of intimacy and separation between man and woman corresponding to the times of the month when the potential for new life is most real, and when that potential is lost. The laws of Family Purity are a profound reflection of the concept of the holiness of the physical, and not the reverse, as is so often not understood. Though the subject requires much further explanation and study, briefly stated, man and wife are forbidden to each other during the woman's menstrual period and for a week thereafter. After her immersion in a *mikvah* (ritual bath), they are permitted to resume relations. These laws were never meant to ostracize women or make them feel unclean. On the contrary, in part they demand that the couple be able to relate on a non-physical as well as physical level. . . . The laws of Family Purity ensure that even the most powerful of physical drives be touched with an awareness of holiness. . . .

7. SOUTHERN BAPTISTS ON WIFELY SUBMISSION (1998, 2002)

In their massive annual conventions, Southern Baptists, the largest Protestant denomination in the United States, pass resolutions indicating the sentiment of the gathering on a variety of issues. The resolutions are not binding on any individual church, but suggest the social beliefs of this important religious group. In recent years the SBC has garnered attention for a variety of controversial resolutions. One recommended a boy-

cott of Disney for its sponsorship of television shows featuring lesbian characters. The most widely discussed resolution, however, came in 1998, when SBC messengers endorsed a conservative reading of Ephesians 5:22, and advocated that wives "graciously" submit to their husbands in the household. Dorothy Patterson, a seminary educator well known nationally for her feisty public presence and for being the wife of a fundamentalist leader of the SBC, authored the resolution, and subsequently spearheaded the addition of an endorsement of wifely submission to the de facto theological creed of the Southern Baptists, the "Baptist Faith and Message Statement." In interviews following the convention, Baptist leaders demonized feminists who attacked the resolution and defended conservative positions generally summarized by the catchphrase "family values." In a piece explicating the resolution further, a Southern Baptist seminary professor explains the biblical meaning of "lordship" and "submission" and espouses their meaning for a materialistic and broken America.

FROM ARTICLE 18, BAPTIST FAITH AND MESSAGE STATEMENT: "THE FAMILY":

God has ordained the family as the foundational institution of human society. It is composed of persons related to one another by marriage, blood, or adoption.

Marriage is the uniting of one man and one woman in covenant commitment for a lifetime. It is God's unique gift to reveal the union between Christ and His church, and to provide for the man and the woman in marriage the framework for intimate companionship, the channel for sexual expression according to biblical standards, and the means for procreation of the human race.

The husband and wife are of equal worth before God, since both are created in God's image. The marriage relationship models the way God relates to His people. A husband is to love his wife as Christ loved the church. He has the God-given responsibility to provide for, to protect, and to lead his family. A wife is to submit herself graciously to the servant leadership of her husband even as the church willingly submits to the headship of Christ. She, being in the image of God as is her husband and thus equal to him, has the God given responsibility to respect her husband and to serve as his helper in managing the household and nurturing the next generation.

Children, from the moment of conception, are a blessing and heritage from the Lord. Parents are to demonstrate to their children God's pattern for marriage. Parents are to teach their children spiritual and moral values and to lead them, through consistent lifestyle example and loving discipline, to make choices based on biblical truth. Children are to honor and obey their parents.

———— ⌾⌾⌾ ————

"BAPTIST FAITH AND MESSAGE: ARTICLE 18: THE FAMILY."

Sep 10, 2002

By William Cutrer
LOUISVILLE, Ky. (BP)— . . . The importance of the marriage relationship unfolds symbolically in the Old Testament with God as husband and Israel as wife, and in the New Testament with Jesus as the bridegroom and the church as the radiant bride. Clearly, marriage and family are distinctly theological.

A healthy home has deep spiritual dimensions, and thus the Bible instructs us concerning the family. We as believers must look first to Jesus Christ, our bridegroom, to engage and understand the divine design for marriage. God's perspective always places greater emphasis on character and motivation than merely on outward conduct. Thus, as Jesus described himself as gentle and humble in heart, always acting in a manner pleasing to the Father, the family provides the altar of transformation where we learn to love and to live like Jesus.

God reveals himself as a relational being, and we are created in his image for lasting, intimate relationships—first with God himself, and then with others. Our love and understanding of God find expression in our love for people, with family relationships being the deepest and most precious.

God's ideal for the home—an intimate relationship that brings deep soul satisfaction to both husband and wife—models grace and faith for the children and proclaims to a lost and lonely world the type of love that God has for his people. This intimacy extends from a spiritual foundation through a relational sphere and culminates in the physical expression within the bounds of marriage. . . .

The Scriptures give unique imperatives—directed to the husband, the wife and the children—that detail the incarnation of submission. The godly husband will nourish and cherish his wife, loving her "as Christ loved the church and gave Himself for her." The spiritual husband is a submissive servant of Christ, humble, gentle, faithfully putting his wife's welfare and needs above his own. The godly wife will respect and honor her own husband, submitting to him "as unto the Lord." Her character and conduct can draw even an unbelieving husband to faith.

For each the Lord Jesus is the motivation and object of an obedient life. Each recreates the very picture of Christ's love for his people as he willingly gave up his life for his beloved. Both husband and wife, absolute equals before the Lord, fix their eyes first upon him and then upon each other. Obedience for the Christian is neither optional, selective, nor conditional upon the spouse's response or behavior.

Should God bless such a household with children, they will witness daily submission and godly love as they are charged to obey their parents "in the Lord." Jesus, the perfect bridegroom and the central focus of each command, radiates his love to the family and through each member to the world.

The family of God operates in direct opposition to our culture and our natural tendency to self-centeredness, self-absorption and self-gratification, and requires the supernatural enablement of the Holy Spirit. The theology of family is characterized by each member outdoing the other in service, in sacrifice, in submission to the Lord, reflecting gratitude for God's faithful, intimate love toward us

8. PAULI MURRAY, "A STUMBLING BLOCK TO FAITH" (FROM *SONG IN A WEARY THROAT*, 1987)

Pauli Murray (1909–1985) lived a remarkable life as a civil rights activist, early feminist, scholar, lawyer, teacher, political candidate, author, professor, and finally, in her last ten years, Episcopalian minister. From the time she wrote a letter of frustration to President Roosevelt in 1938, she was also a correspondent and friend to Eleanor Roosevelt, who was her husband's emissary to the black community. In the 1960s, Murray attended law school at Yale. During the civil rights years, she combined her twin interests in advancing the status of African Americans and of women. In the 1970s, she felt called to take ordination in the Episcopal Church, and entered intensive study in seminary at the age of 63. She and other early female ministerial applicants raised a storm of controversy in the Episcopal Church and other denominations, but Murray was no stranger to such contention, nor to rejected applications and conservative resistance. She had, after all, applied for graduate school training at the University of North Carolina as early as the 1930s, and spent time in jail in 1940 for protesting outrageous treatment of black defendants in court cases in Virginia. Murray received her ordination in 1977, becoming the first female Episcopal minister, all the more remarkable given her status as an African American, her age, and her varied career up to that point. In this selection, Murray reflects on the frustrations she experienced as a believer denied

full privileges in her communion, and on the solace and strength that her faith afford-
ed at the same time.

———◦⦵◦———

Inevitably, my growing feminist consciousness led me to do battle with the Episcopal Church over the submerged position of women in our denomination. Challenging inequalities in religious life was much more difficult than challenging similar inequalities in the secular world, because church practices were often bound up with questions of fundamental faith, insulating them from attack. An aura of immutability surrounded the exclusion of women from the clergy, reinforced by a theology which held that an exclusively male priesthood was ordained by almighty God. Other privileges enjoyed by males—lay participation in the liturgy and governance of the church—carried the weight of centuries of custom.

As a child growing up in the church, I knew that I could never be privileged to carry the cross or serve at the altar as an acolyte. Only boys were permitted to do so. I grudgingly accepted these limitations, suppressing my resentments and serving in the capacities open to me—as choir member, Sunday school teacher, member of the Altar Guild, and occasional organist. I was vaguely aware that women did not serve on vestries or other governing bodies of the church, and I responded to this lack of representation when I became an adult by a studied indifference to church organization. I confined myself to attending worship services and remained aloof from parish life. My feelings toward the church were ambivalent. I could neither stay away entirely nor enter wholeheartedly into Christian community. . . .

I do not know why this familiar spectacle suddenly became intolerable to me one Sunday morning in March 1966. I doubt that Rosa Parks could explain why on December 1, 1955, she rebelled against the segregation she had endured all her life. I remember only that in the middle of the celebration of the Holy Eucharist an uncontrollable anger exploded inside me, filling me with such rage I had to get up and leave. I wandered about the streets full of blasphemous thought, feeling alienated from God. The intensity of this assault at the deepest level of my devotional life produced a crisis in faith. . . .

Similar changes were beginning to come about in other congregations. We had no Episcopal Women's Caucus in the 1960s to exert organized pressure for change, but here and there individual women who felt as I did were speaking out. As in secular life, linkages were being formed, and although we did not define what was happening to us, as we reached out to one another we were finding authentic ministries among ourselves years before they were validated by the official church. In some respects the women's movement was also an ecumenical religious movement, and the term "sisterhood" had religious as well as political meaning. . . .

If in 1966 anyone had spoken of a "call" to the ordained ministry with reference to me, I would have reacted with a feeling akin to terror. At the time, I would even have protested the idea of a lay ministry, for like many people who compartmentalize human experience into separate spheres labeled sacred and secular, I associated ministry with a holiness I could never attain, worldly as I am, and I shrank from any identification with the concept. But in the turbulent decade between the filing of that committee report and the action of the General Convention of the Episcopal Church in September 1976 approving the ordination of women to the priesthood, my own life was undergoing profound changes which nudged me closer to the vocation I dared not acknowledge. . . .

By strange coincidence, when the shattering news of Dr. King's slaying came over the radio on the evening of April 4, 1968, I happened to be reading the final chapters of *The Autobiography of Malcolm X* and had just finished a passage written shortly before Malcolm's own assassination in 1965. Malcolm had observed:

> Sometimes, I have dared to dream to myself that one day, history may even say that my voice . . . helped to save America from a grave, possibly even a fatal catastrophe.
>
> The goal has always been the same, with the approaches to it as different as mine and Dr. Martin Luther King's non-violent marching, that dramatizes the brutality and the evil of the white man against defenseless blacks. And in the racial climate of this country today, it is anybody's guess which of the "extremes" in approach to the black man's problems might personally meet a fatal catastrophe first—"non-violent" Dr. King, or so-called "violent" me.

The prophetic power of Malcolm X's reflection was staggering. I had not been a passionate admirer of Dr. King himself because I felt he had not recognized the role of women in the civil rights movement (Rosa Parks was not even invited to join Dr. King's party when he went abroad to receive the Nobel Peace Prize), but I was passionately devoted to his cause. Beneath the numbness I felt after that fatal evening was the realization that the foremost advocate of nonviolence as a way of life—my own cause—was stilled and those who had embraced Dr. King's religious commitment to nonviolence were called upon to keep his tradition alive and to advance the work for which he gave his life. . . .

[Murray then went to seminary.]

Those three years of seminary subjected me to the most rigorous discipline I had ever encountered, surpassing by far the rigors of my law school training. For most people, I think, seminary is an intensely intellectual and emotional experience of living with others in close quarters while dealing with imponderables and the ambiguities of human existence. It brings to the surface hidden doubts about religious faith as well as fears, insecurities, and unresolved problems. One's personality is under the continuous scrutiny of instructors and schoolmates as well as under constant self-examination. In addition to daily devotions and corporate worship, seminarians have to absorb an immense body of learning. Throughout the process they have to satisfy various layers of the church hierarchy not only that they are academically competent but also that the spiritual formation essential to a priestly calling is plainly evident in their bearing.

Women seminarians were in a peculiarly ambiguous position in the mid-1970s. Although we were formally accepted as candidates for a degree and for ordination to the diaconate, we were the center of bitter controversy, the targets of veiled and sometimes overt hostility. Our numbers were few and our presence in a community designed for men only was more tolerated than encouraged. . . . My legal training was a mixed blessing; when it contributed to clarity of expression, my forensic approach was disturbing in a theological setting. My natural tendency to probe and debate an issue collided with some of the instructors' concepts of being "pastoral," and I soon got a reputation for being "abrasive," a view some professors, believing such a character trait would hinder my ministry, insisted upon expressing in my evaluation report at the end of my first year. . . .

Given my volatile temperament, it was providential that I did not go to the General Convention of 1973. I was too new a postulant to risk a rebuff at the outset of the long road to ordination. By not going I was less battered than the women who went with such fervent hope. This became evident when I attended a weekend conference of women seminarians and deacons shortly after the Convention, to consider future strategy. Many of the women were seething with anger and pain. . . .

The rawness of these wounds was so distressing that in the closing session I felt compelled to say that the church was losing its authority as a Christian body and that it was no longer speaking with an authentic voice if women were treated as outcasts when they sought to answer God's call to the priesthood. At that session we met jointly with a few key men who supported us, and I was struck by the contrast between each group's approach to the issue. While the women stressed the moral wrong of exclusion from ordination, the male priests were pragmatic and toughminded, concerning themselves with ways to enlist the support of influential bishops, clergy, and strategic laypersons to ensure victory for the ordination of women at the next general convention, which would meet in Minneapolis in 1976.

I left the conference troubled because I saw no long-range plan of action directed toward the next convention. But action of a different sort was soon forthcoming. In mid-December, five male deacons were ordained to the priesthood at the Cathedral of Saint John the Divine in New York City. At the ceremony five women deacons whose qualifications were identical to those of their brethren—except for their sex—also presented themselves in vestments to Bishop Paul Moore, Jr., for ordination. Women at General Seminary had been alerted that this public "witness" would take place, and several of us attended the service to give our sisters spiritual and moral support.

It was the first of several dramatic confrontations in the Episcopal Church during the next three years as the women's ordination issue rocketed into the news and almost split the church apart. When the women deacons knelt before Bishop Moore in silent appeal just before the consecration, he told them sadly, "Go in peace, my sisters." Rejected at the altar, they turned and walked with bowed heads in solemn procession down the center aisle. No funeral procession could have been more sorrowful. . . .

The incident had immediate repercussions at General Seminary, where the community divided into warring camps. Heated exchanges took place in the corridors and in the refectory. Some male seminarians condemned the women's action as a scandal. Some who had shown lukewarm support for women's ordination now railed against using a "civil rights demonstration" tactic which, they felt, had no place in the solemn liturgy of the church. Others contented themselves with hostile stares at those of us who supported the women deacons by our presence at the ordination service. I learned that disputes among the faithful, although usually fought with polite words, can be as acrimonious in their language as a street brawl.

At times, when theological arguments were invoked against the ordination of women, I shuttled between faith and inner doubt. These arguments carried the force of a two-thousand-year tribal taboo and were so deeply embedded in the psyche that on the morning of July 29, 1974, when I took the train to Philadelphia to attend the ceremony in which eleven women deacons were ordained priests without the official approval of their own bishops, I experienced sudden terror. . . .

In Philadelphia, we joined a throng of two thousand people from many parts of the country, who crowded into the Church of the Advocate to witness a dramatic turning point in the struggle for women's ordination. None of us knew what to expect, although there were rumors that dissidents might try to disrupt the proceedings by seizing upon a rarely used provision in the order of service, in which the bishop says to the people, "if any of you know any impediment or crime because of which we should not proceed, come forward now, and make it known." When this point was reached in the Philadelphia ordinations, a few male priests fairly screamed their objections. Their hysterical outburst was received calmly, and when they had left the church the ceremony continued with customary beauty and solemnity. By the end of the service the joyous spirit that enveloped the congregation swept away all my doubts as to the rightness of the action taken that day. . . .

This ordination was historic in more than one respect. It took place in a church in the heart of the Philadelphia ghetto, and a Negro congregation was the host. Symbolically, the rejected opened their arms to the rejected. . . .

Several days before [my] ordination, I was suddenly seized by an agony of indecision, as though I had been assaulted by an army of demons. The thought that the opponents of women's ordination might be right and that I might be participating in a monstrous wrong terrified me. As a sister priest put it later, speaking of herself, "I felt that God might strike me dead before it happened." I have since been told by other priests, male and female, that they faced a similar ordeal just before their ordination, but at the time I thought this ambivalence was peculiar to me, so personal that I dared not speak to anyone about it. I prayed fervently for some sign that I was doing God's will.

January 8 was a bitter-cold, gray morning in Washington, with ice and snow covering the ground, but three thousand or more people packed the Washington National Cathedral, a number of them my relatives and close friends. As was customary, a long procession of vested clergy walked down the aisle, followed by the lay presenters (or sponsors) of the ordinands. Then those of us who were being ordained proceeded to our individual prayer desks, which were arranged in a semicircle around the Great Transept, and the participating clergy and elaborately robed bishops continued up into the chancel. The familiar liturgy moved forward majestically through the presentation, declaration of vows, litany for ordination, sermon, examination, and consecration. I was the last of the six to be consecrated, and was told later that just as Bishop Creighton placed his hands upon my forehead, the sun broke through the clouds outside and sent shafts of rainbow-colored light down through the stained-glass windows. The shimmering beams of light were so striking that members of the congregation gasped. When I learned about it later, I took it as the sign of God's will I had prayed for. . . .

All the strands of my life had come together. Descendant of slave and of slave owner, I had already been called poet, lawyer, teacher, and friend. Now I was empowered to minister the sacrament of One in whom there is no

north or south, no black or white, no male or female—only the spirit of love
and reconciliation drawing us all toward the goal of human wholeness.

9. SISTER TERESITA BASSO, "THE EMERGING 'CHICANA'" (1971)

*Like black women, who wrote of the double bind of race and sex, Chicanas (a term for
Mexican American women that came to be preferred among politically active Latinos
in the 1960s) came to realize that they were in a double struggle of race and gender. In
the Catholic Church, home for the large majority of Mexican American Christians,
woman was viewed as "a helpless submissive creature incapable of self-determination."
Mexican American women who entered religious orders could not simply leave behind
their cultural heritage. The politically and culturally aware Mexican American nun,
Basso argues, would be compelled to recognize the urgency of the struggle of La Raza,
even to the point of building her life in the Church around it. Basso was one of the
founding members of Las Hermanas (Sisters), an organization of Spanish-speaking religious women serving in the Church in the United States. Las Hermanas provided a
means to pursue the larger good of the Hispanic community even while serving the
Church as an institution. Basso's struggles within the Church may be compared to
those of Daniel Berrigan, who addressed the question of how to engage in civil disobedience against the Vietnam War even while remaining true to the Church and the order (the Jesuits) that he loved.*

---

*When we are really honest with ourselves we must admit that our lives are all that
really belong to us. So it is how we use our lives that determines what kind of men
we are. It is my deepest belief that only by giving our lives do we find life. I am
convinced that the truest act of courage, the strongest act of manliness is to sacrifice ourselves for others in a totally nonviolent struggle for justice. To be a man is
to suffer for others. God help us to be men.* [quote by César Chávez]

I have chosen the preceding quote by César Chávez because, for me, it
epitomizes the role of the religious sister in the world today. Because I believe in the dignity of the human person, I have chosen to strive to live by
this principal through service to mankind. Since I believe that giving of
oneself is life-giving both for the giver and the receiver, religious life for
me has been the style of life which best allows me to live out this personal conviction.

As a result of my convictions, my experiences, in religious life, and especially my Mexican-American background, I have come to realize my

responsibility to that segment of society known as the Mexican-American people. The impact of this realization has led me to re-evaluate my identity as a "Chicana" religious woman in the decades of the sixties and the seventies and my responsibility as a visible representative of the Roman Catholic Church to the Mexican-American community. . . .

Upon entering religious life the Mexican-American sister just like the barrio child in the educational school system is placed in a middle-class Church oriented organization. If her background is that of a highly acculturated Mexican-American, her adjustment to and acceptance into this life style will not be as difficult as that of a less acculturated Mexican-American young woman. The latter will be placed in a situation where there is very little she can identify with. Those things of relevance in her life, such as, her family, her language, her life style, her work among her people, and her proximity to her environment are very distant in her newly acquired life style.

The Mexican-American sister, however, cannot totally divorce herself from her cultural heritage and whether she is allowed to live out her Mexican-American difference is yet another aspect of this identity conflict. Depending upon the religious congregations' attitude towards the culturally different, certain limitations will be placed on the Mexican-American sister's freedom to live out this difference. . . .

Now it is at this point that the Mexican-American religious woman must choose whether to identify with her people as "Chicana" or remain an acculturated Mexican-American. If she chooses to be known as "Chicana" it is because she is consciously aware of herself, her power of self-determination, as well as proud of her cultural heritage and experiences. Within her religious commitment, the people of La Raza will take priority while she seeks basic institutional changes because she senses the urgency and immediacy of bringing about this change. She begins to recognize who more than her own people, La Raza, are in need of her services. She realizes as the Chicana Sisters Organization in San Jose did:

- that the Church has fallen short in our task of helping provide spiritual and material guidance for our people and that there are hundreds of thousands who need our help.
- that our Mexican-American community has been exploited over the centuries by the established community and has been treated in a paternalistic manner by the Church.
- that the poverty and degradation in which a great number of our Mexican-American population live and the despair and lack of confidence into which they are forced.

- that the demands of social justice and equal rights have not been made available to our Mexican-American population.
- that the time is late—and that it is urgent that we immediately identify ourselves with the Chicano movement.

In recognizing her unique resources as a "Chicana" religious woman she realizes she is the one best able to understand her peoples' basic problems since she comes from the same culture. Necessary to the Chicana sister's reorientation is the simultaneous emerging ethnic awareness of the Mexican-American community. As the local Mexican-American communities become involved in barrio politics, the struggle for community control of health services, schools, welfare, and housing, boycotts for obtaining better wages and working conditions, and Chicano studies programs, the Chicana woman religious finds herself being affected by her people's struggles. She no longer can turn away or wait for the Church or government "structure" to meet these needs. She keenly feels deep distress and hurt at the general insensitivity of these organizations and at their lack of recognition of her peoples' plight. . . .

For the Chicana religious woman, this involvement with the Mexican-American community takes place within the context of her particular religious congregation. Here too, as in the Mexican-American community, the Chicana sister will be a great asset to her particular congregation if her community accepts her in her own culture. For the Chicana woman religious will feel much more loyalty than she would if her congregation restrained her and tried to make her something she is not. She is much more of an asset to her congregation if she feels this confidence in herself, if she feels this pride in herself, if she knows that her people need her because as Chicana she can help her people.

10. WOMEN IN NATIVE AMERICAN RELIGION AND HEALING (1967–69)

While women in Judeo-Christian traditions fought for recognition, ordination, and inclusion, American Indian women often had long and un-selfconsciously been practitioners of their own traditions, especially those involving healing. In the selections below, Native American women interviewed by oral historians recount stories from their own families and tribes about women involved in religious practices around healing (or "special doctoring"), vision quests, and other Indian ceremonial rituals.

THE MEDICINE BUNDLE

The following account of Myrtle Lincoln, an eighty-two-year-old Arapaho woman, was given in an interview December 22, 1969. Her story centers on the special care and taboos of the medicine bundle.

I don't know how many they had, but I know my mother-in-law had one. And we couldn't take the ashes out while that thing was in there. And it had a certain person that was blessed . . . to take it out. Nobody else couldn't touch that thing. My mother-in-law used to take it out before we take the ashes out. And we wasn't supposed to make a noise in there. And every morning when she gets up she'd take a hatchet and hit that tipi pole over there, so when those kids make a noise, well, it wouldn't bother that thing . . . She used to hit it . . . about four times and then . . . when these kids make a noise it wouldn't bother that medicine bag. Used to have to hit that pole every morning.

I don't know how she got it . . . at times she would get maybe tongue and then, you know, them shank bones, and put it on top of that medicine bag . . . She used to say she was feeding the spirit and then the next day she'd take it and cook it and we used to eat it.

It was just wrapped up . . . I never did touch it. I had a respect for that. I used to even keep my kids from running in and out from there.

They [were] not supposed to open them unless they were all together and somebody make a pledge. It took lot of things for them to open them. Never did see it opened. When she handled that thing we had to keep the kids quiet. It wasn't just so you could go over there and pick it up and all that. She used to pray before she touch it. Now when she's going to bring it in she prays . . . to the Lord.

When asked what happened to the mother-in-law's medicine bag, she answered:

I don't know . . . When the old man died and then she died, . . . none of us couldn't handle it. We left it at the house and I don't know who got it. I don't know who it could have went to. But my understanding was that Henry Lincoln and Chase Harrington—and there was a black man that used to stay around here. I guess they went after it and they sold it here in the drugstore. Here in Canton. And just think—all three of them were gone. One had a stroke and one didn't know where he was at. He was just out of his head. And he just talk until he died. And this black man, they had to take him to rest home. I guess he used to just scream and jump. See, that's what got them—because they bothered that medicine bag. . . .

*When asked if there were any reason why the medicine bundle would be
opened, she explained:*

If they made a pledge for some sick people—if their folks would get well,
and they want this one to be painted with whatever paint was in them—in
that bag. And they used to give horses and things and cook big dinner. And
maybe inside of this sweat lodge, that's where they open it. Nobody ever had
anything to do with it. They had a respect for it. They didn't make fun of it
or anything. In a way they had a respect for that and . . . nobody used to talk
about that. And now I'm crazy to be talking about it.

There [are] only two I knew something about. You know, I used to see
them when they take care of them. And when they take them out—when
they walk with them—they didn't walk fast. If you walk fast, well, the storm
used to come up. They used to be easy with them.

VISION QUEST

*Mary Poafybitty Neido, or Sanapia, the Comanche Eagle Doctor, tells about her
vision quest at age seventeen. The four-day ordeal required fasting and solitary
meditation while ghosts attempted to frighten and harass her to the point that she
would renounce her medicine. She relates in this account what was expected of
her. In spite of her failure to stay in the mountains for the required time, she
passed the test and was declared a full-fledged medicine woman.*

Just sit around, don't eat. You have to go out there by yourself and pray.
And then when you pray and then you come back . . . you have to go down
to the creek and wash all your sins away, something bad in you. You have to
go down to the creek and take a bath. And then they paint you . . . all your
face with red paint, you know, that rock paint that they grind, they put it all
over your face and your arms and your feet, from your knees down, they
paint you up like that.

They gave all that medicine to me. They showed me and they told me
how to run it and everything like that. They told me all about that before I
fasted. You supposed to go way up there in the hills and sleep up there by
yourself. But me I was afraid to go up there by myself. I was afraid to go up
there, but you supposed to go up there in the hills, and pray and cry and talk
and . . . somebody come to you. They say,

"Somebody will come to you way in the middle of the night. They going
to push you and kick you and they do things like that, but don't get scared.
Just lay there and let them do what they want to you—just kick you around

and slap you and all that. They fighting you for your medicine. They don't want you to have that. It's ghosts."

That's what they said.

I said, "I don't want to go up there. Them ghosts might catch me."

That's what I told them. I didn't want to go out. I didn't go out there. I was afraid to sleep up there in the mountains by myself. I just go up there and come back.

———— ∞ ————

GHOST SICKNESS

Ghost sickness was not generally prevalent in the Plains area, but ghosts sometimes struck particularly vulnerable Comanche and Kiowa-Apache persons by deforming them. The following account, which was recorded on June 15, 1967, is that of Sanapia, in which she describes the victims of ghost sickness.

[They had a] . . . twisted mouth and twisted eyes. Sometimes their eyes would go up on the left side this way and your mouth would be twisted the other way, and just look like your face get all twisted . . . They would be paralyzed on their arms, or the whole bottom half of their body and be twisted. And do you know what the Indians call that? They call it Ghost-Done-It. Ghost twisted person's face like that. In the night time they come right up on you. If you look at them like that they do that to you. The ghost. The Indians believe that. They believe they're ghosts.

When Sanapia agreed to treat a stricken individual, the person was required to bring a ritual payment consisting of dark green cloth, a commercially obtained bag of Bull Durham tobacco, and four corn-shuck cigarette "papers." She here describes how the contract with the patient was sealed and then gives a detailed account of the treatment. If this treatment failed, she then offered prayers from the Bible. And if this did not get the desired results, she held a special peyote meeting for the patient.

They would get this leaf or corn shuck and they roll their cigarette with that Bull Durham smoke. They wrap it up and light it and they give it to me and say,

"Here take this smoke. Pity me and get me well. I'm tired of this face all twisted up, tired of my legs paralyzed. I can't walk, can't do nothing. I want you to pity me and get me well."

And so I take it. I get a puff on it four times, just four times, and I say,

"Alright, I'll pity you. I'll see what I could do for you . . . Go in there and wash your face and your hands and you come and I'll doctor you."

Chew that medicine and put in on your hands and rub it like that (between the palms) and rub their face with it and their hands—out of my mouth what I chew this medicine . . . Then I would blow this medicine on their face and I would doctor them. Today I doctor three times, and tomorrow I doctor them three times, that's six. And if it's real bad I go ahead and doctor them till I doctor them eight times.

So, I start—tomorrow morning and noon and supper, and the next morning I'm through with them. Take them out there before daylight, and I do all the Indian ways what my mother and my uncle told me to do . . . And in the morning when they get up they ain't a thing wrong with them. They alright. Their face get alright. Their mouth get alright. They don't slobber no more. And then you bring the coals to the front of the house wherever they are, or go to the fireplace and put that cedar on there, and there's another kind of medicine that we mix together and then we just tell whoever it is that's sick—bend over like that. They inhale all that smoke. Take that feather and put it over the fire like that and smoke that feather—that's eagle feather. And take that and smoke that and we fan them all over from head to feet—all over their body. Four this way and four that way and turn around and eight in the back and on top of their head like that. Just fan that bad stuff away from them. That's what that smoke for. And after they do that, they alright. They get well.

11. STARHAWK, "WITCHCRAFT AND WOMEN'S CULTURE" (1977)

Within the Christian and Jewish traditions, feminist theologians challenged patriarchies, broke down barriers to women in the ministry, called for inclusive language in hymns and scriptures, and introduced new rituals more in touch with female ways of knowing the world and encountering the divine. Many women interested in spiritual explorations, however, simply rejected the traditions handed down to them, just as Mary Daly had come to reject the use of the word "God" as so hopelessly masculine as to be beyond repair. These women sought new rituals and symbols to encounter the Spirit; many of them found it in the image of the "Goddess," or what one practitioner summarized as the Goddess symbolizing "the divine within women and all that is female in the universe." Some of them insisted that God was a woman; others suggested that God was not gendered, but human beings inevitably imaged God as gendered. Many women associated themselves with ancient traditions of witchcraft, magic, and astrology, ways that women historically had exerted spiritual authority outside the structures of official religious institutions. Sometimes referred to as "neopagans," they invented new sets of rituals to celebrate women's bodies, connection to the earth, and ways of encountering the divine. Some founded religious organizations that convened annually in special locations, and described what they referred to as "thealogies" (substituting the "a" for the "o" in theology feminized the noun). Here, a well-known neo-pagan writer elaborates on the meaning of the Goddess image and on rituals that celebrate women's bodies.

From earliest times, women have been witches, *wicce,* "wise ones"—priestesses, diviners, midwives, poets, healers, and singers of songs of power. Woman-centered culture, based on the worship of the Great Goddess, underlies the beginnings of all civilization. . . .

Witchcraft, "the craft of the wise," is the last remnant in the west of the time of women's strength and power. Through the dark ages of persecution, the covens of Europe preserved what is left of the mythology, rituals, and knowledge of the ancient matricentric (mother-centered) times. . . .

The Goddess has at last stirred from sleep, and women are reawakening to our ancient power. The feminist movement, which began as a political, economic, and social struggle, is opening to a spiritual dimension. In the process, many women are discovering the old religion, reclaiming the word *witch* and, with it, some of our lost culture.

Witchcraft, today, is a kaleidoscope of diverse traditions, rituals, theologies, and structures. But underneath the varying forms is a basic orientation common to all the craft. The outer forms of religion—the particular words said, the signs made, the names used—are less important to us than the inner forms, which cannot be defined or described but must be felt and intuited.

The craft is earth religion, and our basic orientation is to the earth, to life, to nature. There is no dichotomy between spirit and flesh, no split between Godhead and the world. The Goddess is manifest in the world; she brings life into being, *is* nature, *is* flesh. Union is not sought outside the world in some heavenly sphere or through dissolution of the self into the void beyond the senses. Spiritual union is found in life, within nature, passion, sensuality—through being fully human, fully one's self.

Our great symbol for the Goddess is the moon, whose three aspects reflect the three stages in women's lives and whose cycles of waxing and waning coincide with women's menstrual cycles. . . .

The Goddess is also earth—Mother Earth, who sustains all growing things, who is the body, our bones and cells. She is air—the winds that move in the trees and over the waves, breath. She is the fire of the hearth, of the blazing bonfire and the fuming volcano; the power of transformation and change. And she is water—the sea, original source of life; the rivers, streams, lakes and wells; the blood that flows in the rivers of our veins. She is mare, cow, cat, owl, crane, flower, tree, apple, seed, lion, sow, stone, woman. She is found in the world around us, in the cycles and seasons of nature, and in mind, body, spirit, and emotions within each of us. Thou art Goddess. I am Goddess. All that lives (and all that is, lives), all that serves life, is Goddess.

Because witches are oriented to earth and to life, we value spiritual qualities that I feel are especially important to women, who have for so long been conditioned to be passive, submissive and weak. The craft values independence, personal strength, *self*—not petty selfishness but that deep core of strength within that makes us each a unique child of the Goddess. The craft has no dogma to stifle thought, no set of doctrines that have to be believed. Where authority exists, within covens, it is always coupled with the freedom every covener has, to leave at any time. When self is valued—in ourselves—we can see that self is everywhere.

Passion and emotion—that give depth and color and meaning to human life—are also valued. Witches strive to be in touch with feelings, even if they are sometimes painful, because the joy and pleasure and ecstasy available to a fully alive person make it worth occasional suffering. So-called negative emotion—anger—is valued as well, as a sign that something is wrong and that action needs to be taken. Witches prefer to handle anger by taking action and making changes rather than by detaching ourselves from our feelings in order to reach some nebulous, "higher" state.

Most of all, the craft values love. The Goddess' only law is "Love unto all beings." But the love we value is not the airy flower power of the hippies or the formless, abstracted *agape* of the early Christians. It is passionate, sensual, personal love, *eros*, falling in love, mother-child love, the love of one unique human being for other individuals, with all their personal traits and idiosyncrasies. Love is not something that can be radiated out in solitary meditation—it manifests itself in relationships and interactions with other people. It is often said "You cannot be a witch alone"—because to be a witch is to be a lover, a lover of the Goddess, and a lover of other human beings.

The coven is still the basic structure of the craft, and generally covens meet at the times of full moons and the major festivals, although some meet also on new moons and a few meet once a week. A coven is a small group, at most of thirteen members—for the thirteen full moons of the year. Its small size is important. Within the coven, a union, a merging of selves in a close bond of love and trust, takes place. A coven becomes an energy pool each member can draw on. But, because the group remains small, there is never the loss of identity and individuality that can happen in a mass. . . .

Covens are separate and autonomous, and no one outside the coven has any authority over its functioning. Some covens may be linked in the same tradition—meaning they share the same rituals and symbology—but there is no hierarchy of rule. Elder witches can and do give advice, but only those within the coven may actually make decisions.

Covens are extremely diverse. There are covens of hereditary witches who have practiced rites unchanged for hundreds of years, and covens who prefer to make up their own rituals and may never do the same thing twice. There are covens of "perfect couples"—an even number of women and men permanently paired, and covens of lesbian feminists or of women who simply prefer to explore women's spirituality in a space removed from men. There are covens of gay men and covens that just don't worry about sexual polarities. A few covens are authoritarian—with a high priestess or high priest who makes most of the decisions. (Coveners, of course, always have the option of leaving.) Most are democratic, if not anarchic, but usually older or more experienced members—"elders"—assume leadership and responsibility. Actual roles in rituals are often rotated among qualified coveners.

Rituals also vary widely. A craft ritual might involve wild shouting and frenzied dancing, or silent meditation, or both. A carefully rehearsed drama might be enacted, or a spontaneous poetic chant carried on for an hour. Everyone may enter a deep trance and scry in a crystal ball—or they may pass around a bottle of wine and laugh uproariously at awful puns. The best rituals combine moments of intense ecstasy and spiritual union, with moments of raucous humor and occasional silliness. The craft is serious without being dry or solemn.

Whether formal or informal, every craft ritual takes place within a circle—a space considered to be "between the worlds," the human world and the realm of the Goddess. A circle can be cast, or created, in any physical space, from a moonlit hillside to the living room of a modern apartment. It may be outlined in stones, drawn in chalk or paint, or drawn invisibly with the point of a sword or ceremonial wand. It may be consecrated with incense, salt water, and a formal invocation to each of the four quarters of the universe, or created simply by having everyone join hands. The casting of the circle begins the ritual and serves as a transition into an expanded state of consciousness. The power raised by the ritual is contained within the circle so that it can reach a higher peak instead of dissipating.

The Goddess, and if desired, the Horned God (not all traditions of the craft relate to the male force) can be invoked once the circle is cast. An invocation may be set beforehand, written out and memorized, but in our coven we find the most effective invocations are those that come to us spontaneously, out of the inspiration of the season, the phase of the moon, and the particular mood and energy of the moment. . . .

Chanting, dancing, breathing, and concentrated will, all contribute to the raising of power, which is the essential part of a craft ritual. Witches conceive of psychic energy as having form and substance that can be perceived and directed by those with a trained awareness. The power generated within the circle is built into a cone form, and at its peak is released—to the Goddess, to reenergize the members of the coven, or to do a specific work such as a healing.

When the cone is released, any scattered energy that is left is grounded, put back into the earth, by falling to the ground, breathing deeply, and relaxing. High-energy states cannot be maintained indefinitely without becoming a physical and emotional drain—any more than you could stay high on methedrine forever without destroying your body. After the peak of the cone, it is vital to let go of the power and return to a calm, relaxed state. Silent meditation, trance, or psychic work are often done in this part of the ritual.

Energy is also shared in tangible form—wine, cakes, fruit, cheesecake, brownies, or whatever people enjoy eating. The Goddess is invited to share with everyone, and a libation is poured to her first. This part of the ritual is relaxed and informally social, devoted to laughing, talking, sharing of news and any business that must be done.

At the end, the Goddess is thanked and bid farewell, and the circle is formally opened. Ending serves as a transition back into ordinary space and time. Rituals finish with a kiss and a greeting of "Merry meet, merry part, and merry meet again." . . .

Witches understand that energy, whether it is psychic, emotional, or physical, always flows in cycles. It rises and falls, peaks and drops, and neither end of the cycle can be sustained indefinitely, any more than you could run forever without stopping. Intense levels of energy must be released and then brought down and grounded; otherwise the energy dissipates or even turns destructive. If, in a ritual, you tried to maintain a peak of frenzy for hours and hours, you would find that after a while the energy loses its joyful quality, and instead of feeling union and ecstasy, you begin to feel irritated and exhausted. Political groups that try to maintain an unremitting level of anger—a high-energy state—also run out of steam in precisely the same way. Releasing the energy and grounding out allows the power itself to work freely. It clears channels and allows you to rest and recharge and become ready for the next swing into an up cycle. Releasing energy does not mean losing momentum; rather, real movement, real change, happens in a rhythmic pattern of many beats, not in one unbroken blast of static.

Craft rituals also add an element of drama and fantasy to one's life. They allow us to act out myths and directly experience archetypes of symbolic transformation. They allow us, as adults, to recapture the joy of childhood make-believe, of dressing up, of pretending, of play.

12. KAREN MCCARTHY BROWN, "WHY WOMEN NEED THE WAR GOD" (1984)

In the 1970s and 1980s, scholar Karen McCarthy Brown spent much time among practitioners of neo-African religions in the United States, culminating in the publication of her well-received study Mama Lola: The Life of a Voodoo Priestess in Brooklyn. *Her work coincided with a rapidly rising interest in spiritual possession, from its Protestant expression in Pentecostalism to neo-African religions such as the Cuban practice of Santeria. In this selection, Brown recounts her intellectual history researching Vodou and its close connection to the course of her personal life. She represents what became known as third-wave feminism, in which consciousness-raising and supportive networks gave way to personal quests for claiming internal power and authority. Brown tells of her encounter with (and metaphorical marriage to) the "war god" Ogou, and the way her experience empowered her to resolve internal conflicts and anger. Brown's essay contrasts strikingly with much of contemporary women's theology, which often emphasizes women's natural role as peacemakers and stresses feminine and maternal images of the divine.*

Locating and naming the legitimate sources of authority in our lives is a central and continuing problem for feminists. For those of us involved in religion, the quest for the authoritative is especially problematic. We have had to face the deep misogyny of scriptures, traditions, institutions, and leaders. We cannot easily go back to a naïve acceptance of any of these as authoritative on its own terms. Context and content, we have found, are too bound up with each other. We discovered that the antiwoman bias could not be removed from our religion in a once-and-for-all-time feminist chemical bath. Women have learned that the critique must be ongoing and the watchfulness constant. In order to do this we have had to locate an authoritative voice within ourselves, within our own experience. This is what gives us a place to stand as we carry on that critique. Thus, the authority of experience has emerged as one major tenet of feminism.

Out of this has grown a second: the personal, the political, and the spiritual are understood as dimensions of, or perspectives on, one reality. For me, these first two tenets of feminist thought have led to a third—the need for radical or deep pluralism. By deep pluralism, I refer to a style of understanding that holds multiple truths in dynamic tension. Deeply pluralistic thinkers eschew the grand systems, creeds, and philosophies that Westerners have traditionally used as safety nets under their varying experiences in the world. If truth begins in experience, then there must be many truths, for there are many life stories and many stories within a single life. Furthermore, many truths, held in creative tension and rooted in the deepest parts of one's being, may better equip one to handle the challenges and dangers of contemporary life than those great philosophical, political, and religious systems that, historically, have been able to define themselves only in opposition to other systems. Radical pluralism is not an easy stance toward the world, for there is no place to go "home" to when the crises of one's life demand security before anything else. . . .

With this prologue and in the context of a feminist critique of war, I relate a small, personal story, the story of my marriage to the Haitian Vodou God of war, Ogou. . . .

I have been doing research on Haitian Vodou for ten years. I began as a Ph.D. candidate, questions in mind, paper and pencil in hand. Gradually, I began to put away these things and let the Haitian community formulate questions as well as answers. More gradually I let go of my need to have verbal equivalents at all levels of understanding. . . .

Vodou is an ecstatic religion. It centers on trance and possession by the Gods. . . . In Vodou, one has contact with the Gods. They are available. They give advice, they hug; they can discipline and chastise. They are immediately present in possession-performance. By linking the word performance so closely to possession, I do not intend to signal that I think Vodou trance is not genuine. The trance state the worshiper experiences during possession is quite genuine, but Vodou possession does have a certain theater quality, in the best sense of theater: it is an acting out of a shared tradition. The roles are well known; the personae of the Gods are shared by all who participate. Whoever is possessed by a spirit improvises on a core understanding of who that particular spirit is.

The God I married is Ogou, and he comes from the Yoruba culture of Nigeria. He began as a spirit associated with iron workers. Smiths often had to travel great distances and fend for themselves in foreign territories. Ogou thus became a God associated with "the mobile, the marginal and the isolated," and his shrine, the smithy, became a place of refuge where enemies could not enter and local police forces could not arrest or seize. Out of such practices came the Ogou cult of modern Nigeria, which is perhaps the most rapidly growing traditional religion of contemporary Africa. In addition to

his connection with iron workers and the smithy, the African Ogou has tak-
en on a variety of other areas of life: war and weapons, anything having to
do with metal, and so all machines and modern technology. . . .

The different Ogou explore all aspects of hierarchy, war, and anger; of the
mentality of us-against-them; of the uses and abuses of power, aggression,
and self-assertion. . . . Each and every Ogou, regardless of which dimension
of the war-making spirit is dominant in his character, also embodies something of the other side of the coin. . . .

When people are possessed by Ogou, any of the Ogou, they do a kind of
theologizing with the body that is remarkable. It proceeds in three stages. In
the first stage, the Ogou are handed ritual swords, and they attack, raging
and bellowing around the temple, clanging their swords against pillars and
doorposts. In the second stage, those standing closest to the Ogou become
potential targets. While the Ogou do not actually harm anyone within the
temple in this stage of the possession, they do threaten them by swinging
their weapons perilously close to noses and buttocks. In the third stage, the
Ogou take the sword and turn it toward themselves. The first stage is attack
outward; the second threatens harm to the immediate community; the third
threatens the self. This is the basic choreography of war-making as understood by Haitian Vodouisants, and it is reiterated in myriad guises throughout the various and complex rituals performed for Ogou, God of war.

This is the God I married. Spirit marriages are common events in the
Vodou world. On my wedding day I wore a bright red dress and a red satin
kerchief on my head. There was a wedding cake, a marriage license, and
plenty of champagne. I wear his ring on my left hand as a reminder of the
pledge I made to Ogou that day.

My relationship with Ogou has become a problem for some of my feminist friends. One in particular has pushed hard: "Karen, what are you doing?
How can you have this relationship with—of all things!—a male War God?"
I chose this relationship and it chose me intuitively, for reasons that were
not articulate at the time. I had always said I would not participate in Vodou
out of anthropological curiosity alone. I felt that would show a lack of respect, although that was not the only reason I wanted to find a link between
Vodou and my own life. I knew that the Vodouisant brings her or his life
with all its knots and loose ends to the system, and unless I did the same, I
would not understand anything of its ability to take up a life and weave designs from it. I came to a crisis in my life, an abyss, a dark night. My marriage of eleven years was breaking up, and I was involved in a tenure battle
at my university. I was furious and hurt. I was angry at my husband and at
the institution of marriage. I was angry at some of my colleagues and at the

academic world. I was angry at myself and at women's position in the world. One day I found myself saying: "Karen, stop trying to get rid of this anger. Marry it!" I telephoned a Vodou priestess I knew in Brooklyn and said, "I am ready." And so I married Ogou. I stopped trying to be good, to be understanding, to get over my anger, to be superior to it. I claimed it as mine. It was a transformative experience.

It seems to me that the Gods of war are necessary as long as there is anger in our hearts and war in the world. I am drawn to religious systems that take up all the stuff of life, whole cloth, and bring it into a central, well-lighted place for mutual negotiation. This type of spirituality works for me because it is rooted in an essentially tragic vision of life, and I feel at home there. I do not think humanity is ever going to do away with war, although I can imagine it taking on quite different forms. I fervently hope we can avoid nuclear war. I will work for that. I do not think we are ever going to be rid of hierarchy, another of Ogou's central elements, but I hope we can learn to use hierarchy more responsibly, make hierarchies more flexible, make our critique more trenchant. I doubt we will ever have a world not characterized by some form of us against them thinking, although I hope we can find ways to understand one another better and to have more humane exchanges across the boundaries. I am thankful we will most likely not have to live in a world without self-assertion, anger, and energy. For me, the tragic vision is energizing, but not everyone must experience it my way.

There are idealistic rather than tragic visions; such spirituality can be very moving, very compelling, and of great transformative power. Women working with traditional Jewish and Christian models, as well as those who have recently reclaimed the goddess tradition, most often—although not always—speak from this idealistic, prophetic place, As those who have raised the children who have been victims of war, women are in a good position to condemn the values of the empire builders and assert their own more life-centered value system. The privilege in women's oppression is that we have not been, by and large, those responsible for death and destruction through war. Yet it would be a mistake to think that those who wage war do so out of a humanity essentially different from our own. I have held that particular truth in my own world through my marriage to the male God of war, Ogou. It would be a mistake in a feminist critique of war to paint women as only nurturers, only creative, just as it can be dangerous to attribute only goodness and light to the realm of the spirit. If we go too far in that direction, we put the shadow behind us and put ourselves in a position to be grabbed from behind when we are least suspicious. . . .

While the consequences of nuclear war may be beyond human imagination, the process that made it a possibility is not. We have been brought to the brink of nuclear obliteration by thoroughly human needs, drives, and failings that exist, at least potentially, in all of us. Women simply cannot afford to define the one who makes war as the Other. It will take considerable courage to face the demon of nuclear war and tear off its mask. It will take a strong and large heart to recognize the face beneath the mask as one that resembles our own. Yet I sense this is what we are challenged to do. If women can face this demon and claim its energies as our own, we will be in a far stronger position to suggest how such energies might be turned in more creative, life-supporting directions.

13. RITA GROSS, *BUDDHISM AFTER PATRIARCHY* (1993)

Much of the transmission of Buddhism to Americans came through men, from nineteenth-century Buddhist converts such as Henry Steel Olcott to twentieth-century Buddhist immigrant teachers such as Shunryu Suzuki to "Beat Zen" advocates such as Jack Kerouac and Zen popularizers such as Alan Watts. The monastic practices (such as long periods of meditation and chanting, supervised by a master or teacher) adopted by many American Buddhists favored men in positions of relative wealth and social power. The embarrassing sexism of many popular writings such as Dharma Bums *reflects the history of the largely male practitioners of the American dharma.*

At the same time, nineteenth-century religious innovators and entrepreneurs such as Madame Blavatsky and Mary Baker Eddy had long since shown that borrowings from the East were hardly relevant or relegated exclusively to men. Buddhist precepts soon reached feminist circles, and female Buddhists soon carried on dialogues and conversations about feminism and the Buddhist "tradition" that paralleled the same discussions in Christian and Jewish communities. In the following selection, feminist scholar and Buddhist practitioner Rita Gross outlines the "mutual transformation" that can occur when Buddhism and feminism enter into dialogue. Both have important lessons to teach; in the words of another Buddhist feminist, Sandy Boucher, "both the Dharma and feminism are arrows pointing toward liberation" that can "be brought into harmonious relationship."

―――――― ∞ ――――――

Buddhism and feminism can be brought into relationship with each other through a definition of feminism in Buddhist terms, which I often use when trying to present feminism to Buddhists. According to this definition, feminism involves "the radical practice of the co-humanity of women and men."

To see feminism as a "practice" is not usual in feminist circles because the language is so very Buddhist. Buddhism is at root a "practice," a spiritual discipline; various meditation techniques are the heart of the tradition, and its method for achieving its goals of calm, insight, and liberation. Feminists, more used to the Western predominance of theory over practice, are prone to talk of "feminist theory," but feminism really involves a fundamental reorientation of mind and heart that cannot bear fruit if it is merely theoretical. To be effective, feminism needs to become an ongoing practice of changing one's language, one's expectations, one's ideas of normalcy, which happens as soon as things "click," as soon as one "wakes up," using Buddhist language, to feminisms fundamental and outrageous truth of the *co-humanity* of woman and men. . . . Some women involved in both Buddhism and feminism simply say "Buddhism *is* feminism!" by which they express intuitively the conviction that when Buddhism is true to itself, it manifests the same vision as does feminism. . . .

At least four profound similarities between the fundamental orientations of Buddhism and of feminism strengthen the claim that Buddhism is feminism.

First, contrary to most of the Western philosophical and theological heritage, both Buddhism and feminism begin with experience, stress experiential understanding enormously, and move from experience to theory, which becomes the expression of experience. Both share the approach that conventional views and dogmas are worthless if experience does not actually bear out theory. In other words, in a conflict between one's experience of one's world and what one has been taught by others about the world, both feminism and Buddhism agree that one cannot deny or repress experience.

Allegiance to experience before theory leads to a second important similarity between Buddhism and feminism, the will and the courage to go against the grain at any cost, and to hold to insights of truth, no matter how bizarre they seem from a conventional point of view. In its core teachings about the lack of external salvation (nontheism), about the nonexistence of a permanent abiding self (nonego), and about the pervasiveness and richness of suffering, Buddhism goes against the grain of what religions generally promise. Yet Buddhists continue to see these unpopular religious insights as the only way to attain liberation "beyond hope and fear." . . .

Thirdly, both perspectives use their willingness to hold to experience over convention and theory and their tenacious courage to explore how mental constructs operate to block or enhance liberation. For Buddhism, this exploration has involved the study of conventional ego, its painful habitual tendencies, and the underlying freedom of the basic egoless state. For feminism, this exploration involves looking into ways in which the social conditioning that produces gender stereotypes and conventional gender roles trap both women and men in half-humanity, encouraging mutual incompetence and threatening to destroy the planet. In sum, both Buddhism and feminism explore how habitual ego patterns block basic well-being.

Finally, both perspectives speak of liberation as the point of human existence, the aim toward which all existence strains. . . . Feminism, like Buddhism and like all other visions of the human spirit, looks beyond the immediate and compelling entrapments of easy solutions and conventional perspectives to the radical freedom of transcending those entrapments. . . .

Though it is compelling and accurate to speak of Buddhism as feminism, that statement is not the complete story. Potential mutual transformation between Buddhism and feminism provides an equally significant resource for Buddhist feminism. When mutual transformation, rather than similarity, is focused upon, the emphasis changes from how compatible the two perspectives are to what they might learn from each other. . . .

Mutual transformation is usually thought to result when two partners from different spiritual perspectives interact with each other. In the case of the dialogue and mutual transformation between Buddhism and feminism, the process is usually an internal dialogue within a person seriously committed to both perspectives. That this is an internal dialogue does not make the process less real or less transformative. . . . In my case, feminism was more deeply transformed initially by Buddhist practice than vice versa and this transformation was an ungrounding and profound experience. I continue to believe that Buddhism can make a significant critique of feminism as usually constituted and that Buddhist thought and practice could have a great deal to contribute to feminists.

. . . Buddhist practice has a great deal to offer in helping feminists deal with the anger that can be so enervating, while allowing them to retain the sharp critical brilliance contained in the anger. Buddhist meditation practices can also do wonders to soften the ideological hardness that often makes feminists ineffective spokespersons in their own behalf. Buddhist teachings on suffering help feminists remember that basic human sufferings and existential anxieties are not patriarchy's fault and will not be eliminated in postpatriarchal social conditions. Finally, Buddhist spirituality, with its long-tested spiritual disciplines, can do much to undercut the tendencies towards trippiness and spiritual materialism that often plague feminist spirituality movements.

At this point, however, my main topic is transformation from the other direction, from feminism into Buddhism. This is a feminist history, analysis, and reconstruction of Buddhism, not an assessment of "Feminism from the Perspective of Buddhist Practice." What transformation from feminism to Buddhism involves is, in my view, best summed up by saying that I am taking permission, as a Buddhist, to use the prophetic voice. . . . Feminism, especially the Christian and post-Christian feminist thought with which I am most familiar can, with great cogency, be seen as in direct continuity with biblical prophecy, in its true meaning of social criticism, protest against misuse of power, vision for a social order more nearly expressing justice and equity, and, most importantly, willingness actively to seek that more just and equitable order through whatever means are appropriate and necessary. . . .

"Compassion" is a word that comes easily and naturally in Buddhist discussion of social ethics. The word "righteousness" does not. Compassion for those caught in the ocean of *samsara,* suffering all the indignities inherent in such existence, is a prime motivation for and justification of the Buddhist lifestyle. Living the eightfold path of Buddhist individual and social morality involves nonharming and working for the benefit of all sentient beings on all levels. The method, however, has been individual and somewhat passive, especially when compared with ringing calls for and acts on behalf of overall justice and righteousness common to those who use the prophetic voice. In taking permission to use the prophetic voice as a Buddhist feminist, I am seeking to empower compassion, as understood so well in Buddhist social ethics, by direct infusion of concern for righteousness, for the actual manifestation in Buddhist societies of Buddhism's compassionate vision.

I most certainly am not content to accept the status quo of gender arrangements in most of the Buddhist world. In fact, if I had to be a Buddhist woman under the conditions that exist in most parts of the Buddhist world, Buddhism would not be my religion of choice. Only an auspicious coincidence of Buddhism and feminism, central to my vision, permits the internal dialogue. That internal dialogue has resulted in mutual transformation. The prophetic voice, derived from earlier trainings in Western modalities of the spirit, is coming through loudly and clearly in my Buddhist discussions of women. Furthermore, the permission to use that prophetic voice in Buddhist discourse is perhaps the greatest, most necessary, and most useful resource for a Buddhist feminism.

At the same time, mutual transformation comes through from the other side, for Buddhist meditation training and the Buddhist emphasis on gentleness will modulate the prophetic voice, which can sometimes be strident in expressing its truth and insights. Perhaps we can envision a marriage of compassion and righteousness in social ethics, a gentle and active approach to such issues as gender inequity, privilege, and hierarchy.

Chapter 5

Politics and Religion Since the 1960s

IT SEEMS INEVITABLE. After every election cycle, citizens complain that "this was the dirtiest campaign year yet." In terms of religion, such complaints have been escalating since 1980. That was the year that conservative Protestants and Catholics began getting out the vote more aggressively, highlighting the similarities between their concerns and those of Republican candidates. But much of the resulting explosion of media interest in the relationship between religion and politics was merely stumbling upon a recurring story in American history.

Look back to the election of 1800, when President John Adams faced off against Vice President Thomas Jefferson. Both were so religiously liberal that neither dared share their opinions in public for fear that citizens would never understand their Enlightenment rationalist approach to Scripture and reject them. But that did not stop their supporters from using religion as a club to bludgeon the other side. Adams's "National Day of Prayer" proclamation in 1799 set off riots in Philadelphia, as many feared it was the New Englander's first step toward establishing an official religion for the nation. As the election neared, pamphlets criss-crossed the states claiming Adams sought to make Presbyterianism the federal faith. Jefferson's detractors, on the other hand, painted him as an atheist who sought to bring down organized religion and replace it with temples of reason, like France at the height of its revolution. Actually, both held nearly the same religious opinions and neither had any interest in what the politicos claimed.

Speed forward to 1960, as some Protestant denominational magazines carried stories about the dangers of a Roman Catholic president. Should John F. Kennedy defeat Richard Nixon, they argued, the nation would be plunged into a new Dark Age where the pope controlled both spiritual and temporal powers. If the pontiff gave Kennedy an order he refused to follow, he could excommunicate the president from the Church, cutting Kennedy off from the sacraments and salvation. Could the nation survive putting in its highest position of leadership someone who might be manipulated by an outside power, especially one held in such contempt for centuries by Protestant Americans?

Obviously, the election of 1980 was simply another in a long line of presidential campaigns in which religion played a role. It would once again, time after time. Evangelical darling Ronald Reagan ran against the son (and son-in-law) of mainline Protestants, Walter Mondale, in 1984. In 1988, ordained ministers vied for their parties' nominations. And in 1992 and 1996, the Christian Coalition published millions of voter's guides to influence elections for pro-life candidates. In 2000, Republican candidate George W. Bush spoke at the racially charged religious college, Bob Jones University, and Vice President Al Gore chose a Conservative Jew as his running mate, Connecticut Senator Joseph Lieberman, who made headlines for claiming that Republicans did not own the issue of religion in government and public life.The media's myopic view of religion in politics belies all that took place between 1960 and 1980: black ministers leading the way to the Civil Rights Act, Richard Nixon's appeal in 1968 to the "Silent Majority" who still held to "traditional morality," and the declaration by *Time* magazine of 1976 as the "Year of the Evangelical" after "born again" Southern Baptist Jimmy Carter strode down Pennsylvania Avenue to become the thirty-ninth president.

Religion has been an issue on every level of politics, not just the presidential. From local school boards starting a meeting with prayer to the Ten Commandments posted at a city hall, from high schoolers opening a football game with a student-led prayer to street clashes between pro-life and pro-choice supporters in front of abortion clinics, religion is tied to politics because politics is about the *polis*—the public sphere. And both organized and (often) personal faith are supremely interested in developing policy for society as a whole.

In fact, the broad and complicated relationships between religion and politics in America since 1960 include a number of different playing fields and distinct levels. The interaction can be understood as a multilayered game of chess, where a move on one level can affect both the pieces it faces and those on other levels. For instance, the Christian Coalition gained fame for its role in the nomination and election of national Republican candidates, but perhaps its most important work took place locally, helping to elect potential national leaders to such offices as county commissioner, member of the school board, and mayor.

The relationship between religion and politics is not based merely on elections, although that is where the raw power of each is most often felt. The law is also an important site of interaction between religion and politics because debates over the proper relationship between the spheres are issues related to the polis, and thus political at their core. It is because the laws created by officials are so important that election campaigns gain so much attention. Hundreds of regulations affect religion in American society, including laws governing liquor sales and mail delivery on Sundays, land-use ordinances or exemptions from them for buildings dedicated to religious uses, tax laws for charity to religious organizations, and special tax exclusions for ministers.

Of course, sometimes these laws have become test cases for what should be the proper relationship between government and religion. This was a question that the federal courts faced repeatedly after 1960, a natural outgrowth of earlier Supreme Court decisions holding that both of the religion clauses of the First Amendment ("Congress shall make no law respecting an establishment of religion" and "or prohibiting the free exercise thereof") could be applied to state and local governments via the Fourteenth Amendment, a "reconstruction amendment" that barred lower governments from depriving citizens of their rights as Americans. The court held in *Cantwell v. Connecticut* in 1940 that a state could not bar Jehovah's Witnesses from door-to-door solicitation without a license, thus extending the free exercise clause beyond the federal level. In 1947, in *Everson v. Board of Education,* regarding reimbursement for bus fares for parochial school students, the court ruled that the establishment clause also applied to lower governments. As Justice Hugo Black wrote in the decision, "Neither a state nor the Federal Government can set up a church. Neither can pass laws which aid one religion, aid all religions, or prefer one religion over another. Neither can force nor influence a person to go or to remain away from church against his will or force him to profess a belief or disbelief in any religion. . . . Neither a state nor the Federal Government can, openly or secretly, participate in the affairs of any religious organizations and vice versa. In the words of Jefferson, the clause against establishment of religion by law was intended to erect a 'wall of separation between church and state.'"

Another court decision that became important to the polis, and to those running for elected office to shape it, was *Roe v. Wade,* the 1973 case allowing abortion. The Supreme Court's verdict was based on an implied constitutional "right to privacy," giving women permission to choose whether to give birth. If the decision a decade previous to end prayer in public schools brought the court condemnation, the abortion verdict brought about an organized response to change the composition of the federal courts by first re-

placing or better controlling the elected officials who nominate court justices (the President of the United States) and those who vote to confirm
those nominees (the U.S. Senate). The creation of the Moral Majority, a
coalition of conservative Christians hoping to bring moral reform to the nation through the political process, proved but the first of many attempts to
do so. Along with such other groups as the Christian Coalition, it helped
build a grassroots campaign that brought a conservative revolution to American politics.

Of course, many Americans decried these religiously motivated attempts
to secure regulations based on certain interpretations of the Bible. Citing
the same Jefferson phrase that Justice Black used—a "wall of separation between church and state"—they argued that government should be neutral,
neither religious nor areligious. (To conservative Christians even this sug-
gestion smacked of secularism, as no official recognition of a Supreme Being was tantamount to atheism.) Strict separationists pointed out that keeping high the wall separating the two spheres actually gave religions greater
freedom to operate in society, to proselytize new members. Some conservative Christians, especially those Baptists who remained true to their historic
position on the issue, agreed.

These debates over the proper relationship between religion and state
were so vigorous and rancorous because they went deeper than simply government regulations. Laws are, after all, proposed, debated, passed, and
then challenged by people—and often these people are religious and acting
from religious motivations. The struggle to keep separate such institutions
as government (and its various levels) and religious organizations is far
more difficult to carry out in personal life. How does an individual separate
their religious beliefs from their political beliefs, their religious motivations
for action from their political motivations for action? Justice Black could delineate the separate institutional spheres, but people are not institutions and
often act politically out of religious beliefs.

Every issue before the largely religious public becomes open to religious
critique and action played out in the world of politics. The United States after 1960 saw many such moments. First came the assassination of two religious leaders who used their positions to critique American society and
help bring about the Civil Rights Act. The war in Vietnam further polarized
religious communities, some of whom equated God with country, some of
whom employed the prophetic voice of the church to bring justice to the
helpless at home and abroad. The 1970s saw the Watergate scandal and the
subsequent election of a forthright Southern Baptist who promised a moral
government. Supreme Court decisions during that decade inspired conservative Christians to back the moral and political reforms promised by

Ronald Reagan in 1980 and 1984. Tilting more to the right each year, the majority of American voters rejected the more liberal Democratic presidential candidates in the three national elections of the 1980s by the largest electoral margins ever seen in one decade. Only a Southern Baptist candidate from Arkansas, who attracted moderates while he angered conservatives, could stem the tide by taking many of the previous Republican issues and making them his own. Even then, Bill Clinton was twice elected president with less than half the popular vote.

These changes in politics paralleled transformations in American religion. Religious sociologist Robert Wuthnow noted a "restructuring" of American religion away from institutions and toward liberal or conservative sensibilities. Denominations, the organizational form of most religious institutions, were themselves divided between these two poles, so that a liberal Catholic might have more in common with a liberal Methodist than with a conservative Catholic. In the realm of politics, this restructuring produced a rending of the rhetoric of civil religion—that national iconic language that attributed providential purpose to the nation. Conservative religious folk were likely to emphasize "one nation under God," while the more liberal underlined "with liberty and justice for all."

To understand, then, the relationship between religion and politics since 1960, one must keep in mind the shifting ground during this period. The 1960s were clearly a time of social upheaval, but things did not revert to the status quo thereafter. Whether the motivation was to extend the liberties won during that tumultuous decade or to conserve the traditions that had made America great, religion was the prime motivator of many working for change in the political system. And, most important, it inspired the millions of people who voted, volunteered, donated, and marched. While the separation of religion and state was a legal point debated by experts, it was not a separation that occurred very often in the hearts and minds of Americans.

1. SENATOR JOHN F. KENNEDY, "ADDRESS TO THE GREATER HOUSTON MINISTERIAL ASSOCIATION" (1960)

In August 1960, Senator John F. Kennedy of Massachusetts became the second Roman Catholic to be nominated by a major political party for the presidency of the United States. The previous Catholic presidential candidate, Alfred Smith, Democratic governor of New York, lost to Herbert Hoover in 1928. From the start of his campaign, Kennedy faced questions about his religion. Americans had always preferred Protestant federal executives, as that branch of Christianity had been a sort of de facto established religion since the nation's founding.

With the growth in Catholic numbers throughout the nineteenth and twentieth centuries, however, came increased political power. By the time Kennedy made his run for office, Roman Catholics dominated New England and much of the urban north. But his chances for a national political victory were constantly in doubt, as many regions—particularly those dominated by the evangelical wing of Protestantism—feared a Catholic president would be prone to follow political edicts from the Vatican.

In this speech before a largely Baptist audience in Houston, Texas, the Democratic candidate laid out his vision of the strict separation of church and state in America. Recalling the role Baptists played in creating the freedom of conscience Americans enjoyed, Kennedy made clear that he suffered from no "divided loyalty" as described by some in the religious media. Indeed, his heroic service in World War II and his leadership in the House of Representatives and the Senate the previous fourteen years portrayed a single-minded devotion to the United States. He argued that one's religious beliefs did not affect one's ability to serve in a secular government—"an America that is officially neither Catholic, Protestant, nor Jewish."

Kennedy's narrow victory later that fall has often been held up as a sign of the end of religious politics in the United States. But that was only true for a portion of American voters. Polls showed that many Protestants voted against JFK because of his Catholic background, while many Catholics voted for him simply because of his membership in their church. So although Kennedy won, his election did not prove that voters would rise above the "so-called religious issue" to vote with the critical matters facing the nation in mind. Still, his speech in Houston stands as an eloquent statement for a strict separation between religion and state, and in many ways presaged the Supreme Court decisions in the coming years.

Reverend Meza, Reverend Reck, I'm grateful for your generous invitation to state my views.

While the so-called religious issue is necessarily and properly the chief topic here tonight, I want to emphasize from the outset that we have far more critical issues to face in the 1960 election; the spread of Communist influence, until it now festers 90 miles off the coast of Florida—the humiliating treatment of our President and Vice President by those who no longer respect our power—the hungry children I saw in West Virginia, the old people who cannot pay their doctor bills, the families forced to give up their farms—an America with too many slums, with too few schools, and too late to the moon and outer space.

These are the real issues which should decide this campaign. And they are not religious issues—for war and hunger and ignorance and despair know no religious barriers.

But because I am a Catholic, and no Catholic has ever been elected President, the real issues in this campaign have been obscured—perhaps deliberately, in some quarters less responsible than this. So it is apparently necessary for me to state once again—not what kind of church I believe in, for that should be important only to me—but what kind of America I believe in.

I believe in an America where the separation of church and state is absolute—where no Catholic prelate would tell the President (should he be Catholic) how to act, and no Protestant minister would tell his parishioners for whom to vote—where no church or church school is granted any public funds or political preference—and where no man is denied public office merely because his religion differs from the President who might appoint him or the people who might elect him.

I believe in an America that is officially neither Catholic, Protestant nor Jewish—where no public official either requests or accepts instructions on public policy from the Pope, the National Council of Churches or any other ecclesiastical source—where no religious body seeks to impose its will directly or indirectly upon the general populace or the public acts of its officials—and where religious liberty is so indivisible that an act against one church is treated as an act against all.

For while this year it may be a Catholic against whom the finger of suspicion is pointed, in other years it has been, and may someday be again, a Jew—or a Quaker—or a Unitarian—or a Baptist. It was Virginia's harassment of Baptist preachers, for example, that helped lead to Jefferson's statute of religious freedom. Today I may be the victim—but tomorrow it may be you—until the whole fabric of our harmonious society is ripped at a time of great national peril.

Finally, I believe in an America where religious intolerance will someday end—where all men and all churches are treated as equal—where every man has the same right to attend or not attend the church of his choice—where there is no Catholic vote, no anti-Catholic vote, no bloc voting of any kind—and where Catholics, Protestants and Jews, at both the lay and pastoral level, will refrain from those attitudes of disdain and division which have so often marred their works in the past, and promote instead the American ideal of brotherhood.

That is the kind of America in which I believe. And it represents the kind of Presidency in which I believe—a great office that must neither be humbled by making it the instrument of any one religious group nor tarnished by arbitrarily withholding its occupancy from the members of any one religious group. I believe in a President whose religious views are his own private affair, neither imposed by him upon the nation or imposed by the nation upon him as a condition to holding that office.

I would not look with favor upon a President working to subvert the First Amendment's guarantees of religious liberty. Nor would our system of checks and balances permit him to do so—and neither do I look with favor upon those who would work to subvert Article VI of the Constitution by requiring a religious test—even by indirection—for it. If they disagree with that safeguard they should be out openly working to repeal it.

I want a Chief Executive whose public acts are responsible to all groups and obligated to none—who can attend any ceremony, service or dinner his office may appropriately require of him—and whose fulfillment of his Presidential oath is not limited or conditioned by any religious oath, ritual or obligation.

This is the kind of America I believe in—and this is the kind I fought for in the South Pacific, and the kind my brother died for in Europe. No one suggested then that we may have a "divided loyalty," that we did "not believe in liberty," or that we belonged to a disloyal group that threatened the "freedoms for which our forefathers died."

And in fact this is the kind of America for which our forefathers died— when they fled here to escape religious test oaths that denied office to members of less favored churches—when they fought for the Constitution, the Bill of Rights, and the Virginia Statute of Religious Freedom—and when they fought at the shrine I visited today, the Alamo. For side by side with Bowie and Crockett died McCafferty and Bailey and Carey—but no one knows whether they were Catholic or not. For there was no religious test at the Alamo.

I ask you tonight to follow in that tradition—to judge me on the basis of my record of 14 years in Congress—on my declared stands against an Ambassador to the Vatican, against unconstitutional aid to parochial schools, and against any boycott of the public schools (which I have attended myself)—instead of judging me on the basis of these pamphlets and publications we all have seen that carefully select quotations out of context from the statements of Catholic church leaders, usually in other countries, frequently in other centuries, and always omitting, of course, the statement of the American Bishops in 1948 which strongly endorsed church-state separation, and which more nearly reflects the views of almost every American Catholic.

I do not consider these other quotations binding upon my public acts—why should you? But let me say, with respect to other countries, that I am wholly opposed to the state being used by any religious group, Catholic or Protestant, to compel, prohibit, or persecute the free exercise of any other religion. And I hope that you and I condemn with equal fervor those nations which deny their Presidency to Protestants and those which deny it to Catholics. And rather than cite the misdeeds of those who differ, I would cite the record of the Catholic Church in such nations as Ireland and France—and the independence of such statesmen as Adenauer and De Gaulle.

But let me stress again that these are my views—for contrary to common newspaper usage, I am not the Catholic candidate for President. I am the Democratic Party's candidate for President who happens also to be Catholic. I do not speak for my church on public matters—and the church does not speak for me.

Whatever issue may come before me as President—on birth control, divorce, censorship, gambling or any other subject—I will make my decision in accordance with these views, in accordance with what my conscience tells me to be the national interest, and without regard to outside religious pressures or dictates. And no power or threat of punishment could cause me to decide otherwise.

But if the time should ever come—and I do not concede any conflict to be even remotely possible—when office would require me to either violate my conscience or violate the national interest, then I would resign the office; and I hope any conscientious public servant would do the same.

But I do not intend to apologize for these views to my critics of either Catholic or Protestant faith—nor do I intend to disavow either my views or my church in order to win this election.

If I should lose on the real issues, I shall return to my seat in the Senate, satisfied that I had tried my best and was fairly judged. But if this election is decided on the basis that 40 million Americans lost their chance of being President on the day they were baptized, then it is the whole nation that will be the loser, in the eyes of Catholics and non-Catholics around the world, in the eyes of history, and in the eyes of our own people.

But if, on the other hand, I should win the election, then I shall devote every effort of mind and spirit to fulfilling the oath of the Presidency—practically identical, I might add, to the oath I have taken for 14 years in Congress. For without reservation, I can "solemnly swear that I will faithfully execute the office of President the United States, and will to the best of my ability preserve, protect, and defend the Constitution . . . so help me God."

2. SUPREME COURT DECISION, *ENGEL V. VITALE* (1962)

With America's increased religious diversity came increasing conflicts over public rituals once considered acceptable. Bible reading and prayer in public schools were two. For over a century Catholics had complained about the daily reading from the King James Version of the Bible, used by most Protestant families but not by Catholic ones. Required prayer presented a similar problem, as the two types of Christianity differed considerably.

Engel v. Vitale was the first of the major decisions by the Supreme Court addressing these matters. The court decided, after reviewing the various types of relationships between church and state in English and American history, that the Establishment Clause of the U.S. Constitution forbade mandatory prayer in public schools because such a practice effectively established a religious belief—the existence of God—using tax support. Several important cases would follow in 1963, including Abington v. Schempp *and* Murray v. Curlett *(regarding voluntary Bible reading). In both cases the court ruled that laws must have a secular legislative purpose and that the primary effect must be one that neither advances nor inhibits religion.*

Critics claimed that this series of decisions was hostile to religion. But the court attempted to head off that criticism in its 1962 decision, given below, by indicating that many who helped shape the Constitution were religious men who were interested in keeping religious functions in the hands of the people and prohibiting government from writing or sanctioning certain prayers.

ENGEL V. VITALE

370 U.S. 421

CERTIORARI TO THE COURT OF APPEALS OF NEW YORK

Argued April 3, 1962—Decided June 25, 1962
Mr. Justice BLACK delivered the opinion of the Court.

The respondent Board of Education of Union Free School District No. 9, New Hyde Park, New York, acting in its official capacity under state law, directed the School District's principal to cause the following prayer to be said aloud by each class in the presence of a teacher at the beginning of each school day:

"Almighty God, we acknowledge our dependence upon Thee, and we beg Thy blessings upon us, our parents, our teachers and our Country."

. . . We think that by using its public school system to encourage recitation of the Regents' prayer, the State of New York has adopted a practice wholly inconsistent with the Establishment Clause. There can, of course, be no doubt that New York's program of daily classroom invocation of God's blessing as prescribed in the Regents' prayer is a religious activity. It is a solemn avowal of divine faith and supplication for the blessings of the Almighty. The nature of such a prayer has always been religious, none of the respondents has denied this and the trial court expressly so found:

"The religious nature of prayer was recognized by Jefferson and has been concurred in by theological writers, the United States Supreme Court and State courts and administrative officials, including New York's Commissioner of Education. A committee of the New York Legislature has agreed.

"The Board of Regents as *amicus curiae,* the respondents and intervenors all concede the religious nature of prayer, but seek to distinguish this prayer because it is based on our spiritual heritage. . . . "

The petitioners contend among other things that the state laws requiring or permitting use of the Regents' prayer must be struck down as a violation of the Establishment Clause because that prayer was composed by governmental officials as a part of a governmental program to further religious beliefs. For this reason, petitioners argue, the State's use of the Regents' prayer in its public school system breaches the constitutional wall of separation between Church and State. We agree with that contention since we think that the constitutional prohibition against laws respecting an establishment of religion must at least mean that in this country it is no part of the business of government to compose official prayers for any group of the American people to recite as a part of a religious program carried on by government.

It is a matter of history that this very practice of establishing governmentally composed prayers for religious services was one of the reasons which caused many of our early colonists to leave England and seek religious freedom in America. The Book of Common Prayer, which was created under governmental direction and which was approved by Acts of Parliament in 1548 and 1549, set out in minute detail the accepted form and content of prayer and other religious ceremonies to be used in the established, tax-supported Church of England. The controversies over the Book and what should be its content repeatedly threatened to disrupt the peace of that country as the accepted forms of prayer in the established church changed with the views of the particular ruler that happened to be in control at the time. Powerful groups representing some of the varying religious views of the people struggled among themselves to impress their particular views upon the Government and obtain amendments of the Book more suitable to their respective notions of how religious services should be conducted in order that the official religious establishment would advance their particular religious beliefs. Other groups, lacking the necessary political power to influence the Government on the matter, decided to leave England and its established church and seek freedom in America from England's governmentally ordained and supported religion.

It is an unfortunate fact of history that when some of the very groups which had most strenuously opposed the established Church of England found themselves sufficiently in control of colonial governments in this country to write their own prayers into law, they passed laws making their own religion the official religion of their respective colonies. Indeed, as late as the time of the Revolutionary War, there were established churches in at least eight of the thirteen former colonies and established religions in at least four of the other five. But the successful Revolution against English political domination was shortly followed by intense opposition to the practice of establishing religion by law. This opposition crystallized rapidly into an effective political force in Virginia where the minority religious groups such as Presbyterians, Lutherans, Quakers and Baptists had gained such strength that the adherents to the established Episcopal Church were actually a minority themselves. In 1785–1786, those opposed to the established Church, led by James Madison and Thomas Jefferson, who, though themselves not members of any of these dissenting religious groups, opposed all religious establishments by law on grounds of principle, obtained the enactment of the famous "Virginia Bill for Religious Liberty" by which all religious groups were placed on an equal footing so far as the State was concerned. Similar though less far-reaching legislation was being considered and passed in other States.

By the time of the adoption of the Constitution, our history shows that there was a widespread awareness among many Americans of the dangers of a union of Church and State. These people knew, some of them from bitter personal experience, that one of the greatest dangers to the freedom of the individual to worship in his own way lay in the Government's placing its official stamp of approval upon one particular kind of prayer or one particular form of religious services. They knew the anguish, hardship and bitter strife that could come when zealous religious groups struggled with one another to obtain the Government's stamp of approval from each King, Queen, or Protector that came to temporary power. The Constitution was intended to avert a part of this danger by leaving the government of this country in the hands of the people rather than in the hands of any monarch. But this safeguard was not enough. Our Founders were no more willing to let the content of their prayers and their privilege of praying whenever they pleased be influenced by the ballot box than they were to let these vital matters of personal conscience depend upon the succession of monarchs. The First Amendment was added to the Constitution to stand as a guarantee that neither the power nor the prestige of Federal Government would be used to control, support or influence the kinds of prayer the American people can say—that the people's religions must not be subjected to the pressures of government for change each time a new political administration is elected to office. Under that Amendment's prohibition against governmental establishment of religion, as reinforced by the provisions of the Fourteenth Amendment, government in this country, be it state or federal, is without power to prescribe by law any particular form of prayer which is to be used as an official prayer in carrying on any program of governmentally sponsored religious activity.

There can be no doubt that New York's state prayer program officially establishes the religious beliefs embodied in the Regents' prayer. The respondents' argument to the contrary, which is largely based upon the contention that the Regents' prayer is "non-denominational" and the fact that the program, as modified and approved by state courts, does not require all pupils to recite the prayer but permits those who wish to do so to remain silent or be excused from the room, ignores the essential nature of the program's constitutional defects. Neither the fact that the prayer may be denominationally neutral nor the fact that its observance on the part of the students is voluntary can serve to free it from the limitations of the Establishment Clause, as it might from the Free Exercise Clause, of the First Amendment, both of which are operative against the States by virtue of the Fourteenth Amendment. Although these two clauses may in certain instances overlap, they forbid two quite different kinds of governmental encroachment upon religious freedom. The Establishment Clause, unlike the Free Exercise Clause, does not depend upon any showing of direct governmental compulsion and is violated by the enactment of laws which establish an official religion whether those laws operate directly to coerce nonobserving individuals or not. This is not to say, of course, that laws officially prescribing a particular form of religious worship do not involve coercion of such individuals. When the power, prestige and financial support of government is placed behind a particular religious belief, the indirect coercive pressure upon religious minorities to conform to the prevailing officially approved religion is plain. But the purposes underlying the Establishment Clause go much further than that. Its first and most immediate purpose rested on the belief that a union of government and religion tends to destroy government and to degrade religion. The history of governmentally established religion, both in England and in this country, showed that whenever government had allied itself with one particular form of religion, the inevitable result had been that it had incurred the hatred, disrespect and even contempt of those who held contrary beliefs. That same history showed that many people had lost their respect for any religion that had relied upon the support of government to spread its faith. The Establishment Clause thus stands as an expression of principle on the part of the Founders of our Constitution that religion is too personal, too sacred, too holy, to permit its "unhallowed perversion" by a civil magistrate. Another purpose of the Establishment Clause rested upon an awareness of the historical fact that governmentally established religions and religious persecutions go hand in hand . . . It was in large part to get completely away from this sort of systematic religious persecution that the Founders brought into being our Nation, our Constitution, and our Bill of Rights with its prohibition against any governmental establishment of religion. The New York laws officially prescribing the Regents' prayer are inconsistent both with the purposes of the Establishment Clause and with the Establishment Clause itself.

It has been argued that to apply the Constitution in such a way as to prohibit state laws respecting an establishment of religious services in public schools is to indicate a hostility toward religion or toward prayer. Nothing, of course, could be more wrong. The history of man is inseparable from the history of religion. And perhaps it is not too much to say that since the beginning of that history many people have devoutly believed that "More things are wrought by prayer than this world dreams of." It was doubtless largely due to men who believed this that there grew up a sentiment that caused men to leave the cross-currents of officially established state religions and religious persecution in Europe and come to this country filled with the hope that they could find a place in which they could pray when they pleased to the God of their faith in the language they chose. And there were men of this same faith in the power of prayer who led the fight for adoption of our Constitution and also for our Bill of Rights with the very guarantees of religious freedom that forbid the sort of governmental activity which New York has attempted here. These men knew that the First Amendment, which tried to put an end to governmental control of religion and of prayer, was not written to destroy either. They knew rather that it was written to quiet well-justified fears which nearly all of them felt arising out of an awareness that governments of the past had shackled men's tongues to make them speak only the religious thoughts that government wanted them to speak and to pray only to the God that government wanted them to pray to. It is neither sacrilegious nor antireligious to say that each separate government in this country should stay out of the business of writing or sanctioning official prayers and leave that purely religious function to the people themselves and to those the people choose to look to for religious guidance.

It is true that New York's establishment of its Regents' prayer as an officially approved religious doctrine of that State does not amount to a total establishment of one particular religious sect to the exclusion of all others—that, indeed, the governmental endorsement of that prayer seems relatively insignificant when compared to the governmental encroachments upon religion which were commonplace 200 years ago. To those who may subscribe to the view that because the Regents' official prayer is so brief and general there can be no danger to religious freedom in its governmental establishment, however, it may be appropriate to say in the words of James Madison, the author of the First Amendment:

"[I]t is proper to take alarm at the first experiment on our liberties. . . . Who does not see that the same authority which can establish Christianity, in exclusion of all other Religions, may establish with the same ease any particular sect of Christians, in exclusion of all other Sects? That the same authority which can force a citizen to contribute three pence only of his property for the support of any one establishment, may force him to conform to any other establishment in all cases whatsoever?"

The judgment of the Court of Appeals of New York is reversed and the cause remanded for further proceedings not inconsistent with this opinion.

Reversed and remanded.

3. ABRAHAM J. HESCHEL, "THE MORAL OUTRAGE OF VIETNAM" (1967)

Long known for stunning honesty and clarity in his writings, Abraham Joshua Heschel spoke to, and often for, the American Jewish community on a variety of issues during the third quarter of the twentieth century. As Professor of Ethics and Mysticism at Jewish Theological Seminary from 1945 until 1972, he had opportunity to address many of the moral dilemmas America faced during the turbulent postwar period until the eve of Watergate. During the 1960s, having helped to inspire the participation of Jewish and Christian clergymen in the march on Washington to protest racial inequality, he turned his attention to the war in Vietnam and how it affected the national soul.

In his series of pieces written to express the moral ironies of a superpower being involved in large-scale violence in such a small region, Heschel first employed a biblical-prophetic style to underline the importance of the moment. "For Vietnam's sake I will not keep silent / For America's sake I will not rest," he declares, and moves into a starkly written essay that boils down every point to its barest form of truth. In all, these writings by Heschel—who escaped Nazi persecution in Poland and Germany—sound a particularly prophetic Jewish tone. Moving step by step from the irrationality and immorality of the military action in Southeast Asia to the highest form of human action—peacemaking—Heschel brings his readers to a point of choice, a decision to "unlearn old follies" by recognizing that it is not for humans to decide life or death. The

*human responsibility is always to live in peace with one another. Losing face simply did
not matter as much as losing one's soul.*

⌾⌾⌾

On January 31, 1967, clergymen and laymen concerned about Vietnam assembled in Washington, D.C. At the worship service, I offered the following
meditation on the words of the prophet Ezekiel (34:25–31):

> Ours is an assembly of shock, contrition, and dismay. Who would have be-
> lieved that we life-loving Americans are capable of bringing death and de-
> struction to so many innocent people? We are startled to discover how un-
> merciful, how beastly we ourselves can be.
>
> So we implore Thee, our Father in heaven, help us to banish the beast from
> our hearts, the beast of cruelty, the beast of callousness.
>
> Since the beginning of history evil has been going forth from nation to na-
> tion. The lords of the flocks issue proclamations, and the sheep of all na-
> tions indulge in devastations.
>
> But who would have believed that our own nation at the height of its career
> as the leader of free nations, the hope for peace in the world, whose un-
> precedented greatness was achieved through "liberty and justice for all,"
> should abdicate its wisdom, suppress its compassion and permit guns to
> become its symbols?
>
> America's resources, moral and material, are immense. We have the means
> and know the ways of dispelling prejudice and lies, of overcoming pover-
> ty and disease. We have the capacity to lead the world in seeking to over-
> come international hostility.
>
> Must napalm stand in the way of our power to aid and to inspire the world?
>
> To be sure, just as we feel deeply the citizen's dilemma, we are equally sen-
> sitive to the dilemma confronting the leaders of our government. Our gov-
> ernment seems to recognize the tragic error and futility of the escalation
> of our involvement but feels that we cannot extricate ourselves without
> public embarrassment of such dimension as to cause damage to Amer-
> ica's prestige.
>
> But the mire in which we flounder threatens us with an even greater danger.
> It is the dilemma of either losing face or losing our soul.
>
> At this hour Vietnam is our most urgent, our most disturbing religious prob-
> lem, a challenge to the whole nation as well as a challenge to every one of
> us an individual.
>
> When a person is sick, in danger or in misery, all religious duties recede, all
> rituals are suspended, except one: to save life and relieve pain.

Vietnam is a personal problem. To speak about God and remain silent on
Vietnam is blasphemous.

When you spread forth your hands
I will hide my eyes from you;
Yea when you make many prayers,
I will not hear—
Your hands are not clean.

In the sight of so many thousands of civilians and soldiers slain, injured,
crippled, of bodies emaciated, of forests destroyed by fire, God confronts
us with this question:
Where art thou?
Is there no compassion in the world? No sense of discernment to realize that
this is a war that refutes any conceivable justification of war?
The sword is the pride of man; arsenals, military bases, nuclear weapons lend
supremacy to nations. War is the climax of ingenuity, the object of supreme dedication.
Men slaughtering each other, cities battered into ruins: such insanity has
plunged many nations into an abyss of disgrace. Will America, the promise of peace to the world, fail to uphold its magnificent destiny?
The most basic way in which all men may be divided is between those who
believe that war is unnecessary and those who believe that war is inevitable; between those to whom the sword is the symbol of honor and
those to whom seeking to convert swords into plowshares is the only way
to keep our civilization from disaster.
Most of us prefer to disregard the dreadful deeds we do over there. The atroc-
ities committed in our name are too horrible to be credible. It is beyond
our power to react vividly to the ongoing nightmare, day after day, night
after night. So we bear graciously other people's suffering.
O Lord, we confess our sins, we are ashamed of the inadequacy of our anguish, of how faint and slight is our mercy. We are a generation that has
lost the capacity for outrage.
We must continue to remind ourselves that in a free society, all are involved
in what some are doing. *Some are guilty, all are responsible.*
Prayer is our greatest privilege. To pray is to stake our very existence, our
right to live, on the truth and on the supreme importance of that which
we pray for. Prayer, then, is radical commitment, a dangerous involvement in the life of God.
In such awareness we pray . . .
We do not stand alone. Millions of Americans, millions of people all over the
world are with us.

At this moment praying for peace in Vietnam we are spiritually Vietnamese. Their agony is our affliction, their hope is our commitment.

God is present wherever men are afflicted.

Where is God present now?

We do not know how to cry, we do not know how to pray!

Our conscience is so timid, our words so faint, our mercy so feeble.

O Father, have mercy upon us.

Our God, add our cries uttered here to the cries of the bereaved, crippled, and dying over there.

Have mercy upon all of us.

Help us to overcome the arrogance of power. Guide and inspire the President of the United States in finding a speedy, generous, and peaceful end to the war in Vietnam.

The intensity of the agony is high, the hour is late, the outrage may reach a stage where repentance will be too late, repair beyond any nation's power.

We call for a covenant of peace, for reconciliation of America and all of Vietnam. To paraphrase the words of the prophet Isaiah (62:1):

For Vietnam's sake I will not keep silent,
For America's sake I will not rest,
Until the vindication of humanity goes forth as brightness,
And peace for all men is a burning torch.

Here is the experience of a child of seven who was reading in school the chapter which tells of the sacrifice of Isaac:

Isaac was on the way to Mount Moriah with his father; then he lay on the altar, bound, waiting to be sacrificed. My heart began to beat even faster; it actually sobbed with pity for Isaac. Behold, Abraham now lifted the knife. And now my heart froze within me with fright. Suddenly, the voice of the angel was heard: "Abraham, lay not thine hand upon the lad, for now I know that thou fearest God." And here I broke out in tears and wept aloud. "Why are you crying?" asked the Rabbi. "You know that Isaac was not killed."

And I said to him, still weeping, "But, Rabbi, supposing the angel had come a second too late?"

The Rabbi comforted me and calmed me by telling me that an angel cannot come late.

An angel cannot be late, but man, made of flesh and blood, may be.

MILITARY VICTORY—A MORAL DEFEAT

It is weird to wake up one morning and find that we have been placed in an insane asylum. It is even more weird to wake up and find that we have been involved in slaughter and destruction without knowing it.

What is being done by our government is done in our name. Our labor, our wealth, our civic power, our tacit consent are invested in the production and use of the napalm, the bombs, and the mines that explode and bring carnage and ruin to Vietnam.

The thought that I live a life of peace and nonviolence turns out to be an illusion. I have been decent in tiny matters on a tiny scale, but have become vicious on a large scale. In my own eyes my existence appears to be upright, but in the eyes of my victims my very being is a nightmare.

A sense of moral integrity, the equation of America with the pursuit of justice and peace, has long been part of our self-understanding. Indeed, for generations the image of America has been associated with the defense of human rights and the hope for world peace. And now history is sneering at us.

A ghastly darkness has set in over our souls. Will there be an end to dismay, an end to agony?

The encounter of man and God is an encounter within the world. We meet within a situation of shared suffering, of shared responsibility.

This is implied in believing in One God in whose eyes there is no dichotomy of here and there, of me and them. They and I are one; here is there, and there is here. What goes on over there happens even here. Oceans divide us, God's presence unites us, and God is present wherever man is afflicted, and all of humanity is embroiled in every agony wherever it may be.

Though not a native of Vietnam, ignorant of its language and traditions, I am involved in the plight of the Vietnamese. To be human means not to be immune to other people's suffering. People in Vietnam, North and South, have suffered, and all of us are hurt.

Unprepared, perplexed, uninformed, ill-advised, our nation finds herself in a spiritual inferno. Where do we stand? Where do we go from here? For a long time we suppressed anxiety, evaded responsibility. Yet the rivers of tears and blood may turn into a flood of guilt, which no excuse will stem.

The blood we shed in Vietnam makes a mockery of all our proclamations, dedications, celebrations. We have been moving from obscurity to confusion, from ignorance to obfuscation. Many are unaware, some acquiesce, most of us detest this unfathomable war, but are unable to envisage a way of getting out of this maze. Millions of Americans who cannot close their minds to the suffering and sorrow are stricken with anguish, and form a large fellowship living in a state of consternation.

We are killing the Vietnamese because we are suspicious of the Chinese. The aim is to kill the elusive Vietcong, yet to come upon one soldier, it is necessary to put an end to a whole village, to the lives of civilians, men, women, and children.

Is it not true that Communists are fellow human beings first, antagonists second? Politically, the concept of the enemy is becoming obsolete; yesterday's enemy is today's ally. The state of cold war between the United States and Soviet Russia has given place to a quest of friendly understanding.

The absurdity of this war is tacitly admitted by almost everyone. Our presence in Vietnam has become a national nightmare, our actions are forced, we dislike what we do; we do what we hate to do. Is this a way to bring democracy to Vietnam: more explosives, more devastation, more human beings crippled, orphaned, killed? Is it not clear that military victory in Vietnam would be a tragic moral defeat? That military triumph would be a human disaster?

The choice is clear. We decide either in favor of further escalation that may lead to a world war or in favor of gradual disengagement followed by negotiation. Refusal to embark upon a course of unlimited massacre will redound only to the honor of America. Did not the retreat of France from Algeria, where her involvement was incomparably more important, add to the glory of France? Did President Kennedy's self-restraint during the ill-planned expedition to the Bay of Pigs tarnish in any way the prestige of America?

Is it not the avowed policy of the United States to insist that there is an alternative to war?

We are fully aware of America's moral commitment to give aid to democratic governments all over the world when they are threatened or attacked by tyrants and dictators. However, we do not fight in Vietnam as allies of a freely elected democratic government but rather as fellow-travelers of anti-Communists, as allies of a despotic military oligarchy. Is it the destiny of our youth to serve as mercenaries in the service of military juntas all over the world?

Our major blunder is the fact that our aid and involvement is a government-to-government operation. Driven by our tendency to suspect social change, by our tendency to measure other people's values by our own standards, we have no communication with the people of Vietnam, nor have we sought to relate ourselves to their political understanding. We are in touch with military dictatorship, we ignore the people. We see the power structure, we disregard human beings.

We do not listen to their voice, we are ignorant of their way of thinking, traditions and scale of values. Our failure to convince the Vietnamese that our aim is to save their freedom, to insure their welfare, is not necessarily a sign of their being imbeciles.

Vietnam is a country which has for many decades been the victim of colonial demoralization. Injustice, poverty, exploitation prevail. Revolutionary change is a moral necessity.

Because the government of South Vietnam is corrupt, distrusted by and alienated from the majority of the people, our aid fails to reach the peasants. We are being misguided in maintaining that social revolution can be stopped by military operations. America's identification with Vietnamese juntas not only thwarts any effort to bring aid to the destitute peasants but defames our image in their eyes.

Can an outside power succeed in bringing a recalcitrant heretic community such as the National Liberation Front back to the fold by fire and sword? A major stumbling block to these efforts is our opponents' distrust in our desire for peace. Yet the atmosphere on both sides is infected with suspicion. The Golden Rule seems to be "suspect thy neighbor as thyself."

Indeed, how can there be trust in our desire for peace, if the call for negotiation is consistently followed by further escalation? The groan deepens, the combat burns, the wailing cry does not abate. Every act of escalation has as its effect further aggravation.

For on horror's head horrors accumulate. We are in danger of being swept away—against our will, despite circumspection—by a vehement current and compulsive course which never feels the retiring ebb but keeps on, due to a more violent pace, to an even wider torrent.

War tends to become its own end. Force unleashed moves on its own momentum, breaks all constraint, reaching intensities which man can no longer control. The nation's confidence both in the candor of the Administration and in the policy which it is pursuing in Vietnam is faltering, while the world's respect for American democracy has been profoundly shaken. America's image is tragically distorted.

For many years the world's eyes were directed to Washington, trusting that the White House, the spirit of America would secure peace. Should the world's eyes be directed to Moscow, hoping that the Kremlin may use its influence to bring about peace in Vietnam?

What is it that may save us, that may unite men all over the world? The abhorrence of atrocity, the refusal of the conscience to accommodate to the arrogance of military power. Indeed, it is the power of the human conscience which has in the last twenty years inhibited the use of thermonuclear weapons. Yet the power of the conscience is tenuous and exceedingly vulnerable. Its status is undergoing profound upheavals. We are challenged too frequently, too radically to be able to react adequately.

However, the surrender of conscience destroys first the equilibrium of human existence and then existence itself. In the past, war was regarded as an instrument of politics. Today politics is in the process of becoming an instrument of military technology. How long can total war be avoided?

Militarism is whoredom, voluptuous and vicious, first disliked and then relished. To paraphrase the prophet's words "For the spirit of harlotry is within them, and they know not the Lord" (Hosea 5:4): "Samson with his strong body, had a weak head, or he would not have laid it in a harlot's lap."

4. RESPONSES TO *ROE V. WADE: CHRISTIANITY TODAY,* "ABORTION AND THE COURT" (1973)

JOSEPH F. DONCEEL, S.J., "A LIBERAL CATHOLIC'S VIEW" (1970)

The Supreme Court's 1973 decision about a woman's right to choose an abortion based on the right to privacy proved to be a fault line in American religion and politics. Perhaps no other event caused such an ongoing stir among religious congregations, colleges, and other organizations. Many conservatives became consumed by the thought that roughly 1.5 million unborn children were lost each year. On the other hand, many moderate and liberal people of faith attached abortion rights to women's rights generally, arguing that for centuries men had kept women from controlling their own bodies and so had kept women under their control. If religion is truly about spiritual freedom, they claimed, then women must have the ability to decide these matters for themselves.

Reactions to the court's decision were quick and often very loud. The first selection below exemplifies a common evangelical Christian response. The editors for Christianity Today, the organ of conservative Protestants created by the large following of Billy Graham in the 1950s, claim that the court ruled not merely against the law of God but against the opinion of the majority of Americans. Most followed the traditional teachings of their faiths, which opposed abortion.

In a very different vein, Jesuit Joseph F. Donceel provides a nontraditional Roman Catholic response to Roe v. Wade. Appealing to the writings of Thomas Aquinas, the Church's greatest theologian, Donceel argues that no human being exists in the early stages of pregnancy—the period when nearly every abortion is performed. In fact, he claims, this was the position of the Church for many years until, by employing faulty science, leaders turned their backs on the traditional view in order to follow a particular philosophy that contradicts the Church's own doctrines about humanity. Written a few years before the court's decision, Donceel's piece gave voice to many American Catholic women who believed a deeper and more humane approach to the issue of birth control must include discussion about when life begins—at conception or "infusion" (*the point at which the soul begins to exist, the traditional definition of which the Church has altered*). *In this sense, ironically, many American Catholic women were thrown back upon medieval Church traditions in order to argue for their right to an abortion.*

⊸⊶

ABORTION AND THE COURT

Writing to Christians in Rome about the spiritual condition of the pagan world, Paul diagnosed it in this way: "Although they knew God, they did not honor him as God or give thanks to him, but they became futile in their thinking, and their senseless minds were darkened. Claiming to be wise, they became fools. . . . Since they did not see fit to acknowledge God, God gave them up to a base mind and to improper conduct" (Rom. 1:21, 22, 28). Not only the thinking but often the laws of men, and even the decisions of religious councils, can conflict with the laws of God. That is why Peter and John, called before the Sanhedrin, declared that they must obey God rather than men (Acts 4:19).

In a sweeping decision January 22, the United States Supreme Court overthrew the abortion statutes of Texas, indeed, of all the states that protect the right of an unborn infant to life before, at the earliest, the seventh month of pregnancy. The Court explicitly allows states to create some safeguards for unborn infants regarded as "viable," but in view of the present decision, it appears doubtful that unborn infants now enjoy any protection prior to the instant of birth anywhere in the United States. Until new state laws acceptable to the Court are passed—at best a long-drawn-out process—it would appear impossible to punish abortions performed at any stage.

This decision runs counter not merely to the moral teachings of Christianity through the ages but also to the moral sense of the American people, as expressed in the now vacated abortion laws of almost all states, including 1972 laws in Massachusetts, New York, and Pennsylvania, and recently clearly reaffirmed by statewide referendums in two states (Michigan and North Dakota). We would not normally expect the Court to consider the teachings of Christianity and paganism before rendering a decision on the *constitutionality* of a law, but in this case it has chosen to do so, and the results are enlightening: it has clearly decided for paganism and against Christianity, and this in disregard even of democratic sentiment, which in this case appears to follow Christian tradition and to reject permissive abortion legislation.

The Court notes that "ancient religion" did not bar abortion (*Roe et al. v. Wade*, No. 70–18 [1973], VI, 1); by "ancient religion," it clearly means paganism, since Judaism and Christianity *did* bar abortion. It rejects the "apparent rigidity" of the Hippocratic Oath ("I will give no deadly medicine to anyone if asked, nor suggest any such counsel; and in like manner I will not give to a woman a pessary to produce abortion") on the grounds that it did not really represent the consensus of pagan thinking, though pagan in origin, but owed its universal acceptance to popularity resulting from "the emerging teachings of Christianity" (*ibid.*, VI, 2). To these, the High Court unambiguously prefers "ancient religion," that is, the common paganism of the pre-Christian Roman Empire. Against the official teaching of the Roman Catholic Church that the "life begins at conception" (curious language on the part of the Court, for no one denies that the fetus is human, or that it is alive: the Court apparently means *personal* life), the Court presents "new embryological data that purport to indicate that conception is a 'process' over time, rather than an event, and . . . new medical techniques such as menstrual extractions, the 'morning-after' pill, implantation of embryos, artificial insemination, and even artificial wombs" (*ibid.*, IX, B). It is hard to understand how the contention that conception is a "process" of at most a few days' duration is relevant to the possible rights of the fetus at three or six months, and even harder to comprehend the logic that holds that "new medical techniques" for destroying or preserving the embryo "pose problems" for the view that it was alive before being subjected to those techniques.

Pleading "the established medical fact" that "until the end of the first trimester, mortality in abortion [of course the reference is to *maternal* mortality—fetal mortality is 100 per cent] is less than that in normal childbirth [nine maternal deaths per 100,000 abortions vs. twenty-five per 100,000 live births, a differential of 0.016 percent, of course not counting the 100,000 fetal mortalities]" (*ibid.*, X), the Court decreed that a state may not regulate abortion at all during the first three months, and during the second, only to protect the health of the mother. After "viability," defined as "about six months," when the fetus "presumably has the capability of meaningful life outside the mother's womb," then, "if the State is interested in protecting fetal life . . . it may go *so far* [emphasis added: since abortion is 100 per cent fatal to the fetus it is hard to see the value of "protection" that goes less far] as to proscribe abortion during that period, except when it is necessary to preserve the life or health of the mother" (*ibid.*). Since health is explicitly defined to include "mental health," a very flexible concept, this concession to the protection of the fetus from seven to nine months will, in practice, mean little.

The Court based its abortion decision on the right of privacy, and that without empirical or logical justification. "This right of privacy . . . is broad enough to encompass a woman's decision whether or not to terminate her pregnancy," Justice Blackmun wrote in delivering the opinion of the Court. But the right of privacy is not absolute, and, much more important, no abortion decision can ever be by any stretch of the imagination a purely private matter. The fetus, if not a full-fledged human being, is at least a being owing his existence as much to father as to mother, and is therefore an individual distinct from both. Curiously, fathers are scarcely mentioned in the fifty-one-page majority opinion! The decision would appear to contradict itself when it insists that the "private" abortion decision must be made in conjunction with a physician and/or in line with some kind of medical judgment.

In his concurring opinion, Chief Justice Burger fatuously comments, "I do not read the Court's holding today as having the sweeping consequences attributed to it by the dissenting justices [White and Rehnquist]." The New York state tally stood in 1971 at a ratio of 927 abortions for 1,000 live births; now that abortion has become allowable nationwide, the ratio will presumably change, but the experience of nations with easy abortion suggests that it may very well remain as high as one abortion for every two live births, or even higher. What would the Chief Justice consider sweeping? Mandatory abortion for all those falling into a certain class? Infanticide? Mass extermination of undesirables? Make no mistake: the logic of the high court could be used with like—in some cases with greater—force to justify infanticide for unwanted or undesirable infants; the expression, "capability of meaningful life" could cover a multitude of evils and will, unless this development is stopped now.

In his dissent, Justice White sums up the situation and the Court's action:

> The common claim before us is that for any one of such reasons [he cites convenience, family planning, economics, dislike of children, the embarrassment of illegitimacy, and others], or for no reason at all, and without asserting or claiming any threat to life or health, any woman is entitled to an abortion at her request if she is able to find a medical doctor willing to undertake the procedure. The Court for the most part sustains this position: during the period prior to the time the fetus becomes viable, the Constitution of the United States values the convenience, whim or caprice of the putative mother more than the life or potential life of the fetus. . . .

In arriving at this position, the majority of the Supreme Court has explicitly rejected Christian moral teaching and approved the attitude of what it calls "ancient religion" and the standards of pagan Greek and Roman law, which, as the Court notes in self-justification, "afforded little protection to the unborn" (*ibid.*, VI, 1). It is not necessary to read between the lines for the spiritual significance of this decision, for the Court has made it crystal clear.

In view of this, Justice Rehnquist's dissenting observation that the Court is engaging in "judicial legislation" may seem almost insignificant. Nevertheless, we must ask what remains of the democratic process and the principle of local initiative when not only long-standing older laws but the most recent state laws and even the will of the people expressed in state-wide referendums are swept from the board in a single Court ruling, when the people and their representatives are prohibited forever—or at least until the Constitution is amended—from implementing a higher regard for the life of the unborn than that exhibited by seven supreme judges.·

Having previously seen fit to ban the formal, admittedly superficial, and possibly hypocritical acknowledgment of God that used to take place in public-school prayers and Bible readings, the Court has now repudiated the Old Testament's standards on capital punishment as cruel and without utility, and has rejected the almost universal consensus of Christian moral teachers through the centuries on abortion. Its latest decision reveals a callous utilitarianism about children in the womb that harmonizes little with the extreme delicacy of its conscience regarding the imposition of capital punishment.

Christians can be grateful that the court has not yet made the "right" to abortion an obligation. It is still possible for us to consult the will of God in this matter rather than the laws of the state. The present decision makes it abundantly clear that we are obliged to seek his will and not to be guided only by public law. We should recognize the accumulating evidence that public policy is beginning to display what Paul called "a base mind and improper conduct," and for similar reasons. Will the time come when this nation "under God" is distinguishable from those that are aggressively atheistic only by our currently greater material affluence? Christians should accustom themselves to the thought that the American state no longer supports, in any meaningful sense, the laws of God, and prepare themselves spiritually for the prospect that it may one day formally repudiate them and turn against those who seek to live by them.

———— ⚬⚬⚬ ————

A LIBERAL CATHOLIC'S VIEW

I fully agree with the basic Catholic principle that we are never allowed to kill an innocent human being. Therefore, if there is a real human being from the moment of conception, abortion would have to be considered immoral at any stage of pregnancy. The majority Catholic opinion holds nowadays that there is indeed a real human being from the first moment of conception, or, at least, that we cannot be certain that such is not the case. But there is also a minority Catholic opinion, which has good standing in the church, which was the opinion of her greatest theologian, Thomas Aquinas, and which is now slowly regaining favor among Catholic thinkers. This minority opinion holds that there is certainly no human being during the early stages of pregnancy. I would like to show you briefly why Thomas held this position, how it was given up by his successors on account of erroneous scientific theories, and how, even after these theories had been given up, the Catholic church did not return to her traditional view because of a philosophy which was at variance with her official doctrine of the nature of man.

Traditional Catholic philosophy holds that what makes an organism a human being is the spiritual soul and that this soul starts to exist at the moment of its "infusion" into the body. When is the human soul infused into the body? Nowadays the majority of Catholic thinkers would not hesitate to answer: at the moment of conception. This is known as the *theory of immediate animation*. However, during long centuries Catholic philosophy and theology held that the human soul was infused into the body only when the latter began to show a human shape or outline and possessed the basic human organs. Before this time, the embryo is alive, but in the way in which a plant or an animal is alive. It possesses, as the traditional terminology puts it, a vegetative or an animal soul, not yet a human soul. In more modern terms we might say that it has reached the physiological or the psychological, not yet the spiritual level of existence. It is not yet a human person; it is evolving, within the womb, toward hominization. This is the *theory of mediate or delayed animation*.

Why did Thomas and the great medieval thinkers favor this theory? Because they held the doctrine of hylomorphism, according to which the human soul is the substantial form of man, while the human body is the result of the union of this soul with materiality, with undetermined cosmic stuff, with what was then known as prime matter. Hylomorphism holds that the human soul is to the body somewhat as the shape of a statue is to the actual statue. The shape of a statue cannot exist before the statue exists. It is not something which the sculptor first makes and subsequently introduces into a block of marble. It can exist only in the completed statue. Hylomorphism holds that, in the same way, the human soul can exist only in a real human body.

Although Thomas knew nothing about chromosomes, genes, DNA, or the code of life, he knew that whatever was growing in the mother's womb was not yet, early in pregnancy, a real human body. Therefore he held that it could not be animated by a human soul, any more than a square block of marble can possess a human shape. The medieval thinkers knew very well that this growing organism would develop into a human body, that virtual-ly, potentially, it was a human body. But they did not admit that an actual hu-man soul could exist in a virtual human body. The Catholic church, which had officially adopted the hylomorphic conception of human nature at the Council of Vienne, in 1312, was so strongly convinced of this position that, for centuries, her law forbade the faithful to baptize any premature birth which did not show at least some human shape or outline.

Under the influence of erroneous scientific reports, however, Catholic thinkers gave up this traditional doctrine. In the early seventeenth century, as a result of a combination of poor microscopes and lively imaginations, some physicians saw in embryos which were only a few days old a tiny hu-man being, a homunculus, with microscopic head, legs, and arms. This view of the fetus implied the *preformation theory,* which held that organic de-velopment simply consists of the gradual increase in size of organs and structures which are fully present from the very start. If there really were from the beginning a human body, be it ever so small, there might also from the start exist a human soul. Even a microscopic statue must have a shape. Granted the preformation theory, immediate animation was compatible with the hylomorphic conception of man.

The theory of preformation was eventually replaced by the *theory of epige-nesis,* which maintains that the organism, far from being microscopically preformed from the start, develops its organs through a complex process of growth, cleavage, differentiation, and organization.

Why did the Christian thinkers not return to the delayed animation the-ory, which seems to be demanded by their hylomorphic theory of man? The main reason seems to have been the influence of Cartesian dualism. For Descartes, both man's soul and his body are each a complete substance. The soul is a thinking substance, the body an extended substance. This is no longer hylomorphism. To express it in nontechnical language, this is no longer a "shape in the statue" conception, but rather a "ghost in the ma-chine" conception of the human soul. A full-fledged ghost can manage very well with a microscopic machine. If the soul is no longer the formal cause, the constitutive idea of the body, it might well become its efficient cause, that which produces the ovum's development from the start. Instead of be-ing the idea incarnated in the body, it has turned into the architect and the builder of the body. Just as the architect exists before the first stone of the building is laid, so there can be a real human soul from the first moment of conception, before the emergence of a real human body.

This way of explaining embryogeny is not absurd. The Cartesian outlook, although quite unfashionable nowadays, has been held by many great thinkers. This kind of philosophy calls for immediate animation, which is clearly in conflict with the hylomorphic doctrine of man, solemnly endorsed by the Catholic church at the Council of Vienne.

There have been other influences which explain the shift in Catholic opinion. One of them may have been the long-standing opposition of the church to the idea of evolution. Thomas admitted some kind of evolution of the embryo and the fetus in the mother's womb. How could the church admit this evolution in the womb and reject it in the race? Since the Catholic church has finally come around to admitting the evolution of the human body, it might also be willing to return to Thomas's idea of evolution in the womb.

Moreover, once we give up the idea of immediate animation, we can no longer say when the human soul is infused, when the embryo or the fetus becomes a human person. That is why those who want to play it absolutely safe claim that the human soul is present from the moment of conception. They seem to take it for granted that, since we do not know when the human soul is present, we neither can know for sure when it is not yet present. This assumption is false. Let us consider another case, where we do not know when a certain factor is present, while knowing very well when it is not yet present. Nobody can tell with certitude when a child is capable of performing his first free moral choice, but all of us are quite certain that, during the first months or years of his life, a human baby is not yet a free moral agent. Likewise, I do not know when the human soul is infused, when the embryo becomes human. But I feel certain that there is no human soul, hence no human person, during the first few weeks of pregnancy, as long as the embryo remains in the vegetative stage of its development.

Some people make much of the following objection to my position. They say that from the very first the fertilized ovum possesses forty-six human chromosomes, all the human genes, its code of life—that it is a human embryo. This is undeniable. But it does not make it a human person. When a heart is transplanted, it is kept alive, for a short while, outside of the donor. It is a living being, a human heart, with the human chromosomes and genes. But it is not a human being; it is not a person.

The objection may be pressed. Not only does the fertilized human ovum possess the human chromosomes; unlike the heart, it will, if circumstances are normal, develop into a human being. It is virtually a human being. I admit this, but it does not affect my position. The fertilized human ovum, the early embryo, is virtually a human body, not actually. Correctly understood, the hylomorphic conception of human nature, the official Catholic doctrine, cannot admit the presence of an actual human soul in a virtual human body. Let me use a comparison again. A deflated rubber ball is virtually round; when inflated, it can assume no other shape than the spherical shape. Yet it does not actually possess any roundness or sphericity. In the same way, the early embryo does not actually possess a human soul; it is not a human person. . . .

Throughout my exposition I have taken for granted the hylomorphic conception of human nature. This is in line with the purpose of my essay, which is not only to present a liberal Catholic's view of fetal animation, but also to show that this view seems to be the only one which agrees with the official Catholic conception of human nature. In other words, I submit that Catholics should give up the immediate animation theory, because it implies a Cartesian, dualistic conception of man, which conflicts with the doctrine endorsed by the Council of Vienne. . . .

In my opinion there is a great amount of agreement between the contemporary antidualistic trend of philosophy and the hylomorphic conception of man. It is wise therefore to return to this conception or, at least, to accept the conclusions which follow from it. One of these conclusions is that the embryo is certainly not a human person during the early stages of pregnancy, and that, consequently, it is not immoral to terminate pregnancy during this time, provided there are serious reasons for such an intervention.

Let me insist on this restriction: the opinion which I have defended may lead to abuses, to abortions performed under flimsy pretexts. I would be among the first to deplore and condemn such abuses. Although a prehuman embryo cannot demand from us the absolute respect which we owe to the human person, it deserves a very great consideration, because it is a living being, endowed with a human finality, on its way to hominization. Therefore it seems to me that only very serious reasons should allow us to terminate its existence. Excesses will unavoidably occur, but they should not induce us to overlook the instances where sufficiently serious reasons exist for performing an abortion during the early stages of pregnancy.

5. JESSE JACKSON, "SPEECH AT THE 1984 DEMOCRATIC CONVENTION, SAN FRANCISCO, CA"

Few election years held as much drama as 1988 when it came to religion in the field of American politics. Both major political parties saw ordained ministers seeking the nomination for president—Jesse Jackson, who ran to the political left of his Democratic colleagues; and Pat Robertson, who ran to the political right of his Republican associates. Each represented particularly well their supporters' concerns and hopes as the Reagan presidency moved into its final days.

In many ways, Jackson's energetic and surprising 1988 campaign—in which he won ten of the Democratic primaries and ran strong in most states—began with an electri-

*fying speech at the Democratic National Convention in San Francisco four years earli-
er. Sounding the clarion call of civil rights for all Americans, he fused religious and political language and concerns. His political stances earned him the ire of conservatives
and even many moderates but also galvanized support among the progressives and pop-
ulists in the Democratic Party for the 1988 campaign. This speech exemplifies how liberal Christianity could influence politics at a time when most observers focused solely
on the conservative Moral Majority.*

Tonight we come together bound by our faith in a mighty God, with genuine
respect and love for our country, and inheriting the legacy of a great party,
the Democratic Party, which is the best hope for redirecting our nation on a
more humane, just, and peaceful course.

This is not a perfect party. We are not a perfect people. Yet, we are called
to a perfect mission. Our mission: to feed the hungry; to clothe the naked;
to house the homeless; to teach the illiterate; to provide jobs for the jobless;
and to choose the human race over the nuclear race.

We are gathered here this week to nominate a candidate and adopt a platform which will expand, unify, direct, and inspire our Party and the nation
to fulfill this mission. My constituency is the desperate, the damned, the disinherited, the disrespected, and the despised. They are restless and seek relief. They have voted in record numbers. They have invested the faith, hope,
and trust that they have in us. The Democratic Party must send them a signal that we care. I pledge my best not to let them down.

There is the call of conscience, redemption, expansion, healing, and unity. Leadership must heed the call of conscience, redemption, expansion,
healing, and unity, for they are the key to achieving our mission. Time is
neutral and does not change things. With courage and initiative, leaders
change things.

No generation can choose the age or circumstance in which it is born, but
through leadership it can choose to make the age in which it is born an age
of enlightenment, an age of jobs, and peace, and justice. Only leadership—
that intangible combination of gifts, the discipline, information, circumstance, courage, timing, will and divine inspiration—can lead us out of the
crisis in which we find ourselves. Leadership can mitigate the misery of our
nation. Leadership can part the waters and lead our nation in the direction
of the Promised Land. Leadership can lift the boats stuck at the bottom. . . .

Our party is emerging from one of its most hard-fought battles for the
Democratic Party's presidential nomination in our history. But our healthy
competition should make us better, not bitter. We must use the insight,

wisdom, and experience of the late Hubert Humphrey as a balm for the wounds in our party, this nation, and the world. We must forgive each other, redeem each other, regroup, and move on. Our flag is red, white, and blue, but our nation is a rainbow—red, yellow, brown, black and white—and we're all precious in God's sight.

America is not like a blanket—one piece of unbroken cloth, the same color, the same texture, the same size. America is more like a quilt: many patches, many pieces, many colors, many sizes, all woven and held together by a common thread. The white, the Hispanic, the black, the Arab, the Jew, the woman, the Native American, the small farmer, the businessperson, the environmentalist, the peace activist, the young, the old, the lesbian, the gay, and the disabled make up the American quilt. . . .

From Fannie Lou Hamer in Atlantic City in 1964 to the Rainbow Coalition in San Francisco today; from the Atlantic to the Pacific, we have experienced pain but progress, as we ended American apartheid laws. We got public accommodations. We secured voting rights. We obtained open housing, as young people got the right to vote. We lost Malcolm, Martin, Medgar, Bobby, John, and Viola. The team that got us here must be expanded, not abandoned.

Twenty years ago, tears welled up in our eyes as the bodies of Schwerner, Goodman, and Chaney were dredged from the depths of a river in Mississippi. Twenty years later, our communities, black and Jewish, are in anguish, anger, and pain. Feelings have been hurt on both sides. There is a crisis in communications. Confusion is in the air. But we cannot afford to lose our way. We may agree to agree; or agree to disagree on issues; we must bring back civility to these tensions.

We are co-partners in a long and rich religious history—the Judeo-Christian tradition. Many blacks and Jews have a shared passion for social justice at home and peace abroad. We must seek a revival of the spirit, inspired by a new vision and new possibilities. We must return to higher ground. We are bound by Moses and Jesus, but also connected with Islam and Mohammed. These three great religions, Judaism, Christianity, and Islam, were all born in the revered and holy city of Jerusalem.

We are bound by Dr. Martin Luther King Jr. and Rabbi Abraham Heschel, crying out from their graves for us to reach common ground. We are bound by shared blood and shared sacrifices. We are much too intelligent, much too bound by our Judeo-Christian heritage, much too victimized by racism, sexism, militarism, and anti-Semitism, much too threatened as historical scapegoats to go on divided one from another. We must turn from finger pointing to clasped hands. We must share our burdens and our joys with each other once again. We must turn to each other and not on each other and choose higher ground. . . .

We are often reminded that we live in a great nation—and we do. But it can be greater still. The Rainbow is mandating a new definition of greatness. We must not measure greatness from the mansion down, but the manger up. Jesus said that we should not be judged by the bark we wear but by the fruit that we bear. Jesus said that we must measure greatness by how we treat the least of these. . . .

Rising tides don't lift all boats, particularly those stuck at the bottom. For the boats stuck at the bottom there's a misery index. This administration has made life more miserable for the poor. Its attitude has been contemptuous. Its policies and programs have been cruel and unfair to working people. They must be held accountable in November for increasing infant mortality among the poor. In Detroit, one of the great cities of the western world, babies are dying at the same rate as Honduras, the most underdeveloped nation in our hemisphere. This administration must be held accountable for policies that have contributed to the growing poverty in America. There are now 34 million people in poverty, 15 percent of our nation. 23 million are white; 11 million black, Hispanic, Asian, and others—mostly women and children. By the end of this year, there will be 41 million people in poverty. We cannot stand idly by. We must fight for a change now. . . .

Many say that the race in November will be decided in the South. President Reagan is depending on the conservative South to return him to office. But the South, I tell you, is unnaturally conservative. The South is the poorest region in our nation and, therefore, [has] the least to conserve. In his appeal to the South, Mr. Reagan is trying to substitute flags and prayer cloths for food, and clothing, and education, health care, and housing.

Mr. Reagan will ask us to pray, and I believe in prayer. I have come to this way by the power of prayer. But then, we must watch false prophecy. He cuts energy assistance to the poor, cuts breakfast programs from children, cuts lunch programs from children, cuts job training from children, and then says to an empty table, "Let us pray." Apparently, he is not familiar with the structure of a prayer. You thank the Lord for the food that you are about to receive, not the food that just left. I think that we should pray, but don't pray for the food that left. Pray for the man that took the food to leave. We need a change. We need a change in November. . . .

The victory for the Rainbow Coalition in the Platform debates today was not whether we won or lost, but that we raised the right issues. We could afford to lose the vote; issues are non-negotiable. We could not afford to avoid raising the right questions. Our self-respect and our moral integrity were at stake. Our heads are perhaps bloody, but not bowed. Our back is straight. We can go home and face our people. Our vision is clear.

When we think, on this journey from slave-ship to championship, that we have gone from the planks of the Boardwalk in Atlantic City in 1964 to fighting to help write the planks in the platform in San Francisco in '84, there is a deep and abiding sense of joy in our souls in spite of the tears in our eyes. Though there are missing planks, there is a solid foundation upon which to build. Our party can win, but we must provide hope which will inspire people to struggle and achieve; provide a plan that shows a way out of our dilemma and then lead the way.

In 1984, my heart is made to feel glad because I know there is a way out—justice. The requirement for rebuilding America is justice. The linchpin of progressive politics in our nation will not come from the North; they, in fact, will come from the South. That is why I argue over and over again. We look from Virginia around to Texas, there's only one black congressperson out of 115. Nineteen years later, we're locked out of the Congress, the Senate and the Governor's mansion. What does this large black vote mean? Why do I fight to win second primaries and fight gerrymandering and annexation and at-large [elections]? Why do we fight over that? Because I tell you, you cannot hold someone in the ditch unless you linger there with them. Unless you linger there.

If you want a change in this nation, you enforce that Voting Rights Act. We'll get 12 to 20 black, Hispanics, female and progressive congresspersons from the South. We can save the cotton, but we've got to fight the boll weevils. We've got to make a judgment. We've got to make a judgment.

It is not enough to hope ERA will pass. How can we pass ERA? If Blacks vote in great numbers, progressive Whites win. It's the only way progressive Whites win. If Blacks vote in great numbers, Hispanics win. When Blacks, Hispanics, and progressive Whites vote, women win. When women win, children win. When women and children win, workers win. We must all come up together. We must come up together.

6. U.S. BISHOPS' 1987 PASTORAL LETTER

The Roman Catholic Church in the United States has a long history of remaining objective about the pros and cons of the American free market economy. To some degree, this results from the large number of immigrant Catholics among the lower- and working-class laborers who both bore the brunt of American industrialization and, by taking advantage of the opportunities afforded within that system, rose to middle-class status within a generation or two. The Church that provided spiritual sustenance to these Americans was sensitive to their social and economic plight, and often produced

*official declarations about the harm that runaway capitalism could inflict on the la-
borers who helped build it.*

In 1987, the Council of U.S. Bishops wrote the Pastoral Letter on Catholic Social
Teaching and the U.S. Economy *to address some of the abuses that were harming
those least able to defend themselves politically. The long document called into question
a national acceptance of too-high unemployment rates because of an erroneous belief
that a certain percentage of people do not want to work anyway, of federal spending on
nuclear warheads rather than education, of cutting taxes for the wealthy at the expense
of needed social programs. To some, the letter failed to address the positive aspects of a
capitalist society that granted more rights and opportunities than other economic systems. Still, the Pastoral Letter must be seen in its longer historical context of providing
spiritual underpinnings to social and economic conditions that affect the poor. Re-
minding Americans that Jesus spent more time with the poor than anyone else and that
money was the topic he spoke about more than any other, the bishops call into question
the ambitions that, though they might make a nation powerful, nonetheless cause pain
and hardship for those Jesus most loved.*

A. THE CHRISTIAN VOCATION IN THE WORLD TODAY

327. This letter has addressed many matters commonly regarded as secular,
for example, employment rates, income levels, and international economic
relationships. Yet, the affairs of the world, including economic ones, cannot
be separated from the spiritual hunger of the human heart. We have presented the biblical vision of humanity and the Church's moral and religious
tradition as a framework for asking the deeper questions about the meaning of economic life and for actively responding to them. But words alone
are not enough. The Christian perspective on the meaning of economic life
must transform the lives of individuals, families, in fact, our whole culture.
The Gospel confers on each Christian the vocation to love God and neighbor in ways that bear fruit in the life of society. That vocation consists above
all in a change of heart: a conversion expressed in praise of God and in concrete deeds of justice and service.

1. Conversion

328. The transformation of social structures begins with and is always accompanied by a conversion of the heart. As disciples of Christ each of us is
called to a deep personal conversion and to "action on behalf of justice and
and participation in the transformation of the world." By faith and baptism

we are fashioned into a "new creature"; we are filled with the Holy Spirit and a new love that compels us to seek out a new profound relationship with God, with the human family, and with all created things. Renouncing self-centered desires, bearing one's daily cross, and imitating Christ's compassion, all involve a personal struggle to control greed and selfishness, a personal commitment to reverence one's own human dignity and the dignity of others by avoiding self-indulgence and those attachments that make us insensitive to the conditions of others and that erode social solidarity. Christ warned us against attachments to material things, against total self-reliance, against the idolatry of accumulating material goods and seeking safety in them. We must take these teachings seriously and in their light examine how each of us lives and acts towards others. But personal conversion is not gained once and for all. It is a process that goes on through our entire life. Conversion, moreover, takes place in the context of a larger faith community: through baptism into the Church, through common prayer, and through our activity with others on behalf of justice. . . .

3. Call to Holiness in the World

332. Holiness is not limited to the sanctuary or to moments of private prayer; it is a call to direct our whole heart and life toward God and according to God's plan for this world. For the laity holiness is achieved in the midst of the world, in family, in community, in friendships, in work, in leisure, in citizenship. Through their competency and by their activity, lay men and women have the vocation to bring the light of the Gospel to economic affairs, "so that the world may be filled with the Spirit of Christ and may more effectively attain its destiny in justice, in love, and in peace."

333. But as disciples of Christ we must constantly ask ourselves how deeply the biblical and ethical vision of justice and love permeates our thinking. How thoroughly does it influence our way of life? We may hide behind the complexity of the issues or dismiss the significance of our personal contribution; in fact, each one has a role to play, because every day each one makes economic decisions. Some, by reason of their work or their position in society, have a vocation to be involved in a more decisive way in those decisions that affect the economic well-being of others. They must be encouraged and sustained by all in their search for greater justice.

334. At times we will be called upon to say no to the cultural manifestations that emphasize values and aims that are selfish, wasteful, and opposed to the Scriptures. Together we must reflect on our personal and family decisions and curb unnecessary wants in order to meet the needs of others. There are many questions we must keep asking ourselves: Are we becoming ever more wasteful in a "throw-away" society? Are we able to distinguish

between our true needs and those thrust on us by advertising and a society that values consumption more than saving? All of us could well ask ourselves whether as a Christian prophetic witness we are not called to adopt a simpler lifestyle, in the face of the excessive accumulation of material goods that characterizes an affluent society.

335. Husbands and wives, in particular, should weigh their needs carefully and establish a proper priority of values as they discuss the questions of both parents working outside the home and the responsibilities of raising children with proper care and attention. At times we will be called as individuals, as families, as parishes, as Church, to identify more closely with the poor in their struggle for participation and to close the gap of understanding between them and the affluent. By sharing the perspectives of those who are suffering, we can come to understand economic and social problems in a deeper way, thus leading us to seek more durable solutions.

336. In the workplace the laity are often called to make tough decisions with little information about the consequences that such decisions have on the economic lives of others. Such times call for collaborative dialogue together with prayerful reflection on Scripture and ethical norms. The same can be said of the need to elaborate policies that will reflect sound ethical principles and that can become a part of our political and social system. Since this is a part of the lay vocation and its call to holiness, the laity must seek to instill a moral and ethical dimension into the public debate on these issues and help enunciate the ethical questions that must be faced. To weigh political options according to criteria that go beyond efficiency and expediency requires prayer, reflection, and dialogue on all the ethical norms involved. Holiness for the laity will involve all the sacrifices needed to lead such a life of prayer and reflection within a worshiping and supporting faith community. In this way the laity will bridge the gap that so easily arises between the moral principles that guide the personal life of the Christian and the considerations that govern decisions in society in the political forum and in the marketplace.

4. Leisure

337. Some of the difficulty in bringing Christian faith to economic life in the United States today results from the obstacles to establishing a balance of labor and leisure in daily life. Tedious and boring work leads some to look for fulfillment only during time off the job. Others have become "workaholics," people who work compulsively and without reflection on the deeper meaning of life and their actions. The quality and pace of work should be more human in scale enabling people to experience the dignity and value of their work and giving them time for other duties and obligations. This

balance is vitally important for sustaining the social, political, educational, and cultural structures of society. The family, in particular, requires such balance. Without leisure there is too little time for nurturing marriages, for developing parent-child relationships, and for fulfilling commitments to other important groups: the extended family, the community of friends, the parish, the neighborhood, schools, and political organizations. Why is it one hears so little today about shortening the work week, especially if both parents are working? Such a change would give them more time for each other, for their children, and for their other social and political responsibilities.

338. Leisure is connected to the whole of one's value system and influenced by the general culture one lives in. It can be trivialized into boredom and laziness, or end in nothing but a desire for greater consumption and waste. For disciples of Christ, the use of leisure may demand being countercultural. The Christian tradition sees in leisure, time to build family and societal relationships and an opportunity for communal prayer and worship, for relaxed contemplation and enjoyment of God's creation, and for the cultivation of the arts which help fill the human longing for wholeness. Most of all, we must be convinced that economic decisions affect our use of leisure and that such decisions are also to be based on moral and ethical considerations. In this area of leisure we must be on our guard against being swept along by a lack of cultural values and by the changing fads of an affluent society. In the creation narrative God worked six days to create the world and rested on the seventh (Gn 2:1–4). We must take that image seriously and learn how to harmonize action and rest, work and leisure, so that both contribute to building up the person as well as the family and community.

B. CHALLENGES TO THE CHURCH

339. The Church is all the people of God, gathered in smaller faith communities, guided and served by a pope and a hierarchy of bishops, ministered to by priests, deacons, religious, and laity, through visible institutions and agencies. Church is, thus, primarily a communion of people bonded by the Spirit with Christ as their Head, sustaining one another in love, and acting as a sign or sacrament in the world. By its nature it is people called to a transcendent end; but, it is also a visible social institution functioning in this world. According to their calling, members participate in the mission and work of the Church and share, to varying degrees, the responsibility for its institutions and agencies.

At this moment in history, it is particularly important to emphasize the responsibilities of the whole Church for education and family life.

1. Education

340. We have already emphasized the commitment to quality education that is necessary if the poor are to take their rightful place in the economic structures of our society. We have called the Church to remember its own obligation in this regard and we have endorsed support for improvements in public education.

341. The educational mission of the Church is not only to the poor but to all its members. We reiterate our 1972 statement: "Through education, the Church seeks to prepare its members to proclaim the Good News and to translate this proclamation into action. Since the Christian vocation is a call to transform oneself and society with God's help, the educational efforts of the Church must encompass the twin purposes of personal sanctification and social reform in the light of Christian values." Through her educational mission the Church seeks: to integrate knowledge about this world with revelation about God; to understand God's relationship to the human race and its ultimate destiny in the Kingdom of God; to build up human communities of justice and peace; and to teach the value of all creation. By inculcating these values the educational system of the Church contributes to society and to social justice. Economic questions are, thus, seen as a part of a larger vision of the human person and the human family, the value of this created earth, and the duties and responsibilities that all have toward each other and toward this universe.

342. For these reasons the Church must incorporate into all levels of her educational system the teaching of social justice and the biblical and ethical principles that support it. We call on our universities, in particular, to make Catholic social teaching, and the social encyclicals of the popes a part of their curriculum, especially for those whose vocation will call them to an active role in U.S. economic and political decision making. Faith and technological progress are not opposed one to another, but this progress must not be channeled and directed by greed, self-indulgence, or novelty for its own sake, but by values that respect human dignity and foster social solidarity.

343. The Church has always held that the first task and responsibility for education lies in the hands of parents: they have the right to choose freely the schools or other means necessary to educate their children in the faith. The Church also has consistently held that public authorities must ensure that public subsidies for the education of children are allocated so that parents can freely choose to exercise this right without incurring unjust burdens. This parental right should not be taken from them. We call again for equitable sharing in public benefits for those parents who choose private and religious schools for their children. Such help should be available especially for low-income parents. Though many of these parents sacrifice a great deal for their children's education, others are effectively deprived of the possibility of exercising this right.

2. *Supporting the Family*

344. Economic life has a profound effect on all social structures and particularly on the family. A breakdown of family life often brings with it hardship and poverty. Divorce, failure to provide support to mothers and children, abandonment of children, pregnancies out of wedlock, all contribute to the amount of poverty among us. Though these breakdowns of marriage and the family are more visible among the poor, they do not affect only that one segment of our society. In fact, one could argue that many of these breakdowns come from the false values found among the more affluent—values which ultimately pervade the whole of society.

345. More studies are needed to probe the possible connections between affluence and family and marital breakdowns. The constant seeking for self-gratification and the exaggerated individualism of our age, spurred on by false values often seen in advertising and on television, contribute to the lack of firm commitment in marriage and to destructive notions of responsibility and personal growth.

346. With good reason, the Church has traditionally held that the family is the basic building block of any society. In fighting against economic arrangements that weaken the family, the Church contributes to the well-being of society. The same must be said of the Church's teaching on responsible human sexuality and its relationship to marriage and family. Economic arrangements must support the family and promote its solidity. . . .

C. THE ROAD AHEAD

359. The completion of a letter such as this one is but the beginning of a long process of education, discussion and action; its contents must be brought to all members of the Church and of society.

360. In this respect we mentioned the twofold aim of this pastoral letter: to help Catholics form their consciences on the moral dimensions of economic decision making and to articulate a moral perspective in the general societal and political debate that surrounds these questions. These two purposes help us to reflect on the different ways the institutions and ministers of the Church can assist the laity in their vocation in the world. Renewed emphasis on Catholic social teaching in our schools, colleges, and universities; special seminars with corporate officials, union leaders, legislators, bankers, and the like; the organization of small groups composed of people from different ways of life to meditate together on the Gospel and ethical norms; speakers' bureaus; family programs; clearinghouses of available material; pulpit aids for priests; diocesan television and radio programs; research projects in our universities—all of these are appropriate means for continued discussion and action. Some of these are done best on the parish level, others by the state Catholic conferences, and others by the National Conference of Catholic Bishops. These same bodies can assist the laity in the many difficult decisions that deal with political options that affect economic decisions. Where many options are available, it must be the concern of all in such debates that we as Catholics do not become polarized. All must be challenged to show how the decisions they make and the policies they suggest flow from the ethical moral vision outlined here. As new problems arise, we hope through our continual reflection that we will be able to help refine Catholic social teaching and contribute to its further development.

361. We call upon our priests, in particular, to continue their study of these issues, so that they can proclaim the gospel message in a way that not only challenges the faithful but also sustains and encourages their vocation in and to the world. Priestly formation in our seminaries will also have to prepare candidates for this role.

362. We wish to emphasize the need to undertake research into many of the areas this document could not deal with in depth and to continue exploration of those we have dealt with. We encourage our Catholic universities, foundations, and other institutions to assist in these necessary projects. The following areas for further research are merely suggestive, not exhaustive: the impact of arms production and large military spending on the domestic economy and on culture; arms production and sales as they relate to Third World poverty; tax reforms to express the preferential option for the poor; the rights of women and minorities in the work force; the development of communications technology and its global influences; robotics, automation, and reduction of defense industries as they will affect employment; the economy and the stability of the family; legitimate profit versus greed; securing economic rights; environmental and ecological questions; future roles of labor and unions; international financial institutions and Third World debt; our national deficit; world food problems; "full employment" and its implementation; plant closings and dealing with the human costs of an evolving economy; cooperatives and new modes of sharing; welfare reform and national eligibility standards; income support systems; concentration of land ownership; assistance to Third World nations; migration and its effects; population policies and development; the effects of increased inequality of incomes in society.

D. COMMITMENT TO A KINGDOM OF LOVE AND JUSTICE

363. Confronted by this economic complexity and seeking clarity for the future, we can rightly ask ourselves one single question: How does our economic system affect the lives of people—*all* people? Part of the American dream has been to make this world a better place for people to live in; at this moment of history that dream must include everyone on this globe. Since we profess to be members of a "catholic" or universal Church, we all must raise our sights to a concern for the well-being of everyone in the world. Third World debt becomes our problem. Famine and starvation in sub-Saharan Africa become our concern. Rising military expenditures everywhere in the world become part of our fears for the future of this planet. We cannot be content if we see ecological neglect or the squandering of natural resources. In this letter we bishops have spoken often of economic interdependence; now is the moment when all of us must confront the reality of such economic bonding and its consequences and see it as a moment of grace—a *kairos*—that can unite all of us in a common community of the human family. We commit ourselves to this global vision.

364. We cannot be frightened by the magnitude and complexity of these problems. We must not be discouraged. In the midst of this struggle, it is inevitable that we become aware of greed, laziness, and envy. No utopia is possible on this earth; but as believers in the redemptive love of God and as those who have experienced God's forgiving mercy, we know that God's providence is not and will not be lacking to us today.

365. The fulfillment of human needs, we know, is not the final purpose of the creation of the human person. We have been created to share in the divine life through a destiny that goes far beyond our human capabilities and before which we must in all humility stand in awe. Like Mary in proclaiming her *Magnificat*, we marvel at the wonders God has done for us, how God has raised up the poor and the lowly and promised great things for them in the Kingdom. God now asks of us sacrifices and reflection on our reverence for human dignity—in ourselves and in others—and on our service and discipleship, so that the divine goal for the human family and this earth can be fulfilled. Communion with God, sharing God's life, involves a mutual bonding with all on this globe. Jesus taught us to love God and one another and that the concept of neighbor is without limit. We know that we are called to be members of a new covenant of love. We have to move from our devotion to independence, through an understanding of interdependence, to a commitment to human solidarity. That challenge must find its realization in the kind of community we build among us. Love implies concern for all—especially the poor—and a continued search for those social and economic structures that permit everyone to share in a community that is a part of a redeemed creation (Rom 8:21–23).

7. PATRICK J. BUCHANAN, "1992 REPUBLICAN NATIONAL CONVENTION SPEECH"

Incumbent President George Bush, victorious in the Persian Gulf War and riding high in national polls, found himself surprisingly under attack from the more conservative parts of his Republican Party in early 1992. The leader of this movement was Patrick J. Buchanan, former speechwriter for Richard Nixon and controversial journalist. Arch-conservative Buchanan whipped up his audiences, who were discontented with what they saw as Bush's nonchalance about a deepening recession that included thousands of layoffs as part of corporate restructuring, using many of the populist anti–big business themes announced previously by, ironically, the liberal Jesse Jackson in the 1984 and 1988 Democratic primaries. While Bush held on to win the party's nomination, the damage had been done: he lost the general election to Bill Clinton as the independent candidate Ross Perot drew off support for Bush by sounding many of the concerns Buchanan had highlighted earlier in the year.

Buchanan's campaign used more than populist rhetoric to gain adherents. A devoted Roman Catholic with Jesuit training, Buchanan proclaimed his candidacy was built on moral reform of a nation that had become too secular on account of the liberalism that dominated the 1960s and 1970s. Calling forth his "loyal brigades" like a moral version of the famed Minutemen of the American Revolution, he announced that there existed in the United States a culture war between those who favored morality, strong families, and a more isolated America and those who advocated for individual autonomy, abortion rights, and a foreign policy soft on enemies. His speech at the 1992 Republican Convention, meant to bring his political allies back under the banner of George Bush, is representative of the manner in which his speeches mixed populist themes with calls for moral reform by demonizing the Democrats and anything that smacked of "the L word"—liberalism.

Like many of you last month, I watched that giant masquerade ball at Madison Square Garden—where 20,000 radicals and liberals came dressed up as moderates and centrists—in the greatest single exhibition of cross-dressing in American political history.

One by one, the prophets of doom appeared at the podium. The Reagan decade, they moaned, was a terrible time in America; and the only way to prevent even worse times, they said, is to entrust our nation's fate and future to the party that gave us McGovern, Mondale, Carter and Michael Dukakis.

No way, my friends. The American people are not going to buy back into the failed liberalism of the 1960s and '70s—no matter how slick the package in 1992.

The malcontents of Madison Square Garden notwithstanding, the 1980s were not terrible years. They were great years. You know it. I know it. And the only people who don't know it are the carping critics who sat on the sidelines of history, jeering at one of the great statesmen of modern time.

Out of Jimmy Carter's days of malaise, Ronald Reagan crafted the longest peacetime recovery in U.S. history—3 million new businesses created, and 20 million new jobs.

Under the Reagan Doctrine, one by one, the communist dominos began to fall. First, Grenada was liberated, by U.S. troops. Then, the Red Army was run out of Afghanistan, by U.S. weapons. In Nicaragua, the Marxist regime was forced to hold free elections—by Ronald Reagan's contra army—and the communists were thrown out of power.

Have they forgotten? It was under our party that the Berlin Wall came down, and Europe was reunited. It was under our party that the Soviet Empire collapsed, and the captive nations broke free.

It is said that each president will be recalled by posterity—with but a single sentence. George Washington was the father of our country. Abraham Lincoln preserved the Union. And Ronald Reagan won the Cold War. And it is time my old colleagues, the columnists and commentators, looking down on us tonight from their anchor booths and sky boxes, gave Ronald Reagan the credit he deserves—for leading America to victory in the Cold War.

Most of all, Ronald Reagan made us proud to be Americans again. We never felt better about our country; and we never stood taller in the eyes of the world.

But we are here, not only to celebrate, but to nominate. And an American president has many, many roles.

He is our first diplomat, the architect of American foreign policy. And which of these two men is more qualified for that role? George Bush has been UN ambassador, CIA director, envoy to China. As vice president, he co-authored the policies that won the Cold War. As president, George Bush presided over the liberation of Eastern Europe and the termination of the Warsaw Pact. And Mr. Clinton? Well, Bill Clinton couldn't find 150 words to discuss foreign policy in an acceptance speech that lasted an hour. As was said of an earlier Democratic candidate, Bill Clinton's foreign policy experience is pretty much confined to having had breakfast once at the International House of Pancakes.

The presidency is also America's bully pulpit, what Mr. Truman called, "preeminently a place of moral leadership." George Bush is a defender of right-to-life, and lifelong champion of the Judeo-Christian values and beliefs upon which this nation was built.

Mr. Clinton, however, has a different agenda.

At its top is unrestricted abortion on demand. When the Irish-Catholic governor of Pennsylvania, Robert Casey, asked to say a few words on behalf of the 25 million unborn children destroyed since *Roe v. Wade*, he was told there was no place for him at the podium of Bill Clinton's convention, no room at the inn.

Yet a militant leader of the homosexual rights movement could rise at that convention and exult: "Bill Clinton and Al Gore represent the most pro-lesbian and pro-gay ticket in history." And so they do.

Bill Clinton supports school choice—but only for state-run schools. Parents who send their children to Christian schools, or Catholic schools, need not apply.

Elect me, and you get two for the price of one, Mr. Clinton says of his lawyer-spouse. And what does Hillary believe? Well, Hillary believes that 12-year-olds should have a right to sue their parents, and she has compared marriage as an institution to slavery—and life on an Indian reservation.

Well, speak for yourself, Hillary.

Friends, this is radical feminism. The agenda Clinton & Clinton would impose on America—abortion on demand, a litmus test for the Supreme Court, homosexual rights, discrimination against religious schools, women in combat—that's change, all right. But it is not the kind of change America wants. It is not the kind of change America needs. And it is not the kind of change we can tolerate in a nation that we still call God's country.

A president is also commander in chief, the man we empower to send sons and brothers, fathers and friends, to war.

George Bush was 17 when they bombed Pearl Harbor. He left his high school class, walked down to the recruiting office, and signed up to become the youngest fighter pilot in the Pacific war. And Mr. Clinton? When Bill Clinton's turn came in Vietnam, he sat up in a dormitory in Oxford, England, and figured out how to dodge the draft.

Which of these two men has won the moral authority to call on Americans to put their lives at risk? I suggest, respectfully, it is the patriot and war hero, Navy Lieutenant J.G. George Herbert Walker Bush.

My friends, this campaign is about philosophy, and it is about character; and George Bush wins on both counts—going away; and it is time all of us came home and stood beside him.

As running mate, Mr. Clinton chose Albert Gore. And just how moderate is Prince Albert? Well, according to the Taxpayers Union, Al Gore beat out Teddy Kennedy, two straight years, for the title of biggest spender in the Senate.

And Teddy Kennedy isn't moderate about anything.

In New York, Mr. Gore made a startling declaration. Henceforth, he said, the "central organizing principle" of all governments must be: the environment.

Wrong, Albert!

The central organizing principle of this republic is freedom. And from the ancient forests of Oregon, to the Inland Empire of California, America's great middle class has got to start standing up to the environmental extremists who put insects, rats and birds ahead of families, workers and jobs.

One year ago, my friends, I could not have dreamt I would be here. I was then still just one of many panelists on what President Bush calls "those crazy Sunday talk shows."

But I disagreed with the president; and so we challenged the president in the Republican primaries and fought as best we could. From February to June, he won 33 primaries. I can't recall exactly how many we won.

But tonight I want to talk to the 3 million Americans who voted for me. I will never forget you, nor the great honor you have done me. But I do believe, deep in my heart, that the right place for us to be now—in this presidential campaign—is right beside George Bush. The party is our home; this party is where we belong. And don't let anyone tell you any different.

Yes, we disagreed with President Bush, but we stand with him for freedom to choose religious schools, and we stand with him against the amoral idea that gay and lesbian couples should have the same standing in law as married men and women.

We stand with President Bush for right-to-life, and for voluntary prayer in the public schools, and against putting American women in combat. And we stand with President Bush in favor of the right of small towns and communities to control the raw sewage of pornography that pollutes our popular culture.

We stand with President Bush in favor of federal judges who interpret the law as written, and against Supreme Court justices who think they have a mandate to rewrite our Constitution.

My friends, this election is about much more than who gets what. It is about who we are. It is about what we believe. It is about what we stand for as Americans. There is a religious war going on in our country for the soul of America. It is a cultural war, as critical to the kind of nation we will one day be as was the Cold War itself. And in that struggle for the soul of America, Clinton & Clinton are on the other side, and George Bush is on our side. And so, we have to come home, and stand beside him.

My friends, in those 6 months, from Concord to California, I came to know our country better than ever before in my life, and I collected memories that will be with me always. . . .

There were the people of Hayfork, the tiny town high up in California's Trinity Alps, a town that is now under a sentence of death because a federal judge has set aside 9 million acres for the habitat of the spotted owl—forgetting about the habitat of the men and women who live and work in Hayfork. And there were the brave people of Koreatown who took the worst of the L.A. riots, but still live the family values we treasure, and who still believe deeply in the American dream.

Friends, in those wonderful 25 weeks, the saddest days were the days of the bloody riot in L.A., the worst in our history. But even out of that awful tragedy can come a message of hope.

Hours after the violence ended I visited the Army compound in south L.A., where an officer of the 18th Cavalry, that had come to rescue the city, introduced me to two of his troopers. They could not have been 20 years old. He told them to recount their story.

They had come into L.A. late on the second day, and they walked up a dark street, where the mob had looted and burned every building but one, a convalescent home for the aged. The mob was heading in, to ransack and loot the apartments of the terrified old men and women. When the troopers arrived, M-16s at the ready, the mob threatened and cursed, but the mob retreated. It had met the one thing that could stop it: force, rooted in justice, backed by courage.

Greater love than this hath no man than that he lay down his life for his friend. Here were 19-year-old boys ready to lay down their lives to stop a mob from molesting old people they did not even know. And as they took back the streets of L.A., block by block, so we must take back our cities, and take back our culture, and take back our country.

God bless you, and God bless America.

8. LOUIS FARRAKHAN, "MINISTER FARRAKHAN CHALLENGES BLACK MEN" (TRANSCRIPT FROM REMARKS AT THE MILLION MAN MARCH) (1995)

On October 16, 1995, hundreds of thousands of African American men gathered on Washington, DC's National Mall for a march encouraging "unity, atonement, and brotherhood." Arranged by Louis Farrakhan, leader of the Nation of Islam, as a call for black men to take greater responsibility for their lives and families through personal moral reform and increased economic, political, and social engagement, it produced one of the largest rallies in Washington that decade. Though organized by the prominent black Muslim, the march became a rallying cry for African American men across the country without restriction to any particular faith.

Many African American leaders addressed the huge crowd that day, and even some notable whites, including President Bill Clinton. Some were apprehensive of the plan allowing Farrakhan to speak, as he was a lightning rod not only in regard to black-white relations but also among a number of African Americans. Many disliked his manner of dealing with the political establishment, and some maintained that he was behind the assassination of Malcolm X for personal gain. But there was no denying the fact that he had organized a major event for black men in America—so there was no denying him a spot on the podium.

In his remarks, excerpts of which appear below, he moved freely among a number of topics that included not only the pledge for African American men to commit themselves to a moral, peaceful, and positively engaged life but also the necessity of reparations to blacks for the evils of slavery. His style was vintage Farrakhan, incorporating history, the Bible, the Qur'an, and even numerology. In this passage he begins his speech by teaching the crowd about the influence of Africa's secret wisdom in the founding of the nation, thus laying the basis for his later calls for moral engagement with the country as well as redress for the nation's past treatment of African Americans.

⎯⎯ ∞∞ ⎯⎯

In the name of Allah, the beneficent, the merciful. We thank Him for his prophets, and the scriptures which they brought. We thank him for Moses and the Torah. We thank him for Jesus and the Gospel. We thank him for Muhammad and the Qur'an. Peace be upon these worthy servants of Allah.

I am so grateful to Allah for his intervention in our affairs in the person of Master Farad Muhammad the Great Madi, who came among us and raised from among us a divine leader, teacher and guide, his messenger to us the Most Honorable Elijah Muhammad. I greet all of you, my dear and wonderful brothers, with the greeting words of peace. We say it in the Arabic language, As Salaam Aleikum. . . .

I'm looking at the Washington Monument and beyond it to the Lincoln Memorial. And, beyond that, to the left, to your right, the Jefferson Memorial. Abraham Lincoln was the 16th President of these United States and he was the man who allegedly freed us.

Abraham Lincoln saw in his day, what President Clinton sees in this day. He saw the great divide between black and white. Abraham Lincoln and Bill Clinton see what the Kerner Commission saw 30 years ago when they said that this nation was moving toward two Americas—one Black, one White, separate and unequal. And the Kerner Commission revisited their findings 25 years later and saw that America was worse today than it was in the time of Martin Luther King, Jr. There's still two Americas, one Black, one White, separate and unequal.

Abraham Lincoln, when he saw this great divide, he pondered a solution of separation. Abraham Lincoln said he never was in favor of our being jurors or having equal status with the Whites of this nation. Abraham Lincoln said that if there were to be a superior or inferior, he would rather the superior position be assigned to the White race. There, in the middle of this mall is the Washington Monument, 555 feet high. But if we put a one in front of that 555 feet, we get 1555, the year that our first fathers landed on the shores of Jamestown, Virginia as slaves.

In the background is the Jefferson and Lincoln Memorial, each one of these monuments is 19 feet high.

Abraham Lincoln, the sixteenth president. Thomas Jefferson, the third president, and 16 and three make 19 again. What is so deep about this number 19? Why are we standing on the Capitol steps today? That number 19—when you have a nine you have a womb that is pregnant. And when you have a one standing by the nine, it means that there's something secret that has to be unfolded.

Right here on this mall where we are standing, according to books written on Washington, D.C., slaves used to be brought right here on this Mall in chains to be sold up and down the eastern seaboard. Right along this mall, going over to the White House, our fathers were sold into slavery. But, George Washington, the first president of the United States, said he feared that before too many years passed over his head, this slave would prove to become a most troublesome species of property.

Thomas Jefferson said, he trembled for this country when he reflected that God was just and that his justice could not sleep forever. Well, the day that these presidents feared has now come to pass, for on this mall, here we stand in the capital of America, and the layout of this great city, laid out by a Black man, Benjamin Banneker. This is all placed and based in a secret Masonic ritual. And at the core of the secret of that ritual is the Black man; not far from here is the White House.

And the first president of this land, George Washington, who was a grand master of the Masonic order, laid the foundation, the cornerstone of this capitol building where we stand. George was a slave owner. Now, the President spoke today and he wanted to heal the great divide. But I respectfully suggest to the President, you did not dig deep enough at the malady that divides Black and White in order to affect a solution to the problem.

And so, today, we have to deal with the root so that perhaps a healing can take place.

Now, this obelisk at the Washington Monument is Egyptian and this whole layout is reminiscent of our great historic past, Egypt. And, if you look at the original Seal of the United States, published by the Department of State in 1909. Gaylord Hunt wrote that late in the afternoon of July 4, 1776, the Continental Congress resolved that Dr. Benjamin Franklin, Mr. John Adams, and Mr. Thomas Jefferson be a committee to prepare a device for a Seal of the United States of America.

In the design proposed by the first committee, the face of the Seal was a coat of arms measured in six quarters. That number is significant. Six quarters, with emblems representing England, Scotland, Ireland, France, Germany and Holland, the countries from which the new nation had been peopled. The eye of providence in a radiant triangle and the motto, "E Pluribus Unum" were also proposed for the face of the Seal. Even [though] the country was populated by so-called Indians and Black Slaves were brought to build the country, the official Seal of the country was never designed to reflect our presence, only that of the European immigrants. The Seal and the Constitution reflect the thinking of the founding fathers, that this was to be a nation by White people and for White people. Native Americans, Blacks, and all other non-White people were to be the burden bearers for the real citizens of this nation.

For the back of the Seal the committee suggested a picture of Pharoah sitting in an open chariot with a crown on his head and a sword in his hand, passing through the divided waters of the Red Sea, in pursuit of the Israelites. And, hovering over the sea was to be shown a pillar of fire in a cloud, expressive of the divine presence and command.

And raised from this pillar of fire were to be shown, beaming down on Moses standing on the shore, extending his hand over the sea, causing it to overwhelm Pharoah.

The motto for the reverse was, "Rebellion To Tyrants Is Obedience To God." Let me say it again. Rebellion is obedience to God. Now, why did they mention Pharaoh? I heard the President say today E Pluribus Unum—out of many, one.

But in the past, out of many comes one meant out of many Europeans come one people. The question today is, out of the many Asians, the many Arabs, the many Native Americans, the many Blacks, the many people of color who populate this country. Do you mean for them to be made into the one?

If so, truth has to be spoken to justice. We can't cover things up. Cover them over. Give it a pretty sound to make people feel good. We have to go to the root of the problem. Now, why have you come today?

You came not at the call of Louis Farrakhan, but you have gathered here at the call of God. For it is only the call of Almighty God, no matter through whom that call came, that could generate this kind of outpouring. God called us here to this place. At this time. For a very specific reason. . . .

So, we stand here today at this historic moment. We are standing in the place of those who couldn't make it here today. We are standing on the blood of our ancestors. We are standing on the blood of those who died in the middle passage, who died in the fields and swamps of America, who died hanging from trees in the South, who died in the cells of their jailers, who died on the highways and who died in the fratricidal conflict that rages within our community. We are standing on the sacrifice of the lives of those heroes, our great men and women that we today may accept the responsibility that life imposes upon each traveler who comes this way.

We must accept the responsibility that God has put upon us, not only to be good husbands and fathers and builders of our community, but God is now calling upon the despised and the rejected to become the cornerstone and the builders of a new world. . . .

9. JAMES DOBSON, "AN EVANGELICAL RESPONSE TO BILL CLINTON" (1998)

Few politicians divided postwar Americans as consistently as Bill Clinton, a Southern Baptist from Arkansas. Elected with only 43 percent of the vote in 1992 (4 percent more than the incumbent president), he oversaw the longest peacetime economic expansion in the nation's history, yet was reelected with only 48 percent of the vote in 1996. The reason? Many political conservatives—especially evangelicals—saw in him all the aspects of 1960s and 1970s liberalism they loathed. For some, their denunciation of Clinton turned to demonization, attributing to him such behavior as secret murders and clandestine deals with national enemies.

Clinton's 1998 admission of lewd behavior with a White House intern only added fuel to the fire. Certain the scandal should bring down his presidency, many conservative Protestants called for his resignation, and when that was not forthcoming, they backed his impeachment. James Dobson, host of the popular Christian radio program Focus on the Family and author of books with sales well into the millions, was a particularly vocal critic of the Clinton administration. Having refrained from writing much about the rumors and investigations that riveted the nation through 1998, he broke his silence that September when Clinton admitted to his immoral behavior and public lies in a short televised talk.

While Dobson's piece in his monthly newsletter reviewed the many charges some evangelicals had made against Clinton over the years, he reserved his bewilderment for the opinions of the American people. For despite all the accusations and admissions, Clinton's national approval ratings remained extremely high. Dobson attacked the public's acceptance of a division between private behavior and public service, claiming that no matter how successful a person was at their job, morality mattered. In spite of Dobson's and others' sustained attacks and an impeachment without removal by Congress, Bill Clinton remained in office and left two years later with public opinion about him still divided. Eight months later, Americans were asked in a Harris Poll to name their public figure heroes; Clinton came in number ten, behind the likes of Jesus Christ, Martin Luther King, John F. Kennedy, Mother Teresa, and Abraham Lincoln, and ahead of George Washington, Franklin D. Roosevelt, and the pope. In the same poll, Americans were asked to name public figures no longer considered heroes; Clinton topped a list that included O. J. Simpson and Thomas Jefferson.

⊶⊷

September 1998

Dear Friends:

Greetings to you all. Shirley and I have been visiting the historic city of Boston for the past few weeks while working on a new book called *Coming Home*. . . . Toward the end of our trip, however, we were shocked and dismayed by the admission of the President's affair with "that woman—Miss Lewinsky"—which brought humiliation on himself, his family and our nation. Millions of words have been written and spoken about that sordid story, which I have chosen not to address during these past seven months. But now I want to express some passionate views that are on my heart.

As with many Christians around the country, Shirley and I have been in prayer for our leaders in government who must deal with the fallout from this scandal. They will need great wisdom and discernment in the days ahead. Our most serious concern, however, is not with those in Washington; it is with the American people. What has alarmed me throughout this episode has been the willingness of my fellow citizens to rationalize the President's behavior even after they suspected, and later knew, that he was lying. Because the economy is strong, millions of people have said infidelity in the Oval Office is just a private affair—something between himself and Hillary. We heard it time and again during those months: "As long as Mr. Clinton is doing a good job, it's nobody's business what he does with his personal life."

That disregard for morality is profoundly disturbing to me. Although sexual affairs have occurred often in high places, the public has never approved of such misconduct. But today, the rules by which behavior is governed appear to have been rewritten specifically for Mr. Clinton. We now know that this 50-year-old man had sexual relations repeatedly and brazenly in the White House, with a woman 27 years his junior. Then he spoke on national television while shaking his finger at the camera, and denied ever having a sexual relationship with Miss Lewinsky. He was the most powerful man in the world and she was a starry-eyed intern. That situation would not have been tolerated in any other setting—*ever*. And yet the apologists for the President have said endlessly, "It's just about sex," as though cheating on your wife was of no particular significance. But the majority of the American people replied, "I support the President."

Let me ask, in what other context such behavior would have been acceptable? When a professor is known to have had consensual sex with a student, the university dismisses him or her forthwith. Academic institutions recognize their responsibility to protect the interests of younger and more vulnerable individuals. When a corporate executive is similarly accused, especially if numerous women claim to have been "groped" or abused in the manner of Kathleen Willey or Paula Jones, that man is fired. Period! If a middle-aged physician had sex with a younger patient in his office, he would probably lose his medical license. If a psychiatrist, psychologist or counselor entered into a sexual relationship with a patient of any age, he would be charged with malpractice. It is stated in the code of ethics for these professions. . . .

How did our beloved nation find itself in this sorry mess? I believe it began not with the Lewinsky affair, but many years earlier. There was plenty of evidence during the first Presidential election that Bill Clinton had a moral problem. His affair with Gennifer Flowers, which he now admits to having lied about, was rationalized by the American people. He lied about dodging the draft, and then concocted an incredulous explanation that changed his story. He visited the Soviet Union and other hostile countries during the Vietnam War, claiming that he was only an "observer." Numerous sources reported that he organized and participated in anti-war rallies in the United States, Great Britain, and Norway. Clinton evaded questions about whether he had used marijuana, and then finally offered his now-infamous "I didn't inhale" response. There were other indications that Bill Clinton was untruthful and immoral. Why, then, did the American people ignore so many red flags? Because, and I want to give the greatest emphasis to this point, the mainstream media became enamored with Bill Clinton in 1992 and sought to convince the American people that "character doesn't matter." . . .

Clinton is not the only politician in either party who lacks character, certainly, but he is the only one in American history, to my knowledge, who has been specifically applauded for his deceit. . . .

As it turns out, character DOES matter. You can't run a family, let alone a country, without it. How foolish to believe that a person who lacks honesty and moral integrity is qualified to lead a nation and the world! Nevertheless, our people continue to say that the President is doing a good job even if they don't respect him personally. Those two positions are fundamentally incompatible. In the Book of James the question is posed, "Can both fresh water and salt water flow from the same spring" (James 3:11 NIV). The answer is no.

Speaking again of the First Lady, we're being asked to believe that she knew nothing about the President's escapade. I don't want to be insensitive during her very difficult trial, but there is something strange about that explanation. After all, Hillary has been over this road before with her husband. Remember her appearance on 60 Minutes in 1992 when candidate Clinton admitted he had "caus[ed] pain in [my] marriage" regarding the affair with Gennifer Flowers? Hillary has dealt with infidelity at least once. Wouldn't that have unsettled Mrs. Clinton, especially when she knew about the charges made by Paula Jones, Kathleen Willey and possibly others. Are we to believe that this brilliant woman, a highly respected lawyer, neither saw nor heard anything leading her to conclude that her husband was lying? Did their private conversations reveal anything suspicious to her? How could she not have known about Monica these past seven months when the entire world was digging for information? It doesn't sound believable to me.

This, then, is the key question. If Hillary *did* know about the affair, does that mean she lied too? And if so, was it not inexcusable for her to appear on the *Today Show* in January to blame the "right-wing conspiracy" for trouble that she knew was of her husband's own making?

One thing is certain: Mr. Clinton has betrayed some of his closest friends, many of them being women who were pressed into his defense. Included among them were Senator Dianne Feinstein, Senator Barbara Boxer, Betty Currie, Ann Lewis, Dee Dee Myers, Mandy Grunwald, Secretary of State Madeleine Albright, and Secretary of Health and Human Services Donna Shalala, among others. Columnist Thomas Sowell wrote, "What could be more selfish or more gutless than a man hiding behind a woman, especially a woman young enough to be his daughter." Noted in the President's weak and defensive explanation on August 17 was no mention of Monica Lewinsky and the other cast of characters. The President owes all his defenders an apology. . . .

Well, that brings me back to the issue with which we began. The American people have now heard the President's dramatic confession of adultery. There is no longer any reason to speculate, and yet, the media reports that the majority continues to believe "it doesn't matter." At one point during the shocking revelations last month, Clinton's public approval rating approached 70 percent! I just don't understand it. Why aren't parents more concerned about what their children are hearing about the President's behavior? Are moms and dads not embarrassed by what is occurring? At any given time, 40 percent of the nation's children list the President of the United States as the person they most admire. What are they learning from Mr. Clinton? What have we taught our boys about respecting women? What have our little girls learned about men? How can we estimate the impact of this scandal on future generations? How in the world can 7 out of 10 Americans continue to say that nothing matters except a robust economy?

I am left to conclude from these opinions that our greatest problem is not in the Oval Office. It is with the people of this land! We have lost our ability to discern the difference between right and wrong. Biblical moral principles have guided us since the Pilgrims came to these shores. In his farewell address to the Congress in 1796, George Washington said:

> Of all the disposition and habits which lead to political prosperity, Religion and morality are indispensable supports. . . . And let us with caution indulge the supposition, that morality can be maintained without religion . . . reason and experience both forbid us to expect that national morality can prevail in exclusion of religious principle.

Clearly, this nation has been blessed because it was based on a commitment to biblical morality. But that is changing. Eleven years ago, Gary Hart was forced to withdraw from the Presidential race after a brief tryst, and yet the majority today seems to find nothing wrong with behavior that is too disgusting to be reported on the evening news.

We are facing a profound moral crisis—not only because one man has disgraced us—but because our people no longer recognize the nature of evil. And when a nation reaches that state of depravity—judgment is a certainty.

As for the future of Bill Clinton, who knows where his presidency is headed. Because I'm writing this on September 1, he may or may not still be president by the time you read this. I see the President as a prize fighter who's been staggered by a succession of blows, but he's still standing. One more solid punch and he could go down. Only time will tell. Regardless of his personal future, I hope that Mr. Clinton will, as William Mattox suggested, "choose to follow in the path of Watergate figure Chuck Colson, a man who came clean with the truth, owned up to his misdeeds and found, at the height of his public humiliation, a new life and a new purpose." As with all of us sinners, Jesus Christ is the atonement.

Pray with us for our country, won't you? Nothing short of a spiritual renewal will save us.

Sincerely,
James C. Dobson, Ph.D
President

10. TEACHING EVOLUTION IN PUBLIC SCHOOLS

INTELLIGENT DESIGN NETWORK, "LETTER TO THE BOARD OF EDUCATION OF EACH OF THE UNIFIED SCHOOL DISTRICTS OF THE STATE OF KANSAS" (2000)

KANSAS CITIZENS FOR SCIENCE, "A RESPONSE TO THE INTELLIGENT DESIGN NETWORK'S PROPOSALS TO INCLUDE 'INTELLIGENT DESIGN' IN THE KANSAS SCIENCE STANDARDS" (2001)

It seems appropriate that the twentieth century ended on the note that had produced one of its most well-known battles between religion and secular society. For while the Scopes Trial in 1925 had brought to the fore the cultural debate between those who accepted Darwinism and those who proclaimed the Genesis account of creation, it had hardly settled the issue. Indeed, while many biblical literalists started their own educational institutions in the following decades, they never ceded the intellectual victory to those who taught that science was only about method and not about philosophical underpinnings.

After a number of failed attempts during the late twentieth century to introduce "creation science" alongside the theory of evolution in public schools, anti-Darwinists changed their approach. Arguing instead that scientific facts would support the notion of an "intelligent design" of the universe, they began grassroots campaigns to have local school boards include the possibility of intelligent design (ID) alongside the theory of natural selection when evolution was taught. This movement caught national attention in 1999 when the Kansas State School Board voted to include ID in its science curriculum, having been convinced that Darwinism excluded other forms of good science.

The two letters below illustrate the crux of the debate. The Intelligent Design Network wrote to the local school boards of the state with reasons current science standards were fundamentally flawed. Arguing that logic demands all explanations be explored— rather than philosophically denying theism because of its assumptions rather than because of its evidence—and that the First Amendment requires philosophical naturalism to give up its vaunted role as the official religion of public schools, the letter encourages board members, ironically, to make "origins education" philosophically neutral by including intelligent design in the curriculum.

Kansas Citizens for Science countered these claims by explaining that ID proponents do not understand science, which seeks natural explanations for observable phenomena. Since there is no way to test the hypothesis of intelligent design, to prove or disprove it by observation, they argue, it does not fall into the category of science—so there is no reason to include it in a science curriculum. Indeed, intelligent design relies on gaps in knowledge for its evidence, which in the end discourages true science from ex-

panding into those areas. Denying that Darwinism requires naturalism, which is religious (albeit atheistic) at its base, Kansas Citizens for Science pointed to the many religious scientists involved in the task of natural explanation of observed phenomena. In the end, they carried the day: the new Kansas State School Board rejected the work of its predecessors and reinstated the previous science standards.

⎯⎯⎯⎯ ❈ ⎯⎯⎯⎯

June 8, 2000

BOARD OF EDUCATION OF
EACH OF THE UNIFIED SCHOOL DISTRICTS
OF THE STATE OF KANSAS

Ladies and Gentlemen,

Few are presented with an opportunity to change the course of history. Washington and Lincoln come to mind. The authors of the Declaration of Independence, our Constitution and the Bill of Rights had even greater opportunities. They were faced with the challenge of defining how we should live together.

As you may very well realize, you are now faced with a similar opportunity. You have the chance to make a major mark on history, to let your voice be heard. The decisions that you and your sister Kansas School Boards will be making in the coming months will be watched by the entire nation. Few people enjoy being in the spotlight; however, you are leaders in your community. You have been elected to ensure that our children are prepared to make a positive difference in their lives and the lives of their children. It is now time to seize the opportunity. It is time to change history.

The issue facing you is possibly the most important and fundamental educational issue with which you will ever deal. The issue is: What should our school science teachers tell our children about their origin?

Fundamentally, there are only two answers to this question. The answer presently taught is that life and its diversity results only from the laws of physics and chemistry (a mixture of chance and necessity or "natural law") and not by design. This is the naturalistic explanation. Darwinism (evolution based on the hypothesized natural selection of random mutations) is the mechanism that supports this philosophy. The alternative answer is that life is designed, that some kind of intelligence is responsible for its existence.

Your decision concerns whether you should direct our science teachers to continue to teach only the evidence supporting the naturalistic explanation of life or whether you should also permit them to teach evidence indicating that living systems may be designed. . . .

Why should you put an end to the censorship of design in origins education and open the door to a discussion of all reliable and relevant competing evidence?

Very simply, because logical, scientific, legal and cultural consequences demand it.

1. The Demands of Logic and Science.

Naturalism is a philosophy and not science. The claim of Naturalism that only chemical and physical laws (chance and necessity) are responsible for everything and that design inferences are invalid is not supported by empirical evidence. This is a presupposition, a philosophy, and not an evidence based conclusion.

A scientific conclusion that is driven by philosophy rather than by logic has no evidentiary or logical credibility. Scientific conclusions that are dependent only on evidence that exists within boundaries that have been drawn to exclude other evidence prejudge the issue. Under a naturalistic definition of science, evidence of design is obviously excluded. The exclusion results not from the quality of its evidence, but rather from a philosophical viewpoint. Because design as a cause is excluded, the evidence of design that exists in nature is ignored. When credible evidence is systematically censored, the conclusion that Darwinism adequately explains the existence of life cannot have any logical credibility. . . .

It is also argued that design is not "science" and therefore should not be included in a science curriculum. Obviously if it is philosophically excluded from the definition of science so that science turns into a philosophy rather than a search for the truth, then design is not science. However, according to recent Supreme Court decisions relating to the nature of science, design clearly is science. In fact scientists, such as biochemists, physicists, geologists, biologists, zoologists, mathematicians, statisticians, information theorists, and the like are the only group of professionals that are logically qualified to investigate and scientifically analyze the claims of design. By defining science as the activity of seeking "logical" rather than only "natural" explanations, the New Standards clearly include design within the realm of science. . . .

The Kansas Citizens for Science might argue that they don't see any evidence of design, so why do we have to bring it up at all? This position would be expected from those who have ignored and censored the evidence and refused to give it objective consideration. We are reminded of the saying, "None is so blind as he that will not see."

In fact there is abundant and persuasive scientific evidence of design. Design theory is not new. It ruled science for thousands of years until the advent of Darwinism. Aristotle, Plato, Socrates, Cicero, St. Thomas Aquinas, Kepler, Robert Boyle, William Harvey and Isaac Newton were all design theorists. Even the most ardent Darwinist recognizes that design is apparent in nature. The apparent design exhibited by living organisms is also reflected by the labels put on cellular systems by modern science:

the genetic "code"
the "blueprint" of life
this biological mechanism was "invented"
this biological system uses this "strategy"
"biological information"
"hardware and software" in the cell

But can we readily detect when something has been designed? How can we know with a reasonable degree of certainty? Design detection is simple to understand in concept. First, we find a pattern of events that is functional, carries a message or has some discernable structure, like an automobile, a watch or the six billion bit software program carried in the DNA in each of our cells. Next we ask whether the laws of physics and chemistry could cause the pattern to appear (like a salt crystal or snowflake). Finally, we evaluate the possibility that the pattern was assembled by a chance association of the events. If no known law can explain the existence of the pattern and chance assembly is extremely unlikely, we have reasonably detected design—the product of a mind. . . .

The hallmark of any scientific endeavor is testing. We are taught that science requires that all theories be subjected to the test of competing evidence and competing theories. A naturalistic exclusion of evidence of design violates these fundamental principles of science and logic. . . .

2. Legal and Social Demands.

Any teaching about the cause of life and its diversity has religious and philosophical implications. A naturalistic cause based only on mechanisms of chance and necessity (such as Darwinism) implies the intervention of no intelligent agent or god. Accordingly, the implications of that teaching are consistent with atheism. They are also inconsistent with all theistic religions founded on the belief that a God does exist who designed and can intervene in the material world. A teaching based on the theory that life and its diversity result from design implies the intervention of an intelligent agent. Accordingly, its implications are consistent with theism.

Thus, it is impossible for any science class to promote any theory of origins without implicitly promoting its associated philosophy, religious belief or worldview. This promotion of one theory to the exclusion of the other denigrates the competing theory and its associated philosophical or religious belief or worldview. . . .

The scientific method requires that the evidence on both sides of any issue be considered. There is also a legally compelling reason to do so. If your school board censors the evidence of design and permits only a consideration of evidence that life results only from the the laws of chemistry and physics without design, then we believe that you will be subverting the neutrality mandated by the First Amendment of the Constitution. . . .

As pointed out, although neither design nor "evolution" by natural selection in and of themselves constitute a religion, design and the naturalistic underpinning of Darwinism each have serious religious implications. Although design does not require theism, all theistic religions require design. By excluding design as a possible cause of life and its diversity, naturalism is necessarily hostile to theistic beliefs. Accordingly, if a public school system censors evidence of design that exists in nature due to the naturalistic philosophy of science it will have the "effect" of inhibiting or denigrating the religious beliefs of students who are taught to believe that a designer is responsible for life. Under these circumstances, the parent of such a child would have cause to complain that the School was violating the principle of government neutrality. By the same token, if a school were to censor naturalistic views of origins, the school system would be denigrating atheistic beliefs while promoting theistic beliefs. In that case, atheistic parents would have cause to complain.

The only way any school system can achieve the neutrality required by the Supreme Court is to not censor reliable scientific evidence which supports either causal explanation of the origin of life and its diversity. . . .

As you are well aware, this is an issue that makes many people very uncomfortable. Hold to the truth! Hold to your convictions! Make origins education philosophically neutral as demanded by logic, good science and the First Amendment!

A RESPONSE TO THE INTELLIGENT DESIGN NETWORK'S PROPOSAL TO INCLUDE "INTELLIGENT DESIGN" IN KANSAS SCIENCE STANDARDS

The Intelligent Design network (IDnet) has repeatedly argued that "intelligent design" (ID) should be included in the Kansas science standards.

The IDnet's proposals to insert ID into the standards have been based on two main beliefs: that science embraces the philosophy of Naturalism and that "intelligent design" is a valid "competing hypothesis" to the theory of evolution.

The IDnet's main beliefs are not accepted by the scientific community. They are in fact considered wrong. On that basis alone, the IDnet's proposals should not be included in the state science standards.

Both the nature of science and the specific scientific content described in the 2001 Kansas science standards represent essential, mainstream science as practiced worldwide.

It is not the responsibility of the state BOE to decide what is and is not verified science. If the ideas put forward by the IDnet ever become an essential part of mainstream science, then they may earn a place in the public school science curriculum. At this time, however, the IDnet's quarrel is with the scientific community, not with public education. The IDnet should not be allowed to use the public school curriculum as a means of bypassing the accepted ways for establishing scientific knowledge.

From their two main beliefs, the IDnet concludes that science has atheistic implications, that science has contributed to the moral and cultural decay of society, that the evidence for "design" is censored, and that there are Constitutional reasons why design should be given consideration in the science curriculum. These conclusions, being based on false premises, are also wrong.

"Naturalism" and the Nature of Science

The IDnet believes that science, by limiting itself to "natural" explanations, as stated in Draft 6, inherently embraces philosophical Naturalism [their capitalization], the philosophical belief that "all phenomena result only from natural causes—chance and necessity."

The IDnet is wrong: science neither embraces nor endorses philosophical Naturalism. Science is purposely limited to seeking natural explanations for observable phenomena. Science does not attempt to offer theological explanations for such phenomena. Neither does science attempt to explain our moral, aesthetic, or spiritual experience: these fall outside the realm of science.

Seeking natural explanations has proven to be highly successful in building a universally accessible body of knowledge about how the world works. Explanations involving non-natural causes cannot be investigated empirically with the tools of science, and have not successfully contributed to science.

Nowhere in the practice or teaching of science is there a commitment to the belief that what science studies is all that exists, or that the methods of science are the only valid human ways of seeking knowledge. Science is not a dogmatic philosophy about either the ultimate nature of the world or the full nature of human beings.

It is true that some individuals within the scientific community have used evolution as a vehicle to promote a true "philosophical Naturalism." However, it is equally true that many scientists who accept the evidence for evolution are also committed and outspoken theists. Both groups of individuals see our current scientific understanding of the universe as supporting their philosophical position. However, neither position is an inherent implication of that scientific understanding. Science itself is neutral on issues of the ultimate nature of reality.

Design

The IDnet claims that natural processes are not sufficient to have produced some features of life, and that an additional type of cause, "design," the action of "a mind or some form of intelligence," is necessary to scientifically explain those features. The IDnet writes as if "design" is an obvious and accepted alternative to natural causation, and that a scientific "theory of intelligent design (ID)" exists to compete with the theory of evolution. Neither of these claims is true.

There is no theory of intelligent design. First, ID proposes no testable hypotheses to explain how the alleged design happens—there is no proposed mechanism for design. Second, although ID claims that the identity of the designer is unknown, leaders of the ID movement make it clear the designer is God: the logical alternative to natural causation is obviously supernatural causation. In fact, both William Dembski and Phillip Johnson have recently identified the Word of God as the source and mechanism of "intelligent design."

ID does not explain how to determine precisely when design has taken place, or how to distinguish between what has been designed and what has evolved. ID writers have proposed vague philosophical concepts for use in detecting design ("irreducible complexity" and "complex specified information"), but they offer no empirical means for applying these concepts to actual reality.

There is no ID research. There are no published scientific papers on ID-based experiments that test any specific aspect of the theory of ID nor produce any new, usable knowledge. There just isn't any "theory of ID."

The theory of evolution is truly a scientific theory: "a well-substantiated explanation of some aspect of the natural world that incorporates observations, inferences, and tested hypotheses." (Draft 6) ID, on the other hand, is not even a hypothesis because it makes no testable claims about the world. It is non-empirical speculation.

The IDnet continually calls ID a "competing hypothesis," but this is a claim without merit. The theory of evolution and ID are not remotely equal in their status as scientific explanations. The IDnet's repeated argument that ID should be given equal time throughout the standards is unjustified.

The "evidence for design" and "censorship"

ID relies on gaps in our knowledge for its "evidence," pointing to aspects of the natural world which currently have inadequate scientific explanation. However, since science has a reliable history of narrowing such gaps, this type of design argument is forced to continually emphasize new areas of uncertainty. Dependence on such negative evidence does not establish the claim that a supernatural intelligence must be considered in scientific explanations.

IDnet claims that design, and evidence for it, is "censored" because of science's adherence to Naturalism. The truth is that the propositions of ID and the purported evidence for it have been rejected, not censored, because ID offers neither useful hypotheses nor productive research.

The claim of "censorship" is unfounded. The repeated use of the word, much like that of "competing hypothesis," is a rhetorical tactic meant to elevate ID to a status that it does not have. It is the nature of the scientific enterprise to evaluate new ideas. At this point, ID has made little progress in being accepted as valid science. To acknowledge this lack of acceptance by excluding ID from the science standards is not censorship.

Religious and Cultural Implications

The IDnet believes that science, by embracing Naturalism, is consistent with, and therefore promotes, atheism, while design is consistent with and promotes theism. They conclude that science's adherence to Naturalism has important negative moral and cultural consequences such as the "Naturalistic" belief that people's "ethics and morals can be based on whatever they decide or whatever the scientific elite tells us about nature." The IDnet is wrong about both of these points.

As explained above, science does not embrace Naturalism. Science does not declare that other types of knowledge are invalid, and it also does not presume to add to those other types of knowledge.

All people reach conclusions about morals, values, and spiritual reality by drawing on such non-scientific sources as religious faith, philosophical belief, and personal choice. They may integrate scientific knowledge into their larger belief system, but scientific knowledge itself forces no inherent moral or spiritual conclusions.

The IDnet incorrectly concludes that, in the interest of fairness, a theistic "theory of ID" is needed to balance the atheism they believe is implied by evolution. The appeal to fairness here is misplaced. Religion and science are complementary ways of looking at the universe, not antagonistic ways of knowing between which people must choose. True fairness involves acknowledging and honoring the interrelated complexity of human knowledge, which demands both scientific and other types of knowledge.

ID attempts to drive a wedge between scientific and religious understanding. If anything is unfair, it is the IDnet's insistence that accepting the evidence for evolution is incompatible with both a belief in God and a commitment to moral standards.

Draft 6 presents a religiously neutral science. It is ID that inserts theistic considerations into science. The IDnet places too great a value on scientific explanations as an ultimate arbiter of truth. They make the very mistake they claim others are making: trying to find empirical explanations for truths which must be reached in other than scientific ways. It is they who act like "philosophical Naturalists" as they seek to establish an empirical basis for all aspects of the world, including our beliefs about God and morality.

Constitutional issues

The IDnet claims that Constitutional issues arise because the theory of evolution promotes atheism and the theory of ID promotes theism. However, as we have shown, the theory of evolution does not promote atheism and has no inherent religious implications. Therefore, there are no Constitutional issues of the kind mentioned by the IDnet.

The true Constitutional issue here is that ID, if fully articulated to include the nature of the Designer and the undetectable nature of His interventions, is clearly a religious belief, and thus has no place in the science curriculum.

Conclusion

State standards should reflect science that is considered essential and fundamental worldwide. ID does not meet this criteria. The IDnet's incorrect beliefs about science and its relationship to religious and cultural issues have no place in the Kansas science standards. It is wrong for the IDnet to try to use the public school system as the vehicle to establish these beliefs.

Therefore, for all the reasons outlined in this paper, the proposals made by the IDnet should be rejected, and "intelligent design" ideas should not be incorporated into the Kansas science standards.

Part 3

Religion and American Life in the United States: To the Millennium

Chapter 6

Popular Religion

HAVING ATTENDED CHURCH earlier in the day, the middle-aged divorced woman takes an hour for herself after getting the kids to bed. Lying in a warm bath, surrounded by aromatherapy candles and the strains of New Age music, she reads her horoscope in the newspaper and contemplates who might be the dangerous stranger it instructs her to avoid or proceed around with caution.

"Popular religion" refers to religious beliefs and practices people engage in outside the institutional beliefs and rituals they are taught to follow. These practices are not necessarily contrary to those of their institutional affiliation, but neither are they necessarily in accord: over and above sectarian ideas and behaviors, they help to smooth the rough edges between orthodoxy/orthopraxy and the way individuals personally understand the world to work. The fabricated woman mentioned above might gain meaning for her life by going to Catholic Mass on Sunday mornings, but day-to-day anxieties, including questions about her future, drive her to look for other means of understanding and control, outside her traditional institution. For other believers, popular religion is merely an annex to their faiths—for example, they can worship Jesus or Allah in their cars, whizzing along the highway, to the sounds of praise music. In such cases, popular religion is more consonant with their official statements of faith. Still others might swear off institutional affiliation altogether, but "roll their own religion" by combining religious nonfiction books (often by authors using competing ideas), pop psychology, and several of the popular television ministries, among other available elements.

This sort of religious practice is not new. Virtually every religious tradition can look back to see its adherents even many centuries ago supplementing their faith with folk beliefs and practices usually categorized as "magic." Even those traditions that stood contrary to "popular religion" could not wean members from these practices in their daily lives. For instance, the Puritans who left the Old World to found a "pure" faith in New England held on to folk practices to ward off evil, despite hearing sermon after sermon against them. Tacking horseshoes to their doorsills and pounding metal spikes into their floors—iron was reputed to protect against witches, who lost their power around it—and even erecting frightening anthropomorphic carvings on their property lines to discourage evil beings from entering, the real-life Puritans of New England looked little like the strait-laced orthodox believers portrayed in myth and literature. They supplemented their official doctrines with popular religious practices in order, as they saw it, to gain control of their world.

The last half of the twentieth century certainly had its share of popular religious beliefs and practices. In fact, one might argue that despite the powerful presence of denominations in American religious life, this period saw more developments that encouraged the proliferation of popular religion than any other time in the nation's history. Most important is the development of mass media, which enabled those outside traditional institutional structures to spread their beliefs while giving open access to the masses to hear competing ideas and take part, even in their own living rooms, in competing practices. The anonymity that came with the democratizing effects of mass media created an environment for a variety of popular religions to flourish.

This too had its precedents in American history. The development of quick and cheap mass publishing helped disseminate nontraditional ideas throughout the nineteenth century. While Protestant organizations published inexpensive Bibles and common Sunday School lessons that would be used in all the major Protestant denominations simultaneously—the definition of "mainstream"—religious outsiders were busy printing works about talking with spirits, reading personalities by the bumps on a person's head, or food cures for certain ailments. The progeny of almanacs centuries before, rooted in common beliefs and practices, the mass media in the nineteenth century fed the different forms of popular religion alongside the more mainstream practices.

A number of scholars have studied this phenomenon in its late twentieth-century context. Analyzing radio, television, magazines, the book market, motion pictures, the Internet, and consumer practices, among other things, they have elucidated a long-standing but under-studied aspect of American religious history. One fruitful way to approach the topic is through the lens of popular culture, in relation to which religion situates itself through constant negotiation.

This negotiation is truly two-way: religion appears in popular culture and popular culture appears in religion. An example of the former is trendy films based on religious themes. Some of these are explicitly religious, such as *The Ten Commandments* and *Little Buddha*. In other cases the religious themes might be implicit but touch "cosmic chords" in the audience. The *Star Wars* series, with its eastern religious premises, is a good example, alongside *E.T.*, with its popular healing character from outer space. And of course there are many popular books, especially novels, in which religion and religious characters play a major role.

Examples of popular culture infiltrating religion are legion. This is especially true among proselytizing forms of religion, which tend to make appeals to popular culture in an attempt to save it from its evil ways. The recent phenomenon of "Christian rock" music is but the latest instance of this. A great deal of debate surrounded its birth in the 1970s, including charges by "traditionalists" that it introduced "the Devil's music" into the sacred halls of the church. But evangelical Christianity's long flirtation with popular forms of music (for example, setting doctrinal poems to tavern tunes to create new hymns) probably decided the winner in that debate long before its outcome was apparent. Today, Christian rock musicians and "crossover" artists win Grammy Awards alongside secular musicians whose music sounds very much like that played by Christian artists.

Not only does religion appear in popular culture and vice versa, there is reason to argue that, at times anyway, the two are identical. The immensely popular camp meeting revivals in the nineteenth century helped set the tone for frontier culture, so couldn't they be religion as popular culture, itself? More recently, the cross-shaped jewelry inspired by the singer Madonna, worn first around the neck but later as studs in various body parts, might be understood as a religious symbol that has overtaken the culture. New Age and Taoist symbols worn as jewelry are similar examples. But unless the wearers understand their jewelry as religious symbols, these cases might be popular culture as commodified religion. The fact that many Catholics targeted Madonna for criticism confirms this. Sensing an assault on the things they understood as sacred, these Catholics struck back.

Whatever the case, there is clearly a constant dance of the sacred and secular. For example, Campus Crusade for Christ founder Bill Bright hired the filmmakers who had produced the L.A. crime film *Chinatown* to create a movie on the life of Jesus; the walls between the two spheres are permeable indeed, if not altogether missing. That film, translated into more than 500 languages and seen by over 2 billion people, has become the most watched motion picture in human history. That sort of fact never gets covered in show business media such as *Variety* magazine because it is not considered "entertainment," but it is important for understanding the relationships between religion and popular culture. The examples of cross-fertilization are myriad and becoming ubiquitous. Such recent developments as Christian music videos shown on cable television to rival MTV and "secular" awards for gospel music indicate just how much overlap and synthesis there is.

All of which brings us back to the issue of popular religion—where religion and popular culture meet, outside the institutional walls of the church, synagogue, or temple. This is where people negotiate meaning for their lives. They hear their pastors or priests in weekly sermons, but rather than take those words at face value, they simply put them into the mix of items to choose from as they figure out for themselves what they believe and how they will live.

Popular religion might be where Americans' famed individualism is most apparent in religious life. Clearly, the disestablishment of religion by the Constitution gave rise to denominationalism, the free market of competing faiths in the United States. But the story doesn't end there for most Americans, both historically and today. They have for generations repeated their creeds and then lived according to their individual understandings of the world, sometimes more and sometimes less influenced by popular culture. Clearly fashion, styles, material and intellectual trends, and even good marketing influence the choices people make.

1. NORMAN VINCENT PEALE AND SMILEY BLANTON, "HOW TO MAKE THE MOST OF YOU" (1956)

ROBERT H. SCHULLER, "LIFE CHANGERS" (1981)

Among the most popular mainline Protestant preachers in the twentieth century were those who reflected the positive American spirit exemplified by a sense of progress after World War II. Two in particular, Norman Vincent Peale and his spiritual protégé Robert Schuller, are the best examples. Cloaking Christianity in the language of pop psychology and positive thought, they tethered Christian vision to the American dream to create an immensely popular message for Americans struggling to keep up with their ever faster-paced lives.

Norman Vincent Peale was among the most influential clergy by mid-century, with sermons on positive thinking frequently broadcast first over the radio and then on television. His book The Power of Positive Thinking *was among the best-selling religious books of the century. Smiley Blanton, his coauthor on* The Art of Real Happiness, *was one of the first speech pathologists in the country and ran a free counseling clinic in New York City connected to Peale's church.*

Robert H. Schuller, an ordained minister of the Reformed Church in America, founded the Crystal Cathedral and the Fuqua International School of Christian Communications, and broadcast his sermons live from his church in a television program called The Hour of Power. *He authored more than thirty books, including the one from which the following passage was taken,* Robert Schuller's Life Changers.

Both works excerpted are essentially self-help books. They emphasize the importance of continual optimism, fueled by faith in Christianity and God, to leading a happy and spiritually fulfilling life. Peale and Blanton write, "Take a realistic survey of your God-given talents. Then dedicate these talents to God, praying that He will use them in the best way possible." Likewise, Schuller writes, "What keeps the average person from mining his mind and discovering this power God put in it? . . . You spend your life believing the lowest, instead of beginning to believe the possible." The only general difference between the two works is the date of publication—Peale and Blanton 1956, Schuller 1981.

HOW TO MAKE THE MOST OF YOU

"Am I doing what I really ought to be doing?" "Am I being my real self?" These are the queries of many of us who wonder if we are making the best of our opportunities, or are unhappy about our living conditions, or just generally confused about the complexities of modern life. We all have unfulfilled dreams and yearnings. Each of us feels at times that life has passed us by, and we don't know how to catch up with it.

Twenty years ago a young Negro came to New York City from the South. He was filled with ambition. "My dream was to make a lot of money, own a flashy car, wear expensive clothes and have a pocketfull of fifty-cent cigars," he recalled to friends recently.

But the only job he could find was that of a Red Cap in Grand Central Station. He did not want it. He felt that carrying bags for other people was beneath him. He wanted to give orders, not take them. Only because of financial necessity did he finally take the position. Then, for several years he worked as a Red Cap, seething at the way some people spoke to him, snarling to himself about the smallness of tips, snapping at his fellow workers when they displeased him.

Unhappy, feeling that he was missing something, this Red Cap reluctantly turned, as many do in such a situation, to the church. "I went to find out if God could help me achieve all the things I wanted in life," he admits candidly. "When I prayed, I asked for a better job, success, more money."

His prayers for material things were not answered. This Red Cap might have continued his restless search elsewhere if he had not lingered long enough in church to make contact with the greatest source of power the Christian church has to offer. For the ultimate answers to life's dissatisfactions are not found in the church building itself, nor through church people regardless of how good they may be, nor even in the words and advice of the minister. Jesus Christ is the heart and soul of the Christian church; in Him and through Him do Christians find the real answer to loneliness, frustration, and unhappiness.

The Red Cap was attracted to the Master of Life, and the challenge in these words, "If any man be in Christ, he is a new creature: old things are passed away; behold all things are become new." (II Corinthians 5:17)

The all-important change in the Red Cap's life came when he realized that it was not what Christ could do *for* him that really mattered, but what Christ could do *through* him. For Christ must work *through* people if He is to transform lives. The Red Cap didn't come to this conclusion without much prayer and reading of the Scriptures. The result of months of spiritual searching was this prayer:

"Lord, I asked You before for a better job and more money, I see now that You *did* answer my prayer. The answer was 'No.' Since then I have learned my limitations, but I am not frustrated by this knowledge. I have had the wonderful experience of bringing Christ into my life. 'Old things are passed away.' I no longer want a new job if You think I can serve You best as a Red Cap. Please show me how to use my work for the glory of Your Kingdom."

From that moment Ralston Young, Red Cap 42, started to make the most of his job. His mental attitude changed from "How much of a tip will I get" to "How can I help carry this man's troubles as well as his bags?"

As a result, he started noonday prayer services in a railroad coach on Track 13 in Grand Central Station. The simple, informal inspiration of these meetings soon drew people from all stations in life, regardless of position, color, or faith.

Slowly the lay ministry of this humble Red Cap grew. He was asked to talk to small church groups; more recently he has accepted speaking invitations to such colleges as Yale and Vassar, even though he never had a college education. Always his message is simple yet eloquent testimony of how Christ works through people.

Ralston Young is a remarkable example of a man equipped with average abilities who is making the maximum use of his life. He did it by using a formula for living that is available to all of us. You might call it the "technique of making the most of you." To develop this technique, first, take a realistic survey of your God-given talents. Then dedicate these talents to God, praying that He will use them in the best way possible. Meanwhile go about life normally, alert to every opportunity for service. . . .

Helen Keller was struck with brain fever at the age of two. At first doctors held little hope that she would live, but she did recover. But from that time on she was both deaf and blind. Who would have thought this child could ever amount to anything? What Helen Keller accomplished with a bare minimum of personal assets is one of the greatest stories of our age. When she celebrated her 77th birthday recently, Miss Keller was tirelessly serving the blind and blind-deaf, traveling over the world, writing and lecturing. She had written a dozen books which have been translated into 50 languages. She is the direct inspiration for 50 schools for the blind, 44 state-supported schools, and 48 state programs for the blind.

"I have struggled like everybody else to find myself and enter a field of usefulness," Miss Keller wrote recently in *Guideposts Magazine*. "I believe that we begin heaven now and here if we do our work for others faithfully. There is no useful work that is not part of the welfare of mankind. Even the humblest occupation is skilled labor if it contains an effort above mere self-support to serve a spiritual or social need."

You can get out of life only what you are. As Ernest Holmes stated, "The getting is in the being, and the being always begets the getting; child will be like parent, and men do not gather grapes from cacti. If we want to use the power in our minds, we have to realize it is a spiritual power. We have to realize we are living in a spiritual universe. This means that right now, at the center of everything God is enthroned. And it was Browning who said that our task is to 'loose this imprisoned splendor.'"

In other words, God created man in His Image to achieve great things. But "great things" for the grammar school arithmetic teacher, who inspires children with an excitement to learn, would not be "great things" for the scientific genius Einstein, who delved deeply into the basic mysteries of the universe. Man must accept his limitations and still not dull his incentive to use what abilities he has in a maximum way. . . .

In their search for happiness some individuals steadfastly refuse to accept themselves. They dislike their own personality so much that they try to copy the mannerisms of others. The result is almost always harmful to persons who do this. It stands to reason that if you try to copy someone else, you will never be as good as that person, because you are admitting at the start that he or she is better than you are. But the one thing you can do better than anyone else is to be yourself.

"The Lord gave you certain qualities which are more attractive in you than anyone else," one woman was told by the minister here at our clinic recently. She felt she needed an entirely new personality to be a success. It was pointed out to her that Will Rogers was always an Oklahoma cowboy. He mastered the art of being himself in every situation that came along. People loved him for this very naturalness. But a keenly efficient and methodical man like Douglas MacArthur would have been ridiculed if he acted like Will Rogers. Jimmy Durante would never have achieved success if he had changed from the East Side boy with the big nose. . . .

If you have certain inferiority feelings and have been trying to become someone you are not, why not play this little game with yourself. Set aside one day a week as a "Be Myself Day." Don't try to impress a single person all day long. Don't attempt anything over your head. Take an honest look at your living standards, friends, and activities. Where are you straining yourself? To make the most of yourself, you must learn the difference between honest hard work and neurotic straining for some false goal. The person who has mastered this difference can be relaxed while hard at work; the person who has not mastered it can be full of stress and strain while on an expenses-paid vacation to Bermuda. . . .

Don't try to take on a completely different personality. Spiritual rebirth, however, where one replaces doubtful values with Christ-like qualities is much to be desired. This kind of transformation will do much to bring to the surface hidden creative qualities in an individual. It will not make a good financier out of a mechanic—or vice-versa. But, the miraculous transformations you sometimes see in people are usually the result of the development of latent powers which were in these people all the time.

Be your real self; let your God-given qualities develop naturally and you will make the most out of your life.

LIFE CHANGERS

One Saturday morning I was on a plane flight to Los Angeles and I had to work on my Sunday-morning message. I was not in the mood to communicate with the person who sat next to me—not because I'm unfriendly, but because I have only limited hours left, and nobody else is going to prepare my brain for Sunday morning. My suitcase was open; one of my books was there; and my picture was on the back of the jacket. The man who sat next to me saw it, looked at me, and interrupted my solitude, saying, "Are you an author?" I said, "Yes." He said, "So am I." Then he asked, "What do you write about?" I said, "Possibility thinking. What do you write about?" He answered, "Applied mathematics." I hoped he wouldn't pursue the conversation. Then I had a revelation: "You know, I write about impossibility and possibility thinkers. Obviously possibility thinking doesn't apply in mathematics. I mean, two plus two equals four, and four plus four equals eight."

And he said, "Doctor Schuller, let me tell you a true story: I was a graduate at Berkeley thirty years ago. I came to class late and copied what I believed to be the homework: two problems that were written on the blackboard. Later I said to my professor, 'I haven't been able to solve the homework problems yet, can I have a little more time?' He said, 'Sure, George. When you do, put it on my desk.'

"In due time I did solve them and turned the homework in. Several weeks later, one Sunday morning, there was a great pounding at my door; it was my professor. He was all excited, for it turned out what I mistook for homework were two famous unsolved problems of mathematical statistics.

"Now, Dr. Schuller, do you suppose I would have solved these two problems if I knew that they were two well-known unsolved problems?"

What keeps the average person from mining his mind and discovering this power God put in it? I can tell you, it is preconceived, prejudicial, negative information that's put into us. We think it's impossible. The most dangerous person on planet earth is the negative-thinking expert. Because he's an expert in his field, nobody challenges him. Therefore you accept it as fact. You spend your life believing the lowest, instead of beginning to believe the possible. . . .

Let me ask you a question: Are you a possibility thinker or an impossibility thinker? Here's a test: Tonight the sun will set at approximately 7:30. Suppose it's a beautiful sunset—red, green, purple, blue, orange, and yellow—until twilight and darkness comes and the lights twinkle. Somebody says, "Did you see the sunset?" And you say, "No, I missed it." Is it possible to have a replay? Is it possible to catch the sunset once you've missed it? The answer is no. *Agree?* Wait a minute!

When we left Paris, Mrs. Schuller and I had to get to Honolulu, where I had to deliver the major address to an eight-thousand-member convention. People told me it was impossible to leave Paris and still get to Honolulu on time. There just aren't planes to get you there that fast. Suddenly somebody said, "You can make it if you fly the *Concorde.*" So, Mrs. Schuller and I booked ourselves on the *Concorde.* It was 8:00 p.m. when we were to take off. I was excited because the sun was setting at 9:05 p.m., and I expected it would be glorious to catch the sunset at sixty thousand feet in the air. I was told you could see the curvature of the earth at that altitude.

During the takeoff I made this exciting discovery: I can understand Greek, Hebrew, English, and Dutch, but I didn't know I could understand French. As we were powering down the runway, suddenly there was a screech of brakes, smell of rubber, and a Frenchman rattled something off that I understood. He said, *"Le problem,"* and I knew we had problem. We went back to the gate and we waited. The sun was dropping lower and lower. Finally at

8:45 the sun was horizontal in its beams. We waited until 10:00 p.m. By now it was very dark. We went back with the lights on in the plane, we took off down the runway, and suddenly we were up in the air. It was an exciting, steep, vertical ascent, like a missile. The flight attendant told us that the screen in the front of the fuselage was not a television screen, but we would see a digital dial and the numbers would register our speed. Suddenly, it was 45, 50, 90, 98, 100—meaning Mach 1—then 1, 2, 3, 4, 5, 6, 7 . . . 198, 199, Mach 2. We were now going over 1,400 miles per hour. Then, out of the blackened window, I could see from the west the horizon. Where moments before it was black, it had now turned gold, then orange, and then streaks of pink, purple, red, and blue. And then it happened—sunrise in the west! The sun began to climb. We literally were catching up with the sunset that we had missed! The whole sun was up in the sky sending its late afternoon sunlight into the fuselage. The flight attendant came to me and said, "Doctor Schuller, the pilot would like to invite you to the cockpit." As I went into the cockpit, we were going Mach 2.4. And the cockpit was bathed in golden sunlight.

Today I can tell you it's possible to have a replay of the sunset if you've missed it, given the right circumstances and conditions. A year ago, I would have told you it's impossible. What is my point? My point is: What may be impossible today, may be possible tomorrow. . . .

Not long ago I checked into a hotel back East. It was late in the evening, and the lobby was empty except for the desk clerk. I checked in and began to unpack quickly, so I could get some rest. As I reached for my toothbrush, I realized that I had forgotten to pack my toothpaste. "Well, no problem," I thought to myself. "There's a dispenser down the hall." So I walked down the hall and stood before the machine studying the contents. Enclosed behind the glass were all kinds of goodies—razor blades, pocketbooks, combs, and little tubes of toothpaste! All I had to do was insert two quarters into the slot and my problem would be solved. I had no change, so I went to the desk and got four quarters. When I returned to the dispenser I dropped in the first quarter . . . *cling*. Then I inserted the second quarter . . . *cling*. I pushed the red button below the tube of toothpaste and waited. Nothing happened! It didn't work! So I pressed the coin lever, and my quarters returned.

Okay, I thought, *let's give it another try*. I dropped the first quarter in . . . *cling*. Then the second quarter . . . *cling*. (I even used the other two quarters for good luck!) I pushed the button—again nothing happened! Still no toothpaste! I paused for a moment staring at all the things behind that glass—just out of my reach. "Think positive," I said aloud. So I pressed the button again. Nothing!

A little frustrated at this point, I pushed the coin-return lever, recovered my quarters and stood in front of that stubborn machine. It had what I needed but it wouldn't release what it had to offer! I was willing to cooperate. I had a positive attitude toward it. I was willing to pay the price, but it just would not release the valuable contents it held within.

Some of you are like that dispensing machine. Deep within yourself, you have a lot to give, but you don't know how to give it. You have a lot to offer, but something keeps you tied up—feeling timid, shy, retiring, bashful, and inferior. I challenge you to begin to believe that you have something beautiful and positive to give—it's stored up inside of you. . . .

As I've mentioned before, these days I'm raising fish. Actually I have been for some years. I raise Japanese carp known as koi fish. Several years ago I bought a bunch of little teeny ones for three dollars apiece. Since then, they've grown and reproduced. Today I have a few hundred of these beautiful Japanese koi fish. They're friends of mine, each with a distinct personality. Some are nice; some aren't so nice. In a way, my fish remind me of people.

If I sit at the edge of the pond and watch a leaf fall into the water, I notice that most of the fish will scatter and flee in all directions, as the leaf hits the surface. But there are a few—only a few—who will not flee to hiding places when something hits the water's surface. They are the big fish who make a slow curve around the new object, inspecting it carefully and cautiously. They know that what they find might not be an enemy, but might, in fact, be food.

These are the fish who always find the food. That's why they're the big fish. Frightened fish stay skinny. And a frightened society will soon become an impoverished society. Productivity will stop, and the inevitable conditions of recession and inflation will degenerate into economic depression. There is nothing we need more in the United States today than *possibility thinking*. Possibility thinking works wonders because people dare to take some risks on the odds that if they make it, they can do a lot of good for a lot of people.

2. L. RON HUBBARD, "TWO RULES FOR HAPPY LIVING" (1965)

While "new religious movements" do not usually fall under the category of popular religion—by tradition, new movements are almost always small, sectlike or counterculture groups—the writings of L. Ron Hubbard, founder of Scientology, break down the walls between those typologies. Having started out a fiction writer, Hubbard went on to author dozens of books on his religious philosophies and tape-record more than 3,000 lectures. Scientology, originally a popular expression of individualized religious thought, later sought and obtained status as a church in the United States and abroad.

In Scientology: A New Slant on Life, *Hubbard explains the tenets and principles of his religious movement. The chapter included here, "Two Rules for Happy Living," outlines the evolution of Hubbard's rules from other religions, pointing out their short-comings and explaining how his addresses them. The two rules for happy living are "Be able to experience anything" and "Cause only those things which others are able to experience easily."*

Hitting the book market during the 1950s and free-wheeling 1960s, Hubbard's simple and livable philosophies caught on. Millions of copies of his book Dianetics *sold over the succeeding decades. Growing membership in the Church of Scientology, the large number of books sold, and continued public interest in the Hollywood set who converted to the faith indicate a grassroots following that is difficult to measure but impossible to ignore. The popularity of Hubbard's writings serve as a reminder of the nontraditional philosophical and religious interests and daily practices of millions in America.*

TWO RULES FOR HAPPY LIVING

One: Be able to experience anything.
Two: Cause only those things which others are able to experience easily.

Man has had many golden rules. The Buddhist rule of "Do unto others as you would have these others do unto you" has been repeated often in other religions. But such golden rules, while they served to advance man above the animal, resulted in no sure sanity, success or happiness. Such a golden rule gives only the cause-point,[1] or at best the reflexive effect-point.[2] This is a self-done-to-self thing and tends to put all on obsessive cause. It gives no thought to what one does about the things done to one by others not so indoctrinated.

How does one handle the evil things done to him? It is not told in the Buddhist rule. Many random answers resulted. Amongst them are the answers of Christian Science[3] (effects on self don't exist), the answers of early Christians (become a martyr), the answers of Christian ministers (condemn all sin). Such answers to effects created on one bring about a somewhat less than sane state of mind—to say nothing of unhappiness.

After one's house has burned down and the family cremated, it is no great consolation to (1) pretend it didn't happen, (2) liken oneself to Job,[4] or (3) condemn all arsonists.

So long as one fears or suffers from the effect of violence, one will have violence against him. When one *can* experience exactly what is being done to one, ah, magic, it does not happen!

How to be happy in this universe is a problem few prophets or sages have dared to contemplate directly. We find them "handling" the problem of happiness by assuring us that man is doomed to suffering. They seek not to tell us how to be happy but how to endure being unhappy. Such casual assumption of the impossibility of happiness has led us to ignore any real examination of ways to be happy. Thus, we have floundered forward toward a negative goal—get rid of all the unhappiness on Earth and one would have a liveable Earth. If one seeks to get rid of something continually, one admits continually he cannot confront[5] it—and thus everyone went down hill. Life became a dwindling spiral[6] of *more* things we could not confront. And thus we went toward blindness and unhappiness.

To be happy, one only must be *able* to confront, which is to say, experience, those things that are.

Unhappiness is only this: the inability to confront that which is.

Hence, (1) *Be able to experience anything.*

The effect side of life deserves great consideration. The self-caused side also deserves examination.

To create only those effects which others could easily experience gives us a clean new rule of living. For if one does, then what might he do that he must withhold from others? There is no reason to withhold his own actions or regret them (same thing) if one's own actions are easily experienced by others.

This is a sweeping test (and definition) of good conduct—to do only those things which others can experience.

If you examine your life, you will find you are bothered only by those actions a person did which others were not able to receive. Hence a person's life can become a hodgepodge of violence withheld, which pulls in, then, the violence others caused.

The more actions a person emanated which could not be experienced by others, the worse a person's life became. Recognizing that he was bad cause or that there were too many bad causes already, a person ceased causing things—an unhappy state of being.

Pain, misemotion,[7] unconsciousness, insanity—all result from causing things others could not experience easily. The reach-withhold phenomenon is the basis of all these things. When one sought to reach in such a way as to make it impossible for another to experience, one did not reach, then, did he? To "reach" with a gun against a person who is unwilling to be shot is not to reach the person, but a protest. All *bad* reaches never reached. So there was no communication, and the end result was a withhold by the person reaching. This reach-withhold became at last, an inability to reach—therefore, low communication, low reality, low affinity.

Communication is one means of reaching others. So, if one is unable to reach, one's ability to communicate will be low; and reality will be low, because if one is unable to communicate, he won't really get to know about others; and with knowing little or nothing about others, one doesn't have any feeling about them either, thus one's affinity will be low. Affinity, reality and communication work together; and if one of these three is high, the other two will be also; but if one is low, so will the others be low.

All bad acts, then, are those acts which cannot be easily experienced at the target end.

On this definition, let us review our own "bad acts." Which ones *were* bad? Only those that could not be easily experienced by another were bad. Thus, *which* of society's favorite bad acts are bad? Acts of real violence resulting in pain, unconsciousness, insanity and heavy loss could at this time be considered bad. Well, what other acts of yours do you consider "bad"? The things which you have done which you could not easily, yourself, experience were bad. But the things which you have done which you, yourself, could have experienced, had they been done to you, were *not* bad. That certainly changes one's view of things!

There is no need to lead a violent life just to prove one can experience. The idea is not to *prove* one can experience, but to regain the *ability* to experience.

Thus, today, we have two golden rules for happiness:

1. Be able to experience anything; and
2. Cause only those things which others are able to experience easily.

Your reaction to these tells you how far you have yet to go.

And if you achieve these two golden rules, you would be one of the happiest and most successful people in this universe, for who could rule you with evil?

1. **cause-point**: the originator of something; the point from which something was begun or dreamed up.
2. **effect-point**: the receipt-point of an idea, particle or mass.
3. **Christian Science**: a church founded by Mary Baker Eddy (1821–1910), American religious leader, editor and author.
4. **Job**: the central character in the Book of Job, an ancient Indian work, later incorporated into the Bible. In this story, Job endures much suffering but does not lose his faith in God.

5. **confront**: face without flinching or avoiding. *Confront* is actually the ability to be there comfortably and perceive.

6. **dwindling spiral**: a phenomenon of ARC (ARC is a word from the initial letters of Affinity, Reality, and Communication which together equate to Understanding), whereby when one breaks some affinity, a little bit of the reality goes down, and then communication goes down, which makes it impossible to get affinity as high as before; so a little bit more gets knocked off affinity, and then reality goes down, and then communication. This is the dwindling spiral in progress, until it hits the bottom—death—which is no affinity, no communication and no reality.

7. **misemotion**: a coined word used in Dianetics and Scientology to mean an emotion or emotional reaction that is inappropriate to the present time situation. It is taken from *mis-* (wrong) + *emotion*. To say that a person was *misemotional* would indicate that the person did not display the emotion called for by the actual circumstances of the situation. Being misemotional would be synonymous with being irrational. One can fairly judge the rationality of any individual by the correctness of the emotion he displays in a given set of circumstances. To be joyful and happy when circumstances call for joy and happiness would be rational. To display grief without sufficient present time cause would be irrational.

3. TOM GEARHART, "JESUS CHRIST SUPERSTAR: A TURNING POINT IN MUSIC" (1971)

Toward the end of the 1960s, a curious phenomenon occurred, particularly on the West Coast (especially around San Francisco): the Jesus Movement. Spurred by the antiauthoritarian attitudes taking deeper root in America's youth culture, many began to see Jesus as a Roman-era revolutionary hippie who was cut down by an authoritarian government. This movement took many forms, from an evangelical counterculture (led by Chuck Smith, whose ministry established the Calvary Chapel movement) to a sort of "Jesus is just alright by me" rock-and-roll outlook. One example of this new fascination was Jesus Christ Superstar, *a hit musical written by Tim Rice and Andrew Lloyd Webber.*

Premiering on stage in New York in fall 1971 and released as a motion picture in 1973, Jesus Christ Superstar *covered the final week in the life of Jesus through the eyes of Judas Iscariot. Some loved it, others hated it. In this piece written for a Toledo, Ohio publication in 1971, a Roman Catholic journalist reacts to the popularity of the musical and the ensuing outcry from religious groups. Tom Gearhart describes* Jesus Christ Superstar *as "a rock opera that retells the story of the Passion with immense feeling and power."*

The article embodies the popular reception of the musical in the 1970s by a generation who wanted the love of Jesus but didn't want the church. Jesus Christ, changed from his traditional portrayal to a very human man loved by crowds, becomes "a person who, like modern man, is trapped in doubt and mortally afraid that he has no legacy to leave."

⊶⊷

SANNA HO SANNA HEY SUPERSTAR

I was born and reared a Roman Catholic, went to Catholic elementary and high schools, and I was told about Jesus—at Mass, in religion classes, at CYO dances. I wanted to be his friend.

In the grade school choir I sang his praises, while as a torch-bearer and acolyte I participated in the Mass itself. Along about the third or fourth grade, after long rehearsals and much praying, a great honor was bestowed upon me: I became an altar boy.

If there are cherubs here on earth, then surely I was one—a small, red-cheeked boy with a Hopalong Cassidy tie tucked under my cassock and surplice. I went to confession often, received Holy Communion daily, and cared deeply about the parish priests—mixing their incense, pouring their wine, clanging the bells at the Consecration. And doing it all gladly in the name of this Jesus they had so often told me about.

But I also remember something that my first-grade teacher had told us one morning during religion instruction, and it haunted me throughout my pristine childhood. She told us that we had better not die with a mortal sin on our souls, because if we did, at the Last Judgment our faces would turn black in fear of meeting God. Of meeting Jesus.

Those words troubled me terribly, with the result that I never could focus my feelings toward Jesus very clearly. Was my desire to please him attributable to love or wordless fear? Was he a benevolent Saviour, or was he waiting for me to trip up, just once, then snatch me away for good and abandon me in flames?

I finally gave up searching for answers to these questions, deciding instead that Jesus was, if not an ogre, then certainly not the kind of person you'd sidle up to and exchange confidences with. You're not supposed to fear a friend.

The notions of a first-grade teacher notwithstanding, it is time to resume the search. It is time to inquire into lost and long-ago relationships, to ask more questions. Was Christ on earth a sometimes reluctant Saviour who also suffered his share of uncertainty and doubt? Was he as human and in need of a friend as you and I?

That is the proposition put forth in "Jesus Christ Superstar." Two Englishmen, composer Andrew Lloyd Webber and librettist Tim Rice, have fashioned a rock opera that retells the story of the Passion with immense feeling and power, revealing Christ to be a person who, like modern man, is trapped in doubt and mortally afraid that he has no legacy to leave.

But Webber and Rice also paint him as a man with sensitivity and the courage to believe in himself in the face of frightful odds. And in the end, Christ surfaces as a hero, as a Superstar.

RELEVANT AND IRREVERENT

Considering the sacred nature of the subject, "Superstar" could have been a colossal flop, a sophomoric rock-'n'-roll venture that would only rouse the ire of Christians everywhere crying blasphemy. That it emphatically is not is evidenced in the opera's overwhelming popularity since its release. It has racked up more than $1 million in sales, and most radio stations in the country are playing its refrain.

But the real measure of "Superstar's" success is in the variegation of the music and the contemporary wisdom of the lyrics. Eleven characters, backed by an 85-piece orchestra and several choirs, unravel the story of Christ's last three years on earth, using a broad range of rhythmic forms, from baroque to soul, from electrifying rock to bawdy vaudeville: ya-ya girls fading into Fillmore East fading into booming overtures, etc.

If there is one thing that distinguishes Webber's score, it is melody. Whether heralding the majesty of the "King of the Jews" with lush orchestral flourishes, or pondering his grief in the Garden of Gethsemane with low choral moans, the music spins with such good, gorgeous melody that it is hard not to carry the songs with you long after hearing them.

Although Jesus occupies center stage in the two-record pop opera, the other players are well-characterized, and each has a chance to present his own point of view in Rice's brilliantly relevant, and often irreverent, libretto.

Judas is not the blank-faced betrayer of the New Testament, but a throbbing human who, while accusing Christ of having too much ambition, is tormented by odd stirring of emotion for this strange man. Solicitously Judas, transported, counsels:

> "You'd have managed better if you had planned,
> Why'd you choose such a backward time and such a strange land?

If you'd come today you would have reached a whole nation,
Israel in 4 BC had no mass communication."

In a rollicking barroom ditty, Herod, the Establishment fat cat, challenges the great Jesus Christ to "walk across my swimming pool." And Pontius Pilate, an obvious victim of circumstances, tosses fitfully over the question of whether to condemn the broken King to the cross. He dreams seeing "thousands of millions crying for this man, and then I heard them mentioning my name . . . and leaving me the blame."

Such vivid description puts new faces on characters who have become all too tired and familiar, and revitalizes the gospels in a way that no updated Gideon could. In "Superstar," the apostles no longer are bearded reflections on a kitchen wall, but know the value of laughter and companionship, getting plastered at the Last Supper and singing, "Then when we retire we can write the gospels, so they'll talk about us when we've died."

Even the crowd, Jesusmaniacs all, has a personality. They are movie house popcorn-munchers, smug in their belief that Christ, like John Wayne, will "escape in the final reel," and copy-hungry sports writers asking Jesus, "Do you plan to put up a fight? Do you feel you've had the breaks? What would you say were your big mistakes?"

Aside from Ian Gillian's portrayal of Jesus, the most penetrating performance is by Yvonne Elliman as Mary Magdalene. When she sings "I Don't Know How To Love Him," the confusion of emotion which Mary Magdalene feels toward Christ—pain, bewilderment, and melancholy love—is exquisitely transmitted and touches deeply.

And there is Jesus. Jesus with beckoning eyes and a troubled brow, suddenly a human, with human instincts and foibles. "There's too little of me," he cries to the crowd begging to be healed.

His supreme agony at Gethsemane is beautifully conveyed by Gillian, baring the heart and spirit of a lamenting Redeemer. "I'm not as sure as when we started," Jesus says to God, and: "You're far too keen on where and how and not so hot on why."

Christ is capable of vanity as well, and greedy. "Would I be more noticed than I ever was before? What will be my reward?"

As his emotions pitch and roll within him, he hesitates, and points angrily to the crowd. "I must be mad thinking I'll be remembered—yes, I must be out of my head! Look at your blank faces! My name will mean nothing 10 minutes after I'm dead!"

But finally he succumbs, in weariness and near despair. "I will drink your cup of poison, nail me to your cross and break me. Bleed me, beat me, kill me, take me now—before I change my mind."

ON RECORD

"Jesus Christ, Jesus Christ, Who are you, what have you sacrificed?"

"Superstar" is a historic occasion in music, begging to be staged and brought before live audiences.

The altar boy of years past feels a flicker of recognition in the Jesus Christ seen by Webber and Rice.

And if "Superstar" provides no answers, at the very least it assures him that many are asking the same questions.

4. KENNETH TAYLOR, PREFACE TO *THE LIVING BIBLE* (1971)

Since one of the tenets of the Protestant Reformation was "sola scriptura" (only scripture), it is not surprising that Christians of that persuasion put such emphasis on biblical translations. The earliest reformers had, after all, made a point of translating the Bible into local languages so people could read it for themselves.

Readability, then, became important every few generations, as language continued to evolve and change. By the 1960s, as evangelicals distrusted the Revised Standard Version (largely the product of mainline Protestant scholars) and continued to use the beautiful but increasingly archaic King James Version, some felt the need for a friendlier Bible that average folk could relate to. Kenneth Taylor, the editor of His magazine, spent seven years paraphrasing the New Testament epistles. His idea for a book of "Living Letters" was rejected by publishers, so Taylor published it privately. After a recommendation by Billy Graham, however, the book was in such demand that Taylor founded Tyndale House and eventually also published The Living Bible.

A paraphrase of several versions of the Bible, The Living Bible *was meant "to simplify the deep and often complex thoughts of the Word of God." Whether Taylor meant it to or not, his publication entered a stream that was widening into a mighty river of individual interpretation that often ran contrary to official statements of faith. It was the same problem Martin Luther encountered with his German translation of the Bible: once people had it in their own hands, in their own idiom, there was no controlling interpretation.*

In this wonderful day of many new translations and revisions we can greet another new one with either dread or joy! Dread that "people will become confused" or joy that some will understand more perfectly what the Bible is talking about. We choose the way of joy! For each new presentation of God's

Word will find its circle, large or small, of those to whom it will minister strength and blessing.

This book, though arriving late on the current translation scene, has been under way for many years. It has undergone several major manuscript revisions and has been under the careful scrutiny of a team of Greek and Hebrew experts to check content, and of English critics for style. Their many suggestions have been largely followed, though none of those consulted feels entirely satisfied with the present result. This is therefore a tentative edition. Further suggestions as to both renderings and style will be gladly considered as future printings are called for.

A word should be said here about paraphrases. What are they? To paraphrase is to say something in different words than the author used. It is a restatement of an author's thoughts, using different words than he did. This book is a paraphrase of the Old and New Testaments. Its purpose is to say as exactly as possible what the writers of the Scriptures meant, and to say it simply, expanding where necessary for a clear understanding by the modern reader.

The Bible writers often used idioms and patterns of thought that are hard for us to follow today. Frequently the thought sequence is fast-moving, leaving gaps for the reader to understand and fill in, or the thought jumps ahead or backs up to something said before (as one would do in conversation) without clearly stating the antecedent reference. Sometimes the result for us, with our present-day stress on careful sentence construction and sequential logic, is that we are left far behind.

Then too, the writers often have compressed enormous thoughts into single technical words that are full of meaning, but need expansion and amplification if we are to be sure of understanding what the author meant to include in such words as "justification," "righteousness," "redemption," "baptism for the dead," "elect," and "saints." Such amplification is permitted in a paraphrase but exceeds the responsibilities of a strict translation.

There are dangers in paraphrases, as well as values. For whenever the author's exact words are not translated from the original languages, there is a possibility that the translator, however honest, may be giving the English reader something that the original writer did not mean to say. This is because a paraphrase is guided not only by the translator's skill in simplifying but also by the clarity of his understanding of what the author meant and by his theology. For when the Greek or Hebrew is not clear, then the theology of the translator is his guide, along with his sense of logic, unless perchance the translation is allowed to stand without any clear meaning at all. The theological lodestar in this book has been a rigid evangelical position.

If this paraphrase helps to simplify the deep and often complex thoughts of the Word of God, and if it makes the Bible easier to understand and follow, deepening the Christian lives of its readers and making it easier for them to follow their Lord, then the book has achieved its goal.

5. BILLY GRAHAM, "ANGELS IN OUR LIVES TODAY" (FROM *ANGELS: GOD'S SECRET AGENTS*, 1975)

When the most popular preacher in the world writes about one of the most popular topics in Christianity, the result is almost certainly a best-seller. And that is exactly what Billy Graham's Angels: God's Secret Agents *proved to be. The book sold over one million copies within ninety days of its release in 1975.*

While long a belief in virtually all forms of Christianity, the topic of the existence and role of angels became increasingly popular in the United States after World War II. Perhaps it was a response to the growing secular view of the world in the latter half of the twentieth century, sort of an infusion of the divine into everyday life. After all, if Christians were assured that angels were part of their daily existence, it could raise the meaning of what people did to heavenly levels. Likewise, belief in angels assured people they were not alone in their constant struggles against evil. "We know that God has given His angels charge over us so that without their help we could never get the victory over Satan," Graham writes. "Let's consider how we can gain help from God through angels."

Graham's book helped spur this popular belief in angels and spiritual warfare. Pentecostals were especially quick to react, using small gold-colored lapel pins to mark their belief in angels for others in the know. But the phenomenon was more widespread than that, as polls indicated more Americans believed in angels than attended church. Millions tuned in to watch a TV series in which Michael Landon play an angel who wandered the Earth helping strangers. By the end of the millennium, Americans were still deeply immersed in the angel trend, with many watching Touched by an Angel, *another popular television show, still wearing angel pins, reading books about their guardian angels, and, in some cases, using spiritualist techniques to contact their personal angel. While none of these expressions might have been in Graham's mind when he penned his popular book, they are part of the widespread belief in supernatural beings that his work represented and advanced.*

In the early days of World War II, Britain's air force saved it from invasion and defeat. In her book, *Tell No Man*, Adela Rogers St. John describes a strange aspect of that weeks-long air war. Her information comes from a celebration held some months after the war, honoring Air Chief Marshall Lord Hugh Dowding. The King, the Prime Minister and scores of dignitaries were there. In his remarks, the Air Chief Marshall recounted the story of his legendary conflict where his pitifully small complement of men rarely slept, and their planes never stopped flying. He told about airmen on a mission who, having been hit, were either incapacitated or dead. Yet their planes kept flying and fighting; in fact, on occasion pilots in other planes would see a figure still operating the controls. What was the explanation? The Air Chief Marshall said he believed angels had actually flown some of the planes whose pilots sat dead in their cockpits.

That angels piloted planes for dead men in the battle for Britain we cannot finally prove. But we have already seen from Scripture some of the things angels have certainly done, can do, and are yet going to do as history approaches its climax. The important question for each of us is how angels can assist *us* in our lives here and now: How do they help us attain victory over the forces of evil? What is our continuing relationship to them?

We know that God has given His angels charge over us so that without their help we could never get the victory over Satan. The Apostle Paul said, "For we wrestle not against flesh and blood, but against principalities, against powers, against the rulers of the darkness of this world, against spiritual wickedness in high places" (Ephesians 6:12). Let's consider how we can gain help from God through angels.

THE GOD OF THIS AGE

Lucifer, our archenemy, controls one of the most powerful and well-oiled war machines in the universe. He controls principalities, powers and dominions. Every nation, city, village and individual has felt the hot breath of his evil power. He is already gathering the nations of the world for the last great battle in the war against Christ—Armageddon. Yet Jesus assures us that Satan is already a defeated foe (John 12:31, 16:11). In II Timothy 1:10 Paul says that Jesus Christ has abolished death and brought life and immortality to light through the gospel. Peter declares that Jesus "has gone into heaven, and is at the right hand of God, with angels, authorities, and powers subject to him" (I Peter 3:22 RSV).

THE DEFEAT OF SATAN

While Satan is a defeated foe in principle, obviously God has not yet eliminated him from the world scene. The Bible teaches, however, that God will use angels to judge and totally eliminate him from the universe. In Revelation 12 we read of Satan's earlier defeat: "Michael and his angels fought against the dragon; and the dragon fought and his angels, And prevailed not; neither was their place found any more in heaven. And the great dragon was cast out, that old serpent, called the Devil, and Satan, which deceiveth the whole world: he was cast out into the earth, . . . " (verses 7–9). In chapter 20 John describes how Satan's present earthly rule will be temporarily restricted: "And I saw an angel come down from heaven, having the key of the bottomless pit and a great chain in his hand. And he laid hold on the dragon, that old serpent, which is the Devil, and Satan, and bound him a thousand years, And cast him into the bottomless pit, and shut him up, and set a seal upon him, that he should deceive the nations no more, . . . " John then tells us that after a temporary release followed by the last great battle, God will cast Satan into the lake of fire and brimstone, there to be tormented for ever (Revelation 20:10).

Some will say, "It is well and good to talk about the final defeat of the devil but until that happens it doesn't help me because I have to contend with him every day." But this is not the whole story. We have been given specific instructions in Scripture about how to get victory over the devil.

We are told, for example, "Give no opportunity to the devil" (Ephesians 4:27 RSV). In other words, don't leave any vacant places in your heart for him. The Apostle Peter taught, "Be sober, be vigilant; because your adversary the devil, as a roaring lion, walketh about, seeking whom he may devour" (I Peter 5:8). Thus, we cannot be too careful. This includes the injunction to join God's resistance movement: "Whom resist stedfast in the faith" (I Peter 5:9). And James says "Resist the devil, and he will flee from you" (James 4:7).

But these admonitions to be vigilant and to resist tell only part of the story. In addition we can count on the powerful presence of angels many times more numerous and powerful than Satan and his demons. As Increase Mather wrote centuries ago in *Angelographia*, "Angels both good and bad have a greater influence on this world than men are generally aware of. We ought to admire the grace of God toward us sinful creatures in that He hath appointed His holy angels to guard us against the mischiefs of wicked spirits who are always intending our hurt both to our bodies and to our souls." . . .

We must not get so busy counting demons that we forget the holy angels. Certainly we are up against a gigantic war machine. But we are encompassed by a heavenly host so powerful that we need not fear the warfare—the battle is the Lord's. We can boldly face Satan and his legions with all the confidence of the old captain who, when told that his outfit was completely surrounded, shouted, "Good, don't let any of them escape." If your valley is full of foes, raise your sights to the hills and see the holy angels of God arrayed for battle on your behalf.

When Abraham sent his eldest servant back to his blood relations to look for a bride for Isaac he urged him to go confidently because of God's angel: "he shall send his angel before thee, . . . and prosper thy way" (Genesis 24:7, 40). Isaiah the prophet said, "In all their affliction he [the Lord] was afflicted, and the angel of his presence saved them" (63:9). God promised Moses in the midst of all his exasperations, "Mine Angel shall go before thee" (Exodus 23:23). The Bible also says we may see the angels God has sent, but fail to recognize them: "Be not forgetful to entertain strangers: for thereby some have entertained angels unawares" (Hebrews 13:2). Angels, whether noticed by men or not, are active in our twentieth-century world too. Are we aware of them?

It was a tragic night in a Chinese city. Bandits had surrounded the mission compound sheltering hundreds of women and children. On the previous night the missionary, Miss Monsen, had been put to bed with a bad attack of malaria, and now the tempter harassed her with questions: "What will you do when the looters come here? When firing begins on this compound, what about those promises you have been trusting?" In his book, *1,000 New Illustrations* (Zondervan, 1960), Al Bryant records the result. Miss Monsen prayed, "Lord, I have been teaching these young people all these years that thy promises are true, and if they fail now, my mouth shall be forever closed; I must go home."

Throughout the next night she was up, ministering to frightened refugees, encouraging them to pray and to trust God to deliver them. Though fearful things happened all around, the bandits left the mission compound untouched.

In the morning, people from three different neighborhood families asked Miss Monsen, "Who were those four people, three sitting and one standing, quietly watching from the top of your house all night long?" When she told them that no one had been on the housetop, they refused to believe her, saying, "We saw them with our own eyes!" She then told them that God still sent angels to guard his children in their hour of danger.

We have also noted the provision of angels. On occasion they have even given food, as we know from the life of Elijah, following his triumph over the priests of Baal. Fearful, tired and discouraged, "As he lay and slept under a juniper tree, behold, then an angel touched him, and said . . . Arise and eat" (I Kings 19:5–7). God has promised, "Are they not all ministering spirits, sent forth to minister for them who shall be heirs of salvation?" (Hebrews 1:14). Need we think this provisioning by angels ceased thousands of years ago?

When I was visiting the American troops during the Korean War, I was told of a small group of American marines in the First Division who had been trapped up north. With the thermometer at twenty degrees below zero, they were close to freezing to death. And they had had nothing to eat for six days. Surrender to the Chinese seemed their only hope of survival. But one of the men, a Christian, pointed out certain verses of Scripture, and taught his comrades to sing a song of praise to God. Following this they heard a crashing noise, and turned to see a wild boar rushing toward them. As they tried to jump out of his way, he suddenly stopped in his tracks. One of the soldiers raised his rifle to shoot, but before he could fire, the boar inexplicably toppled over. They rushed up to kill him only to find that he was already dead. That night they feasted on meat, and began to regain their strength.

The next morning just as the sun was rising they heard another noise. Their fear that a Chinese patrol had discovered them suddenly vanished as they found themselves face to face with a South Korean who could speak English. He said, "I will show you out." He led them through the forest and mountains to safety behind their own lines. When they looked up to thank him, they found he had disappeared.

ANGELS IN JUDGMENT

As we continue to study how to gain the help of angels in our lives today, we need to look soberly once again at the relation of angels to judgment.

Just before fire and brimstone fell on Sodom because of its sins, the angel said, "For we will destroy this place . . . the Lord hath sent us to destroy it" (Genesis 19:13).

In Daniel 7:10 the Word of God says, "A fiery stream issued and came forth from before him . . . the judgment was set, and the books were opened." In scores of places in the Bible God tells us that He will use angels to execute His judgments on all those who have refused to obey His will by failing to receive Christ as Savior and Lord. As Jesus said, "The Son of man shall send forth his angels, and they shall gather out of his kingdom all things that offend, and them which do iniquity; and shall cast them into a furnace of fire: there shall be wailing and gnashing of teeth" (Matthew 13:41, 42). Jesus also said, "It shall be more tolerable for Tyre and Sidon at the day of judgment, than for you" (Matthew 11:22). And again, "every idle word that men shall speak, they shall give account thereof in the day of judgment" (Matthew 12:36). "For there is nothing covered, that shall not be revealed; neither hid, that shall not be known" (Luke 12:2).

God is recording not only the words and actions but all the thoughts and intents of our hearts. Someday you and I will have to give an account, and at that time our final destiny will be determined by whether we have received or rejected Jesus. Paul said that God would give "to you who are troubled rest with us, when the Lord Jesus shall be revealed from heaven with his mighty angels, in flaming fire taking vengeance on them that know not God and that obey not the gospel of our Lord Jesus Christ" (II Thessalonians 1:7–8). . . .

ANGELS REJOICE IN THE SALVATION OF SINNERS

. . . Just what must you do to cause the angels to rejoice? How do you become reconciled to God? How do you repent of your sin? A simple question demands a simple answer. Jesus made everything so simple, and we have made it so complicated. He spoke to people in short sentences, using everyday words, illustrating His message with never-to-be-forgotten stories. He presented the message of God in such simplicity that many were amazed at what they heard. They could hardly believe their ears, because the message was so simple.

In the Acts of the Apostles, the Philippian jailer asked the Apostle Paul, "What must I do to be saved?" Paul gave him a very simple answer, "Believe on the Lord Jesus Christ, and thou shalt be saved" (Acts 16:30, 31). This is so simple that millions stumble over it. The one and only way you can be converted is to believe on the Lord Jesus Christ as your own personal Lord and Savior. You don't have to straighten out your life first. You don't have to try to give up some habit that is keeping you from God. You have tried all that and failed many times. You can come "just as you are." The blind man came just as he was. The leper came just as he was. The thief on the cross came just as he was. You can come to Christ right now wherever you are and just as you are—and the angels of heaven will rejoice!

Some of the greatest and most precious words recorded in all of Scripture were spoken by Satan himself (not that he intended it to be so). In his discussion with God about Job, he said, "Hast not thou made an hedge about him, and about his house, and about all that he hath on every side? thou hast blessed the work of his hands, and his substance is increased in the land" (Job 1:10).

As I look back over my life I remember the moment I came to Jesus Christ as Savior and Lord. The angels rejoiced! Since then I have been in thousands of battles with Satan and his demons. As I yielded my will and committed myself totally to Christ—as I prayed and believed—I am convinced that God "put a hedge about me," a hedge of angels to protect me.

The Scripture says there is a time to be born and a time to die. And when my time to die comes an angel will be there to comfort me. He will give me peace and joy even at that most critical hour, and usher me into the presence of God, and I will dwell with the Lord forever. Thank God for the ministry of His blessed angels!

6. CAROL FLAKE, *REDEMPTORAMA* (1984)

For years journalists either ignored or lampooned conservative Protestants. Over time, it seemed, the only public image of evangelicals was a caricature—Puritans, holy rollers, snake oil salesmen, hypocrites—left over from the poor showing of a certain type of fundamentalist at the Scopes Trial in 1925. Little did most people realize that conservative Protestants spent the next fifty years laying the groundwork—through their own publications, education, and grassroots efforts—to reenter the public fray. The election of 1980 announced their arrival. Many journalists then attempted to understand the phenomenon, but few did so with quite the verve of Carol Flake.

Carol Flake was a founding editor of Vanity Fair, *a writer for* The New Yorker, *cofounder and editor of a literary journal, and author of numerous nonfiction books. In* Redemptorama: Culture, Politics, and the New Evangelicalism, *published in 1984, she explored the causes and effects of the growing emergence of a "new conservative alliance," the evangelicals.*

This excerpt is a journalist's account of a transdenominational movement, driven by politics, which led to the explosion of conservative Christianity on the pop culture scene. Flake traces the appearance of the new evangelicalism back to the general sense of American moral and political unrest during the 1980s, with the implication that these new conservatives capitalize on that unrest to their own benefit. She uses sermons and her own conversations with evangelical leaders to support her point, as well as to outline the ideas and goals of the new movement.

The prayerful throngs of the 1980 Washington for Jesus rally heralded a turning point for conservative evangelicals in their quest for national recognition. If the Jonestown massacre in 1978 had demonstrated the dangers of fanatic isolationism for charismatic preachers, WFJ dramatized the benefits of public involvement for ambitious ministers. Although the rally had drawn only a quarter of the million marchers its leaders had expected to heed the call, the gathering was one of the largest in the capital's history.

Even more significant than the size of the gathering was its display of handclasping, back-pounding brotherhood. With WFJ, fundamentalist leaders had transformed the world of conservative evangelicalism from a dispersed, isolated subculture into a highly visible counterculture. They drew their strength from the two great religious movements that had shaped the American way: Puritanism and revivalism. Their passion for reform compounded a neo-Puritan demand for discipline and law and order with a revivalist call for immediate, emotion-wracked repentance. The repentance, however, was not for themselves but for the religious and political establishment.

Despite the narrow parochialism displayed by many fundamentalists in their dealings with public life, they managed to join some rather unlikely allies in the formation of a powerful new conservative coalition. So formidable did this new alliance appear that the fundamentalist constituency was greatly inflated by the news media. However, fundamentalist leaders not only made some influential new friends; they made some new foes and rekindled some old feuds. Antagonizing leaders of mainstream Protestant churches, they managed to polarize the already divided world of Protestantism into warring camps. The fundamentalist crusade created a backlash among secular and religious liberals alike.

THE COMMON ENEMY

In order to transform fundamentalism in America from a cranky subculture into an effective counterculture, fundamentalist leaders had to translate sectarian issues into ideological issues and ideological issues into political issues. They had to create unity among themselves by identifying a common enemy before they could find common cause with the conservative political leaders who courted them.

Church leaders who could never have agreed on the finer theological issues, such as demonology and the Rapture, found themselves united, for the first time, against a common enemy—secular humanism. And they found themselves united in a common cause—the family. For the fundamentalist crusader, secular humanism had become the source of all the sins of America, the multiformed beast of modern liberalism: the cold idol of godless science; the brazen serpent of pornography and homosexuality; the unpainted temptress of women's liberation; the meddling giant of big government.

By the time Washington for Jesus had gotten under way, secular humanism had taken on the familiar resonance of Godless communism in fundamentalist sermons. But whereas communism had been an unseen menace, whose subversive triumphs in America were evident primarily to the CIA, the threat of secular humanism was right next door, its effects felt in the schools, on TV, and on the newsstands. Preachers fused faith, the flag, and the family, repeating the now-standard tropes of conservative Christianity: *Let there be prayer in the schools, Christians in Congress, and missiles in the silos. Lead us not into temptation, but deliver us from secularism. Lock the homosexuals in the closet, the wives in the kitchen, and the baby-killers behind bars.*

Recharging the old symbols of civil religion with apocalyptic urgency, preachers decried the decay of American might and morality, many citing the foiled rescue mission to Tehran as yet another warning flare before the major conflagration of Armageddon. Most fundamentalists were agreed on the imminence of the Second Coming, and most of them were premillennialists. They believed that the end-time prophecies were coming true, and that Jesus would soon descend from the heavens with a great fanfare of trumpets prior to the earthly shocks of the Tribulation, the showdown at Armageddon, and the golden age of the Millennium when Satan would be safely chained in a bottomless pit.

In the popular millenarian view, every global event, from the fluoridation of water to the Six-Day War, signified another crucial moment in the countdown to Armageddon. If earlier prognosticators had foolishly stuck their necks out with exact dates and were thus left waiting in vain on lonely mesas or their own rooftops, this new crop of seers were only slightly more cautious in their specifics. Preachers peered breathlessly into the Scriptures for new clues, certain that the curtain of the quotidian was about to rise to reveal a supernatural technicolor epic of disaster, judgment, and redemption. That America's own stockpile of nuclear weapons might be the means by which the earthly slate was to be wiped clean was an idea that led, paradoxically, to a position of militancy rather than pacifism.

As each lurid prophecy was unveiled, the smell of brimstone wafted around the edifices of government, and the fundamentalist sense of common cause quickened like the instant camaraderie of soldiers under siege, of survivors in a catastrophe. But there was something new in the chosen-tribe mentality of this gigantic revival meeting that was sweeping the country. The criterion for membership in this private club of the elect was not so much how one stood with God but how one stood on key moral, political, and economic issues. It was not enough to be a Christian, a Protestant, or even a fully dunked Baptist; it was necessary to proclaim oneself a born-again, no-fault, no-doubt, family-loving Bible-believer. In a new form of inquisition, a kindly member of Moral Majority had questioned me about the certainty of my own faith: "But do you know that you know that you know?" A conundrum of election that might have baffled even John Calvin.

TONGUE-SPEAKERS, ISRAELITES, PAPISTS, AND LATTER-DAY SAINTS

In their battle to save the American family, fundamentalists left a number of faithful out in the cold, but welcomed as kin some rather distant relatives in the religious kingdom. During WFJ, all those hands uplifted in prayer, in the traditional pentecostal *orans* posture, signified a breakthrough in conservative evangelicalism: the acceptance of pentecostalism. WFJ marked the first time tongue-speaking, palms-up pentecostals and more tight-lipped, palms-together evangelicals, represented by Bill Bright and his flock, had cooperated in such numbers without sectarian one-upmanship. In fact, some leading conservative evangelicals, including the rock of fundamentalism, Bob Jones III, chancellor of Bob Jones University, had objected to WFJ because of the creeping ecumenism the event portended. And some pentecostals theorized that Jerry Falwell's lack of interest in the gathering reflected his Baptist bias against tongue-speakers.

Historically, since the first stirrings of modern pentecostalism during the early years of the century, fundamentalists and mainstream Protestants alike had tended to regard pentecostals as holy-rolling, snake-handling hicks, despite the fact that the movement had originated in Los Angeles and spread rapidly in urban areas. Scholars had categorized pentecostals as marginal groups seeking emotional consolation for the social or cultural deprivations that had constricted their lives. Theoretically, the babbling tongues and quaking bodies liberated in pentecostal worship would compensate for the lack of culture and comfort in the daily lives of the worshipers. Ironically, pentecostals were the strictest of denominations when it came to one's behavior outside of church. Dancing, drinking, movies, the wearing of makeup, and even sports were all heavily frowned upon.

Generally, tongue-speakers were relegated to the lunatic fringes of Protestantism, with the more exotic forms of worship found in the hills and hollers of Appalachia. In my church, for example, if anyone had tried speaking in tongues or holding out their arms like TV antennae, they probably would have been doused with a bucket of cold water—no baptism intended. And a favorite pastime among bored teenagers in the Bible Belt was cutting the ropes on a pentecostal revival tent while a service was in progress or sitting on a back pew trying to control snorts of laughter at all the strange carryings-on. When healer Oral Roberts abandoned the Pentecostal Holiness church and his portable revival tent for the permanent respectability of Tulsa, Oklahoma, and the United Methodist church, it was regarded as an opportunistic move in spiritual upward mobility. . . .

Unlike the rural and lower-income members of older pentecostal denominations, who prided themselves on their isolation from secular culture and mainstream religion, the new pentecostals tended to be middle class, Republican, suburban, and well connected in business, social, and political circles. "Imagine their surprise, these tax-paying people . . . these veterans of patio barbecues, when they learned they were carriers of ecstasy."

Pentecostalism had come to mean for the conservative Christian middle class what the Human Potential movement had meant to the secular middle class: a source of immediate community and emotional rebirth. Popular pentecostal speaker General Ralph Haines, Jr., a retired cavalry officer who had become the comedian of the charismatic circuit, liked to describe his staid, complacent role as traditional Episcopalian, before he was "zapped" by pentecostalism: "I was sacramentalized but not evangelized. I was one of God's frozen chosen." Whereas evangelical worship services tended to be predictable and nonparticipatory, except for occasional antiphonal readings and approving amens uttered to punctuate a good sermon, pentecostal prayer meetings were spontaneous and personal, encouraging voluntary testimonials, prayers, and prophecies from the congregation. . . .

Fundamentalists seemed to be hopping into the bunker with almost any ideologues they found to be lodging in the same conservative camp. Even though many fundamentalists still regarded Catholics as the legions of Babylon and the Mormons as members of a demonic cult, pro-family fundamentalist tacticians joined forces with leaders of the long-standing Roman Catholic crusade against abortion and the discreetly organized Mormon campaign against the ERA. In fact, many of the principal strategists of the new conservative right turned out to be Catholic. Clearly, for fundamentalist leaders, it had come down to choosing the lesser of evils—the Pope and Joseph Smith being currently less dangerous than the sybarites of secular humanism.

This ex officio ecumenism indicated that the fundamentalist identity had become more ideological than theological. If one ignored such troublesome issues as the status of the Virgin Mary and the authority of the Pope, fundamentalists seemed to have more in common with conservative Catholics than they did with liberal Protestants. The key to such ideological unity amid serious religious differences was placing the big, symbolic issues—abortion, prayer in the schools, etc.—on a Manichaean battleground of good and evil, and talking about unity of purpose without sounding overly ecumenical. Thus politics would become a morality play, and the embattled family a rallying point for conservative Protestants, Catholics, and Jews alike.

The crusade by conservative Christians to "save" America had in fact become a last-ditch attempt to preserve their traditional values and carry out their obligations as God's people in an increasingly pluralistic society. The coincidental resurgence of the political and religious right—two discrete if overlapping movements—pointed to common causes of discontent. Conservative middle-class Americans, once complacent in their status within the moral and social—if silent—majority, had come to feel like voices in the wilderness. Upward-bound evangelicals who had moved into suburban respectability from farms or factories felt like second-class citizens whose concerns were being either ignored or assaulted by the government at every level.

These were not the grievances of a marginal group, as the Far Right had been perceived in the fifties and sixties, when Billy James Hargis was raving about Communist conspiracies and Richard Hofstadter was writing about the paranoid style in American politics. Such factors as "status anxiety" put forth by Daniel Bell and Seymour Martin Lipset no longer seemed entirely adequate to account for the growing restiveness and power of conservative Christians. By the late seventies, evangelicals had come a long way from revival tents, streetcorner pamphleteering, backwoods camp meetings, and Bible-verse billboards. Their churches had grown, and they had prospered, as had the fundamentalist faction within the loosely allied National Association of Evangelicals.

Even as conservative Christians consolidated their numbers and their power, the quality of life around them continued to deteriorate, and the stench of corruption was everywhere. As they saw it, their hard-earned prosperity was being eaten away by taxes that were redistributed as handouts to the idle or as contributions to the legal-services funds for the flagrantly sinful. Unless good Christian people shelled out non-tax-exempt tuition for private Christian schools, their sons and daughters would be taught values in the classroom that assailed the book of Genesis and mocked the strict morality of their parents. Even sheltered parochial-school students were being lured into a corrupt secular world with the switch of a TV channel or the flip of a magazine page. There was crime in the streets, lenience in the courts, mutiny in the home, apathy on the job, abortion on demand. One did not have to be paranoid to perceive that the close-knit family, the tightly woven fabric of community, had frayed into loose ends.

The time was ripe for another Great Awakening, or at least another eruption of the scapegoating populism that had been popping up on the American scene since the Know-Nothings set out to curb the Catholics in the mid-nineteenth century. The fact that America had entered the age of high technology was no assurance that primitive religious instincts would die out like the dodo bird. Popular religious movements, in fact, often flourish within a context of rationalism. The first Great Awakening in America coincided with the first rays of the Enlightenment.

7. JASON E. MCBRIDE, "GOTHS FOR JESUS" (1999)

MICHAEL L. KEENE, "THE CHURCH ON THE WEB" (1999)

Popular culture can affect religion every bit as much as religion can influence pop culture. From the market-oriented language of evangelist George Whitefield in the 1740s to the mass-produced handbills of the Charles Finney revivals of the 1840s and the zoot suited, staccato delivery of Billy Graham in the 1940s, style, fashion, and even technology have helped shape religion, especially at its most popular, least institutional levels. *The following two pieces, both from* The Christian Century *in 1999, show that this continued to be the case at the century's end.*

In the article "Goths for Jesus," a so-called "alternative witness" discusses how subcultures, like Goths, integrate themselves into Christian religious practice. It focuses primarily on the Cornerstone Festival, an annual five-day celebration of alternative Christian music replete with "intra-Christian encounter[s]." But the true theme of the article is the idea of using secular (i.e., pop culture) sources to promote religious values—the efficacy of which the author finds difficult to assess.

Meanwhile, Michael L. Keene, a professor of English at the University of Tennessee and a journalist, outlines the growing role of religion on the Internet, exploring the benefits of the technology for religious organizations as well as worshippers. "While the image of hundreds or thousands of people sitting in front of their computer screens praying may make many shudder, the Web does offer interesting resources for personal prayer," he writes. This article represents the growing practice of "Web worship" as the newest form of individual faith, independent from institutional religions.

⸛⸛⸛

GOTHS FOR JESUS

His black-dyed hair, shaven at the base, was pulled up into a bun pierced by thin black sticks. All of his clothing was black: an ankle-length skirt accompanied by a zip-down leather vest with fishnet sleeves. Six silver rings of various shapes cluttered his fingers, and his nails were painted pale green to match both his eye shadow and the jewel set in the large Celtic cross hanging from his neck. With his hands folded and held just below his chest, this slight, pale young man seemed to float into view while a high school girl and a college-aged woman tried to explain the culture of Christian Goth to two adults.

One of the adults pointed to the elaborately dressed young man and commented that, no offense, but this guy looks, well, not like a guy, and well, that's a problem for me. The college-aged Goth offered: "I look at him and I think, 'He's beautiful.'"

This intra-Christian encounter was one of many fascinating scenes that took place at the Cornerstone Music Festival, probably the largest venue for Christian alternative music (and alternative culture) in the nation. The festival is sponsored by *Cornerstone* magazine, whose masthead challenges readers "to look out the window of biblical reality and break the 'normal Christian' mold with a stance that has cultural relevancy." The magazine is a publication of Jesus People USA (known as JPUSA, and pronounced "ja-poo-za"), based in Chicago. The first Cornerstone festival was held in 1984 with 5,000 participants. In early July, close to 22,000 campers, most of them evangelical Christians, converged on the 579-acre *Cornerstone*-owned campground in western Illinois.

Cornerstone is a strange melange of music, costume and consumerism. For five days a lightly wooded plot of land surrounded by farm fields is transformed into a tent city, complete with fast-food trailers, a grocery store and an art gallery. Musicians perform nearly around the clock at six music tents, and festival participants gather every night at the main stage for four-hour concerts. The festival also features seminars on a variety of hot topics, including pluralism, New Age philosophy, sexuality, "neo-theism" and women's roles in the church. Festival-goers can even take drawing lessons at Art Rageous workshops.

The campground reminded me of the East Village in New York, where body parts are pierced with rings, bars and chains; skin is painted with tattoos; and hair is dyed all colors imaginable. Plenty of young people also brandished cigarettes—a new trend, I learned, among young evangelicals exercising their "freedom in Christ" to flout the old taboos. Not everyone donned chain and padlock necklaces or lit up, however. There were plenty of clean-cut youth-group types as well. And the families in the RV sites, with their yard torches and makeshift pavilions, brought a suburban feel to this temporary community.

Over a hundred bands were on hand, representing music ranging from folk to ska swing, punk to metal. In a tent featuring hip-hop I ran into Keith, whose braided hair competed with his bushy beard for length. On his right calf was a tattoo of big red Rolling Stones lips. He called himself "just an old hippie trying to spread the gospel," and said he was at the festival mainly for the hip-hop music. He said he and a pastor run a coffeehouse in inner-city St. Louis, and he wanted to make hip-hop contacts. Hip-hop, he hoped, would attract black urban youth, who evidently were not being drawn by other Christian musicians. I left the tent soon after the hip-hoppers started the chant, "Go, Jesus, go, Jesus, go!"

Later in the night I ventured into the "hard music" tent to observe some moshing. This was not watered-down moshing, with people merely bumping against each other in an overcrowded room. The space cleared in the center of the tent looked like a charged field. The moshers threw their bodies into the field and thrashed violently, gaining momentum before hurling themselves to the fringe. The crowd at the edges couldn't always hold them, and when I saw a blur of leather, ripped denim and silver spikes hurtling toward me, I raised my flashlight as a shield. Better bring my own spikes next time.

"Does the gargoyle belong on the cathedral?" This question about the place of the grotesque in the Christian worldview was the theme of Imaginarium, a tent dedicated to the discussion of film and literature. My first night I decided to watch both films that were playing: Todd Browning's *Freaks* (1932) and William Dieterie's *Hunchback of Notre Dame* (1939). The discussion that followed touched on monstrosities, the human form and our general fascination with the freakish.

The next day the freaks came out in full force to attend a panel discussion on Goth. On my way to the tent I passed a fellow whose eyes were framed in black diamonds, painted over a white face. He wore a black T-shirt that declared "Jesus loves Marilyn Manson too." OK. And the point? Is this Christian Goth?

The answer, apparently, is not exactly. I gathered from the panel discussion that for these young adults, being a Goth was simply a "cultural preference" for things sad, quiet and mournful. And of course it entails a liking for Goth music, which embodies that somber mood. Begun as a component of punk rock, Goth music shares similarities with industrial music, with its vocal distortions, and may be seen as a backlash to upbeat and colorful disco. One panelist said the Goth outlook is aligned with the Christian perspective in many ways—like Christianity, Goth culture acknowledges human fallenness and suffering.

One person said that she had been born a Goth, and that it was a comfort to come to a place where Christian Goth was recognized as a possible strategy for evangelism. In fact, the young man who was dressed in the elaborate black costume told me he serves as a missionary in London to its underground community.

Still, unsavory associations due to mainstream stereotyping have their cost. One girl tearfully related how, after the shootings at Columbine High School, where the murderers were identified with Goth-style clothing, her church had shunned her. (The original crosses that were built as memorials for the dead at Columbine had been reassembled at the festival, adding further to its eerie mix of cultural symbols.)

Attracted to its style, proponents of Christian Goth resisted admitting that there might be serious incompatibilities between the cultural props and meanings of Goth (like its bleak posturing and macabre fascination with death) and the ultimate message of Christianity. As with hard-metal moshers—whose violence makes them even more unpalatable—their tendency was to think that inserting the gospel into any musical form redeemed that form for Christian use.

There are precedents, of course, for the Christian use of secular sources. Renaissance composers used popular folk songs as cantus firmi for their masses, and Luther adapted familiar drinking songs as hymn tunes. Fin-de-siècle evangelicals employ all styles of popular music and its attendant culture to spread the gospel. But many seem surprisingly uninterested in the relation of form and content, and satisfied merely with reproducing forms of popular culture, however questionable. Like the cathedral gargoyles, whose phantasmagoric appearance still remains a curiosity, the Christian Goths are unsettling forms in the artifice of Christian pop.

THE CHURCH ON THE WEB

Sunday School teachers say that the toughest question kids ask is, "But what's a virgin?" While my class of 13-year-olds hasn't asked me that, they certainly can stump me with other questions. After the bishop accepted my wife as a candidate for seminary, I mentioned to the class that she had to send him a status-report letter four times a year—during Ember Days. I should have been prepared for "But what are Ember Days?" Where can you go for quick answers to such questions? To the Internet, of course. In my office or at home, the answer is only a click away. . . .

The World Wide Web is playing an important and rapidly growing role in helping laypeople think about their faith. For starters, it helps us look up all kinds of church history and other theologically oriented reference information. But the Web also helps build the community of God both by increasing the flow of information from denominational organizations to churchpeople and by helping like-minded believers find and connect with each other. And the Web provides additional opportunities for people to engage in private, or not-so-private, prayer. Finally, and perhaps uniquely, the Web can bring a refreshing wind of serendipity into our faith lives, making more concrete the line that "the spirit blows where it wills." Access to the World Wide Web gives us access to a richer church life.

My Education for Ministry class at the cathedral has "the quest for the historic Jesus" as one of its topics. As usual, in the hours before the class meets I'm looking for additional ways to illuminate and update the subject matter. Typing "quest for historic Jesus" into my favorite search engines produced a mishmash of odd sites, and a quick look at the first five or ten of them (this takes only five minutes with a fast connection) suggests I'm not getting the kind of thing I want. Having just finished rereading *The God We Never Knew*, I take a chance and type in the author's name, "Marcus Borg."

The second site that comes up on AltaVista is Cam Linton's "A Portrait of Jesus" . . . which contains an amazingly detailed summary of Borg's work, complete with an audio of Borg and links to his speaking schedule for the year, to a list of his publications, to the Jesus seminar and to Westar Institute. It takes only a couple of minutes to browse the site's main pages and select a few to print out for my class. The printer puts the Web address on each copy so that students can go straight to the source I used.

That scenario shows just one of the many ways that the Web helps me find additional information on church-related topics. When I'm puzzling over a particular Bible passage, such as the one I always remember (incorrectly) as "the spirit blows where it will," I like to read other people's interpretations. Of course, the first problem is that I don't remember exactly where that phrase occurs. Not having my pocket concordance with me at the office, I go to the "Bible Gateway" . . . which has a very forgiving search engine—if I give it an approximate phrase, the computer will do the rest. (The Bible Gateway also offers seven different versions of the Bible in ten different languages.) I choose to search the RSV for "spirit blows," and the site gives me back information more accurate than my search phrase had been. The source is John 3:8: "The wind blows where it wills, and you hear the sound of it, but you do not know whence it comes or whither it goes; so it is with every one who is born of the Spirit." If I feed "John 3:8" back into the search engine, it will offer me the whole chapter so I can see the context (or the same text in any of the other six versions).

Once I have the right chapter and verse, I can start looking for sermons and commentaries on that text. I can check Richard Fairchild's enormous "Sermons & Sermon-Lectionary Resources" site . . . or John Kapteyn's "Sermon Central" . . . but there are so many sermon sites, nearly all of which will let me search for sermons by a particular chapter and verse or a particular key phrase, that I may decide simply to type "John 3:8" into the AltaVista search engine, which itself yields me over 1,800 "hits."

Or maybe it's music I want. My home church's choir normally focuses on music by 18th- and 19th-century European composers, so when they launched into the spiritual "Steal Away" a few weeks ago, I was really struck by it. But on Monday I couldn't remember the words. A quick visit to Frank Petersohn's "Hymns, Gospel Songs, & Spirituals" site . . . takes me right to the words, and the site will play me the melody (both versions) as well.

Why is my favorite hymn often called "The breastplate of St. Patrick"? I can find the answer at Diarmuid O'Laoghaire's "Introduction to Celtic Spirituality" . . . which I found by putting "breastplate of St. Patrick" into the AltaVista search engine. This search took longer than usual, not because I did not find an answer in under five minutes, but because the search led me to so many good Celtic spirituality sites, most of which I could not resist skimming.

Was the answer I found authoritative? That's always an important question to ask on the Web, where the mad ravings of pizza-crazed computer programmers and the wise musings of English professors are often initially indistinguishable. I would have to look up Diarmuid O'Laoghaire to find out how authoritative his answer is. On the Web, the fact that it looks good and sounds good may not count for much. With a little help from the search engine, I find that O'Laoghaire, who turns out to be a Jesuit, publishes in *Milltown Studies* and *Celtic Studies*, has translated and published a collection of short stories by Welsh writers, and has contributed an essay to James Mackey's *Introduction to Celtic Christianity*—probably enough information on which to base a decision about the authoritativeness of this reading of the breastplate.

Of course, there are official sources of information as well. If I'm interested in the demographics of seminarians in the Episcopal Church (my denomination), I can find that information from the Episcopal Church's Standing Commission On Ministry Development page. . . . In fact, if I go to the Episcopal Church's own home page . . . , I can learn things about the church this lifelong Episcopalian never suspected. . . .

While the notion of looking things up more quickly and easily is appealing, there's another important and growing function of the Web: building community. Here we will go from the biggest to the smallest features, but without implying that the biggest is most important or that the smallest is least important.

Every three years the Episcopal Church comes together in its annual convention. Like most Episcopalians, I have never attended. So it is hard for me to appreciate just what goes on at the convention—socially, politically, theologically, or in any other way. Some delegates bring a reasonably full report back to their congregations; many do not. Most of us have to make do with the vague rumblings we hear—"rumble rumble rumble *women;* rumble rumble rumble *gays;* rumble rumble rumble *budget*" and so on. Usually local discussions take place on the basis of such meager information. So during the 1997 General Convention it was a delight to find on the Web a complete account of each day's happenings, compiled by volunteers and the church's news service and posted by the morning of the next day. This account was in the form of a complete newspaper done anew every day. . . . For perhaps the first time, I felt part not just of the larger spiritual body, but also of the larger political body of the church. Now, because I have subscribed via my computer to the mailing list of the Episcopal News Service, I receive daily news stories and bulletins, not just the once-a-month summary offered by the denomination's newspaper.

So far I have talked only about one-way communication, but on the Web communication goes a multitude of ways at once. Consider the example of listserves, electronic (e-mail) mailing lists that allow any number of people to stay in touch with each other regularly—all one has to do is subscribe. Here are two examples: I am one of perhaps six mentors in the Education for Ministry program, within a 50-mile radius. But in many places, EFM mentors live far apart. So what does someone do who has a problem, question or epiphany to share? The answer is a listserve called "Reflections-L" that enables mentors everywhere to "talk" with each other daily. Typical postings might include questions about how to lead a particular lesson in the program, how best to deal with a particular kind of meeting problem, or how to find additional resources for, say, graduation ceremonies or recruiting new students or dealing with the departure or illness of a group member. . . .

If you want a great example of what building the community of Christ on the Web can be like, visit "Saint Sam's Cyberparish." . . . Yes, it's a church that exists on the Web. (Its motto is "Via Media Via Modem.") You can spend a considerable amount of time wandering the site, but if you've never been part of a listserve before, I recommend that you first view the last 48 hours of posts . . . there you'll see Christian community—warts, halos and all—alive and at work. This list has not just created a cyberchurch, it has also spun off the Society of Archbishop Justus. . . . The society states its purpose as follows: "The particular good works that we focus on are Internet information services: Web and e-mail servers that help Anglicans be one body. Our members help install, operate and maintain the computers and networks that enable our online communication, and they help educate the Anglican public about how best to use those computers."

The Web builds the community of God by allowing even local groups to communicate better. My parish, St. John's Cathedral in Knoxville, Tennessee, is a downtown church with a nongeographic membership. We live all over the city and in the surrounding hills, and we tend to see each other only at church events. So we have to work to stay in touch. In my EFM group, seven of this year's ten members have e-mail. When someone misses a meeting, I send that person a short e-mail summary of what went on (the other three, when they miss, receive the same summary by regular mail). Of the 15 young people in my Sunday morning class, 13 have e-mail. We send out e-mail announcements of program activities each week. (Our 13-year-olds seem to pay attention to what they receive electronically but throw away anything they receive on paper!)

While the image of hundreds or thousands of people sitting in front of their computer screens praying may make many shudder, the Web does offer interesting resources for personal prayer. One of my favorite sites is the "Daily Office" . . . (also available in Spanish), a function of Elisheva Barsabe at the Mission of St. Clare. This site offers a liturgical calendar, liturgical music and complete texts—including texts of the readings for each day—for morning prayer, noonday prayer, evening prayer and compline, plus the daily devotions for families and individuals. You can use these for your own worship anywhere you have a computer, and you can print them out for use in groups.

Like most Web sites, this one also offers a list of links to other sites. If you have time, these lists are always worth following. For instance, it was from the Daily Office site that I learned that Forward Movement Publications' *Forward Day by Day* is now available on the Web (only the current day's entry, though). . . . So if I don't make it to church for morning prayer, I can read the service right here in my office. And if I don't have time for that, I can surely take a minute after lunch to read the day's entry.

One of the best things for me about life in the church is the way grace seems to shower on me. I find that our new canon pastor used to live in my hometown, a thousand miles away from here; or a faculty colleague with whom I've often had minor squabbles becomes a good and warm friend because we have dinner together so often at church on Wednesday nights, or on retreat I meet someone who teaches at my daughter's college and knows her and I say, "Gee, it sure would be nice if she would go ahead and make the decision to be confirmed," not knowing he's a catechist in that diocese— and four months later she's confirmed.

Little epiphanies like these play a major role in our faith lives. Perhaps because the World Wide Web is so enormous and so constantly changing, working through the Web's religious sites seems to increase the flow of that kind of grace. So there I am on the Web, again on a Wednesday afternoon, hoping to find something appropriate to share with my EFM group for the beginning of Lent, but also thinking about my own Lenten discipline. I'm at one of those points when giving up dessert or beer or even pizza seems not much of a response, and I used "giving up giving up things" as last year's discipline. . . .

Then there was the day I had been listening to too much gossip among church friends about how the denomination is tearing itself apart. By coincidence, that day I also discovered the Web presence of the Society of Archbishop Justus (mentioned above) and found in its list of resources the reference to a "collection" of prayer books. Clicking to that page . . . I found *The Book of Common Prayer* from 1549, 1552, 1559, 1662, 1786, 1789, 1892, 1928 and (the current one) 1979. Somewhere in my browsing through those intriguing, faith-filled documents, I lost the hard edge of my anxiety about today's church. Perhaps concern is appropriate, but looking at that 450-year history convinced me that panic is not.

Finally, there is humility. How do you feel when you visit a different church? What if you could visit not five churches, not 50, but 500 or 5,000? Would you not feel humbled and awed by the splendor and variety of God's creation? I have already mentioned Web search engines such as Yahoo! or AltaVista (but not multisearch engines, such as Dogpile . . . which search more than one search engine at once), but I have not mentioned subject trees, which are hierarchically organized lists of resources that have already been looked up and categorized by subject. Yahoo! maintains a comprehensive subject tree, with categories such as Education, Entertainment, Government and so on.

Under the category "Society & Culture" there is "Religion," and under "Religion" are over 40 subheadings ranging from Angels, Arts and Crafts, Ask an Expert, and Bibliographies to Software, Symbols, Television, Theology, Theosophy, Tours and Tour Operators, Web Directories, Women and Usenet. Under each of these headings there are more delightful, more bizarre and more spirit-filled sources than any of us could take in. But the biggest subheading is "Faiths and Practices," with over 16,000 entries, within which we find "Christianity," with over 11,000 entries, under which is "Denominations and Sects," with over 7,000 entries. The main list under Denominations and Sects includes more than 100 variations—Amish, Armenian Evangelical, Association of Vineyard Churches, Cell Church, Charismatic Episcopal Church, Free Methodists, Free Presbyterians, the International Church of the Foursquare Gospel, Knanaya, the Plymouth Brethren, Rastafarians, the Two-by-Twos and the Waldensian Church, among others. Click onto any one of those entries in this subject tree, and you're immediately into that church's world. . . .

8. ZAIN BHIKHA, "PRAISE THE PROPHET" (2000)

JONATHAN SCHORSCH, "MAKING JUDAISM COOL" (2000)

Perhaps the most fruitful area for cross-fertilization between the religious and the secular is music. Rhythm and blues finds its roots in African American gospel music, while the "Christian rock" that has become a standard fixture in American society puts traditional doctrine into the sounds of what was once considered "the Devil's music." Perhaps lesser known but no less important are recent experiments in religious music by Muslims and Jews.

"Praise the Prophet," written by Zain Bhikha of South Africa, is part of a compilation of songs on an album entitled In Praise of the Last Prophet. *Drawing upon numerous musical traditions, the songs center around the work and person of Muhammad, the last Prophet of Allah and founder of Islam. Bhikha's song outlines Muhammad's ministry and indicates his place as the role model of faith. Having come to the attention of Muslim music producers after winning a local singing contest broadcast by radio, Bhikha went on to record his first album in 1994, at the age of twenty. By 2000, when "Praise the Prophet" was released, he was well known through the American Muslim world for his remixed songs teaching about the faith.*

In "Making Judaism Cool," Jonathan Schorsch discusses how Judaism—even Orthodox Judaism—has gained entrance into pop culture through music. He explores the struggle to find "authentic" Judaism and the sense of pride felt by young people participating in this newly "cool" religion. Schorsch concludes that while this new brand of Judaism may help teenagers escape the dangers of secular pop culture, it threatens to dilute the religious meaning, sometimes unrecognizably so. And so, the debate goes on—can the sacred and the secular dance together without the sacred being seduced?

<hr />

Praise the Prophet

ZAIN BHIKHA

TAKEN FROM THE ALBUM *TOWARDS THE LIGHT*

Taken from the album *Towards the Light*
Amid the confusion, the chaos and the pain
a man emerged and Muhammad was his name
And walking with nothing but Allah as his aid
and the mark of a prophet between his shoulder blades

In a cave in Mount Hira, the revelation came:
Read o Muhammad, read in Allah's name
May the blessings of Allah be on al-Mustafa
none besides him could have been al-Mujtaba

Chorus:
Muhammad, peace be upon his soul
The greatest of prophets, Islam was his only goal
Muhammad, salla allahu 'alayhi wa sallam

From among all the prophets, Muhammad was the last
as his was a mission of the greatest task

There was only moral degeneration
people clung to idol adoration

For all nations, he was al-Mukhtaar
so was he praised by Allah, al-Ghaffaar
The bearer of glad tidings, al-Basheer
leading into light, as-Seeraj-al-Muneer

Chorus

In handling the wicked, he had the best of skill
He pacified with tolerance and goodwill
The best of morals he aimed to attain
All he accomplished through suffering and pain

Reviving imaan as al-muthakkir
He is known in the Qur'an as al-mud-dath-thir
Only he was given the honour of miraaj
Unique was this glory to Muhammad as-seeraj

Chorus

He was ad-da'ee illallah hil azheem
al hadi elaa seerauteem mustakeem
His mission complete, he's held in great esteem
Allah praised him as bil-khuluqil azeem

May the blessings of Allah be on al-Mustafa
none besides him could have been al-Mujtaba
So perfect were his morals, so justly did he rule
darkness had vanished and the word was full of noor

Chorus

—————❈❈❈—————

MAKING JUDAISM COOL

I sit listening to the newest and skankiest dub beat, bass thumping, high reverb shimmering, cool horns sliding around the syncopation, the chorus droning:

Slaughter, slaughter, they want to slaughter em
Slaughter, slaughter, watch out murderer.

The "em" is slurred enough to be "us." The singer drawls in deep Jamaican accents, the words strobe-lighted by the heavy reverb:

> I want to tell you sometin about my granfader,
> my granfader was a concentration camp survivor
> taken from his home in the second world war
> separated from his family by the Nazis mister
> and herded like an animal into a cattle car.

Is this some Rasta philosemite? No, only a recent CD by a collection of New York's hottest Jewish musicians. Doing the holocaust as Jamaican dub, it struck me, marked the quintessence of a near decade of making Judaism cool.

Already in the mid-1990s, when living in Jerusalem, I noticed that the ultra-religious radio stations played all sorts of updated songs that were little more than covers of tunes from cool genres—usually from Africa or its diaspora—with words from the Bible or the like. The last decade has also witnessed the rise of the heavy metal Hasidic rock of Yossi Piamenta, the Jewish rap of Blood of Abraham, Rebbe Soul, the New Orleans Klezmer All-Stars, and the whole lower East side avant-garde Jewish music scene: the Klezmatics, John Zorn, the Radical Jewish Culture/Tzadik label, etc. A Reggae Passover disk came out a few years back, while an announcement for a Reggae Chanukah disk popped up recently in my e-mail. Even the stodgy Israeli Duo Re'emim did a hip-hop/DJ-mix cover of the traditional Ashkenazic Rosh Hashanah melodies.

This borrowing approach has a long history in music, Jewish and otherwise, and especially so in Ladino and Hasidic music, many of whose tunes originated in secular, non-Jewish contexts (for instance, as drinking songs). The Hasidim sought to elevate the fallen sparks hidden within the melodies by attaching them to words that called forth the holiest qualities. In the twentieth century, popular Jewish music also went in search of the newest fashion, in search of making the old new and the global local, like the tangos played by Polish Jewish orchestras in the 1920s, or the American "klezmer" musicians in the first part of this century who invented "authentic" old world Jewish music by updating it with thoroughly American instruments and styles.

Today, post-baby-boomers, alive to ethnicity and the rise of religiosity since the 1980s, have come around to appreciating the arts of their own ethnic culture. The movement of *ba'alei teshuvah* (those who have "returned" to Jewish observance) has shifted the demographics of the institutional orthodox world such that the young yeshivah-bochers can groove quite easily to the secular, cool, ethnic *riddims* of their sinful youths.

Indeed, such grooves typify the general trend of making Judaism cool. Just think of Madonna and Roseanne studying kabbalah, radical Jewish culture (Tatooed Jew, etc.), Carlebach followers and fans, the hip currency of Sephardi and Mizrahi music, the style of Chabad missionizing (not to mention the popularity of the Chabad telethon), a Jewish lounge club in New York named Makor (Source). It's not just that Judaism and things Jewish are "in," though that is part of it. No, we are being told that things Jewish—traditionally very uncool—are actually cool. Some Jews are even acting as if it's cool to be Jewish. An Upper West Side paper reported that Friday nights at shul are as popular now as discos! People are converting to Judaism right and left; in some synagogues on the West coast converts to Judaism make up 30 percent or more of the congregation. Indeed, if one looks closely one sees that Jewish cool signifies a kind of amusing and perverse but much needed tikkun or repair for Judaism and our culture at large.

Still, isn't there something a little wrong here? Cool marks ironic distance, detachment, and anti-establishmentarianism, an overemphasis on style. "Mama, I wanna make rhythm, don't wanna make music," crooned Cab Calloway in 1937 New York, as he slid into a mock ethnic voice and scenario (a boy playing rhapsodies on a violin), before exploding into a crescendo of scat ("noise" according to the contemporary mainstream understanding of music and taste). "Pop" music, television and Hollywood host, if not breed, irony and sarcasm as a weltanschaung. Meanwhile, observant Judaism for the most part entails utter seriousness, without much room for humor, sarcasm, or irony, especially in the ultra-orthodox world. There would seem to be some tension, to say the least, between hip-hop and *tehillim* (psalms), no? Doesn't some inherent semiotics of heavy metal preclude it from serving the seriously sacred?

According to the Jerusalem-based paper Kol Ha-Ir some years ago, many ultra-orthodox rabbis of Me'ah She'arim thought so and came out against the rock and roll religious music, which had become popular enough to keep open a large, allegedly disruptive music store on one of the ultra-orthodox neighborhood's main streets. It made sense that many of the late-night religious DJs in Israel broadcast while obviously stoned. Though supposedly radically different in content, the fit between the pre- and post-teshuvah life-styles appeared stylistically continuous. They had traded in their black leather for the stylistics of black suits and fedoras; mohawks for the myriad of specific pe'ot styles, each representing a different Hasidic group. The ornate, patterned, textured chintz vests of the Hasidic rebbes—the fabric origin of the derogatory adjective "chintzy"—now signified the height of cool. (Remember the haute-fashion rip-off of Hasidic garb from a few years back?) No surprise that the rebbes worried that the seepage of the pre-teshuvah life into the ba'al-teshuvah life would threaten to undermine the entire point of the transformation.

A close look at two of the recent releases by John Zorn's Tzadik label provides a fascinating glimpse into the paradoxes of cool Judaism. Trumpet player Steven Bernstein's disc *Diaspora Soul* (1999) features a small postmodern Latin jazz ensemble belting out versions of Ani Ma'amin, Manishtanah, Rock of Ages, Roumania, Roumania, and others. The playing is both straight and ironic, funky and funny; Bernstein blows a mean trumpet. In a revealing chain of associations, Bernstein describes the sound he sought:

> Not just the rhythms, but the phrasing and air flow of the R&B players are a continuation of the [New Orleans] marching style [. . .] This led me to thinking not just about a New Orleans sound, but rather the Gulf Coast sound, encompassing Texas and Cuba—and the last part of the Gulf Coast was Miami. And who retired to Miami? The most popular Cuban export of the '50s was the cha-cha [. . .] who loves a cha-cha more than the Jews? And the final piece of the grail—the hora bass pattern—one, two-and, and-four-and—is the first half of the clave, the heart of Afro-Cuban music.

Bernstein's music is clearly a loving tribute. Note, however, that Jews here are only the recipients, the listeners to the great ethnic musics, not their creators.

The tension between the disparate elements in Bernstein's music parallels the tension in the problematic of ethnic identity itself at play in the production of this music and the manufacture of this disk. The Cuban percussion, languid dance-groove bass, vibe-like electric piano, or swelling organ underpin the Jewish melodies which make up the horn themes. These melodies, however, are more icing than cake; Bernstein's soloing, for instance, only occasionally takes up allusions to Jewish music.

Bernstein has (purposefully? ironically?) recreated the overall feeling of exactly those Fifties and Sixties Jewish groups (Mickey Katz, the Barry Sisters) who incorporated "exotic" elements. He makes fun of (and pays respect to) them just as these groups had had fun with (and made fun of?) the "exotic" musics they were borrowing and even the Jewish music they were simultaneously transforming, down to the cheapo arrangements, "tacky" production values, often uninspired lounge-music tracks—amusing and almost desperate efforts to make cheesy songs cool. Is this the music that Jews who love cha-cha produced? Yet the playing is great and the concept often works; Bernstein has forged a unified sound and it constitutes convincing Jewish music. But the effect cannot be listened to unironically. Perhaps all this has to do with Bernstein's comment about being asked to do a "Jewish" album:

How does a Jewish musician who has spent his entire life studying "other" musical cultures make a "Jewish" record? How does one make a "Jewish" record, when by nature, all of one's music is already "Jewish"?

Another new Tzadik release provides one answer to Bernstein's question.

Keter (1999), the first disc from Zohar, an ensemble made up of eclectic pianist Uri Caine, singer/hazzan Aaron Bensoussan, and other adept players of cutting-edge music scenes in the States and Israel, presents a seamless DJ-mix of Mizrahi and Sephardi trance music over extended renditions of standards such as Eli Eli, Avraham Avinu, and many more. The Arabic improvisational singing, ladino ballads, deep syncopated percussion, throbbing bass lines, avant-garde jazz piano, samples, and tape manipulation all come and go in the overarching mix, constituting equal, interchangeable elements from the databank of world music sounds. Yet this music does not sound ironic. The titles, intensity, and ecstasy all aim to produce a Jewish answer to Nusrat Ali Fatah Khan, Yoruba street percussion, or techno: Jewish music is the primal thang, the oldest and most up-to-date, connected to the grooves of the universe.

The disc's unintended irony resides in the degree to which the music's features come from "other" musical cultures. This shouldn't surprise: the Zohar and Kabbalah itself represent utterly miscegenated texts, a seamless mix of Hellenistic, Arabic, Christian, and Jewish elements. Another unintended irony is that normalizing Jewish music, making it just one among all other ethnic grooves/styles, is done at the cost of accepting the marketing of multiculturalism, the manufacture of cultures. In some ways the music on *Keter* is what I imagine the just-opened Jewish "club" Makor in New York must be like—I've only heard from a sister-in-law who was there herself—with its three stories of Jewish happenings, a bar and strictly kosher food, hip world music imported via the mavens from the lower East side, mosh pit above, shiurim below, a mind-body *yosher* (balance) that would do the Maharal proud.

Convivencia, man! Judaism for the new millennium! But what does it really mean when lyrics yearning for the speedy rebuilding of the Temple float over the beautiful explosions of Afro-Cuban drumming, a drumming (with its own lyrics, by the way) whose rhythms, like those of Haiti, Brazil, and elsewhere, derive from worship devoted to deities/heroes of Yoruba or Fon or Nago origin, and energize the Afro-Cuban religion known as Santeria. The ironies here abound. Does using this beat imply that the artists condone the Santeria practice—so controversial in parts of the United States—of animal sacrifice? They should, since they sing for the revival of the Temple-based cult of animal sacrifice in Judaism. Do they really want the speedy rebuilding of the Temple and return of the sacrificial system? (Do we, when we sing this song at wedding parties?) One can certainly dance to it, but I wonder . . .

The cool Jewish trip could only be American. On one side, the roots of Jewish cool lie in New Age terminology and attitude: positivity and openness to the non-modern, to the non-rational. But New Age was never cool. It is a pretend religion for people with pretend traditions. The homogenized, boundaryless music of New Age well reflects its sanitized, denatured, fake solution to personal and world problems. New Age is goofy, yet self-serious, with *no* sense of irony. On the other side, Jewish cool derives from cool aesthetes, from the beat poets to their progeny of the Sixties. These were self-serious, adolescent rebels with a cause, goofy only unintentionally. But their extreme anti-establishment cool left no escape from alienation and anomie.

One brand of Jewish cool that seems to escape this existential angst is the ecstatic neo-Hasidic style developed by the late Shlomo Carlebach. That Carlebach style is a variety of cool can readily be seen from its staunch hippie anti-fashion hierarchy, its rainbow people politics, and its ease with way-long ecstatic praying and dancing, a product of its followers' affection for way-long guitar and drum solos. Carlebach style owes much to the optimistic, cheerful searching of New Age religiosity, but it derives as well from white working class rebellion and from a hippie back-to-the-land spirit, with roots in serious personal and political tikkun: Bob Dylan, Grateful Dead, Gil Scott Heron. It's more a whole-person Jungian-balance, caring-people kind of trip. (This might be particularly true for Jewish boys and men, whose self-involved energies adulating cool can thus be channeled into community-oriented, world-healing activities. A great deal of overlap binds Jewish renewal with the men's movement.) Carlebach followers favor a Sephardi/kabbalistic/neo-hasidic *nusach* for prayer, a rebellion against the insipid Protestant harmonies of American Conservative and Reform synagogues and homes. Carlebach followers are very sincere. A Carlebachey approach maintains interest in the ritual efficacy of particular traditions, all of them, and is never mocking. . . .

A recently-released anthology of previously-untranslated stories of the Ba'al Shem Tov contains a tale in which the wonder rabbi cures a Jew who was passing as a hedonistic Polish noble of his "negativity and insidious addictions." The tale explains to some degree the relationship between cool and Judaism, at least in ba'al teshuvah circles. In his healing speech, addressed both to and not to the disguised Jew, the Besht says:

> Anybody who really wants to progress on the spiritual path must look into his very own soul and see clearly what is stopping him from getting close to God.

> In my experience there are two traits that obstruct one from truly proceeding on the path. The first one is irrational anger, and the other is sarcasm.

In this Hasidic view, sarcasm, a form of irony, simply must be eliminated. It is easy to understand why. Irony and especially sarcasm imply disdain, haughtiness, mockery, negation, and act as corrosive agents. Spiritual Judaism, even of the cool variety inspired by pseudo-kabbalah, entails a voluntary move away from irony. There is to be no more camp for Madonna, who made her name camping and vamping Catholicism. Now, I am told in all seriousness, Roseanne gives *shiurim* at the Kabbalah Learning Center. Even cool Jewish culture that is openly ironic seems to be so these days only affectionately (I'm thinking of the Bay Area group Charming Hostess' cover of eastern European and Klezmer tunes or even of Israeli comedian Gil Kopetch).

It all makes sense. People are desperate to escape the postmodern condition, which is fundamentally marked by an ironic stance toward the world. Neo-hasidism's vision of traditional Judaism's no nonsense approach to the world offers Jewish kids who grew up in the most assimilated, up-to-date, worldly spheres a means of maintaining the stylistics of cool while escaping cool's alienation and disinterest. A world in which nothing matters or can be done is replaced by one in which every action makes a difference and saves worlds.

Cool Judaism has enabled young Jews to express ethnic pride in themselves and in Judaism, now that they've discovered that the "true" Judaism repressed by their bourgeois parents is ethnic, oppressed and Other. Such "ethnicity" has allowed young Jews to express sincerity in acceptable cool fashion (reggae, hip hop, cutting-edge klezmer) since, unlike whites, oppressed Others are permitted to be sincere, oppositional, searching and positive while fighting for cultural survival. And it has allowed Jews who have discovered the transcendent in "other" cultures to be open enough to themselves and others about their finding the transcendent "at home."

Through the stylistics of cool Judaism, the rebellion manufactured and harnessed for marketing the rebel youth culture is channeled into a rebellion against the very things producing these styles and attracting young people to them in the first place: the secular culture industry, bourgeois living, individualism, emotional deadness. Hopefully. One cannot forget the extent to which even seemingly authentic efforts of cultural resistance, "the relics of counterculture," as Thomas Frank writes, "reek of affectation and phoniness, the leisure-dreams of white suburban children." All too often cool Judaism harnesses transgression for the sake of mere posture, even for profits. It remains to be seen whether cool Judaism is just another style to

consume or whether it helps lead to an authentic and lasting personal rebellion against materialism, against abused worldly power, against the destructive cult of the individual and the ego, the source of the need to be cool.

Judaism will survive cool. Cool might just survive Judaism. After all else
is said, the two new Tzadik disks make fantastic music for simchas! The
question of whether they can survive together, however, depends in each
case on the fundamental formula contained in Pierre Bourdieux' theory of
the "habitus," as articulated by Duke Ellington: it ain't what you do but the
way that you do it. Passion and the search for "authenticity" cannot become
a substitute for thinking, for the eternal effort to juggle the necessary opposites of God and human, devotion and critique, self-confidence and humility. Planning for the third Temple is not merely a larger equivalent of the
drumming circles of men's groups. The dangers of soul without mind continue to be very real. This said, however, the potential power of cool Jewish
culture remains strong. If cool Judaism helps young people to avoid the Or-
wellian carelessness, ignorance and idiocy induced by the culture industry,
it makes a damn good noble lie.

9. LOU CARLOZO, "JABEZ: BIBLICAL BIT PLAYER TO POP-CULTURE PHENOM" (2001)

*"And Jabez called on the God of Israel saying, 'Oh, that You would bless me indeed,
and enlarge my territory, that Your hand would be with me, and that You would keep
me from evil, that I may not cause pain.' So God granted him what he requested."*

*So reads the innocuous prayer of Jabez, a heretofore unnoticed figure in the Old Tes-
tament. In the following article, Lou Carlozo, a Chicago Tribune staff writer, explores
the phenomenon of Jeff Wilkinson's best-selling* The Prayer of Jabez, *a short book that
claims this small prayer found in the Bible, repeated frequently, can bring about success
and good fortune. It was an outgrowth of the "Name It and Claim It" theology espoused
increasingly by Pentecostal and Charismatic preachers teaching that God wishes to materially bless his children in this world. By naming their needs and claiming them in
the name of Jesus, believers would convince God to fulfill them. This movement reached
its apex at the end of the century with Wilkinson's immensely popular book.*

*The Jabez phenomenon indicates the intersections of religion and commercial cul-
ture—the book is a prayer to get rich, which is exactly what its publishers have done.
"Americans expect results," as the religion editor for Publishers Weekly told Carlozo.
"They expect their religion to work. Americans are very oriented towards success." This
form of "the gospel of wealth" drew millions of hopeful readers by the new millennium,
marking a transition in emphasis from the suffering Son of God to the wealth of the Father, poured out on his children.*

As *biblical* figures go, Jabez is a walk-on.

The Old Testament devotes only three sentences to his life story, which has been buried in obscurity since before the time of Christ.

Only in pop culture's pantheon could Jabez (JAY-bez) (pronounced JAY-bez) rise from the dead. Today, he's as hot or hotter than Tiger Woods. He's in vogue with White House insiders. And as millions recite his prayer, they report miracles from marriages restored to sick dogs saved (physically, not spiritually).

All this attention comes via Atlanta preacher Bruce Wilkinson and his 92-page volume—"The Prayer of Jabez: Breaking Through to the Blessed Life" (Multnomah Publishers). A year and a half after its release, "Jabez" has sold close to 9 million copies and remains perched atop national best-seller lists, outselling such books as Woods' "How I Play Golf."

At the book's core is what Wilkinson calls "a daring prayer that God always answers." He challenges readers to recite it for 30 days while watching the blessings roll in.

The full text, from First Chronicles 4:10, reads: "And Jabez called on the God of Israel saying, 'Oh, that You would bless me indeed, and enlarge my territory, that Your hand would be with me, and that You would keep me from evil, that I may not cause pain.' So God granted him what he requested."

Not in Wilkinson's wildest dreams, or prayers for that matter, could he have imagined the reach and impact of his book.

"It's been an unending surprise," said Wilkinson, 54, president and founder of Walk Thru the Bible Ministries. "Somebody said to me, 'You got out-Jabezed with the book on Jabez.'"

As even the best Bible students might not recall, Jabez only appears in a long-winded list of genealogies in First Chronicles. All that is known about him is that he "was more honorable than his brothers" and that his mother named him Jabez, meaning pain, because his birth was no picnic. Other than that—and the prayer—he's a blip on the *biblical* radar screen.

Wilkinson has changed all that, perhaps for good. Yet for all its success, the book has its critics, who assail the Jabez phenomenon as a symptom of materialistic, bumper-sticker faith. "The problem is that if you take any passage out of the Old or New Testament and turn it into a mantra, that scares me," said Robert Darden, senior editor of The Door, a Christian satire magazine. "The wiser course would be to focus on the words of Jesus—but Jesus doesn't say to acquire more territory. He says to give it away."

The Door published a parody, "The Prayer of Job." "When our son totaled our car the other day," it begins, "my wife and I should have been dismayed. But we weren't. . . . We knew it was 'The Prayer of Job,' coming to pass."

"Americans want a formula to find blessings from God," said Mark Talbot, an associate philosophy professor at Wheaton College. "I don't think he (Wilkinson) means to be doing harm here, but there is no such formula. The main blessing we get from God is reconciliation through his Son."

Wilkinson is aware of the salvos fired at his book—many by other evangelicals such as Talbot. "Oftentimes, whatever goes really large gets shot at," Wilkinson said. "You know, I've been preaching this for 30 years all over the nation and there has never been a negative comment. Then when it becomes a best seller, it's a moving target."

To be sure, Wilkinson has his supporters. Howard Hendricks, a professor at Dallas Theological Seminary (Wilkinson's alma mater) and former Dallas Cowboys chaplain, has called "Jabez" "a must read." Christian radio host James Dobson has also extolled the book to his "Focus on the Family" audience. Meanwhile, "Jabez" continues to expand its territory, if you will. Besides inspiring the masses, it has also inspired a marketing blitz worthy of a Hollywood blockbuster (and a sequel, "Secrets of the Vine," also high on the best-seller lists). To date, licensed Jabez products include golf shirts, baseball caps, calendars, mugs, backpacks, mouse pads, neckties, a Christian music CD, key rings and Bible covers.

"We've had a lot of requests from jewelry (makers) too," said Leslie Nunn Reed, who oversees licensing of Jabez products. "A lot of people are so touched by the book and they have a small cottage business and want to do something. But they don't have the distribution"—or, in one case, a palatable proposal. "The most surprising idea was a Jabez candy bar. It was chocolate, but it could also come with krispies or nuts."

"It's become a franchise," said Lynn Garrett, religion editor for Publisher's Weekly. "You've not only got the original book, but the sequel, the audio book, the devotional. As soon as they (Multnomah) saw the first signs of success, the marketing machine went into high gear." As for why Jabez has caught on so big, "One point is its pricing and the format," Garrett said. "It's $10, so people are buying multiple copies to give out as gifts." That includes President Bush's senior counselor Karl Rove, who keeps a small stack of the "Jabez" book in his White House office, according to a recent New Yorker piece.

"Its self-help orientation is also part of its popularity," Garrett said. "Americans expect results; they expect their religion to work. Americans are very oriented towards success."

Wilkinson explains the runaway popularity this way: "It's an uplifting, encouraging spiritual experience. The second reason is that people try it and it works. People are stunned—not shocked but stunned—that God answers that prayer for them."

Several Web sites—including the official http://prayerofjabez.com/—record the hundreds of testimonies attributed to the prayer. They include the lifesaving ("Son saved from 12-story fall"), the profit-making ("PR executive enlarges territory at alumni breakfast") and those that defy easy categorization ("Irish bagpiper witnesses at club").

Wilkinson's introduction to Jabez came in 1970 or '71, at a sermon by Richard Seume, then the chaplain at Dallas Theological Seminary. "He preached that Jabez was more honorable (than his brothers) and challenged us to be more like Jabez," Wilkinson recalled. "So I went to the library afterwards and was disappointed that there wasn't anything (else) on Jabez." And little wonder: With its long list of names, First Chronicles 4 reads like a phone book.

"Then I looked at the prayer and said, 'There must be something there.'" He began to recite it in the library, then stopped himself. "I couldn't pray it," he said, laughing at the memory. "It felt selfish, to ask God to bless me. It felt entirely wrong."

Still, Wilkinson stuck with it daily, and claims that it helped him to get Walk Thru the Bible off the ground. Later in the '70s, he wrote a 270-page book about Jabez but decided that "it was so boring that I wouldn't let the publisher publish it."

Wilkinson went on to pen other books, racking up only modest sales. But that would change in late 1999, when Christian radio host Dobson and his wife heard a tape of a Wilkinson sermon on Jabez. Dobson invited him to deliver the keynote address at the National Day of Prayer in May of last year.

Approached by Multnomah to do a Jabez book in time for the event, Wilkinson at first declined. But, with help from editor David Kopp, a manuscript was fashioned from Wilkinson's notes and sermons. The result: a breezy, pocket-size tome that's easy to read in one sitting. (It begins with the young Wilkinsons reading the Bible, with "Texas-sized raindrops pelting the window" of their Dallas kitchen.)

"The first time I saw the book was at the banquet the night before," Wilkinson said. "We had a dinner with senators and congressmen, and I gave them each a copy." But the real power broker turned out to be Dobson, who repeatedly urged his listeners to buy the little book with the big promise.

In a May newsletter he billed as "maybe the most important I have written," Dobson plugged "Jabez" heartily, saying Wilkinson had inspired him to expand his own ministry (a lengthy fundraising pitch followed).

In "Jabez," Wilkinson doesn't shy from defining "expanded territory" in material terms. He writes: "When Christian (businessmen) ask me, 'Is it right for me to ask God for more business?' my response is, 'Absolutely!' If you're doing business God's way, it's not only right to ask for more, but he is waiting for you to ask."

Wilkinson says critics have taken that passage out of context, and he is quick to note that he isn't just talking about money, but any sphere of life. "The amazing thing is that I've never had one person share with me that 'The Prayer of Jabez' got them into the 'health and wealth' gospel," he said, referring to the Pentecostal prayer movement. "I would say by your fruits you'll know, and the fruits are indisputable."

Still, the dissenters—who insist it's not sour grapes—fear that "Jabez" could do more harm than good, especially if the prayer becomes the equivalent of wishing on a star.

"Much of modern Christianity makes people feel worse, that you need to do it more and need to do it better," said Mike Yaconelli, owner of Youth Specialties, a California company that supplies and trains youth pastors. "Jesus gave us a pretty good prayer. I don't think we need Jabez's."

Chapter 7

Revitalization Movements in American Christianity

PENTECOSTALISM, MEGACHURCHES, CHARISMATIC MOVEMENTS,
THE NEW RELIGIOUS RIGHT, AND THE NEW SOCIAL GOSPEL

AFTER THE APPARENT halcyon days of the 1950s, the high point of church membership and attendance in American history (with over 60 percent of Americans claiming some church affiliation, and over 96 percent professing belief in God), mainstream American Protestantism went into decline in the 1960s. With attendance decreasing, contributions plummeting, urban churches struggling in a new context of neighborhoods in rapid racial transition, and the intelligentsia proclaiming a "death of God" theology, observers soon began to wonder about the future of American Protestantism, and to puzzle over what to do with mammoth church buildings and denominational infrastructures that now seemed superfluous and even arrogant. Applications to theological seminaries and divinity schools dropped as young white men (and, with increasing frequency, women) who might formerly have gone into the ministry chose careers in academia, law, politics, or the nonprofit sector instead.

But that view told only part of the story. In comfortable Presbyterian and Congregationalist churches in northeastern urban centers, "religion" appeared to be in decline—and God, if not dead, at least in failing health. But in a (seemingly) ever-expanding Southern Baptist Convention empire, headquartered in Nashville, all trends pointed upward, as this group assumed its place as the nation's largest Protestant denomination, with members and churches in all fifty states. From the perspective of American Pentecostals, gradually emerging from smaller-town and lower-class shadows to respectable places in suburban and middle-class America, things had never seemed so promising. To Christians renewed by the call of the "charismatic" movement (the importation of Pentecostal ideas and practices into mainstream denominations), the present era seemed an exciting time. And viewed through the lens of "megachurches," nondenominational religious centers, primarily in suburbs, that offered church services patterned after theatrical performances, contemporary America seemed full of anxious seekers waiting to be evangelized in language they could understand, and eager to worship in ways they could "relate to" easily.

American Christianity, then, was not so much in decline as in transition. Put in economic terms, the older established "firms"—such as Congregationalists and Episcopalians—had stagnated while the more innovative upstart entrepreneurs—such as Pentecostals and the interdenominational megachurches—took off. Noting this phenomenon, church bureaucrats, journalists, and scholars attempted to explain, as the title of one early scholarly study put it, "why conservative churches are growing"—and, implicitly, why mainstream or "liberal" churches were losing members and social power. Later scholars updated and improved this thesis. They argued that religious groups and organizations drew adherents most readily when they were truly countercultural, that is, when they demanded commitment from their members and defied rather than espoused dominant cultural norms. In the free market of American religion, consumers would "buy into" religious expressions that gave the psychic rewards that came with commitment. Thus, "establishment" religions inevitably would stagnate precisely because they were mainstream, while religious insurgents would consistently experience higher rates of growth and expansion.

Skeptics of this thesis raised questions about its applicability. Churches in the Southern Baptist Convention, for example, were hardly "countercultural." More nearly, they were captives to white southern culture. Likewise, the most rapidly growing and successfully institutionalized expression of Pentecostalism, the Assemblies of God, seemed perfectly situated in the Ozarks of Arkansas and Missouri from where it drew its primary strength; the denomination's headquarters (as well as several denominational colleges and seminaries) could be found in downtown Springfield, Missouri. But the argument did at least provide some context for understanding what religious commentators saw happening all around them—the rise of the "new" evangelicalism, including Pentecostalism, megachurches, guitar masses, political activism concentrated on the Right, and the intense interest in conservative Christian explanations of the coming millennium, memorably summarized in Hal Lindsey's 1972 classic exposition of popular premillennialism, *The Late Great Planet Earth*.

Evangelicals, Pentecostals, and megachurchers alternated between visions of America as a "Christian nation," founded by God as a city set upon a hill, and as Sodom and Gomorrah, a decadent civilization seemingly at the height of its power but actually in moral ruin. Evangelicals early in the Reagan years, for example, enthused that one of their sympathizers, a master politician who spoke their language, was in power. The selection from Ronald Reagan in the chapter on mainline religion and the Cold War shows "The Great Communicator" at the height of his power: lambasting secular liberals, defending "the rights of the unborn," and connecting the future of Christianity and the fate of the world in the struggle between freedom and communism. The legacy of this "New Religious Political Right" was carried on in the 1990s by Ralph Reed, a savvy and well-educated strategist. Reed placed himself and the group he helped to form, the Christian Coalition, in the context of previous marriages of activist religion and politics, including the civil rights movement and abolitionism. The Christian Coalition cobbled together religious folk from a variety of traditions—Protestants, conservative Catholics, Mormon leaders, and others who shared a common faith in "family values" and a political agenda of lower taxes, less government, school prayer, increased military spending, and opposition to abortion and "secular humanism" in public schools. Meanwhile, however, many of the former activists of the new religious-political Right gave up on politics, insisting that the war for America's soul was cultural and that the profanity and sexually immoral behavior that pervaded American popular culture (movies, music, television programs) showed that Christian conservatives were losing.

Patrick Buchanan brought these two concerns together, becoming known for his speech at the 1992 Republican convention (see chapter 5) advocating all-out effort in the "culture war." As a television political pundit, candidate for president on the Republican ticket and third-party tickets, newspaper columnist, and conservative firebrand, Buchanan carried forward a tradition of conservative Catholic populism. He was the 1990s counterpart to Father Charles Coughlin, the "radio priest" of the 1930s who denounced large financial institutions, communism, Jewish bankers, and salacious popular culture with equal vigor. Buchanan, like Couglin, fell prey to charges of anti-Semitism, which he denied. This chapter provides an excerpt from Buchanan's autobiography of growing up a feisty and conservative Catholic in the suburbs of Washington, DC in the 1940s and 1950s. The moral rectitude enforced on him in his Catholic education, he suggests, might serve as a model for saving America's kids today.

Accompanying the other fighters for equal rights and social justice—participants in the civil rights movement and feminism—gay Americans also pushed for equal protection under the law. In the 1980s and 1990s, rights of homosexuals to marry, receive medical and other benefits as domestic partners, receive ordination to the ministry, and assume positions of church leadership incited controversies in American churches. Many church groups, seeing the struggle for gay rights as following along the lines of other movements for equal rights from African Americans and women, admitted gays into full membership. Gay Christians formed their own organizations and fellowships, including Dignity, a group of Catholics who conducted their own masses and dissented from the official Church position on homosexuality. Conservative Protestants and Catholics resisted these moves, believing that the Bible declared homosexuality to be a sin. The issue came to a head in Colorado in 1992, when conservative Christian groups, led by a large organization known as Focus on the Family, headed by conservative Christian psychologist James Dobson, pushed for an amendment to the state constitution denying special status under the law for homosexuals as a class. Proponents of the measure argued that gays should not receive special treatment and protection from discrimination; gays did not need such protection in the way that other minority groups did.

Moderate and liberal evangelicals also joined in the discussion. Since the civil rights movement had opened up possibilities for religiously inspired political activism, Social Gospel evangelicals such as Ronald Sider and left-wing liberation theologians associated with *Sojourners* magazine insisted that evangelical fire did not have to be co-opted by the political Right. They applied religious values in political ways as well, demonstrating against nuclear weapons and capital punishment, creating "alternative budgets" that would redirect federal spending from defense and corporate welfare to individual and social needs such as jobs and housing, and defending First Amendment rights of Native Americans and others against increasingly restrictive interpretations set down by the Supreme Court. As unapologetically Christian and Jewish believers made their way into academia, moreover, they decried the tendency of secular liberals to ban all "God-talk" from the political realm and to associate Christian social thought with far-Right political agendas. In his work *The Culture of Disbelief* (excerpted in chapter 9), Stephen Carter, law professor and practicing evangelical Episcopalian, denounced the way in which many Americans "trivialize" religious expression, implying that belief may be fine as a private "hobby" but certainly should not influence the way one thinks or acts in the public realm. Much like evangelicals from both the Right and the Left, Carter insisted that religious belief was a legitimate force in the broader American political scene, and that Christians could act from religious motives without breaching the separation of church and state. Secular intolerance of true religious commitment represented the most pressing threat to the First Amendment.

The rise of neo-evangelicalism and the increasing popularity of New Age religious thought were strikingly parallel in their motivations. On the surface, many evangelicals denounced New Agers as agents of a satanic conspiracy, while New Agers stereotyped Christians as conservative conformists. On a deeper level, however, both groups were fundamentally interested in the "re-enchantment" of the world, in reattuning spiritual and human life to supernatural forces. If the scientific revolution and the Enlightenment had "disenchanted" the world, contemporary believers sought to reconnect with the supernatural forces that pervaded (so they believed) the universe. Conservative Christians thought that secularists had denied the active role of God's spirit in ordering human affairs. New Agers were convinced that the rise of a scientific techno-rational culture had destroyed ancient and profound understandings of the interconnectedness of all things. For New Agers, neopagans, and religious ecologists, nature was a living ecosystem that contained myriad portions of the divine, a view bordering on pantheism. For Christians, the air was alive with angels and demons, divinely and demonically appointed agents of supernatural forces, who fought for supremacy and directly intervened in worldly affairs for good and ill. Just as neo-evangelicals were fundamentally split on the prospects for a "Christian America," so they seemed undecided about whether angels or demons were truly supreme in the nether spiritual world just outside the realm of this one. Popular works such as evangelist Billy Graham's book *Angels* and the CBS television series *Touched by an Angel* presented a positive and sentimental view of benign spiritual forces who brought comfort and joy to distressed and ailing humans. But popular evangelical works such as Peter Wagner's *Wrestling with Dark Angels* insisted that Christians and their supernatural allies were at war with powerful forces of the demonic, fighting battles in the very real day-to-day contemporary world of international politics as well as more private struggles with demonic possession. The "re-enchantment" of the world, then, was itself complicated and scary. For conservative Christians, it involved acknowledging the very real power of satanic minions that sometimes won out over the divine (even as these believers assured themselves of the eventual, ultimate victory of God over evil).

Pentecostals, one of the fastest growing groups of religious Americans, also felt the active influence of the Spirit and contributed to re-enchanting the spiritual universe. Pentecostalism arose as a small and interracial movement of working-class Christians in the early twentieth century; its distinctive doctrine was the "baptism of the Holy Spirit," which many believed to be evidenced by "speaking in tongues." Over the course of the century, Pentecostals subdivided into dozens of groups, the two largest of which were the Assemblies of God (a predominantly white denomination headquartered in Springfield, Missouri), and the Church of God in Christ (the largest black Pentecostal denomination). The Church of God (Cleveland, Tennessee) and the International Pentecostal Holiness Church (headquartered in Oklahoma City) also represent sizable Pentecostal populations. The son of poor Pentecostal parents in rural Oklahoma, Oral Roberts grew up to manage one of the largest religious empires in the United States, including radio and television shows, a university (Oral Roberts University, in Tulsa), a medical complex, and a number of other enterprises. Roberts made his name originally as a "faith healer," barnstorming the country in the 1940s and 1950s in large-scale tent revivals and healing crusades. He preached the Pentecostal message that the Holy Spirit empowered individuals to defeat forces both natural (such as illnesses) and supernatural (such as demonic possession). As a boy, Roberts had experienced a severe bout of tuberculosis, which he believed was healed by divine intervention. He subsequently advocated a "health and wealth" theology, the notion that health and prosperity were the natural results of following God's word. Roberts served as the model for future big-time Pentecostal evangelists such as Jimmy Swaggart and James Bakker, who shared his penchant for elaborately costumed and choreographed religious productions staged for mass media, for a theology that emphasized the worldly blessings that should fall on God's followers, and for unabashedly maudlin techniques of fund raising.

Although predominantly white, Swaggart's and Bakker's Pentecostal denominations claim considerable numbers of black and Hispanic members. Pentecostalism originated as an interracial movement, with many early white converts bowing to the baptism of the Spirit under the preaching of a black minister from Louisiana named William Seymour, who headed up the famous Azusa Street revivals in Los Angeles in 1906. But by World War I, Pentecostalism was nearly as strictly segregated as American religion generally. In 1994, white and black Pentecostals came together in Memphis for healing and reconciliation, a meeting quickly dubbed the "Memphis Miracle." White leaders bowed to wash the feet of the bishop of the black Church of God in Christ, a ceremonial ritual indicating humility and brotherly love on the part of the foot-washer. Despite these occasional moments, however, 11:00 on Sunday morning remains the most segregated hour in America, and the solid institutionalization of "white" and "black" denominations seems sure to perpetuate an American Christianity largely separated by race.

The "death of God" theology fashionable in the 1960s now appears a rather quaint anachronism in comparison to the continued enthusiasm of Americans for religious expression that commands personal commitment in belief, time, and money. Nowhere is this more true than in American evangelicalism and Pentecostalism, which seem to thrive the most in places where one would least expect it—the entertainment industry center of Los Angeles, the military-industrial complex hub in Colorado Springs, and the Disneyfied fantasy world of Orlando, Florida. As groups that feed on "spiritual war," the more beleaguered—and combat-ready—conservative evangelicals feel, the more successful they are.

1. BILLY GRAHAM, "WATERSHED: LOS ANGELES, 1949"

Billy Graham was a tall, golden-haired preacher from North Carolina who had assumed the presidency of an evangelical college near Chicago in the 1940s. After World War II, he began his career as an evangelist who would bring the word of God to the masses, through every means necessary and available. Graham perfected the modern-day version of the tent revival, a respectable and made-for-television traveling show held in football and baseball stadiums, large auditoriums, convention centers, and other venues for mass meetings. While other evangelists came and went, and many succumbed to scandals financial and sexual, Graham's careful and above-board dealings won him respect, and his preaching—full of evangelical unctuousness yet careful to avoid bathos—gained him a large audience. Graham's early years featured full-bore assaults against communism and an easy declaration of America as God's chosen country, themes he toned down later. His primary concern, however, always remained bringing the lost to salvation. In this excerpt from his autobiography, he explains how he stumbled on his first great mass evangelistic success in Los Angeles, a crusade that began his career as the national evangelist.

⎯⎯∞⎯⎯

The invitation to hold meetings in Los Angeles originally came from a group of businessmen who called themselves "Christ for Greater Los Angeles," representing about two hundred churches. They had already sponsored several such Campaigns with other evangelists, all of which were reasonably successful. Now they wanted me to preach and to bring Cliff Barrows and George Beverly Shea. I agreed but insisted on several stringent conditions.

First, they were to try to broaden church support to include as many churches and denominations as possible. Second, they were to raise their budget from $7,000 to $25,000, in order to invest more in advertising and promotion. Third, they were to erect a much larger tent than they had planned; our limited experience in citywide Campaigns had already taught us that the crowds seemed to grow as the days went on. . . .

To many of those seasoned, older Christians, I came across as brash. But I found myself drafting a Los Angeles scenario bigger and bolder than anything I had imagined before. Besides insisting on the budget increase, I set yet another seemingly impossible condition: the committee had to put the public leadership and the platform duties of the Campaign entirely in the hands of local clergy. The committee, I felt, represented too limited an evangelical constituency to make an impact.

I consulted with Cliff, and he agreed. I wrote back to our hosts and told them we would be forced to cancel if they could not see their way clear to step out in faith and take that financial risk.

"I stand upon the brink of absolute fear and trembling when I think we might come to Los Angeles with only a small handful of churches," I wrote in February 1949. "The city of Los Angeles will not be touched unless the majority of the churches are actively back of this campaign."

My limited experience had already shown me that without the cooperation of the local churches and their pastors, not only would attendance suffer but so would the follow-up of new Christians.

One of my objectives was to build the church in the community. I did not simply want the audience to come from the churches. I wanted to leave something behind in the very churches themselves.

Even as I imposed these conditions on the long-suffering committee, I doubted that they could comply. Yet I burned with a sense of urgency to move forward. . . .

Just before the Campaign began, Henrietta Mears invited me to her home in Beverly Hills to speak to the Hollywood Christian Group. That occasion gave me an opportunity for lengthy discussions with well-known actors and actresses.

One man at the meeting, Stuart Hamblen, impressed me tremendously. He was rough, strong, loud, and earthy. Every inch of his six-foot-two frame was genuine cowboy, and his 220 pounds seemed all bone and muscle. His name was legendary up and down the West Coast for his popular radio show, heard every afternoon for two hours. He said he would invite me on as a guest. I took an instant liking to him and coveted him for Christ. Only half-jokingly, he said he could fill the tent if he gave his endorsement.

In the months ahead, I would meet other Hollywood celebrities of the time, especially in visits to Miss Mears's "out of this world" home, as Ruth described it—people such as Tim Spencer (who wrote a number-one song on the hit parade, "Room Full of Roses"), Mickey Finn, Jon Hall, Connie Haines, and Jane Russell. Edwin Orr led these meetings, so they were both intellectually stimulating and spiritually stirring. Many of these stars were so earnest about learning the Word of God and translating it into daily living that Ruth felt they put to shame our Thursday afternoon prayer meetings back home in the Bible Belt. . . .

The attendance at our early Los Angeles meetings averaged about 3,000 each night and 4,000 on Sunday afternoons, so the tent was never filled to capacity.

I sensed that interest was building, though, and the crowds were getting larger. However, I found that I was preaching mainly to Christians. As Ruth observed in a letter home to her folks in October, "It isn't easy to get unconverted to a tent."

Nevertheless, I was preaching with a new confidence and fervor. I had always been loud and enthusiastic (and some said authoritative). But since my pivotal experience in the mountain woods at Forest Home, I was no longer struggling internally. There was no gap between what I said and what I knew I believed deep in my soul. It was no coincidence that the center-piece of the 150-foot platform in the tent, right in front of the pulpit, was a replica of an open Bible—twenty feet high and twenty feet wide. . . .

We were approaching the scheduled closing-night meeting—Sunday, October 16—of our three-week Campaign. . . .

Should the Campaign be extended? It was not simply for the committee to decide. We needed a clear sense of direction from the Lord. Grady, Cliff, Bev, and I prayed together over and over again as the last week wore on. At last we decided to follow the example of Gideon in the Old Testament and put out a fleece, asking God to give us a decisive sign of His purpose.

It came at four-thirty the next morning.

I was awakened in my room at the Langham Hotel by the jangling of the telephone. In a voice broken by tears, a man begged to see me right away. It was Stuart Hamblen. I woke up Grady and Wilma Wilson, and they went with Ruth into another room to pray.

By the time I was up and dressed, Stuart and his praying, godly wife, Suzy, were at my door. We talked together and prayed, and the rugged cow-boy gave his life to Christ in a childlike act of faith. He came forward in the next service. The first thing he did after he received Christ was to call his fa-ther, who was an old-fashioned Methodist preacher in west Texas. I could hear his father shout with joy over the phone! . . .

When I arrived at the tent for the next meeting, the scene startled me. For the first time, the place was crawling with reporters and photographers. They had taken almost no notice of the meetings up until now, and very little had appeared in the papers. I asked one of the journalists what was happening.

"You've just been kissed by William Randolph Hearst," he responded.

I had no idea what the reporter was talking about, although I knew the name. Hearst, of course, was the great newspaper owner. I had never met the man, but like most Americans I had read his papers. The next morn-ing's headline story about the Campaign in the *Los Angeles Examiner,* fol-lowed by an evening story in the *Los Angeles Herald Express*—both owned by Hearst—stunned me. The story was picked up by the Hearst papers in New York, Chicago, Detroit, and San Francisco, and then by all their competitors. Until then, I doubt if any newspaper editor outside the area had heard of our Los Angeles Campaign.

Puzzled as I was, my curiosity was never satisfied. Hearst and I did not meet, talk by phone, or correspond as long as he lived. Supposedly, he had sent a message to his editors, "Puff Graham," but there were so many sto-ries about how we might have come to his notice and about why he might have been interested in promoting us that I did not know which, if any, was true. One of the more intriguing ones was that Hearst and his controversial partner, Marion Davies, disguised themselves and attended a tent meeting in person. I doubted it.

Time magazine pulled out all the rhetorical stops in its November 14, 1949, issue: "Blond, trumpet-lunged North Carolinian William Franklin Graham Jr., a Southern Baptist minister who is also president of the Northwestern Schools in Minneapolis, dominates his huge audience from the moment he strides onstage to the strains of *Send the Great Revival in My Soul.* His lapel microphone, which gives added volume to his deep, cavernous voice, allows him to pace the platform as he talks, rising to his toes to drive home a point, clenching his fists, stabbing his finger at the sky and straining to get his words to the furthermost corners of the tent."

The newspaper coverage was just the beginning of a phenomenon. As more and more extraordinary conversion stories caught the public's attention, the meetings continued night after night, drawing overflow crowds. Something was happening that all the media coverage in the world could not explain. And neither could I. God may have used Mr. Hearst to promote the meetings, as Ruth said, but the credit belonged solely to God. All I knew was that before it was over, we were on a journey from which there would be no looking back. . . .

When the train stopped briefly in Kansas City, we were met by a couple of reporters. When we got to Minneapolis, the press was again there to interview us, along with some Twin Cities pastors and faculty and students from Northwestern Schools. Until then it had not fully registered with me how far-reaching the impact of the Los Angeles Campaign had been. I would learn over the next few weeks that the phenomenon of that Los Angeles tent Campaign at Washington and Hill Streets would forever change the face of my ministry and my life. Overnight we had gone from being a little evangelistic team, whose speaker also served with Youth for Christ and Northwestern Schools, to what appeared to many to be the hope for national and international revival. Everywhere we turned, someone wanted us to come and do for them what had been done in Los Angeles. What they didn't know, however, was that *we* had not done it. I was still a country preacher with too much on my plate. Whatever this could be called and whatever it would become, it was *God's* doing.

2. HARVEY COX, *FIRE FROM HEAVEN* (1994)

Cox's 1994 work Fire from Heaven *begins with the paradox that in the 1960s religion seemed in permanent decline, while three decades later it seemed that secularity was on its way to extinction. He traveled the world attempting to understand the fastest growing portion of contemporary Christianity, Pentecostalism, which derived originally from a group of lower-class black and white worshippers in a converted horse stable in Los Angeles who conducted a series of revivals and spoke in tongues in 1906. Cox argues that Pentecostalism answers the human need for an experiential, primal, carnal spirituality. Pentecostalism is a characteristic American contribution to Christianity in the same way that jazz is the characteristic American music: both invoke spirits and encourage individual spontaneity and improvisation within a group theme context. At the end of this book, Cox worries about whether Pentecostalism will betray its true calling and become another rigid, orthodox theology in line with fundamentalism, or a "health-and-wealth" theology that simply provides a spiritual imprimatur to materialism and consumerism.*

Nearly three decades ago I wrote a book, *The Secular City,* in which I tried to work out a theology for the "postreligious" age that many sociologists had confidently assured us was coming. Since then, however, religion—or at least some religions—seems to have gained a new lease on life. Today it is secularity, not spirituality, that may be headed for extinction. . . . I decided to find out what I could about pentecostals, not just by reading about them but by visiting their churches wherever I could and by talking with both their ministers and with ordinary members. . . .

Even before I started my journey through the world of pentecostalism it had become obvious that instead of the "death of God" some theologians pronounced not many years ago, or the waning of religion that sociologists had extrapolated, something quite different has taken place. Perhaps I was too young and impressionable when the scholars made those sobering projections. In any case I had swallowed them all too easily and had tried to think about what their theological consequences might be. But it had now become clear that the predictions themselves had been wrong. The prognosticators had written that the technological pace and urban bustle of the twentieth century would increasingly shove religion to the margin where, deprived of roots, it would shrivel. They allowed that faith might well survive as a valued heirloom, perhaps in ethnic enclaves or family customs, but insisted that religion's days as a shaper of culture and history were over.

This did not happen. Instead, before the academic forecasters could even begin to draw their pensions, a religious renaissance of sorts is under way all over the globe. Religions that some theologians thought had been stunted by western materialism or suffocated by totalitarian repression have regained a whole new vigor. . . . But why were the predictors so wrong? Why has this unanticipated resurgence of religion occurred? . . .

I set out, accompanied by the college psychotherapist and a professor of philosophy, both of them impelled in part by curiosity and in part by a reluctance to have their guest get lost in a strange city. We were off to visit the Sheffield Family Life Center in Kansas City, Missouri.

Although its name makes it sound like a counseling clinic, the Family Life Center is actually a pentecostal congregation affiliated with the Assemblies of God, the largest predominantly white Pentecostal denomination in America. Like many other pentecostal congregations recently, however, the building it meets in is called a "family life center," in part because it provides the space for many of the church's other programs in addition to worship, and also because—I was beginning to learn—many pentecostals have attached themselves so enthusiastically to the recent religious celebration of "traditional family values" that the words have even found their way into the names of their churches. . . .

Inside, the building seemed utterly cavernous. Rows of metal folding seats, about 600 of them by my estimate, faced a wide stage on which an immense off-white curtain was presently drawn. From behind it we could hear the chirps and roars of invisible clarinets and trombones tuning up. There was an air of expectation in the crowd. We sat down about halfway back and looked around. People nodded pleasantly, but—as in most pentecostal churches—no one handed us a bulletin or a hymn book, not because they were not glad to see us but because the order of service is supposed to be spontaneous and the songs are flashed on a screen. I noticed that to our right there was a large balcony equipped with facilities for preparing and serving food. The railing of the balcony was decked with dozens of flags representing—as we learned later—the countries where the Assemblies of God has missionaries.

The auditorium was filling up rapidly but people were still arriving. Our earlier phone call, answered by a recorded voice, had informed us that there were 9 o'clock and 11 o'clock services in the morning as well as this one. I asked the smiling woman in the pew in front of me who welcomed us if she had been present that morning and she said she had. "And it was terrific," she added, "we really had *church*." From behind the curtain the tuning-up sounds, trumpet runs, and flute trills, were becoming more clamorous. The people seated around us did not appear well to do. Their clothes might have come from discount stores or rummage sales. Some of the young people sported bright message t-shirts. Many of the men wore no ties. The women seemed to favor print dresses and pants suits.

Most of the people were white, and—listening carefully to the accents I heard around me—I speculated that many had found their way to Kansas City from Appalachia and the Ozarks. But there was a scattering of blacks

and Latinos, and a few Asians. Only slightly more than half those in attendance were women. . . .

The curtain was still closed when a very friendly middle-aged woman in
purple slacks, green blouse, and yellow sweater leaned over from the row of
seats behind us and laughed heartily as she shook our hands and welcomed
us. . . . I seized the opportunity, however, to ask her some questions. No, she
had not been here this morning, she had had to work, cleaning an office
building. But she had certainly been here last week, she said, "and we really *got down* here. I mean we really *had church.*"

It was the second time I had heard that expression in ten minutes. I had
heard it previously among African Americans but not among whites, so I
asked her what "really having church" meant. "You'll see," she said smiling,
"in just a minute." She told me she had been coming to this church for
three years, ever since she moved here from a small town in southern Missouri. When I asked her if most of the people in the church had recently
moved to town she said, "No, everybody's coming here," adding with what
seemed a note of pride that this was a new building because the congregation had overflowed the last one. As she was talking a man in olive-drab
slacks and an open-necked flannel shirt joined her. He nodded to me, but
our conversation was cut off as the lights dimmed and the curtain parted
dramatically on a towering swell of music to reveal about fifty people on
stage producing an eruption of joyous sounds.

Now all eyes were directed to the wide stage, bathed in spots and footlights. On the left sat five ministers, including the one in the crimson sus-
penders. In the middle a good-sized band perched on risers between two
choirs, one on either side of a magnificent set of gleaming drums and cym-
bals. There were two lead singers. One was a very pretty, slim young white
woman in her early twenties, wearing a semiclinging vivid red dress that
reached just below her knees, with a stylish gold chain around her waist.
She moved and swayed as she sang, and led a song called "Whose Report
Do You Believe?" Her brown hair fell well below the shoulders and swirled
as she turned back and forth, first pointing up to the ceiling on "whose,"
then to the congregation on "you." . . .

I turned back to watch the band. Pentecostal churches almost always
have them, but they are usually four- or five-piece affairs. This was the
biggest one I had ever seen: flute, two trumpets, a trombone, three saxo-
phones, a violin equipped with an amplifying device, a clarinet, keyboard,
piano guitar, electric bass, and drums. A dark-skinned man dressed in a
carefully tailored light-blue suit and a canary necktie seemed to be actually leading the singing. At least he was waving his arms while holding a
cordless mike now in one hand, now in the other. I later learned he was a

Filipino. The racial and ethnic mix of both the congregation and leader-ship seemed very impressive to me; and yet I would not hear the word "multicultural" all night. . . .

We sang another song, with the same glamorous lead singers and the arm waver in the canary tie back in action. Then, just as the song ended, I heard a staccato burst of glossolalia. I looked around but then saw that it was coining from the drummer and was amplified by the clip-on microphone on his jacket. He went on for only about twenty seconds in a high monotone. As soon as he had finished, the pastor said through his own microphone, "That was speaking in tongues. Just as we read about it in Acts 2." Then the service proceeded apace.

I was bothered. I had heard tongue speaking in pentecostal churches many times before, and had never been annoyed. It can show how close the worshippers feel to God, and can provide a way of praying that goes beyond normal linguistic limitations. But there was something about this instance that disturbed me. It had not come from the heart of the congregation, but from behind the footlights. It had been followed so quickly by the pastor's smoothly packaged explanation. This was not glossolalia as protest or as prophecy. It was glossolalia as performance, and—at least to me—it sound-ed counterfeit.

As soon as the minister's peroration on money was over, something else happened that only deepened my already uneasy mood. He started talking excitedly about how *big* the Assemblies of God denomination was and how fast it was growing. Why, the Lord was adding *thousands* and *thousands* of souls every day. . . . My hunch is that they had much more immediate prob-lems, and that whether or not the church they were attending tonight was part of a worldwide religious bandwagon was not of pressing interest to them. I had heard a lot of boasting from pentecostals about their staggering growth statistics and it was beginning to irritate me: it sounded like more health-and-wealth theology. They seemed to be saying, in effect, "God must be on our side." But this is a somewhat ironic claim to be made by a move-ment that early in its life maintained that the proof that God was with them was that they were so small and so despised. . . .

As I watched the preacher pace the stage and heard his breath reverber-ate through the microphone, I was carried back to a visit I had made five years earlier to another pentecostal family life center, the one located on the 279-acre headquarters estate of Jimmy Swaggart Ministries in Baton Rouge, Louisiana. What was it that had called forth the mental association? Maybe it was the flags. That was the last time I had seen so many of them in a church setting. Only there they represented not the mission fields of a de-nomination, but the 195 nations reached by Swaggart's own sprawling world ministry. I remembered that I had been shown a state-of-the-art television production center, a private Christian elementary school, and an impressive printing plant. Swaggart's Family Worship Center itself is a modern eight-sided building whose lobbies are decorated with gigantic world maps showing where his television evangelism is carried. At that time the statistics were spectacular, even for a pentecostal televangelist. At the height of his fame, before his widely publicized "fall," it is estimated that Swaggart was reaching 500 million people, the largest television audience ever to watch a regularly scheduled program of any kind. . . .

On television at least, Swaggart was something of a shaman. By putting himself into an ecstatic state of consciousness, with hundreds of millions of people watching, he conveyed a wildly dissonant note from a register that is somewhere within us, but that we do not hear from very often. . . .

I had also sensed some of that power on television. But at Swaggart's church it was diluted. He seemed almost puny. It was clearly one of those instances in which the power of the television medium transforms and magnifies the ordinary. . . .

I have not seen Jimmy Swaggart on television for a long time now. After his tearful confession of his various rendezvous with prostitutes, and his defrocking by the Assemblies of God, many stations stopped carrying his program. He is also—along with Jim and Tammy Faye Bakker—a severe embarrassment to many pentecostals who wish they could have been spared the shoddy saga of the rise and fall of such celebrities. But Swaggart remains an important figure for anyone who seeks to understand the appeal of the pentecostal impulse. For me he represented not only the unprocessed harshness of primal spirituality, but also how easily it can be manipulated and misused in the hands of a skilled practitioner.

3. PENTECOSTAL "RACIAL RECONCILIATION MANIFESTO," "MEMPHIS 1994: MIRACLE AND MANDATE" (1994)

In 1994, representatives from a variety of Pentecostal denominations, black and white, gathered in Memphis. Out of that emotional meeting, recounted by Vinson Synan below, came a "racial reconciliation" manifesto and a number of articles by Pentecostal leaders urging their constituents to recapture the spirit of interracial fellowship that had characterized the very earliest days of their movement. Black Pentecostal bishop George McKinney reminded his white brethren of the reality of structural and institutional racism, while Pentecostal historian Harold Hunter added a white voice expressing many of the same sentiments. The articles here reflect a broader emphasis among recent evangelicals on recognizing the painful legacy of racism within the evangelical community, seen in such events as the "Memphis Miracle" and the Promise Keepers meetings at huge venues, where white men were exhorted to reconcile with black men.

⊶⦵⊷

RACIAL RECONCILIATION MANIFESTO

Challenged by the reality of our racial division, we have been drawn by the Holy Spirit to Memphis, Tennessee, October 17–19, 1994, in order to become true "Pentecostal Partners" and to develop together "A Reconciliation Strategy for the 21st Century Ministry." We desire to covenant together in the ongoing task of racial reconciliation by committing ourselves to the following agenda.

I. I pledge in concert with my brothers and sisters of many hues to oppose racism prophetically in all its various manifestations within and without the Body of Christ and to be vigilant in the struggle with all my God-given might.

II. I am committed personally to treat those in the Fellowship who are not of my race or ethnicity, regardless of color, with love and respect as my sisters and brothers in Christ. I am further committed to work against all forms of personal and institutional racism, including those which are revealed within the very structures of our environment.

III. With complete bold and courageous honesty, we mutually confess that racism is sin and as a blight in the Fellowship must be condemned for having hindered the maturation of spiritual development and mutual sharing among Pentecostal-Charismatic believers for decades.

IV. We openly confess our shortcomings and our participation in the sin of racism by our silence, denial and blindness. We admit the harm it has brought to generations born and unborn. We strongly contend that the past does not always completely determine the future. New horizons are emerging. God wants to do a new thing through His people.

V. We admit that there is no single solution to racism in the Fellowship. We pray and are open to tough love and radical repentance with deep sensitivity to the Holy Spirit and Liberator.

VI. Together we will work to affirm one another's strengths and acknowledge our own weaknesses and inadequacies, recognizing that all of us only "see in a mirror dimly" what God desires to do in this world. Together, we affirm the wholeness of the Body of Christ as fully inclusive of Christians regardless of color. We, therefore, commit ourselves "to love one another with mutual affection, outdoing one another in showing honor" (Romans 12:10).

VII. We commit ourselves not only to pray but also to work for genuine and visible manifestations of Christian unity.

VIII. We hereby commit ourselves not only to the task of making prophetic denouncement of racism in word and creed, but to live by acting in deed. We will fully support and encourage those among us who are attempting change.

IX. We pledge that we will return to our various constituencies and appeal to them for logistical support and intervention as necessary in opposing racism. We will seek partnerships and exchange pulpits with persons of a different hue, not in a paternalistic sense, but in the Spirit of our Blessed Lord who prayed that we might be one (John 17:21).

X. We commit ourselves to leaving our comfort zones, lay aside our warring, racial allegiances, respecting the full humanity of all, live with an openness to authentic liberation which is a product of Divine Creation, until the shackles fall and all bondage ceases.

XI. At the beginning of the twentieth century, the Azusa Street Mission was a model of preaching and living the Gospel message in the world. We desire to drink deeply from the well of Pentecost as it was embodied in that mission. We, therefore, pledge our commitment to embrace the essential commitments of that mission in evangelism and mission, in justice and holiness, in spiritual renewal and empowerment, and in the reconciliation of all Christians regardless of race or gender as we move into the new millennium.

MANIFESTO COMMITTEE:

Bishop Ithiel Clemmons   Dr. Cecil M. Roebeck, Jr.

Dr. Leonard Lovett   Dr. Harold D. Hunter

MEMPHIS 1994: MIRACLE AND MANDATE

DR. VINSON SYNAN

It was a day never to be forgotten in the annals of American Pentecostalism—October 18, 1994—when the Spirit moved in Memphis to end decades of racial separation and open doors to a new era of cooperation and fellowship between African-American and white Pentecostals. At the time, it was called the "Memphis Miracle" by those gathered in Memphis as well as in the national press which hailed the historic importance of the event.

It was called a miracle because it ended decades of formal separation between the predominantly black and white pentecostal churches in America. In its beginnings, the Pentecostal movement inherited the interracial ethos of the Holiness Movement at the turn of the century. One of the miracles of the Azusa Street revival was the testimony that "the color line was washed away in the blood." Here in the worldwide cradle of the movement a black man, William J. Seymour, served as pastor of a small black church in Los Angeles, where from 1906 to 1909, thousands of people of all races gathered to receive the baptism in the Holy Spirit with the accompanying evidence of speaking in tongues. . . .

In the beginning, practically all the Pentecostal movements and churches in America were inter-racial with many having thriving black leaders and churches. But from 1908 to 1924, one by one, most churches bowed to the American system of segregation by separating into racially-segregated fellowships. In "Jim Crow" America, segregation in all areas of life ruled the day. Gradually Seymour's Azusa Street dream of openness and equality faded into historical memory. . . .

The Memphis Miracle

When the delegates arrived in Memphis on October 17, 1994, there was an electric air of expectation that something wonderful was about to happen. The conference theme was "Pentecostal Partners: A Reconciliation Strategy for 21st Century Ministry." Over 3,000 persons attended the evening sessions in the Dixon-Meyers Hall of the Cook Convention Center in downtown Memphis. Everyone was aware of the racial strife in Memphis where Martin Luther King, Jr. was assassinated in 1968. Here, it was hoped, a great racial healing would take place. . . .

The morning sessions were remarkable for the honesty and candor of the papers that were presented by a team of leading Pentecostal scholars. . . . In these sessions, the sad history of separation, racism and neglect was laid bare before the 1,000 or more leaders assembled. These sometimes chilling confessions brought a stark sense of past injustice and the absolute need of repentance and reconciliation. . . .

The climactic moment, however, came in the scholar's session on the afternoon of October 18, after Bishop Blake tearfully told the delegates, "Brothers and Sisters, I commit my love to you. There are problems down the road, but a strong commitment to love will overcome them all." Suddenly there was a sweeping move of the Holy Spirit over the entire assembly. . . .

Immediately, a white pastor appeared in the wings of the backstage with a towel and basin of water. His name was Donald Evans, an Assemblies of God pastor from Tampa, Florida. When he explained that the Lord had called him to wash the feet of a black leader as a sign of repentance, he was given access to the platform. In a moment of tearful contrition, he washed the feet of Bishop Clemmons while begging forgiveness for the sins of the whites against their black brothers and sisters. A wave of weeping swept over the auditorium. Then, Bishop Blake approached Thomas Trask, General Superintendent of the Assemblies of God, and tearfully washed his feet as a sign of repentance for any animosity blacks had harbored against their white brothers and sisters. This was the climactic moment of the conference. Everyone sensed that this was the final seal of Holy Spirit approval from the heart of God over the proceedings.

4. ALBERT CLEAGE, "LET'S NOT WASTE THE HOLY SPIRIT" (1972)

Black Pentecostals, like their white counterparts, grew rapidly in the post–World War II era. While the Church of God in Christ, based in Memphis, was the largest black Pentecostal denomination, dozens of smaller groups and sects dotted the black religious landscape. In this selection, a minister who founded the Shrine of the Black Madonna in Detroit, Michigan, connects black Pentecostal theology to the larger currents of black theology. If James Cone and others argued that God is black, Cleage suggests that the Holy Spirit is too—"The Holy Spirit gives us a sense of identification with the rage of suffering oppressed people everywhere. . . . It is the mystery of a magic moment when we are touched by a power which we cannot understand." Cleage suggests that this spiritual force that truly speaks to humans has moved world events, such as the Montgomery bus boycott, by empowering individuals to act courageously in the face of oppression. Cleage's piece shows that Pentecostalism, often seen as concerned only with speaking in tongues and supernatural talk, also may connect with contemporary social and political concerns.

The Holy Spirit is the revolutionary power which comes to an exploited people as they struggle to escape from powerlessness and to end the institutional oppression forced upon them by an enemy.

At Pentecost the Disciples were together as usual, eating, drinking, talking, and trying to remember and to understand the things Jesus had said and the things he had done. Suddenly it seemed that the room was filled with the rush of a mighty wind. It seemed as though tongues of fire came and rested over each head. The writer was trying to describe a deeply moving inner experience. Another person might have described the experience in a different way. There need not necessarily have been tongues of fire and the rush of a mighty wind, but there was the feeling that some great power was there and that the Disciples had suddenly been caught up and were being acted upon by a force outside themselves. Each individual was touched and they began to talk. . . . Here again we have the symbolic language of the Bible. Suddenly caught up in the power of the Holy Spirit, they began to speak in such a way that people from everywhere except Galilee could understand them. Whether they were speaking strange languages in a literal sense, or whether the simple message of the Black Messiah calling men to struggle against oppression could be understood by the exploited and despised from every land, we do not know. This is the same simple message that oppressed nonwhite peoples understand everywhere in today's world. . . .

The Holy Spirit gives us a sense of identification with the rage of suffering oppressed people everywhere, and so at Pentecost the remnant of the Nation Israel, so soon to be humiliated and dispersed by the fall of Jerusalem and Masada, could be understood by all. It is rage, anger, hatred, commitment. It is divine discontent. It is the mystery of a magic moment then we are touched by a power which we cannot understand.

Only a people can feel the Holy Spirit. God does not speak to individuals. Ordinary Black men and women came together in Montgomery, Alabama, and decided that they could no longer sit in the back of the bus. We wonder what at that moment made the back of the bus so much more irksome than it was a week before or a decade before. Why did Black people suddenly decide to walk? What happened? The most reasonable explanation is the simple one. In this time and in this place, these Black people were touched by the Holy Spirit. The conviction that God had created them equal gave them a new sense of dignity. They were no longer able to ride in the back of the bus. They had been touched by the Holy Spirit. They were forced to walk, and so they walked for more than a year. How can we say what touched a Black mother, whose child had been going to an inferior segregated school, who suddenly decided that she would take her child to an integrated school where the child could get a decent education? Where did she get the courage to face a mob? It was the Holy Spirit. How can we explain the rage of Black people in cities all across America in 1965, '66 and '67, Black people who were accustomed to being oppressed and exploited, who had grown calloused to brutality by white police officers, to injustice in white courts, to misinterpretations by white newspapers and the mass-communications media, and who were accustomed to the hostility of white people? Why did all these things suddenly become unbearable? Black people in city after city rose up against oppression, saying, "We will no longer tolerate these conditions." Why the sudden violence and the upheaval which still shakes America? It was as though the cities were filled with the rush of a mighty wind and tongues of fire rested over each Black head. We can't say it any better than the Bible says it. . . .

We accept Jesus as the Black Messiah sent by God to lead men in a revolutionary struggle for liberation because his life testifies to the validity of our faith. We can accept the beautiful mythology with which men have surrounded his birth because we can believe that the advent of a man like this, obviously sent by God, must have been attended by miraculous signs and wonders. Of course the heavens sang and a star came to rest over the lowly stable in which he lay. But we find it difficult to associate God with the church which bears the name of Jesus Christ. The institutional Christian church has never spoken for God nor mediated His spirit. Certainly God has tried through the person and teachings of Jesus and through the Holy Spirit made manifest at Pentecost. . . . The spirit of God came to followers of Jesus, *the church potential*, at Pentecost with power but found them apostate. They had lost contact with the life and teachings of Jesus. They wasted the Holy Spirit. To understand, we have but to turn back to the Disciples' own account of Pentecost and ask, What did the Disciples do with the Holy Spirit? They tell you, "We began to speak in tongues." They talked. "People listened so we told them about Jesus." Then what did you do? "We devoted ourselves to the Apostles' teaching and fellowship." That sounds like the church! They sat down together, listened to the Disciples preach, and enjoyed a beautiful fellowship. They wasted the Holy Spirit! They didn't really harness it to any kind of constructive program. The Holy Spirit comes. All God can do is give us a sense of togetherness, a sense of power, and a sense of commitment. If we waste it, it is gone.

Recently I spoke in Harlem at a mass meeting honoring Brother Malcolm. All through the meeting I was conscious of the fact that we were wasting the Holy Spirit. It was a beautiful program. It was one of those spectaculars which can only be gotten together in Harlem, which is still the artistic capital of Black America. There are so many talented people doing so many things and they come together once in a while for a spectacular, and this was that kind of occasion. . . .

Everything had been beautiful, but we had wasted the Holy Spirit just as the early Christians had wasted it. We had gone through empty motions. We had not even recruited for the Black Muslims. No one had said anything about the problem. No one had identified the enemy. No one had mentioned a program. We had enjoyed the Holy Spirit. We had enjoyed ecstasy. No one had said anything about putting the Holy Spirit to work. We had burned it all up right there! There seemed nothing left to do but get drunk. Neither program nor direction had been either suggested or implied. It had been exactly like a Sunday-morning service of worship in a Black church. I said, "You are a funny people here in Harlem. I always thought I'd love to participate in a Malcolm memorial, here where you understood him best and loved him most. But I fear that you have forgotten the things he taught and the meaning of his life."

"This program has been all in honor of Brother Malcolm. Brother Malcolm taught us that the white man is the enemy. It is the white man's system of oppression that is destroying us. While we are here screaming that Black is Beautiful, our brothers are starving to death in Mississippi and being driven off farms in Georgia and Alabama. Black people are being beaten to death in Detroit, and Black children are being denied a decent education all over this land. We are 'niggers' because the white man has deliberately and systematically 'niggerized' us. Let's not waste the Holy Spirit in a poem, a song, or a dance of self-hate. The day of the 'nigger' is drawing to a close. The era of the Black man has already begun to dawn. Let us look not backward but forward into our new day. Black culture must be an expression of our Liberation Struggle. It must express our hope and determination in poem, song, dance, and drama. It must express our total commitment to the liberation of Black people. There can be no Black art apart from the revolution in which we are engaged. Everything in the Black community must serve the Black Liberation Struggle."

5. PETER WAGNER, "WE ARE AT WAR" (FROM *WRESTLING WITH DARK ANGELS*, 1990)

New Agers, Wiccans, and adherents of eastern religions were not the only religious believers who were uncovering energy fields, spirits, ghosts, and demons in the late twentieth-century world. Conservative Christians, especially Pentecostals, were as well. For them, however, the re-enchantment of the world was considerably more dark, mysterious, and dangerous than the relatively positive emanations seen in works such as James Redfield's The Celestine Prophecy *or the benignly powerful goddess invoked by Wicca Webmasters. For the Christian authors of the work* Wrestling with Dark Angels: Toward a Deeper Understanding of the Supernatural Forces in Spiritual Warfare, *the devil had appointed demon-ambassadors to inhabit various parts of the world and work evil in particular ways. Much of this literature came from evangelical missionaries, who dealt with witches, conjure men, apparent demonic possession, bloodthirsty genocidal rulers, famine, and tribal war. They explained the chaos of the world as a result of sin—an "active, dynamic, negative spiritual energy field that seeks to carry away everything with it." The re-enchantment of the world envisioned by these conservative Christians, then, was the flip side of the utopian visions spun by New Age practitioners, and was directly tied to the chaos, war, and strife that still characterized much of the world.*

∽∾∽

We are at war. That war will not end until the final judgment of evil supernaturalism. . . .

The flesh and the world are the channels through which evil supernaturalism oppresses and seeks to destroy the human race, both believers as well as unbelievers.

THREE LEVELS OF SPIRITUAL WARFARE

We are all to be involved in spiritual warfare on at least three levels. First, there is the objective level, reaching unbelievers with the gospel. Next is the subjective level, protecting ourselves and our families from succumbing to the demonic warfare directed against us. Finally, there is the Christian level, helping to free demonized Christians from demonization.

THE OBJECTIVE OFFENSIVE LEVEL OF SPIRITUAL WARFARE

The Church is not only the community of the redeemed, it is also the redeeming community. We are both commanded by our Lord and impelled by the indwelling Holy Spirit to declare the message of God's redeeming love in Jesus Christ to all peoples. That task is easier stated than it is accomplished. Not only do we face the overwhelming logistical complexities of such a mission and the incredible cross-cultural and cross-linguistical barriers involved; something even more tenacious challenges our best efforts.

Satan holds the nations in bondage to himself and will not easily let them go. Indeed, he will resist us each step of the way. World evangelism is spiritual warfare.

The Scriptures are emphatically clear at this point. All human beings who live without the true God are in bondage to evil supernaturalism. . . .

Therefore, all of those we seek to bring to Christ are potentially demonized to one degree or another, most only mildly so, but some severely so. They are not demon possessed. They are not all demonized. All are potentially demonized, however. . . .

By *demonization* I mean that *Satan, through his evil spirits exercises direct partial control* over one or more areas of the life of a human being. The exact location of these attached demons is not always as important as some believe it to be. That is, partial control can be exercised from without as well as from within the victim.

It is true that most demons seem to want to enter the body of their victim. They are evidently more effective working from within. Yet some demons seem to prefer to remain attached to their victim from outside. They may be more difficult to detect in this manner. Others are able to slip in and out of the more severely demonized, almost at will.

It is important to stress five facts at this point.

One, while all unbelievers live under demonic dominion, *not all unbelievers are demonized.*

Two, some unbelievers, however, *are demonized,* and should be set free from these demons when they are brought to faith in Christ.

Three, demonization can range from very severe to very mild. There are many complex factors leading to this difference in demonization which cannot be mentioned in this brief study.

Four, when dealing with the potentially demonized, the typical Western, analytical, reasoned approach toward evangelism will be ineffective. Only a gospel of power will set them free.

Finally, to evangelize the demonized we must learn how to bind demonic activity from the minds of demonized unbelievers. Demons cause confusion and resistance, hindering unbelievers from understanding then responding to the gospel. We can take control over these demons, allowing the unbeliever to exercise his or her will to accept or reject Christ without direct demonic interference. . . .

While Satan and his demonic hosts are totally defeated, they are not dead. They are very much alive and continually active in promoting evil wherever they can find responsive hearts and/or ignorance of their schemes of deception. Thus, the title of Hal Lindsay's popular 1974 best-seller is accurate, *Satan Is Alive and Well on Planet Earth.*

Contrary to popular opinion, true believers are the main objects of Satan's subtle deceptions.

6. MYRTLE LINCOLN, "A PENTECOSTAL CONVERSION" (1970)

In the early twentieth century, Pentecostalism had a particularly interracial character. When William Seymour, a black minister originally from Louisiana, attracted a motley congregation of blacks, whites, and Mexican Americans to his pioneering services in Los Angeles in 1906, Pentecostal churches were almost the only racially integrated religious institutions of the time. As the twentieth century progressed, Pentecostalism appealed to a wide variety of poorer and working-class Americans of all races, including

some Native Americans. Here a Native American woman talks about her own Pente-
costal conversion, and astutely compares practices from her native tradition (such as the
Ghost Dance) and the kind of spirit possession that characterized Pentecostalism. The
document also evidences the interracial character of the Pentecostal movement, and the
way whites engaged in behavior that blacks and Indians recognized as religious trances.

It seem like it's same way with this Pentecostal way. You know, they say they get the spirit and all that—that's the way these Ghost Dances used to do. There would be some jumping around shaking their hands—holding their hands up in the air. It's just like a Pentecostal. We always think it might be the same thing.

I heard these songs ever since I used to sing. I used to sing with my grandpa and my grandma—Sitting Bull . . . There was three men that used to dance with my grandfather—they used to have white sheets, you know—white sheets.

And the longer they dance—somebody over there be shaking, and they say, "She's getting the Spirit." They shake around, you know, just like these Pentecostals always hold their hands when they shake hands. That's the way it was. And they always fall. And when they get up, they always tell the story about heaven.

"I've seen my people . . . It's a good place, over there. Everything is green. Everything shines like gold."

That's the way they used to tell. They used to, when they fall, when they get up again they used to tell their story, what they seen, but you might as well say their "dream". And it's just like—the way I look at it—it's just like this Pentecostal way. I seen one of these white women, you know, in Pentecostal, holler and just yell and jump around, and then pretty soon they fall to the floor and talk in tongues. And I think it's a wonderful way—the way they talk in tongues.

Now one time, over here, we had a church and my boy was preaching. There was a man by the name of Reed, Park Reed. They were singing together. They were singing a special song. Boy, here was just like—just like popcorn, these women just pop up. We were way in there, and they just circle around and dance around and praise the Lord and everything. One woman fell. She's living yet. Down south there where she fell, and start talking. Oh, she was hollering, "Glory, Hallelujah!" And then pretty soon she talk Arapaho.

In Arapaho she said, "Father in Heaven, give us a blessing here. Bless our Indians. Show them the way."

That's what she said. I never will forget that.

I used to go to the Mennonite Church. That's where I was baptized. And when he (my son) start preaching over here, I used to go Sunday mornings, and sometimes some service at night. You know on Wednesday they have service and on Saturdays. And I'd go on Saturday night instead of Wednesday night. They used to have good services. And when they start, you know, start praising the Lord and everything, somebody getting the Holy Ghost, it was wonderful the way they used to do.

And when my second oldest boy got killed, I lost my voice. I couldn't talk. I used to just try to make signs for what I want. And I used to try to talk but I couldn't talk. So one Sunday, about a month after that, my son said, "Well, Mama, I'm going to take you Wednesday night. I done asked the people, the group, to pray for you. We're going to pray for you. So you will get your voice."

And I didn't want to go. "No," I shook my head. Then when he got ready, he told me to come on. And without me knowing it, I was already out, going with him. So we all went, my girls and my old man went.

And they start having their service. And then they told me to come to the altar and sit down. They said, "Come sit down."

They prayed for me, and oh, gosh, I tell you, I don't know when I went down, I guess I fell off the bench. They prayed for me, and I breathe and my boy was at the head and they said, "Say, glory, glory."

I try to talk—I couldn't talk. Then the longer I laid there, I said, "Glory, glory."

And they got me up and they told me to get up and tell how it was with me. And I thought I couldn't talk, but I come out of it and talk, and ever since then I can talk. And oh, that foam was just running out of my mouth, and boy had a handkerchief, and he used it to wipe it off. And every time he wipe it off he used to say, "Heal, heal, heal, Lord," you know.

And my throat was clear and I could talk and I been talking every since.

Yeah, I did. You know, now a lot of people, they deny this Holy Ghost, but it's real. You can feel the spirit when the Lord is in the church with you. You can just imagine things how it is up in heaven. And when I got that Holy Spirit, I seen things that they preach about . . .

And they were singing a song you know—"there's an unseen eye watching you."

And I try to hold myself, you know, I start shaking. Try to hold on and I ask the Lord,

"I live my life up here, whatever you think it should be for me."

And I kept praising Him you know, and thanking Him, you know, for answering my prayers, so finally I fell. I was laying there. And well, they said

I talk in tongues. But I didn't know what I said in tongues. But I seen where I was at—everything was green. Just green. And I look west and it was just like sunset, you know. Just kind of gold color like. I kept on, you know. So finally I guess I come to and I praised the Lord and thanked Him for giving me the Holy Ghost. He's done to me what the world couldn't do. That's what I said when I first got up. And then they told me to testify. I got up and testify. I told them that I was thankful that the Lord seen fit to give me the Holy Ghost, and give me the feelings he has given me.

7. PATRICK J. BUCHANAN, "BLESSED SACRAMENT" (FROM *RIGHT FROM THE BEGINNING*, 1990)

As a political warrior, speechwriter, adviser to President Nixon, television commentator, orator, and presidential candidate first for the Republican Party, later for the Reform Party, Patrick Buchanan engaged in a kind of no-holds-barred rhetoric uncommon in American politics. In this book, part autobiography and part political memoir, Buchanan tells of his years growing up in Maryland, near Washington, DC. Coming from a family of diehard Catholics, Buchanan was raised in a world of stable moral verities and an even more certain faith: "Why compromise when you have the true Faith?" he rhetorically asks in this selection. His early education included drilling on the Blessed Sacrament first, then in the basics. During high school and college, Buchanan continued his classical education, even while engaging in a little harmless carousing on the town.

Buchanan's autobiography also serves as a political primer for those like himself "who wish to see Judeo-Christian values ascendant again in American society and undergirding American law." Buchanan's campaign featured fiery political rhetoric, including a controversial call for a "culture war" at the 1992 Republican presidential convention, a speech widely credited for tarring the Republican Party as having been captured by the religious Right. His memoir tells us much not only about Buchanan as a political figure but also about growing up as a conservative Catholic in post–World War II America.

"What parish are you from?"

When one Catholic asked another whence he or she came, that is how the question was framed in the 1940s and '50s.

The answer might be "Blessed Sacrament," or "We're out in Saint Michael's," or "We belong to Lourdes." . . .

The Buchanans "belonged" to Blessed Sacrament, as did the Flynns and Lillys and McCalebs and O'Neills and Warners and Keegans. Even during the war years, when the public schools were experiencing the birth dearth of the Depression, Blessed Sacrament was a booming parish. . . .

Between 1941 and 1961, the Catholic population of the United States virtually doubled, from 22 million to 42 million; and between 1955 and 1960, 56 percent of the population growth in the United States was among Catholics.

While still a minority and subjects of suspicion to our Protestant neighbors (we were forbidden, under pain of sin, from entering their churches, and their children were told not to enter ours), Catholics manifested a self-confidence in those years that was extraordinary. By conscious choice, we inhabited a separate world of our own creation; we built and occupied our own ghettos. And not only were we content to live within, the outside world was powerfully attracted to what we had. . . .

There was an awe-inspiring solemnity, power, and beauty within the old Church, which attracted people who were seeking the permanent things of life—after having tasted of the unfulfilling affluence of the postwar. There was something within that Church that said to the open heart and mind, "What you have been searching for may be found here."

Not only did we proclaim ours to be the "one, holy Catholic and Catholic Church," under the watchful eye of the Holy Ghost—with all others heretical—we were gaining converts by the scores of thousands, yearly. On Sunday mornings at Blessed Sacrament, there were six Masses—at seven, eight, nine, ten, eleven, and noon—to accommodate the parish faithful; and daily Masses were at 6:30, 7:30 and 8:30 a.m. The Presbyterian church, across from the school on Patterson Street, had services on Sunday—and that was it. Ecumenism was not what we were about; we were on the road to victory. Why compromise when you have the true Faith? Conversions were the order of the day. Regularly, non-Catholic mothers and fathers of Blessed Sacrament children were taken into the Church.

"The parish" was the hub of our existence. . . .

For eight years, all my teachers were nuns, the Sisters of the Holy Cross; they lived in a cloistered convent that separated church from school. The remarkable success of Blessed Sacrament, and the other parochial schools in the city—with fifty children in a classroom taught from nine to three by the same nun—persuades me that much of modern educationist theory is self-serving hokum. . . .

Those parish schools were enclaves of Americanism as well as Catholicism. America was God's country; there was no conflict then between nation and church. The United States, after all, had been consecrated to the Blessed Virgin Mary. Every noon, after lunch hour, the whole school assembled—each grade and class in its designated position and line—and, following several minutes of prescribed prayers, turned on signal, faced the flag, and made, hand over heart, the Pledge of Allegiance to the United States. Then, we were marched back into school. . . .

Our indispensable textbook was the Baltimore Catechism. Containing hundreds of questions and answers—all of which had to be learned by rote—the catechism instructed us on the central tenets of the Faith contained in the Apostles Creed, on each of the Ten Commandments (what they required and what they forbade), and on the Seven Sacraments (their precise purpose, and the spiritual conditions required for their worthy reception). For a grounding in Catholicism, it was unsurpassed. . . .

Twenty-five years after I went through that preparation for Penance, Holy Communion, and Confirmation, I was heading a delegation of young political leaders in the Soviet Union, in one of the final "exchanges" before formalization of Mr. Nixon's "detente." In Kiev, the capital of the Ukraine, we were taken to a Young Pioneer Palace, to watch dozens of six- and seven-year-olds inducted into the Young Octobrists. Having spent six to ten hours a week being indoctrinated in the Communist faith, they were now making their formal profession of faith—in the gospel according to Lenin. Watching those fresh faces, full of anticipation and delight, took me back a quarter century. With all the formality, if not the solemnity and beauty, attendant to my own First Holy Communion, these children were being formally received into the Church of Marxism-Leninism. . . .

It confirmed for me what I had already come to believe: The war between West and East is not between the economic systems of capitalism and Marxism; it is a religious war for control of the soul and destiny of mankind, the outcome of which cannot be arbitrated or negotiated.

Supplementing the catechism were the lives of the saints, as embellished by the piety and enthusiasm of the Sisters of the Holy Cross. . . .

I never understood what harm was supposed to have been done by the telling, and occasional embellishing, of these stories of martyrdom and virtue. Every one of us grew soon to an age when we knew what was true and what was mythical, and what was on a par with the Easter bunny. Yet, the same trendy Catholics most exercised over "superstitious" myths and "outright falsehoods," from which children had to be protected, turned out to have their own little hagiographies.

In recent years, politicians and the secular clerisy of the national press, who succeeded the routed Christian clergy as our Lords Spiritual, have not hesitated to use the power of law to insist that all Americans, including us "heretics," set aside as a day of reflection and remembrance the birthday of the late Dr. Martin Luther King, a secular saint whose interests appear to have been somewhat broader than peace and civil rights. The Church of yesterday never insisted that nonbelievers observe our feast days or Holy Days of Obligation; yet, the triumphant humanists have no reservations about imposing their household gods upon us. . . .

The idea of education that pervaded at Blessed Sacrament, four decades ago, is utterly antithetical to the view that dominates public education today.

Modern theory holds that children should be presented with facts, shown a menu of values and beliefs, and be permitted to make up their minds, at maturity, as to what is right and wrong, and what they wish to believe. We held to the opposite view.

We already had the truth. For two millennia Catholics had lived it; and the best of them had died for it. Now it was being handed down to us from the ages; the Church was there to impart it; and we were there to receive it, and to be its custodians and defenders for the next generation. The notion that children should decide for themselves what they should believe would have been considered scandalous if not laughable. Indeed, instruction in the truths of the Catholic faith was considered infinitely more important at Blessed Sacrament than learning the facts of mathematics and spelling and geography. After all, that is why the Catholic schools existed; that is why parents, priests, and nuns were making such immense personal sacrifices.

All ideas were not equal at Blessed Sacrament; and heresy had no rights. Parents did not send their children to Blessed Sacrament to have them come home spouting heretical nonsense. . . .

Because saving one's soul was more important than saving one's life, the nuns did not wait until the upper grades to begin teaching right and wrong. If the child became a scientist or composer or scholar, that was ancillary to the central task of the parochial school, the making of good Catholics. If, however, the child turned out at twenty-one to be a brilliant student, but lost the Faith and left the Church, then the nuns had not succeeded; they had failed in the mission to which, after all, they had dedicated their lives.

Those nuns and priests were in no more doubt as to what they were about then, than the secularists, who control public education today, are in doubt as to what they are about. "Indoctrination" is the derisory term secular critics use to disparage the Catholic education of four decades ago. Yet, even by secular standards, those Catholic schools "worked." If, today, however, parents asked that their own children receive a like education in the public schools, they would be told by the Supreme Court that this is unconstitutional, and by the education industry that this is outrageous. But, Catholic or Protestant or Jewish or Moslem, it is parents' rights that are paramount in early education, not the ideology of bureaucrats, judges, or Supreme Court justices. And there is nothing wrong with parents' demanding that schools—attended by their children and paid for by their tax dollars—turn their children into good men and good women, by *their* standards of morality . . . even if those standards are the ones written down in the Old and New Testaments. Nor is there anything wrong with the government insisting that the literature and history taught in public schools be tailored to inculcate in children a reverence for their national past, a respect for their democratic institutions, and an unabashed love of country.

If the current Supreme Court says such ideas are not constitutional, it is not the ideas that need changing. . . .

Men seek certitude. That is what the Catholic Church of the midcentury offered—and the modern Church in America does not seem to understand. We had the Way, the Truth, and the Light. Other ways were not equally valid; they were false.

While Catholicism made hard demands, it offered to those who kept the Commandments of God and the Commandments of the Church an iron-clad guarantee: eternal life. Agnostics, atheists, and Protestants of the war generation accepted the offer by the tens of thousands, and signed on. But the legacy was squandered by those to whom it was entrusted. The coffee-house clerics of the 1960s and '70s who sought to make Catholicism "relevant" to a hedonistic age found themselves irrelevant to youngsters searching for meaning in life. After you've "witnessed" for civil rights and peace, and the Voting Rights Act has been extended and "peace" has been brought to Cambodia and South Vietnam, what do you do next?

What people seek in religion today is what people sought then: answers to the questions that keep one awake at night. They want to believe that this life has meaning beyond the day-to-day, that there is life after death; and they want to be told what they have to do to attain that eternal life. They have neither the desire nor the time to sit down and "rap" like college students in an all-night bull session about whether God exists; nor are they going to be satisfied with a "social gospel" some trendy Catholic cleric seems to have picked up in the vestibule of the First Church of Christ, Socialist.

While one hears endlessly from Catholic pulpits today of the need to give food to the poor, in America's suburbs and inner cities, the true hunger that needs feeding is not physical at all. Fundamentalist and Evangelical Protestant denominations, whose preachers speak with conviction and authority of sin and salvation and Heaven and Hell, today gather the converts that in the 1950s were fighting their way into the Catholic Church. At some Catholic parishes today, not in a month of Sundays can you hear the subject of Hell even mentioned; the sermons are all about being considerate and kind and nice. The Church Militant has been superseded by the Church Milquetoast.

While teenagers give themselves up to drugs and despair, leading to appalling crime and violence in the inner cities and to indiscriminate sex, suicide pacts, and even satanic cults in the suburbs, the National Conference of Catholic Bishops labors away on pastoral letters to manifest the American Church's impatience with the most successful economy in human history. Remarkable. Today's clergy seem to be casting about blindly for economic and political solutions to problems of the human heart—to which they once had the answer. The moral capital of the Catholic Church in the United States, piled high over two centuries, has been squandered in two decades, invested in such fly-by-night secular stocks as boycotting lettuce and saving the Sandinistas.

To the Catholic youth of my generation, the death of Pius XII in 1958 was as great a jolt as the death of FDR was to Americans who had known no other president. With the coming of John XXIII and Vatican II came the "reformers." With Pius XII dead and buried, it was their time now; and, brimming with new ideas, they were going to "throw open the windows," to modernize the Church, to make it "relevant" to the outside world. Lord, what a mess they made of it. . . .

The old Church, which was always there, unchanged and unchanging, seems to have disappeared. Visiting the modern churches today is like coming back to the town where you grew up and finding that the oldest landmark, the great mansion on the hill, has been gutted and rebuilt to fit in architecturally and devotionally with the bustling suburban scene. Outside a sign reads UNDER NEW MANAGEMENT.

8. RALPH REED, *ACTIVE FAITH* (1996)

As the "New Religious Political Right" sprang up in the 1970s, some political commentators dismissed it as a kind of fundamentalist revival movement destined to die when brought into the real world of American politics. These pundits underestimated the impact of a new generation of Christian activists with considerable experience in campaign politics and first-class education in the nation's premier schools. One exemplar of the savvy Christian conservative politico was Ralph Reed. After developing a taste for hard-core political combat in his high school and college days, Reed took his Ph.D. in American history from Emory University. Rather than follow a conventional academic career, he plunged into the political world again at the behest of his new mentor, Pat Robertson, Yale-trained lawyer and Virginia-based host of the 700 Club television show. Robertson tapped Reed to organize what soon became the Christian Coalition, a broad-based conservative activist group that energized formerly apolitical evangelical Christians in a way unprecedented in twentieth-century American history. In Reed's autobiography, memoir, and historical treatise Active Faith, he explains himself and the Christian Coalition to the general public, placing his work in the context of the long tradition of religiously inspired activism in American public life (from stok-

ing the fires of revolutionary sentiment in the 1770s to abolitionism and temperance in
the nineteenth century to Social Gospel progressive crusades in the early twentieth cen-
tury). Perhaps most important, Reed validates the Christian Coalition by placing it in
the tradition of Martin Luther King and the civil rights movement, "forcing politicians
to confront troubling issues and social injustice that they would have otherwise ig-
nored." Reed represents the politically experienced and historically sophisticated face of
the religious Right.

Over the past six years, as executive director of one of the nation's leading
public policy organizations, I have traveled an average of 200,000 miles a
year, living out of a suitcase in a string of anonymous hotels and byways,
crisscrossing the country and delivering hundreds of speeches to the faithful in hotels, churches, and meeting halls. . . . On this frenetic schedule I
have been sustained by the inescapable conclusion that our time as people
of faith has finally come.

The reasons are clear: To look at America today is to witness a nation
struggling against forces as dangerous as any military foe it has ever faced
The threats, however, come not from without but from within. Families are
disintegrating, fathers are abandoning their children, abortion is the most
common medical procedure in the nation, and young people attend schools
that are not safe and in which they do not learn. In the inner city illegitimacy
is rampant, drug deals are openly conducted on streetcorners, hopelessness
is the norm, and children are shot by marauding carloads of juvenile gang
members. There is no economic solution to this social chaos—it is a collection of moral problems that require moral solutions.

The pro-family movement grows and prospers by addressing these problems. Our solutions are so morally compelling that we can no longer be denied our place in the conversation we call democracy. We shall experience
triumph and disappointment, victory and defeat, leaps of progress followed
by frustrating setbacks, but we will not be denied what is right. I believe in
the unforgettable words of the abolitionist preacher Theodore Parker: "The
curve of the moral universe is long, but it leads towards justice." . . .

The American revolutionaries in their day, the Communists in their
time, and the left in the 1960s all possessed a unique and powerful conviction that history was on their side. Today that conviction no longer belongs
to liberals or their allies, but to the right and, more particularly, to religious
conservatives. The once morally persuasive and politically powerful left has
lost its voice. Where once it was a vanguard on behalf of minorities and the
downtrodden, today it is a special-interest polyglot of quotas and set-asides.

Its eloquent defense of voting rights and economic equality for women has been drowned out by the extremist demands of the abortion lobby. Its voice for the have-nots has been garbled by a shameful defense of a bloated and unresponsive poverty industry.

But more than any other failure, it is their myopic rejection of religion as a "fanatical" intrusion into politics that has paved the way for the success of the pro-family movement. For today, religious conservatives are poised to enter an era of American life in which moral issues, and the pro-family agenda, will predominate. . . .

My arrival at this position of responsibility and leadership was the culmination of a long personal odyssey. It all began in Miami, where I grew up. My childhood was hardly spent in the Bible Belt. Miami was an international city in which whites were a bare majority, with a large population of Cubans, Nicaraguans, Haitians, and African-Americans. It also had a large Jewish population, and I attended more bar mitzvahs than baptisms as I grew up. My father was an ophthalmologist and surgeon, and my mother worked at home. I grew up in a fairly typical middle-class neighborhood, where I attended public schools, joined a local swim club, learned to play golf, and followed the Miami Dolphins. But from an early age my greatest passion was reading. . . .

Despite my involvement in Christian groups like the YMCA, my faith was not an important dimension in my political involvement until some years later. I had been raised in the Methodist church and generally held to conservative views on most issues because of my upbringing in a Republican household. . . .

As a lifelong Methodist, I believed intellectually in the tenets of the Christian faith but had gradually drifted away from the church. In the rough-and-tumble of politics, I began to sense the need for spiritual roots. While I found much that was good and honorable in politics, I recognized instinctively that the allure of fame and power could not satisfy my hunger for a transcendent meaning for my life. I needed more. . . .

In 1983 I made a faith commitment and began to attend an evangelical church in Washington. My religious beliefs never changed my views on the issues to any great degree, because my political philosophy was already well developed. As a conservative, I believed in less government, lower taxes, tougher laws against crime and drugs, and policies to strengthen the family. After my faith experience, I became more skeptical of government's ability to legislate morality or reform people's souls. But I did believe that government should protect children and strengthen families. . . .

What does it mean to be a person of faith in the political arena? It is no different from being a Christian in any other vocation. If a Christian is an attorney, he seeks to win his case as aggressively and fairly as possible. If he is the starting middle linebacker for a professional football team, he tries to stop the other team. Politics is a contact sport. I have a job to do, and it involves trying to advance my agenda. In that combat, I play hard and I try to win. But I never hit below the belt, I play according to the rules of fairness and courtesy, and after the game is over, I always help my opponent up off the turf. My faith is not a function of my politics. When the last tackle is over and the game ends, I kneel on the field with other players of both teams and ask for God's blessings. That is the proper perspective of faith in politics—not that I am right and you are wrong, or that I have all the answers and you are an enemy of God, but that we are both flawed human beings in an imperfect world in search of the truth who are asking for His guidance in the struggle.

During the past few years we have heard a lot about the dangers of Christian political activism. The argument goes that we are claiming the imprimatur of God and implicitly damning all of our foes. Some have said that since we call ourselves the "Christian Coalition," we believe it is implicitly "un-Christian" to oppose anything in our legislative agenda—from a balanced budget to restricting abortion. That is nonsense, of course. We can win these issues on their merits; we need not impugn the religious beliefs of our opponents. Others have said that we care more about political power than the traditional Christian concerns of charity, love, and caring for the poor. Our critics scrawl a harsh caricature of conservative people of faith as uneducated boobs who live in trailer parks, wear overalls, drive pickup trucks, eat moonpies, and hate women and minorities—the final and ugly backwash of George Wallace's and David Duke's politics of rage. . . .

Those claims are not only untrue, but their tone shows a lack of understanding about the central—I believe essential—role that religion has played in our political affairs from the earliest days of our republic. Nor is the demonic image of the pro-family movement matched by the demographics of its supporters. It is a predominantly middle-class, highly educated, suburban phenomenon of baby-boomers with children who are motivated by their concerns about family and a sense of values. The religious conservative community has greatly matured in recent years by broadening its message and narrowing its aspirations to those that are appropriate for any other group in a pluralistic society. Unlike fundamentalist political movements in the Middle East, religious conservatives in the United States are properly understood as an interest group within a democratic order. If they gained power, they would not repeal the Constitution or attempt to impose their religion on others through the state. Yet that process of maturation and growth has gone largely unreported. . . .

As a community of faith, we stand at a crossroads. Down one path lies the fate of many other great religiously-inspired political movements of the past: irrelevance and obscurity. It is a path defined by its spiritual arrogance and by its faulty assumption that the most efficacious way to change the hearts of men and women is through the coercive power of the state. This is the path taken by the prohibitionists, the Social Gospel advocates, the New Dealers, and the architects of the Great Society. It is not the right path for our movement. . . .

We begin with a principle of the Social Gospel. Reinhold Niebuhr said, "The purpose of politics is to establish justice in a fallen world." In attempting to right wrongs and ameliorate social evils, people of faith should use the political system wherever possible and advisable. The state clearly has a role both in executing the will of God and society by punishing wrongdoers and in protecting the innocent and vulnerable. But we must never lose sight of the fact that the sinful nature of mankind means that the power of the state, even when seasoned by love, is a corrupting instrument to those who wield it. In Niebuhr's unforgettable phrase, "Goodness, armed with power, is corrupted." Therefore, all attempts to use government to establish justice must be tempered by an equally strong impulse to keep government small, limited in its functions, and diffuse in its operations. . . .

A second important principle in a theology of Christian political involvement is the notion of citizenship as a spiritual obligation. For years, conservative people of faith have resisted direct political activity because they thought it was "dirty," "worldly," and a distraction from the call to evangelism. There is simply no biblical basis for such a belief. . . .

There are two contradictory qualities that faith should bring to politics. The first is an uncompromising sense of right and wrong and a willingness to speak out against injustice and immorality. The second is mercy. Our political witness should reflect not only God's judgment but also His forgiveness. For He loves everyone—including our political foes. . . .

Unlike some of our predecessors, our deepest hopes for restoring and renewing America do not rest solely on our political involvement. In fact, though it may come as a surprise to some, I believe there are strict limits to what politics can accomplish. In many cases our best agenda may not be a political agenda at all.

That is not a limiting admission but a vital affirmation. It is an affirmation of Christ's pronouncement that "my kingdom is not of this world." Only after we acknowledge how little government and politics can accomplish are we free to roll up our sleeves and enter the fray with a realistic view of what politics can achieve. . . .

And yet social movements have an obligation to resist injustice and advance what is right regardless of public sentiment. Martin Luther King asserted in his famous "Letter from a Birmingham Jail," "A just law is a manmade law that corresponds with the law of nature and the law of God." Public opinion alone cannot dictate the political program of people of faith. It is undeniable that the pro-life movement, the temperance struggle, and the civil rights movement have all called us back to the "better angels of our nature," forcing politicians to confront troubling issues and social injustice that they would have otherwise ignored. The difficult question is how to balance moral suasion with the force of law. . . .

As it happens, I draw much of my own inspiration from the example of Martin Luther King, Jr. He faced this difficult dilemma of balancing a movement's passionate faith with the requirements of political sophistication. His response varied, but one of the things he did say in no uncertain terms was that his must be a movement defined by love. To ensure that everyone was clear about what this meant, each and every volunteer in his SCLC signed a pledge card mandating that they would:

1. *Meditate* daily on the teachings and life of Jesus.
2. *Remember* always that the . . . movement . . . seeks justice and reconciliation, not victory.
3. *Walk* and *talk* in the manner of love, for God is love.
4. *Pray* daily to be used by God in order that all men might be free.
5. *Sacrifice* personal wishes in order that all men might be free.
6. *Observe* with both friend and foe the ordinary rules of courtesy.
7. *Seek* to perform regular service for others and for the world.
8. *Refrain* from the violence of fist, tongue, or heart.

With this solemn promise in place, King and his army were able to move out in love, transforming the country and bringing to fruition the dreams of tens of millions of Americans—a transformation whose spirit has outlived both King and the movement he led. I am not comparing our movement to King's. We can never know the indignity, suffering, violence, and death that the civil rights pioneers experienced. But we can seek to make this creed our own, and hope to wield a fraction of the influence that they had on the hearts of their fellow citizens.

9. RONALD SIDER, "A STATEMENT OF INTENT" (FROM *EVANGELICALS AND DEVELOPMENT*, 1981), "OUR HISTORIC MOMENT" (FROM *ONE-SIDED CHRISTIANITY*, 1993)

In the nineteenth century, evangelicalism and social action were closely connected. In the 1830s and 1840s, many Christians participated avidly in the Second Great Awakening (the great revival movement of that time) while throwing themselves into causes such as abolitionism and temperance. In the twentieth century, however, the Social Gospel increasingly became the province of mainstream and liberal Protestants, while evangelicals emphasized personal salvation and the relative futility of reforming this world. Historians use the term "great reversal" to describe this move of evangelicals from the progressive mainstream to the antiprogressive right wing.

In recent years, evangelicals from both the Left and the Right have attempted to bridge this gap. Ralph Reed and the Christian Coalition lead evangelicals on the Right who are intimately involved in antiabortionism and other social causes. Ronald Sider, a socially concerned evangelical and author of many books on social Christianity, well represents evangelicals on the Left who seek an equal emphasis on personal and social transformation. Sider first became known for his book Rich Christians in an Age of Hunger, *a stinging indictment of the complacency of First World Christians in the face of the poverty and desperation of so much of the planet's population. The selection from his compilation* Evangelicals and Development *below documents the thinking of many socially concerned evangelicals on the issue. In the 1990s, Sider became involved in efforts to bridge the divide between socially concerned evangelicals and those suspicious of the Social Gospel. The second piece, from* One-Sided Christianity, *illustrates his attempts to reconcile the century-old split between salvationists and Social Gospelers.*

A STATEMENT OF INTENT

As we stand at the threshold of the 1980s we are deeply disturbed by much of what we see in the contemporary world.

We are deeply disturbed by the human suffering present in the agonizing realities of hunger, malnutrition, disease, unemployment, illiteracy, deprivation and starvation.

We are deeply disturbed by the inability or unwillingness of the governments of the world to grapple with this injustice and tragedy.

We are deeply disturbed by the rising occurrence of violence and conflict within many of our societies and between many of them. The growth in the international arms trade gives particular cause for acute concern.

We are deeply disturbed that the difference in standards of living between the rich and the poor continues to increase.

We are deeply disturbed by many activities undertaken in the name of development which are leading to further injustices and suffering.

We are deeply disturbed that many of the social, economic and political structures of our societies are pervaded by injustice and violence.

We are deeply disturbed by the gross violation of human rights that continues to be committed in many of our societies.

We are deeply disturbed by the extent of apathy within the Christian church in the face of widespread suffering and injustice in the world.

We recognize that the Bible teaches that the mission of the church includes the proclamation of the gospel and the demonstration of its relevance by working for community development and social change.

We recognize that the church is called to work for that justice in society which God wills and to help people to enjoy the fullness of life which is God's purpose for all people.

We recognize that in order to engage in social change and model the relationships it commends for society, the church must exhibit total dependence on the transforming power of the Holy Spirit of God.

In the light of this understanding of scripture we resolve with God's help to live out the full Christian gospel and to apply it to the needy situations in which we find ourselves.

We resolve, in the company of others within the church, to study more deeply the current social, political and economic issues, which are so heavily influencing the lives of the world's population.

We resolve to change many of the attitudes that we find within ourselves which contribute to poverty and injustice.

We resolve to place greater trust in God and greater trust in each other in order to build relationships which will encourage and strengthen us in our common task to relieve poverty and injustice.

We resolve to encourage, by all the peaceful and constructive means available to us, the poor and oppressed who are seeking to establish a position of dignity and self-worth.

Finally we resolve to reconsider the use of the resources which God has given us, in order that such resources may contribute more effectively to God's kingdom and righteousness, love and justice.

OUR HISTORIC MOMENT

Christians privileged to live in the last decade before the year 2000 face a historic opportunity.

The number of Christians worldwide is growing at unprecedented rates. A shrinking global village and new technology make it easier to get the message of Christ to those who have never heard. Growing agreement on both the urgency of evangelism and the importance of a wholistic approach encourages optimism. And historic political changes have opened more doors to the Gospel. The last decade of the second Christian millennium is a breathtaking time to be a disciple of Jesus Christ.

Reasons for Hope

Global Christianity is on the move. Considerably more people have become Christians in the twentieth century than in any previous century. In 1900, there were about 558 million Christians. In 1992, there were 1,833 million. Experts predict that in eight years—by the year 2000—there will probably be 2,130 million.

One must quickly add that this explosive expansion is almost exactly parallel to the total global population growth There are also vastly more non-Christians today. In 1900, Christians represented 34.4% of the global population. Christian statistician David Barrett estimates that Christians will be 34.1 percent in 2000 A.D. There is still much to do. . . .

Pentecostals and charismatics today are the most successful at evangelism, and their numbers are growing at explosive rates. In 1970 there were seventy-two million. Twenty-two years later (1992), they had increased more than 500% to 410 million. Barrett estimates that by the year 2000, Pentecostal and charismatic Christians alone will number 560 million.

The tremendous growth of the church in the Third World is another reason for joy and hope. In 1900 at least 75% of all Christians were white folk living in places like Europe, North America, and Russia. By 2000, 56% of all Christians will be Third World Christians living outside those traditionally "Christian" countries. The number of Christians in Africa, Asia, and Latin America will have increased 1300% in 100 years to almost 1.2 billion people. . . .

Another reason for hope is the growing agreement in many parts of the church that evangelism and social concern must go hand in hand. Evangelicals in the Lausanne movement and The World Evangelical Fellowship have increasingly affirmed the importance of social concern. And ecumenical Protestants and Roman Catholics have recently made strong statements about the importance of evangelism. . . .

The Problems

Our optimism, however, must be guarded. Satan has not been converted. Human sin continues its stupid, destructive rampage. There are many reasons for deep concern. . . .

While most Christians live in affluence or at least comfort, one-quarter of our world suffers grinding poverty. Each day, over 100,000 people die of starvation and malnutrition. Each day, too, 55,000 people die without even having heard about Jesus.

One of four people (1.4 billion) in our hurting world live in near absolute poverty. Starvation and malnourishment torment and deform their bodies and dreams. Many are starving or malnourished. One of four people in our broken world also live and die without ever being told about the Gospel. They enter eternity without hearing even once about God's incredible love in Christ.

And the two groups largely overlap. Most of the desperately poor are un-evangelized. Does that matter? Is that important to people who are follow-ers of the One who said that he came to bring good news to the poor and of-fer eternal life to the perishing? It should! . . .

It is both biblically heretical and strategically stupid for rich Christians to neglect the world's poor. With the collapse of communism, one of the great-est threats to global peace will come from North-South hostility grounded in the growing gap between rich and poor. Ethnic hostility, racial prejudice, and environmental destruction will also pose terrible dangers for our chil-dren and grandchildren.

As we cast probing, expectant eyes toward the twenty-first century, Chris-tians have many reasons for optimism and many reasons for concern. Wholistic mission, a faithful biblical combination of the things we so often divide, offers the best hope for reducing the dangers and maximizing the opportunities.

Incarnational Kingdom Christianity for the Third Millennium

Our world desperately needs committed Christians who do both evangelism and social concern—who both think and strategize vigorously as well as pray increasingly for the renewal, presence, and power of the Holy Spirit—who both build the church and transform society. Our world desperately needs incarnational kingdom disciples committed to wholistic mission.

Think of the impact if wholistic mission became central to every institu-tion of the church. Our Christian schools and colleges would send forth a steady stream of talented Christian leaders equipped to change the world by building the church and transforming society. Our evangelistic and church planting programs and structures would nurture a concern for social trans-formation. Our organizations devoted to relief, development, and structural change would integrate prayer, the work of the Holy Spirit, and evangelism into their social agendas. Our seminaries would train pastors eager and able to lead wholistic congregations that have an equal concern for inward nur-ture in the local congregation and outward action in the world for evangel-ism and social transformation. More and more local congregations would become powerful demonstration projects of the coming kingdom. . . .

We can transcend one-sided Christianity!

What would happen if Christians most identified with evangelism would join with Christians most engaged in social action and Christians most concerned with renewal in the power of the Holy Spirit in city-wide crusades? We could call the meetings shalom revivals. The Old Testament word *shalom*, as we saw earlier, means wholeness in every way—right relationship with God, neighbor, and earth.

Shalom revivals would include the clear evangelistic invitation to accept Christ of the typical Billy Graham Crusade. But shalom revivals would also feature a vigorous call to Christians to share with the poor and seek justice for the oppressed. Equally central would be an invitation to all Christians to deepen their walk with the Lord by opening themselves unconditionally to the fullness of the Holy Spirit. . . . Christians would be urged to come forward if they sensed God calling them to make new concrete commitments for Christian service—whether in new evangelistic efforts or a new engagement to solve the tragedies of world hunger, broken inner cities, and a devastated environment; whether in new programs of Christian renewal, or concrete political engagement. . . .

I wonder how the secular intellectual community would respond to that kind of apologetics and evangelism. Some, of course, would still prefer the immediate pleasures of relativistic, individualistic secularism. But more and more people in the universities realize that Enlightenment secularism, like its offspring atheistic Marxism, has failed. Tragically, however, these people often turn to Eastern religion rather than to Christianity—in part because they think that Christianity does not help us solve the terrible problems of global hunger, economic injustice, racial oppression, militarism, and ecological destruction. So they turn to the old monistic gods marketed under a modern, New-Age label. Full-orbed biblical Christianity is what they need. And the best way to help them to see that is by wholistic discipleship and wholistic apologetics. . . .

Worldwide, we need widespread political engagement by committed Christians grounded in thoroughly biblical assumptions. Such a movement would know that politics is important but limited in what it can do. Only God through transforming grace can create new persons although wholesome social structures can encourage good and discourage evil. Intermediate institutions like churches, schools, the media and businesses are crucial to prevent the growth of despotic, all-powerful governments. Such a movement would renounce political ideologies of left and right and seek to develop concrete political proposals that are thoroughly grounded in biblical ethical principles and careful factual analysis. Because it was shaped by God's agenda, such a movement would be concerned with strengthening the family and empowering the poor, with both peace and freedom, with both the sanctity of human life, and the preservation of the environment. Such a movement would offer the world an alternative social vision.

Such a movement would also challenge the tragic materialism and self-ishness of contemporary Christians. Nominal "Christians" control about two-thirds of the worlds' wealth. They control the politically dominant nations in Europe and North America. Tragically, precisely this "Christian" world refuses to make the costly sacrifices that would help poor nations both to solve their environmental problems and nurture a decent life for all their people.

10. STEVE CHARLESTON, "THE OLD TESTAMENT OF NATIVE AMERICA" (1990)

Native Americans have had a tortured relationship with Christianity. On the one hand, it was the religion of the colonizers, the exploiters; it was often used as a justification for displacement of and genocide against Indian peoples. On the other hand, Christian missionaries, from the Franciscans in sixteenth-century New Mexico and John Eliot in seventeenth-century New England forward, made significant inroads among Native Americans. In some cases, notably including missionaries to the Cherokees in the 1820s and 1830s, Christians defended Native American rights against the encroachments of the United States government.

Today, more Native Americans claim Christianity as their belief than practice any other religion. At the same time, during the Indian renewal movement of the last thirty years, Native American believers and ministers have coped with both the demands of their faith and what they know of the history of Indians and Christianity. In this piece, Steve Charleston, a Native American Presbyterian minister from Oklahoma, investigates whether there can be a "Native People's Christian theology" or an "indigenous theology." He finds it in the Old Testament, noting a close similarity between the religious worldviews of ancient Israel and ancient Native America. The truths of the Bible and of Indian oral tradition, he concludes, can complement each other. The result, Charleston hopes, is that "the Traditional and the Christian People will once again become whole."

CONTEXT AND COMMITMENT

I come from Oklahoma. I was born in the southern part of the state in a small town called Duncan. My grandfather and great-grandfather were Presbyterian ministers. Like most people in our tribe, the Choctaw Nation, they were Presbyterians who preached and sang in Choctaw. My own family was tied up with the oil fields. We moved out of Duncan and went up to

Oklahoma City as the jobs changed. That means that I experienced a number of different churches. I was baptized a Southern Baptist, but I've known everything from Roman Catholic to Unitarian to the Baha'i faith. I think that's partly because Oklahoma Indian life can be so eclectic. There are dozens of tribes to go along with dozens of churches. Things are very mixed in Oklahoma. It's a cultural patchwork quilt laid down over ranch land, red dirt, and eastern timberland. I've inherited some of that mixture and it's followed me around wherever I've gone.

I am an Indian. I am a Christian. Being both wasn't always easy. Like many other Native People, I've known my share of confusion, frustration, anger, and struggle. But I've also known a lot of hope, joy, and visions. So the two balance each other out. Today I feel comfortable talking about Christianity as a faith that emerges from Native America. I came to that feeling after many years of travel through different Native communities. I would credit a great many Native men, women, and children (Traditional, Christian, and a little of both) as being my real teachers. They helped me to grow up and find the sense of spiritual balance that I think is central to life. Of course, keeping the balance takes a lifetime, but at least I have a place to stand.

The place I stand is in the original covenant God gave to Native America. I believe with all my heart that God's revelation to Native People is second to none. God spoke to generations of Native People over centuries of our spiritual development. We need to pay attention to that voice, to be respectful of the covenant, and to be unafraid to lift up the new covenant as the fulfillment of the ancient promise made to the Native People of North America. That means seeing Jesus not as a white plastic messiah taken off the dashboard of a car and dipped in brown to make things look more Indian, but a living Christ that arises from the Native covenant and speaks with the authority and authenticity of Native America.

I have been talking about what I call a Native People's Christian theology for over fifteen years. I started out when I was one of only four Native People in seminary and I am still doing it today. So I feel a deep commitment to this new theology. I want to do all that I can to help bring Native People together. That means healing the false divisions brought into our tribes by Western colonialism. It means helping Native People who think of themselves as being either Traditional or Christian find common ground, a common center. In time, it will mean carrying the voice of Native America around the world to join with millions of other Christians in a second reformation. I may not be around for that time, but I want to help make it happen by proclaiming the indigenous theology of this continent. . . .

CONSTRUCTION

Imagine a supermarket: not one of the small local convenience stores, but a really big supermarket, the kind of place with aisle after aisle of things from which to choose. . . .

Now imagine that instead of groceries, this supermarket sells theologies. As you roll your cart along the aisles, what do you see? Dozens of different brands: a theology for every taste. There is a department for basic Western theologies, the old standbys. There are sections reserved for feminist theology, for Black theology, for liberation theology. There are shelves for African theology and Asian theology. There is even a gourmet section for New Age theologies. At first glance, it seems that this supermarket has a Christian theology from every culture and community. Almost. But not quite. Something is missing. As strange as it may seem, the Great American Religious Supermarket is incomplete. It has some shelves that are standing empty. Go down the aisles and try to find the section for a Native People's Christian theology. It isn't there. Look for a department called Native American or American Indian Christian theology. Still not there. . . .

Why? That's the simple but profound question that needs to be answered. Why have Native People not entered visibly into the Christian debate? Why is there no quickly recognizable Christian theology from Native America? Why not several brands for Native Americans to choose from? Why not a whole shelf of theologies from Native Christian theologians? Is it because they are content to let others do the talking for them? Or are there other reasons that need to be examined, understood, proclaimed? . . .

If we tackle that question first, we may find that we are starting to surface some clues to the more fundamental reasons for Native America's silence in the Christian debate. Here is a place to begin: many people may have overlooked the absence of a Native People's Christian theology because they assumed it was covered by the supermarket sections reserved for spirituality. I think that's a fair guess. After all, there are many shelves these days loaded with works on Native American spirituality. Some are historical, others are anthropological or biographical; some are journalistic accounts by white authors who went to live with the Indians and returned to share the exotic secrets they discovered. In fact, there has been something of a minor gold rush in Native American "spirituality," with lots of people writing about it. What is described as Native American spirituality crops up in all kinds of places, especially in the gourmet section of the theological supermarket. In a style not too far removed from the 1960s and early 1970s, it's become chic to be Indian again, or, at least, to know an Indian, particularly if that Indian is a medicine person. It's romantic, earthy, "creation-centered." . . .

THE OLD TESTAMENT OF NATIVE AMERICA

So far, we've said that the answer to why most people have ignored the absence of a Native People's Christian theology is because they thought they were getting it through Native "spirituality." But that still doesn't explain why the theology itself is missing. Now, we have a clue to follow. What would happen if instead of speaking about Native American spirituality we began speaking of an Old Testament of Native America? What would that do for us? . . .

As a result, attitudes toward Native People and their Tradition would alter. Naming that Tradition an "Old Testament" is a powerful statement of recognition for Native America. It says that Native People are not just historical curiosities, footnotes for Western colonial expansion, but the living members of a world-class religious heritage. Since the first Western missionary or anthropologist walked into a native community, the Tradition of Native America has been called everything but an Old Testament. It has been named by others. It has been named by the West, not the People themselves. It has been called "superstition," "tribal religion," "nature worship," "animism," "shamanism," "primitive," "Stone Age," "savage," "spirituality," anything and everything, but never an Old Testament. The namers themselves have had mixed motives, some innocent, some racist, some just ignorant. But the results have been the same: the names attached to the Old Testament of Native America have consigned that Tradition to the backwaters of serious Christian scholarship. Native American spiritual tradition has been considered the proper study of historians, ethnologists, anthropologists, or even the gourmet writers of the New Age, but not for most Christian theologians. There is a big difference for Western theologians between a "spirituality" and a "theology," just as there is between a "tradition" and the "Old Testament." By claiming the right to name the Tradition an Old Testament, Native America would be walking into the private club of Christian theology, even if that means coming in uninvited. . . .

Why? Because Native People also have an "old" testament. They have their own original covenant relationship with the Creator and their own original understanding of God prior to the birth of a Christ. It is a Tradition that has evolved over centuries. It tells of the active, living, revealing presence of God in relation to Native People through generations of Native life and experience. It asserts that God was not an absentee landlord for North

America. God was here, on this continent among this people, in covenant, in relation, in life. Like Israel itself. Native America proclaims that God is a God of all times and of all places and of all peoples. Consequently, the "old" testament of Native America becomes tremendously important. It is the living memory, the living tradition of a people's special encounter with the Creator of Life. . . .

My own awareness of a Native American Old Testament began to grow while I was sitting in an introductory Old Testament class during my first year of seminary. The professor described what was unique about the religious worldview of ancient Israel. He said that Israel, unlike its neighbors, had a special understanding of the relationship between God and humanity. This was the covenant between a single God and a particular People. It involved the promise of a homeland. It was sustained by the personal involvement of God in history. It was communicated through the prophets and the Law. It made Israel a nation. It brought them together as a People.

It was the most simple, important, understanding of the Old Testament that we share as Christians. And yet, during that lecture, I couldn't help but make a list of comparisons in my mind. Each time the professor mentioned some aspect of the Old Testament story that was "unique" to early Israel, I was reminded of my own Tradition and People. To help you understand what I mean, I will repeat that list in abbreviated form:

1. God is one.
2. God created all that exists.
3. God is a God of human history.
4. God is a God of all time and space.
5. God is a God of all People.
6. God establishes a covenant relationship with the People.
7. God gives the People a "promised land."
8. The People are stewards of this land for God.
9. God gives the People a Law or way of life.
10. The People worship God in sacred spaces.
11. God raises up prophets and charismatic leaders.
12. God speaks through dreams and visions.
13. The People maintain a seasonal cycle of worship.
14. The People believe God will deliver them from their suffering.
15. God can become incarnate on earth.

These fifteen items for comparison each merit more discussion, but the point I wish to make is simply that the religious worldviews of ancient Israel and ancient Native America have much in common. This is not to say that their understandings were identical. There are many variations on the theme not only between the two communities, but within them as well. What is striking, however, is that for many key concepts the two traditions run parallel. Like Israel, Native America believed in the oneness of God; it saw God as the Creator of all existence; it knew that God was active and alive in the history of humanity; it remembered that the land had been given to the people in trust from God. Native People accepted the revelation from God as it was given to them through prophets and charismatic leaders; they recognized sacred ground and holy places in their worship; they maintained a seasonal liturgical calendar; they had a highly developed belief in the incarnational presence of God and expected that presence to be revealed in times of strife or disaster. Is it strange, therefore, that Native Americans would consider themselves to be in a covenant relationship to their Creator or that they would think of themselves as a People "chosen" by God? Take the names which the People used for themselves in their own languages and you get a clear sense of this: in the tribal languages, the many nations of Native America announced their identity as "The People" or "The Human Beings." Moreover, they tied this identity to the land given to them by God. It was this land-based covenant that gave them their identity as "The People," as the community special to a loving God. . . .

As with Israel, this memory was transmitted through all of those channels that make up any Old Testament: through stories, histories, poetry, music, sacraments, liturgies, prophecies, proverbs, visions, and laws. The mighty acts of God in North America were witnessed and remembered. They were interpreted and passed on. Taken all together, they constitute an original, unique, and profound covenant between God and humanity.

If this is true then we are confronted with a problem. Suppose that we do allow Native People to claim an "Old Testament" status for their Tradition. Then what do we do with "the" Old Testament? What is the relationship between the two? What is the relationship to the "New" Testament?

An immediate answer is that we will have to be more concise when we speak of the original covenant with ancient Israel. We won't be able to use that word *the* in quite the same way. As Christians, we're going to have to make some elbow room at the table for other "old testaments." Not only from Native America, but from Africa, Asia, and Latin America as well. That's another door that is opening up in Christianity, and I doubt that anyone is going to be able to close it again. The fact is, Christians must permit the same right for other peoples that they have claimed for themselves. . . .

At the same time, I can stand on my own Old Testament Tradition and let it speak to me just as clearly about the person, nature, and purpose of the

Christ. I maintain that this Christ fulfills both Old Testaments. In the Pauline sense, I can assert that while as a man Jesus was a Jew, as the risen Christ, he is a Navajo. Or a Kiowa. Or a Choctaw. Or any other tribe. The Christ does not violate my own Old Testament. The coming of the Christ does not erase the memory banks of Native America or force me to throw away centuries of God's revealing acts among my People. But let me be careful about this: I am not glossing over the Old Testament of Native America with the Western whitewash of a theology that gives out a few quick platitudes about the "Christ of all cultures." When I speak of a fulfillment of Native America's Old Testament, I mean just that: a Christ that emerges from within the Native Tradition itself; that speaks of, by, and for that Tradition; that participates in that Tradition; that lives in that Tradition. . . .

THE SECOND REFORMATION

In the next century, the Christian church is going to experience a second major reformation. It will be far more powerful than the one we knew in sixteenth century Europe. For one thing, it will be international, not just regional. It will cross over not only denominational lines, but also over lines of color, class, gender, and age. It will be more important than the last reformation because it will change the way people think and feel about themselves. While the West will participate in this reformation, it will not play a dominant role. The leaders of the coming reformation will be women. They will be from Africa, Asia, Latin America, and Native America. They are being born right now.

One of the guiding theologies of the second reformation will be the Christian theology of Native America. The emergence of that theology is already taking place. Not that too many people have noticed yet. . . .

The Native People's Christian theology is being overlooked, because it is being born in silence. That silence is so strong, so pervasive, so smothering that even the shout of a human voice cannot escape it. Not alone. But with each day that passes, more and more voices are beginning to take up the cry. In little backwater reservation chapels. In urban slums. In Arizona and Alaska and Minnesota and California and Manitoba. In sweat lodges and camp meetings, in Christian homes and Traditional homes. In Cheyenne homes and Mohawk homes. In Tribes all across Native America.

Native People are shouting into the silence of Western colonialism. They are shouting their names. They are saying that they are still the Tribe of the Human Beings. The Memory is coming back and with it the voice of a whole nation. Against that kind of power, no silence will long endure.

11. DONALD E. MILLER, "THE REINVENTED CHURCH: STYLES AND STRATEGIES" (1999)

In the 1980s and 1990s, observers began to note the proliferation of new kinds of churches—variously dubbed "new paradigm" or "megachurches." Oriented toward suburban baby boomers dissatisfied with or alienated from conventional denominational Christianity, these churches generally took a generic-sounding name and met in places that more resembled theatrical halls or auditoriums than conventional congregations. Services were oriented to entertainment, with professional musical numbers setting the stage for an informal address-sermon, and with money raising kept as low-key as possible. The megachurches deliberately avoided the trappings of "church" or denominationalism, the kinds of stuffiness that drove people away from traditional services. Growing rapidly in suburban areas in Los Angeles, Chicago, Denver, and other cities, these new congregations appealed to a market segment underserved by conventional Christian institutions.

For all their unconventional trappings, these new churches were decidedly evangelistic, and grew rapidly from their proselytizing. Some of them became involved in sociopolitical causes (such as antiabortionism) associated with the evangelical right wing. Donald Miller analyzes the growth of the new paradigm churches, and suggests what spiritual nourishment they provide for baby-boomer seekers—as well as what established religious traditions still have to offer the boomers.

My personal religious pilgrimage is not exceptional. I grew up in a community church in southern California that had evangelical leanings. It was a strong and caring group of people, even though the leadership of the church circumscribed the Christian faith with a relatively strong dose of moral legalism. In college I joined the InterVarsity Christian Fellowship and discovered that some people actually think about their faith and write rather sophisticated arguments defending their beliefs. Then I read Marx, Freud, Weber and Durkheim and decided that Christianity is a social construction that sometimes operates as a crutch, is sometimes politically repressive, and in its finer moments is a source of moral challenge and social cohesion.

When my wife and I moved to Pasadena, California, we joined a group of well-educated couples who were meeting in a local Baptist church on Sunday mornings for a freewheeling discussion of life, social issues and various cultural challenges to the Christian faith. This was the early 1970s, and the countercultural revolutions launched in the '60s were in full bloom.

One Sunday morning while the 40 of us were in heated discussion, a deacon delivered an ultimatum: conclude your Sunday school class in time to attend the 11 o'clock worship service, or meet on other premises. We started shopping for a new meeting place. At All Saints Episcopal Church, Rector George Regas issued our group the same invitation that he did every Sunday morning as he stood before the eucharistic table: "Wherever you are on the journey of faith, you are welcome." We could use a room free of charge and come to worship services if we wanted.

The first few times that I went to church at All Saints, I didn't know when to stand or sit. I fumbled my way through the Book of Common Prayer. The music was too sophisticated for my taste. But the preaching was riveting. The Vietnam war was raging and Regas was birthing the Interfaith Center to Reverse the Arms Race.

Furthermore, I grew to love the liturgy. Unable to accept the creed literally, I nevertheless recited it as a statement of my heritage and found myself deeply moved—often to tears—in a way that I had never experienced in evangelical churches. Clearly, something rather mystical and self-transcending was occurring. A few years later I was on the vestry, and learned about organizational management from a dedicated cadre of men and women. At a Sunday Rectors Forum, I listened to thoughtful people speak about the most pressing social issues of our time. In the early 1980s I wrote *The Case for Liberal Christianity* and dedicated it to the people of All Saints Church. In this community I had come to a new commitment and understanding of the Christian faith.

Meanwhile, through conversations with my undergraduate students, I became intrigued with a movement of churches that had roots in southern California and was spreading across the country—churches that appealed especially to unchurched baby boomers and baby busters. With the assistance of a grant, I visited dozens of rapidly growing churches associated with the Vineyard Christian Fellowship, Calvary Chapel and Hope Chapel and interviewed several hundred clergy and lay leaders.

On the basis of my research, I wrote *Reinventing American Protestantism* (1997), which argued that a reformation is transforming the way Christianity will be experienced in the new millennium. Unlike the one led by Martin Luther, this reformation is challenging not doctrine but the very medium through which the message of Christianity is articulated. Like upstart religious groups of the past, these "new paradigm" churches have discarded many of the attributes of establishment religion. They are appropriating contemporary cultural forms and creating a new genre of worship music. They are restructuring the organizational character of institutional religion and democratizing access to the sacred by radicalizing the Protestant principle of the priesthood of all believers. They are harbingers of postdenominational Christianity.

In the typical new paradigm church, most members are relatively young. The church meets in a building that has no stained glass, steeple or pews. In fact, most of these worship spaces are either converted warehouses, theaters or rented school auditoriums. People (including the pastors) come dressed as if on their way to a picnic. The music is what one might hear on a pop radio station, except the lyrics are Christian. The sermon is informal and focused on exposition of a passage of scripture. The pastors are not required to have a seminary education. Typically they are individuals whose lives have been radically transformed by God and who wish to share the good news of their Christian convictions. They view God as capable of supernatural intervention in our lives; hence, they have no difficulty affirming the miracles described in the Bible and they hold to a fairly literal view of scripture.

But the worship environment is not legalistic or rigid. Sunday morning is a time of celebration. The focus is not on theological doctrines but on finding analogues in one's life to the biblical narratives. During the week, members meet in small groups where they worship, study the Bible and care for each other. For many, this small group is the extended family that they never had. These churches also offer a myriad of programs that deal with everything from divorce recovery to child rearing, money management, social outreach ministries to prisoners and unwed mothers, and food distribution. Far from being fundamentalistic, new paradigm churches tend to be tolerant of different personal styles, even while members hold to rather strict moral standards for themselves.

This type of church is culturally hip. Lay members are given tremendous freedom to develop programs. The pastor is a teacher, visionary and trainer, but the people do the basic work of ministry. Many of these churches are independent, and if they do have a denominational affiliation they are part of a movement, not of a church bound by rules and policies. Many of these churches grow too large to manage, but they constantly give away members and young clergy to start new churches on the outskirts of their city and throughout the world. This makes room for more people and new leadership. . . .

I found that these new paradigm congregations exist throughout the U.S. and the world. Currently, Ted Yamamori, of Food for the Hungry, and I are studying churches throughout the developing world that 1) are large and fast growing and 2) have well-defined social and community outreach ministries. During the first year of this four-year project, we were in Manila, Bangkok, Nairobi, Kampala, Buenos Aires, Santiago and São Paulo. The churches that are fast growing and have active social ministries are by and large charismatic or Pentecostal. Furthermore, almost everywhere we went we were told that mainline churches were in decline, although one can ob-

viously always find the notable exception if one searches for it. And, surprising to us, old-line Pentecostal groups—those started through missionary activity in the first half of this century—are often not as vital as charis-
matically inclined churches that were started in the past two decades.

Because our sample of churches includes some that are socially active, I
hesitate to make any sweeping generalizations about *all* rapidly growing Pentecostal churches. What I can conclude is that being charismatic does not
negate the possibility of highly creative engagement with social issues. . . .

Many of the things that I observed in U.S. churches are multiplied in
these developing countries. First, these movements are led by people with
immodest vision. They are not limiting themselves to doing what seems hu-
manly possible given their resources and capacity. . . .

Second, these visions are typically not the result of megalomania, although the human element can never be fully removed. Rather, these
dreams have come, quite literally, during periods of extended prayer and
fasting. People have seen visions of what God is going to do in their city.
Sometimes God even speaks audibly to them. In short, the very visitations
that are described in the Hebrew scriptures and the New Testament seem
still to be happening.

Third, the ministry is being done by the people, not the pastor. Most of
these churches are radically decentralized, with small fellowship groups
meeting in homes. Common people are studying the Bible for themselves,
praying together and taking care of each other's needs on a highly informal
level. And fourth, when they gather to worship, you can't keep people from
dancing in the aisles, raising their hands in praise, embracing each other
and having an exuberant good time. Do they speak in tongues? Are people
healed? Yes. But unlike the typical media-take on such churches, this is not
the focus of their life together. It is a byproduct of what they believe to be
the Holy Spirit's presence in their community.

These new paradigm churches are, I believe, cultural pioneers of sorts.
They are attempting to reintegrate bodily experience into religious life. Worship is not simply a matter of the head, affirming various creeds or acknowledging normative beliefs. Beliefs are important, especially when an-
chored in the retelling of biblical stories—but beliefs in themselves are
sterile. Religion is a full-bodied experience that includes all the receptors—
all the senses—with the rational mind being only one locus of information
about reality.

Is there any way to reconcile the insights manifest in new churches, as
well as the changes occurring in postmodern society, with mainline traditions such as that of my own Episcopal Church? To answer, I would first of
all suggest that there are inherent strengths of the Episcopal tradition that

will continue to be significant because they are strengths that the new paradigm churches lack.

For example, some members of new paradigm churches will probably grow tired of the radical contemporaneity of their worship. While these churches are effective in attracting a nonchurchgoing population, the worship experience may begin to seem shallow after a while. Hence, spiritual seekers may shop for something that has more depth and complexity to it. The Episcopal Church will be a prime alternative.

Second, while many people may desire a religious option that offers concrete answers to life's problems, there will be a minority of well-educated people who will find new-paradigm Christianity to be simplistic in its affirmation of Jesus as the exclusive path to truth.

Third, many members of evangelical churches are tired of the narrow-minded, legalistic, anti-intellectualism that they encounter there. I know dozens of people who have become Episcopalians rather than drop out of church altogether—I am one of those individuals.

One of the wonderful things about the Episcopal Church and other mainline traditions is their affirmation of reason and their willingness to see both sides of an argument and be open to ambiguity. The growth of evangelical churches will create a market for open-minded churches that are ready to wrestle with complex issues.

At the same time, mainline churches can learn from new paradigm churches. They can learn, first of all, the importance of religious experience. We need to bring the magic back into our worship and back into our personal lives. We need to acknowledge that the Holy Spirit reflects the feeling and experiential dimension of the religious life. We should reach deep within our tradition and rediscover those practices that connect us to God in direct ways.

In the 21st century, people will be seeking spiritual pathways to balance the flat secularism of the Enlightenment metaphysic. They will seek for something beyond the physical world and beyond the bottom line of financial accounting. It should not surprise us that young people are more inclined to believe in angels than are their grandparents. Nor should it shock us that hard-nosed rationalism and empiricism are empty methodologies for many young people. One commentator on the worldwide explosion of Pentecostalism states that there is an "ecstasy deficit" in our culture. I would add that there is also a "hope deficit." The challenge to the church is to tap its tradition for those practices that will enable people to move beyond the utilitarian ethic of our individualistic, materialistically oriented world.

Chapter 8

New Immigrant Communities

LOS ANGELES began the twentieth century as the whitest and most Protestant sizeable city in the United States. Compared both to larger cities—New York, Chicago, San Francisco—and to those of similar size, the "City of Angels" could have been renamed the "City of White Protestants." Its entire public structure exhibited the power of the mainline churches, as the powerful denominations claimed 93 percent of all elected offices and 87 percent of all appointed positions in the city government.

By the end of the century, everything had changed. Los Angeles had been transformed into the most ethnically and religiously diverse metropolis in the world. With more than six hundred identified faith groups represented among its citizens, the city exhibited all the trends that had begun to show up throughout the nation at large: the majority of Christians were found not in Protestant churches but in Roman Catholic parishes; Muslims outnumbered Episcopalians; and evangelical Protestants, especially those of the Pentecostal/charismatic variety, had made impressive gains next to heavy losses by the old mainline Protestant establishment.

What could cause such a change? The Immigration Act of 1965.

Certainly, immigration had always been part of the American experience—and particularly the American religious experience. The narrative myth of the nation was the story of immigrants arriving on American shores seeking religious freedom and economic opportunity. The developing American diversity throughout the nineteenth and early twentieth centuries came by way of (largely) European migrations: first Germans, then Irish, Italian, Jewish, and Polish waves of settlers approached the American dream by crossing dangerous waters and Anglo-American biases that proved difficult to overcome, even after several generations.

As important as those migrations were, the modern United States is the result of a new immigration—a broader, more global relocation of millions of people since World War II. Some of the players were familiar: Europeans of several nationalities and ethnic groups (including Jews who had survived the Holocaust) moved soon after the war. But changes within the Western Hemisphere brought more "Americans"—broadly defined—than had been absorbed in previous generations. Puerto Ricans, with U.S. citizenship, enjoying higher status in the eyes of the U.S. government than most other Latinos, began moving in large numbers to New York City in the postwar period. Tens of thousands of Cubans, meanwhile, fled particularly to South Florida in the shadow of Fidel Castro's Marxist revolution in 1959. The population growth and agricultural advances of the American Southwest, in the meantime, called for a larger and cheaper labor force. Initially Mexican migrant workers filled the bill, but over time more Central Americans began to cross the border to provide this valuable service along the agricultural sunbelt.

The changes in immigration law were partially the result of increasing tensions in Southeast Asia, as communist revolutions or the threat of them moved Congress to drop the longtime ban on Asian immigration. Slow to begin, the influx of Asians to the United States picked up steam through the 1970s and 1980s and exploded in the 1990s when the American economy called for more high-tech workers. These changes in the law also enabled more people of Middle Eastern background to migrate to the United States. The fall of Iran's Shah in 1979, for instance, led to the emigration of many thousands of middle- and upper-class Muslims. Thirty-five years later, the face of religion in America has been utterly changed by this worldwide movement of people. By 2000 Islam was poised to surpass Judaism as the second largest religion in the nation. Meanwhile, aspects of Hinduism and Buddhism had so permeated American culture that such terms as "karma" and "meditation" rolled off citizens' tongues without a second thought.

Hinduism is an amalgam of beliefs and rituals going back thousands of years in India. Because the deities worshipped are so plentiful and so different, Hindus have a variety to choose from. In India devotees of Shiva, Kali, or Brahma might be found in separate temples dedicated to each god. But in the United States they did not have the luxury of such numerous facilities. Forced by necessity to alter the way they practice, Hindu immigrants have created thousands of "garage temples" dedicated to particular deities. But balkanization is not the story here. Indeed, Indians have come together not only in the obvious cities of Los Angeles and Chicago but also in Indianapolis and Jackson, Mississippi, to build cultural centers where they meet to enjoy common aspects of their heritage and to worship jointly several of the more prominent deities in their religion. In many ways, these cultural centers are merely interim measures, meeting the cultural and religious needs of Indians until a real temple can be built. By 2000, some two hundred Hindu temples had been raised, at great expense, across the country. These structures might look similar to those in India, but a closer inspection reveals that they are far more inclusive than those dedicated to specific deities in the old country. Reflecting the reality of Hindu life in America, where approximately one million Hindus must share, the temples contain images of numerous gods and goddesses. America might promote individualism in spirit, but it has produced community pluralism for Hindu worshippers.

Buddhism also flourished in the United States once immigration restrictions were lifted. Limited previously to a few Japanese faithful on the West Coast and Anglo dilettantes in urban areas, Buddhism had arrived in all its varieties by the late twentieth century. Japanese Zen Buddhism, with its emphasis on individual meditation, had already caught the imagination of many American literary types in the 1950s. But the coming of D. T. Suzuki and the founding of the San Francisco Zen Center gave many Americans their first real taste of the ancient practice. Zen was soon followed by the Nichiren Shoshu sect, founded in the twelfth century, emphasizing chanting and the Lotus Sutra scripture, and by Tibetan Buddhism, known for its sacred texts and belief in bodhisattvas, saviors who forgo final enlightenment in order to enlighten humanity. The Tibetan spiritual leader, the Dalai Lama, is understood to be the sum of the compassion of all previous buddhas. Tantric Buddhism also came from Tibet, and numerous other local flavors of Buddhism arrived with the Vietnamese, Laotians, and Cambodians who fled the communist wars in their countries.

It is difficult to measure precisely how many Buddhists live in the United States. Like Hindus, Buddhists practice their faith largely alone and in silence. Meditation, after all, would be impossible in a religious meeting replete with singing and preaching. Sociologists studying religion in America estimate there are more than 1,500 temples in the United States, about a fifth of them in Los Angeles alone. That city also boasts the largest Buddhist temple in the Western Hemisphere. The Hsi Lai Temple in Hacienda Heights was built by a Taiwanese sect of Buddhism that is particularly missionary minded. The massive structure, which sits on a hill overlooking a largely Latino Catholic neighborhood, does not seem so out of place in the most religiously diverse city in the world. Its parking lots remain constantly busy, even if rarely filled, as Buddhists of all ethnic and national backgrounds visit the temple to make their prayers to the bodhisattvas and meditate quietly.

While it was possible for both Hindus and Buddhists to blend somewhat into the background of American life since neither faith is prone to large public meetings or noticeable proselytization, the growth of Islam has attracted a good bit of attention. Of course, much of this awareness is political in nature. Since the Ayatollah Khomeini's commandeering of the U.S. embassy in Iran in 1979 and the holding of American hostages there for over a year, many Americans have harbored mistrust toward Muslims. Of course, there are as many different types of Muslims as there are Christians, Hindus, or Buddhists, and many were repulsed by the Ayatollah's actions as well as by subsequent acts of terrorism. But once the Pandora's Box of religious bias has been opened, it is difficult to close.

Nonetheless, Muslims of many nationalities have flourished in the United States. Not interested in the militant Nation of Islam led first by Elijah Muhammad and later by Louis Farrakhan, immigrant Muslims have quietly built lives for themselves and mosques in which to continue their worship traditions. They are fairly evenly split in their regional origins, coming from such Middle Eastern nations as Lebanon, Syria, and Iran, and from Southeast Asia, particularly Pakistan. Some also hail from Malaysia, which is predominantly Muslim. Approximately one third of American Muslims are African American.

All these nationalities worship side by side in the mosques that now dot the American map. By 2000, approximately 1,200 mosques scattered across the country claimed about 2 million members. Many "cultural Muslims," however, lived in the United States by this point but did not belong to a particular mosque. Some estimates put their number near 3 million. With rapid growth via conversion of African Americans and immigration from traditionally Muslim countries, Islam was poised by the end of the century to overtake Judaism as the second most populated religion in the United States.

Post–1965 immigration might have brought new religious forms, but it also highlighted an old and familiar form of Christianity: Roman Catholicism. The earliest type of Christianity to hit the New World was a stringent Spanish Catholicism that arrived with the earliest European explorers. Eventually, nearly all of Latin America would be converted, while in North America other versions dominated. Quebec maintains its colonial French Catholic character. The northeastern United States, meanwhile, became the destination of millions of Irish Catholics, whose characteristics can still be read in the religious landscapes of Boston, New York, and Baltimore. German Catholics helped settle the Midwest. Spanish Catholicism still existed in parts of California, throughout Texas, and in pockets of Florida. But changes in immigration law enabled millions of Mexican, Puerto Rican, and Central and South American Catholics to enter the country.

The results of this influx of Latino Catholics were becoming clear by the end of the century. Again, Los Angeles serves as a good example. By the mid-1990s, Latin American migration made the L.A. archdiocese the largest in the country, with some 5 million adherents. Politics felt this shift as well. For the first time since the mid-nineteenth century, whites no longer constituted at least 50 percent of the population. With a strong Latino Catholic presence in the city, the Church could voice its social concerns and immediately receive the attention of politicians and the press.

The rest of the country began to experience the upsurge in Latino congregations as millions migrated to urban areas for work. Nearly every sizeable city now has a considerable Latin American presence. In many places this has meant the creation of Latino parishes to meet the needs of the Catholics. Some of these migrants, however, have left the Catholic fold for evangelical and Pentecostal Protestant congregations. Polls indicated that these individuals recognized the still largely Protestant nature of American culture and understood their adopted denominations as a door to greater acceptance by the mainstream.

Another group of Christian immigrants has complicated matters further. Asian Christians, converted by American foreign missions from decades ago, moved to the United States in record numbers. Vietnamese Catholics who fled their war-torn homeland in the mid-1970s settled in numerous middle-sized American cities. Korean Presbyterians have churches in every major city. In fact, studies showed the number of Korean Christian congregations by century's end at between 2,000 and 2,500, and growing. Often these congregations began meeting in other churches during off hours. Once a critical mass of like-minded Koreans was gathered, they built their own structure (but not until it was absolutely necessary, in order to save time and money).

Of course, all these changes in such a short period of time brought a backlash from some elements of American society. Early impressions of Buddhism (the beat generation), Hinduism (the Hare Krishnas, a sect of Hinduism devoted to the god Krishna), and Islam (the Nation of Islam, then Middle Eastern terrorists) gave each of these traditions difficult hurdles to overcome. Common racial profiling, meanwhile, affected the American experience for Latin American and Asian Christians. Clearly, the "nativism" that marked American life in antebellum America was not dead. But neither were the Puritans' dreams of religious freedom and economic prosperity, lived out now by America's new immigrant groups.

1. D. T. SUZUKI, "WHAT IS ZEN?" (1959)

CHOGYAM TRUNGPA, *MEDITATION IN ACTION* (1969)

While to many Americans in the 1960s Buddhism was a new player on the religion scene, it is in fact a very ancient religion, older even than Christianity, which most Americans claimed as their faith. For years many in intellectual communities across America knew something of its beliefs and practices, but the average person not only never knew a Buddhist, they didn't even know someone who knew a Buddhist.

Two individuals stand out as Buddhist "missionaries" to the United States. Daisetz Teiraro Suzuki was trained in a Japanese monastery but never went on to become a monk. Instead, he moved to the United States in 1897 at the age of twenty-seven and worked in publishing for over a decade. Returning to Japan, he married a Theosophist, with whom he founded an English-language journal about Buddhism. He came back to the United States in the 1950s and founded the Cambridge Buddhist Association in Massachusetts, where he influenced many intellectuals over the coming decade to incorporate Zen practices into their lives. Chogyam Trungpa, meanwhile, was representative of Tibetan Buddhism. Having studied with several masters in Tibet before its takeover by the Chinese, he went on to study philosophy and religion in England and moved to the United States in 1970. Founding the Naropa Institute in Colorado, he became the leading voice in America for Buddhist contemplative wisdom through meditation.

WHAT IS ZEN?

(1) Zen discipline consists in attaining enlightenment (or *satori*, in Japanese).

(2) *Satori* finds a meaning hitherto hidden in our daily concrete particular experiences, such as eating, drinking, or business of all kinds.

(3) The meaning thus revealed is not something added from the outside. It is in being itself, in becoming itself, in living itself. This is called, in Japanese, a life of *kono-mama* or *sono-mama*. *Kono-* or *sono-mama* means the "isness" of a thing, Reality in its isness.

(4) Some may say, "There cannot be any meaning in mere isness." But this is not the view held by Zen, for according to it, isness is the meaning. When I see into it I see it as clearly as I see myself reflected in a mirror.

(5) This is what made Hō Koji (P'ang Chü-shih), a lay disciple of the eight century, declare:

How wondrous this, how mysterious!

I carry fuel, I draw water.

The fuel-carrying or the water-drawing itself, apart from its utilitarianism, is full of meaning; hence its "wonder," its "mystery."

(6) Zen does not, therefore, indulge in abstraction or in conceptualization. In its verbalism it may sometimes appear that Zen does this a great deal. But this is an error most commonly entertained by those who do not at all know Zen.

(7) *Satori* is emancipation, moral, spiritual, as well as intellectual. When I am in my isness, thoroughly purged of all intellectual sediments, I have my freedom in its primary sense.

(8) When the mind, now abiding in its isness—which, to use Zen verbalism, is not isness—and thus free from intellectual complexities and moralistic attachments of every description, surveys the world of the senses in all its multiplicities, it discovers in it all sorts of values hitherto hidden from sight. Here opens to the artist a world full of wonders and miracles.

(9) The artist's world is one of free creation, and this can come only from intuitions directly and immediately rising from the isness of things, unhampered by senses and intellect. He creates forms and sounds out of formlessness and soundlessness. To this extent, the artist's world coincides with that of Zen.

(10) What differentiates Zen from the arts is this: While the artists have to resort to the canvas and brush or mechanical instruments or some other mediums to express themselves, Zen has no need of things external, except "the body" in which the Zen-man is so to speak embodied. From the absolute point of view this is not quite correct; I say it only in concession to the worldly way of saying things. What Zen does is to delineate itself on the infinite canvas of time and space the way flying wild geese cast their shadow on the water below without any idea of doing so, while the water reflects the geese just as naturally and unintentionally.

(11) The Zen-man is an artist to the extent that, as the sculptor chisels out a great figure deeply buried in a mass of inert matter, the Zen-man transforms his own life into a work of creation, which exists, as Christians might say, in the mind of God.

MEDITATION IN ACTION

Prajna. Wisdom. Perhaps the English word has a slightly different sense. But the word used in Tibetan, *sherab*, has a precise meaning: *she* means knowledge, knowing, and *rab* means ultimate—so primary or first knowledge, the higher knowledge. So sherab is not specific knowledge in any technical or educational sense of knowing the theology of Buddhism, or knowing how to do certain things, or knowing the metaphysical aspect of the teaching. Here knowledge means knowing the situation, *knowingness* rather than actual knowledge. It is knowledge without a self, without the self-centered consciousness that one is knowing—which is connected with ego. So this knowledge—prajna or sherab—is broad and far-seeing, though at the same time it is tremendously penetrating and exact, and it comes into every aspect of our life. It therefore plays a very important part in our development, as does upaya, method, which is the skillful means for dealing with situations in the right way. These two qualities, in fact, are sometimes compared to the two wings of a bird. Upaya is also described in the scriptures as being like a hand, which is skillful, and prajna as being axlike, because it is sharp and penetrating. Without the ax it would be impossible to cut wood: one would simply hurt one's hand. So one may have the skillful means without being able to put it into effect. But if there is also prajna, which is like an eye, or like light, then one is able to act properly and skillfully. Otherwise the skillful means might become foolish, for only knowledge makes one wise. In fact upaya by itself could make the greatest of fools, because everything would still be based on ego. One might see the situation up to a point and be partially able to deal with it, but one would not see it with clarity and without being affected by past and future, and one would miss the immediate nowness of the situation.

But perhaps we should examine how to develop this knowingness, or sherab, before we go into any further details. Now, there are three methods which are necessary for the cultivation of sherab, and these are known in Tibetan as töpa, sampa, and gompa. Töpa means to study the subject, sampa means to contemplate it, and gompa means to meditate and develop samadhi through it. So first töpa—study—which is generally associated with technical knowledge and the understanding of the scriptures and so on. But true knowledge goes much further than that, as we have already seen. And the first requirement for töpa is to develop a kind of bravery, to become a great warrior. We have mentioned this concept before, but perhaps it would be as well to go into it in more detail. Now, when the true warrior goes into battle he does not concern himself with his past and with recollections of his former greatness and strength, nor is he concerned with the consequences for the future and with thoughts of victory or defeat, or pain and death. The greatest warrior knows himself and has great confidence in himself. He is simply conscious of his opponent. He is quite open and fully aware of the situation, without thinking in terms of good and bad.

What makes him a great warrior is that he has no opinions; he is simply aware. Whereas his opponents, being emotionally involved in the situation, would not be able to face him, because he is acting truly and sailing through their fear and is able to attack the enemy with effect. Therefore töpa, study and understanding, demands the quality of a great warrior. One should try to develop theoretical knowledge without being concerned with the past or the future. At first one's theories may be inspired by reading books, so we do not altogether dismiss learning and studying, which are very important and can provide a source of inspiration. But books can also become merely a means to escape from reality; they can provide an excuse for not really making an effort to examine things in detail for oneself. Reading can be rather like eating food. Up to a point one eats from physical necessity, but beyond that one is doing it for pleasure, because one likes the taste of food, or possibly just to fill up time: it is either breakfast time or lunch time or tea time or time for dinner. In the development of sherab it is clear that we do not read merely to accumulate information. We should read with great openness without making judgments, and just try to receive. . . .

This is the first stage of töpa, where one develops theory. And it often happens at a certain point that this theory appears almost in the guise of experience, so that one may feel one has reached a state of spiritual ecstasy or enlightenment. There is a great excitement and one almost feels one has seen Reality itself.

Of course this theoretical knowledge is very interesting. One can talk so much about it—there are a great many words involved—and there is great pleasure in telling other people all about it. . . .

But that is still theory. And from there we come to sampa, which is reflective meditation, or contemplating and pondering on the subject. Sampa is not meditating in the sense of developing mindfulness and so on, but meditating on the subject and digesting it properly. In other words what one has learned is not yet sufficiently developed to enable one to deal with the practical things of life. For example, one might be talking about one's great discovery when some catastrophe occurs; say, the milk boils over or something like that. It might be something quite ordinary, but it seems to be rather exciting and terrible in a way. And the transition, from discussing this subject to controlling the milk, is just too much. The one is so elevated and the other is so ordinary and mundane that somehow one finds it very difficult to put one's knowledge into effect on that level. The contrast is too great and, as a result, one becomes upset, suddenly switches off and returns to the ordinary level of ego. So in this kind of situation there is a big gap between the two things, and we have to learn to deal with this and somehow make the connection with everyday life, and to identify our activities with what we have learned in the way of wisdom and theoretical knowledge. Of course our theory is something far beyond just ordinary theory, which one might have worked out mathematically to produce a feasible proposition. One is involved and there is great feeling in it. Nevertheless this is only theory, and for that very reason one finds it difficult to put it into effect. It seems true, it seems to convey something, when you only think on that subject, but it tends to remain static. So sampa, reflective meditation, is necessary because one needs to calm down after the initial excitement of discovery and one has to find a way of relating one's newfound knowledge to oneself on a practical level.

. . .

Finally we come to gompa, meditation. First we had theory, then contemplation, and now meditation in the sense of samadhi. The first stage of gompa is to ask oneself, "Who am I?" Though this is not really a question. In fact it is a statement, because "Who am I?" contains the answer. The thing is not to start from "I" and then want to achieve something, but to start directly with the subject. In other words one starts the real meditation without aiming for anything, without the thought, "I want to achieve." Since one does not know "Who am I?" one would not start from "I" at all, and one even begins to learn from beyond that point. What remains is simply to start on the subject, to start on what *is*, which is not really "I am." So one goes directly to that, directly to the "is." This may sound a bit vague and mysterious, because these terms have been used so much and by so many people; we must try then to clarify this by relating it to ourselves. The first point is not to think in terms of "I," "I want to achieve." Since there is no one to do the achieving, and we haven't even grasped that yet, we should not try to prepare anything at all for the future.

There is a story in Tibet about a thief who was a great fool. He stole a large sack of barley one day and was very pleased with himself. He hung it up over his bed, suspended from the ceiling, because he thought it would be safest there from the rats and other animals. But one rat was very cunning and found a way to get to it. Meanwhile the thief was thinking, "Now, I'll sell this barley to somebody, perhaps my next-door neighbor, and get some silver coins for it. Then I could buy something else and then sell that at a profit. If I go on like this I'll soon be very rich, then I can get married and have a proper home. After that I could have a son. Yes, I shall have a son! Now what name shall I give him?" At that moment the moon had just risen and he saw the moonlight shining in through the window onto his bed. So he thought, "Ah, I shall call him Dawa" (which is the Tibetan word for moon). And at that very moment the rat had finished eating right through the rope from which the bag was hanging, and the bag dropped on the thief and killed him.

Similarly, since we haven't got a son and we don't even know "Who am I?," we should not explore the details of such fantasies. We should not start off by expecting any kind of reward. There should be no striving and no trying to achieve anything. One might then feel, "Since there is no fixed purpose and there is nothing to attain, wouldn't it be rather boring? Isn't it rather like just being nowhere?" Well, that is the whole point. Generally we do things because we want to achieve something; we never do anything without first thinking, "Because . . . " "I'm going for a holiday *because* I want to relax, I want a rest." "I am going to do such-and-such *because* I think it would be interesting." So every action, every step we take, is conditioned by ego. It is conditioned by the illusory concept of "I," which has not even been questioned. Everything is built around that and everything begins with "because." So that is the whole point. Meditating without any purpose may sound boring, but the fact is we haven't sufficient courage to go into it and just give it a try. Somehow we have to be courageous. Since one is interested and one wants to go further, the best thing would be to do it perfectly and not start with too many subjects, but start with one subject and really go into it thoroughly. It may not sound interesting, it may not be exciting all the time, but excitement is not the only thing to be gained, and one must develop patience. One must be willing to take a chance and in that sense make use of will power.

One has to go forward without fear of the unknown, and if one does go a little bit further, one finds it is possible to start without thinking "because," without thinking "I will achieve something," without just living in the future. One must not build fantasies around the future and just use that as one's impetus and source of encouragement, but one should try to get the real feeling of the present moment. That is to say that meditation can only be put into effect if it is not conditioned by any of our normal ways of dealing with situations. One must practice meditation directly without expectation or judgment and without thinking in terms of the future at all. Just leap into it. Jump into it without looking back.

2. MAHARISHI MAHESH YOGI, *TRANSCENDENTAL MEDITATION* (1963)

The 1960s saw the first full-scale exposure of the American public to Hinduism through mass media. Among the earliest examples was Maharishi Mahesh Yogi, who not only became "spiritual advisor to the stars" but also spoke to national audiences as the guest of Johnny Carson on The Tonight Show. *His influence on the Beatles, the defining rock group of the period, only further enhanced his role as the leading spokesman for Hinduism, even if his thoughts were truly but one branch—the meditative branch—of an ancient tradition.*

Maharishi Mahesh Yogi published his book Transcendental Meditation *(original title:* The Science of Being and the Art of Living*) in 1963. It was an immediate success in the United States and marked the origin of the TM program, considered by its followers to be the application of his "Vedic Science and Technology," which is based on the idea of improving society by improving individual consciousness. In 1970 both* Science *and* Scientific American *published articles dealing with some of his themes, and many believed the pieces validated aspects of Maharishi's theories of TM.*

In this excerpt from Transcendental Meditation, *Maharishi expands upon the reasons for and advantages of understanding the "art of living." The piece particularly emphasizes the importance of the individual to society, echoing oddly the post–World War II rhetoric of preachers like Billy Graham. It describes all aspects of human life as connected through "Being," an abstract state of understanding, and explains how individuals can realize their full potential "on all levels of life, physical, mental, and spiritual" through meditation on this universal connectivity.*

———— ∞ ————

"Art" implies a graceful and skillful method of accomplishment. The art of living any phase of life is to master that phase. The only way one can master any or all phases of life is by using latent potentialities and applied techniques.

The art of living enables a man to live full values of life, accomplish the maximum in the world, and at the same time, live a life of external freedom in God consciousness. The art of living is the art of letting the life stream flow in such a manner that every aspect of living is supplemented with intelligence, power, creativity, and the magnificence of the whole life. As the art of making a flower arrangement is to glorify every flower by the beauty and glory of every other flower, in a similar way the art of living is such that every aspect of life is supplemented by the glories of every other aspect. It is in this way that the transcendental aspect of life supplements the subjective and objective aspects of existence, so that the entire range of subjectivity and objectivity enjoys the absolute strength, intelligence, bliss, and creativity of the eternal Being.

When the power of the absolute supplements all aspects of subjectivity, the ego is full, the intellect is profound, sharp, and one-pointed, the mind is concentrated and powerful, thought force is great, and the senses are fully alert. When the ego, intellect, mind, and senses are fully supplemented by the absolute Being, experience is more profound, activity is powerful, and, at the same tune, the intellect, ego, mind, and senses are useful in all spheres of life, in all spheres of action and experience in the individual life in society and in the entire cosmos.

We have seen earlier that it is the sap which is the basis of the root and the entire tree. In this example, we find the root lying between the transcendental area of the tree and the outer tree. Likewise, the subjective aspect of life, the inner man (ego, mind, and senses) lies between the transcendental Being (the basis of our life) and the outer gross field of objective existence. The art of living demands proper and effective existence. The art of living demands the proper and effective intake of the Being in the subjective aspect of life, and Its infusion in all the fields of objective existence; the art of living requires that the mind draw the power of the Being and pass it on to the body and surroundings.

For a tree to grow to maturity, efficiency is demanded on the part of the root so that the nourishment from the surrounding area is properly absorbed by the root and given out to all the different aspects of the outer tree. This provides the key to the art of living.

The inner man should be such that it absorbs the value of the transcendental absolute state of life and passes it on to the outer gross relative state of life, enriching each aspect and supplementing it with the power of the absolute Being. This technique amounts to thinking in such a way that each individual thought enjoys the strength of cosmic intelligence of the absolute Being. Every action enjoys the power of the absolute unlimited Being, as the experience is supplemented by the bliss of the transcendental Being. The individual creative energy is supplemented by the unlimited, unbounded creative energy of the cosmic Being.

Thus we conclude that the art of living demands that the mind be in constant communion with the absolute state of life, so that whatever the mind is thinking, in whatever action of experience it is engaged, it is never away from the influence of the eternal absolute Being.

The art of life demands that the mind cultivate within itself the eternal state of absolute Being. For without constant and continuous infusion of the absolute into the very nature of the mind, the mind can never be all-comprehensive and all-powerful.

If a businessman does not invest all his wealth in his business, he does not gain the most profit possible. If the individual mind does not bring out the bliss of the absolute Being and experience things in the outside relative field of life while remaining saturated with that bliss, then nothing that is experienced will bring contentment. The mind will always be searching for greater happiness. But if the mind is saturated with the bliss of absolute Being, it derives joy from the variety of multiple creation and remains well established in contentment. Only then does the mind fully enjoy variety.

If it is left without the basis of the bliss of unity within, the mind is as though it were being tossed about like a football, from one point to the other, having no stable status of its own. That is why, in order that the experiences in life give the maximum charm and the world of variety prove itself to be of real value, it is necessary that the bliss of the absolute Being remain infused into the very nature of the mind.

The variety of the world can be enjoyed only when the mind has gained an unshakable status in the bliss of the absolute Being. Otherwise, the very purpose of the multiplicity of joyful, glorious variety of creation is undermined. If experience is only one-sided, if the mind experiences only the variety of relative, gross fields of life, then it is clear that the values of the relative life are not being supplemented by the absolute state of life. Such a one-sided life is due only to the lack of knowledge of the art of living.

Thus, the art of living demands that, for life to be lived in all its values, the subjective aspect of life be infused with the power of the Being. Then only will it be possible to make use of one's full potential for glorification of all aspects of life.

In order to make this clear, we shall first analyze what man's full potential is and then see how the power of Being can be infused on the various different levels of life so that one may take advantage of all aspects of the art of living.

MAN'S FULL POTENTIAL

We have seen that the nervous system of man is the most highly developed nervous system in creation. With such a highly developed nervous system the full potential of man indicates that man should be able to live the supreme state of life—at the least, a life without suffering and, at its best, a life of absolute bliss in God consciousness.

The full potential of man means that—on all levels of life, physical, mental, and spiritual—one should live to one's maximum capacity.

The full potential of man on the physical plane means the ability to have a healthy body in which all the limbs, the senses, and the nervous system are functioning normally and in good coordination with each other. The full potential on the mental plane of life means the ability of man to make use of his full mental capacity. The full potential on the spiritual plane of life means man's ability to live the value of the spiritual Being in all fields of daily life.

Man's full potential on the physical, mental, and spiritual levels of existence also implies that there should be a perfect coordination between these planes of life. The physical plane of life should be in perfect coordination with the mental plane; the mental plane should be in perfect coordination with the spiritual plane.

The full potential means a perfect coordination of the divine with the physical levels of man's life, the full functioning capacity of the mind, perfect health, and the value of divine life being infused in the day-to-day material life of man.

Man generally does not use his full mind. The conscious mind is only an insignificant part of the total mind that a man possesses, and, as long as man functions on only the ordinary level of conscious mind, he is not using his full mental potential. The conscious capacity of man should be the normal functioning capacity of the full mental potential.

Over and above these considerations, the use of full potential should enable a man to think, speak, and act in such a manner that every thought, word, and action not only accomplishes the maximum in material life, but also becomes a means of remaining in tune with almighty God, thereby bringing the blessing of the almighty on all levels of human life.

We have seen that the human mind has the ability of taking within its consciousness the field of the transcendental absolute divine Being. This shows that the whole range of creation and the field of the ultimate creator, the almighty universal Being, lies within the scope of human life. The full potential of man in this sequence is the full cosmic life open to each individual. The full potential of man is the unlimited potential of the universal Being.

A normal human life means living a life of divine consciousness; a normal human mind is one that should function on human levels but should also have the status of universal cosmic mind.

Cosmic consciousness should not be considered as something far beyond the reach of normal man. The state of cosmic consciousness should be the state of normal human consciousness. Any state below cosmic consciousness can only be taken to be subnormal human consciousness. The human mind should be a cosmically conscious mind. The potential of human life should mean the potential of the almighty divine on earth. The normal life of man should be a God-realized life, in divine consciousness, a fruitful life in universal Being.

The full potential of man is such that it can bring to every man this blessed and graceful state of divine life in a natural and easy manner with no struggle and maintain it in all phases of daily life.

A direct and simple technique for beginning to express one's full potential in a natural way is the practice of transcendental deep meditation, which unfolds all the divine in man and brings human consciousness to the high pedestal of God consciousness. It brings the life to a state of eternal freedom, supplementing it with unlimited creative energy and harmonizing the abstract absolute values of divine Being with the concrete physical material values of day-to-day human life.

HOW TO USE ONE'S FULL POTENTIAL

In "Individual and Cosmic Life" we have seen that "the boundaries of individual life are not restricted to the boundaries of the body, and not even to those of one's family or one's home; they extend far beyond that sphere to the limitless horizons of cosmic life."

And in "Man's Full Potential," we have seen that man's full potential means that "man should be able to live the supreme state of life—at the least a life without suffering, and at best a life of absolute bliss in God consciousness."

In view of this, the art of using one's full potential means that the wave of individual life should not be confined only to the surface value of the ocean of eternal absolute Being, but should also extend to the depths of the unbounded ocean of Being, so that all the potentialities are unfolded, and life becomes strong and powerful.

When one's full potential is unfolded, then every phase of life supplements every other phase, strengthens it and makes life more substantial, more glorified, more useful, and more worthwhile on all levels for oneself and for others. A small wave on the surface of the ocean would not be a very powerful wave, but the same wave becomes powerful when it connects with deeper levels of water. So, the art of improving and strengthening a wave is to enable it to contact directly deeper levels of water.

If the wave is to rise high to accomplish more and be more powerful, then the act of rising high should be supplemented by drawing in more water at the base. When the wave is able to supplement the act of rising high by drawing in more water at its base, it is possible for it to rise up in an integrated and powerful manner. Otherwise, if it failed to draw more water at its base while rising higher, it would become weak at the crest, and even a slight breeze could disintegrate it.

The art of using one's full potential necessitates that the surface value of relative life be supplemented by the power which lies at the depth of the ocean of absolute Being. It means that the relative life should be supplemented with the absolute state of life. The art of using one's full potential is the art of deepening the stream of individual life to the maximum depth possible by taking the wave of relative experience and existence to the limit of absolute experience and existence. The art of using one's full potential lies basically in supplementing the wave of individual life with the power of the ocean of Being.

The art of living is the ability to supplement and reinforce individual life with the power of the absolute cosmic Being. It is within the reach of every individual to fathom the great depth of the absolute Being, thereby supplementing and reinforcing the individual life with the life of eternal cosmic Being.

Every wave on the sea has the opportunity to embrace within itself as great an amount of water at its base as it likes. The whole ocean could be drawn in a single wave; it is possible that one wave could draw upon the strength of the entire ocean and rise with infinite power.

Similarly, every individual has an opportunity available to gain for himself the strength of the unlimited, eternal, absolute Being and thus, be powerful to the maximum extent possible.

When there is a possibility for a wave to enjoy the limitless strength of the ocean, does it not amount to a sheer waste to be tossed about by the breeze in a weak and powerless manner? When there is open to every man the opportunity of gaining unlimited power, energy, existence, intelligence, peace, and happiness, then is it not a waste of life to remain in a limited, weak, and powerless state?

The art of using one's full potential demands that life as a whole should have a solid basis for itself. For without a strong basis, life will be just as unstable as a building without a strong foundation. In the first place, the building cannot be properly built and will not be stable. Thus, a solid foundation for life is the first requisite for an all-comprehensive and powerful life.

Life in its relative stages is ever-changing. The ever-changing phases of life leave no stable status of life. Therefore, in order to be able to use one's full potential, the first step will be to infuse stability into the ever-changing phases of relative life.

Stability belongs to the absolute status. Stability is attributed to that factor of life which never changes, and that which never changes is the truth of life, the ultimate reality, the eternal Being. Life, then, in its absolute state alone is stable. And when stability is gained by the mind and retained through all the mind's activity of experience and action, the whole field of activity is supplemented by the power of the never-changing absolute Being. This forms the basic platform for using one's full potential; it reinforces and enriches the ever-unstable phases of relative existence.

If the basis of life is weak, if the life is not based on the eternal and stable status of absolute Being, then apart from being ever-changing in its character, it will always remain weak.

The art of using one's full potential is the same as the art of shooting an arrow ahead; one begins by pulling the arrow back on the bow. As the arrow is drawn back, it gains the maximum strength for going forward. A useless shot will result if the arrow is not first pulled back.

The art of using one's full potential demands bringing the mind back to the field of absolute Being before it is brought out to face the gross aspect of the relative fields of life. Fortunately, this art of living has been developed to bring most effective results in life and all its glory has been centered in a technique of bringing the mind to the field of the Being in a simple and effective way.

The ever-changing phase of relative existence must remain ever-changing all the time. This ever-changing phase cannot be transformed into a never-changing status. This is relative life. But the subject within, the inner man, could gain a simultaneous status in the eternal, absolute Being. For, while it is maintaining its status in the ever-changing phenomenal phases of life, it is not devoid of its status in the absolute, never-changing Being.

This is how the never-changing absolute might supplement the ever-changing phenomenal phases of life, and these two, together, go to make life complete.

This absolute stable factor in life, the Being of the transcendent, is always out of the field of the ever-changing phenomenal creation and experience.

The art of using one's full potential is in harmonizing the absolute and the relative which is easily accomplished through the simple system of transcendental deep meditation.

A man has two sides, left and right, and the art of living demands that the left and right sides both be used to full advantage. If only the left side is used and the right remains unused, the latter might become immobile and the left side would be over-strained in action. The right side too, will be over-strained, being in a state of inactivity. Therefore, in order to live all values of life, it is necessary that we should have the left and right working together in good coordination, working together for the same cause.

The absolute and the relative are the two phases of one's existence. It is the art of living that brings these two together, enabling all values of life to be lived. Otherwise, on the one hand, the absolute remains transcendental, out of the field of activity, out of sight, and as if of no practical value. On the other hand, it leaves the field of the relative life to be overstrained, due to constant activity, and the relative life remains weak in the unstable, ever-changing field.

That is why the art of living brings together the never-active absolute of transcendental nature with the ever-changing field of relative existence and links them together. Both are brought together on the level of the mind, just as in the life of the tree the surrounding area of the nourishment and the outer sphere of the tree are brought together by the instrumentality of the root, which draws nourishment from one side and supplies it to the other.

The art of using one's full potential is to live a life supplemented by the power of the unlimited eternal absolute Being. It is easy to learn this art because, as we have seen in "Transcendental Deep Meditation," when the mind proceeds on the experience of subtler states of thought and experiences the transcendental Being, the full potentiality of the mind is unfolded, and one naturally begins to make use of one's full mental potential in one's daily activities. By this process one also begins to make full use of one's potential in the fields of one's senses, body, and surroundings. . . .

Thus we find it is easy to learn the art of using one's full potential. It is easy to live a life of full values of power, intelligence, creativity, peace, and bliss of the eternal absolute Being through the regular practice of the simple system of transcendental deep meditation.

3. RICHARD RODRIGUEZ, "THE 'MINORITY STUDENT'" (1982)

Richard Rodriguez came from a Mexican American Catholic family and was raised in the United States. An editor for the Pacific News Service, a contributing editor for Harper's, and a winner of the Peabody Award for his essays on The NewsHour with Jim Lehrer, *he received critical acclaim for his autobiography* The Hunger of Memory: The Education of Richard Rodriguez, *published in 1982. The book explores his feelings of alienation from his Mexican culture and heritage caused by success in American society, what he gained and lost in his journey from being a "socially disadvantaged child" to a major public figure in the United States.*

In this excerpt from The Hunger of Memory, *Rodriguez discusses how his religious upbringing affected his perception of American life: "I would remain a Catholic, but a Catholic defined by a non-Catholic world." He presents a picture of a world unfamiliar to many Americans, in which religion truly defines and shapes the events of every day. And he describes how the "gringo" culture began to infiltrate his own, first through the Church and then through all other aspects of his life.*

Rodriguez's deft description of the ethnic practice of Catholicism in the United States is a reminder of the powerful influence of religious traditions carried here by immigrant populations. The first generation often virtually transplants the beliefs and practices in a new environment. The second generation, however, is often trapped be-tween two worlds—one familiar and familial, the other exotic and enticing. Finding ways to remain connected to their ethnic and religious heritage in a rapidly changing American society is a task immigrants face daily, for the rest of their lives.

---◌◎◌---

The steps of the church defined the eternal square where children played and adults talked after dinner. He remembers the way the church building was at the center of town life. She remembers the way one could hear the bell throughout the day, telling time. And the way the town completely closed down for certain feastdays. He remembers that the church spire was the first thing he'd see walking back into town. Both my parents have tried to describe something of what it was like for them to have grown up Catholic in small Mexican towns. They remember towns where everyone was a Catholic.

With their move to America, my mother and father left behind that Mexican Church to find themselves (she praying in whispered Spanish) in an Irish-American parish. In a way, they found themselves at ease in such a church. My parents had much in common with the Irish-born priests and nuns. Like my parents, the priests remembered what it was like to have been Catholic in villages and cities where everyone else was a Catholic. In their American classrooms, the nuns worked very hard to approximate that other place, that earlier kind of religious experience. For a time they succeeded. For a time I too enjoyed a Catholicism something like that enjoyed a generation before me by my parents.

I grew up a Catholic at home and at school, in private and in public. My mother and father were deeply pious *católicos*; all my relatives were Catholics. At home, there were holy pictures on a wall of nearly every room, and a crucifix hung over my bed. My first twelve years as a student were spent in Catholic schools where I could look up to the front of the room and see a crucifix hanging over the clock.

When I was a boy, anyone not a Catholic was defined by that fact and the term *non-Catholic*. The expression suggests the parochialism of the Catholicism in which I was raised. In those years I could have told you the names of persons in public life who were Catholics. I knew that Ed Sullivan was a Catholic. And Mrs. Bob Hope. And Senator John F. Kennedy. As the neighborhood newspaper boy, I knew all the names on my route. As a Catholic, I noted which open doors, which front room windows disclosed a crucifix. At quarter to eight Sunday mornings, I saw the O'Briens and the Van Hoyts walking down the empty sidewalk past our house and I knew. Catholics were mysteriously lucky, 'chosen' by God to be nurtured a special way. Non-Catholics had souls too, of course, and somehow could get to heaven. But on Sundays they got all dressed up only to go to a church where there was no incense, no sacred body and blood, and no confessional box. Or else they slept late and didn't go to church at all. For non-Catholics, it seemed there was all white and no yolk.

In twelve years of Catholic schooling, I learned, in fact, very little about the beliefs of non-Catholics, though the little I learned was conveyed by my teachers without hostility and with fair accuracy. All that I knew about Protestants was that they differed from Catholics. But what precisely distinguished a Baptist from a Methodist from an Episcopalian I could not have said. I surmised the clearest notion of Protestant theology from discussions of the Reformation. At that, Protestantism emerged only as deviance from Catholic practice and thought. Judaism was different. Before the Christian era Judaism was *my* religion, the nuns said. ('We are all Jews because of Christ.') But what happened to Judaism after Christ's death to the time the modern state of Israel was founded, I could not have said. Nor did I know a thing about Hinduism or Buddhism or Islam. I knew nothing about modern secular ideologies. In civics class a great deal was said about oppressive Soviet policies; but at no time did I hear classical Marxism explained. In church, at the close of mass, the congregation prayed for 'the conversion of Russia.'

It is not enough to say that I grew up a ghetto Catholic. As a Catholic schoolboy, I was educated a middle-class American. Even while grammar school nuns reminded me of my spiritual separateness from non-Catholics, they provided excellent *public* schooling. A school day began with prayer—the Morning Offering. Then there was the Pledge of Allegiance to the American flag. Religion class followed immediately. But afterward, for the rest of the day, I was taught well those skills of numbers and words crucial to my Americanization. Soon I became as Americanized as my classmates—most of whom were two or three generations removed from their immigrant ancestors, and all of whom were children of middle-class parents.

When we were eleven years old, the nuns would warn us about the dangers of mixed marriage (between a Catholic and a non-Catholic). And we heard a priest say that it was a mortal sin to read newspaper accounts of a Billy Graham sermon. But the ghetto Catholic Church, so defensive, so fearful of contact with non-Catholics, was already outdated when I entered the classroom. My classmates and I were destined to live in a world very different from that which the nuns remembered in Ireland or my parents remembered in Mexico. We were destined to live on unhallowed ground, beyond the gated city of God.

I was in high school when Kennedy's picture went up on the wall. And I remember feeling that he was 'one of us.' His election to the presidency, however, did not surprise me as it did my father. Nor was I encouraged by it. I did not take it as evidence that Catholics could, after all, participate fully in American public life. (I assumed that to be true.) When I was a senior in high school, consequently, I did not hesitate to apply to secular colleges.

It was to be in college, at Stanford, that my religious faith would seem to me suddenly pared. I would remain a Catholic, but a Catholic defined by a non-Catholic world. This is how I think of myself now. I remember my early Catholic schooling and recall an experience of religion very different from anything I have known since. Never since have I felt so much at home in the Church, so easy at mass. My grammar school years especially were the years when the great Church doors opened to enclose me, filling my day as I was certain the Church filled all time. Living in a community of shared faith, I enjoyed much more than mere social reinforcement of religious belief. Experienced continuously in public and private, Catholicism shaped my whole day. It framed my experience of eating and sleeping and washing; it named the season and the hour.

The sky was full then and the coming of spring was a religious event. I would awaken to the sound of garage doors creaking open and know without thinking that it was Friday and that my father was on his way to six-thirty mass. I saw, without bothering to notice, statues at home and at school of the Virgin and of Christ. I would write at the top of my arithmetic or history homework the initials Jesus, Mary, and Joseph. (All my homework was thus dedicated.) I felt the air was different, somehow still and more silent on Sundays and high feastdays. I felt lightened, transparent as sky, after confessing my sins to a priest. Schooldays were routinely divided by prayers said with classmates. I would not have forgotten to say grace before eating. And I would not have turned off the light next to my bed or fallen asleep without praying to God.

[I]

The institution of the Church stood an extraordinarily physical presence in my world. One block from the house was Sacred Heart Church. In the opposite direction, another block away, was Sacred Heart Grammar School, run by the Sisters of Mercy. And from our backyard, I could see Mercy Hospital, Sacramento's only Catholic hospital. All day I would hear the sirens of death. Well before I was a student myself, I would watch the Catholic school kids walk by the front of the house, dressed in gray and red uniforms. From the front lawn I could see people on the steps of the church, coming out, dressed in black after funerals, or standing, the ladies in bright-colored dresses in front of the church after a wedding. When I first went to stores on errands for my mother, I could be seen by the golden-red statue of Christ, where it hovered over the main door of the church.

I was *un católico* before I was a Catholic. That is, I acquired my earliest sense of the Church—and my membership in it—through my parents' Mexican Catholicism. It was in Spanish that I first learned to pray. I recited family prayers—not from any book. And in those years when we felt alienated from *los gringos*, my family went across town every week to the wooden church of Our Lady of Guadalupe, which was decorated with yellow Christmas tree lights all year long.

Very early, however, the *gringo* church in our neighborhood began to superimpose itself on our family life. The first English-speaking dinner guest at our house was a priest from Sacred Heart Church. I was about four years old at the time, so I retain only random details with which to remember the evening. But the visit was too important an event for me to forget. I remember how my mother dressed her four children in outfits it had taken her weeks to sew. I wore a white shirt and blue woolen shorts. (It was the first time I had been dressed up for a stranger.) I remember hearing the priest's English laughter. (It was the first time I had heard such sounds in the house.) I remember that my mother served a *gringo* meat loaf and that I was too nervous or shy to look up more than two or three times to study the priest's jiggling layers of face. (Smoothly, he made believe that there was conversation.) After dinner we all went to the front room where the priest took a small book from his jacket to recite some prayers, consecrating our house and our family. He left a large picture of a sad-eyed Christ, exposing his punctured heart. (A caption below records the date of his visit and the imprimatur of Francis Cardinal Spellman.) That picture survives. Hanging prominently over the radio or, later, the television set in the front room, it has retained a position of prominence in all the houses my parents have lived in since. It has been one of the few permanent fixtures in the environment of my life. Visitors to our house doubtlessly noticed it when they entered the door—saw it immediately as the sign we were Catholics. But I saw the picture too often to pay it much heed.

I saw a picture of the Sacred Heart in the grammar school classroom I entered two years after the priest's visit. The picture drew an important continuity between home and the classroom. When all else was different for me (as a scholarship boy) between the two worlds of my life, the Church provided an essential link. During my first months in school, I remember being struck by the fact that—although they worshipped in English—the nuns and my classmates shared my family's religion. The *gringos* were, in some way, like me, *católicos*. Gradually, however, with my assimilation in the schoolroom, I began to think of myself and my family as Catholics. The distinction blurred. At home and in class I heard about sin and Christ and Satan and the consoling presence of Mary the Virgin. It became one Catholic faith for me.

Only now do I trouble to notice what intricate differences separated home Catholicism from classroom Catholicism. In school, religious instruction stressed that man was a sinner. Influenced, I suspect, by a bleak melancholic strain in Irish Catholicism, the nuns portrayed God as a judge. I was carefully taught the demands He placed upon me. In the third grade I could distinguish between venial and mortal sin. I knew—and was terrified to know—that there was one unforgivable sin (against the Holy Ghost): the sin of despair. I knew the crucial distinction between perfect and imperfect contrition. I could distinguish sins of commission from sins of omission. And I learned how important it was to be in a state of grace at the moment of death.

Death. (How much nearer it seemed to the boy than it seems to me now.) Again and again the nuns would pull out the old stories of death-bed conversions; of Roman martyrdoms; of murdered African missionaries; of pious children dying of cancer to become tiny saints; of souls going immediately to heaven. We were taught how to baptize in case of emergency. I knew why some souls went to Limbo after the death of the body, and others went for a time to Purgatory, and why others went to heaven or hell—'forever and ever.' . . .

Sin remained, nevertheless. Confession was a regular part of my grammar school years. (One sought forgiveness through the ritual plea: 'Bless me, father, for I have sinned. . . .') Sin—the distance separating man from God—sin that burdened a sorrowful Christ; sin remained. ('I have disobeyed my parents fourteen times . . . I have lied eight times . . . I am heartily sorry for having offended Thee. . . .') God the Father judged. But Christ the Son had interceded. I was forgiven each time I sought forgiveness. The priest murmured Latin words of forgiveness in the confessional box. And I would leave the dark.

In contrast to the Catholicism of school, the Mexican Catholicism of home was less concerned with man the sinner than with man the supplicant. God the Father was not so much a stern judge as One with the power to change our lives. My family turned to God not in guilt so much as in need. We prayed for favors and at desperate times. I prayed for help in finding a quarter I had lost on my way home. I prayed with my family at times of illness and when my father was temporarily out of a job. And when there was death in the family, we prayed.

I remember my family's religion, and I hear the whispering voices of women. For although men in my family went to church, women prayed most audibly. Whether by man or woman, however, God the Father was rarely addressed directly. There were intermediaries to carry one's petition to Him. My mother had her group of Mexican and South American saints and near-saints (persons moving toward canonization). She favored a black Brazilian priest who, she claimed, was especially efficacious. Above all mediators was Mary, *Santa María*, the Mother. Whereas at school the primary mediator was Christ, at home that role was assumed by the Mexican Virgin, *Nuestra Señora de Guadalupe*, the focus of devotion and pride for Mexican Catholics. The Mexican Mary 'honored our people,' my mother would say. 'She could have appeared to anyone in the whole world, but she appeared to a Mexican.' Someone like us. And she appeared, I could see from her picture, as a young Indian maiden—dark just like me.

On her feastday in early December my family would go to the Mexican church for a predawn high mass. The celebration would begin in the cold dark with a blare of trumpets imitating the cries of a cock. The Virgin's wavering statue on the shoulders of men would lead a procession into the warm yellow church. Often an usher would roughly separate me from my parents and pull me into a line of young children. (My mother nodded calmly when I looked back.) Sometimes alone, sometimes with my brother and sisters, I would find myself near the altar amid two or three hundred children, many of them dressed like Mexican cowboys and cowgirls. Sitting on the floor it was easier to see the congregation than the altar. So, as the mass progressed, my eye would wander through the crowd. Invariably, my attention settled on old women—mysterious supplicants in black—bent deep, their hands clasped tight to hold steady the attention of the Mexican Virgin, who was pictured high over the altar, astride a black moon.

The *gringo* Catholic church, a block from our house, was a very different place. In the *gringo* church Mary's statue was relegated to a side altar, imaged there as a serene white lady who matter-of-factly squashed the Genesis serpent with her bare feet. (Very early I knew that I was supposed to believe that the shy Mexican Mary was the same as this European Mary triumphant.) In the *gringo* church the floors were made not of squeaky wood but of marble. And there was not the devotional clutter of so many pictures and statues and candle racks. 'It doesn't feel like a church,' my mother complained. But as it became our regular church, I grew to love its elegant simplicity: the formal march of its eight black pillars toward the altar; the Easter-egg-shaped sanctuary that arched high over the tabernacle; and the dim pink light suffused throughout on summer afternoons when I came in not to pray but to marvel at the cool calm.

4. ANDRÉS TAPIA, "VIVAN LOS EVANGELICOS!" (1991)

Andrés Tapia grew up in Lima, Peru and was interested in Peruvian culture and politics as well as race relations in the evangelical church. This article, published in Christianity Today in 1991, explores the effects of growing Latin American immigration on American culture, economy, politics, and, most important, religion—what some have referred to as "the browning of the church." This article particularly looks at the growing Latin American population in the evangelical community.

According to Tapia, the evangelical church is particularly appealing to Latino immigrants for a number of reasons—the emphasis on a personal relationship with God, the idea of intimacy at a divine level, and the opportunities for service, among others. The article also discusses how Hispanic immigrants have transformed traditional evangelical services from la iglesia fria (the "frigid" church) to la iglesia caliente (the "hot and spicy" church). Finally, the article discusses how the Catholic Church ran into problems retaining these lifelong Catholics once they were in the United States. Many evangelical and Pentecostal congregations made concerted efforts to appeal to these newcomers, to such a degree that many thousands have left behind their childhood Catholic Christianity for a form of Protestantism thoroughly shaped by the American experience.

On the two-mile stretch between the Montrose and Foster Avenue beaches on Chicago's lakefront—with pricey condominiums to the west and showcase architecture to the south—thousands of Hispanics celebrate Memorial Day. Salsa, Latin America's contemporary beat, shimmies out of huge Sony boom boxes; the staccato of Spanish punctuated with an occasional "hey man" fills the air; the smell of tortillas grilling on Weber Smokey Joes wafts across the park; and wiry soccer players elicit cheers from huge families that include parents, siblings, grandparents, aunts, uncles, first, second, and third cousins, and the boy next door.

As an Anglo couple whizzes by on their 10-speeds, the man comments, "I feel like I'm in another country!"

THE BROWNING OF AMERICA

According to the Census Bureau, by 2070 the 21 million Hispanics legally in the U.S. today (there are estimates of up to 10 million here illegally) will have multiplied to 57 million, making them the largest minority in the U.S. Currently, in some Texan cities, Hispanics make up the majority (in Laredo, 95 percent; in El Paso, 68 percent; and in Corpus Christi, 51 percent), and in some important regions they make up a substantial number of residents

(37 percent of Los Angeles County and 24 percent of California). In the seventies, the Hispanic population grew by 61 percent, says the U.S. Department of Commerce, while the entire U.S. population grew only 11.5 percent. In the eighties, the Hispanic growth rate was 34 percent.

This Latin explosion is spicing up nearly every sphere of mainstream North American life. Jews in Skokie, Illinois, are heard humming "La Bamba" as they leave movie theaters; yuppies dance away their stock-portfolio worries to Miami Sound Machine's "Conga Beat" in discos; teenagers go nuts over Latin heartthrob Esai Morales; and everyone, including Scandinavians in Willmar, Minnesota, are eating tacos.

But the changes go beyond *People* magazine editorial copy. Numbers bring power.

Political candidates court the Hispanic vote. Michael Dukakis gave part of his acceptance speech in Spanish, while candidate Bush, in an effort to reach out to the Hispanic vote that backfired, referred to his Mexican-American grandchildren as "my little brown ones." In Chicago, with their 20 percent of the population, Hispanics hold the balance of power between the polarized white and African-American communities, each representing 40 percent of the city.

Madison Avenue, in the meantime, courts the Hispanic dollar. With a purchasing power of $130 billion, Hispanics are getting the attention of companies such as Procter & Gamble, which spent $30 million in 1990 advertising to Hispanics. P&G, Anheuser-Busch, Campbell's, and myriad other companies spent over $628 million last year targeting Hispanics (sometimes in tortured translations) on any of the two national Hispanic TV networks, 145 Spanish-language magazines, 30 bilingual or English publications, or 450 Spanish radio stations.

The numbers also bring fear.

The Immigration Reform and Control Act passed four years ago granting amnesty to certain illegal aliens has also made it a crime to hire knowingly those who do not qualify for amnesty, making some employers hesitant to hire anyone of Hispanic descent. Former U.S. Sen. S. I. Hayakawa of California, founder of the English Only movement, is so concerned with Hispanic growth that he wants English to be declared the United States' official language. And once a month, frightened white southern Californians hold a Light Up the Border rally by shining their pickups' headlights across the Mexican-U.S. border to help nab illegals.

THE BROWNING OF THE CHURCH

In addition to being the fastest-growing ethnic group in the U.S., Hispanics are also the fastest-growing segment of the Protestant church. According to various polls, more than 20 percent of Hispanics are Protestant—an astounding figure given the virtual assimilation of Catholicism into Hispanic culture. In the past two decades, the growth has occurred at a dizzying rate. According to studies conducted in part by Clifton Holland, executive director of In-Depth Evangelism Association, the number of Hispanic Protestant congregations in Southern California jumped from 320 in 1970 to 1,022 in 1986 to 1,450 in 1990.

Factors contributing to the surge are the influx of legal and illegal immigration, the highest birth rate among all ethnic groups, and massive defections from the Catholic church. It is in the reasons for the defections that the story of Hispanics and the evangelical church lies.

Defections from the Catholic church in the U.S. to Protestant denominations are occurring at a pace of 60,000 a year, or 1 million in 15 years. This is according to a report presented in 1987 by Allan Figueroa Deck, a Catholic theologian and specialist in Hispanic studies, to the National Conference of Catholic Bishops. Sociologist of religion Father Andrew Greeley refers to this exodus as an "ecclesiastical failure of unprecedented proportions."

Deck and others point to studies demonstrating that Hispanics will constitute the majority of Catholic faithful in the United States by the year 2000. However, as Roberto González and Michael LaVelle observed in *The Hispanic Catholic in the U.S.*, fewer than 23 percent of Hispanic Catholics are practicing. This has Catholic leaders worried. As Deck told the nation's Catholic bishops, "If we miss this historic moment, the window of opportunity may close on us for many centuries to come."

In fact, the Vatican is worried. In the spring of 1987, Pope John Paul II made his second visit to the U.S. His stops: Miami, San Antonio, Los Angeles—three cities with significant Hispanic populations.

As in all major demographic changes, both push and pull factors are at work in the exodus from a church that in this century has traditionally served the nation's immigrants. These factors can be summarized as intimacy, opportunity, and expression.

INTIMACY

The emphases at evangelical churches on a personal relationship with God and on the fellowship of believers are an invitation for intimacy at a divine and human level.

Jesse Miranda, president and founder of AHET (a research institute in Pasadena, California, dedicated to examining issues affecting Hispanics in the U.S. church) and trustee of Fuller Theological Seminary, explains that the need for intimacy among Hispanics is especially acute. Not only is Latin culture relationship-oriented, but as with any recent immigrant group, Hispanics are in a state of uncertainty and flux. "The upheaval of immigration creates a need for familiarity and intimacy." The evangelical focus on small groups and accessibility to God meets this need.

In addition, says Miranda, "the Catholic church has neglected Hispanics." Catholic officials concur by saying that the church has driven away some minorities through apathy and insensitivity. Meanwhile, evangelicals are busy knocking on doors, presenting their message, and inviting people to church. Allan Deck writes in his book *The Second Wave: Hispanic Ministry and the Evangelization of Cultures*: "A mature and creative response to the Hispanic presence requires a great deal of energy. Frankly, there are some signs that the energy is not there [in the Catholic church]. The vigorous and often effective outreach of evangelical Protestant groups to Hispanics compared to the sometimes lackluster outreach of Catholic parishes and schools to the same group is a case in point."

H. O. Espinoza, founder and president of Promesa, a parachurch organization dedicated to training second-generation Hispanics to serve in the church and integrate into U.S. society, points to another reason Hispanics feel less attached to the Catholic church: "The Latin American Catholic church, which was virtually left untouched by Vatican II, is very different from its U.S. counterpart. The result is that the U.S. Catholic church feels foreign to many Latin American immigrants."

Isaac Canales, who is currently pastoring an inner-city church while completing his doctorate in New Testament at Fuller's Center for Advanced Theological Research, adds, "By already being in a milieu of change—new neighborhood, new language, new jobs—and dealing with a lot of fear and trepidation, immigrants begin to question fundamental traditional religious values. Hence their openness to the evangelical church down the street." . . .

EXPRESSION

It is the difference between *la iglesia fria* (the frigid church) and *la iglesia caliente* (the hot and spicy church). While worship in most parishes is muted and private, gatherings in many Hispanic evangelical congregations rock and sway to loud and effusive music—expressions of the Latin spirit of *fiesta*. At Hope Christian Fellowship, a multiethnic Christian Reformed Church in Chicago's predominantly Puerto Rican Humboldt Park, the Afro-Latin beat of the conga accompanies both Spanish *coritos* and traditional North American hymns such as "Amazing Grace."

The freedom to pray and preach in a style true to their cultural background is also inviting to Hispanics. "While Anglos are afraid of emotion, for us it's a way of life," says Miranda. Sermons by Hispanics have a certain level of intensity that speaks to the Latin heart. Writes Alex Montoya in his book *Hispanic Ministry in North America*: "A typical Hispanic speaks with his soul not just with his mouth. Hands wave in the air, feet move back and forth, the eyes are aflame and penetrating, and there's an urgency in the tone of his voice. This is the way he speaks about everyday life. Can we imagine him accepting the truths about God with any less energy?"

Because of these factors—intimacy, opportunity, and expression—it is no wonder that the churches with the greatest Hispanic growth are the Pentecostal churches, the Southern Baptist Convention, and the American Baptist churches. Hispanic membership in the Southern Baptist Convention climbed 54 percent in the eighties while it climbed 35 percent in the Assemblies of God. Holland observes that if it weren't for the Hispanic explosion, the Assemblies would actually have, after accounting for demographics, a flat growth curve. Miranda says that nationally, 15 to 20 percent of all Hispanic evangelicals consider themselves Pentecostals, while the Latin America Mission found that 58 percent of all Latin Protestants in Florida's Dade County are Pentecostals.

AGGRESSIVE EVANGELISM

The message of what evangelicalism offers is spreading through aggressive evangelism within the U.S. and Latin America. According to Manny Ortiz, a professor in the practical theology department at Westminster Theological Seminary, many Latin immigrants are pre-evangelized either in Latin America, which is experiencing a Protestant explosion of its own, or in the charismatic renewal sectors of the Catholic church, which stimulate excitement in people for a living relationship with Jesus but often cannot nurture them further.

Canales sensitively, yet unabashedly, extends invitations to accept Jesus at funerals for gang members in his church near East Los Angeles. One time a whole gang came forward, made a circle around the coffin of their fallen comrade, and accepted Jesus.

Protestant evangelism, not surprisingly, is causing tensions between Catholics and evangelicals. Archbishop John L. May of St. Louis, Missouri, says Protestant groups have a deceptive plan for recruiting Hispanics that includes churches featuring Catholic art and music to draw Hispanics in to hear anti-Catholic teaching.

The Catholic church is trying to make parish life more Protestant in appearance. *The National Pastoral Plan for Hispanic Ministry*, published a few years ago, lays out a strategy to make parish life more intimate and inviting by increasing lay leadership and developing small groups. It also suggests emulating the more personal, emotional, and mystical style of the Pentecostals.

Canales remembers Pope John Paul II's mass at the Los Angeles Memorial Coliseum a few years ago. "It could've been a Billy Graham crusade. The mass included a popular liturgy, Protestant hymns such as 'How Great Thou Art,' and a focus on Jesus rather than on the Virgin of Guadalupe." And Saint Louis Catholic Church in Miami, Florida, which has 3,500 Hispanic parishioners, effectively uses evangelical programs such as James Kennedy's Evangelism Explosion.

But Catholic efforts have little chance of stemming the exodus. As Pablo Sedillo, coordinator of the pastoral plan for Hispanic ministry told the *Chicago Tribune*, "When dioceses meet to balance their budgets, one of the first things to get axed is the Hispanic Ministries office. This is a dangerous action. Their congregations become a prime prize for fundamentalists." . . .

LEARNING FROM EACH OTHER

The Hispanic influx is changing both the Hispanics coming in and the evangelical church as a whole. If partnership can be achieved, the church will end up much richer and stronger.

According to the leaders interviewed, each culture has something the other needs. The white church, long one that has served more with its head than its heart, has the potential to lose many of its inhibitions as it experiences the freer, more soulful styles of Hispanics. Hispanic culture, long fatalistic to the extent that even its language reflects a sense of powerlessness (for example: *"el avión me dejó,"* which translates as, "the plane left me," rather than, "I missed the plane"), can learn from the Anglo can-do attitude.

In the same vein, the focus on management in Anglo America can help Hispanics more efficiently serve their communities. And Anglos, who have come to run churches like Fortune 500 corporations, can imitate the Hispanic reliance on the spontaneous and the inspired leading of the Holy Spirit—perhaps even catching the spirit of *siesta* by focusing more on relationships than on productivity.

George Muñoz, a lay Catholic and partner at the prestigious Mayer, Brown, and Platt law firm in Chicago, describes another contribution Hispanics are making to U.S. society in general: "What made this country strong were the values of the Protestant ethic: deep religious faith, strong families, loyalty to the country, and a hardworking ethic. With the breakdown of the American family and the declining significance of religion among North Americans, it's no coincidence that the U.S. economy is not strong. Hispanics have what it takes to carry the banner of the American Dream into the twenty-first century—not just for themselves, but for all Americans."

It is this new blood in evangelicalism that can bring renewed vitality to the North American church to reach out with more relevance and conviction to its inner cities and to the *pueblos* across the oceans. A popular Mexican saying goes, "*Pobre Mexico—tan lejos de Dios y tan cerca de los Estados Unidos.*" Poor Mexico, so far from God and so close to the United States. The paradox today is that by coming to the U.S., millions of Mexicans, and other Latin Americans, are getting the opportunity to come closer to God.

5. MOISES SANDOVAL, "HUDDLED MASSES: THE HISTORY OF OUR IMMIGRANT CHURCH" (2000)

The first Christian prayer said in what would later become the United States was a Catholic one. The Spanish explorers who settled along the Gulf Coast and later moved in an arc across Texas, New Mexico, Arizona, and up the California coastline carried with them Catholic priests who were to spiritually counsel the soldiers and convert the local natives. These Catholic territories were later complicated by the Protestant Anglo culture as it moved west across the American landscape.

But the Catholic Church in America was hardly finished. In this article from U.S. Catholic, Moises Sandoval discusses the growing Latin American population in the Church. He says "the history of the Catholic Church in the United States is one of immigrant people creating a new spiritual home for themselves while seeking to maintain links to their religious traditions." Using the new Hispanic immigrants as a starting point, Sandoval explores the history of the Catholic Church as an essentially immigrant church, also including German, Polish, and Italian immigrants.

Longtime editor of Maryknoll *magazine and* Revista Maryknoll *magazine, which he also founded, Sandoval was for years in a position to assess Catholic life in the United States. He authored several books on American Hispanics, including* On the Move: A History of the Hispanic Church in the United States.

Lady Liberty has seen many tempest-tossed generations set foot upon these shores. With each new wave of immigrants, the American Catholic Church has become a harbor that gets wider and deeper by the year.

One night in 1967, Marcelino Ramos entered the United States illegally in the trunk of a car. Crammed with him as the smuggler's car crossed the border without incident from Tijuana, Mexico were his wife, Maria, his 7-year-old son, Humberto, and his 5-year-old daughter, Rosa. It is the heat that Humberto, now the assistant director of Hispanic ministry for the Archdiocese of Los Angeles, most remembers. "I always tell people that I am a wetback, not from swimming the river but because I was wet with sweat."

The Ramos family is among those immigrants whom Jesuit Father Allan Figueroa Deck, a leading authority on Hispanic ministry, classifies as "the second wave": the millions from Latin America and from the Asian Pacific region who have come to the U.S. since World War II. Though they are not the "teeming masses" who arrived in the 19th and 20th centuries, they are like the millions of immigrants who, from colonial days, have revitalized the Catholic Church in this country. They arrived poor but hardworking—and filled with an indomitable faith in God and in their own possibilities.

Those qualities can be seen in the success of the 10 children of Marcelino and Maria Ramos. Sergio is a Norbertine priest; Hector, a physician; Rosa, a city corrections officer; Ricardo, an architect; Ramiro, a state corrections officer; Jaime, a doctoral candidate in economics; Estella, a psychologist; Gloria, a teacher with a master's degree from Harvard; and Lorena, still in college.

Encuentro 2000, the U.S. bishops' official Jubilee Year celebration held in July, invited the "many faces in God's house"—whites, blacks, Asians, Native Americans, and all shades in between—"to come together to cherish the histories of all our peoples and discover Christ in each other's stories, so that in solidarity we may cross into the new millennium."

The history of the Catholic Church in the United States is one of immigrant people creating a new spiritual home for themselves while seeking to maintain links to their religious traditions. It is the story of outsiders becoming insiders and then failing to welcome those who come after them, a process that repeats itself again and again with each succeeding group. It is the slow, often painful, process of coping with diversity.

Religion has always been important for the peoples of the Americas, whether they arrived 30 or 30,000 years ago. Deck wrote that the most notable feature of the Mesoamerican world was the importance given religion in every sphere of life. Native American reverence for the earth and its ecology has become an important element of modern-day theology. For Christopher Columbus, Hernan Cortes, or John Calvert—the Catholic founder of the Maryland colony—planting the faith went hand-in-hand with exploration, conquest, or settlement. Missioners from various nations left a beautiful saga of dedication, bravery, sacrifice, and martyrdom.

Perhaps because of all these influences, and irrespective of country of origin, Americans take their religion more seriously than do the inhabitants of their motherlands. The Ramoses knelt down every night as a family to pray the rosary. In 1913, Japanese immigrant Leo Hatekeyama went all over Los Angeles looking for a priest who spoke Japanese to hear his Confession. Finding none, he wrote to the bishop of Japan asking permission to send his Confession by registered mail, and to receive absolution and penance by the same means. As a result, Japanese missions were begun in Los Angeles, San Francisco, and Seattle.

Whether they came to New Mexico in 1598 or to the East Coast 200 years later, immigrants organized around their religion. Parishes were the center of religious, social, and even political activity. In the former 13 colonies, immigrants organized national parishes, often led by priests who came with them from the mother country. Historian Jay Dolan writes that the church building itself was so important to an Irish neighborhood in Detroit in the 1850s that, when the population began to shift, they "jacked up the building and rolled it 15 blocks northwest."

Similarly, Marcelino Ramos, being too poor to buy a car—even by working as a janitor by night and a gardener by day, rented a two-room house five blocks from a parish church in San Gabriel, California. He led his family there every Saturday for Confession and every Sunday for Mass. "The church represents a familiar institution [for Hispanic immigrants]," writes Deck. "It is one of the few with which they can identify in an otherwise inhospitable land."

In 1820, Catholics were the smallest denomination in the United States, with only 195,000 members. By 1860, they were the largest, with 3.1 million members. The churches had increased from 124 to 2,385 and the number of clergy from 150 to 2,235. Fed by wave upon wave of immigrants—mainly Irish and German—Catholicism had gone a long way toward becoming the church of immigrants, says Dolan. . . .

By the end of the 19th century, however, the Catholic population had increased to the point where Protestants were concerned about a papist takeover. Out of that concern came the Know-Nothing political party, whose platform was explicitly antiforeign and anti-Catholic. To the nativist mind, Catholics could not be good Americans because of their religion and foreign birth. The nativists feared that in being loyal to the pope, Catholics could not be completely loyal U.S. citizens.

Orestes Brownson, in an 1884 essay titled "Native Americanism," wrote that the Irish and all other immigrants "must ultimately lose their own nationality and become assimilated in general character to the Anglo-

American race." A convert, he insisted that a person could be both a good American and a good Catholic.

To counter anti-Catholic prejudice, the bishops promoted Americanization. "What I mean by Americanization is the filling of the heart with love for America and her institutions," said Archbishop John Ireland of St. Paul, Minnesota. "It is the harmonizing of ourselves to our surroundings, so that we will be as to the manner born, and not as strangers in a strange land, caring but slightly for it, and entitled to receive from it but meager favor. It is the knowing of the language of the land and failing in nothing to prove our attachment to our laws and our willingness to adapt, as dutiful citizens, all that is good and lovable in its social life and civilization." . . .

Americanization helped to create a church with an Irish identity. Early on, the Irish gained control in every section of the country and, by the end of the 19th century, two thirds of the bishops were Irish. Germans, Poles, and, more recently, Hispanics fought—with meager success—for more bishops. Appeals to Rome had little effect. Even in St. Louis, where German clergy were in the majority, all but one of the 12 priests elevated to bishop between 1854 and 1922 were of Irish birth or descent. Only about 15 Polish priests were ordained bishop in the 70 years after a protest to Rome led to the appointment of Paul Rhode as auxiliary in the Archdiocese of Chicago in 1908. Mexican Americans in the Southwest, territory seized by the United States from Mexico in 1846, waited 124 years before one of their own priests, Patricio Flores, was ordained a bishop in 1970.

Worse, as the first groups assimilated, they rejected those who came after them. When Italians began to arrive in St. Paul, Minnesota toward the end of the 19th century, Archbishop Ireland invited Father Nicola Carlo Odone from Genoa to take charge of the Catholic mission in St. Paul. For several years the Italians worshiped in the dark, humid basement of the cathedral. It was a humiliating experience for "we children of Catholic Italy," bemoaned Odone, "to have to meet under the feet of a different people [the Irish] which looks at us from above with contempt."

Half a century later, Puerto Rican leader Encarnacion Armas complained that Puerto Ricans in New York were forced to worship in the basement and that they had to file through the alley to get there. In New Jersey, Puerto Ricans in one parish had to worship in a chicken house. Mexicans in Texas, as blacks everywhere in the South, had separate churches or chapels. In San Francisco, historian Jeffrey Burns reported "intense racial prejudice and hatred of Asians." A pastor said, "Americans will leave if a Japanese comes in their pew." Blacks were not welcomed in white parishes when, in well-meaning efforts to end segregation, the bishops closed the separate black churches. Now, however, those who were rejected fill the churches, though not at the same time as those who assimilated long ago.

In the interim, cultural pluralism has flourished. The civil-rights movement of the 1960s raised awareness about the importance of ethnic identity and pride. Court decisions and civil-rights laws defended the rights of minorities. All that was part of a wider movement. Karl Rahner wrote that Vatican II was the beginning of a "world church" equally at home everywhere, as Asian and African in its self-understanding as it is European. Tolerance for diversity increased.

Furthermore, Catholic loyalty to the nation was no longer in doubt. Recent immigrants have found it easier to maintain their culture, and some of those who had assimilated reclaimed their heritage. The church has made greater efforts to serve the special needs of newcomers. The Archdiocese of New York alone has sent hundreds of priests to Puerto Rico to learn Spanish, now required in many seminaries.

As a result, ethnic Catholicism flourishes as never before. The rejected have found a home. The Puerto Ricans who worshiped in the chicken house are now in the main church. In St. Ann Parish in Ossining, New York, the Mass is celebrated each week in English, Spanish, Portuguese, and Italian. It is celebrated in 52 languages in the Archdiocese of Newark, says Sister Maria Iglesias, S.C., Hispanic RENEW Coordinator for New Jersey-based RENEW International. The Mass is celebrated in more than 40 languages in Los Angeles.

The melting pot church is giving way to a multicultural model in which Hispanics will soon be the majority. Hispanic bishops are leading the move to embrace the multicultural paradigm. This is entirely fitting, says Alejandro Aguilera-Titus, assistant director of the bishops' Secretariat for Hispanics, "because the blood of many cultures runs in our veins."

6. BARBARA BROWN TAYLOR, "VISHNU'S ALMONDS" (2000)

The immigrants who arrived in the United States after 1965 were very different from those who had moved to America previously. While Protestants might have had some difficulty accepting Catholics in the nineteenth century, at least they could recognize some aspects of those Europeans' Christianity. Likewise with Jewish immigrants: they held to a different faith, but parts of it (the Hebrew Scriptures as the Christian "Old Testament") were familiar. But Asians and Middle Easterners arriving after the Immigration Act of 1965 baffled some Christians. Not surprisingly, reactions varied.

Barbara Brown Taylor, an Episcopal priest in Atlanta, taught religion and philosophy at Piedmont College. In this article, published in The Christian Century *in 2000,*

Taylor recounts her experience taking her World Religions class to a Hindu temple in Atlanta. She describes a particular ceremony dedicated to the god Vishnu, after which it is traditional to eat offerings of prasad or holy food, including coconuts, bananas, oranges, and almonds. She uses her personal experiences as a starting point from which to ponder whether the Christian faith couldn't make use of the same spiritual generosity she experienced in the Hindu temple, concluding, "Is this really what Jesus had in mind?" The article considers the ecumenism of mainline Protestantism in its larger context of the world community within the United States.

This week I am headed to the Hindu Temple in Atlanta so that the students in my World Religions class may see a living faith in action. When they fill out their final evaluation forms, many of them will say that the field trips were the best part of the class, and I will agree with them. While our textbook does a good job of explaining bhakti yoga—the devotional way—it is no substitute for the smell of fresh almond and coconut offerings, or the sight of a hundred sesame oil lamps burning in front of a dazzling Hindu deity.

We are going for Sri Lakshmi Abhishekam, the weekly bathing and dressing of the statue of Lakshmi. Like all other Hindu deities, she is but one visible face of the invisible Brahman, the source of all being, before whom all words recoil. Hindus have no problem with the Christian idea of divine incarnation. Their only problem is with the exclusivity of it. "If God can have children," Gandhi said, "then we are all God's children." The great variety of deities reminds Hindus how many different forms divinity may take.

Along with her husband, Vishnu, Lakshmi is revered as the protector of life, the defender of home and family. In gratitude for her benevolence, the priests treat her as they would treat a most honored guest. First they remove her old clothes, which they will give to her devotees. Then they bathe her, applying yogurt, honey and spices to her skin. Finally they pull a curtain in front of her alcove while they dress her. When the curtain opens again some 30 minutes later, Lakshmi draws gasps from the little children who are present. Clothed as the queen she is, she is resplendent in a new red silk and gold brocade sari, with so many garlands of fresh flowers around her neck that her placid face floats above them like the moon.

Offerings are then placed around her feet—halved coconuts and bananas, oranges and heaps of whole almonds. Once this food has been blessed in Lakshmi's presence, the priests will offer it back to the people again, along with sips of camphor-scented water. In some times and places, this prasad, or holy food, is the only meal poor worshipers will eat all day, so the priests make sure that no one goes away empty-handed. They walk around the circle of people who stand near Lakshmi, handing each one a piece of fruit or a spoonful of almonds.

The first time this happened, I was caught by surprise. I had asked a Hindu colleague from the college to go with us on the field trip. She had gladly agreed and had also, apparently, asked for special prayers for our group. When we arrived, we followed her around the central room of the temple as if she were a museum docent, listening intently to her stories about Hanuman, Ganesha and Durga.

When she reached the antechamber of Vishnu's alcove we followed her inside, where she and a priest conversed briefly in a language we did not understand. Then the priest turned to the image of the god before us and began a sonorous chant as he tossed flower petals and pinches of turmeric at the statue's feet. Slowly it dawned on us that we were no longer observers but participants. He was asking Vishnu to protect us—to give us long life and prosperity—while we stood there awkwardly with our hands clasped in front of us.

Then the chant ended and the priest turned toward us. As he started around the circle with the prasad, I watched each student decide how to handle the curveball. Some stuck out their left hands—a terrible blunder, since this hand is considered unclean in Indian culture—but instead of slighting them the priest tried to help them. "Other hand," he whispered, as he held a spoonful of almonds out in front of them. Although we clearly did not know what we were doing, he went out of his way to offer every person a portion of the holy food. Some students made faces at him and waved him away, while others simply stepped back behind their classmates and dropped their heads.

As the priest rounded the bend toward my side of the circle, I was caught in a cognitive thunderstorm. My students were watching me to see what I would do. I wanted to do the right thing, but what was it? My mind sped from the first commandment to Paul's advice about eating food offered to idols. I tried to imagine what Jesus would do. Meanwhile, the person next to me refused the almonds, and I saw the priest step back as if he had been pushed.

I did not have time to make a carefully considered theological decision, so I made an instinctive one. I bowed to the priest, held out my right hand and received the prasad. As I did it, I thanked the One God, both for the blessing and for the opportunity to pray in another tongue. Then the priest moved past me and returned to the altar with most of his almonds still in his bowl, while I waited to be struck by lightning.

Now, when I prepare my students for a field trip to the Hindu Temple, I tell them when to bail out if they want to remain observers. I also remind them that there is no barrier from the Hindu side to prevent them from becoming participants. As far as the temple priest is concerned, they can be perfectly good Christians and still eat Vishnu's almonds. The barrier to communion comes from the Christian side, where creedal differences divide not only Christians from Hindus but also Catholics from Orthodox Christians, Catholics from Protestants, and some Protestants from one another. My cognitive thunderstorm is still going on. Is this really what Jesus had in mind?

7. ADITI BANERJEE, "HINDU-AMERICANS: AN EMERGING IDENTITY IN AN INCREASINGLY HYPHENATED WORLD" (2003)

With changes in immigration laws in 1965 came an influx of educated workers from Southeast Asia. By the end of the century, over one million Asian Indians lived in the United States. Moving from a pluralistic society where thousands of Hindu gods and goddesses are worshipped to a society that is pluralistic but nonetheless primarily characterized by an Anglo Christian culture, many second- and third-generation Hindu Americans have sought ways to negotiate dual understandings of themselves. Religion, naturally, is part of the mix. As religious studies scholar Raymond Williams pointed out, it is an important identity marker that can "preserve individual self-awareness and cohesion in a group."

In this piece by Aditi Banerjee, a law student at Yale University, the topic is revealed in both its highly personal and its social natures. How does one create personal meaning between two worlds, especially Hinduism (a highly individualistic religion) in America (a highly individualistic society)? The author faces head on the crisis that many immigrants of faith have felt upon entering American society. Understanding that this is an issue unique to American Hindus (as compared to Indian Hindus) because religious groups can only be created in relation to the "other," not in a homogenous society, Banarjee concludes that religion must be reinterpreted to adapt to new societies and lifestyles in order for the individual to find meaning and the religion to survive.

My parents came to Chicago from Calcutta in the 1960's. They associated with Bengalis and their closest friends have remained Bengali—it is with the Bengalis of Chicago that we have celebrated and to this day celebrate

Thanksgiving, New Year's, Durga Puja, Kali Puja, and Saraswati Puja (excuse my Bengali pronunciation!). What binds them together is not just the language but also the shared memories of the home they left behind—a fragmented India, where Bengal was distinctive from the rest of the country. They saw themselves as Bengalis, not Indians.

The India they left behind is drastically different from the India I found this summer when I spent a few months there. This is an India where Bengalis speak Hindi as much as they speak Bengalis, while many in my parent's generation cannot follow a Hindi movie without subtitles. This is an India where my cousins listen to national pop stars and Hindi film music rather than Bengali renditions of Rabindra sangeet. This is an India where the anthem being sung is the national anthem, not Tagore's homage to a unified Bengal. This is an India where Indians finally see themselves as Indians.

So, the new immigrants who are coming from India are identifying themselves not as members from a particular region, but members of an increasingly unified nation. They are more apt to celebrate Diwali rather than Kali Puja when both celebrations fall on the same weekend. They are more likely to talk to their friends in Hindi than Bengali.

This shift is similar to the changes in identity prevalent among the second generation, the so-called ABCDs, American Born Confused Desis like myself. While I learned to speak Bengali before English, and while I bonded with the children of my parents' Bengali friends, what drew us together wasn't our ethnicity, it was our shared experience of being brown folk in a white world, of weekend get-togethers with other immigrant families and eating Indian food, of being dragged to pujas celebrated in local high schools rented out for the weekend. It was our shared experience of being perceived as the dorky nerds in school, of teachers and parents expecting us to excel in math and science and be at the top of our class, of teachers and parents expecting us to be engineers or doctors, of being asked whether we spoke Indian. In short, what bound us together wasn't being Bengali American or even necessarily Indian American; it was the experience of being foreigners born in this country, an affinity we felt with each other and even Asian Americans in general.

I first heard the term South Asian when I came to Tufts. I was told that the differences between Pakistanis, Indians, and Bangladeshis was negligible—in short, since other Americans couldn't distinguish between us, why should we? Eventually, I was told that we should think of ourselves as Asian Americans—we shared common experiences and came from the same general continent, after all. The underlying premise beneath each of these movements was the idea that what formed a group identity was based largely on how others perceived us and on what would give us the most political clout and coherence.

This is a fundamentally flawed approach. Of course, it is valuable and necessary to have communities of Indian-Americans, South-Asian-Americans, and Asian-Americans. But communities and group affiliation are different from what constitutes social identity. Identity cannot be based on political expedience or social convenience—it cannot be based on circumstances of birth or geographical origin or even race/ethnicity. Even culture is not enough, though it is a closer approximation of what matters—it is our values, our worldview, our beliefs about ourselves and the world we live in, it is the way we think, the way we conduct ourselves, the philosophy behind our actions.

Bengali-Americans, Asian-Americans, South-Asian-Americans function well as communities but cannot suffice as identities. They will shed and morph over time as migration patterns and political realities shift. The same way the Bengali identity has given way to an Indian identity, the current South Asian vogue will give way to something else in the coming years. These identities are inherently unstable, based on external circumstances not innate characteristics of personality that are necessary to constitute any real or permanent identity.

For example, while I may go for months without uttering a word of Bengali or even without speaking to another Indian, not a day would pass by where I wouldn't pray to Krishna or recite the Gayatri mantra. While I would be as amenable to marrying a Punjabi as a Rajasthani as a Bengali, I would find it very difficult to marry a man who didn't believe in reincarnation or karma or dharma. While I might be equally happy at a South Indian temple or a Chinmaya Mission or an ISKCON center, all three share fundamental characteristics of the faith dear to me. While I may not take my children to the local Durga puja celebrated by Bengalis in the future, I would tell them the stories I know from the Ramayana and the Mahabharatha.

These are aspects of my self that do not alter regardless of which country I'm in or what people surround me. They are aspects of my most fundamental beliefs and values that do not shift the same way my personality adapts to the society that surrounds me. When in Rome, we should do as Romans do, but that does not necessarily mean we become Romans or believe the things Romans believe.

You may ask, why do we need a Hindu American identity at all? Why don't we practice this most individualistic of all religions individually? Isn't mixing religion and politics a disaster in the making?

Well, first of all, to think religion and politics aren't mixed to begin with is a naive and dangerous presumption. Politics does not happen in a vacuum; all actors, especially political actors, are motivated by convictions based on ideology and morality which comes from social norms as well as religious beliefs. The debate over slavery was inextricably intertwined with Christianity; the universal recognition of human rights is based on a consensus of religious viewpoints on basic values common to us all; the partition that tore through the subcontinent was a bitter battle raging over whether the soul of the new India was to be based on one religion or a plurality of religions. The more conscious we are of how religion affects our identities and viewpoints, the more we can try to be broadminded and fair. If we deny the religious component of our identity, we just become blinded to what is going on in our subconsciousness and it makes it harder to understand ourselves.

Before debating the merits of adopting a Hindu-American identity, we have to understand what it means to be a Hindu-American; how is it distinctive from being any other type of American or any other type of Hindu? I've touched a bit on how Hindu-Americans are distinctive from the groupings of Indian-Americans or Asian-Americans, etc. It's an identity that looks at the individual rather than broad categories of ethnicities or race; it's an identity that is chosen rather than assigned.

But how are American Hindus different from other Hindus, principally Hindus from India? It is admittedly difficult to separate the two; India is Hinduism's birthplace and tradition homeland for a religion that has done little proselytizing beyond its geographic borders. However, we must understand that the faith and philosophy of Hinduism is distinctive from the social customs and religions that have come to plague it through the years. Just as Christianity is not about the crusades or slavery or sexual abuse perpetuated by priests, Hinduism is not fundamentally about dowry, or the current caste system, or the subordination of women in the name of religion.

Those are social practices caused more by the situation of Indian society at those times than by the philosophy of the religion. What does it mean to be a Hindu? Not so long ago, people identified themselves as followers of Shiva or Vishnu or the Vedanta philosophy, not as Hindus. When we began to call ourselves Hindu, it came from an acknowledgment that despite the diversity of the faith, a diversity of beliefs and practices that we cherish, there is an underlying unity—an acceptance that though there is one truth, we call it by different names, that we are all taking different paths to the same God, the same destination, an acceptance of the truths of the Vedas that we may never have ever read.

Though we in America may never understand a word of Sanskrit or celebrate pujas on the weekend for convenience rather than the actual day it is supposed to be held, though our vision of Hinduism may be more colored by the popularization of yoga and meditation than teachings from the Puranas, we still subscribe to the same beliefs that allowed Shaivites and

Vaishnavas to bridge the gaps between themselves and forge a common identity as Hindu. These beliefs are strong enough to bridge the geographical distance that separates American Hindus from Hindus of other nations.

It is this unity that matters the most, that we need to recognize and acknowledge. Whether we pray to Kali or Krishna, Rama or Ramakrishna, whether we revere the words of Swami Vivekananda or Aurobindo, there is a unity of belief underlying it all. However, we must understand that American Hindus are also distinctive from other Hindus around the world. These distinctions are based on the society in which we are living. Think of people like Deepak Chopra, who has brought Ayurvedic science into this country and repackaged it for a western audience, or Krishna Das, who has taken traditional bhajans and fused it with western music. Think of the hundreds of yoga teachers who have combined traditional hatha yoga with aerobics or Pilates or even martial arts. Think of Hindu weddings as they happen in America today, three days' worth of ceremonies compressed into an hour or two with English translations for those non-Sanskrit speakers like me.

The issues we face as American Hindus are different from, say, the issues facing Indian Hindus. Instead of Ayodhya, students in campuses wonder whether Ramadan should be celebrated alongside Diwali. Instead of banning cow slaughter, we worry about whether McDonalds' fries are purely vegetarian. Instead of battling communalism, we battle stereotypes of dotheads and elephant gods.

I am not as Indian as my parents or others of their generation are. I date, I would probably not consent to an arranged marriage, I drink at social gatherings, I do not speak Bengali as frequently or as well as I should. But does that make me less Hindu? I pray, I meditate, I do yoga, I read books on the Gita and other scriptures, I believe in the philosophy they hold dear, I value the same things they do: family, caring for others, and honor. I just express those values differently. I practice the religion differently. I am Hindu, just not in the Indian way but in a new American way. When I think of a Hindu-American, I think of myself.

I have reinterpreted my religion to adapt to the society and lifestyle I have adopted as my own. Some would call this deviating from the authentic religion. I disagree. I think it is healthy to reinvent and reinterpret and reform any philosophy or religion. That is how people and societies and religions survive and evolve. It is this process of adaptation and assimilation that has preserved Hinduism for so long. It is the reforms that preserve the essence of the faith while accommodating social changes and modernization that have added to the richness and wisdom of the religion.

As American Hindus, we have the opportunity to contribute to that process. It is something we should not shy away from, it is a responsibility we should accept and honor. Why? Why have and adopt a Hindu-American identity? First, because it is necessary for the survival of the religion. Religions that are stagnant and refuse to change with the times, to adapt to the society in which they are living, die away. Christianity has been so successful in its appeal to people around the world for so many centuries precisely because it has been more flexible than most in accepting the tide of the times.

Why should we care about whether Hinduism survives as a religion? This reminds me of an article I read a while ago in *National Geographic*. There are languages that are dying by the thousands every year. Sure, in some ways it is effective and efficient to have fewer languages to ease communication between groups. But, one problem is that as these languages die out, vocabulary vanishes that identifies the medicinal properties of herbs and plants. Without this vocabulary, we lose the knowledge of potential cures for cancer and other illnesses.

Religions contain invaluable knowledge. Whether one is a Hindu or not, there is an interest in preserving as many traditions of the religions of the world—preserving not as in maintaining status quo but in encouraging the growth and evolution of such traditions and faiths while staying true to its roots.

More specifically, as Hindus ourselves, we have a particular interest in formulating and articulating a Hindu-American Identity. I believe that the "confused" in ABCD (American Born Confused Desi) comes from being confused about what it means to be a desi in America. Of course, there are things that we share in common with all Indians, but the lasting impact of being born as an Indian-American comes from the rift between the values our parents taught us and the values we find ourselves surrounded by in the U.S. Some of these differences are based on social norms and cultures, some on religion. In order to better understand these differences and our own coherence, we need to examine our religious identity, what we accept from our heritage and what we reject.

Doing that in a group or community format is preferable to each of us doing it for ourselves, because having the support of others going through similar experiences helps, as many heads are always better than one. And in the end, we are not islands isolated from one another—we are all members of communities, of a subcommunity as Hindus, but also of a larger community of Americans and global citizens. And in order to contribute to the important dialogue between civilizations and faiths, we must begin with the discussions and dialogues within our faith and religion.

How do we do this? The best and most important way is through education. The only way we can get to think of ourselves as Hindu is to understand first what it means to be Hindu. We need to learn more about our religion. I've read so little of the scriptures, and all of it has been in poorly translated English, not the original Sanskrit. My knowledge is fragmented, bits and pieces of the Puranas, selected verses of the Gita. But imagine the possibilities if we could all get together and put together our own fragments of knowledge—we'd be so many steps closer to a coherent understanding of the fundamentals of the religion. There are so many resources out there, and they're best used if shared and the products of collaboration.

Interaction and dialogue are also key. Conferences like this and forums encouraging widespread community participation and input are invaluable. Forums based on being Hindu rather than being of a certain ethnicity or nationality are important and necessary. Also, open-ended discussions on topical issues such as what our views as American Hindus are on social issues such as women's rights or interfaith marriages would be great.

These are just my thoughts. This is just one voice in what I hope is a massive dialogue and discussion about what unites and distinguishes us as Hindus living in America.

Darwinism is not just for living beings. Survival of the fittest applies to religions, societies, civilizations. To succeed not just as individuals, Americans, or Indian Americans, but as Hindu Americans, we need to understand better both sides of the hyphen—what does it mean to be Hindu and what does it mean to be American? As really the first significant generation of American Hindus, we have the unique opportunity to frame, formulate, and generate the dialogue and debate needed to give birth to an identity that will hopefully stand the test of time and generations.

8. MUZAMMIL H. SIDDIQI, "HUMAN RIGHTS IN ISLAM" (2003)

SARAJI UMM ZAID, "MAKE WAY FOR THE WOMEN! WHY YOUR MOSQUE SHOULD BE WOMAN FRIENDLY" (2003)

Of all the growing immigrant religious communities in the second half of the twentieth century, none faced stiffer odds than Islam. Distrusted by many Jewish Americans because of geopolitics in the Middle East and disliked by many Christians, who were angered by the claim that the Qur'an displaced Christian scriptures as the final revelation from God (despite, ironically, the same Christian claims about Hebrew scriptures), practicing Muslims in the United States were watched suspiciously by others in the Abrahamic traditions. The seizure of the American embassy in Iran and subsequent terrorism sponsored by radical Muslim groups over the next quarter century exacerbated the situation.

American Muslims face various tensions. One problem is how to loyally follow the laws in each of their nations—the United States of America and the larger Muslim "nation," or Ummah (community). How could one remain both a good Muslim, committed to Islam's laws and practices based on the good of the community, and a good American, committed to individualism in law, economics, and religion? Other issues spring out of that, including how people who want to enjoy American freedoms negotiate their roles in their faith tradition. Can one use moral principles outside Islam to critique religious practices?

The following two pieces reflect those tensions. Muzammil H. Siddiqi was among the most famous scholars writing about Islam in North America after 1970. Holding a doctorate in comparative religion from Harvard University, he led the way in discussions about Islam in interfaith dialogues and served as President of the Islamic Society of North America from 1996 to 2000. In "Human Rights in Islam," Dr. Siddiqi is careful to trace how many of the rights Americans and westerners hold dear are inherent within Islam, based on human dignity and ideals of justice. While not claiming an organic connection between Islamic and American notions of rights, he clearly indicates their overlap for American Muslims.

Saraji Umm Zaid reflects the diversity of Muslims in America. President of the Latino American Dawah Organization in New York City, she is a freelance writer who grapples with a number of issues facing Muslim converts, particularly those dealing with the role of women in Islam. Tired of being prevented from attending prayers at the mosque, she sounds particularly "American" in criticizing those of her faith who are unwilling to make room for women. This piece reflects an important segment of the American Muslim population—those who attempt to be faithful to the traditions of the religion, but are willing to speak out against "Old World" attitudes in the United States.

HUMAN RIGHTS IN ISLAM

We have indeed honored the children of Adam; provided them with transport on land and sea; given them for sustenance things good and pure; and conferred on them special favors, above a great part of Our Creation. (al-Isra' 17:70)

We sent aforetime Our Messengers with Clear Signs and sent down with them the Book and the Balance (of Right and Wrong), that humankind may stand forth in justice; and We sent down Iron, in which is (material for) mighty war, as well as many benefits for humankind, that Allah may test who it is that will help, unseen, Him and His Messengers: for Allah is Full of Strength, Exalted in Might (and able to enforce His Will). (al-Hadid 57:25)

The concept of human rights in Islam is based on two important principles: dignity of human beings and justice. Islam emphasizes that all human beings are honored by Allah subhanahu wa ta'ala. Allah wants all human beings to live in peace and harmony and for this reason He wants us to establish justice in this world. Without justice there is no dignity and without dignity and justice there cannot be any peace.

There are four important principles that we must keep in mind when talking about human rights in Islam:

1. Rights are given by Allah.
2. Rights are governed by duties.
3. There is a hierarchy in rights.
4. There are priorities in human relations.

1. Rights are given by Allah: The rights in Islam are not just human conventions, or so-called "natural rights" or "social contracts." They are Allah's orders. They should be considered as "permanent values," "universal and eternal standards." They should not be given only to those who shout most or who lobby most, but they should be given even to those who are not yet empowered to speak for themselves, or who are not even aware due to social circumstances to know what rights they should have. The rights are rights even when no one asks for them.

2. Rights are governed by duties: The Shari'ah is the network of rights and responsibilities. There are Huquq (rights) and there are Wajibat (duties). Muslim scholars have debated this issue whether the Huquq come first or the Wajibat come first. Some have emphasized duties and some have emphasized rights. However, both of them are important. It is not possible to have rights without duties. Also there is mutuality between rights and duties. Someone's right is another person's duty and someone's duty is another person's right.

3. Hierarchy in rights: The Shari'ah has special objectives (maqasid). Imam Ghazali, Imam Shatibi and many other scholars have mentioned five basic objectives of the Shari'ah. The Shari'ah came to preserve: 1. Din, 2. Life, 3. Progeny, 4. Intellect, 5. Wealth. But within the Shari'ah there are certain rules that are called Darurat (necessities) and some that are called Hajat (needs) and some that are called Tawassu' and Taysirat (ease and facilities). Preservation of Din is at the top. Life is second most important thing and so on and so forth. Similarly there are things that are Fard (obligatory) and there are things that are Nafl (recommended) and then there are those that Mubah (permissible). In a similar fashion there are some rights that are on the top and then other rights come after them.

4. Priorities in relations: Islam has a detailed scheme in its priorities. All people have rights but no one has a right above Allah's rights. Among the people there are rights of parents, rights of spouses, rights of children, rights of other relatives. There are rights of neighbors. There are rights of employers and employees. There are rights of Muslims and there are rights of other human beings. There are rights of animals, resources and objects. Sometimes there are conflicts between one right and another right and so the question comes what is my first duty. It is for this reason the issue of rights becomes very complex and difficult. The most important thing is to have the fear of Allah in all relations.

Following are some of the rights emphasized in Islam:

1. Protection of life including the right of life of the unborn
2. Protection of property including use, investment and transfer
3. Protection of honor, no defamation, slander or calling of names
4. Protection of privacy
5. Individual freedom
6. Right to obtain justice, Due process of law
7. Freedom from guilt by association
8. Freedom of opinion and expression of opinion
9. Freedom of conscience, belief and worship
10. Right to be equal
11. Right to economic security
12. Right to assembly
13. Right to abstain from sin
14. Right of political involvement
15. Freedom of movement and settlement
16. Right to just wages

MAKE WAY FOR THE WOMEN! WHY YOUR MOSQUE SHOULD BE WOMAN FRIENDLY

"Do not stop the maid servants of Allah from going to the mosques of Allah." (Muwatta of Imam Malik)

"When the wife of one of you asks about going to the mosque, do not stop her." (Bukhari)

I recently took a trip with my family to the state of Colorado, and I was look-ing forward to visiting a different Muslim community. To my great dismay, when we went to an (unnamed) Colorado city to pray Jumu'ah in their masjid (mosque), we were told that there were no women in that masjid, and that I would be unable to pray there. With my children and (non Mus-lim) mother in tow, I went off to a park while my husband prayed. As a Mus-lim, I felt humiliated and angry, and I was embarrassed for the Ummah that my non Muslim mother should have to see Muslims barring me from Bait Ullah (house of God) for no reason other than my gender. Nothing like re-inforcing negative stereotypes, is there? Later, the brothers there told my husband that it was nothing against me, there just "wasn't room" for wo-men in this masjid.

A few years ago, I visited a masjid in New York, intending to perform 'asr prayer while I was out shopping for things for my new home with my daughter and a friend. Instead, the sister and I were greeted at the door by a very angry teenager, who railed at us to return to our homes, that women have no place in the masjid, and that we were a fitna (a trial, calamity or af-fliction) upon the brothers who were there (all three of them). Mind you, we were a group consisting of a small child, a sister in hijab and jilbab (a loose-fitting garment covering the entire body), and a sister in niqab (face veil). Subhan'Allah, if a small child and two sisters in hijab are a fitna upon these men, then whatever do they do as they walk around New York City and en-counter women who cover nothing more than what they are legally required to cover (meaning the genitalia)? As we were leaving, one of the brothers caught up to us, and apologized for the incident. Then he said, "It's not that women aren't allowed, just that there isn't any room for you in this masjid." I fail to see how a two bedroom apartment with a living room converted into a masjid where there are only three brothers present at the time doesn't "have enough room."

I don't know. Maybe it's just me, but the "we don't have room for you" ex-cuse is getting old. I visited a masjid in Monterey, California that was about the size of my living room. If any masjid had a valid reason to use this ex-cuse it was this place. However, the brothers here had the foresight to cur-tain off a corner in the back for women. If no women showed up, they would keep the curtain drawn to the side, and there would be more room for men. If a sister or two did show up, they would close the curtain, and the men would have to make do with the space they had left.

Yes, some spaces for masajid are very small, but to use that as an excuse to bar women from praying there is unacceptable. Proof of that is offered in the example of the Monterey masjid. Because the Prophet, aleyhi salatu wa

salaam, specifically forbade keeping women from the masjid, no one is going to come right out and say that they bar women from entering. "We don't
have room" becomes code for "We don't want you here. Go home." If people were really interested in keeping with the Sunnah of ar Rasul, aleyhi
salatu wa salaam, they should make sure that their masjid doesn't aid them
in violating the Prophet's command, aleyhi salatu wa salaam.

People in these communities who speak out against this injustice are often labeled as "troublemakers." When I wrote a letter to that New York
masjid, giving reasons from Qur'an, Sunnah, and the writings of our es-
teemed scholars as to why it is haram to block women from the masjid, I
was labeled a "radical feminist." Subhan'Allah. Is anti-feminism so in-
grained in our community now that any speech for the rights of women
should be dismissed, even when that speech comes directly from Allah and
His Messenger?

Besides the inconvenience such masajid pose to women who are traveling, or working, or in some other way unable to be at home or another
masjid to pray, these masajid also detract from the community as a whole.
There is a void in that community. A multitude of viewpoints, ideas, and energy have been eliminated. More than 50% of the local community is invisible and excluded. I say more than 50%, because it is almost always the case
that when a masjid excludes women, it automatically excludes children as
well. Is this the face of our da'wa? A face that is exclusively male? How can
we tell non Muslim women that Islam is a sheltering peace for them if we
show them a community wherein women are virtually invisible?

It was not the face of the da'wa of the Sahaba, and it was not the Sunnah
of the Prophet, aleyhi salatu wa salaam, to exclude women. Not from the
masjid, and not from the community as a whole. Much is made of the hadith wherein the Prophet, sallalahu aleyhi wa salaam, told a woman that
prayer in her home is better than prayer in the masjid. (Ustadh Abdullah
Adhami has taught this hadith from a common sense, traditional point of
view, and discusses misinterpretations that people have made of this hadith to justify banning women from the masajid, and you can hear this on
his tape set "Ibadah of Women," from Ihya Productions.) The point that I
am making here is that while the Prophet, aleyhi salatu wa salaam, told the
woman that the prayer in her home is better for her, he did not forbid her
from coming to the masjid at all. In fact, we know that the contrary is true,
that he forbad men from preventing women to go to the masjid, as seen in
the ahadith cited at the top of the page. If you are in a masjid that does not
have a space for women, you are preventing them from entering this
masjid. If you stand by while another brother tells a woman to go home,

you are preventing her from entering the masjid. Do you really want to take that position?

If your masjid space truly is very small, there are very easy ways for you to make it available to women who need to pray there, while opening up the entire space for the men when no women are present. Many home improvement and home decorating stores sell decorative screens (like the rice paper ones seen in Japan), for a relatively low price. They fold up and are easy to store when not in use. Office supply stores sell cubicle walls with wheels. They also fold up for easy storage. If your masjid doesn't have enough of a budget for these items, take up a special collection. In the meantime, you can install an extended curtain rod across the intended space for women and put up floor length curtains. You can use a table or chairs to mark the space reserved for women. Or you can do as masajid have done for hundreds of years, and just designate a space behind the men as women's space, without hijab (barriers) or walls. However, be aware that some women (and men) might not be comfortable with this style, since they may need to breastfeed an infant or adjust their coverings in the course of a Jumu'ah khutba.

If you have been blessed by Allah subhannahu wa ta'ala to have a larger amount of space for your masjid, then do the right thing by your sisters. Make sure that the space reserved for them is adequate. Make sure the floor is clean. Make sure it is heated in the winter, and has air in the summer. Make sure the roof doesn't leak when it rains. Are there shoe racks and coat hangers? Make sure copies of the Qur'an are on hand for them to read. Make sure that the women's bathroom has hooks for their hijabs (when they are making wudhu), paper towels for them to dry with, slippers to wear, and soap to wash with. Make sure the bathroom is clean. If you have the room, you should add a changing table. It is a fact of life that where there are Muslim women, there are bound to be Muslim children, and the smallest of those children will need to have their diapers changed. Should the mother change it on the musallah floor, or on a wet, dirty, bathroom floor?

When you ensure that women are included in the masjid, you are ensuring that the entire community has access to the teachings of Islam. You are showing non Muslims that Islam does not stand for the exclusion of women and children, that Islam is not a "man's religion." You are showing non Muslims that a woman can be modest, can be religious, and can still participate in community life. You are showing the next generation of Muslims that cultural ideas about excluding women and keeping them in the home are not from Islam. And you are following the teachings and example of our beloved Prophet, aleyhi salatu wa salaam. It is time for us to start undoing the damage done to our communities by pre-Islamic cultural ideas about "women's places." It is time for us to erase the misconceptions and misunderstandings of the diyn (religion) that many still cling to. The only way that we can be sure that the next generation understands Islam as it was truly taught by the Prophet, sallalahu aleyhi wa salaam, is to be sure that women and children are fully included in the masjid.

Chapter 9

Religion, the New Age, and the New Millennium

AS THE TWENTIETH CENTURY came to a close, religious prophesiers, seers, and skeptics alike vigorously debated what the new millennium would bring. Conservative Christians searched contemporary history for signs that would validate their ideas of the imminent end of the world and triumphant return of Christ. Liberal Christians, chastened by a century that started with the optimistic prognostications of Social Gospelers and postmillennialists but in fact was dominated by two cataclysmic world wars, the Holocaust, and the threat of nuclear annihilation, searched for ways to renew a lost faith in humanity. They banded together with Muslims, Hindus, and others at the Parliament of the World's Religions Centennial in 1993 to enunciate a new "global ethic," marrying religious and environmental concerns. They articulated concern about "a world in agony" while calling for a renewed commitment to a global golden rule. At the same time, they drew a critical response from some American Buddhists, who objected to the emphasis on the existence of a Supreme Being in the document. New Agers, neopagans, and religious humanists exulted in a kind of secularized (and orientalized) postmillennial thought that placed faith in harmonic convergences, positive energy fields, the seven chakras, and utopian visions.

This chapter presents a variety of documents that suggest the diversity and intensity of interest generated by millennialism, broadly defined as expressions of philosophy concerning the eventual fate of the world and humankind. The continued predominance of Christianity in the United States can be seen in the simple fact that the year 2000 C.E. was counted as a "millennial" year. It was that, of course, only for those who counted their calendars from the birth of Christ; it was not the millennium for Jews, Muslims, Buddhists, or members of any other religious tradition. But American Jews,

Muslims, and Buddhists celebrated the millennium along with the Christian (and nonbelieving) majority, for the Christian calendar had long since been established as the norm and had in fact been "de-Christianized" by the substitution of the term C.E. (Common Era) for B.C. (Before Christ) and A.D. (*Anno Domini*, "the year of our Lord").

Conservative Christians historically have expressed a deep ambivalence within their millennialist thinking. On the one hand, of course, the millennial age is defined as the time of Christ's return, so it must be the ultimate occasion of rejoicing and victory for Christians. On the other hand, many varieties of evangelical millennial thought predict a "time of tribulation" and the thousand-year reign of the Antichrist, "the beast," for those left on Earth after the "Rapture" of Christians. For example, some conservative Christians plastered bumper stickers on their cars, IN CASE OF RAPTURE, THIS VEHICLE WILL BE UNOCCUPIED, indicating their belief that Christ would redeem his chosen prior to the time of tribulation and Armageddon that would close out human history. Christian writers such as Hal Lindsey popularized premillennialist thought. In Lindsey's *The Late Great Planet Earth* (published originally in 1972), the world is depicted as in its final days leading up to the great conflict between God and the forces of the Antichrist. The restoration of the state of Israel and rebuilding of the Jewish temple signified the beginning of the end times, Lindsey argued, as prophesied in the Old Testament eschatological texts, including the books of Daniel and Ezekiel. The massive success of Lindsey's work indicates how well he popularized formerly esoteric and theologically complex concepts drawn from obscure and mysterious biblical texts, and summarized them in a programmatic form that could be repeated not only in books but in hymns, bumper stickers, movies (such as *Left Behind*, a wildly popular set of evangelical movies and novels concerning what happens to those "left behind" after the Rapture of Christians), comic books, and tracts. One of the most popular contemporary Christian hymns, sung with great fervor at countless youth crusades, was "I Wish We'd All Been Ready," the lyrics of which are included here. The hymn appealed to Christian young people who would not wish to see their friends "left behind" in the millennium. A darker version of millennialism was enacted in the conflagration that burned up dozens of Branch Davidian believers in Waco, Texas, in 1993, a tragic incident of desperate religious fervor and governmental misunderstanding discussed in the essay by Michael Barkun reprinted below.

In 1999 Jerry Falwell, Virginia Baptist minister and founder of the political group Moral Majority, made headlines and sparked controversy (not for the first time) in a sermon about the millennium that featured speculative identification of the Antichrist with a Jewish male presently living. After a firestorm of criticism, Falwell (weakly) apologized. This episode was unusual only for the public outcry it provoked, as similar sermons and rhetoric had pervaded evangelical thought for decades. Indeed, had it not been for the coming of the millennium and attention given to millennial themes, it is likely that Falwell's sermon would have gone unnoticed. Liberal Christians countered with skeptical essays pointing out how often in the past Christians had made fools of themselves with attempts to apply biblical prophecy to the contemporary world. Christian writers historically associated with the evangelical Left, such as Ronald Sider, sought to join the emphasis on personal salvation among conservative Christians with the social ethic of liberal Christians, correcting what he called "one-sided Christianity." Sider and others attempted to turn the millennial discussion back to this-worldly concerns.

But evangelicals were hardly the only ones to issue millennial prophecies and pronouncements. Quasi-religious millennial themes abounded in popular literature as well. Few works reached such heights of popular success as James Redfield's *The Celestine Prophecy*, a novel that employed a rather flimsy plot in order to serve as a forum for the author's own vaguely New Age ideas. Redfield's hero goes to Peru and joins others there on a quest for an ancient manuscript dating from 600 B.C. that outlines "insights" concerning a transformation of the world to begin "in the last decades of the twentieth century." The manuscript prophesied "a renaissance in consciousness" that was "not religious in nature, but it is spiritual." The manuscript was organized sequentially, with each insight building on the previous one, showing how to move "from where we are not to a completely spiritual culture on earth." In the process of searching for it, the characters battle authoritarian religious and governmental figures who want to prevent discovery of the text and dissemination of antiauthoritarian ideas. The search for the manuscript thus serves as a metaphor for the broader "revolution in consciousness" seen by New Age authors. Redfield's work is conveniently described on numerous Web sites (including Redfield's own, at http://www.celestinevision.com) that paraphrase and summarize the "Nine Insights" and reveal the dates on which readers may purchase the texts that will reveal future revelations. Christian authors responded to Redfield, condemning him as a "New Age fraud." "Were it not for the fact that this book is a best-seller, I would be tempted to write it off as a silly piece of harmless fluff," wrote one such critic, while also acknowledging that for many people "it is an explanation of life's mysteries." Popular reaction ranged from wildly enthusiastic to contemptuously dismissive. But most of those who dismissed it were not resistant to millennialism per se, but rather to the particular form of it purveyed in Redfield's text.

Millions of Americans experimented with, dabbled in, or plunged head-first into the New Age. Much of this investigation followed directly from the counterculture, explored by the documents in chapter 2. In the 1970s, especially, the social consciousness characteristic of the 1960s receded, scarred by the tumult of the period 1968–1975, which included urban race riots, the American withdrawal from Vietnam, and the energy crisis. Spiritual seekers influenced by the counterculture increasingly went on individual quests, far less inclined than in the 1960s to seek a kind of social salvation or utopianism. While some proclaimed the ideas of the New Age to be new, scholarly authors quickly traced their sources back centuries, to Renaissance texts on esoterica and late nineteenth-century American religious phenomena such as psychical research, Theosophy, and New Thought. Religious studies scholar Mary Ferrell Bednarowski defines New Age religion this way:

> An insistence on the need for a new cosmology that will embrace and restore to wholeness the dualisms that are considered the products of outmoded Enlightenment worldview—science/religion, body/spirit, matter/consciousness, thinking/feeling, male/female, etc. Another is the insistence on the immanence of the divine or the Absolute in every atom of the universe along with its correlative proposition—the interrelatedness of all things. A third is an intense optimism about the possibilities for individual and social transformation. A fourth is a concern with ecology and the need for planetary rather than a national or even international consciousness. Underlying all these themes is an assumption of the cosmic pervasiveness of the evolutionary process, however defined and interpreted by particular groups. ("Literature of the New Age: A Review of Representative Sources," *Religious Studies Review* 17 [July 1991]: 209)

New Age thought emerged in philosophical texts, works on the intersection of science and religion, and serious fiction. But its real impact came through more popular outlets and vehicles, such as *The Celestine Prophecy*, a staggering variety of other self-help and consciousness-raising books and groups, and scripts in television series (such as the friendly Native American shamans and trickster figures and the whimsical philosophizing disk jockey of the fictional radio station KBER in the CBS series *Northern Exposure*). New Age author Marilyn Ferguson summarized much of the "buzz" of the movement in her popular treatise *The Aquarian Conspiracy*. She argued that a huge variety of social trends that seemed to be disconnected in fact all emerged from similar impulses, parallel drives for unity in the world and harmony with the cosmos. These united self-help seminars, astrological interests, New Age philosophical treatises, environmental activism, the recovery of Native American traditions, feminist consciousness raising, and the rise of neopaganism.

Reflections on religion at the millennium, then, were enormously varied, alternately utopian and dystopian, and often disputatious. This chapter and this book conclude with a series of excerpts from the works of Harvey Cox, one of the deans of American religious studies; reflections on "twenty-first century spirituality" from a variety of contemporary thinkers and practitioners of various traditions; a lament by law professor Stephen Carter about the "culture of disbelief" in modern American life and politics; and a more personal account from the spiritual autobiography of Elizabeth Lesser.

A professor at Harvard Divinity School, Harvey Cox long has been a widely read author of studies of American religion. Coming from a rather conservative midwestern Baptist background, Cox soon moved onto the wider stage of the religious establishment, liberal Protestantism, but in more recent years has focused on studying the efflorescence of religions at the margins (fundamentalism, Pentecostalism, liberation theology) rather than at the center. He made his name with the 1965 classic *Religion and the Secular City*, a work squarely in the dominant progressive, pragmatic, and optimistic intellectual trends of the time. He suggested that secularization should be welcomed rather than condemned, that anonymity in the city was not "loneliness" as it had been portrayed in so much contemporary literature, but rather freedom. The subsequent selection shows his rethinking and, in some cases, 180 degree reversals of positions outlined in *The Secular City*. In *Religion in the Secular City: Toward a Postmodern Theology*, he first addressed the question of why in the 1960s it seemed that religion was dead, whereas by the 1980s one could wonder if it was secularism that was dying.

The chapter finishes with two strikingly different pieces. The first, by Elizabeth Lesser, is both an autobiography and a self-help text, outlining her own spiritual journey and quests from the 1960s to the present. The second is a *cri de couer*, a work of poetry by the Palestinian American writer Suheir Hammad, whose confusions and affirmations capture much of the experience of Middle Eastern immigrants in the wake of the terrorist attacks of September 11. With her deep pragmatism and optimism, her engagement in social causes and resulting burnout, her desire for community and yet deep yearning for a more individualized family life, and her ability to piece together fragments of a multitude of diverse traditions, Lesser comes as close as anyone to the paradigmatic religious American. Hammad's work, written just after 9/11, suggests alternative ways to view the American social and religious experience in the new millennium, highlighting the pluralism of the American past and future.

American religion at the millennium was characterized by deeply personal quests in which elements of diverse traditions were combined—an evolving spirituality exciting for its freedom and flexibility and dangerous for its frequent lapses into hyperindividualism and narcissism. As Alexis de Tocqueville had noted in his 1831 classic *Democracy in America*, Americans remained at once the most materialistic and the most spiritually inclined people in the western world. Their openness to religious innovation and entrepreneurship created the dynamism and market responsiveness of American religion that continues to puzzle and fascinate outsiders.

1. HARVEY COX, "THE BIBLICAL SOURCES OF SECULARIZATION" (FROM *THE SECULAR CITY*, 1965), *RELIGION IN THE SECULAR CITY* (1984)

One of the most widely read and influential authors in the field of religious studies over the last thirty years, Harvey Cox first made his name as author of a seminal text in the 1960s, The Secular City. *In this work, Cox argued for a new religious "exorcism, to scrape off the stubborn deposits of town and tribal pasts" and leave men free to face the concrete issues of this world: "The church should be ready to expose the fallaciousness of the social myths by which the injustices of a society are perpetuated." The first selection shows Cox's thinking in 1965, as a pragmatic, optimistic, and modernist intellectual.*

Twenty years later, in Religion in the Secular City: Toward a Postmodern Theology, *Cox reversed course, writing about "the unexpected return of religion as a potent social force in a world many thought was leaving it behind." The work addressed the rapid rise of religious movements since the 1960s, ranging from liberation theology to fundamentalism. New theologies, he believed, would come to people and regions who had been "largely left out of participation in the centers of modern theological discourse" (such as the Third World poor and the fundamentalists with their "redneck religion").*

<hr />

THE BIBLICAL SOURCES OF SECULARIZATION

We have defined secularization as the liberation of man from religious and metaphysical tutelage, the turning of his attention away from other worlds and toward this one. But how did this emancipation begin? What are its sources? . . .

The discussion is designed to make amply clear that, far from being something Christians should be against, secularization represents an authentic consequence of biblical faith. Rather than oppose it, the task of Christians should be to support and nourish it. But before we deal with these matters let us look briefly at the word *secularization* itself. . . .

From the very beginning of its usage, secular denoted something vaguely inferior. It meant "this world" of change as opposed to the eternal "religious world." . . .

More recently, secularization has been used to describe a process on the cultural level which is parallel to the political one. It denotes the disappearance of religious determination of the symbols of cultural integration. Cultural secularization is an inevitable concomitant of a political and social secularization. Sometimes the one precedes the other, depending on the historical circumstances, but a wide imbalance between social and cultural secularization will not persist very long. In the United States there has been a considerable degree of political secularization for many years. The public schools are officially secular in the sense of being free from church control. At the same time, the cultural secularization of America has come about more slowly. The Supreme Court decisions in the early 1960s outlawing required prayers pointed up a disparity which had continued for some years. In Eastern Europe, on the other hand, the historical process has been just the opposite. . . .

In any case, secularization as a descriptive term has a wide and inclusive significance. It appears in many different guises, depending on the religious and political history of the area concerned. But wherever it appears, it should be carefully distinguished from secularism. Secularization implies a historical process, almost certainly irreversible, in which society and culture are delivered from tutelage to religious control and closed metaphysical world-views. We have argued that it is basically a liberating development. Secularism, on the other hand, is the name for an ideology, a new closed world-view which functions very much like a new religion. While secularization finds its roots in the biblical faith itself and is to some extent an authentic outcome of the impact of biblical faith on Western history, this is not the case with secularism. Like any other ism, it menaces the openness and freedom secularization has produced; it must therefore be watched carefully to prevent its becoming the ideology of a new establishment. It must be especially checked where it pretends not to be a world-view but nonetheless seeks to impose its ideology through the organs of the state. . . .

Secularization signifies the removal of religious and metaphysical supports and putting man on his own. It is opening the door of the playpen and turning man loose in an open universe. . . .

The ministry of exorcism in the secular city requires a community of persons who, individually and collectively, are not burdened by the constriction of an archaic heritage. It requires a community which, if not fully liberated, is in the process of liberation from compulsive patterns of behavior based on mistaken images of the world. In performing its function the church should be such a community and should be sensitive to those currents in modern life which bear the same exorcising power. The church should be ready to expose the fallaciousness of the social myths by which the injustice of a society are perpetuated and to suggest ways of action which demonstrate the wrongness of such fantasies. . . .

Where in all this do theologians and preachers fit? Sociologically speaking, they represent the victims both of historical change and of social differentiation. Most people perceive them as cultural antiques and may have the same fondness for them they have for *deuxième empire* furniture. Especially when they dress up and strut about occasionally in their vivid ecclesiastical regalia, clergymen give people a welcome sense of historical continuity, much like old soldiers in the dress uniform of some forgotten war. Or clergy are perceived as the custodians of a particular in-group lore, and as such are usually granted an expansive deference in a culture which has been taught to be meticulously tolerant of the beliefs of others, however quaint. But this dual role of personification of the past and preserver of a subcultural ethos, a role clergymen play quite avidly, takes its toll when they speak of God. Because of the role they have been willing to play, when they use the word *God* it is heard in a certain way. It is heard, often with deference and usually with courtesy, as a word referring to the linchpin of the era of Christendom (past) or as the totem of one of the tribal subcultures (irrelevant). The only way clergy can ever change the way in which the word they use is perceived is to refuse to play the role of antiquarian and medicine man in which the society casts them, but this is difficult, because it is what they are paid for.

<hr />

RELIGION IN THE SECULAR CITY

The current reappearance of religion does not, however, make the message of *The Secular City* obsolete. . . . If the challenge modern theology took on was to define and defend the faith in an era of religious decline, the task of a postmodern theology is to interpret the Christian message at a time when the rebirth of religion, rather than its disappearance, poses the most serious questions. . . .

Politics always makes strange bedfellows, especially when mixed with religion. If the conservative wing of the uprising against modern theology is a

potpourri, the radical party is also a choir of mixed voices. It brings together not only Latin American Catholics but an increasing number of Asian
and African Christians; a growing group of feminist religious thinkers;
black American theologians; a scattering of white American inner-city
Catholics and Appalachian Protestants, and—more recently—voices from
the Asian American and Mexican American subcultures. Like the pope's division, this list includes people who until recently might have crossed the
street to avoid meeting each other.

At first the convergence of the traditionalists and radicals seems odd. The
conservatives dismiss the radicals and their liberation theology either as a
collapsing of the faith into a political ideology or as just the latest sellout to
modernity. The Latin Americans and their allies in the radical camp lump
the sophisticated conservatives along with the fundamentalists as variations
of the same religiously tinctured bourgeois ideology. But when it comes to
evaluating modern theology, the two warring schools agree: they both find
it a failure. Can a postmodern theology arise out of such cacophony?

I think it will, but one should not try to answer this question at the theological level alone. Theologies, unlike philosophical schools or scientific par-
adigms, do not make much headway in the world unless they are borne
along by vigorous religious movements. They need a social base. The emergence of a postmodern theology from the bottom and the edges of the modern world will happen only as religious movements incorporating powerful
critiques of modern theology and the religious sensibility on which it is
based come more and more into prominence. . . .

I have chosen to examine two representative antimodernist religious
movements, one traditional and one radical, in considerable detail:

1. The dramatic reappearance of political fundamentalism and its recent marriage to the electronic media in the United States and, even more recently,
   in other countries as well; and,
2. The equally dramatic appearance of the Christian base communities and of
   liberation theology, which has occurred in many places, but chiefly in Latin
   America.

Both movements are growing rapidly. Both are profoundly antagonistic to
modern theology, especially what they call "liberal" or "progressive" theology, though in quite different ways. Both are shattering the institutional
forms of religious life that came to birth during and after the Reformation.
Both are uniting people who once fought each other and dividing people
who once felt united. Both are creating new forms of religious association
that are rendering denominations, the most characteristic social expression

of modern Christianity, obsolete. Both emphasize the Bible and claim to be recalling people to the Original Message, away from the errors and idols of modernity. Both emphasize increased participation of Christians in political life. Both rely on leaders whose authority has more to do with personal charisma than with academic degrees or ecclesiastical ordinations.

Yet despite these similarities, the differences between the burgeoning mass media religion of the United States and the fast-growing base-community liberation Christianity in other parts of the world could not be greater. The two open a schism in the church that runs far deeper than the occasional bickering that still divides Catholics from Protestants. Mass media fundamentalism, though it varies in tone and tenor, presents a theology that celebrates patriotism, individual success, and a political spectrum ranging from moderately conservative to the far, far right. The base communities on the other hand, though they also vary immensely from place to place, exemplify a theology that affirms social justice, the rights of the poor, a communal understanding of salvation, and a politics that stretches from moderately reformist to revolutionary. Still, both movements are strongly antimodernist; to understand them is to understand why "modern religion" and its theological rationale seem fated for dissolution. . . .

2. HAL LINDSEY, *THE LATE GREAT PLANET EARTH* (1970)

Hal Lindsey spent years as a traveling lecturer for Campus Crusade for Christ, a large conservative evangelical organization that focused on college students. He collected some of his lectures and speculations into his 1970 book The Late Great Planet Earth, *a surprise runaway best-seller. Lindsey provided an easy-to-read analysis of the course of contemporary human events interpreted through the lens of biblical prophecy. Mixing verses from the Bible's eschatological books—chiefly Daniel, Ezekiel, and Revelation—he provided readers with an updated version of premillennialism, the theological innovation from the nineteenth century that suggested a period of tribulation and apocalyptic world conflict, culminating in the triumphant Second Coming of Christ. To this he added a twentieth-century notion of the "Rapture," when Jesus would take up his followers to heaven prior to the final earthly cataclysm that would engulf the unbelievers.*

As was typical of conservative evangelical prophesiers, Lindsey focused on Israel and the Middle East, especially the reestablishment of the state of Israel that was a prerequisite to the final playing out of the human drama. His book appealed to a generation of evangelicals affected by, but also deeply suspicious of, the social changes brought by the 1960s, searching for a biblical explanation for the tumult they saw all around them.

⊛

REVIVAL OF MYSTERY BABYLON

. . . We are told in the Bible that before the seven-year period of tribulation there will be an all-powerful religious system which will aid the Antichrist in subjecting the world to his absolute authority. For a time this religious system will actually have control of the Dictator.

There are several names given to this one-world religion, all of them drawing a perfect analogy in meaning. It is called the Great Harlot, or prostitute; the "harlot" represents a religion which prostitutes the true meaning of being wedded to Christ, and sells out to all the false religions of man. . . .

As pieces of the prophecy puzzle appeared to fall into place there was one important part that was lost to me. The Bible outlines very specifically that there would be a one-world religion which would dominate the world in the time before the return of Christ. However, this seemed so remote, with so many different religions competing for the minds and hearts of men, how on earth could people unite in allegiance to just one religion?

Five years ago, for instance, as I surveyed the college campuses where I ministered, it seemed that most of the intellectual community was alienated by any concept of the supernatural. . . .

But the scene has changed rapidly in the intellectual community in the past few years. Many of those who scoffed at "religion" have become addicted to the fast-moving upsurge in astrology, spiritualism, and even drugs. What does all this mean? Does it have any significance in Biblical prophecy?

We believe that the joining of churches in the present ecumenical movement, combined with this amazing rejuvenation of star-worship, mind-expansion, and witchcraft, is preparing the world in every way for the establishment of a great religious system, one which will influence the Antichrist. . . .

The Scripture says that a Great Dictator is coming and he will be boosted to power, and strengthened in his grasp upon the world with the assistance of the ancient religion, called Mystery, Babylon. This is the very religion which started in the Genesis account and made possible the first world dictator. . . .

The Latin word for "1000" is "millennium" and down through history the teaching concerning this earthly kingdom came to be known as the "millennial kingdom." Those who reject that Christ will establish a 1000 year kingdom after His return are known theologically as "amillennialists," meaning "no millennium." Those who believe that Christ will return and set up a 1000 year kingdom are called "premillennialists," meaning Christ returns first, then establishes the kingdom on earth.

There used to be a group called "postmillennialists." They believed that the Christians would root out the evil in the world, abolish godless rulers, and convert the world through ever increasing evangelism until they brought about the Kingdom of God on earth through their own efforts. Then after 1000 years of the institutional church reigning on earth with peace, equality, and righteousness, Christ would return and time would end. These people rejected much of the Scripture as being literal and believed in the inherent goodness of man. World War I greatly disheartened this group and World War II virtually wiped out this viewpoint. . . .

We are "premillennialists" in viewpoint. The real issue between the amillennial and the premillennial viewpoints is whether prophecy should be interpreted literally or allegorically. As it has been demonstrated many times in this book, all prophecy about past events has been fulfilled literally, particularly the predictions regarding the first coming of Christ. The words of prophecy were demonstrated as being literal, that is, having the normal meaning understood by the people of the time in which it was written. The words were not intended to be explained away by men who cannot believe what is clearly predicted. . . .

With increasing frequency the leadership of the denominations will be captured by those who completely reject the historic truths of the Bible and deny doctrines which according to Christ Himself are crucial to believe in order to be a Christian. In some of the largest Protestant denominations this has already taken place. The few remaining institutions which are not yet dominated by the disbelievers will go downhill in the same manner.

There will be unprecedented mergers of denominations into "religious conglomerates." This will occur for two reasons: first, most denominations were formed because of deep convictions about certain spiritual truths. As more of these truths are discarded as irrelevant because of unbelief in Biblical authority, there will be no reason to be divided. Unity is certainly important to have, but never, according to the teachings of Christ, at the expense of the crucial truths of Christianity.

Secondly, as ministers depart from the truths of the Bible they lose the authority and power that it has to meet real human needs, and as many ministers are not truly born spiritually themselves and are consequently without the illumination of God's Spirit, they no longer will be able to hold their present congregations, much less attract others. So they resort to "social action gimmicks," super-organization, and elaborate programs as a substitute.

Young people will continue to accelerate their exodus from the institutional churches. Several surveys taken by church leaders indicate this. Youth today reject impersonal, highly structured organizations with their emphasis upon buildings and material affluence. In talking with many young people from various backgrounds I have found that the institutional churches are viewed by them as a reflection of all they despise in what they consider materialistic, hypocritical, and prejudiced elements within our American culture. . . .

There will be an ever-widening gap between the true believers in Christ and those who masquerade as "ministers of righteousness." I believe that open persecution will soon break out upon the "real Christians," and it will come from the powerful hierarchy of unbelieving leaders within the denominations. Christians who believe in the final authority of the Bible, salvation through the substitutionary atonement of Christ alone, the deity of Jesus Christ, etc., will be branded as prime hindrances to "the brotherhood" of all men and the "universal Fatherhood of God" teaching. . . .

Look for vast and far-reaching movements toward a one-world religious organization, spearheaded mostly by the unbelieving leaders of the institutional churches; also look for this movement to become more politically oriented than it is now.

Look for movements within Israel to make Jerusalem the religious center of the world and to rebuild their ancient Temple on its old site.

3. JERRY FALWELL, "A BIBLICAL LOOK INTO THE 21ST CENTURY" (1999)

LARRY NORMAN, "I WISH WE'D ALL BEEN READY" (1970S)

As pastor of an enormous Baptist church in Virginia and a spokesman for many conservative and fundamentalist Protestants, Jerry Falwell made his name as creator and leader of the Moral Majority in the 1970s, an influential political group in the rise of the "New Religious Political Right." After receding from public view for a time in the 1980s and 1990s, vowing to return to preaching the gospel and ministering to his flock, Falwell rose to prominence again in the late 1990s, this time as a vitriolic and polemical critic of President William Jefferson Clinton (whom Falwell accused of everything from drug dealing in the White House to murder of a top aide who had committed suicide). Falwell drew intense interest again in early 2000 with a series of sermons on the meaning of the millennium. Mostly the sermons repackaged themes familiar to Protestant premillennialism—the imminent Second Coming of Jesus, the Rapture of the believers, the dark days of Armageddon, and the key role of the Israeli-Arab conflict in the fate of the world. But Falwell also garnered attention for a very specific prophecy concerning the Antichrist—that this biblically prophesied figure was probably now living, and was most likely a Jewish male. Jewish organizations immediately decried Falwell's state-

ments; he apologized, but stood by his interpretation of the biblical prophecies. The following sermon, typical of thousands delivered by conservative Protestants as the year 2000 approached, summarizes some key tenets of Falwell's millennialism.

Following the sermon is the text of a hymn familiar to conservative Protestants since it was written in the late 1960s, "I Wish We'd All Been Ready." A generation of evangelical youth grew up singing this song, set to a popular tune and accompanied by guitar, often at church camps or youth services. The lyrics depict what will happen at the time of the rapture of Christians.

INTRODUCTION: Today I am going to suggest to you 16 things that I believe will occur in the next century. Even though this seems like a "sensational" sermon topic, what I am predicting is not based on sensationalism or on a "Jeanne Dixon" type prophecy. I cannot predict the future. Three things you or I cannot do:

> We can't read tea leaves.
> We don't have a crystal ball.
> We can't predict the future.

There is only One Who can predict the future—God. He is without beginning, without end.

> He knows what's in the final chapter of life's book.
> He knows how things will turn out.
> He has given us a few signs that point to the end times.

From what I know of the Bible, and from my limited knowledge of signs, here is a list of things I expect in the next century:

1. I expect the Lord to return in the 21st Century to rapture out His church.

While I said before that I am not predicting when He will come, I expect the Lord will probably come in this century for three reasons:

Everything is in place that needs to happen before He can return. There are no more predicted events that need to happen for Jesus to return. Jesus said He would be gone a long time (Matthew 25:19) and it has been a long time (approximately 2,000 years) since His departure. We are commanded to "watch" and "be ready" for His return (Matthew 24:42–44), so if I expect him to return this century, I am only following His orders by watching and waiting.

2. I expect the preaching of the gospel to reach every ethnic group in the world.

Jesus commanded His church, "Go into all the world and make disciples of all nations" (Matthew 28:19). The word "nations" means people groups or ethnic groups. We are closer to getting this done than ever before. "This gospel of the kingdom shall be preached in all the world for a witness unto all nations; then shall the end come" (Matthew 24:14).

3. I expect Jesus to return when He is least expected. . . .

"Behold I come quickly" (Matthew 22:7).

4. I expect many to set dates and make predictions about His return, but they will be all wrong. . . .

5. I expect increased conflict in the Middle East, primarily focused around the State of Israel.

The Bible is full of illustrations that tell that Israel shall return to the land (Ezekiel 37) and those nations inspired by Anti-Christ will oppose Israel.

6. I expect the European nations to further consolidate themselves as a revived Roman Empire.

This is the prediction of the revived Roman Empire (Daniel 2). Daniel predicted four nations would rule the known world; first Babylon, second Medo-Persia, third Greece and fourth, Rome. This has happened as he predicted; then Daniel said the Roman Empire would be revived in the last days. I believe this will happen in this century, although I don't know what form it will take.

7. I expect a global economy which first manifests itself by a cashless society.

When the Rapture takes place, Anti-Christ will step into the picture and create a one-world government, a one-world economy, a one-world religion. Therefore, I expect the world to move towards global economy in preparation for a one-world government.

8. I expect the nations of the world to work together rapidly towards a one-world government.

While a functional one-world government will not be operative before the Rapture, I believe that the infrastructure for one-world government will be in place when Jesus comes. While I do not approve of America giving up her sovereignty to the United Nations in the area of military, judicial and legislative matters; nevertheless, this will be obvious as we move into the 21st century.

9. I expect a great increase of wars globally, even though there is more and more talk of peace.

Jesus said to us, "And ye shall hear of wars and rumours of wars: see that ye be not troubled: for all these things must come to pass, but the end is not yet. (24:7) For nation shall rise against nation, and kingdom against kingdom: and there shall be famines, and pestilences, and earthquakes, in divers places."

We have a media industry that is first driven on reporting crises and calamity, but worse, they are fanatical in their speculation and prediction of gloom, impending disaster, weather storms, etc.

10. I expect the apostate church to become more powerful as it departs farther from the fundamentals of the faith. . . .

11. I expect the prophetic picture to become clearer to the true church as we get closer to His return.

Five hundred years ago there were many factors about the Lord's return that we did not understand in Scriptures; but certain "signs" have appeared in the world, giving us evidence that God is preparing the world stage for His appearing. Notice the following:

> The return of Israel to the land and the establishment and recognition of the State of Israel.
> The revival of the old Roman Empire.
> The creation of a one-world economy and one-world government.

12. I expect wickedness to become more prevalent in the next 100 years.

I think one of the things that surprises me most in the last fifty years, is not the scientific advances nor all the electronic marvels we have seen occur. What surprises me most is the moral free fall of our society. America has forgotten God. . . .

I once wondered if sin could become any blacker. I once doubted if homosexuality would become an accepted way of life in America, but it has. I would have never thought that Americans would kill its unborn, but they do.

13. I expect the explosion of knowledge to continue, while fewer persons obtain wisdom.

Daniel predicted "knowledge shall increase" (Daniel 12:4). The Internet has made the knowledge of the world available to anyone who will go online, but today everyone (including the young) has access to all knowledge. Timothy said, "that people would be ever learning and never able to come to the knowledge of truth" (II Timothy 3:7).

14. I expect more and more disruption to the family and raising of children.

Paul predicts, "This know also, that in the last days perilous times shall come. (3:2) For men shall be lovers of their own selves, covetous, boasters, proud, blasphemers, disobedient to parents, unthankful, unholy." . . .

15. I expect more prosperity with people becoming wealthier while succumbing to materialism and hedonism. . . .

16. I expect a soul-winning, sin-crushing, Holy Ghost revival which will sweep millions into the Kingdom of God.

While the Bible promises "perilous days" and "evil days" at the end of this age, I believe . . . God loves people and wants to save as many as possible. God is powerful enough to stop evil at any time. God will respond to the repentance and prayers of His people.

I Wish We'd All Been Ready

1. Life was filled with guns and wars,
and all of us got trampled on the floor,
I wish we'd all been ready.
Children died, the days grew cold,
a piece of bread could buy a bag of gold.

I wish we'd all been ready.
There's no time to change your mind,
the Son has come and you've been left behind.

2. A man and wife asleep in bed,
she hears a noise and turns her head he's gone.
I wish we'd all been ready.
Two men walking up a hill,
one disappears and one's left standing still.
I wish we'd all been ready.
There's no time to change your mind,
the Son has come and you've been left behind.

The Father spoke the demons died,
how could you have been so blind?

There's no time to change your mind,
the Son has come and you've been left behind.

4. MICHAEL BARKUN, "REFLECTIONS AFTER WACO: MILLENNIALISTS AND THE STATE" (1993)

In the winter and spring of 1993, a formerly obscure religious millennialist sect known as the Branch Davidians came to national prominence. Led by a man originally named Vernon Howell, renamed David Koresh, the Davidians had built a compound just outside of Waco, Texas, where they sat awaiting the end days. The Bureau of Alcohol, Tobacco, and Firearms (ATF) became involved with this group because of allegations of child abuse and weapons stockpiling raised by officials of the Justice Department as well as by groups such as the Cult Awareness Network. On February 28, 1993, ATF agents, with assistance from the FBI, attacked the compound, resulting in the deaths of 4 lawmen and the injury of 14 others. For the next two months, the government laid siege to the area, trying negotiations and psychological tactics to force the Davidians out. Finally, on April 19, 1993, government agents moved in. Soon, the Davidian complex was engulfed in flames. In the fire, nearly all the remaining believers—more than 80 in number—perished, in a horrific scene televised for a national viewing public. Controversy, argument, and recrimination followed this incident for years. Two years later, 169 people were murdered in an explosion at a federal building in Oklahoma City, a bombing committed by a young man obsessed with avenging the deaths of the Davidians.

In the following selection, an academic authority reflects on the events in Waco, arguing that the government fundamentally failed to enforce its own principles of religious freedom, and, by not taking seriously the Davidians' own apocalyptic ideas, almost inevitably forced the group to its tragic denouement.

Not since Jonestown has the public been so gripped by the conjunction of religion, violence and communal living as they have by the events at the Branch Davidians' compound. All that actually took place near Waco remains unknown or contested. Nonetheless, the information is sufficient to allow at least a preliminary examination of three questions: Why did it happen? Why didn't it happen earlier? Will it happen again? . . .

The single most damaging mistake on the part of federal officials was their failure to take the Branch Davidians' religious beliefs seriously. Instead, David Koresh and his followers were viewed as being in the grip of delusions that prevented them from grasping reality. As bizarre and misguided as their beliefs might have seemed, it was necessary to grasp the role these beliefs played in their lives; these beliefs were the basis of their reality. The Branch Davidians clearly possessed an encompassing worldview to which they attached ultimate significance. That they did so carried three implications. First, they could entertain no other set of beliefs. Indeed, all other views of the world, including those held by government negotiators, could only be regarded as erroneous. The lengthy and fruitless conversations between the two sides were, in effect, an interchange between different cultures—they talked past one another.

Second, since these beliefs were the basis of the Branch Davidians' sense of personal identity and meaning, they were non-negotiable. The conventional conception of negotiation as agreement about some exchange or compromise between the parties was meaningless in this context. How could anything of ultimate significance be surrendered to an adversary steeped in evil and error? Finally, such a belief system implies a link between ideas and actions. It requires that we take seriously—as apparently the authorities did not—the fact that actions might be based on something other than obvious self-interest. . . .

Federal authorities were clearly unfamiliar and uncomfortable with religion's ability to drive human behavior to the point of sacrificing all other loyalties. Consequently, officials reacted by trying to assimilate the Waco situation to more familiar and less threatening stereotypes, treating the Branch Davidians as they would hijackers and hostage-takers. . . .

The perpetuation of such stereotypes at Waco, as well as the failure to fully appreciate the religious dimension of the situation, resulted in large measure from the "cult" concept. Both the authorities and the media referred endlessly to the Branch Davidians as a "cult" and Koresh as a "cult leader." The term "cult" is virtually meaningless. It tells us far more about those who use it than about those to whom it is applied. It has become little more than a label slapped on religious groups regarded as too exotic, marginal or dangerous.

As soon as a group achieves respectability by numbers or longevity, the label drops away. Thus books on "cults" published in the 1940s routinely applied the term to Christian Scientists, Jehovah's Witnesses, Mormons and Seventh-day Adventists, none of whom are referred to in comparable terms today. . . .

In the Waco case, the "cult" concept had two dangerous effects. First, because the word supplies a label, not an explanation, it hindered efforts to understand the movement from the participants' perspectives. The very act of classification itself seems to make further investigation unnecessary. To compound the problem, in this instance the classification imposed upon the group resulted from a negative evaluation by what appear to have been basically hostile observers. Second, since the proliferation of new religious groups in the 1960s, a network of so-called "cult experts" has arisen, drawn from the ranks of the academy, apostates from such religious groups, and members' relatives who have become estranged from their kin because of the "cult" affiliations. Like many other law-enforcement agencies, the FBI has relied heavily on this questionable and highly partisan expertise—with tragic consequences. It was tempting to do so since the hostility of those in the "anti-cult" movement mirrored the authorities' own anger and frustration.

These cascading misunderstandings resulted in violence because they produced erroneous views of the role force plays in dealing with armed millenarians. In such confrontations, dramatic demonstrations of force by the authorities provoke instead of intimidate. It is important to understand that millenarians possess a "script"—a conception of the sequence of events that must play out at the end of history. The vast majority of contemporary millenarians are satisfied to leave the details of this script in God's hands. Confrontation can occur, however, because groups often conceive of the script in terms of a climactic struggle between forces of good and evil.

How religious prophecy is interpreted is inseparable from how a person or a group connects events with the millenarian narrative. Because these believers' script emphasizes battle and resistance, it requires two players: the millenarians as God's instruments or representatives, and a failed but still resisting temporal order. By using massive force the Bureau of Alcohol, Tobacco and Firearms on February 28, and the FBI on April 19, unwittingly conformed to Koresh's millenarian script. He wanted and needed their opposition, which they obligingly provided in the form of the initial assault, the nationally publicized siege, and the final tank and gas attack. When viewed from a millenarian perspective, these actions, intended as pressure, were the fulfillment of prophecy.

The government's actions almost certainly increased the resolve of those in the compound, subdued the doubters and raised Koresh's stature by in effect validating his predictions. Attempts after the February 28 assault to "increase the pressure" through such tactics as floodlights and sound bombardment now seem as pathetic as they were counterproductive. They reflect the flawed premise that the Branch Davidians were more interested in calculating costs and benefits than in taking deeply held beliefs to their logical conclusions. Since the government's own actions seemed to support Koresh's teachings, followers had little incentive to question them.

The final conflagration is even now the subject of dispute between the FBI, which insists that the blazes were set, and survivors who maintain that a tank overturned a lantern. In any case, even if the FBI's account proves correct, "suicide" seems an inadequate label for the group's fiery demise. Unlike Jonestown, where community members took their own lives in an isolated setting, the Waco deaths occurred in the midst of a violent confrontation. If the fires were indeed set, they may have been seen as a further working through of the script's implications. . . .

Just as the authorities in Waco failed to understand the connections between religion and violence, so they failed to grasp the nature of charismatic leadership. Charisma, in its classic sociological sense, transcends law and custom. When a Dallas reporter asked Koresh whether he thought he was above the law, he responded: "I am the law." Given such self-perception, charismatic figures can be maddeningly erratic; they feel no obligation to remain consistent with pre-existing rules. Koresh's swings of mood and attitude seemed to have been a major factor in the FBI's growing frustration, yet they were wholly consistent with a charismatic style.

Nevertheless, charismatic leaders do confront limits. One is the body of doctrine to which he or she is committed. This limit is often overcome by the charismatic interpreter's ingenuity combined with the texts' ambiguity (Koresh, like so many millennialists, was drawn to the vivid yet famously obscure language of the Book of Revelation).

The other and more significant limit is imposed by the charismatic leader's need to validate his claim to leadership by his performance. Charismatic leadership is less a matter of inherent talents than it is a complex relational and situational matter between leader and followers. Since much depends on followers' granting that a leader possesses extraordinary gifts, the leader's claim is usually subject to repeated testing. A leader acknowledged at one time may be rejected at another. Here too the Waco incident provided an opportunity for the authorities inadvertently to meet millennialist needs. The protracted discussions with Koresh and his ability to tie down government resources gave the impression of a single individual toying with a powerful state. While to the outer world Koresh may have seemed besieged, to those in the community he may well have provided ample evidence of his power by immobilizing a veritable army of law-enforcement personnel and dominating the media. . . .

The universe of American communal groups is densely populated—they certainly number in the thousands—and it includes an enormous variety of ideological and religious persuasions. Some religious communities are millenarian, and of these some grow out of a "posttribulationist" theology. They believe, that is, that Armageddon and the Second Coming will be preceded by seven years of turmoil (the tribulation), but they part company with the dominant strain of contemporary Protestant millennialism in the position they assign to the saved. The dominant millenarian current (dispensational premillennialism) assumes that a Rapture will lift the saved off the earth to join Christ before the tribulation begins, a position widely promulgated by such televangelists as Jerry Falwell. Posttribulationists, on the other hand, do not foresee such a rescue and insist that Christians must endure the tribulation's rigors, which include the reign of the Antichrist. Their emphasis upon chaos and persecution sometimes leads them toward a "survivalist" lifestyle—retreat into defendable, self-sufficient rural settlements where they can, they believe, wait out the coming upheavals.

Of all the posttribulationists, those most likely to ignite future Wacos are affiliated with the Christian Identity movement. These groups, on the outermost fringes of American religion, believe that white "Aryans" are the direct descendants of the tribes of Israel, while Jews are children of Satan. Not surprisingly, Identity has become highly influential in the white suprema-cist right. While its numbers are small (probably between 20,000 and 50,000), its penchant for survivalism and its hostility toward Jews and non-whites renders the Christian Identity movement a likely candidate for fu-ture violent conflict with the state.

When millenarians retreat into communal settlements they create a com-plex tension between withdrawal and engagement. Many communal soci-eties in the 19th century saw themselves as showcases for social experi-mentation—what historian Arthur Bestor has called "patent office models of society." But posttribulationist survivalist groups are defensive commu-nities designed to keep at bay a world they despise and fear. They often deny the legitimacy of government and other institutions. For some, the reign of Antichrist has already begun. . . .

These and similar groups will receive a subtle but powerful cultural boost as we move toward the year 2000. Even secularists seem drawn, however ir-rationally, toward the symbolism of the millennial number. The decimal sys-tem invests such dates with a presumptive importance. We unthinkingly as-sume they are watersheds in time, points that divide historical epochs. If even irreligious persons pause in expectation before such a date, is it sur-prising that millennialists do so?

5. JAMES REDFIELD WEB SITE, "THE CELESTINE INSIGHTS"; READER RESPONSES FROM AMAZON.COM; DENNIS POLLOCK, "*THE CELESTINE PROPHECY*: HEAVENLY INSIGHT OR NEW AGE FRAUD?" (1999)

In 1994, James Redfield's The Celestine Prophecy *topped best-seller lists for weeks and spurred a national following for the "Nine Insights" it presented. Redfield's novel follows the story of an anthropologist who is dissatisfied with his life and the strictures of mod-ern society. Through a series of apparent coincidences, he travels to Peru to search for a missing manuscript, one supposedly containing the key to unlock the mysteries of the future of humanity. While there he meets with other journeyers on the same quest, as well as government officials and religious authorities who forcibly attempt to prevent publication of the manuscript. They fear that the insights of the ancient text will un-dermine all current forms of hierarchy and authority.*

Redfield's "Nine Insights," summarized on numerous Web sites (including the one excerpted below), summarize much conventional New Age thought about the necessity of a personal mystical experience to overcome conflict in the world. Also included is a biting critique from a Christian evangelist's response not only to Redfield but also to New Age thinking generally.

THE CELESTINE INSIGHTS

1. A Critical Mass
A new spiritual awakening is occurring in human culture, an awakening brought about by a critical mass of individuals who experience their lives as a spiritual unfolding, a journey in which we are led forward by mysterious coincidences.

2. The Longer Now
This awakening represents the creation of a new, more complete world view, which replaces a five-hundred-year-old preoccupation with secular survival and comfort. While this technological preoccupation was an important step, our awakening to life's coincidences is opening us up to the real purpose of human life on this planet, and the real nature of our universe.

3. A Matter Of Energy
We now experience that we live not in a material universe, but in a universe of dynamic energy. Everything extant is a field of sacred energy that we can sense and intuit. Moreover, we humans can project our energy by focusing our attention in the desired direction . . . where attention goes, energy flows . . . influencing other energy systems and increasing the pace of coincidences in our lives.

4. The Struggle For Power
Too often humans cut themselves off from the greater source of this energy and so feel weak and insecure. To gain energy we tend to manipulate or force others to give us attention and thus energy. When we successfully dominate others in this way, we feel more powerful, but they are left weakened and often fight back. Competition for scarce, human energy is the cause of all conflict between people.

5. The Message Of The Mystics
Insecurity and violence ends when we experience an inner connection with divine energy within, a connection described by mystics of all traditions. A sense of lightness—buoyancy—along with the constant sensation of love are measures of this connection. If these measures are present, the connection is real. If not, it is only pretended.

6. Clearing The Past
The more we stay connected, the more we are acutely aware of those times when we lose connection, usually when we are under stress. In these times, we can see our own particular way of stealing energy from others. Once our manipulations are brought to personal awareness, our connection becomes more constant and we can discover our own growth path in

life, and our spiritual mission—the personal way we can contribute to the world.

7. Engaging The Flow

Knowing our personal mission further enhances the flow of mysterious coincidences as we are guided toward our destinies. First we have a question; then dreams, daydreams, and intuitions lead us towards the answers, which usually are synchronistically provided by the wisdom of another human being.

8. The Interpersonal Ethic

We can increase the frequency of guiding coincidences by uplifting every person that comes into our lives. Care must be taken not to lose our inner connection in romantic relationships. Uplifting others is especially effective in groups where each member can feel energy of all the others. With children it is extremely important for their early security and growth. By seeing the beauty in every face, we lift others into their wisest self, and increase the chances of hearing a synchronistic message.

9. The Emerging Culture

As we all evolve toward the best completion of our spiritual missions, the technological means of survival will be fully automated as humans focus instead on synchronistic growth. Such growth will move humans into higher energy states, ultimately transforming our bodies into spiritual form and uniting this dimension of existence with the after-life dimension, ending the cycle of birth and death.

10. Holding The Vision

The Tenth Insight is the realization that throughout history human beings have been unconsciously struggling to implement this lived spirituality on Earth. Each of us comes here on assignment, and as we pull this understanding into consciousness, we can remember a fuller birth vision of what we wanted to accomplish with our lives. Further we can remember a common world vision of how we will all work together to create a new spiritual culture. We know that our challenge is to hold this vision with intention and prayer everyday.

11. Extending Our Prayer Fields

The Eleventh Insight is the precise method through which we hold the vision. For centuries, religious scriptures, poems, and philosophies have pointed to a latent power of mind within all of us that mysteriously helps to affect what occurs in the future. It has been called faith power, positive thinking, the power of prayer. We are now taking this power seriously enough to bring a fuller knowledge of it into public awareness. We are finding that this prayer power is a field of intention and moves out from us and can be extended and strengthened, especially when we connect with others in a common vision. This is the power through which we hold the vision of a spiritual world and build the energy in ourselves and others to make this vision a reality.

The Twelfth Insight is to be released in 2001.

————— ∞∞ —————

READER RESPONSES FROM AMAZON.COM

★★★★★   **Life can now change**

Reviewer: **A reader** from Portugal   November 30, 1999

If you want to change your life, and start facing its problems with another perspective, read this book immediatelly. Yet, this only applies for the open-minded. All those out there who are simply not prepared to a new reality, although being able to read and comprehend its messages, can't fully reach the true objective of this book. Apart from giving a sympathetic and optimistic view of the world, it introduces new notions, new dimensions that most of us didn't fully give credit to. So, this one is to be read with an open-mind, with a spirit ready to hear and receive different perspectives, and not to be taken as some sort of Bible or dogmatic book. Nevertheless, those who aren't inserted in this faction should read it, just for the enriching experience.

★   **Redfield Unbound**

Reviewer: **[a reader]** from Hollywood, USA   November 30, 1999

Bland writing, flat characters, tedious pacing—some might forgive all this, if the insights were, well, insightful in some way. Alas, they begin with the obvious, and then lurch off into nonsense about plants having energy fields, etc. Come on, folks—do you really think you're more likely to find spiritual growth by loafing on some mountain peak in Peru, surrounded by coca fields, than by volunteering at a battered women's shelter near the edge of town, or a soup kitchen on skid row? A run-down warehouse district may not be pretty, but the truth—even with a capital T—rarely is.

★★★★★   **The Spiritual Journey**

Reviewer: **[a reader]** from Colorado   November 29, 1999

I knew someone who had this book and I borrowed it. It caught my interest and I bought one of my own, which I read twice. The energy is what caught my attention in this book. In time I began to practise the energy seen in plants and trees. I caught myself more involved in information about Aura's. At that time this book also lead me toward meditation. Eventually I found myself destined to seek deeper. I held a pen in my hand and asked what my destiny was? Why do these things happen and who is behind all this? Though this method did reveal answers, I thought Satan was behind it. Little do we know about the unknown . . . until we understand the love and understanding of our creator. God's techniques work mysterious in way's that are not commonly understood. Therefore, you need to understand the barricade that separates you from many hidden truths which is available for you to direct your destiny. If you are not rooted in what you believe to be true, critics can turn you toward doubt and fear. God is not fear nor is he punishing. . . . The soul is connected to the internal world where it knows peace and wisdom with God. The true characteristics of humankind develop these truths from within this realm. It is only known to that individual in spirit with spirit, whereas, beyond the means of God is Ego against spirit. Celestine Prophecy is a book that enhanced my hidden abilities to get me where I am today. . . .

❧❧❧

THE CELESTINE PROPHECY: HEAVENLY INSIGHT OR A NEW AGE FRAUD?

For almost a year it has been on the best seller list. It is being taught in churches, and has developed a cult-like following in a very short time. Study classes have gathered all over the country to discuss its precepts and implement its "insights." *The Celestine Prophecy*, written by James Redfield, is the latest New Age oracle which has managed to transcend the boundaries of the crystal gazers and navel meditaters [sic], and reach out to large numbers of mainstream Americans.

The book makes some pretty pretentious claims for itself. From the inside flap of the book cover, we read:

When you find and understand all 9 of the insights you will have an exciting new image of human life, and a positive vision of how we will save this planet, its creatures, and its beauty . . . And you will suddenly recognize the quantum leap forward humankind is preparing to make as we approach the new millennium. . . .

The Nine Insights
This novel centers around nine insights which humans will begin to grasp sequentially, one insight then another, as they move from their present state to a completely spiritual culture on earth. The attaining and comprehending of these insights is the salvation offered by Mr. Redfield. None of them relate to Jesus Christ. Nothing is said about forgiveness of sins or reconciliation to God. Instead we are told that by learning and applying these insights, our lives will be spiritual and fulfilling, and all will be well. Obviously the cross of Jesus has no place here.

The insights are a curious hodgepodge of homespun philosophy, borrowed pop-psychology, and new age rhetoric. The first step is to realize that all of life's coincidences are for a purpose. The second one is to realize that man has left traditional religion, tried materialism, and now must find true spirituality (through the insights, of course). The third insight is that there is an invisible energy which people must learn to perceive, and that the universe is energy that responds to our expectations. The fourth reveals that the world is a vast competition for energy, and the fifth says that the "universe" can provide all the energy we need if only we can open up to it. I could go on, but I think you get the idea. . . .

If there is one word that gets run into the ground in the story, it is energy. According to the insights, life is all about energy. The manuscript reveals that "eventually humans would see the universe as comprised of one dynamic energy, an energy that can sustain us and respond to our expectations. Yet we would also see that we have been disconnected from the larger source of this energy, that we have cut ourselves off and so have felt weak and insecure and lacking." Although God is mentioned a few times in the book, **the real god of this book is energy**. . . .

So as a Christian I am not opposed to the idea of spiritual energy. However the Scriptures make plain that God's energy is only available through Jesus Christ and the filling of the Holy Spirit. This is not some universal power available to people of all religions. . . .

What this tale fails to take into account is that there is an evil energy that is at work in the world. This is the very energy that will one day empower the Antichrist. . . . Those who would desire to open themselves up to universal energy, without bothering to make Jesus Christ the Lord of their lives, may find that the energy they receive comes from a most malicious source. . . .

What a vast difference there is between *The Celestine Prophecy*'s "Life is energy" nonsense, and the revelation of God's plan of salvation for man, as revealed in the Holy Scriptures! **The one thing Mr. Redfield dares not touch is the cross.** No mention whatever is made of the cross of Jesus in his book. No doubt he realizes that the message of the cross is somehow incongruous with his religion of universal energy.

6. 1993 PARLIAMENT OF THE WORLD'S RELIGIONS, "TOWARDS A GLOBAL ETHIC"; RESPONSE FROM BUDDHISTS AND FRIENDS

In 1993, Americans celebrated the hundredth anniversary of the World's Columbian Exposition of 1893, a mammoth event in Chicago that symbolized for many at that time America's coming of age. At the exposition, religious leaders gathered at the World's Parliament of Religions, an event that introduced many Americans to religions outside the Judeo-Christian orbit, especially Hinduism and Buddhism. The event as a whole, however, was ultimately a celebration of liberal Protestantism. In 1993, religious figures gathered again, this time in a Chicago now inhabited by practitioners of virtually all the faiths of the world.

Representatives at the Parliament worked for two years prior to the 1993 meeting to draft the following statement of global ethics, "those rules for living on which the world's religions agree." The most comprehensive and ecumenical statement to that point, it did not meet the approval of all religious leaders, including Buddhists who added a protest to the Parliament indicating that Buddhism does not hold Buddha to be a divine creator. Thus, the document symbolizes both the hopes for unity among the world's major religions and the difficulties involved in such megacooperative endeavors.

TOWARDS A GLOBAL ETHIC (AN INITIAL DECLARATION)

1993 PARLIAMENT OF THE WORLD'S RELIGIONS

CHICAGO, ILLINOIS, USA

This interfaith declaration is the result of a two-year consultation among scholars and theologians representing the world's communities of faith. . . .

The Declaration of a Global Ethic

The world is in agony. The agony is so pervasive and urgent that we are compelled to name its manifestations so that the depth of this pain may be made clear.

Peace eludes us . . . the planet is being destroyed . . . neighbors live in fear . . . women and men are estranged from each other . . . children die.

This is abhorrent!

We condemn the abuses of Earth's ecosystems.

We condemn the poverty that stifles life's potential: the hunger that weakens the human body; the economic disparities that threaten so many families with ruin.

We condemn the social disarray of the nations; the disregard for justice which pushes citizens to the margin; the anarchy overtaking our communities; and the insane death of children from violence. In particular we condemn aggression and hatred in the name of religion.

But this agony need not be.

It need not be because the basis for an ethic already exists. This ethic offers the possibility of a better individual and global order, and leads individuals away from despair and societies away from chaos.

We are women and men who have embraced the precepts and practices of the world's religions.

We affirm that a common set of core values is found in the teachings of the religions, and that these form the basis of a global ethic.

We affirm that this truth is already known, but yet to be lived in heart and action.

We affirm that there is an irrevocable, unconditional norm for all areas of life, for families and communities, for races, nations, and religions. There already exist ancient guidelines for human behavior which are found in the teachings of the religions of the world and which are the condition for a sustainable world order.

We Declare:

We are interdependent. Each of us depends on the well-being of the whole, and so we have respect for the community of living beings, for people, animals, and plants, and for the preservation of Earth, the air, water and soil.

We take individual responsibility for all we do. All our decisions, actions, and failures to act have consequences.

We must treat others as we wish others to treat us. We make a commitment to respect life and dignity, individuality and diversity, so that every person is treated humanely, without exception. We must have patience and acceptance. We must be able to forgive, learning from the past but never allowing ourselves to be enslaved by memories of hate. Opening our hearts to one another, we must sink our narrow differences for the cause of the world community, practicing a culture of solidarity and relatedness.

We consider humankind our family. We must strive to be kind and generous. We must not live for ourselves alone, but should also serve others, never forgetting the children, the aged, the poor, the suffering, the disabled, the refugees, and the lonely. No person should ever be considered or treated as a second-class citizen, or be exploited in any way whatsoever. There should be equal partnership between men and women. We must not commit any kind of sexual immorality. We must put behind us all forms of domination or abuse.

We commit ourselves to a culture of nonviolence, respect, justice, and peace. We shall not oppress, injure, torture, or kill other human beings, forsaking violence as a means of settling differences.

We must strive for a just social and economic order, in which everyone has an equal chance to reach full potential as a human being. We must speak and act truthfully and with compassion, dealing fairly with all, and avoiding prejudice and hatred. We must not steal. We must move beyond the dominance of greed for power, prestige, money, and consumption to make a just and peaceful world.

Earth cannot be changed for the better unless the consciousness of individuals is changed first. We pledge to increase our awareness by disciplining our minds, by meditation, by prayer, or by positive thinking. Without risk and a readiness to sacrifice there can be no fundamental change in our situation. Therefore we commit ourselves to this global ethic, to understanding one another, and to socially beneficial, peace-fostering, and nature-friendly ways of life.

We invite all people, whether religious or not, to do the same.

TO THE COUNCIL FOR A PARLIAMENT OF THE WORLD'S RELIGIONS:

August 31, 1993

We the undersigned Buddhists and friends are deeply concerned with the following and urge the Parliament to take proper measures in order to rectify the situation.

Having listened to invocations, prayers and benedictions offered by religious leaders of different host committees during the Opening Plenary and having attended the evening Plenary on Interfaith Understanding, we could not help but feel that the 1993 Parliament of the World's Religions is being held for the worshippers of Almighty and Creator God and efforts are being made towards "achieving oneness under God."

Further, with great astonishment we watched leaders of different religious traditions define all religions as religions of God and unwittingly rank Buddha with God. We found this lack of knowledge and insensitivity all the more surprising because we, the religious leaders of the world, are invited to this Parliament in order to promote mutual understanding and respect, and we are supposed to be celebrating one hundred years of interfaith dialog and understanding!

We would like to make it known to all that Shakyamuni Buddha, the founder of Buddhism, was not God or a god. He was a human being who attained full Enlightenment through meditation and showed us the path of spiritual awakening and freedom. Therefore, Buddhism is not a religion of God. Buddhism is a religion of wisdom, enlightenment and compassion. Like the worshippers of God who believe that salvation is available to all through confession of sin and a life of prayer, we Buddhists believe that salvation and enlightenment is available to all through removal of defilements and delusion and a life of meditation.

However, unlike those who believe in God who is separate from us, Buddhists believe that Buddha which means "one who is awake and enlightened" is inherent in us all as Buddhanature or, Buddhamind.

Our concern is threefold:

1. We feel that mutual understanding and appreciation of different approaches to spirituality and salvation should be a prerequisite for an inter-religious gathering like A Parliament of the World's Religions.
2. We feel that we the religious leaders of the world gathered here at this historic Parliament of the World's Religions must establish strong guidelines for religious tolerance and cooperation and serve as inspirations for the different religious communities in the world.
3. Language and communication skills are important elements in bringing about agreement and cooperation. We must train ourselves to be sensitive to each other and learn to use language that is inclusive and all embracing. We suggest we use "Great Being" or "power of the transcendent" or "Higher Spiritual Authority" instead of God in reference to the ultimate spiritual reality.

Today we religious leaders and teachers of the world are facing unprecedented new opportunities for our future together in the global village as well as severe challenges from the secular world. In order to seize upon these opportunities for our common future we must change. We would have to depart from our traditional religious attitudes and open our hearts in order to introduce to the world community a new religious consciousness and vision for peace, happiness and ecological justice. And we believe that Buddhism can contribute to this new vision with the message that we can practice religion with or without God. In other words, we must broaden our religious base in order to meet the challenges of our secular world, so that the civilizing influence of the liberal religious traditions would prevail over secular forces.

We the undersigned respectfully request that Mr. Daniel Gomez-Ibanez, Executive Director and members of the Executive Board of the Council for a Parliament of the World's Religions bring this matter to the attention of the Parliament and respond to us.

Respectfully,

Venerable Samu Sunim, Buddhist Society of Compassionate Wisdom, Zen Buddhist Temple, 1710 West Cornelia, Chicago 60657

Venerable Maha Ghosananda, Supreme Patriarch of Cambodian Buddhism, Inter-Religious Mission for Peace in Cambodia

Zen Master Seung Sahn, Founder and head, Kwan Um Zen School, International

Venerable Walpola Piyananda, Abbot, Dhamma Vijaya Temple Buddhist Temple, Chief Sangha Nayaka, Sri Lankan Buddhism U.S.A.

Rev. Chung Ok Lee, Head, Won Buddhists (Korea) in the U.S.A., Vice-chair, Committee on Religious NGOs at U.N.

Dr. Chatsumarn Kabilsingh, Professor, Thammasat University, Bangkok, Thailand

7. STEPHEN CARTER, *THE CULTURE OF DISBELIEF* (1993)

In the 1990s, religious intellectuals and activists increasingly made their voice heard in the public sphere. In this selection, Stephen Carter, a law professor at Yale, a practicing Episcopalian, and former clerk to Supreme Court Justice Thurgood Marshall, addresses a broad (and presumably politically moderate or liberal) audience. He insists that American culture has turned God into a "hobby" to be pursued by well-meaning but naive people in their spare time. Americans increasingly are implicitly told that it is fine to believe in religion as long as they don't take it too seriously or bring such views in the public realm: "We have created a political and legal culture that presses the religiously faithful to be other than themselves, to act publicly, and sometimes privately as well, as though their faith does not matter to them." His work seeks to "discover whether there might be a way to preserve the separation of church and state without trivializing faith as we do today." His real audience is political liberals, who hypocritically (in his view) excoriate the activism of the religious Right while praising the religiously inspired activism of the civil rights era, thus suggesting that religious people can apply their faith to politics only as long as it is the right kind of politics. He warns against an "antireligious fervor" that he sees as too prevalent, and insists on the right of believers to take stands on political issues based on their religious and moral convictions.

---∽∾∞∾∽---

THE CULTURE OF DISBELIEF

Contemporary American politics faces few greater dilemmas than deciding how to deal with the resurgence of religious belief. On the one hand, American ideology cherishes religion, as it does all matters of private conscience, which is why we justly celebrate a strong tradition against state interference with private religious choice. At the same time, many political leaders, commentators, scholars, and voters are coming to view any religious element in public moral discourse as a tool of the radical right for reshaping American society. But the effort to banish religion for politics' sake has led us astray: In our sensible zeal to keep religion from dominating our politics, we have created a political and legal culture that presses the religiously faithful to be other than themselves, to act publicly, and sometimes privately as well, as though their faith does not matter to them. . . .

Yet religion matters to people, and matters a lot. Surveys indicate that Americans are far more likely to believe in God and to attend worship services regularly than any other people in the Western world. True, nobody prays on prime-time television unless religion is a part of the plot, but strong majorities of citizens tell pollsters that their religious beliefs are of great importance to them in their daily lives. Even though some popular histories wrongly assert the contrary, the best evidence is that this deep religiosity has always been a facet of the American character and that it has grown consistently through the nation's history. And today, to the frustration of many opinion leaders in both the legal and political cultures, religion, as a moral force and perhaps a political one too, is surging. Unfortunately, in our public life, we prefer to pretend that it is not.

Consider the following events:

- When Hillary Rodham Clinton was seen wearing a cross around her neck at some of the public events surrounding her husband's inauguration as President of the United States, many observers were aghast, and one television commentator asked whether it was appropriate for the First Lady to display so openly a religious symbol. But if the First Lady can't do it, then certainly the President can't do it, which would bar from ever holding the office an Orthodox Jew under a religious compulsion to wear a yarmulke.

- Back in the mid-1980s, the magazine *Sojourners*—published by politically liberal Christian evangelicals—found itself in the unaccustomed position of defending the conservative evangelist Pat Robertson against secular liberals who, a writer in the magazine sighed, "see[m] to consider Robertson a dangerous neanderthal because he happens to believe that God can heal diseases." The point is that the editors of *Sojourners*, who are no great admirers of Robertson, also believe that God can heal diseases. So do tens of millions of Americans. But they are not supposed to say so.

- In the early 1980s, the state of New York adopted legislation that, in effect, requires an Orthodox Jewish husband seeking a civil divorce to give his wife a *get*—a religious divorce—without which she cannot remarry under Jewish

law. Civil libertarians attacked the statute, as unconstitutional. Said one critic, the "barriers to remarriage erected by religious law . . . only exist in the
minds of those who believe in the religion." If the barriers are religious, it
seems, then they are not real barriers, they are "only" in the woman's mind—
perhaps even a figment of the imagination.

• When the Supreme Court of the United States, ostensibly the final refuge
of religious freedom, struck down a Connecticut statute requiring employers
to make efforts to allow their employees to observe the Sabbath, one Justice
observed that the Sabbath should not be singled out because all employees
would like to have "the right to select the day of the week in which to refrain
from labor." Sounds good, except that, as one scholar has noted, "It would
come as some surprise to a devout Jew to find that he has 'selected the day of
the week in which to refrain from labor,' since the Jewish people have been
under the impression for some 3,000 years that this choice was made by
God." If the Sabbath is just another day off, then religious choice is essentially arbitrary and unimportant; so if one Sabbath day is inconvenient, the
religiously devout employee can just choose another. . . .

These examples share a common rhetoric that refuses to accept the notion that rational, public-spirited people can take religion seriously. . . .

What matters about these examples is the language chosen to make the
points. In each example, as in many more that I shall discuss, one sees a
trend in our political and legal cultures toward treating religious beliefs as
arbitrary and unimportant, a trend supported by a rhetoric that implies that
there is something wrong with religious devotion. More and more, our culture seems to take the position that believing deeply in the tenets of one's
faith represents a kind of mystical irrationality, something that thoughtful,
public-spirited American citizens would do better to avoid. If you must worship your God, the lesson runs, at least have the courtesy to disbelieve in the
power of prayer; if you must observe your Sabbath, have the good sense to
understand that it is just like any other day off from work.

There are, we are taught by our opinion leaders, religious matters and
important matters, and disaster arises when we confuse the two. Rationality, it seems, consists in getting one's priorities straight. (Ignore your religious law and marry at leisure.) Small wonder, then, that we have recently
been treated to a book, coauthored by two therapists, one of them an ordained minister, arguing that those who would put aside, say, the needs of
their families in order to serve their religions are suffering from a malady
the authors call "toxic faith"—for no normal person, evidently, would sacrifice the things that most of us hold dear just because of a belief that God so

intended it. (One wonders how the authors would have judged the toxicity of the faith of Jesus, Moses, or Mohammed.)

We are trying, here in America, to strike an awkward but necessary balance, one that seems more and more difficult with each passing year. On the one hand, a magnificent respect for freedom of conscience, including the freedom of religious belief, runs deep in our political ideology. On the other hand, our understandable fear of religious domination of politics presses us, in our public personas, to be wary of those who take their religion too seriously. This public balance reflects our private selves. We are one of the most religious nations on earth, in the sense that we have a deeply religious citizenry; but we are also perhaps the most zealous in guarding our public institutions against explicit religious influences. One result is that we often ask our citizens to split their public and private selves, telling them in effect that it is fine to be religious in private, but there is something askew when those private beliefs become the basis for public action. . . .

Religions that most need protection seem to receive it least. Contemporary America is not likely to enact legislation aimed at curbing the mainstream Protestant, Roman Catholic, or Jewish faiths. But Native Americans, having once been hounded from their lands, are now hounded from their religions, with the complicity of a Supreme Court untroubled when sacred lands are taken for road building or when Native Americans under a bona fide religious compulsion to use peyote in their rituals are punished under state antidrug regulations. . . .

The problem goes well beyond our society's treatment of those who simply want freedom to worship in ways that most Americans find troubling. An analogous difficulty is posed by those whose religious convictions move them to action in the public arena. Too often, our rhetoric treats the religious impulse to public action as presumptively wicked—indeed, as necessarily oppressive. But this is historically bizarre. Every time people whose vision of God's will moves them to oppose abortion rights are excoriated for purportedly trying to impose their religious views on others, equal calumny is implicitly heaped upon the mass protest wing of the civil rights movement, which was openly and unashamedly religious in its appeals as it worked to impose its moral vision on, for example, those who would rather segregate their restaurants. . . .

The First Amendment to the Constitution, often cited as the place where this difficulty is resolved, merely restates it. The First Amendment guarantees the "free exercise" of religion but also prohibits its "establishment" by the government. There may have been times in our history when we as a nation have tilted too far in one direction, allowing too much religious sway over politics. But in late-twentieth-century America, despite some loud fears about the influence of the weak and divided Christian right, we are upsetting the balance afresh by tilting too far in the other direction—and the courts are assisting in the effort.

8. MICHAEL LERNER, "THE FOUNDING EDITORIAL STATEMENT," *TIKKUN* (1986)

In 1986, a rabbi from San Francisco named Michael Lerner began a magazine entitled Tikkun, *a Hebrew word meaning "to heal, repair, and transform the world." The meaning of the word was the motto of the magazine itself, a bimonthly periodical that featured extended commentaries and reviews by leading Jewish (and non-Jewish) intellectuals and activists. Much as Ronald Sider had done with socially conscious evangelicals and Rabbi Abraham Heschel had preached and practiced through his involvement in the civil rights movement, Lerner tried to marry the historic strands of personal piety and devotion to the word of God with the equally strong Jewish tradition of activism to address the very real injustices of this world. Lerner remained committed to Jewish faith, belief, and practice traditions. He took inspiration especially from the prophets of the Torah. By starting* Tikkun, *he hoped to "provide a voice for those who still dare to hope, for those who are not embarrassed to dream." In the excerpt below, Lerner attempts to define the meaning of the Jewish tradition at the new millennium.*

The notion that the world could and should be different than it is has deep roots within Judaism. But in the late 1980s it is an idea that seems strangely out of fashion—and those who still dare to hope often view themselves as isolated, if not irrelevant. In the context of Western societies too often intoxicated with their own material and technological success, in which the ethos of personal fulfillment has the status of "common sense," those who talk of fundamental transformation seem to be dreaming.

"Dreaming" has a different meaning for people rooted in Jewish history and culture. It is a phrase that was used to dismiss the Prophets and their message, and it was a phrase Jews applied to themselves when they first hoped for the return to Zion. For Jews who built a culture and religion out of the experience of slavery, it has always seemed possible to imagine that the dominant regimes of the moment might pass. . . .

It is this refusal to accept the world as given, articulated in the Prophetic call for transformation, that has fueled the radical underpinnings of Jewish life. The great idol-smashers of the last 150 years, Karl Marx and Sigmund

Freud, articulated a fundamentally Jewish sensibility—at the very moment that they developed a universalist perspective. The universalist dream of a transformation and healing of the world, the belief that peace and justice are not meant for heaven but are this-worldly necessities that must be fought for, is the particularistic cultural and religious tradition of Jews. . . .

Keeping the Prophetic tradition alive, as our spiritual mentor Abraham Joshua Heschel pointed out in his book *The Prophets*, means immersion in the details of daily life. The Greek philosophers spent much of their time talking about abstract concepts of goodness, virtue and justice. Eastern spirituality led its practitioners to the mountains, forests, and caves for meditation, and directed their energies away from ordinary, daily life—a life often dismissed as "illusory." But to the Prophets, God's message directed attention to daily life, to the marketplace, to the family and to the state. To the Prophets, each time the powerless were oppressed was a fresh outrage, each time religion was used as a cover for economic immorality was a new affront to God.

The commitment to change the world, to demand justice and love in a world that has given up on these ideals, is not some pious sentiment clouding one's eyes to a hard-nosed look at reality. On the contrary, the rejection of moral neutrality, the committed stance on behalf of the oppressed, makes possible a deeper understanding of the dynamics of culture and society. It is precisely in the process of acting to transform the world that the world reveals its deeper structures and meanings. Yet we shall insist that any social transformation requires a systematic and deep intellectual inquiry—we may get inspiration from the Torah, but we shall also engage in critical thinking that requires intellectual integrity, innovation and sustained analysis. . . .

The Liberal and Radical Traditions in Politics

Jewish religion is irrevocably committed to the side of the oppressed. Jewish history began with a slave rebellion and the success of that rebellion shapes our historical memory and our religious sensibility. Shabbat, our weekly celebration of the creation of the universe, is also a celebration of our liberation from Egypt. The message of our historical experience is a revolutionary message: The way the world is can be radically different—we know, because we were slaves who thought that we would always be in slavery, and then overcame our bondage.

There are many religions that celebrate the grandeur and splendor of the physical universe. Yet the message of the Sabbath is unique: that we not only must stand in radical amazement and awe in the face of creation, but we must remember that the world needs to be and can be transformed; that history is not meaningless but aimed at liberation; that the struggle of one people to move beyond slavery (retold each week in the Torah reading) is still a drama with universal meaning through which we can understand contemporary reality.

No wonder then, that Jews are deeply involved in politics, and strongly committed to both the radical and liberal traditions. Yet our historical memory and religious ideals also give us an independence from these traditions, and a vantage point from which to assess some of their limitations.

Jews have a deep commitment to the fundamental liberties. The insistence on respect for alternative views, the openness that the framers of Rabbinic Judaism encouraged in their endless debate and consideration of a wide range of possibilities, the spirit of dialectical inquiry, the notion that there will always be three opinions on any given matter where there are two Jews discussing it—all these express a Jewish approach that encourages tolerance and diversity. Through much of Jewish history, these attitudes guided the debate among the religious elite, although much of Jewish society did not partake in this pluralism and was closed, rigid and illiberal in its actual practices. In the past several hundred years, as Jews grappled with the modern world, we have become strong partisans of liberal values. . . .

But we are not uncritically committed to liberalism. When liberal values are used as a cover for materialism and individualism, we say clearly that these are not our values. We stand for tolerance, but not for ethical relativism which is sometimes seen as either the primary justification for, or the logical consequence of a commitment to tolerance. We stand for freedom—but not for giving unlimited freedom to corporations so they can exploit the people and resources of the planet. Nor do we necessarily take at face value the claim of Western societies to be the living embodiments of the liberal ideals that they so proudly proclaim. If radically alternative policies to those held by the dominant parties are systematically excluded from serious public consideration, if anti-nuclear and antiapartheid forces must use civil disobedience to have their views noticed (and even then not given a serious public airing), if U.S. military interventions can be financed despite the opposition of a majority of Americans, if freedom of the press actually amounts to freedom only for those with vast economic resources to buy media time or space, if economic power concentrated in the hands of the few pre-shapes the options so that the range of serious political choices becomes dramatically narrowed, then we can get a different kind of unfreedom—an unfreedom that celebrates itself as the paradigm of liberal ideals.

Jews are also drawn to the radical tradition in politics. Radical politics has often adopted the idealism and commitment to justice that are central to the Jewish tradition. The articulation of the needs of the oppressed, the unwillingness to compromise with unfair distributions of power and wealth, the historical link between the Left and the underdog, have brought many Jews into the world of radical politics. The Utopian demand for transformation is something we proudly identify with—it remains a central ingredient in Jewish vision.

9. *TIKKUN* MAGAZINE WRITERS, "RELIGIOUS VISIONS FOR THE NEW MILLENNIUM" (2000)

The following selections feature several writers prominent in contemporary discussions of spirituality, who provide brief essays on the meaning of religious traditions in the twenty-first century. They write from a variety of perspectives—New Age, Quaker, evangelical, Jewish—but converge remarkably on a number of points. Perhaps most significantly, they find common ground in foreseeing a more open, flexible, adaptable spirituality, one that draws on tradition but is not limited or stultified by it. These pieces come from a special issue of Tikkun *magazine.*

⸺ ∞ ⸺

SPIRIT IN THE NEW MILLENNIUM

Judaism for a New Age
Zalman Schachter-Shalomi

A new consciousness is emerging among the Jewish people which will flourish in the coming millennium.

• This millennium will bring a new ecumenism to Judaism and to the Jewish people. I've already seen a growing centrism in the Orthodox world, an openness to including in clal Yisra'el (the community of the Jewish people) everyone from the Orthodox to the Reform—and secular Jews as well. Of course, there will be some tension between those who want a more flexible definition of Judaism and those who want to insist on more rigid paths. But all this is part of what it is to be a living organism. You need some part that is brittle and stiff like the skeleton to give shape and hold up the other parts.

• There are many signs that the ceiling that locked Judaism into a halachic behaviorism (a focus on specified rules and behaviors) is lifting. We have people learning meditation in all corners of the Jewish world and people who are interested in the somatic area of serving God, so that religious services not only are about addressing the cortex, but can include sensation and bodily movement.

- A new generation is arising in Israel and in Islamic countries that seeks a renewal of religious traditions in positive ways that will bring greater openness and greater respect for "the other." There is more energy toward peacemaking that speaks to the mythic and shadow regions of people's feelings. . . .
- Even the information superhighway is being sacramentalized by various religious groups. In the future the Web will have an impact on the consciousness of even the most fundamentalist elements of the religious world.
- The world is speeding up, and that speedup has hurtful consequences for many. The world needs Shabbat—our Jewish Sabbath—in its fullness. There's much to learn from our calendar and its focus on the celebration of the seasons, and in our notion of having a monthly moment of inner repentance and correction. . . .
- The world needs a new understanding of food, one that incorporates the notion of eco-kosher that we developed in Jewish renewal: eating only those foods that have been grown in ecologically sensitive ways that promote sustainability and ethical industry behavior.
- People are beginning to open to a new way of approaching sacred texts, "myth-rush," that has emerged from the Jewish tradition of midrash. This is the rush that we get out of the myth when people personally grapple with possible elaborations of the text, filling in the blanks and creating contexts that incorporate their own deepest psychological and spiritual wisdom as they interpret ancient material. Many people worry about Jews leaving Jewish arenas and being "lost" to other spiritual traditions like Buddhism—but these people don't realize that in some ways these Jews are spiritual ambassadors to these other traditions and that Judaism is also learning from these other traditions.

Light the Spark
Jim Wallis
How do Christians receive the new millennium? Is it with the expectation of a "Second Coming"?

First, on that Second Coming thing. Not a big issue at the moment. The religious right doesn't seem to think the Second Coming of Christ is imminent, seeing how much money they all are putting into their houses and the stock market. Plus, they're still trying to take over the Republican Party in several states and who would be left to run things if the Christians were suddenly all caught up together in the clouds? . . .

As far as progressive Christians are concerned, we've generally held to the theology that says you should live by the values of the kingdom of God right now, rather than worrying about when and how it's all finally going to be implemented. In fact, that's the best way to implement it. So, not much Second Coming discussions going on during or after church.

Are we optimistic? Well, optimism is just bad theology. You know—the cup is half full, look on the bright side, let a smile be your umbrella, etc. It's hard to ask that of the mother we saw in the Burger King the other day helping her three children with their homework, between serving cars at her drive-in window. The politicians boast about her as the success story of welfare reform, but she's poorer than she was before, having to decide now between paying her rent or taking her kids to the doctor. So far, the rising tide has lifted all yachts and hasn't gotten to her boat yet.

But hope is a different matter altogether than optimism. And yes, there is talk about that. Theologically, hope is more a decision based upon what we know and trust about God's purposes. Archbishop Desmond Tutu used to say, "As Christians, we are prisoners of hope." Many just thought he was an eccentric old man, but he turned out to be right in South Africa. And Rosa Parks wasn't just tired that day in Montgomery, Alabama, in 1956 when she refused to give up her seat on a bus. No, she had been going to retreats and training conferences. She was part of a network all over the South, of people who believed that history was about to change. Mrs. Parks had been getting ready for the change, and just happened to be the one who lit the spark. You didn't think that the civil rights movement began in Montgomery, did you?

That's exactly what a lot of us are doing now.

We're getting ready.

We actually believe that the growing gap between the rich and the poor is like a 900-pound gorilla just waiting to be recognized.

We think that shopping can't satisfy the deepest longings of the human heart, and we're listening to the middle-class students who are volunteering far beyond what is necessary for a balanced resume when they tell us they're looking for "connection" and "meaning."

Many of us are reading Isaiah when he tells us that sharing your bread with the hungry will cause your light to rise like the dawn and your healing to come quickly.

So we're not predicting the Second Coming, but we are getting ready for a new movement (now that's a word we've been afraid to use for a while), a movement of both justice and healing, led in large part by people of faith. We can't tell what the "movement time" is. It's not 1956 yet, but is it 1955, '53, '48, or '49? We don't know, but we feel something is coming.

SOCIETY IN THE NEW MILLENNIUM

Utopia: An Abiding Presence
Douglas Guryn

Utopia: the word literally means "no place." Utopia has never been more "nowhere" than it is today. The twentieth century began with burgeoning utopian expectations, but two horrendous world wars, the Holocaust, the advent of atomic warfare, and accelerating environmental degradation (to name only a few crises) have greatly darkened that prospect. What's more, these disasters have not been unexpected detours along the road to utopia, but the product of various utopian agendas and movements themselves. Now, with the defeat of Nazism and Marxist-Leninism, the victorious forces of liberal capitalism have pronounced utopianism anathema in all its forms. Instead, political pragmatism, an abiding confidence that the ruling technocracy can "fix" whatever messes it creates, and a blind faith in the benign "hidden hand" of the global market—all anti-utopian expectations—have dominated the last years of the twentieth century. If there is a utopianism in good standing today, it is only in the electronic "nowhere" of cyberspace, or the private "no-mind" of meditation.

The anti-utopia teaches us that Oz is a dangerous place, that "there's no place like home." Indeed, home, identity, and tradition are reassuring verities amid the permanent revolution of capitalist development (and there is nowhere to stand outside that revolution today). Over the past thirty years, many have delved deeper into adopted or inherited religious traditions for comfort and stability. But that search has led many of us into a renewed confrontation with utopia. Studying my own inherited faith, Quakerism, has revealed to me what a fiercely utopian faith and politics might look like. Far from the gentle, reforming peacemakers of the modern Religious Society of Friends, the earliest Friends were confrontational, apocalyptic prophets who were beaten and imprisoned by the thousands for their witness, notwithstanding their pacifism. Certainly, these "Children of the Light" did not see the realization of their egalitarian dream for England and the world. But their utopian agitation helped shape the future of religious liberty and multiparty politics.

One lesson I have learned from the early Friends is that, while a utopian vision can never be adequate, it can open the popular imagination to new possibilities within the present. Certain criteria for a constructive utopianism must be rigorously observed, however. First, the utopia envisioned must neither exclude nor scapegoat anyone. The power of "nowhere" is in its presence everywhere and its availability to everyone. (In the early Quaker case, the preaching of a universal inward Light asserted utopia's hidden omnipresence.) Second, and by implication, violent tactics of attaining, and coercive means of maintaining, any envisioned utopia must be utterly renounced. The End, the "nowhere," envisioned cannot be realized anywhere by means that defeat it. Third, utopian communities perform an essential mediating function, nurturing the spirituality and social values of participating individuals while constituting collective actors in political struggle. Finally, each community must qualify its vision through provisional collaborations with other communities, where common ground is found and common aims can be pursued. Through the fulfillment of these criteria, utopia begins to take shape here and now.

Utopian faith and politics are essential to any twenty-first century worth living. Transcendent hope is vital to any future that is more than an extension of the present regime, which has no future, which is destined to consume the earth and everything upon it. Any hope that is true hope is the presence of something not yet seen. And any true faith substantiates something of that hope here and now. Utopia, the free and reconciling Shalom of God, is nowhere to be seen, yet everywhere present by its effects upon the hearts of women and men foolish enough to hope. . . .

The path to utopia begins in the heart.

———— ∞∞∞ ————

For the Love of Life
David C. Korten

> By his constant rituals, trances, ecstasies, and "journeys," the tribal shaman
> ensures that the relation between human society and the larger society of be-
> ings is balanced and reciprocal, and that the village never takes more from
> the living land than it returns to it.
>
> —DAVID ABRAMS, *THE SPELL OF THE SENSUOUS*

. . . We, the people of planet Earth, face our moment of truth. Our future, indeed our very survival, depends on awakening and channeling these latent energies toward the creation of a life-affirming human civilization that embodies the values and inspiration of a *new story* given practical expression by a *new politics* and a *new economy*. . . .

The foundation of the Great Work is a new story of the miracle of cosmic creation narrated by the great storytellers of our time. . . .

The new story calls on us to reexamine our most basic understanding of the nature or reality. Its cosmic metaphor is not the machine, but the organism. Its irreducible building block is not a particle, but a thought. Rather than banishing the spiritual intelligence and energy we know as God to some distant place beyond our experience, it recognizes God as integral to all being. . . .

The new story opens the way to healing the centuries-old breach between science and religion that has left us with an artificial and often schizophrenic separation of our intellectual and spiritual lives—torn between a theology that denies the evidence of logic and observation and a science that denies our experience of consciousness and spirit. It allows us to recognize sin as that which is destructive of life and the actualization of its potential. Equally, it allows us to recognize our own capacity for goodness, compassion, and creative engagement in the unfolding drama of creation. And in revealing life's ability to self-organize with a mindfulness of both self and whole, this story further affirms our potential to create truly democratic, self-organizing human societies that acknowledge and nurture our individual capacity to balance freedom with responsibility.

10. ELIZABETH LESSER, *THE NEW AMERICAN SPIRITUALITY* (1999)

As Americans continued spiritual explorations at the end of the twentieth century, a number of "veterans" of these quests produced spiritual autobiographies (long a tradition of American literature), often combined with self-help manuals and tie-ins to Web sites, cassette tapes, and workshops to market them. One of the most thoughtful books of this genre was Elizabeth Lesser's The New American Spirituality, *in which she catalogued her spiritual explorations from the 1960s forward. She recounts a relatively religionless childhood, participation in countercultural communal groups, divorces and other personal crises, the alternative spiritual therapies popular in the 1970s, and finally her own eclectic brand of spiritual practices drawn from eastern and western traditions. She wrote her book as a "realistic and practical synthesis of the American spiritual traditions of our times—a seeker's guide to forging a personal path that honors who you are as an American, even as it honors your unique religious roots, your need for discipline and morals, and your desire to belong to a community of fellow seekers." The key point of her philosophy is that "you can decide which of your religious customs work for you, and which ones may need to be revitalized." This combination of Emersonian self-reliance, Unitarian idealism, and pragmatic synthesizing represents a deep-rooted strain of American religious expression, and serves well to summarize much of American religion at the new millennium. In this excerpt from the beginning of her work, Lesser serves up her own spiritual autobiography, culminating in her formation of the Omega Institute as a sort of clearinghouse for American spiritual quests.*

I had been actively searching for God since childhood. My path wove through the peaks and valleys of many different traditions: organized religion, disorganized mysticism, psychotherapy, philosophy, mythology, science. My search had all the signs of being an American one: it was diverse, individualistic, open-minded, free. It included ten years of discipleship with an Eastern meditation master; a deep immersion into Christian, Jewish, and Islamic mysticism; extended work with a psychotherapist; study of Jungian psychology and Western schools of philosophy; and exposure, from my work at Omega Institute, to the world's wisdom traditions, from ancient healing systems to modern consciousness research. For more than twenty-five years I had been searching—not to become a Christian or a Jew or a Muslim; a Buddhist or a Sikh or a Hindu—but to become a spiritual person, here in America, at the beginning of the twenty-first century. . . .

In democratizing the spiritual life, the burden is on you, the seeker. You are entitled to your own beliefs and practices, but you are also accountable for your own morality and enlightenment. Your path is your own, but you must walk side by side with others, with compassion and generosity as your beacons. You don't have to join a religion or a school of thought or a community of seekers to be part of the American spiritual tapestry. You can do this, and you may benefit tremendously if you do; but you don't have to. If anything is required it is this: fearlessness in your examination of life and death; willingness to continually grow; and openness to the possibility that the ordinary is extraordinary, and that your joys and your sorrows have meaning and mystery. . . .

America is just the place for spiritual seekers to be lamps unto themselves. Throughout our history, revolutionaries who worshiped God and the individual, a higher order and democracy, the One and diversity, have made America a land of many lamps. There is room enough for everyone on God's mysterious path, and millions of lamps light the way for the benefit of all. . . .

When I was a child, God was dead. I was raised in a family and a culture that were hooked on science and progress, and suspicious of spirituality and introspection. *Time* magazine put the nail in the coffin in 1966, when I was fourteen: "Is God Dead?" ran the headline on the cover. . . .

Without some kind of religious institution, my life in the 1950s and 1960s was based almost entirely on material values. Suburbia bred isolation from community and the shared rituals that bring a sense of mythic proportion to life. Age-old rites of passage such as birth, coming of age, and death were no longer part of the fabric of life, but instead were relegated to "experts" in hospitals or institutions. The same society that revered the rational and the scientific held the intuitive, the magical, the unmeasurable, and the wild in disdain. It seemed that every year the natural world was shrinking, as huge housing developments covered remaining tracts of wilderness. . . .

My own yearning for a spiritual life and the sense of belonging to something greater than my personal world followed me through childhood and grew stronger in adolescence. Around the same time that God was declared dead by *Time*, I began listening to the music of the Beatles, Joan Baez, and Bob Dylan, and taking an interest in the society around me, especially the civil rights and anti-Vietnam War movements. My adventurous older sister went to great pains to introduce me to anything unusual she discovered in college. The first time I saw her in a Volkswagen van filled with long-haired hippies was a watershed moment in my young life; here were people with a belief system that I could embrace. With the intuitive understanding of cultural change that each generation seems to be born with, I identified with what the hippies stood for even before I knew what it was. Something about these people, and their dress and music and books and language, thrilled me just as the dress and music and books and language of the Catholic Church had thrilled me when I was younger. By the time I left high school for college I had done more than admire the hippies. I had wholeheartedly become one. . . .

In 1970 I entered Barnard College, across the street from Columbia University in New York City—a haven for intellectuals, feminists, and political activists. It was also my mother's alma mater. Although I had always known that my experience at college was not going to be very similar to my mother's, I was not prepared for what I found at Barnard and Columbia. In high school I had imagined that college was going to be like one long Grateful Dead concert, punctuated by classes. But a few weeks after my first semester began, Columbia University students joined students across the country and went on strike to protest the continuation of the Vietnam War. Since half of my classes were at Columbia, I went on strike too. . . .

For a while, filled with the passionate desire to be "part of the solution, not the problem," I devoted my days to protesting the war, disrupting Columbia's business-as-usual, and working with disenfranchised people in New York's Upper West Side. My hunger to belong to something greater than myself was temporarily satiated by my wish to see an unjust war ended. Of course, I was also fueled by the typical longings of an eighteen-year-old, and I found plenty of opportunities to participate in the general unraveling of the established order. Those were the days when sexual freedom and drug experimentation were explored with a naiveté that seems inconceivable today. Yet to us, children of middle-class, middle-twentieth-century America, free expression took precedence over conventional mores.

One spring evening in Manhattan, I met my father at the Cornell Club for dinner. Waiting for him in the stuffy lounge, amid gray-suited businessmen and their properly attired wives, I glanced at my own outfit: ripped bell-bottom jeans, a Mexican peasant blouse, no bra, and hair down to the middle of my back. I was suddenly made aware, by the cool stares of the club members, that everything about me, from the sheerness of my blouse to the dirt on my work boots, represented an attack on the values they held sacred. . . .

What I didn't tell my father was that I was scared of the increasing violence emanating from a movement that had started with dreams of harmony and freedom. For all of the real peace and love of the times, an equally real sense of turmoil and intolerance shadowed the years that have become known as the sixties. It was a confusing time to be leaving home and setting out into the world. I had turned to the anti-war movement because my political conscience was too troubled by the war not to stand up and be counted. But now the movement had adopted a harshness that was not my own. I was too proud to tell my father this. The alternative looked like the people sitting around me at the Cornell Club, drinking martinis and talking about the stock market. . . .

In my disillusionment with politics I began reading Thomas Merton's autobiography, *The Seven Storey Mountain*. I felt a personal connection with Merton since he had been a student at Columbia when he began his lifelong search for spiritual wholeness. His sense of alienation within his own religious order reawakened my childhood hunger for a relevant spiritual path and community. Through his words, and the books of other Christian mystics I found in the Columbia library, I reconnected with my childhood forays into Catholicism, when I went to Mass with my best friend's family. I mimicked a ritual that Merton had secretly performed in college—getting off the subway at random stations, just to sit in a new church. Like Merton, I kept this strange behavior from my friends, who, I imagined, would find my mystical leanings incongruous with radical politics. It was in one of Merton's books that I was led to Zen Buddhism and then to other Eastern religious traditions.

Zen was an appropriate first step into Eastern spirituality for the existentially raised post-war generations. Its lack of pretense and dogma was appealing to the Western mind, and it is no surprise that Zen was one of the first of the Eastern religious practices to take serious hold in America. . . .

I was introduced to Zen practice by a medical student I met as I pulled away from radical politics. When I first walked into the New York zendo, or practice hall, I was struck by the smell and the colors and the stillness. Outside the city was a swarming hive of exertion and commotion. Inside the zendo not much was happening. Somber men and women sat on brown cushions (*zafus*), staring at the bare wooden floor. Incense, as subtle as wood smoke on an autumn day, drifted in the stillness. Every now and then a tiny Japanese man in black robes would shuffle behind the meditators and whack them on the shoulders with a long stick. I couldn't imagine what the point of any of this was. But my friend had been sitting at the zendo for a year. I trusted him, and I gave meditation a try.

I remember when I first took my seat on a *zafu* at the Zen Center. The simple gesture of folding my legs beneath the cushion and resting my palms in my lap felt powerfully familiar, as if I had sat like that, in that posture, smelling that same incense for a thousand years. A strange sense of peaceful dignity overcame me. The instructions were simple: Become aware of the breath rising and falling in the stomach; keep a straight back; let thoughts come and go without focusing on them. Merely by following these directions I would experience a novel state of self-containment and inner strength. . . .

It wasn't long after I began sitting zazen that I heard of a strange-sounding weekly gathering called Sufi dancing, held on the Columbia campus. While Zen stressed a solitary, unsentimental, and orderly progression toward enlightenment, Sufism was at the other end of the spiritual spectrum. At my first gathering I fluctuated between wanting to leave immediately and feeling as though I had come home. Forty young people, dressed in flowing clothes, held hands and danced in circles chanting the names of God from a variety of religious traditions. At the end of each dance the leader would instruct us to look into each other's eyes and to "see through the eyes with which God sees us." That simple act of exchanging glances spoke to me. It challenged me, in a nonaggressive, loving way, to connect— with myself, and with my fellow seekers; to see the world—its beauty and its pain—through God's eyes. . . .

I met Pir ("revered teacher") Vilayat Inayat Khan in the summer of 1972. The people leading Sufi dancing at Columbia urged me to study with Pir Vilayat, as he was called by his students. They were all planning to caravan out to "Sufi camp" in the golden hills of Northern California. My boyfriend had to stay in medical school that summer, and I was tired of New York City. California sounded like heaven to me; so did a tribal gathering of spiritual seekers. When school was over I crowded into a van and drove for four days straight across the United States.

For a month, a few hundred students camped out in the hills of Mendocino County, ate together, and practiced the wisdom traditions that Pir Vilayat taught. To a nineteen-year-old, sprung from New York and hungry for spiritual teaching, this was indeed a divine adventure. Pir. Vilayat, dressed in flowing robes and with long white hair and a graying beard, fit the part of a guru perfectly. Everything that had struck me as solemn and severe at the Zen Center was dramatically missing from Pir Vilayat's teachings. He taught us to sing and dance, encouraged us to read and learn from the great sacred and mythological texts of the world, and led a variety of meditation exercises. We arose early and meditated as the sun rose over the hills, and stayed up late sharing poetry and chants around the campfire. . . .

This immersion in religious tradition was thrilling to me. My childhood curiosity and hunger were being addressed in ways I had never even imagined. What I had intuited—that it is human nature to hunger for the sacred—was being revealed in a rich tapestry of myth and traditions from around the world. God may have died in mainstream culture, but spirituality was being revived in my life through the traditional and proven practices of world religions. To an outsider, and especially to the American press, *traditional* is not a word that would have been used to describe the spiritual communes of the 1970s. But in contrast to many Americans in those years, from the "radical chic" to the expanding consumer culture, we were busy studying sacred texts, worshiping together each Sunday, and adhering to moral codes set to secure our marriages and families, much as early Americans had done in the founding years of the country. . . .

Pir Vilayat specifically did not want to be in California. Most of us were living in Northern California at that time, but we started to search in the Southeast for land. Just as we were about to purchase a few hundred acres in North Carolina, a friend named Wavy Gravy, the celebrated master of ceremonies at the Woodstock festival, put us in touch with some friends of his who needed to sell part of the land they had inherited from their parents. It was the New Lebanon Shaker Village, nestled in the Berkshire mountains of New York State, and charged with the spirit of the devout people who had built it in the 1700s. While the cold winters and the antiquated buildings (that needed more money for repair than we would ever have) were intimidating, the Shaker doctrines of communal sharing of possessions, equality of the sexes, and consecrated labor attracted us to the structures and land.

In their well-organized, self-sufficient communities segregated from the outside world, the Shakers had worshiped in unusual ways—ecstatic dancing and singing that led to direct contact with the Holy Spirit. We were struck by the similarities between the Shakers' manner of worship and our own and by their sincere desire to live a genuine, spiritual life. Before purchasing the land, we went as far as asking for the blessings of the eight remaining Shaker sisters who lived in a remote village in Maine. I can only now, in retrospect, imagine the shock that these elderly, reserved women must have endured when we arrived at their home. At the time I thought it quite reasonable for six young people dressed in hippie garb, traveling with a white-bearded Indian guru, to ask for their permission to carry on the spiritual legacy of the land in New Lebanon. . . .

We settled into the Shaker village, renamed it the Abode of the Message, and started families, a school, businesses, a farm, and a loose system of governance. Soon the difficult realities of communal life emerged, like the weeds in our organic gardens. The two hundred remarkable men and women—doctors, businessmen, teachers, artists, builders, farmers, even a pilot—whose combined talents had sounded so promising began to bicker about everything. To debate whether a "family member" could have a dog or to decide how we should divide resources from community-held businesses, we convened endless family meetings. My understanding of political process and my compassion for anyone involved in governance grew in those years. . . .

For six years I did just what the old Shaker adage advised: I put my hands to work and my heart to God. . . .

Eventually the strain of combining the intensity of communal life with the responsibilities of family life became too difficult. I understood why the Shakers had forbidden nuclear families to exist within their community. They believed that the devotion to one's own family would compete with devotion to God and the community. They were right about the community part; my path to God was now centered around my children, and I felt too divided to do both. . . .

[The birth of the Omega Institute] coincided with my own need to expand out of what had become a limiting experience for me at the Abode and a troubling one within an organized religious group. The exclusivity of belonging to a particular religion—complete with foreign mantras, spiritual names, and ways of behaving that were endearing only to us—had become unappealing. I no longer wanted to separate myself from the world. Relegating my spirituality only to practice, prayer, and meditation created a split within myself. I needed to find ways to incorporate my sense of the sacred into my family life and my psychological and physical well-being. Was there a way to bring the peace I had found through inner spiritual practice out into my daily life? Were other people already experimenting with this? What about my social and political conscience, which had been slumbering as I meditated and prayed? And why, if God is love, and I had spent so much time searching for God, was I so unhappy in my marriage?

A few of us from the community put our heads together and researched any and everything in which we were interested and that spoke to the combination of spirituality and everyday life. We invited a small faculty of health practitioners, psychologists, artists, and spiritual teachers to join us for Omega Institute's first summer program in 1977. We then rented the campus of a nearby boarding school, sent out a few thousand brochures, and waited to see if anyone would respond. No market research could have prepared us for Omega's immediate success. . . .

The interest in Omega grew; each year more than fifteen thousand guests would participate in our programs. I began to understand that God had not died in America, but rather that our culture was in the birth pangs of a new kind of spirituality. My childhood hunger had convinced me of the need for the sacred in one's life. My experience as a disciple of an organized religion was my first step on the spiritual path. It provided me with a meaningful framework and community. But it also narrowed my experience of the sacred and exposed the pitfalls of the group mind. Now I was witnessing something else, something more wide-ranging, inclusive, and humane. Whether people came to Omega to study nutrition or self-awareness, Native American spirituality or African dance, what they were really interested in was a spirituality that could infuse the totality of their daily lives. If Omega's curriculum seemed like a spiritual smorgasbord, we simply were forging new territory and needed all the input we could get. Experimenting with the mistakes and the wisdom of the past, the marriage of East and West, the crossbreeding of religion and psychology, and the alliance of science and mysticism, we were searching for a new American spirituality. . . .

WHAT IS SPIRITUALITY?

As you search, keep in mind that religion and spirituality are not necessarily synonymous. Religions are like cookbooks and guidebooks: they are not the food or the foreign country; rather, they suggest ingredients and point us in the right direction. "Do not be idolatrous or bound to any doctrine, theory, or ideology," says Thich Nhat Hanh, a Vietnamese Zen monk. "All systems of thought are guiding means; they are not absolute truth." Many people are so turned off by religions—their seemingly arbitrary moral codes, the boundless hypocrisies between word and deed, the arcane rituals—that they have acquired a resistance to spirituality itself. I sympathize with those intellectuals who equate spirituality with sanctimoniousness or sentimental nonsense, and who turn a disgusted back on the whole topic. Many who call themselves spiritual seekers are so irrational and hold so rigidly to their beliefs that, if their way is the only way, count me out as well. But in truth, spirituality and intelligence are not in competition. They are one and the same if we affix a definition to spirituality that is inclusive and forgiving enough to hold the full human condition. . . .

A formidable resistance that arises when modern people approach the spiritual path is a cultural bias in favor of intellectualism, as well as a devaluing of other human modes of perception: emotions, intuition, sensation. An unnatural divide between intellectual development and the development of our other capacities has evolved in the twentieth century to the point where many who consider themselves thinking people will have nothing to do with anything that smacks of mysticism. Intellectuals scorn spirituality, as if pondering our very existence is not as valid as researching science or history. The modern reverence for the mind has obscured a profoundly natural yearning—one that is as basic as hunger and as near to us as our breath.

Another misconceived notion about spirituality that alienates the modern seeker is the association of sacredness with saintliness. It is erroneous to separate spirituality from everyday life. To equate holiness only with celibacy, or solitude, or poverty is to deny most of us a spiritual life. Enlightenment can be nurtured in a monastery or in a family, alone or in a relationship, in prayer or at work. The bliss of the world is no less spiritual than the bliss of transcendence. We can indeed "follow our bliss" as we follow the spiritual path, whether that bliss is raising our consciousness or raising children, reading a holy text or running a marathon. But be warned! There's a fine line between bliss and narcissism. . . .

Rather, spirituality is a long, slow process—a patient growing into wisdom. It is no wonder that this kind of spirituality seems foreign to many Americans. It is much more like cooking a fine meal of many courses—picking the fresh herbs from the garden, waiting for the yeasted rolls to rise, marinating the meat, rolling the pie crust—than like driving up to the fast food window and drumming your fingers for two minutes while a stranger wraps your burger.

Inviting spirituality into your life is like packing for a long journey. As you search for your own definition, here are some of the most important things to pack: an openness to things you may have been conditioned to reject, a comfortableness with the unknown, and fearlessness.

11. SUHEIR HAMMAD, "FIRST WRITING SINCE" (2001)

On September 11, 2001, American life—and religion—changed forever, with the simultaneous attacks on the World Trade Center and the Pentagon, and the downing of another plane possibly intended for a target in Washington, DC. The result of a suicide mission by nineteen young Islamic men (almost all from Saudi Arabia) directed by the organization Al Qaeda and its messianic leader Osama bin Laden, the mass murder of over 3,000 people perpetrated on that day radically altered the course of American society and politics.

In the immediate aftermath of these events, artists and intellectuals struggled to comprehend and respond. One of the earliest writings from that period, one that immediately attracted public attention, was this poem by a Palestinian American woman named Suheir Hammud. In the poem, read before enthusiastic audiences, Hammad portrays the confusion and despair provoked by the attacks; the anger felt by many Muslim Americans who were singled out for detention, scrutiny, and sometimes deportation; the feeling among some that American might and hubris defied the gods; and, at last, the resolution to "affirm life" even in the face of the mass violence that greeted the coming of the new millennium.

First Writing Since

1. there have been no words.
i have not written one word.
no poetry in the ashes south of canal street.
no prose in the refrigerated trucks driving debris and dna.
not one word.

today is a week, and seven is of heavens, gods, science.
evident out my kitchen window is an abstract reality.
sky where once was steel.
smoke where once was flesh.

fire in the city air and i feared for my sister's life in a way never
before, and then, and now, i fear for the rest of us.

first, please god, let it be a mistake, the pilot's heart failed, the
plane's engine died.
then please god, let it be a nightmare, wake me now.
please god, after the second plane, please, don't let it be anyone
who looks like my brothers.

i do not know how bad a life has to break in order to kill.
i have never been so hungry that i willed hunger
i have never been so angry as to want to control a gun over a pen.
not really.
even as a woman, as a Palestinian, as a broken human being.
never this broken.

more than ever, i believe there is no difference.
the most privileged nation, most americans do not know the difference
between indians, afghanis, syrians, muslims, sikhs, hindus.
more than ever, there is no difference.

3. the dead are called lost and their families hold up shaky
printouts in front of us through screens smoked up.

we are looking for iris, mother of three. please call with any
information. we are searching for priti, last seen on the 103rd
floor. she was talking to her husband on the phone and the line
went. . . .

i am looking for peace. i am looking for mercy. i am looking for
evidence of compassion. any evidence of life. i am looking for
life. . . .

if i can find through this exhaust people who were left behind to
mourn and to resist mass murder, i might be alright.

thank you to the woman who saw me brinking my cool and blinking back
tears. she opened her arms before she asked "do you want a hug?" a
big white woman, and her embrace was the kind only people with the
warmth of flesh can offer. i wasn't about to say no to any comfort.
"my brother's in the navy," i said. "and we're arabs." "wow, you
got double trouble." word.

5. one more person ask me if i knew the hijackers.
one more motherfucker ask me what navy my brother is in.
one more person assume no arabs or muslims were killed.
one more person assume they know me, or that i represent a people.
or that a people represent an evil. or that evil is as simple as a
flag and words on a page.

we did not vilify all white men when mcveigh bombed oklahoma.
america did not give out his family's addresses or where he went to
church. or blame the bible or pat robertson. . . .

and when we talk about holy books and hooded men and death, why do we
never mention the kkk?

if there are any people on earth who understand how new york is
feeling right now, they are in the west bank and the gaza strip.

. . .

i feel like my skin is real thin, and that my eyes are only going to get darker. the future holds little light.

my baby brother is a man now, and on alert, and praying five times a day that the orders he will take in a few days time are righteous and will not weigh his soul down from the afterlife he deserves.

both my brothers—my heart stops when i try to pray—not a beat to disturb my fear. one a rock god, the other a sergeant, and both palestinian, practicing muslim, gentle men. both born in brooklyn and their faces are of the archetypal arab man, all eyelashes and nose and beautiful color and stubborn hair.

what will their lives be like now? over there is over here.

7. all day, across the river, the smell of burning rubber and limbs floats through. the sirens have stopped now. the advertisers are back on the air. the rescue workers are traumatized. the skyline is brought back to human size. no longer taunting the gods with its height.

i have not cried at all while writing this. i cried when i saw those buildings collapse on themselves like a broken heart. i have never owned pain that needs to spread like that. and i cry daily that my brothers return to our mother safe and whole.

there is no poetry in this. there are causes and effects. there are symbols and ideologies. mad conspiracy here, and information we will never know. there is death here, and there are promises of more.

there is life here. anyone reading this is breathing, maybe hurting, but breathing for sure. and if there is any light to come, it will shine from the eyes of those who look for peace and justice after the rubble and rhetoric are cleared and the phoenix has risen.

affirm life.
affirm life.
we got to carry each other now.
you are either with life, or against it.
affirm life.

—SUHEIR HAMMAD

Acknowledgments

Every effort has been made to trace copyright holders and give proper credit for all copyrighted material used in this book. The editors regret if there are any oversights. The publisher will be pleased to hear from any copyright holders not acknowledged in this edition so that a correction might be made at the next opportunity.

CHAPTER ONE

Harold John Ockenga, "Convocation Address for Fuller Theological Seminary," 1947. Reprinted with permission.

Fulton J. Sheen, D. D., *Peace of Soul* (New York: McGraw-Hill Book Company, 1949), 12–25. Reprinted with the permission of The Society for the Propagation of the Faith.

Reinhold Niebuhr, *The Irony of American History* (New York: Charles Scribner's Sons, 1952), excerpts from 17–35. Reprinted with the permission of the Estate of Reinhold Niebuhr.

A Letter to Presbyterians Concerning the Present Situation in Our Country and In the World, Unanimously Adopted by the General Council of the General Assembly of the Presbyterian Church in the United States of America, October 21, 1953 (Philadelphia, n.d.,), 2–8. Reprinted by permission of the Office of the General Assembly, Presbyterian Church (U.S.A.).

Dorothy Day, from *Dorothy Day, Selected Writings*, edited by Robert Ellsberg. Copyright © 1983, 1992, by Robert Ellsberg and Tamar Hennessey. Published in 1992 by Orbis Books, Maryknoll, New York, 10545.

Will Herberg, from *Protestant, Catholic, Jew*, copyright © 1955 by Will Herberg. Used by permission of Doubleday, a division of Random House, Inc.

Church League of America, "A Manual for Survival" (Illinois: The Church League of America, 1961), 9–14.

J. B. Matthews, *Certain Activities of Certain Clergymen* (Illinois: The Church League of America, 1963).

J. William Fulbright, from *The Arrogance of Power*, copyright © 1966 by J. William Fulbright. Used by permission of Random House, Inc.

National Conference of Catholic Bishops, excerpts from *The Challenge of Peace*, © 1983 United States Conference of Catholic Bishops, Inc., Washington, DC. Used with permission. All rights reserved.

Ronald Reagan, speech to the National Association of Evangelicals, 8 March 1983.

CHAPTER TWO

Allen Ginsberg, "A Blake Experience," from *Paris Review*, Spring 1966. Reprinted by the permission of Regal Literary, as agents for the *Paris Review*. Copyright © 1966 by The Paris Review.

"Grace," "The World is Watching," and "The Etiquette of Freedom," from *The Practice of the Wild* by Gary Snyder. Copyright © 1990 by Gary Snyder. Reprinted by permission of North Point Press, a division of Farrar, Straus, and Giroux, LLC.

"Beginning a Counterculture," from *In My Own Way: An Autobiography*, by Alan Watts. Reprinted by the permission of Russell & Volkening as agents for the author. Copyright © 1972 by Alan Watts.

"Psychedelics and Religious Experience," from *Does It Matter?* by Alan Watts. Reprinted by the permission of Russell & Volkening as agents for the author. Copyright © 1971 by Alan Watts.

Charles Reich, *The Greening of America*. Copyright © 1970 by Charles A. Reich. Reprinted with the permission of the author.

Timothy Leary, "Interpretations of Religious Experience." Copyright 1982, by Timothy Leary, Ph.D., 2001 by the Futique Trust, from *Your Brain Is God*, Ronin Publishing, by permission. All rights reserved. Roninpub.com/rn_learlylib.html.

Ram Dass, *Be Here How: Cookbook for a Sacred Life* (1971). Used by permission of the Hanuman Foundation, San Cristobal, New Mexico.

Shirley MacLaine, "Going Within," from *Going Within*, by Shirley MacLaine, copyright © 1989 by Shirley MacLaine. Used by permission of Bantam Books, a division of Random House, Inc.

Medicine Story Manitonquat, "Somewhere Under the Rainbow." Reprinted with the permission of the author.

Hiley Ward, *The Far-out Saints of the Jesus Communes* (New York: Association Press, 1972). Reprinted with the permission of the author.

Duane Pederson, *Jesus People* (Pasadena: Gospel Light Books, 1971). Reprinted with the permission of the author.

Shunryu Suzuki, "Posture," from *Zen Mind, Beginner's Mind: Informal Talks on Zen Meditation and Practice*. Reprinted by permission of Weatherhill Press, Inc.

Keith Harrary, "The Truth About Jonestown: Giving Away Power." *Psychology Today*, March/April 1992. Reprinted with permission from *Psychology Today* Magazine, Copyright © (1992) Sussex Publishers Inc.

Fritjof Capra, "Modern Physics," from *The Tao of Physics*, by Fritjof Capra. © 1975, 1983, 1991, 1999 by Fritjof Capra. Reprinted by arrangement with Shambhala Publications, Inc., Boston, www.shambhala.com.

CHAPTER THREE

Martin Luther King, "Letter from a Birmingham Jail." From *Why We Can't Wait.* Reprinted by arrangement with The Heirs to the Estate of Martin Luther King., Jr., c/o Writers House, Inc. as agent for the proprietor. Copyright 1963 by Martin Luther King., Jr., copyright renewed 1991 by Coretta Scott King.

"Woke up This Morning," additional lyrics by Robert Zellner. © Copyright 1963 (renewed) by Sanga Music, Inc. All rights reserved. Used by permission.

"Hallelujah, I'm A-Traveling" by Harry Raymond. © Copyright 1947 by Stormking Music Inc. All rights reserved. Used by permission.

"We Shall Overcome," by Zilphia Horton, Guy Carawan, Frank Hamilton, Pete Seeger (Ludlow Music CAE/IPI # 18683174). All rights reserved. Used by permission of Ludlow Music, Inc.

James Lawson, "Address from a Lunch Counter Stool," and "SNCC Manifesto," reprinted with permission of the Reverend James Lawson Jr.

Mary King, *Freedom Song: A Personal Story of the 1960s Civil Rights Movement* (New York: William Morrow, 1987). Copyright Mary King, reprinted with the permission of the Gerard McCauley Agency, Inc.

The Autobiography of Malcolm X, by Malcolm X with the assistance of Alex Haley. Copyright © 1964 by Malcolm X and Alex Haley. Copyright © 1965 by Alex Haley and Betty Shabazz. Reprinted by permission of Random House, Inc.

James Cone, "Black Theology and the Black Church," *CrossCurrents* (Summer 1977), reprinted by permission of *CrossCurrents*.

James Cone and Gayraud Wilmore, "Introduction," from *Black Theology: A Documentary History* (Orbis Books, 1979), reprinted with permission of Orbis Books.

"Black Power and the American Christ," by Vincent Harding. Copyright 1967 Christian Century Foundation. Reprinted with Permission from the Jan 4, 1967 issue of *Christian Century*.

"Black Manifesto Declares War on Churches." *Christianity Today*, May 23, 1969. Reprinted courtesy of *Christianity Today*.

César Chávez, "The Mexican American and the Church," originally from Octavio I. Romano V., ed., *Voices: Readings from El Grito* (Berkeley: Quinto Sol, 1973); Luis Fontánez, "The Theology of Social Justice," from an Address to the Northeast Regional Encounter, November 29, 1974, both reprinted by permission from Anthony Stevens-Arroyo, ed., *Prophets Without Honor: An Anthology on the Hispano Church of the United States* (New York: Maryknoll, 1980).

God is Red: A Native View of Religion, by Vine Deloria, Jr. Copyright 1994. Fulcrum Publishing, Inc., Golden, Colorado, USA. All rights reserved. Used by permission of Fulcrum Publishing, Inc.

Jacquelyn Grant, "Black Theology and the Black Woman." Reprinted with the permission of the author.

James Cone, "The White Church and Black Power," reprinted from James Cone, *Black Theology and Black Power* (New York: Seabury Press, 1969). Used with permission.

"The Black Manifesto" and Committee of Black Churchmen, "Black Power," reprinted from Gayraud Wilmore and James Cone, eds., *Black Theology: A Documentary History, 1966–1979* (Maryknoll: Orbis Books, 1979), pp. 80–93.

CHAPTER FOUR

Gyn/Ecology, by Mary Daly. Copyright © 1978 by Mary Daly. Reprinted by permission of Beacon Press, Boston.

Audre Lorde, "Open Letter to Mary Daly." Reprinted with permission from *Sister Outsider* by Audre Lorde, copyright 1984. Published by the Crossing Press, Freedom, California.

Cynthia Ozick, "Notes Toward Finding the Right Question: Fifteen Brief Meditations," *Lilith* 6 (1979): 19–29; Elsye Goldstein, "Take Back the Waters: A Feminist Reappropriation of the Mikvah," *Lilith* 15 (Summer 1986): 15–16; both reprinted with the permission of *Lilith* magazine.

Beverly Harrison, "The Power of Anger in the Work of Love." From *Feminist Theology: A Reader*, edited by Ann Loades. Used by permission of Westminster John Knox Press.

William Cutrer, "Baptist Faith and Message: Article 18, The Family." From www.sbc.net. Reprinted with the permission of the author.

Shaina Sara Handelman, "Modesty and the Jewish Woman," from the *Uforatzo Journal*, 1979, and reprinted in *The Modern Jewish Woman: A Unique Perspective*, ed. Raizel Schnall Friedfertig and Freyda Schapiro (Brooklyn: Lubavitch Educational Foundation for Jewish Marriage Enrichment, 1981). Reprinted with the permission of the author.

Pauli Murray, "Stumbling Block to Faith," from *Proud Shoes: The Story of an American Family* (New York: Harper & Row, 1978). Copyright by Pauli Murray. Reprinted by permission of Sterling Lord Literistic, Inc.

Teresita Basso, "The Emerging Chicana," *Review for Religious* 30 (6) (1971): 1019–28. Used by permission.

Myrtle Lincoln, "The Medicine Bundle," and other documents on Native American women's religion from Doris Duke Indian Oral History Collection, Western History Collections, University of Oklahoma Libraries. Used by permission.

Karen McCarthy Brown, "Why Women Need the War God." From *Women's Spirit Bonding*, ed. Janet Kalven and Mary I. Buckley. Copyright Pilgrim Press, 1984. Reprinted with permission.

Judith Plaskow, "The Right Question is Theological." From *On Being a Jewish Feminist: A Reader*, ed. Susannah Heschel (New York: Schocken Books, 1983). Reprinted with the permission of the author.

"Witchcraft and Women's Culture," by Starhawk, from *Womanspirit Rising: A Feminist Reader in Religion*, edited by Carol P. Christ and Judith Plaskow. Copyright © 1979 by Carol P. Christ and Judith Plaskow. Reprinted by permission of HarperCollins Publishers, Inc.

Rita Gross, "Buddhist Feminism," from *Buddhism After Patriarchy: A Feminist History, Analysis, and Reconstruction of Buddhism*, by Rita Gross. Reprinted by permission of the State University of New York Press, © 1993, State University of New York. All rights reserved.

CHAPTER FIVE

John F. Kennedy Jr., "Address to the Greater Houston Ministerial Association," 12 September 1960.

Engle v. Vitale, 370 U.S. 421, Certiorari to the Court of Appeals of New York, Argued April 3, 1962—Decided June 25, 1962.

Abraham J. Heschel, excerpts from "The Moral Outrage of Vietnam," from *Vietnam: Crisis of Conscience*, ed. National Board of Young Men's Christian Association Church (1967), 48–60. Copyright © 1967 by Abraham Joshua Heschel. Copyright renewed 1994 by Susannah Heschel. Reprinted by permission.

"Abortion and the Court," Editors of *Christianity Today* (1973). Used by permission, *Christianity Today*, 1973.

Joseph F. Donceel, S.J., "A Liberal Catholic's View." From *Abortion in a Changing World, vol. I*, ed. Robert E. Hall (New York: Columbia University Press, 1970). Used by permission.

Jesse Jackson, "Speech at the 1984 Democratic Convention," San Francisco, CA, 18 July 1984. Used with the permission of the author and the Rainbow Push Coalition.

National Conference of Catholic Bishops, "Pastoral Letter by Council of American Bishops," excerpts from *Economic Justice for All* © 1986 United States Conference of Catholic Bishops, Inc., Washington, D.C. Used with permission. All rights reserved.

Patrick J. Buchanan, "1992 Republican National Convention Speech," August 17, 1992. Reprinted with the permission of the author.

Louis Farrakhan, "Minister Farrakhan Challenges Black Men" (1995). Used with permission.

James C. Dobson, "Dobson on Clinton" (1998). From *Family News from Dr. James Dobson*, September 1998 edition, published by Focus on the Family. Copyright © 1998, Focus on the Family. All rights reserved. International copyright secured. Used by permission.

Intelligent Design Network, Inc., *Letter to Board of Education of Each of the Unified School Districts of the State of Kansas* (Kansas: 8 June 2000) available from http://www.Intelligentdesignnetwork.org. Used by permission.

Kansas Citizens for Science, *A Response to the Intelligent Design Network's Proposals to Include "Intelligent Design" in the Kansas Science Standards* (Kansas: 9 February 2001) available from http://www.kcfs.org. Reprinted with permission.

CHAPTER SIX

Norman Vincent Peale, D.D. and Smiley Blanton, M.D., *The Art of Real Happiness*, Revised Ed. (Carmel, New York: Guideposts Associates, Inc., 1956), 248–262. Used with permission.

Robert Schuller's Life Changes, ed. Robert A. Schuller (New Jersey: Fleming H. Revell Company, a division of Baker Book House Company, 1981), 136–150. Used with permission.

L. Ron Hubbard, "Two Rules for Happy Living" © 1965 by L. Ron Hubbard Library from *Scientology; A New Slant on Life* published by Bridge Publications, Inc., All Rights Reserved. Grateful acknowledgment is made to L. Ron Hubbard Library for permission to reprint a selection from the copyrighted works of L. Ron Hubbard.

Tom Gearhart, "Jesus Christ Superstar: A Turning Point in Music." Reprinted from *The Blade*, Toledo, Ohio, May 2, 1971, Sec. C, pp. 1, 2, 4. Used with permission.

Kenneth Taylor, Preface to *The Living Bible* (Illinois: Tyndale House Publishers, 1971). Used with permission. All Rights Reserved.

Billy Graham, *Angels: God's Secret Agents*. W. Publishing, Nashville, Tennessee, 1975, 163–175. Reprinted by permission.

Carol Flake, *Redemptorama: Culture, Politics, and the New Evangelicalism* (Virginia: Anchor Press/Doubleday & Company, Inc., 1985), 215–225. © 1984 by Carol Flake. Used with permission of Doubleday, a division of Random House, Inc.

Jason E. McBride, "Goths for Jesus." Copyright 1999 *Christian Century*. Reprinted by permission from the July 28–Aug. 4, 1999 issue of *Christian Century*. Subscriptions: $49/yr. from P.O. Box 378, Mt. Morris, IL 61054. 1–800–208–4097.

Michael L. Keene, "The Church on the Web." Copyright 1999 *Christian Century*. Reprinted by permission from the Aug. 11–18, 1999, issue of *Christian Century*. Subscriptions: $49/yr. from P.O. Box 378, Mt. Morris, IL 61054. 1–800–208–4097.

Zain Bhikha, "Praise the Prophet" (2000). Used with the permission of Mountain of Light.

Jonathan Schorsch, "Making Judaism Cool" (2000). Used with the permission of *Tikkun: A Bimonthly Jewish Critique of Politics, Culture, and Society. Tikkun* is a project of the Institute for Labor and Mental Health, a nonprofit organization.

Lou Carlozo, "Jabez: Biblical Bit Player to Pop-Culture Phenom" (11/28/2001). Used with the permission of the author and *Chicago Tribune*, article published November 28, 2001.

CHAPTER SEVEN

Billy Graham, "Watershed," from pages 167–185 of *Just as I Am* by Billy Graham. Copyright © 1997 by Billy Graham Evangelistic Association. Reprinted by Permission of HarperCollins Publishers, Inc.

Harvey Cox, "Fire from Heaven," from *Fire from Heaven*. Copyright © 1995 by Harvey Cox. Reprinted by permissions of Perseus Books Publishers, a member of Perseus Books, L.L.C.

"We are at War," from C. Peter Wagner and Frederick Douglas Pennoyer, *Wrestling with Dark Angels: Toward a Deeper Understanding of the Supernatural Forces in Spiritual Warfare*. Ventura, CA: Regal Books, 1996. Reprinted with the permission of the author.

"Racial Reconciliation Manifesto" and Vinson Synan, "Memphis 1994," from *Reconciliation*, Summer 1998. Reprinted with permission of the International Pentecostal Holiness Church and the Pentecostal Charismatic Churches of North America.

Albert Cleage, "Let's Not Waste the Holy Spirit," from Albert B. Cleage Jr., *Black Christian Nationalism*. Copyright 1972 by Albert B. Cleage Jr.

Myrtle Lincoln, "A Pentecostal Conversion," from Doris Duke Indian Oral History Collection, Western History Collections, University of Oklahoma Libraries. Used by permission.

Patrick Buchanan, "Blessed Sacrament," from *Right from the Beginning*. Copyright © 1990 by Patrick Buchanan. All rights reserved. Reprinted with special permission by Regnery Publishing Inc., Washington, D.C.

Ralph Reed, *Active Faith: How Christians Are Changing the Soul of American Politics*. Copyright 1996 by Ralph Reed. Reprinted and abridged with the permission of the Free Press, a Division of Simon and Schuster, Inc.

Ronald Sider, "A Statement of Intent" and "Our Historic Moment," from Ronald Sider, *Good News and Good Works* (Grand Rapids, MI: Baker Book House Company, 1996). Reprinted by permission of Baker Book House.

Steve Charleston, "The Old Testament of Native America," from *Lift Every Voice*, ed. Susan Brooks Thistletwaite. Copyright © 1990 by Harper and Row, Publishers, Inc. Reprinted by permission of HarperCollins Publishers, Inc.

"The Reinvented Church: Styles and Strategies," by Donald Miller. Copyright 2000 Christian Century Foundation. Reprinted by permission from the March 15, 2000 issue of *Christian Century*. Subscriptions: $49/yr. from P.O. Box 378, Mt. Morris, IL 61054. 1–800–208–4097.

CHAPTER EIGHT

D. T. Suzuki, *Zen and Japanese Culture*. Copyright © 1959 by Bollingen, © 1987 renewed by Princeton University Press. Reprinted by permission of Princeton University Press.

Chogyam Trungpa, from *Meditation in Action*. © 1991 by Diana Mukpo. Reprinted by arrangement with Shambhala Publications, Inc., Boston, www.shambhala.com.

"Transcendental Meditation" by Maharishi Mahesh Yogi, from *The Science of Being and the Art of Living: Transcendental Meditation* by Maharishi Mahesh Yogi, © 1963 by Age of Enlightenment Publications. Used by permission of Dutton Signet, a division of Penguin Group (USA) Inc.

Richard Rodriguez, "The 'Minority Student'" from *Hunger of Memory* by Richard Rodriguez. Copyright © 1982 by Richard Rodriguez. Reprinted by permission of David R. Godine, Publisher, Inc.

Andres Tapia, "Vivan Los Evangelicos!" ©1991 Andres Tapia. Reprinted with the permission of the author.

Moises Sandoval, "Huddled Masses: The History of Our Immigrant Church." Copyright 2000 by *U.S. Catholic*. Reproduced by permission from the July 2000 magazine issue of *U.S. Catholic* (http://www.uscatholic.org). *U.S. Catholic* is published by the Claretians. Call 1–800–328–6515 for subscription information.

Barbara Brown Taylor, "Vishnu's Almonds." Copyright 2000 Christian Century Foundation. Reprinted with permission from the March 22–29, 2000 issue of *Christian Century*.

Aditi Banerjee, "Hindu-Americans: An Emerging Identity in an Increasingly Hyphenated World," published 2003, available from www.hvk.org/articles/1102/25.html. Reprinted with the permission of the author.

Muzammil H. Siddiqi, "Human Rights in Islam," available from http://www.isna.net/Library/khutbahs/HumanRightsinIslam.asp. Reprinted with the permission of the Islamic Society of North America.

Saraji Umm Zaid, "Make Way for the Women! Why Your Mosque Should be Woman Friendly," available from http://www.islamfortoday.com/ummzaid04.htm. A shortened version of this essay appeared in *Taking Back Islam*, ed. Michael

542 *Acknowledgments*

Wolfe, Rodale Press/Beliefnet, 2002. Reprinted with the permission of the author.

CHAPTER NINE

Harvey Cox, "Biblical Sources of Secularization," from *The Secular City: Secularization and Urbanization in Theological Perspective* (New York: Macmillan, 1965). Reprinted with the permission of the author.

Harvey Cox, "Religion in the Secular City," from *Religion in the Secular City: Towards a Postmodern Theology*, by Harvey Cox. © 1984 by Harvey Cox. New York: Simon and Schuster. Reprinted by permission.

Hal Lindsey, excerpts from *The Late Great Planet Earth*. © 1970, 1977, Zondervan Publishing House, Rand Rapids, Michigan. Used by permission.

Jerry Falwell, "A Biblical Look into the 21st Century." Reprinted with permission from http://www.jerryfalwell.com.

Larry Norman, "I Wish We'd All Been Ready," lyrics cited courtesy of Hal Leonard Corporation, 1969.

"Reflections After Waco: Millennialists and the State," by Michael Barkun. Copyright 1993 *Christian Century* Foundation. Reprinted by permission from the June 2, 1993 issue of *Christian Century*.

"*The Celestine Prophecy*: Heavenly Insight or a New Age Fraud?" by Dennis Pollock, Evangelist with Lamb and Lion Ministries. http://www.lamblion.com/Web08–11.htm. Reprinted with the permission of the author.

"Towards a Global Ethic (An Initial Declaration)," 1993 Parliament of the World's Religions, Chicago, Illinois, USA. Reprinted by permission of Council for a Parliament of the World's Religions.

The Venerable Samu Sunim, et al., "To the Council for a Parliament of the World's Religions," unpublished document, 31 August 1993. By the Venerable Samu Sunim, President, Buddhist Society for Compassionate Wisdom, North American Buddhist Order. Used by permission.

Stephen Carter, *The Culture of Disbelief*. Copyright © 1993 by Stephen L. Carter. Reprinted by permission of Basic Books, a member of Perseus Books, L.L.C. Used by permission.

Michael Lerner, "The Founding Editorial Statement," *Tikkun* 1 (Fall 1986): 3–5; Michael Lerner, Peter Gabel, "Why We're Hopeful About the New Millennium," *Tikkun* 14 (November/December 1999), 9–10, 53–56; Zalman Schachter-Shalomi, "Judaism for a New Age," Jim Wallis, "Light the Spark," Douglas Gwyn, "Utopia: An Abiding Presence," and David C. Korten, "For the Love of Life," all from *Tikkun* 15 (January February 2000). All reprinted with the permission of *Tikkun: A Bimonthly Jewish Critique of Politics, Culture, and Society. Tikkun* is a project of the Institute for Labor and Mental Health, a nonprofit organization.

Elizabeth Lesser, *The New American Spirituality*. Copyright © 1999 by Elizabeth Lesser. Reprinted by permission of Random House, Inc.

Suheir Hammad, "First Writing Since." Reprinted with the permission of the author.